**Financing the
1980 Election**

Financing the 1980 Election

Herbert E. Alexander
Citizens' Research Foundation,
University of Southern California

with the assistance of
Brian A. Haggerty

LexingtonBooks
D.C. Heath and Company
Lexington, Massachusetts
Toronto

Library of Congress Cataloging in Publication Data

Alexander, Herbert E.
     Financing the 1980 election.

     Includes bibliographical references and index.
     1. Campaign funds—United States. 2. Presidents—United States—
Election—1980. 3. United States. Congress—Elections, 1980. I. Haggerty,
Brian A. II. Title.
JK1991.A685   1983   324.7′8′0973   82-48863
ISBN 0-669-06375-4

Published simultaneously in Canada

Printed in the United States of America

International Standard Book Number: 0-669-06375-4

Library of Congress Catalog Card Number: 82-48863

*To the memory of William H. Vanderbilt
who had the prescience to know many years
ago that political finance was an important
subject to study*

Contents

Tables

Preface and Acknowledgments

This is my sixth quadrennial book on the financing of presidential-election campaigns. The 1972 study reflected a dimension differing from the 1960s because vast amounts of data regarding political receipts and expenditures—more than in any previous presidential election in American history—were available. New laws, voluntary disclosure, and official and media exposures, particularly about Watergate, produced a new data base. A re-examination of research and analytical techniques used previously was undertaken, and considerable modifications were made to cope with the new data. The first experience with presidential public funding occurred in 1976. New laws and court cases affected the 1976 elections in dramatic fashion also. The 1980 elections constituted the second experience with public funding, adding new dimensions and leading to new ways of dealing with and thinking about the subject. Each successive study is an educational experience for me; 1980 was notable in the diversity of ways and means found to raise, handle, and spend the large amounts of money used.

A new agency, the Federal Election Commission (FEC), came into being in 1975, producing immense amounts of data and information and affecting greatly the contours and analyses of this 1980 study. Some amounts reported in this book as spent by a given candidate may differ from other figures because audit totals of the FEC do not agree with totals in its published compilations or with direct or later information that the Citizens' Research Foundation (CRF) received. The CRF made certain adjustments that the FEC did not. Close-off dates for some CRF analyses differed from FEC or other compilations, thus affecting totals. Some definitions of categories differ, affecting which groups are included or excluded in certain totals. For certain purposes, independent expenditures, compliance costs, and communication costs were included, unlike compilations by others. Moreover, the FEC compilations often give totals only for general-election candidates, going back to January 1 of the election year or previous year, without separating primary-election from general-election spending, and not accounting for primary loser totals of dollars raised and spent. Of course, the FEC disclosure forms are not designed to differentiate accurately primary-election from general-election spending.

So many events and facts required description independently by topic that it was difficult to organize the book efficiently. There would have been so many notes cross-referencing topics such as fund raising or public financing within the confines of the book that for the most part we dispensed with these. Accordingly readers should use both the contents and the index for cross-referencing.

This study attempts to update and to keep active analyses and categories of data developed over the years by Professors James Pollock, Louise Overacker, and Alexander Heard and by the Senate Subcommittee on Privileges and Elections (under the chairmanship of Sen. Albert Gore of Tennessee) in 1956.

Acknowledgments

The data in this study were collected by the CRF. Special appreciation is due to many individuals for providing information in personal interviews, through correspondence, and by telephone. Many finance managers and others preferred to remain anonymous. Because it would be unfair to name some and not others, I regretfully will not list the many persons in such capacities who graciously cooperated. For example, some of the information for the tables in chapter 5 were provided by various anonymity-seeking campaign staff members and hence are not indicated by source in the book.

Two special acknowledgments are in order. In December 1980 I gave a lecture at Sangamon State University in Springfield, Illinois. That lecture, "Financing the Campaigns and Parties of 1980," is published, in revised and updated form, in *Presidential Election and Transition, 1980-81*, edited by David Everson and published by Southern Illinois University Press.

Another brief version of this book is contained in my article, "Making Sense about Dollars in the 1980 Presidential Campaigns," in a book, *Parties, Interest Groups and Money in the 1980 Elections*, edited by Michael J. Malbin, and published by the American Enterprise Institute for Public Policy Research, Washington, D.C., 1983.

I am happy to give special acknowledgment to Brian A. Haggerty, who helped write first drafts of substantial portions of the book and who rewrote, reorganized, shortened, and edited every chapter, adding style and clarity to the entire manuscript. Brian's invaluable help is accorded due recognition on the title page of the book.

Special thanks are due to Caroline Lyons and Robert Lyons for their major contribution to analyzing data and writing a draft of chapter 4. Caroline Lyons has been CRF's research associate in Washington, D.C., for eighteen years, and her talents in making sense of the mass of figures contained in filings made under federal law were joined by Robert Lyons's research and editing abilities.

At the University of Southern California, major analyses and redrafting were done by three research assistants who are graduate students in the Department of Political Science: Mike Eberts, who is responsible for the analyses in and preparation of chapter 8 and part of chapter 9 and whose fine writing style emanates from his journalistic experience; Craig Holman, who prepared major parts of chapters 2 and 3 and whose growing command of the subject is evident; and Patricia Gibson, who admirably drafted and reworked the litigation and suits sections of the book.

I appreciate the typing under deadline by Jacqueline Sanchez and the fine indexing done by Cheryl Newton.

Throughout, CRF's assistant director, Gloria N. Cornette, was a constant source of strength, lightening my administrative responsibilities, providing continuity, and minimizing disruptions, thus enabling me to devote more time to the book. Gloria managed superbly the preparation of the manuscript at all stages.

None of those who were so helpful is responsible for errors of omission or commission; for those, as for interpretations, I bear sole responsibility.

I am happy to acknowledge the encouragement and forbearance of my wife, Nancy, and the good cheers of my children, Michael, Andrew, and Kenneth.

I always appreciate the cooperation and encouragement received from officers and members of the board of trustees of the Citizens' Research Foundation and of my colleagues at the University of Southern California, but the presentation is mine and does not reflect their views.

Without the contributions of numerous supporters of the Citizens' Research Foundation, this study would not have been possible.

Financing the
1980 Election

1 Introduction

Whether the 1980 national election results represent the end of an era and a fundamental realignment of political power in the United States remains for history to determine.[1] Yet the elections clearly brought many changes: in the occupant of the White House, the composition of the Congress, and the direction of our politics. The 1980 election campaigns also signaled changes in the ways in which campaigns are financed and regulated. Those changes and their significance for our political system are the subject of this book.

The most-notable elements of change in political finance and campaign regulation may be sketched as follows:

Total political spending at all levels—for candidates, for the maintenance of the political-party system, and on ballot issues—was more than $1 billion. That amount includes all party and elective activity in the 1979-1980 election cycle, although most of the spending took place in 1980. It represents a dramatic increase, well beyond the inflation rate, compared with such political spending in 1976, estimated at $540 million. The $1.2 billion political bill needs to be put in perspective. In fiscal year 1980, governments at all levels—national, state, county, and municipal—spent a total of $958,657,000,000 in taxpayer money. The $1,203,000,000 spent on election campaigns, whose outcomes determined who will make decisions on, among other things, how such enormous sums of tax money are spent, amounts to only about one-tenth of 1 percent of that total.

The costs of electing a Congress ($239 million) were almost as high as those of electing the president ($275 million). In all some $514 million was spent to elect the national government, a substantial increase over the $340 million spent four years earlier. Lest the federal total appear inordinately high, the nation's leading commercial advertiser, Procter and Gamble Company, spent $649 million promoting its products in 1980.

Although money was an important factor in the election, the size and breadth of the Reagan victory and the ability of the Republicans to gain control of the Senate indicate that factors other than money played key roles in most election outcomes. The increased significance of nonmonetary factors involved in campaigning, such as the availability of time to engage in long campaigns, the talents of the candidates, the extent of family and surrogate support, the voluntary actions of many individuals, and the impact of the issues, are worthy of mention.

1

The unprecedented political spending in 1980 was highlighted by political-party renewal and by increases in the importance of political action committees and in the uses of independent expenditures.

Political-party renewal was most notable in the organizational and fund-raising successes achieved by the Republican party nationally and in the revival of partisan Republicanism reaching down to the state and local levels. Republican party committees contributed large amounts to various candidates at all levels, and provided important services and training. The Republican National Committee used television as a political instrument by spending $9.5 million on "anti-Democrat" advertising urging voters to "vote Republican for a change" and to elect "the Republican team." This strategy benefited federal as well as state and local candidates across the country in a first effort to nationalize the party ticket and to speak on its behalf with a single voice.

The Republicans raised more money and spent more at every level than did the Democrats. Essentially the Republicans outdistanced the Democrats, both in developing broad-based financial constituencies at the national level and in applying national-party expertise to help the state parties develop stronger financial bases. The trend toward the nationalization of campaign funding, spurred to a significant degree over the past decade by use of party direct-mail solicitations and telethons (and through political action committee and lobbyist giving at the national level), may be counterbalanced to the extent that state and local political parties improve their funding.

Following defeats in the contest for the presidency and the Senate, the Democrats undertook serious rethinking and regrouping. In the many years the Democrats controlled the Congress, and occasionally the White House, they failed to build stable financial constituencies, depending mainly upon their incumbency, labor support, and contributors of large sums. Only following the 1980 election defeats did the Democrats begin serious efforts to broaden their financial bases. Interestingly, the reappearance of a highly contested two-party system in congressional elections came on the heels of a major effort by an important independent candidate for president.

The importance of political action committees (PACs) as a source of funding, particularly for senatorial and congressional campaigns, was magnified as PACs raised and spent more money than in the two previous election cycles—1975-1976 and 1977-1978—combined. By the end of 1980, there were 2,551 PACs registered with the Federal Election Commission (FEC), of which 2,146 made contributions to federal candidates. A historical first occurred when corporate PACs raised and spent more money than labor PACs, although the combination of corporate and trade association PACs—often termed business-oriented PACs despite wide diversity—has been outspending labor PACs since 1976.

The political activities of the New Right PACs and their evangelical allies achieved high levels of publicity and significant amounts of funding. The effectiveness of these interrelated phenomena remains uncertain.

The use of independent expenditures escalated dramatically in both the presidential and congressional elections, generating controversy particularly with respect to negative spending against certain U.S. Senate candidates but also because the massive use of independent expenditures did violence to the tightly drawn systems of Federal Election Campaign Act-imposed contribution and expenditure ceilings in the presidential elections and to contribution limits in congressional elections. Litigation led to a Supreme Court decision upholding independent expenditures in publicly funded presidential elections, including those made by groups established for the single purpose of pooling contributions in order to make such expenditures.

The system of public funding did not discourage important potential presidential candidates from running and in fact probably encouraged some who otherwise would not have been able to do so. Certainly public money helped George Bush and John Anderson, who were not well known nationally and did not have ready access to large amounts of private money, to stay the course of primaries and caucuses until the outcome was decided. In this second election in which public funding was available for presidential candidates, John Connally, whose fund-raising success qualified him to receive the government matching subsidies, became the first major candidate to refuse to accept them, and John Anderson, whose percentage of the popular vote total made him eligible, became the first independent or minor-party candidate to receive postelection public financing.

The 1979 amendments to the Federal Election Campaign Act (FECA) permitted state- and local-party committees to participate meaningfully in the presidential general election. The Republicans outspent the Democrats by large amounts in these categories.

The lengthy and exhausting presidential selection process became the subject of considerable criticism and triggered a large number of postelection studies by the political parties and by many academics and organizations. Suggestions for change include proposals for strengthening the roles of the parties, ensuring that the process is representative and responsive, and upgrading the deliberative role of the conventions in choosing nominees who are electable and able to govern once elected. Other aspects of the process being studied deal with the roles of the media and the campaign finance systems and with the methods by which state legislatures choose each state's procedure for selecting convention delegates or indicating presidential preference in the prenomination period.

The 1980 elections dealt political campaign reform a telling blow. For the foreseeable future the main activities of political reformers will be efforts to forestall counterreform, which threatens to reverse the policies adopted during the past decade. Reform was a priority issue of the 1980s. Reform policies, catalyzed but not originated by Watergate events, consisted of comprehensive and timely disclosure of political funds, limitations on contributions, campaign expenditure limitations (when constitutional), public funding of presidential campaigns, and the establishment of the FEC to administer and enforce the law.

Counterreform has taken the form of efforts to reduce the extent of government regulation of the electoral process, to lighten the burdens the law has imposed on candidates and political committees by reducing paperwork, to raise contribution limits to more-realistic levels or to repeal them, and to restrict some of the powers of the FEC. Indeed some critics have been trying to abolish that agency.

No action may reasonably be anticipated in the immediate future on the two remaining goals of campaign-reform advocates: the extension of public financing to senatorial and congressional campaigns and restrictions on the amounts of money federal candidates may receive from PACs. In an era of fiscal restraint, the Congress certainly will not enact public funding of more campaigns. At a time of budget reductions, a new spending program to help fund political campaigns would be unthinkable to many. And in the permissive atmosphere, the nonregulatory mode, which currently prevails at the federal level, restrictive legislation regarding PACs is not to be expected.

Beyond the efforts to deregulate the election law, various post-Watergate reform laws, including the Government in Sunshine Act, the Freedom of Information Act, and the Ethics in Government Act, have come under similar attack. Efforts to revise lobbying disclosure law have been unsuccessful. The election of Ronald Reagan, an advocate of less government regulation, confirmed the trend toward mitigating the political reforms of the 1970s.

Supreme Court cases possibly approaching the magnitude of *Buckley* v. *Valeo* (1976) were either decided or were in process, some beginning as a result of events in the 1979-1980 election cycle. Of particular note are those cases relating to the autonomy of the political parties in the presidential selection process, the role of broadcasters in political advertising, the use of independent expenditures by groups especially formed for the purpose, and the constitutionality of limitations on contributions to ballot issue campaigns.

The election laws of the 1970s have brought a number of changes, some of which profoundly affect the nature of campaigning. The legislation has led to new campaign strategies using high technologies, particularly in political communications: computers for targeting and direct mail, and recording and telephoning devices for reaching voters. The professionalization of politics has continued apace, creating an environment with important consequences for voluntarism. Politics in a democracy is properly animated by the voluntary efforts of individuals, political parties, groups, and organizations. As federal election law is increasingly refined, it resembles tax law, with the FEC doing for politics what the Internal Revenue Service does for taxes. This development has two effects: it increases the need for professionals—accountants, lawyers, and other skilled individuals—to help candidates and their staffs comply with increasingly complex regulations, and it may chill enthusiasm for citizen participation since so many campaign functions require skillful use of limited resources, and since non-knowledgeable amateurs may easily violate the law.

The FECA and its state equivalents also may be compared to the Securities Exchange Act of 1934. That act required public corporations to systematize and publicize their bookkeeping, which led private lawyers and accountants to set standards that in turn brought about a far greater degree of voluntary compliance than the Securities and Exchange Commission alone would have been able to command. Labor unions felt a similar disciplining effect when the Landrum-Griffin Act was passed. The new election laws and the professionals dealing with them have exerted a comparable influence on politics. But a higher price must be paid for effective governmental regulation of politics because politics is so dependent upon voluntary action. Corporations and labor unions can use money from their treasuries, assigning paid workers to cope with regulations and passing along the cost in higher prices or lower stockholder yields or increased dues. In politics, however, money is a scarce resource. Candidates, parties, and political committees cannot as readily pay salaries to ensure compliance, nor can they pass along the cost. As they allocate financial resources to compliance, their campaigning capability is reduced and financial pressures grow. Moreover, when expenditure limits are in effect, compliance costs increase, although in federal election campaigns, compliance costs are exempted from the statutory limits on campaign spending. Of course, public funding works to relieve some major financial pressures, but at the same time it causes new pressures because it imposes additional compliance requirements.

The role of fund raisers has changed. For example, the election reforms have placed a premium on those who, no longer able to give $50,000 themselves, can attract from among their social contacts, business associates, and political acquaintances fifty donors of $1,000 each. Focus also is shifting to fund raisers who can organize and solicit membership groups or tap into existing networks or persons.

In addition, the reform laws of the 1970s led to an institutionalization of the special-interest influence the laws sought to eliminate. Following the 1974 FECA amendments, the key role of the large donor was replaced by that of the effective fund raiser. No longer could someone like W. Clement Stone contribute millions of dollars or a Stewart R. Mott hundreds of thousands, so candidates were forced to broaden their financial bases. Persons who had access to networks of contributors from other campaigns or who possessed mailing lists that might yield potential donors became critically important because they could raise big money in smaller sums. But elite solicitors who can bring in large amounts of money are few, and direct-mail solicitation of campaign funds is expensive and not feasible for most candidates. Further, the number of fund-raising events—dinners, cocktail parties, breakfasts—donors will pay to come to is limited.

PACs helped to fill the void. Sponsored by corporations or unions or membership groups with political interests, these committees share characteristics essential to fund raising: access to large aggregates of like-minded people and internal means of communication. PACs began to collect numerous small contributions, aggregate them, and make contributions in larger, more-useful amounts, all at no cost to the favored candidates. In the process, corporations and membership groups of all kinds have been politicized further, establishing PACs as a supplement to lobbying activity.

The 1980 election campaigns, then, represent some significant departures from earlier practices in campaign finance and regulation, as well as confirmation of a number of trends that may be traced to previous elections. In the chapters that follow, events and data from the 1980 campaigns for federal office, particularly for the office of the presidency, are described and analyzed in an effort to illuminate the role money plays in our uniquely American system of choosing political leaders.

Note

1. For provocative views of the significance of the 1980 election results and the questions they raise, see Theodore H. White, *America in Search of Itself: The Making of the President, 1957-1980* (New York: Harper and Row, 1982), especially pp. 410-433; "Face Off: A Conversation with the Presidents' Pollsters, Patrick Caddell and Richard Wirthlin," *Public Opinion* (December-January 1981):7, 64; Arthur Schlesinger, Jr., "The End of an Era?" *Wall Street Journal,* November 20, 1980; Morton Kondracke, "A Doubtful New Order," *New Republic,* November 15, 1980, pp. 11-13.

2 The Course of Election Reform

After decades of relative inattention, political campaign reform came into its own in the first half of the 1970s. Under pressure from reformers upset by what they perceived as years of neglect and dissatisfied with what they considered an antiquated system of political finance, Congress in 1971 passed two far-reaching measures designed to open campaign financing to public scrutiny and to encourage political giving from a broader constituency. The FECA of 1971 required fuller disclosure of political campaign contributions than ever before, and the Revenue Act of 1971 provided tax incentives for political contributions and enacted a tax checkoff to subsidize presidential general-election campaigns.

In 1974, spurred by campaign-finance abuses revealed in the course of investigations surrounding the Watergate break-in and its aftermath, Congress strengthened the law through enactment of a series of amendments. The 1974 FECA amendments established a number of contribution and expenditure limits for federal candidates and political committees, made provision for government funding of presidential prenomination campaigns and national nominating conventions, and created a bipartisan Federal Election Commission (FEC) to administer election laws.

The amended law, however, quickly created a controversy that led to court-mandated efforts to temper the new election code. A lawsuit—*Buckley* v. *Valeo*—challenging the constitutionality of the major provisions of the FECA, as well as the existence of the FEC, resulted in a 1976 Supreme Court decision overturning expenditure limitations except in publicly funded campaigns, protecting independent expenditures by individuals and groups, and requiring that the law be rewritten to reconstitute the FEC. The Court, however, upheld the law's individual and group contribution limits, as well as its public-disclosure and public-funding provisions. Later in 1976 Congress amended the FECA once again, in part to make the campaign law conform to the Court's ruling. The 1976 amendments reconstituted the FEC and reopened the door to the use of substantial sums of money through independent expenditures and through the activities of PACs.

Experience with the law during the 1976 and 1978 elections led to further amendments designed to eliminate some obstacles critics maintained the law posed to free and open political debate and effective political campaigning. The 1979 FECA amendments lightened the burden the law imposed on candidates and political committees by reducing reporting requirements

7

and gave greater leeway to state and local political-party committees to participate in presidential-election campaigns.

The movement to reform political finance laws began strongly early in
the 1970s but reached its high point with the post-Watergate enactment of
the 1974 FECA amendments. During the latter half of the decade, political
finance regulation was dominated by reactions to the reforms and by efforts
to relax some of the constraints they imposed on the electoral process.
Thus, over the course of the decade, the initiative passed from the reformers
and the media supporting them to the courts and to those most directly affected by the regulations: incumbents, political parties, and major interest
groups.

Events surrounding the enactment of the FECA and its 1974 and 1976
amendments have been described in earlier books.[1] This chapter picks up
where the previous book left off: with events leading to enactment of the
1979 FECA amendments and to additional efforts at campaign finance
legislation.

1979 FECA Amendments

Throughout the 1976 campaigns there was considerable discussion about
the effects of the 1974 and 1976 FECA amendments on the conduct of the
campaigns and on election outcomes. After the election, the FEC commissioned a survey that systematically questioned those directly affected and
regulated by the FECA: the candidates who ran for the Senate and the
House in 1976 and their campaign staff. Although the survey did not yield a
consensus about the act or what should be done about it, there was general
agreement among all but a handful of those regulated by the FECA that
changes of some kind should be made in the law.[2]

From 1976 through 1979, the FEC made annual recommendations to
the Senate Rules Committee regarding legislative revisions to the FECA,
many of them consistent with the recommendations made by participants in
the 1977 survey.[3] Among the commission's recommendations were proposals to simplify reporting requirements and to encourage local-party and
grass-roots political activity.

The desire for additional changes in the FECA also was expressed by the
White House. On March 22, 1977, Vice-President Walter F. Mondale,
speaking for the Carter administration, announced the most comprehensive
election-reform package a president ever submitted to Congress.[4] Among
the administration's election-reform proposals was one supporting extension of public funding to congressional campaigns and a series of proposals
regarding presidential campaigns based on the 1976 presidential candidates'
experience of the effects of the FECA.

Even before the president's March 22 message had been sent to Congress, action had been taken to amend the FECA. In the Senate, a bill providing public funds for senatorial primary and general elections was introduced by a bipartisan coalition of senators. In June the Senate Rules Committee reported a revised version of the bill, with public financing of primary campaigns deleted to reduce costs and make the legislation more acceptable to the House.[5] The bill also contained many amendments to the FECA. When the bill came to the Senate floor, opponents launched a successful filibuster that led the Democratic leadership to drop the public-funding provisions from the bill. The amendments to the FECA, which remained, were passed by a vote of eighty-eight to one, but they never were acted on by the House.

Institute of Politics Study

In August 1978 the House Administration Committee commissioned Harvard University's Institute of Politics to study and report on the impact of the FECA and its amendments. The study, the first congressionally commissioned review of the laws, took nearly a year to complete. It concluded that the FECA and its amendments had brought about major, long-overdue changes in the funding of congressional-election campaigns.[6] According to the research report, "The overall impact of the act has added to the honesty and efficiency of the political system."[7] Nevertheless, the researchers found that the laws had had a number of unintended consequences. The study sought to identify problems in funding election politics that either were caused by the laws or remained in spite of them and to suggest a number of legislative remedies.

The study report singled out three problems caused by the implementation of the act and its amendments: the individual contribution limits were set too low; a further weakening of political parties resulted; and the laws imposed burdensome reporting requirements on election campaigns.

According to the study report, since candidates have been unable to raise sufficient funds due to the FECA's individual contribution limits, they have had to seek campaign funds from other sources, particularly from PACs and, in the case of wealthy candidates, from their own assets. The study group's analysis indicated that contributions to House candidates from PACs increased from 14 percent of all contributions in 1972 to more than 25 percent in 1978. In addition, although complete figures were not available, the analysis indicated a significant increase in the amounts candidates loaned or contributed to their own campaigns. It appeared to the researchers, then, that although the contribution limits were intended to curtail the influence of special-interest groups, they actually served to increase that influence. The researchers also concluded that the laws gave an unfair advantage to wealthy candidates whose personal funds could help them finance their own campaigns.

The study group found that legal restrictions on the amount political-party committees can contribute to candidates, as well as the laws' regulations and burdensome reporting requirements, served to discourage many local-party committees from contributing to senatorial or congressional campaigns. In addition, the laws' expenditure limits prevented those committees from helping their parties' presidential candidates. According to the study group's analysis, 17 percent of the money available to House candidates in 1972 came through their political parties. Only about 4.5 percent came from that source in 1978.

Finally, the study group found that the threshold above which both contributions and expenditures had to be disclosed under the law increased the cost of campaigning without providing a corresponding benefit to the public. The group found that the laws' compliance and reporting requirements imposed a particularly heavy burden on smaller campaigns and committees.

In order to alleviate the problems it cited, the study group recommended numerous legislative changes. Foremost, it believed that the individual contribution ceiling should be raised from $1,000 to $3,000. This change would help provide funds for candidates during the early phases of their campaigns, thus facilitating political dialogue, which would be particularly beneficial to unknown candidates who require an early start in campaigning. A higher contribution ceiling also would lessen the pressures on candidates to seek contributions from PACs and other organized interest groups. Furthermore, it would allow candidates to give less time to fund raising and more time to political campaigning.

The study group recommended that the role of political parties be augmented in order to take into account "the special position of parties within the electoral process."[8] National- and state-party committees should be allowed to contribute more to congressional and senatorial candidates than nonparty committees, concluded the study, and state- and local-party committees should be allowed to spend up to $5,000 and $2,000, respectively, in behalf of federal candidates without having to report these contributions and expenditures to the FEC.

Finally, the group recommended reducing the volume of reports candidates and committees would have to file, and the FEC would have to process, by raising the threshold for itemized reporting of contributions and expenditures from $100 to $500. Additionally, it was recommended that the FEC establish a computer data-transmission system for filing reports and that candidates be allowed to designate banks or accounting firms as their campaigns' official reporting agencies. Finally, the study group concluded that a four-year term for an FEC chairperson to be appointed by the president would provide greater consistency and efficiency in the administration of the commission.

The study group considered the wisdom of enacting lower contribution limits on PACs in order to diminish "the growing torrent of money channeled through political action committees."[9] But it rejected that proposal for several reasons. According to the study group report, campaign funds should be expanded, not limited further. In addition, the report went on, lowering the contribution limits probably would lead to proliferation of PACs and "further diffusion of accountability within the electoral process."[10] Finally, according to the study group, such a legislative change also probably would lead to coordinated giving by like-minded PACs, as well as an increase in independent expenditures in behalf of candidates.

The Harvard study was intended to provide the House Administration Committee with information and suggestions for a reform of the federal election camapaign laws. Soon after the study was released, however, it became apparent that not all of the study group's suggestions would be acted upon by the House committee. Robert Moss, the committee's chief counsel, said the committee would put off any attempt to change the contribution ceilings.[11] According to Moss, Republicans and Democrats in both houses felt that any consideration of that change would produce a "cat and dog" fight that could impair the possibility of any other changes being made.

One criticism of the Harvard study came from Common Cause, which had been instrumental in reform efforts. According to the lobby's vice-president, Fred Wertheimer, the Harvard study group had "one [hand] tied behind its back" when it considered legislative remedies for the problems it cited.[12] Wertheimer maintained the Harvard Study Group had been "explicitly barred" by the House Administration Committee from proposing public financing to remedy any problems it found in the financing of congressional elections.[13] He reaffirmed Common Cause's support for partial public financing of congressional races and said such a move should be accompanied by a "substantial reduction in the amount PACs can contribute" to congressional campaigns.[14]

Congressional Action

Although not all of the recommendations made by the study group were acceptable to Senate and House members for immediate action, several of its recommendations were influential in mid-1979, when the matter of revising the FECA was taken up by the Senate Rules Committee and the House Administration Committee. On July 26, the Senate committee approved a draft of amendments intended to ease candidate and political-committee reporting requirements, give political parties an expanded role in federal elections, and change other procedural matters.

On August 1, the House Administration Committee approved its own draft of amendments, which not only included many of the provisions of the Senate committee draft but also made important changes in FEC enforcement procedures. The House bill, HR 5010, was intended to propose only noncontroversial changes in the law; all twenty-five members of the House Administration Committee were listed as cosponsors.

Since neither bill was tied to proposals for public financing or proposals to make controversial changes in the roles of interest groups, political parties, or PACs, sponsors were certain the bills would be quickly approved. And since the differences between the Senate and House versions appeared to be relatively minor, proponents of additional changes in the political finance law were confident that amendments to the FECA would be enacted by the end of the session.

In order to hasten the passage of HR 5010, House Administration Committee chairman Frank Thompson (D-N.J.) brought the bill to the House floor on the suspension calendar, a device that allows noncontroversial bills to be passed quickly without amendment, provided they receive a two-thirds vote. On September 10, by a voice vote, the House passed HR 5010.

Once HR 5010 had passed the House, the Senate had the choice of continuing work on its own bill amending the FECA (S 1757) or taking up the House bill. Passage of the Senate bill would have required a House-Senate conference to resolve the differences between the two versions. To avoid the delay separate consideration of the Senate bill and the subsequent conference would have caused, the Senate Rules Committee decided to introduce the House bill in the Senate. Although the two bills were similar, there were enough significant differences to indicate that the Senate would seek to amend the House proposal.

Three matters were of particular concern to Senate members: Senate support for a proposal to ensure that the FEC's Clearinghouse Division retain an election administration role rather than be restricted to matters of political finance and disclosure, as proposed in HR 5010; support for retaining for the FEC the power to conduct random audits of campaigns, a power not included in the House bill; and Senate opposition to the conversion of excess campaign contributions to personal use by the candidates. The last was a particularly sensitive issue. House rules prohibited sitting members from converting campaign funds to personal use. Retired House members, however, or candidates who never won elections were allowed to make personal use of excess campaign funds. Senate rules prohibited personal use of campaign contributions by both sitting and retired members. Since legislative redistricting would take place after the 1980 census, it was presumed that more incumbents than usual would be defeated. Some congressional incumbents apparently looked forward to the excess campaign contributions to cushion their possible defeat. Thus no provision to exclude the personal use of such funds had been included in the House bill.

Senate Version: To hasten the passage of the new FECA amendments, the Senate Rules Committee consulted with the House Administration Committee on compromise amendments to HR 5010 that would be acceptable to the House. Initially the process of consultation appeared to proceed smoothly. On October 17, however, the House passed a controversial bill, HR 4970, that placed a ceiling on PAC contributions to House candidates and on the total amount a House candidate could receive from PACs in a two-year election cycle. Although the bill would not directly affect members of the Senate, many Republican senators saw it as a threat to future GOP congressional strength. All work on HR 5010 came to a halt as opponents of HR 4970 focused their efforts on preventing Senate approval of that bill. By November 1979, it was clear that the Senate would not act upon HR 4970 until 1980. Once the bill was sidetracked, the Senate once again took up the process of amending HR 5010 in consultation with the bill's principal cosponsors.

By early December it was reported that the Senate Rules Committee and the House Administration Committee had reached agreement on all but two matters: the personal use of excess campaign funds and amending the criminal code to allow receipt of unsolicited campaign contributions by mail on federal property providing the money is delivered to the appropriate campaign committee within seven days.[15] By mid-December, however, a compromise had been reached on those issues too.

On December 18, the Senate approved HR 5010 with a number of amendments worked out with the House leadership.[16] On December 20, the Senate's amended version of HR 5010 passed the House without objection, becoming the FECA amendments of 1979.[17] According to Rep. William Frenzel (R-Minn.), the changes included in the amendments would "simplify and make life easier for candidates, for the parties, for volunteers, and for everybody."[18]

New FECA Provisions: The most-significant changes in the FECA enacted by the 1979 amendments dealt with reporting requirements, the power and activities of the FEC, and the activities of political-party committees. The 1979 act:

1. Raised the reporting threshold for contributions and expenditures from over $100 to over $200 and for independent expenditures from $100 to $250.

2. Reduced the maximum number of reports to be filed by a member of the House from twenty-four to nine during a two-year election cycle and by a member of the Senate from twenty-eight to seventeen during a six-year election cycle.

3. Changed the preelection filing date from twenty to twelve days before an election.

4. Exempted candidates who do not receive or spend more than $5,000 from filing disclosure reports.

5. Permitted political committees to include on each disclosure report ten fictitious names, provided the committees submit to the FEC a separate list of those names that would not be made public. (This device is intended to allow the committees to determine if their donors are being solicited by other committees, an action that would violate the law.)

6. Allowed audits of any political committee but only when there is indication of significant violations.

7. Allowed any person to request an advisory opinion from the FEC ''with respect to a specific transaction or activity by the person.''[19]

8. Imposed a sixty-day time limit within which the FEC must answer requests for advisory opinions and reduced the time limit to twenty days after receipt of a written request if a candidate makes such a request within sixty days prior to an election.

9. Required the FEC to notify any person accused of a violation within five days after receipt of the complaint and to allow the accused fifteen days within which to respond in writing.

10. If the FEC determines that there is reason to believe a violation has occurred, it is required to notify the accused and to ''set forth the factual basis for such alleged violation.''[20] Only then may an investigation begin.

11. Exempted local political-party committees from registering with or reporting to the FEC if they do not receive more than $5,000 in contributions during a calendar year; if, in a calendar year, they do not make more than $1,000 in contributions or expenditures in connection with a federal election; or if they do not spend more than $5,000 for activities, such as certain voter-registration activities, exempted by the 1979 act from the definition of expenditure.

12. Allowed state and local political-party committees to pay for voter registration or get-out-the-vote activities provided such activities are primarily on behalf of the party's presidential nominee.

13. Allowed state- and local-party committees to purchase, without limit, certain campaign materials, such as buttons, pins, and stickers, for use in volunteer activities, and permitted the purchase of such materials to be used in volunteer activities in behalf of any federal candidate provided the funds used did not come from contributions designated for a particular candidate.

14. Increased the amount that volunteers can spend on travel and home entertainment in behalf of a candidate without reporting it from $500 to $1,000, and in behalf of a political party from $1,000 to $2,000.
15. Prohibited the conversion of excess campaign funds to personal use by anyone except a current member of Congress. (Since Senate rule 46 prohibiting senators and former senators from converting campaign funds to personal use remained in force, this provision applied only to House incumbents.)
16. Required that a candidate's principal campaign committee contain his or her name.
17. Increased from $2 million to $3 million the amount each major political party would receive from the presidential income tax checkoff fund to finance its presidential nominating conventions.
18. Amended the Criminal Code so that the prohibition against soliciting campaign contributions on federal property not apply when unsolicited contributions are received on federal property by persons on the staff of a senator or representative provided those contributions are transferred within seven days to the officeholder's authorized campaign committee.
19. Continued the ban on solicitation of campaign contributions by congressional candidates, members of Congress, and federal employees from any other such officer, employee, or person, but amended the existing law to permit federal employees to make voluntary contributions to federal officials other than their own employers.

Presidential Signature: On January 8, 1980, President Carter signed HR 5010 into law.[21] Upon signing, he said that the new law improved the FECA because it eliminated burdensome regulation of candidates and political committees and increased the opportunity for grass-roots political participation. But the president expressed strong objections to the provision in the bill that allowed federal employees to make campaign contributions to federal officials as long as they did not contribute to their immediate employers. He called the provision a "severe infringement of Federal employees' First Amendment rights" and noted that the attorney general had advised him that it raised "grave constitutional concerns."[22]

The letter of the law prior to enactment of HR 5010 actually prohibited any campaign contributions from one federal employee to another. Justice Department advisory letters in 1974 and 1977, however, suggested that if such contributions were voluntary, they were not prosecutable offenses.

The president was concerned that the language of the provision he objected to might prohibit a large number of federal employees from contributing to his reelection campaign. Reps. Thompson and Frenzel and Sens. Claiborn Pell and Mark Hatfield, however, sent letters to the president assuring him that the provision in question was intended to be interpreted narrowly. It would, they said, prohibit only employees of the White House Office from contributing to an incumbent president's reelection campaign. They told the president that legislation to clarify the provision to that effect would be introduced. Given that assurance, President Carter signed the FECA amendments of 1979 into law; they became effective on January 8, 1980. Despite congressional assurances, however, both the Senate and the House were slow to make the alterations promised, and President Carter's primary campaign reportedly suffered the consequences. In the last half of 1979, Carter's primary-campaign committee received more than $70,000 from members of the White House staff, cabinet officers, ambassadors, and other federal employees.[23] Checks from White House aides and other public employees that arrived after the effective date of the 1979 FECA amendments, however, were either returned to the contributors or placed in escrow by the campaign committee. By late October 1980, long after the primary campaigns had been completed, the Senate and the House had each enacted legislation to clarify the law, but the legislation still had to be considered by a conference committee.[24]

Congressional Public Financing

Since it was first considered by the Senate in July 1973, the issue of public financing of congressional campaigns has been debated and defeated in Congress several times, most recently in the House in 1979.[25] Although advocates of congressional public financing have laid claim to considerable popular support for the proposal, the results of public-opinion polls on the matter have been mixed at best. For example, in a major national poll in 1977, pollster Louis Harris told respondents that President Carter had proposed that all House and Senate primary- and general-election campaigns be "publicly financed, as presidential primaries and elections are now financed."[26] When asked their opinions of this proposal, the respondents overwhelmingly supported the idea, with 49 percent in favor and 28 percent opposed. In 1977 and 1979 Gallup polls arrived at similar findings. The Gallup Poll asked, "It has been suggested the government provide a fixed amount of money for the election campaigns of candidates for Congress and that all private contributions from other sources be prohibited. Do you think this is a good idea or a poor idea?"[27] In 1977, 57 percent of respondents approved of public funding of congressional campaigns and 32 percent disapproved; in 1979, 57 percent approved and 30 percent disapproved.

   The conclusion that popular support existed for public financing of congressional campaigns appeared well substantiated until Harris reworded his survey question in January 1980. This time Harris asked respondents if they would approve of having "all federal elections financed out of public funds contributed by taxpayers."[28] The respondents were overwhelmingly opposed. Only 39 percent supported public funding when the proposal was worded in this manner compared with 58 percent who disapproved. The negative response probably was generated by the phrase "contributed by taxpayers" and by considerations of fiscal restraint. Although public funds for election campaigns have always been paid out of tax dollars, the latter description may have carried a negative connotation that influenced the survey's results.

Just as emotive words may have influenced the 1980 poll results, wording may also have affected the results of the earlier surveys. The 1977 Harris poll told respondents that President Carter had endorsed the plan. Carter's popularity, which was high at the time, may have helped to increase the favorable response rate. Similarly, the Gallup polls asked the respondents if they liked a system that prohibits all private contributions. If "private contributions" had a negative connotation, that wording choice may have affected the outcome.

Civic Service Polls

The Civic Service, Inc., a St. Louis-based survey research group, has been tracking national public opinion since 1977 on assorted political issues, particularly public financing. These surveys, worded differently from the earlier Harris and Gallup polls, also produced different results. The Civic Service finding regarding public attitudes toward public financing has been one of consistent and resounding disapproval by respondents. A 1978 survey drawn from a nationwide sample found that a majority of those polled agreed that changes were needed in the electoral campaign system, but public financing of all federal elections gained the support of only 4 percent of the respondents.[29]

The results of the Civic Service polls of February 1980, March 1981, and March 1982 were not much different.[30] The benchmark question in all of the surveys also remained constant: "It has been proposed in Congress that the federal government provide public financing for congressional campaigns for the U.S. House of Representatives and Senate. Would you approve or disapprove of the proposal to use public funds, federal money, to pay the costs of congressional campaigns and how strongly do you feel?" The results of the March 1982 poll showed that 4.2 percent of respondents strongly approved of the proposal; 21.2 percent approved of it; 36.9 percent disapproved of it; 28.3 percent strongly disapproved of it; and 9.4 percent expressed no opinion.

The 1982 results conform with those of the Civic Service surveys conducted in the previous five years. Variations of approval for extending public financing to congressional campaigns were registered by 25.4 percent of the 1982 sample. Disapproval of such public financing was indicated to some degree by 65.2 percent of the respondents. Further, in the survey results throughout the period, opposition to public financing of congressional campaigns dominated every subgroup in the sample.

The 1981 and 1982 Civic Service polls also discovered that the dissatisfaction expressed by a majority of respondents at the prospect of public financing of congressional campaigns also applied to presidential-campaign public financing. By more than a two-to-one margin, respondents did not approve of the existing public-funding system for the presidential general election. Upon evaluating alternatives, the bulk of respondents favored returning to the system of private contributions. Substantial support was indicated, however, for maintaining the present campaign-contribution ceilings.

Judging from the Civic Service survey results, the American public does not appear to be in the mood for any fundamental reforms of congressional campaign finance. There is overwhelming support for the voluntary system of campaign finance in both congressional campaigns and presidential general-election campaigns. But the contradictory findings of the Harris and Gallup polls cannot be dismissed outright. Perhaps Americans are disturbed by the idea of using federal money to pay the costs of campaigns, but the Harris and Gallup polls suggest that public attitudes may be altered through the endorsement of an opinion leader or through the manner in which the proposal is made.

1979 Efforts

Despite setbacks in all of the previous efforts to enact legislation to provide public funding for congressional campaigns, several factors encouraged proponents of congressional public financing to try again in 1979. First, an effort to enact such legislation in the House in 1978 was defeated by a relatively narrow margin—213 to 196—the closest the House had ever come to enactment. Further, although final figures were not yet available, it was apparent that the amount of money spent on 1978 congressional elections far exceeded that spent in 1976. Early reports on 1978 spending not only highlighted the increase in comparison with previous congressional election years but also pointed out that a growing percentage of the money spent was raised from special-interest PACs and that candidates who outspent their opponents generally won their races.[31] Many of these spending trends reported before final figures had been tabulated later proved to be correct.[32]

Proponents of congressional public funding thought reaction against spending and the growing influence of special interests would make public financing more attractive as an alternative means of financing campaigns.

Finally, potentially influential voices continued to be heard in favor of congressional public financing. Late in 1978 and early in 1979 both Vice-President Mondale and President Carter made clear that the Carter administration was not abandoning its efforts to have public financing extended to congressional campaigns. The House Democratic Caucus also came out in support of congressional public financing, and both Common Cause and organized labor continued to advocate it.

Other factors, however, were working against enactment of public-financing legislation by the Ninty-sixth Congress. Sen. Dick Clark (D-Iowa), public funding's chief spokesman on the Senate Rules Committee, had been defeated in the November 1978 election. Although the November elections gave the Democratic leadership of the House the opportunity to replace a House Administration "no" vote on public financing with a public-financing supporter, that change would not be enough to establish a committee majority in favor of public financing, given the fifteen to ten vote against the measure in 1978. Most Republican party members remained opposed to public funding, maintaining among other things that the expenditure limits in most public-funding proposals favored incumbents—the majority of whom were Democrats—since challengers generally need to outspend incumbents in order to mount effective campaigns. A number of conservative Democrats, particularly those representing safe seats, were not interested in public-funding proposals that would encourage potential challengers. Finally, some members of Congress were reluctant to vote an appropriation that would reduce their efforts to raise money privately, fearing it would be as unpopular as voting themselves a salary increase.

HR 1: Against this backdrop, the Ninety-sixth Congress convened on January 15, 1979. Supporters of public financing of congressional election campaigns wasted no time in proposing a congressional public-funding bill, which was awarded the symbolically prestigious designation HR 1, a sign of the House leadership's interest in the measure.[33] If passed, HR 1, which had 132 cosponsors, including some Republicans, would apply only to House general-election candidates and candidates in special or runoff elections beginning in 1980. Its cost was estimated to be $25 million in each congressional election year.

According to its provisions, candidates who accepted public funding would be limited to spending $150,000 overall, plus 20 percent for fund raising and 10 percent for one mailing within the district. Candidates and members of their immediate families would be limited to contributions or loans of no more than a total of $25,000 in personal funds.

Public funding would be distributed to eligible candidates in the form of matching grants. Grants would be authorized to match individual contributions of $100 or less received by the candidate during the election year (or within ninety days before the date of a special or runoff election). Total matching-fund payments could not exceed 40 percent of the overall spending limit ($60,000), and at least 80 percent of the contributions matched would have to come from persons residing within the district.

Aggregate matching payments to all candidates in an election could not exceed three times the maximum amount payable to any candidate. (No candidate could receive more than $60,000; thus no more than $180,000 could be made in matching payments to all candidates in an election.)

The FEC would conduct random postelection audits of 10 percent of the participating candidates. Audits also could be conducted, even before the election, if four members of the FEC found reason to believe a violation of the law had occurred.

The overall spending limit of the law would be suspended if a participating candidate's nonparticipating opponent spent more than $25,000 in personal or family funds, received more than $75,000 in private contributions, and/or made more than $75,000 in expenditures. Nonparticipating candidates who exceeded those amounts would be required to notify the FEC within forty-eight hours of the time the amount was exceeded. In that case, participating candidates would be eligible for up to $60,000 more in matching funds. They also would be allowed to solicit new contributions, to be matched by federal payments, from persons who already contributed the matchable maximum of $100.

If the aggregate of independent expenditures and costs of union, membership group, or corporate political communication in an election exceeded $50,000 and the benefit of not more than one-third of this sum accrued to an eligible candidate, that candidate's overall spending limits would be waived, if the candidate so requested.

Matching funds would come from a new House of Representatives Election Campaign Account, an additional account in the Presidential Election Campaign Fund. Money for the fund would continue to come from the voluntary federal income tax checkoff. Eligible House general-election candidates would receive payments only after it had been determined that the fund contained money adequate to meet the costs of financing presidential-election campaigns.

Responsibility for coordinating efforts to enact HR 1 was assumed by the Democratic majority on the Administration Committee, to which the bill was referred, and the House Democratic Study Group. Both groups were supported by the House leadership.

Strong Opposition: Despite the initial impressive and well-organized support for HR 1, there were several indications that, as in previous years, the public-funding proposal would meet stiff opposition. The makeup of the Administration Committee itself did not appear to have changed sufficiently to ensure that a public-funding proposal would be reported out of committee. Further, a Common Cause poll of incoming members of Congress indicated that, in comparison with the Ninety-fourth and Ninety-fifth Congresses, the Ninety-sixth Congress was moving away from public financing.[34] The number of "no" votes on the issue of congressional public funding had increased steadily from 1974, while the number of "yes" votes leveled off. Finally, opponents of congressional public financing were mobilizing their own forces and making their voices heard.

S 623: Shortly before the House Administration Committee began hearings on HR 1, Sen. Edward Kennedy (D-Mass.) and seven other senators introduced a bill in the Senate that would provide for partial public financing of Senate general-election campaigns beginning in 1980.[35] Under the bill, S 623, senators who raised a threshold amount of money in private contributions and who agreed to limit their spending to $250,000 plus 10 cents per eligible voter in their states would receive federal matching payments for individual contributions of $100 or less. The threshold amount specified was equal to 10 percent of the candidate's spending limit or $100,000, whichever was lower. Contributions from outside the state exceeding 20 pecent of the total contributions would not be matched. Candidates who accepted public funding would be limited to expenditures of $35,000 in family funds. The overall spending limit would be waived if it was exceeded by an opposing candidate. Matching payments would be drawn from funds available from the voluntary tax checkoff. The maximum amount that a candidate could receive in public funds would be 50 percent of the spending limit. It was estimated that the cost of the public-funding proposal would be $18 million in Senate election years.

Administration Committee Hearings: On May 15 the House Administration Committee began hearings on HR 1. Witnesses who appeared before the committee over the course of several days included representatives of the FEC and the Treasury Department, congressmen, members of the academic community, state campaign-finance-law officials responsible for administering public-financing laws, and representatives of political parties and interest groups. Few witnesses clearly endorsed the proposed legislation. Most questioned the merits of specific provisions in the bill.

Damaging testimony against HR 1 was offered by the first witness, FEC chairperson Joan D. Aikens. Aikens estimated that the total amount of matching payments under HR 1 would range from $35 million to $44 million in each congressional-election year, considerably more than the estimates of $22 million to $30 million offered by the bill's supporters. The FEC estimates later were revised after the bases upon which they were made were called into question. Aikens also criticized the bill's procedures for certifying the eligibility of candidates for matching funds within forty-eight hours of their application as inadequate and the procedure for determining when expenditure limitations would be suspended as unworkable.

On the first day of testimony, committee member Frenzel suggested the bill had another problem. He noted that under the $180,000 ceiling imposed by the bill on the total amount of matching payments that could be made in any election, two minor-party candidates and a major-party candidate who qualified early could prevent the other major-party nominee from receiving any federal support. As drafted, HR 1 contained no provision for prorating funds in such cases; instead money would be distributed on a first-come, first-served basis.

Later in the hearings a number of congressmen criticized the public-funding bill under scrutiny. House minority leader John Rhodes (R-Ariz.) called HR 1 the "Tenure of Office Act" and said, "I can think of no measure better designed to ensure permanent tenure for Members than by discouraging challenges to them, as this legislation certainly does."[36] He maintained that the proposed bill failed to take into account the advantages of incumbents over challengers in the form of staff, allowances, subsidized mailings, and taxpayer-financed radio and television facilities. Further, according to Rhodes, by imposing uniform spending limits, HR 1 failed to recognize that the nation's 435 congressional districts "are not pieces of a homogenous whole, nor are campaign requirements and situations all identical."[37]

Criticism of HR 1 also came from a variety of sources outside Congress. John T. Dolan, chairman of the National Conservative Political Action Committee (NCPAC), recommended that the bill be scrapped even though, he told moderate Republican Bill Frenzel, it would present NCPAC and other conservative groups "with a delightful opportunity to harass you and dozens of others like you" by providing the group with the incentive—public financing—to recruit candidates to run against incumbents.[38]

Richard B. Berman, vice-president for human resources for Steak and Ale Restaurants of America, testified that "potential corruption of elected officials by a conspiracy of PACs is a hypothetical scenario that has no supporting evidence."[39] Joseph J. Fanelli, president of the Business-Industry Political Action Committee, objected to much of the criticism of PACs as an unfair and unwarranted "attempt to tar all such groups with a reputation of greed, selfishness and a disregard of the general good."[40] According to Fanelli, the average corporate PAC contribution to House candidates in 1978 was only $485.

Impact on Parties: A number of political-party officials and political scientists expressed concern that HR 1 would further diminish the influence of political parties. On behalf of the Association of State Democratic Chairpersons, Morley Winograd, association president and Michigan Democratic state party chairman, proposed that public funding be channeled to the candidates through the state-party organizations. Under his plan, the party organizations would be allowed to retain 25 percent of the public monies received to support federal-election activities such as voter registration and voter turnout. The parties would have no discretion in the distribution of funds to eligible candidates. Winograd noted that HR 1 seemed to encourage candidates to hold themselves above party, thus making them easy prey to single-interest politics. The Iowa Republican and Democratic party state chairmen both supported public financing and agreed with Winograd that the political parties should oversee the allocation of public funds, although they proposed giving greater discretion to the parties in distributing the funds. B. Allen Clutter, executive director of the Minnesota Ethical Practices Board, also favored public financing but suggested, on the basis of his state's experience, that expenditure limits set too low might discourage candidates' participation in the program. Lewis B. Thurston III, executive director of the New Jersey Election Law Enforcement Commission, proposed, on the basis of New Jersey's publicly financed 1977 gubernatorial election, that "expenditure limits are undesirable because they are unfair, unwise, unnecessary and unenforceable."[41] Finally, representatives of the Committee on Party Renewal urged that a public-financing system be adopted that provided for public funding through the parties and that allowed the parties to retain a portion of the funds to aid their general development and maintenance.

Support for Public Funding: Not all of the testimony presented to the Administration Committee criticized HR 1 or proposed alternatives. A panel of congressional supporters—Reps. Abner J. Mikva (D-Ill.), John B. Anderson, Thomas S. Foley (D-Wash.), Barber B. Conable, Jr. (R-N.Y.) and Morris Udall (D-Ariz.)—urged passage of the bill. Rep. Mikva declared, "Unless we are prepared to reverse the trend of congressional campaign spending, we will increase the spectre of government by auction, the spectre of the best government money can buy. . . . HR 1 moves us in the right direction."[42] Rep. Anderson called the current manner of financing congressional elections a "national disgrace" and maintained that HR 1 would provide challengers with "a basic floor of support," which would give them a chance at defeating incumbents.[43]

Common Cause vice-president Fred Wertheimer testified that "public financing does not mean victory for challengers nor defeat for incumbents. It simply means more competition in an arena where it has been woefully lacking."[44] He expressed the lobbying organization's belief that the partial public-financing system established by HR 1 would "enhance the role of the small individual contributor, curtail the influence of special interest groups . . . increase electoral competition [and] go a long way toward restoring the people's confidence in their government."[45] Mitchell Rofsky of Ralph Nader's Congress Watch recounted a number of episodes he said indicated that "the very organizations opposing [HR 1] operate under the assumption that campaign contributions provide leverage with their elected officials."[46] In response to those who maintained that public financing is too expensive, Rofsky said, "Either we pay a little now or we pay a lot later—through special interest legislation that benefits only the few."[47]

Supporters of HR 1 also were encouraged by developments regarding the testimony given before the Administration Committee by Joan Aikens. After it was discovered that the bases upon which the FEC estimated costs for the proposal were faulty, Aikens agreed to comply with a request by Administration Committee chairman Thompson to revise the cost estimates. On April 23, the FEC submitted its revised estimates based, according to Aikens, "upon the methodology specified by the House Administration Committee."[48] According to the new estimates, the cost of funding House candidates under HR 1 would range from $22.2 million to $29.7 million, a range in line with estimates by the bill's supporters. HR 1's backers hoped the revised estimates would help them recover from the negative publicity that the bill received from Aikens's original testimony.

Rep. Thompson also sought to counter another element of the original FEC testimony that criticized the proposed procedure for certifying the eligibility of candidates for matching funds. He requested the American Institute of Certified Public Accountants (AICPA) to evaluate HR 1's certification procedures. In a letter to Thompson, the AICPA responded: "We believe those provisions of HR 1 could be effectively administered without a large increase in permanent personnel or expenditures by the Federal Election Commission . . . if the use of normal audit sampling and test-checking procedures is acceptable rather than the verification of every transaction in every campaign."[49] The AICPA letter added, "We would urge the Congress to accept techniques, in wide use today, that rely upon sampling and test-checking to provide a reasonably reliable result. Any alternative is just too costly."[50] Thompson made the contents of the AICPA letter known to the Administration Committee members before the committee hearings on HR 1 had concluded.

Once the hearings were completed, the bill's backers began revising the proposed legislation to win additional support. The process of revising the measure focused on raising the eligibility threshold for participating candidates and on bypassing the frequently criticized FEC by transferring control for the certification process to the state parties or to state secretaries of state or independent boards responsible for state election administration.

During markup of HR 1, which took place between May 15 and May 24, a variety of amendments were made in an effort to accommodate criticisms of the bill. The eligibility threshold was raised to $10,000, although some Republicans argued that the new figure was too high and discriminated against challengers. The amount of individual contributions that could be matched was raised from $100 to $150, to make it easier for challengers because fewer contributors would be required. Secretaries of state or independent state-election commissions were to be given $6,000 per district to distribute the matching payments and to pay certified public accountants to certify the eligibility of candidates for the payments. This procedure bypassed the FEC in an effort to win support of members critical of the commission.

Committee Vote: Despite passage of amendments to make HR 1 more palatable to critics, the closeness and the makeup of the votes on those amendments as well as on some that were defeated indicated that proponents had been unable to construct a majority in favor of the bill. Supporters claimed they had commitments from twelve of the committee's Democrats but were unable to find the needed thirteenth vote on the twenty-five-member committee to report the bill out.[51] When their inability to garner the support they needed became apparent, they released several Democrats who had agreed to vote for the bill if their support would make a difference. On May 24 the Administration Committee voted seventeen to eight not to report HR 1 to the House floor. All nine Republicans on the committee opposed the bill. After the vote Rep. Thompson said, "In my judgment, it is probably dead for this Congress."[52]

Despite the setback in the Administration Committee, supporters of HR 1 still hoped their bill would be able to reach the House floor. Sponsors, led by Reps. John Anderson and Morris Udall, announced they would ask the House Rules Committee to allow the amended version of the bill to be offered on the floor as an amendment to campaign finance-related legislation. Speaker Thomas P. O'Neill and Rules Committee chairman Richard Bolling (D-Mo.), however, were not keen on the idea. O'Neill said his supporting such a move would be a "bad precedent" but noted he would not object if the Rules Committee took action on its own.[53]

Shortly after the Administration Committee vote against reporting out HR 1, majority whip John Brademas (D-Ind.) conducted a poll of all House

Democrats to determine whether the House leadership should send a request to the Rules Committee to report the public-funding legislation to the floor. The count indicated that public funding did not have enough support, and Speaker O'Neill said he would not pursue the matter. In the meantime, the Senate Rules Committee postponed indefinitely hearings on S 623. According to Senate aides, there would be no Senate action on public financing unless it was evident the House was ready to approve the legislation. After the House leadership's decision to shelve HR 1, it was apparent that action on public financing would not take place in either house. Some proponents of revising spending laws then turned their attention to a related matter: limiting the contributions of PACs to House candidates.

Limits on PACs

A major purpose of the supporters of HR 1 was to reduce reliance of House candidates on contributions from perceived special-interest groups. Since it had become apparent that efforts to extend public financing to congressional campaigns had reached an impasse, opponents of the growing influence of interest-group PACs chose another approach to curbing that influence. On July 26, 1979, a bipartisan coalition led by Reps. David R. Obey (D-Wis.) and Tom Railsback (R-Ill.) filed a bill that would reduce the amount of money PACs could give candidates for the House of Representatives and would impose a ceiling on the total funds House candidates could receive from PACs.

The Obey-Railsback Bill

As introduced, the Campaign Contribution Reform Act of 1979, also known as HR 4970 or the Obey-Railsback bill, would reduce the maximum PAC contribution to a House candidate from $5,000 to $2,500 per election (primary, runoff, or general election), impose a $50,000 ceiling on contributions that a House candidate could receive in a two-year election cycle from all PACs, and prohibit PACs, media advertising, or direct-mail fundraising consultants from extending to House candidates credit in excess of $1,000 for more than thirty days.

In a letter to their colleagues explaining their proposed legislation, Congressmen Obey and Railsback acknowledged the legitimate role played by PACs. But that role, they said, had to be kept in balance "to preserve the integrity of the Congressional process."[54] The Congressmen expressed their concern that unless some limits were imposed on the size and numbers of PAC contributions, "special interests would soon dominate the legislative process."[55]

Although the Carter administration did not take part in the debate on the Obey-Railsback bill, the proposed legislation did elicit strong responses from legislators and other interested parties. Support for the bill was coordinated by the Democratic Study Group (DSG), an organization of House liberals chaired by Rep. Obey that had played a major role in support of HR 1. Much of the data on PAC contributions and influence gathered by the DSG and other supporters of that bill were refined and used in the campaign in favor of HR 4970. Obey-Railsback also attracted more than twenty Republican cosponsors, as well as the support of the AFL-CIO and reform advocates including Common Cause.

Among opponents of HR 4970 was the Republican Policy Committee, which maintained that the bill "restricts full participation in our election process."[56] According to a policy committee statement, the Obey-Railsback bill left candidates "no defense against rich competitors," raised the cost of political fund raising, and penalized challengers, who customarily have to spend heavily to gain identity equal to incumbents.[57]

Also opposing HR 4970 were many organizations that interpreted the emergence of PACs as a positive development in American politics, including the National Association of Manufacturers, the American Medical Association, and the Business-Industry Political Action Committee. *Public Affairs Report*, a publication of the U.S. Chamber of Commerce, noted that of the $199.4 million given to all House and Senate candidates in 1978, PAC contributions represented only 16 percent and corporate PAC contributions only 4 percent of the total.[58] The publication observed that opponents of HR 4970 cited those figures when asking whether any significant degree of influence or access could be obtained "with only 16 percent of the contributions candidates receive."[59]

Legislative Action

As with any other controversial legislation, a good deal of scrimmaging took place among supporters and opponents. In an effort to gain more support for the bill and to hold on to wavering supporters, the bill's sponsors agreed to make a number of changes in the original bill. The changes raised the amount a PAC could contribute to a House candidate from $2,500 to $3,000 per election and increased the total amount a House candidate could receive from all PACs from $50,000 to $70,000 per election cycle. The sponsors agreed to increase the time limit for the extension of credit to a House candidate by a consultant or vendor for mass-media political advertising from thirty to sixty days and to drop the original $1,000 limit. The changes agreed to, however, prohibited any extension of credit by a supplier of direct-mail services. Finally, the sponsors consented to add a requirement that House candidates use no more than $35,000 from political contributions to repay themselves for personal expenditures in their campaigns.

In addition, realizing that the House Administration Committee had failed to report out many pieces of campaign legislation in the past, sponsors of HR 4970 sought a waiver from the House Rules Committee that would allow them to bypass the Administration Committee and bring the bill up on the floor as a nongermane amendment to the FEC appropriations bill (S 832). On September 19, the Rules Committee voted to permit the bill to be offered directly on the floor.

Opposition to the Bill: Opponents of the bill stepped up their opposition both within and outside the House. Rep. Bill Frenzel, one of the bill's most vocal critics, wrote that PACs had "encouraged and expanded political participation by the public."[60] Frenzel listed a number of negative effects he was convinced the proposed legislation would have, including discriminating against Republicans. Frenzel explained that fourteen of the sixteen Republican challengers who defeated incumbent Democrats in 1978 received more contributions from PACs than would be allowed under HR 4970. He suggested that under the Obey-Railsback bill, many of those Republicans may not have won.

Within the House, opponents made moves that appeared to threaten the bill's future. In late September, Obey-Railsback supporters maintained they had enough votes to pass the bill, scheduled for consideration at the end of the week of September 24. Events on the House floor, however, upset that schedule. A week earlier, House members had defeated the budget bill for fiscal 1980, which began on October 1. Since the Columbus Day recess was fast approaching, it was imperative that the budget resolution be passed to avoid disruption of the budget process. On the morning of September 27, Rep. Mendel J. Davis, a long-time opponent of public financing, told House Budget Committee chairman Robert N. Giaimo (D-Conn.) that a postponement of consideration of HR 4970 until after the recess would gain eleven votes for the budget bill. Giaimo took the Davis proposal to House Speaker O'Neill, who promptly agreed. The budget bill passed 212 to 206.

Obey-Railsback's supporters, predictably, were concerned. Davis's action, said Obey in a press statement, amounted to "legislative blackmail."[61] It was, he said, a desperate attempt by PAC supporters to gain additional time "to pressure and arm-twist members" into reneging on their commitment to the bill.[62]

The cosponsors' concern about lobbying against the bill during the recess proved justified, but their pessimism regarding the bill's chances proved unnecessary. After two weeks of intense lobbying on both sides, the House reconvened on October 9, and on October 17, HR 4970 came to the floor for a vote. Floor debate was long—the better part of the six hours devoted to the FEC authorization bill—and often heated. In the end supporters of the bill prevailed. The vote to adopt HR 4970 was 217 to 198, with 29 Republicans joining 188 Democrats in favor and 74 Democrats and 124 Republicans opposed. Among the bill's supporters were 22 incumbents who had each received more than $70,000 in contributions from PACs.[63]

Senate Consideration: Although Obey-Railsback applied only to House elections, it required Senate approval. Customarily such approval would be a routine matter. If the Senate voted in favor of Obey-Railsback, however, pressure certainly would build up for passage of similar legislation applying to campaigns in the Senate. Alternatively, if the Senate permitted the House bill to become law but failed to enact legislation applicable to itself, campaigns for the two Houses of Congress would be conducted under different rules.

Immediately after the bill's passage in the House, many Republicans who interpreted the bill as a threat to future GOP congressional strength redoubled their opposition to it. House opponents of the bill as well as a number of PACs asked senators to refer the bill to committee, hoping that it would be amended or killed. As an alternative, opponents urged senators to filibuster efforts to send the bill to a House-Senate conference or efforts to seek its passage on the Senate floor. The interest groups that opposed action in the House regrouped to assist a filibuster if one developed. They saw the passage of the bill as an opening wedge to advance the cause of congressional public financing, because inflation and rising campaign costs would continue to create demand for alternative sources of funds.

The DSG leadership wrote to all Democratic senators soliciting their support. The DSG also asked those House members who had supported HR 4970 to discuss the proposal with their senators and, in particular, to emphasize that it had nothing to do with the Senate. Rep. Railsback and other Republican House members who supported the proposal wrote to Republican senators asking for help.

For a time it appeared that one of the casualties in the battle over Obey-Railsback would be HR 5010, the noncontroversial reform bill amending the FECA that had passed the House on September 10. Once Obey-Railsback passed the House, work on HR 5010 in the Senate came to a halt as attention was directed at the controversial measure.

By November 1979, it became clear that Obey-Railsback would not be acted upon by the Senate until 1980. Backers of the bill expected a long, drawn-out fight on the Senate floor. Since several major items remained on the 1979 agenda, backers preferred to hold off on the bill until the next session. Opponents of the bill expressed confidence that it would be killed in the Senate Rules Committee or by filibuster on the Senate floor. Sens. Gordon Humphrey (R-N.H.), Mark Hatfield, and Paul Laxalt (R-Nev.) were in the forefront of opposition to the bill. Sen. Humphrey counted thirty-three to thirty-five Republicans who would join in a filibuster if the House proposal made it out of the Rules Committee.[64] Senate minority leader Howard Baker declared, "If it comes up, there will be a filibuster," and added that if that happened he would be in the forefront.[65]

Once the controversial Obey-Railsback bill was sidetracked, Senate attention was returned to HR 5010. The Senate, in consultation with the bill's principal House sponsors, added a number of amendments. On December 18 the bill passed the Senate, and on December 20 the Senate's amended version passed the House without objection. It was signed into law by President Carter on January 8, 1980. Meanwhile, the Obey-Railsback bill remained stalled, and with it the hopes of its supporters to curtail perceived PAC influence in congressional-election campaigns.

In 1981 and 1982 several proposals similar to the Obey-Railsback bill were introduced in the Ninety-seventh Congress, including a proposal by Senate minority leader Robert Byrd of West Virginia, which differed only slightly from HR 5010, as well as an additional proposal by Rep. Obey. The new Congress, however, was decidedly more conservative than the previous one and did not look favorably either on restrictive legislation regarding PACs or on new spending programs. Nevertheless Democratic gains in the House in the 1982 midterm elections suggested there might well be further efforts to curb PACs through legislation restricting the amount of money candidates may accept from them.

Miscellaneous Election-Law Proposals

A number of legislative proposals were offered during the Ninety-seventh Congress that would have a far-reaching effect on the FECA and the FEC. In addition several other proposals were offered that would alter the FECA's contribution-limit provisions, extend its disclosure provisions, restrict the political use of union dues money, make tax-code provisions more favorable to candidate campaign committees, and change elements of the presidential selection process. Of those proposals, only a proposal cosponsored by Sens. Robert Packwood (R-Ore.) and Wendell Ford (D-Ky.) to lower the tax rate on the earnings campaign committees derive from investments was successful. The Packwood-Ford legislation, an amendment to the Economic Recovery Act of 1981, establishes a sliding scale for tax rates on campaign committees that matches the new progressive corporate rates. Previously interest earned on campaign funds invested in a savings account or money-market fund had been taxed at the top corporate rate of forty-six cents out of every dollar. The new rates appear to be most beneficial to senatorial incumbents preparing for reelection, since incumbents may begin effective fund raising well in advance of a reelection campaign and since Senate campaign committees are more likely to have large amounts of money deposited in bank accounts.

Another proposal offered in the Ninety-seventh Congress was of particular interest in light of the constitutional questions it raised. Sen. Robert Kasten Jr. (R-Wis.) offered a bill designed to extend the FECA's disclosure provisions to include the Communist party and any other group exempted from the disclosure requirements because of possible harassment of its contributors. In its *Buckley* decision, the Supreme Court permitted exemptions from the law's disclosure requirements for minor political parties that could demonstrate their contributors might thereby be subject to harassment by either the government or private organizations or individuals. In January 1979 the Socialist Workers party was granted such an exemption. The Communist party, USA, also claimed such an exemption when, citing the Supreme Court's ruling, it refused to comply with FEC demands that it disclose the names and addresses of the 424 contributors who had each made donations of $100 or more to its 1976 presidential campaign. Instead the Hall-Tyner Election Campaign Committee, the presidential-campaign committee for the party's 1976 presidential and vice-presidential nominees, Gus Hall and Jarvis Tyner, listed the contributors as anonymous. The FEC filed suit against the party to force disclosure of its contributors but received an adverse ruling from the U.S. District Court for the Southern District of New York in September 1981. The commission appealed, but the appeals court upheld the lower court ruling. In May 1982 Second Circuit Chief Judge Irving Kaufman ruled that the FEC's vigorous pursuit of the names and addresses of the committee's contributors exhibited "an appalling disregard for the needs of the free and open political process" guaranteed by the First Amendment.[66]

Kasten's bill would have required all campaign committees and political parties to comply with the act's disclosure provisions. In order to protect groups that fear harassment, the bill would have imposed stiff penalties against any person who "knowingly and willfully" used the disclosed information for harassment purposes.

Presidential-Campaign Financing

Throughout the 1980 presidential primary and general-election campaigns, candidates and campaign officials criticized the FECA for having a harmful effect on the conduct of the campaigns. In general the criticisms held that the act imposes burdensome accounting and reporting requirements on the campaigns and often forces candidates to make campaign decisions on the basis of accounting considerations rather than politics. Following the general election, the impact of the FECA on presidential campaigns was examined in a variety of forums, and recommendations were made for additional amendments to the election law.

Citizens' Research Foundation Conference

The first of these examinations took place only a month after the general election. On December 5, 1980, the Citizens' Research Foundation (CRF) sponsored a Presidential Finance Officers Conference in Washington, D.C. The conference brought together some thirty finance chairmen, finance directors, and treasurers of major- and minor-party and independent-candidate presidential campaigns for 1976 and 1980. Conference participants examined the contribution and expenditure limits of the FECA as they affect presidential-prenomination and general-election campaigns and developed a number of proposals recommended as worthy of prompt action.[67] The proposals that received such support were the following:

1. Raise the individual contribution limit from the current $1,000 per candidate per election and repeal the $25,000 calendar-year limit on aggregate contributions made by an individual. If the individual contribution limit is indexed to take account of rising costs and the decreased buying power of the dollar, the formula should provide for rounding off the indexed limit to the nearest $500 amount.
2. Eliminate the prohibition on private contributions to the campaign committees of presidential candidates in the general-election period in order to increase citizen participation in the general-election process and discourage potentially harmful independent expenditures on behalf of presidential candidates.
3. Retain existing provisions for matching funds for presidential candidates in the prenomination period.
4. Maintain an overall spending limit for candidates in the presidential-prenomination period but replace the current method of indexing the expenditure limit according to rises in the consumer price index by a method that would better reflect increases in those items that relate specifically to campaign costs, such as television costs, air travel, and mailings.
5. Eliminate individual state expenditure limits but continue to require of candidates full and timely disclosure of expenditures on a state-by-state basis.
6. Remove from federal regulations governing independent expenditures any presumption of coordination between candidates and their campaign committees and those making independent expenditures.

Several other proposals did not receive the same level of support as those recommended for prompt action but nevertheless were noted by the conference participants as worthy of further consideration because of the concerns they raised about federal-election law:

1. Eliminate contribution and expenditure limits as well as public funding for presidential-prenomination and general-election candidates but require full and timely disclosure of contributions and expenditures as a means of preventing political money from having an undue influence on electoral outcomes.
2. Provide federal matching funds to all independent, new-party, and minor-party candidates who reach the fund-raising threshold required of major-party candidates who want to qualify for the matching grants: $5,000 raised in amounts of $250 or less in each of twenty states. This formula would apply to minor-party and independent candidates in their general-election period.
3. Raise the individual contribution limit to independent, new-party, and minor-party candidates to twice that of major-party candidates.
4. Eliminate the limits on contributions by individuals to independent committees supporting either a single candidate or a number of candidates.
5. Eliminate the limits placed on the amounts national-, and state-, and local-party committees are allowed to spend on behalf of their presidential ticket, including spending for media, direct mail, and other forms of communication and voluntary grass-roots activity.

In April 1981 the CRF sponsored another national conference on the impact of the FECA. Unlike the December 1980 conference, the 1981 conference did not limit itself to considering the effect of the election law on presidential campaigns, nor did conference participants seek to draw up a list of recommendations for amending the FECA. Nevertheless many of the recommendations made at the earlier conference were supported by participants in the April meeting, including increasing the law's individual contribution limits and abolishing state-by-state expenditure limits.[68]

Harvard Study

In July 1981 the Senate agreed to a resolution providing up to $115,000 to pay for research into the financing of presidential election campaigns. The results of the research were to be delivered to the Senate Committee on Rules and Administration by January 1982. The Rules Committee hired the Campaign Study Group affiliated with Harvard University's Institute of Politics to conduct the research and prepare the analysis called for in the

Senate resolution. In 1979 the study group had prepared a widely circulated analysis of the FECA's impact on the electoral process for the House Administration Committee.

The study group completed its research and presented its analysis to the Senate committee in January 1982, but the study's release was delayed by nearly two months and was greeted with less enthusiasm than the Harvard group's earlier study. Although the research report found that the FECA had fulfilled many of its stated objectives, it also concluded that under the law, presidential candidates do not have enough money to conduct their campaigns effectively and that despite the law's expenditure limits, "those involved in presidential politics" had discovered means of raising and spending unlimited amounts of money in conjunction with presidential campaigns through channels outside the control of the candidates' campaign committees.[69]

Among the most important of the study group's specific recommendations were proposals to provide two-for-one matching grants to qualified candidates for the presidential nomination up to the first $5 million raised and a dollar-for-dollar match thereafter up to $15 million; eliminate prenomination-campaign state expenditure limits; raise the individual contribution limit to $5,000; provide a 100 percent income tax credit for contributions made to candidates and political parties up to a maximum of $50; index public funding to major-party nominees according to the growth of the voting-age population, as well as the cost of living; provide national-party committees with a modest level of public funding at the start of the election year to pay the costs of party-building activities; allow national-party committees to make unlimited expenditures on behalf of their nominees during the general-election campaigns; and provide two-for-one matching funds in general-election campaigns for third-party nominees and independent candidates who pass a significant threshold test and to provide block grants in advance of subsequent general-election campaigns to nominees of genuine political parties on the basis of performance in the prior election.

When the report was released on March 8, 1982, at an informal meeting of the Senate Rules Committee, ranking committee Democrat Wendell Ford of Kentucky criticized both the kind of research upon which he thought the study group relied and the research recommendations. The study, said Ford, appeared to rely largely on "opinions, impressions and recommendations" and did not sufficiently emphasize original research.[70] The Kentucky senator also maintained that some of the report's recommendations were "clearly at odds with the basic purposes of the law" and were impractical because they did not take account of the realities of political campaigning.[71] Criticism by Ford and others notwithstanding, it was clear that Congress had relatively little time to act if it wished to change the laws regulating presidential-campaign financing in time for the 1984 election campaigns.

Alleged Campaign-Related Violations

After the 1976 elections, a number of cases came to light (not resolved in time for inclusion in the previous volume) involving the possible missuse of campaign money or suspicion of financial misconduct by prominent public officials. Some of those cases involved the Carter administration; others involved senators and congressmen.

Investigations of the Carter Administration

During his term in office, President Jimmy Carter suffered political damage from lengthy, well-publicized investigations into alleged financial misconduct by his friend and political appointee Bert Lance; alleged financial misconduct and possible violation of federal campaign finance laws by himself, Lance, the president's brother Billy, and presidential media adviser Gerald Rafshoon; and alleged influence peddling by Billy Carter. Lance, who in September 1977 had been forced to resign his post as director of the Office of Management and Budget (OMB) following federal investigations of his questionable banking practices, was indicted in May 1979 for allegedly violating a series of federal banking laws.[72] He was charged with twenty-two felony counts, including conspiracy, defrauding the government, making false entries in bank records, falsifying personal financial statements, and misapplying bank funds. In April 1980, after a lengthy trial, Lance was acquitted of most of the charges against him, and the jury deadlocked on the remaining charges. The Justice Department eventually decided not to retry Lance on the charges on which the jury had not been able to reach a verdict.

The investigations of Lance's banking practices spawned separate investigations by the Securities and Exchange Commission and the Justice Department into a complex financial relationship between the National Bank of Georgia, of which Lance had served as president prior to his appointment as director of the OMB, and the Carter family peanut business. Specifically, investigators sought to determine whether loans made by Lance's bank in 1975 and 1976 to the Carter peanut warehouse—then managed by Billy Carter—had been diverted to Carter's presidential campaign, possibly with the advertising agency of Carter's media adviser, Gerald Rafshoon, serving as a conduit or cover. In time, media and opposition-party pressure led to the appointment of Paul Curran, a former U.S. attorney and a Republican, as special counsel to investigate the Carter warehouse loans. After nearly seven months of investigation, Curran concluded that although the warehouse records were disorganized and the loans were frequently out of bond, there was no evidence to

establish that Jimmy Carter had committed any crimes or that any indictment should be brought against anyone.[73]

The third case involving the Carter administration focused on Billy
Carter's dealings with the radical government of Libya, particularly on
$220,000 that the president's brother received from the Libyan govern-
ment in late 1979 and early 1980 after two Libyan-initiated visits by Billy
Carter to the North African country. Although the younger Carter insisted
the money was a loan, a Justice Department investigation sought to determine whether he had accepted the money in return for a promise to try to
influence Carter administration policy regarding Libya. Also at issue was
the wisdom of the administration's decision in November 1979 to use Billy
Carter as an intermediary with his new Libyan friends in an effort to persuade Muammar Qaddafi to intervene with Iran's Ayatollah Khomeini to
release the Americans taken hostage at the U.S. embassy in Tehran. Finally, questions were raised about whether Billy Carter benefited in the
Justice Department investigation from inside information from the White
House.

The Carter administration took extraordinary steps to defuse the controversy, including issuing a lengthy white paper on the matter in mid-July
1980 and calling an hour-long televised news conference with President
Carter in early August. Both the Senate and the House initiated investigations, and the president's brother testified before the Senate investigating
panel denying he had committed any crimes but regretting the trouble his
dealings had caused. On October 4, after eight weeks of investigation and
just four weeks before the general election, the Senate Judiciary Subcommittee investigating the Billy Carter-Libya connection issued a report concluding there was no evidence that anyone at the White House had done
anything illegal to help Billy Carter and that the Justice Depatment had conducted its investigation honestly and conscientiously.[74] The report,
however, declared that the younger Carter merited "severe criticism" for
his conduct in the matter and that President Carter should have taken steps,
publicly or privately, to make clear to the Libyan government that Billy
Carter did not represent the United States and would be unable to exercise
any influence in their favor. The report also called the decision to use Billy
Carter in the hostage crisis "ill-advised."

As with the investigations of Bert Lance's financial dealings and the
warehouse loan investigation, the precise political effect of Billy Carter's
dealings with Libya is difficult to determine. Nevertheless, the net effect of
all of the investigations, which together stretched out over most of the
Carter presidency, must be judged negative and adverse. At the very least
they called into question the president's judgment in choosing his advisers
and his competence in managing his own and his family's affairs.

Investigations of Legislators

Other investigations after the 1976 elections into alleged misuse of campaign money or violations of campaign finance laws involved two senators, Birch Bayh of Indiana and Herman Talmadge of Georgia, and two congressmen, Charles Wilson of California and Buddy Leach of Louisiana. In October 1978 the Senate Ethics Committee found that Sen. Bayh (D-Ind.) was in "neglect of his duties" for having failed to inform the committee in a written statement he had submitted a year earlier that he had been offered a substantial campaign contribution by Tongsun Park, a wealthy Korean businessman who was a central figure in efforts by Korean nationals to buy influence with elected officials of the United States government.[75] The Senate committee concluded, however, that there was insufficient evidence to establish that Bayh, who maintained he had forgotten Park's offer, had actually accepted any contribution from Park. It also found no evidence to suggest Bayh had ever acted officially at Park's bidding. In an unrelated matter, in March 1980 the Senate Select Ethics Committee ruled Bayh had violated Senate franking regulations when, in December 1979, he sent out a mass mailing to 15,000 Chrysler employees setting out his views on federal aid to the ailing automobile firm. The Senate panel made its ruling in response to a request from Bayh regarding the legality of the mailing, and accepted from the senator $2,250 that Bayh had given to the committee to cover the cost of postage in the event the mailing was found in violation of Senate rules.[76]

On September 14, 1979, after a thirteen-month investigation spawned by information uncovered by lawyers for Sen. Herman Talmadge's estranged wife during the course of divorce proceedings,[77] the Senate Ethics Committee announced its recommendation that Sen. Talmadge (D-Ga.) be "denounced" for conduct that was "reprehensible and tends to bring the Senate into dishonor and disrepute."[78] The committee concluded that Talmadge had improperly collected more than $43,000 in Senate reimbursements, including nearly $13,000 that had been placed in a secret Washington bank account. It called for Talmadge, who had repaid $37,000 of the money when the discrepancy between his actual reimbursable expenses and the reimbursements he had received became public, to repay the entire amount. It concluded that Talmadge had filed inaccurate financial-disclosure reports with the Senate from 1972 through 1977. Finally, the committee concluded that the senator had failed to report more than $10,000 in campaign contributions that had been deposited in the secret account. On October 11, the full Senate followed the Ethics Committee's recommendation, voting eighty-one to fifteen, with four members replying "present," to denounce Sen. Talmadge for financial misconduct.

Talmadge, who denied any intentional wrondoing and blamed much of his difficulties on negligence and unwise delegation of financial responsibility to his aides, was the first senator ever to be denounced and only the eighth in the history of the Senate to be disciplined for improper conduct.

In April 1980, after four months of formal investigation, the House Ethics Committee recommended that Rep. Charles Wilson (D-Calif.) be censured for financial misconduct. The committee concluded that Wilson had accepted $10,500 in gifts from a person with a direct interest in legislation before Congress and had improperly converted almost $25,000 in campaign funds to personal use. On June 10 the full House voted 308 to 97 to censure Wilson, despite an emotional address by Wilson himself protesting his innocence, and a proposal by Rep. Paul N. McCloskey (R-Calif.) that the penalty be reduced to a reprimand. Wilson became the third congressman in the century to be censured.

Finally, on November 3, 1979, Rep. Claude (Buddy) Leach (D-La.) was acquitted by a trial jury of charges of vote buying in the November 1978 general election, despite sworn testimony against him. The charges originally had been made by Leach's opponent, Republican Jimmy Wilson. On December 20, 1979, a House Administration Committee task force recommended that a challenge of the election results registered by Wilson with the House be dismissed. The following February the committee itself, by a party-line vote of 11 to 8, also recommended dismissal, maintaining that "Wilson failed to sustain his burden with [sufficient] evidence."[79] On March 4 the House upheld the Administration Committee vote by a nearly exact party-line vote of 241 to 153. House Democrats responded to Republican charges that they were trying to sweep the vote scandal under the rug by pointing out that Leach had been acquitted of general-election vote-buying charges and that the number of alleged fraudulent votes still at issue after investigations had been conducted would not account for the congressman's margin of victory.

Both senators and both congressmen sought reelection in 1980. All four were defeated, Wilson in a June 1980 primary and Bayh, Talmadge, and Leach in 1980 general elections.

Notes

1. See Herbert E. Alexander, *Financing the 1976 Election* (Washington, D.C.: Congressional Quarterly Press, 1979), pp. 11-43; and *Financing the 1972 Election* (Lexington, Mass.: Lexington Books, D.C. Heath and Co., 1976), pp. 1-38. See also Alexander, *Financing Politics: Money, Elections and Political Reform*, 2d ed. (Washington, D.C.: Congressional Quarterly Press, 1980), pp. 25-44. Summaries of the provisions of the FECA

and its 1974, 1976, and 1979 Amendments, as well as of the Revenue Act of 1971, are included as appendexes A-E to this volume.

2. For more detailed information about the FEC survey, see Alexander, *Financing the 1976 Election*, pp. 43-55.

3. See ibid., pp. 80-84; 87-88; see also "FEC Testifies on Amendments to Act," *Federal Election Commission Record*, September 1979, p. 1.

4. See Alexander, *Financing the 1976 Election*, pp. 645-646.

5. U.S. Congress, Senate, *Public Financing of Senate General Elections Act and Federal Election Campaign Act Amendments of 1977*, Report 95-300, Report of the Committee on Rules and Administration, 95th Cong., 1st sess., 1977.

6. U.S. Congress, House, House Administration Committee, *An Analysis of the Impact of the Federal Election Campaign Act, 1972-78*, from the Institute of Politics, John F. Kennedy School of Government, Harvard University (Washington, D.C.: Government Printing Office, 1979).

7. Ibid., p. 1.

8. Ibid., p. 13.

9. Ibid., p. 11.

10. Ibid.

11. Fred Barbash, "Study Faults Election Financing 'Reforms,' " *Washington Post*, July 20, 1979.

12. "CC Finds 'Hands Tied' in Harvard Study," *Common Cause Front Line* (July-August 1979):11.

13. Ibid.

14. Ibid.

15. *AICPA Washington Report*, December 10, 1979.

16. "Federal Election Campaign Act Amendments of 1979," *Congressional Record*, December 18, 1979, S19089-S19100.

17. "Federal Election Campaign Act Amendments of 1979," *Congressional Record*, December 20, 1979, H12356-H12366.

18. Ibid., H12366.

19. Ibid., H12362.

20. Ibid.

21. PL 96-187.

22. "FECA Amendments," *Congressional Quarterly Weekly Report*, January 12, 1980, p. 107.

23. Warren Weaver, Jr., "Carter's Campaign Hurt by Curb on Contributors," *New York Times*, February 24, 1980.

24. *Campaign Practices Reports*, October 27, 1980, p. 8.

25. For information about congressional efforts to enact legislation to provide public funding for congressional campaigns from 1973 through 1978, see Alexander, *Financing the 1976 Election*, pp. 654-660.

26. Louis Harris, *The Harris Survey* (New York: Tribune Company Syndicate, May 1977), p. 4.

27. George H. Gallup, *The Gallup Poll: Public Opinion 1972-1977* (Wilmington: Scholarly Resources, 1978), 2:1060-1061; and *The Gallup Poll: Public Opinion 1979* (Wilmington: Scholarly Resources, 1980), pp. 103-104.

28. Louis Harris, "Limit on Political Action Committee Campaign Contributions Favored," *ABC News-Harris Survey* (New York: Chicago Tribune-N.Y. News Syndicate, April 3, 1980), p. 2.

29. See Roy Pfautch, "Campaign Finance: The Signals from the Polls," *Public Opinion* (August-September 1980), p. 52.

30. The following is a condensation of the February 1980, March 1981, and March 1982 reports by the Civic Service, Inc., "Attitudes toward Campaign Financing" (St. Louis, Mo.: Civic Service).

31. "Candidates Spend $138 Million—So Far," *Washington Post*, November 4, 1978; Warren Weaver, Jr., "Spending on Senate Campaigns Averaged $900,000," *New York Times*, January 9, 1979; "Bigger Spenders Won 85 Pct. of Senate Contests," *Washington Post*, November 16, 1978; "Cash Big Factor in Senate Races," *Los Angeles Times,* November 16, 1978. See also FEC, news release, November 2, 1978.

32. See, for example, FEC, news release, May 10, June 29, 1979.

33. *Congressional Record*, 96th Cong., 1st sess., 1979, vol. 125, H57.

34. See "Advocates of Public Financing Optimistic, But Others Envision Many Obstacles," *Campaign Practices Reports*, January 22, 1979, p. 8.

35. *Congressional Record*, 96th Cong., 1st sess., 1979, vol. 125, S2530.

36. U.S. Congress, House, Committee on House Administration, *H.R. 1 and Related Legislation*, Hearings, 96th Cong., 1st sess., March 15, 20, 21, 22, 27, 1979, p. 243.

37. Ibid., p. 244.

38. Ibid., p. 325.

39. Ibid., p. 328.

40. Ibid., p. 351.

41. Ibid., p. 421.

42. Ibid., p. 214.

43. Ibid., p. 216.

44. Ibid., p. 292.

45. Ibid., p. 293.

46. Ibid., p. 439.

47. Ibid., p. 441.

48. Letter to the Honorable Frank Thompson, Jr., Chairman, Committee on House Administration, from Joan D. Aikens, Chairman, Federal Election Commission, April 23, 1979.

49. *H.R. 1 and Related Legislation*, Hearings, p. 356.

50. Ibid.

51. Alan Ehrenhalt, "Panel Deals Blow to Campaign Finance Bill," *Washington Star*, May 24, 1979.

52. Mary Russell, "Campaign Financing Bill Rejected by House Panel," *Washington Post*, May 25, 1979.

53. Cited by ibid.

54. Cited by Warren Weaver, Jr., "Bill Seeks Limits on Interests' Gifts in House Races," *New York Times*, July 16, 1979.

55. Ibid.

56. Cited by Mary Russell, "Democrats Push Bill to Cut Special Interest Election Gifts," *Washington Post*, September 13, 1979.

57. Ibid.

58. "Obey-Railsback Action Expected in September," *Public Affairs Report* (August 1979):1.

59. Ibid.

60. Bill Frenzel, "On the Bill Curbing Interests' Gifts," *New York Times*, September 27, 1979.

61. Cited by John M. Berry and Mary Russell, "Budget Plan Voted after Bill Tradeoff," *Washington Post*, September 28, 1979.

62. Cited by "Backers of Obey-Railsback Bill Pessimistic as House Delays Bill Until after Recess," *Campaign Practices Reports*, October 1, 1979, p. 2.

63. "New Limits on PAC Contributions Advanced," *Congressional Quarterly Weekly Report*, October 20, 1979, p. 2337.

64. "PAC Bill Dead Issue until Next Year," *Political Action Report* (November 1979):6.

65. Cited by Alan Ehrenhalt, "Senators to Fight House PAC Limits," *Washington Star*, October 26, 1979.

66. Quoted in "Appeals Court, with Rebuke to FEC, Upholds Communist Disclosure Decision," *Political Finance/Lobby Reporter*, May 19, 1982, p. 132.

67. The full Statement of Recommendations by Former Presidential Campaign Finance Officers is reprinted in Herbert E. Alexander and Brian A. Haggerty, *The Federal Election Campaign Act After a Decade of Political Reform* (Los Angeles: Citizens' Research Foundation, 1981), appendix B, pp. 131-135.

68. See ibid.

69. *Financing Presidential Campaigns: An Examination of the Ongoing Effects of the Federal Election Campaign Laws Upon the Conduct of Presidential Campaigns*, Research Report by the Campaign Finance Study Group to the Committee on Rules and Administration of the United States Senate (Cambridge, Mass.: Institute of Politics, John F. Kennedy School of Government, Harvard University, January 1982).

70. Quoted in "Finance Study Greeted on Hill with Skepticism," *Campaign Practices Reports*, March 15, 1982, p. 2.

71. Ibid.

72. For a more detailed description of the investigations and allegations leading to Lance's resignation, see Alexander, *Financing the 1976 Election*, pp. 686-699.

73. "Investigation of Carter's Warehouse and the National Bank of Georgia: Report to the Congress of the United States, Paul J. Curran, Special Counsel" (mimeo.).

74. See Nadine Cohandas, "Administration Faulted on Billy Carter Case," *Congressional Quarterly Weekly Report*, October 4, 1980, p. 2895.

75. Alan Berlow, "Senate Ethics Committee Details Evidence against Bayh and Aide Berman," *Congressional Quarterly Weekly Report*, October 28, 1978, p. 3136.

76. "Bayh Franking Violation," *Congressional Quarterly Weekly Report*, April 5, 1980, p. 912.

77. For a more detailed description of allegations against Senator Talmadge and of the course of investigations leading to Senate hearings on his alleged financial misconduct, see Alexander, *Financing the 1976 Election*, pp. 743-745.

78. Edward T. Pound, "Panel Urges Senate to 'Denounce' Talmadge on Financial Misconduct," *New York Times*, September 15, 1979.

79. Cited by "House Dismisses Challenge against the 1978 Elections of Reps. Leach and Daschle," *Congressional Quarterly Weekly Report*, March 8, 1980, p. 656.

3 The FEC and the FECA

Since beginning operations early in April 1975 as a result of the 1974 FECA amendments, the FEC has been a focus of considerable controversy.[1] It has suffered from uncertainty about its mandate, both on Capitol Hill and at times among the commissioners and staff, and consequently has been unable to achieve clarity of purpose. The agency has had to spend substantial time and resources defending itself, which has detracted from its primary responsibility of administering and enforcing the election law.

Following the 1980 elections, criticism of the FEC increased, and it became apparent, with the arrival of a new administration pledged to reduce federal regulation, that the electoral process would not escape selective deregulation. In fact, activities related to the transition period between the Carter and Reagan administrations indicate that the new administration and its supporters were seriously considering changes in the election law and its administration. Robert Visser, who had been counsel to George Bush's prenomination-campaign committee, prepared a report for the Reagan transition team on the role of the commission. The report, however, was not published. The Heritage Foundation, a conservative think tank, published a series of proposals regarding the FEC and the FECA as part of a conservative agenda meant to assist the transition to a new administration in the event that a conservative was elected president in 1980.[2] Among the recommendations for legislation were proposals to make the FEC the point of entry for filing all candidate and committee reports; to limit the commission's hearing, investigation, and enforcement authority; to limit volunteer fund-raising activities by performers and artists on behalf of candidates; to allow any group to publish candidates' voting records without FEC interference; and to increase the law's contribution limits.

The prospect of selective deregulation of the electoral process promises greater freedom of action for practitioners but also includes the possibility of new campaign abuses. The electoral process is a sensitive mechanism that requires carefully calibrated regulation. Revisions of the FECA and modifications in the manner in which it is administered and enforced may be salutary or harmful, depending upon how well and how cautiously Congress proceeds. Some change now appears certain, but the impact of reforming earlier reforms is not.

An Agency under Fire

Poised in the difficult position of regulating the regulators, the FEC has occasioned a great deal of criticism since its inception in 1975 and at times has
even been threatened with legislative extinction. Efforts to curb the FEC
have accelerated since the 1980 elections. Disgruntled members of Congress, lobbyists, and practitioners have joined in the mounting effort to
reduce the authority of the FEC, if not eliminate the agency.

Some criticism of the FEC is inevitable, for inherent in the idea of
creating an agency to regulate elections rests a philosophical dilemma: how
closely can elections be regulated in order to preserve the integrity of the
election system and still allow for free and untrammeled political exchange?
The actual criticisms leveled at the commission, however, do not address the
philosophical dilemma directly. Instead they take the form of allegations of
violations of due process by the agency in its enforcement procedures; administrative inefficiency, particularly regarding its conduct of campaign
audits; favoritism in hiring and appointment practices and in enforcement
procedures; and excessive zeal in enforcing the letter of the law. Resentment
arising from these perceived inadequacies of the agency has been expressed
in recent years by reductions in appropriations for the agency and by the in-
troduction of legislation that would alter, sometimes substantially, the
agency's mandate, or even transfer its functions to new or existing government offices.

FEC Enforcement Powers

The FECA of 1971, as amended in 1974, 1976, and 1979, vests the FEC with
its powers and designates its responsibilities as a watchdog over federal-
election campaign practices. The FEC has jurisdiction over civil enforcement of federal-campaign finance laws, including reporting and record
keeping, contribution limits, corporate and union political activities, and
public financing of presidential campaigns.

The FEC has no formal authority to act as a court of law. Like other
regulatory agencies, it cannot compel a party into a conciliation agreement,
to admit a violation, or to pay a fine. The commission can levy a fine upon a
party voluntarily participating in conciliation, or it can pursue forcible
litigation in the courts. Nonetheless, civil complaints regarding federal election finance must first be acted upon by the FEC; only later can redress and
nonvoluntary enforcement be sought through litigation.

The role of the Justice Department in pursuing violations of campaign
finance laws has been whittled away steadily. Prior to the inception of the
commission, the Department of Justice had sole authority in all such cases.

From 1975 to 1979 the FEC and the Justice Department divided jurisdiction by mutual agreement. All "serious and substantial" violations of the act were the responsibility of the Department of Justice, and the commission was left to clear up less serious civil violations.[3] The 1979 amendments, however, changed the wording of enforcement responsibilities. The commission was given "exclusive jurisdiction" over all civil matters relating to the act. The Justice Department can unilaterally pursue criminal enforcement matters or follow through on referrals from the commission. Such referrals, which usually require the commission's determination of a "knowing and willful" violation that cannot be resolved through the agency's own resources, have not been common. Only twenty-two investigations had been referred by the commission to the Justice Department prior to 1982.

For an FECA offense to be considered a criminal matter, and hence a Justice Department enforcement responsibility, there must be evidence that the would-be defendant planned on breaking the law or that the violation was made with "evil" motive. Generally such cases are confined to two situations: those in which surreptitious means, such as cash payments or false documentation, are employed to generate conduct that violates the act and/or those in which the violation takes place as a means to a felonious end. Most provisions of the act do not easily lend themselves to criminal violation. Thus the Department of Justice regularly refers reporting and organizational offenses to the commission.

Although the commission can initiate civil actions to enforce the act or refer litigation to the Justice Department, the act specifically mandates the commission to encourage voluntary compliance. The commission, wrote former FEC chairman Thomas B. Curtis, "must make every endeavor . . . to correct or prevent violation by informal methods of conference, conciliation, and persuasion, and to enter into a conciliation agreement with the person involved."[4] And in its 1975 *Annual Report*, the commission resolved that civil-enforcement action was to be used only when necessary.

When civil-enforcement action does become necessary, violation of federal-campaign laws can lead to penalties of up to $25,000 or 300 percent of the amount of campaign funds involved in the violation, whichever is greater. A study conducted by Orlando Potter, a former FEC staff director, has shown that from 1975 to 1981, the commission and the courts imposed fines for 377 violations.[5] The fines, which ranged from $100 to $75,000, totaled more than $413,000. To the credit of the commission's emphasis on conciliation, 319 of the 377 violations in which fines were levied were handled outside the courts. Nearly half of these conciliation penalties were moderate fines of less than $250, and 257 of the penalties were less than $1,000. Of the civil penalties imposed by the courts, 76 were for $1,000 or more—62 imposed through conciliation and 14 by litigation.

According to Potter, budgetary pressures have changed the patterns of civil-enforcement proceedings over the years. For the FEC, as for most other federal government agencies, 1981 marked a new era of fiscal restraint. Actual appropriations were unable to keep up with inflation, and proposed congressional reductions in the commission's budget for the following fiscal year forced it to become more selective. Before February 1981, the commission and courts levied 169 penalties of less than $250. In the remainder of that year, only five more such penalties were imposed. Most of the commission's compliance resources were directed at more-important violations.

Although Congress requires the FEC to seek conciliation whenever possible, candidates and committees may agree to conciliation for a variety of reasons. The exceptional pressures of time and publicity may make a candidate under investigation by the FEC reluctant to choose any other course. Further, fines levied by the FEC are regularly less than the anticipated costs of litigation. Finally, although the FEC does not formally adjudicate, the commission does interpret matters of law, determine matters of fact, and publicly declare violations of law. These powers cannot be easily ignored. Voluntary compliance for the FEC in actuality is much more than that: pressures of time, costs, and potentially unfavorable publicity are important factors in strengthening the clout of the agency.

Enforcement and Due Process

The constitutionality of the FEC was put to a test in the *Buckley* case. Although the U.S. Supreme Court deemed certain features of the FEC's makeup unconstitutional, it did not strike down the concept of regulating elections. Recently, however, a new constitutional challenge has emerged. Although the agency seeks voluntary compliance, the time, cost, and publicity pressures accompanying electoral activity provide the FEC with an advantage over those it is investigating. Given the actual authority of the FEC, one study suggests that the commission violates due process of law in the way it conducts investigations and handles public hearings.[6]

According to this study, there are two fundamental principles of due process: promotion of accurate determinations and avoidance of unnecessary defense costs. The study suggests that the commission violates both principles in its enforcement proceedings by withholding evidence in its investigations, providing those under investigation with insufficient opportunities to respond to the charges, failing to disclose its legal reasoning, even after closing a case, and placing an unfair burden on those under investigation to accept the FEC's terms in order to avoid further publicity and/or costs in time and money to seek vindication in the courts.

A task force of the American Bar Association (ABA) found similar problems with the FEC's enforcement procedures. Composed primarily of Washington lawyers who have been directly involved in FEC enforcement actions, the task force recommended that civil penalties for minor violations be eliminated, that the requirement for an admission of guilt in conciliation agreements also be eliminated, and that those under investigation be provided an opportunity for oral rebuttal of all charges.[7]

In response, the commission contends it is free from due-process constraints because it is not vested with the power of a court. The FEC does not formally adjudicate; its authority comes from an agreement with candidates and committees to participate in compliance proceedings as established by the agency. Furthermore, the commission says its approach is not adversarial but conciliatory; the FEC attempts to generate a mutual understanding on the nature of a mistake and to encourage its rectification.

The fact that voluntary compliance is based upon consent, however, does not necessarily mean that those involved are protected from the exercise of authority. Students of the subject claim that superior resources of money and skill, as well as familiarity with court proceedings, provide a substantial advantage to a regulatory agency. Given such resources, the power to prosecute or withhold prosecution frequently is sufficient to induce compliance. A variety of regulatory agencies wield this power to obtain "voluntary" substantive action, often without the procedural safeguards of a court. Observers point out that the due-process complaint is a challenge to the concept of voluntary compliance, questioning whether such compliance is indeed voluntary. If the enforcement powers of regulatory agencies are, in fact, judged to be coercive and if due-process constraints consequently are mandated for the enforcement proceedings of such agencies, the nature of independent regulatory agencies needs to be reconsidered. Either an agency may have to operate in a manner similar to a court of law, or its enforcement powers may have to be reduced, or both.

For reasons other than the issue of the constitutionality of FEC enforcement procedures, a far-reaching regulatory reform bill took shape in the Ninety-seventh Congress. On March 24, 1982, the Senate unanimously approved legislation that would provide the first major changes in the Administrative Procedures Act of 1946. The House version of the reform bill, which has not yet been reported out of committee, has remained distinct from the Senate bill thus far, but convergence seems likely in light of congressional disenchantment with the independent operations of regulatory agencies.

The Senate measure (S 1080), introduced by Sen. Paul Laxalt (R-Nev.), would curb the power of federal independent regulatory agencies by making them directly accountable to Congress, subjecting all major new regulations to a cost-benefit analysis under review of the president, and weakening the agencies' status in court. Accountability to Congress would be achieved by granting the power of a two-house legislative veto over most newly proposed regulations; the Senate bill preserves the current one-house Senate veto over FEC regulations. The president, presumably through the OMB, would have the authority to establish guidelines for a cost-benefit test of regulations proposed by an independent agency and to review the cost-benefit analysis within thirty days of submission.

The House bill (HR 746), sponsored by Rep. George Danielson (D-Calif.), also would require a regulatory analysis but would not require agencies to select the least-costly method. And the House measure proposes a one-house legislative veto over the regulations of all independent agencies.

The concept of a congressional veto over independent regulations currently is being reviewed by the Supreme Court and may be ruled unconstitutional. President Reagan, though supportive of the Senate bill, is opposed to the legislative veto provision and has encouraged Congress to delay passage of the regulatory reform bill until the courts have acted.

A more important provision of the Senate bill states that in court proceedings stemming from actions of a regulatory agency, judges should not accord any presumption of validity to the agency's interpretation of the law. This would have a major impact on the influence of all regulatory agencies in the courts by reversing a 1965 Supreme Court ruling granting deference to agency interpretations of law. The House bill has no similar provision.[8]

Such curbs on the enforcement powers of regulatory agencies would certainly take some of the wind out of the constitutional objections to the FEC, primarily because these limits would weaken significantly the role of the FEC in regulating the election process. These regulatory reforms, however, still would not respond to the due-process complaints voiced by the ABA task force.

Alleged Administrative Inefficiency

From its inception, the FEC administration has been faulted on a wide variety of counts—sometimes inconsistently. Frequently leveled criticisms include a lack of professionalism in auditing procedures,[9] consuming too much time in completing audits,[10] and failing to maintain the agency's investigative role.[11] At the same time, others complain that the agency enforces the law too strictly and requires costly accuracy in its reporting requirements.[12] Some believe that the FEC does not act enough like a court of law,[13] and others complain that it acts with too much legal authority.[14] And one Capitol Hill watcher rates the FEC as the "most incompetent" regulatory agency.[15]

No one claims the commission is free from administrative problems. Robert Tiernan, 1980 chairman of the commission, noted that the FEC is structurally handicapped by its political nature. Congress, he concluded, was worried about "a runaway commission. They said, 'We want some reform, but on the other hand . . .' "[16]

Critics are not so likely to blame Congress for the FEC's shortcomings; they see many of the problems resting with the inadequacy of the agency's members and staff. For instance, although a major role of the agency is to audit financial statements, often it has not had a certified public accountant on its staff. Elmo Allen, the principal FEC auditor of Jimmy Carter's primary campaign, resigned, complaining that the audit was "badly flubbed." In an interview he said, "I just believe that those people don't know what the hell they're doing."[17]

Another criticism of administrative operations was expressed in May 1979 by Harvard University's Institute of Politics whose Campaign Finance Study Group found "inefficiency and a lack of clarity and consistency in policy making" due in large part to the FEC's rotating chairmanship.[18] And, the study suggested, with that lack of direction in leadership has come low morale among the staff. Staff turnover, between 20 and 30 percent annually, has made it exceedingly difficult to maintain experience and expertise within the agency.

Charges of Favoritism

The FEC consists of six voting members appointed by the president and confirmed by the Senate for six-year terms. To prevent political favoritism, no more than three commissioners may be of one party. The chairman and vice-chairman are chosen by the commission. The two officers cannot be of the same party, and the positions are for one year only.

The three-three split between the parties on the commission has not led to the inefficiency one might expect. Although a majority of commissioners must approve agency policy, partisan squabbling between commissioners apparently has not occurred often enough to pose a significant problem. Said Max L. Friedersdorf, a commissioner from February 1979 to December 1980, "If we have differences, it's usually over the interpretation of the law, not due to partisanship."[19]

A 1979 Congressional Quarterly study found only one deadlock in a full year's sixty-five advisory opinions. Fifty of those advisory opinions were unanimous decisions.[20] The one tie vote came when the commission had to decide whether the Texas Voter Participation Project, affiliated with the Democratic party, could help pay for five congressional-campaign debts. With a straight party split, no decision was made. In its written opinion, however, the failure to reach a decision was presented as less a partisan than a procedural matter. The main point of contention was how permission should be sought—through an advisory opinion or through regulation—rather than whether the decision would benefit one or the other of the parties.

Despite structural safeguards that appear to have prevented one form of political favoritism, allegations of other forms of favoritism have been directed against the commission, some involving hiring practices, others involving appointments to the commission itself, and still others involving commission enforcement procedures. In the matter of hiring, former commission director Orlando Potter estimates that somewhat fewer than half the people employed by the FEC have prior connections with politicians, especially with members of Congress.

One example that received considerable publicity was that of Kenneth A. Gross, an assistant general counsel hired in 1979 to advise auditors, including those conducting the Carter campaign audit. Previously Gross had worked with the Atlanta law firm of Robert Lipshutz, treasurer of the Carter campaign.[21] Although some objections were raised to the appointment due to the relationship, Potter defended the hiring of Gross, noting that he did not directly participate in decisions pertaining to the Carter campaign audit.

Similar complaints of favoritism in hiring and promotion may have been a contributing factor to the employees' low morale. Phillip Kellet, president of the agency's recently established independent labor union National Treasury Employees Union (NTEU), echoed this resentment toward the commission's hiring practices, suggesting that it helped stir support for creation of the union.[22]

In the matter of enforcement procedures, the National Right to Work Committee (NRWC) long has argued that the commission has a pro-union bias and claims it has prevailed in two separate lawsuits charging the FEC with favoritism toward labor unions. The right-to-work group took the commission to court to force action against both the AFL-CIO and the National Education Association (NEA). The AFL-CIO had been illegally mingling dues money with contributions to its political education arm, the Committee on Political Education (COPE); NEA's PAC had been funded by automatic payroll deductions. The NRWC claimed the commission was acting too slowly in these cases. The right-to-work group won a federal court order requiring the NEA to change its fund-raising procedures,[23] and, although the commission eventually did fine the AFL-CIO $10,000 for commingling funds, a federal appeals court scrapped the fine, ruling that the federation had not broken the law knowingly.[24] An FEC spokesman responded to the charges of foot-dragging in both disputes by maintaining that the commission was attempting to pursue a conciliatory approach, which tends to be more time-consuming.[25]

Some critics of the FEC have suggested that the agency's refusal to look into Linda Ronstadt's benefit concert for the reelection of Sen. Gary Hart (D-Colo.) is another example of a partisan tilt.[26] The act established ceilings on direct contributions to federal candidates but exempted the donated services of volunteers from limitation. Consequently entertainers, among others, emerged as a major source of campaign fund raising; some can raise as much as $500,000 for a candidate at a single concert. Rock concerts have proved to be among the most profitable of benefits conducted by entertainers and generally favor candidates from the Democratic party. The commission has not pursued complaints over such benefit concerts, reasoning that the FEC had no legal authority to impinge upon the voluntary donation of professional services. But in its 1982 legislative recommendations to Congress, the commission suggested the law be amended to permit the agency to circumscribe the use of volunteer services when they are donated solely for fund-raising purposes rather than for actual campaigning.

Nonincumbents often have cited statistics to demonstrate alleged commission favoritism toward incumbents. Indeed, a *Congressional Quarterly* examination of FEC records for the first three months of 1979 found that most enforcement actions were taken against nonincumbents.[27] Of sixty-eight investigations of congressional candidates, only eight focused on incumbents: two senators and six congressmen. The remaining sixty cases involved eight nonincumbent Senate candidates and fifty-two nonincumbent House candidates.

Most of the investigations were dismissed without charges or uncovered minor infractions such as late filing. The conciliation and occasional litigation procedures were costly to the defendants nonetheless, and this burden generally fell on those candidates least able to afford the expense. The agency, for example, filed civil suits against the Communist party, USA, the Socialist Workers party, La Raza Unida, and the Prohibition party.

The FEC maintained that there was no effort to be soft on incumbents and that nonincumbents simply were not as familiar with election law and often could not afford costly legal consultants. Consequently, nonincumbents tended to make more mistakes than the seasoned incumbents. According to the agency, most of the infractions were not of grave significance, but the integrity of the law had to be upheld.

Excessive Zeal?

By far the justification most frequently heard on Capitol Hill for abolishing the FEC is what critics perceive as the agency's relentless pursuit of petty campaign violations. A commonly cited example of the commission's perceived tendency to engage in needless litigation is the 1980 case, *FEC* v.

Central Long Island Tax Reform Immediately (CLITRIM). The commission charged that CLITRIM violated federal-election law by failing to report an estimated $135 spent on printing a pamphlet criticizing the voting record of Rep. James Ambro (D-N.Y.). After four years and $35,000 in legal expenses, the case was thrown out of court. Judge Irving Kaufman criticized the FEC for violating freedom of speech and added, "I find this episode somewhat perverse."[28]

The commission defended its actions by arguing that CLITRIM was an important test case in spite of the minimal expenditures involved in the violation. The pamphlet distributed by CLITRIM did not explicitly encourage voters to vote against James Ambro, but the commission viewed the materials as expressly advocating Ambro's defeat. The term *express advocacy* had not been defined by the FECA, and the resolution of this issue, according to agency officials, was to set a precedent because other related organizations were undertaking similar activities.[29]

Politicians are well aware of the FEC's concern with detail. In one instance, Rep. Cecil Heftel (D-Hawaii) was hesitant to give macadamia nuts to other congressmen without the FEC's approval. The commission determined that the gift would not count as a campaign contribution. In another instance, Sen. Ted Stevens (R-Ala.) wanted to postpone his daughter's wedding until after his 1978 election to avoid any potential conflict with the FEC. Judging from past concerns of the FEC, Stevens suspected the agency might consider the wedding a campaign event because of the publicity that would be generated. In yet another instance, the FEC claimed to have uncovered $43,000 of unreported expenditures in Morris Udall's unsuccessful 1976 presidential bid. The Udall campaign was organized heavily around college campuses, with each campus branch staffed by students who often are sincere but unprofessional in their approach to the administration of campaigns. Ed Coyle, Udall's campaign staff director, complained that the commission's ruling failed to take account of the college volunteers' lack of sophistication. "We were nickled and dimed to death," he said.[30]

Some critics believe the agency's alleged obsession with the letter of the law not only is wasteful but also hinders the election process. According to election-law attorney H. Richard Mayberry, the commission's literal interpretation of the act has a chilling effect on constitutional rights.[31] The FEC's actions in the Rexnord case illustrate the problem for such critics. In that case, the agency initially refused to allow Rexnord, Inc., a Milwaukee-based industrial corporation, to use corporate funds to pay for advertisements encouraging the general public to register to vote. Later, after Rexnord pursued the issue, the commission reversed its decision.

In defending some of its controversial policies, the FEC blames Congress for overly restrictive legislation and maintains that it merely interprets, but does not write, the law. Commission defenders maintain further that the agency's propensity for strictly literal interpretations—and, hence, petty enforcement practices—may actually spur voluntary compliance. If the FEC deals firmly with even minor infractions, this reasoning holds, candidates and committees will work harder at voluntarily meeting the law's many requirements. Critics are not satisfied, however, and hold that the FEC, like any other enforcement agency, has some interpretive prerogative. Literal interpretations of the law, they claim, subvert the intent of the law.

Reduced Appropriations

As congressional authorization for the FEC approached its September 30, 1981, expiration date, resentments against the agency's alleged administrative shortcomings surfaced, first in the form of congressional committee reduction of the agency's requested appropriations by $4 million and then in a concerted effort to abolish the agency.

The proposed reductions in appropriations for FEC functions for fiscal year 1982 were received with great alarm by members of the commission. In an October 1, 1981, memorandum to the House Appropriations Committee, then chairman John McGarry said the pending fiscal reductions would have a potentially "devastating effect on commission operations."[32] McGarry outlined several probable consequences of the proposed budget reductions, including obstructing fulfillment of a recently implemented pay raise of 4.8 percent, hindering preparation for the 1982 congressional elections, laying off 106 of the agency's 229 full-time employees, leading to an understaffing of all divisions in the agency, severely reducing outreach activities, cutting back the amount of information that could be coded and made available to the public, and conjoining several divisions into broader, less specialized branches.

Despite McGarry's warning, the reductions in appropriations were implemented, and the FEC appropriation for fiscal year 1982 was set at $8,990,000. The actual consequences to the FEC were far milder than McGarry had proposed. Twenty-three permanent employees were laid off, and a larger number of part-time employees also were dismissed, including approximately sixteen auditors.[33] The National Clearinghouse on Election Administration, an informational service to federal, state, and local election agencies, was cut back, and the activities of the outreach program were curtailed. Specialization within the various divisions was not sacrificed, and disclosure activities were not hampered significantly. Enforcement activities were made more selective but probably not to the detriment of the agency's function.

During the process leading up to a decision about FEC appropriations for fiscal year 1982, dissatisfaction with the agency had led to initiatives that posed a far greater threat to the commission than the budgetary limits. The FEC budget request initially was reduced to $9,655,000 in committee when it was attached to the House appropriations bill for the Treasury and Postal Service (HR 4242). The measure passed the House July 30.

The appropriations bill then moved into the Senate Appropriations Committee where it faced stiff opposition. Senate majority whip Ted Stevens, with a fistful of Republican proxies, offered an amendment to delete FEC funds from the bill, arguing that Congress had not reauthorized the agency yet. Sen. Dennis DeConcini (D-Ariz.) countered Stevens's effort with enough Democratic proxies to meet the challenge. DeConcini argued that the amendment should be considered by the Senate Rules Committee, which has jurisdiction over election matters. The amendment to delete was rejected on a twelve-to-twelve party-line vote. Ultimately the FEC's survival at this stage was decided by three Republican members, including Arlen Specter of Pennsylvania, who left the session without leaving their proxies behind.

Sens. Roger Jepsen (R-Iowa) and William Armstrong (R-Colo.) later led a floor fight to amend the 1982 authorization bill to limit FEC funding to a six-month period. They realized there was substantial sentiment among congressional members to weaken the agency, if not abolish it, and by setting an early expiration date for commission funding, the amendment would force Congress into deliberating proposed changes in the FEC and the act before the 1982 elections.

The Reagan administration expressed interest in the Republican effort to abolish the FEC, but only if the attempt could garner bipartisan support. Initially there seemed to be bipartisan support; complaints about the agency came from all sides. But the Democrats, particularly in the House, were not prepared to make fundamental changes in the FEC under pressure of the impending 1982 elections. Democrats made it clear they would oppose halving the FEC's authorization but were willing to discuss new legislation through proper channels.

A stalemate between Democrats and Republicans on the Jepsen-Armstrong amendment persisted for several months. Finally, faced with the possibility of failing to approve appropriations for the U.S. Treasury, on November 20, 1981, the Senate voted sixty-five to thirty-one to table the Jepsen amendment. The motion to table—and thus kill—the amendment came from Sen. Alan Cranston (D-Calif.).

Consideration of the future of the FEC subsequently took place in the Senate Rules Committee. The 1982 campaign season began before legislation to revamp the agency could reach the Senate floor. Since there was a widespread feeling that changes in the law halfway through the election cycle would be unfair, consideration of revisions in the law was tabled until 1983.

In spite of President Reagan's possible interest in abolishing the FEC, the administration requested $9,880,000 for the commission for fiscal year 1983, about a $1 million budget increase. The increase, however, was deceptive. The commission anticipated a 10 percent increase in the number of campaign finance disclosure reports to be received and reviewed in 1983; the presidential-election cycle, including the additional activities required to manage the public funding program, was scheduled to begin late in the year; and the work load for auditing and compliance matters was expected to increase.

Officials of the FEC addressed the committee hearings in both the House and Senate, pleading for a larger budget for fiscal year 1983. The commission's 1982 chairman, Frank Reiche, argued that Congress had destabilized FEC functions by failing to provide authorizations in three of the previous four years. Each budget since 1979 decreased in terms of real dollars, he said, and in 1982 decreased in actual dollars as well. Furthermore Reiche requested an additional $184,000 to complete the fiscal year; otherwise, he said, the commission might have to close down for eight to ten days before September 20. The supplemental request (HR 6863) was reported out of committee and then tacked onto a more inclusive government appropriations bill, which was passed by the Congress. President Reagan vetoed the bill but was overridden by Congress by a narrow margin of one vote on September 10, 1982. Total FEC funding for fiscal year 1982 was $9,174,000.

Congress appeared to be heading toward approval of an appropriations bill for the FEC that approached Reagan's request. In May 1982, the House Administration Committee approved legislation to authorize $9,787,408 for the commission for fiscal year 1983. The amount represented a compromise between the administration's request and a proposal by Rep. Bill Thomas (R-Calif.) for $9.6 million plus a cost-of-living increase.

The fiscal year 1983 authorization bill received approval in the Senate Rules and Administration Committee on May 20. Since several senators were absent from the committee hearing, chairman Charles Mc. Mathias (R-Md.) ordered a polling of those not present. The objection of a single committee member would have prevented the bill from passing out of committee. There were no objections.

Despite approval of the 1983 authorization bill in the relevant committees of both houses of Congress, the Congress found itself unable to agree on a budget prior to the beginning of a new fiscal year on October 1, 1982. A stopgap funding resolution (HJ Res 599) was introduced to keep the government running during the first part of the 1983 fiscal year. On October 1, both houses approved the continuing funding resolution, which authorized the FEC to spend at an annual rate of $9.7 million through December 15, 1982, pending further congressional action on the final budget.

Legislative Debate

The Senate Rules and Administration Committee began its long-awaited hearing on the FEC and the FECA on November 20, 1981. The earlier appropriations controversy had been moved into Sen. Mathias's committee and had taken the form of a legislative debate. In the course of the debate, differences became apparent among those who wanted to fine-tune the agency and the law, those who wanted to streamline them, and those who wanted to abolish the FEC. Sen. Mathias offered a measure that would not fundamentally alter the FEC but would change certain disclosure, procedural, and judicial-review features of the law. Sen. Arlen Specter proposed legislation that would leave most of the FECA intact but would alter the nature of the commission by making commissioners part-time officers in an agency that would emphasize disclosure and deemphasize compliance and enforcement. Sen. Jepsen offered a bill that would abolish the FEC and transfer some of its functions to the General Accounting Office (GAO) and would establish an administrator of federal elections as part of the GAO to investigate complaints of violations and seek to resolve them through conciliation. None of those measures was acted on during the Ninety-seventh Congress, nor was a measure proposed in the House by Rep. Bill Frenzel that would revise the way federal election laws are enforced and increase the spending ceilings for political parties.[34]

It does not seem likely that Congress will abolish the FEC in the near future. As Sen. Mathias notes, criticism of the agency may be widespread, but "very few people" want to scrap it altogether.[35] Many of the commission's most ardent Republican critics apparently do not want to be responsible for undoing the Watergate reforms only a decade after the event. And other moderate Republicans and Democrats see some continuing need for an independent election agency. Many of the agency's functions are viewed with favor, regardless of perceived administrative and enforcement problems. For instance, the FEC's disclosure activities have decreased suspicion of and secrecy in campaign finance, and the agency's compilations of data are considered by knowledgeable observers to be invaluable. Many observers also believe the FEC and the act have provided politics with a cleaner image. "It saved us" observes Archibald Cox, chairman of Common Cause; the post-Watergate campaign reforms made clear that "government should be open and not only honest, but honorable."[36]

But there also are strong sentiments that something is wrong with the FEC, in spite of the agency's attempts to improve its image and field criticisms with a full-time congressional liaison. The FEC likely will be tolerated in the immediate future, though it is not clear in what form the agency will continue its operations.

FEC Audit Authority

When the FEC was created by the 1974 FECA amendments, the commission was directed "to make from time to time audits and field investigations with respect to alleged failures to file any report or statement required under the provisions of the [act]."[37] The commission's exercise of its audit authority has been a matter of contention almost from the beginning. Both the slow pace of its audits, particularly of presidential campaigns, and the conduct of random audits of congressional campaigns were the focus of controversy and criticism during and after the 1976 elections.[38] Following the 1980 elections, criticism of the commission's audit policy and procedures focused on the agency's alleged insensitivity to the realities of presidential campaigning.

The Arthur Andersen and Accountants for the Public Interest Studies

In June 1979, in light of the criticisms it had received from Congress for the slow pace of its audit procedures and from some of its own staff for the narrow focus of its audits, the FEC voted to hire Arthur Andersen & Co., a major accounting firm, to study its political campaign auditing process. In addition, since Arthur Andersen had prior involvement with political campaigns, candidates, and committees, the FEC voted to hire Accountants for the Public Interest (API), a nonprofit association of volunteer CPAs and accountants, to monitor the Andersen study from a public-interest viewpoint—to avoid any conflict of interest or charges of partisan bias—and to review certain aspects of the FEC's audit process and reporting systems that have public-interest implications. The Andersen study cost $90,000 and the API study an additional $20,000.

The two studies were conducted over the course of the summer of 1979, and on September 13, both Arthur Andersen and API presented their findings to the commission. The Andersen study concluded there were a number of major problem areas.[39] It found that FEC audits were not completed on a timely basis, that the commission planned for more audits than its staff could complete, and that too much effort was expended on "very small contribution and expenditure problems."[40] It also found that the categories into which the commission divided audit reports confused the public, that the FEC audit division was understaffed and inexperienced, and that the management information system employed did not allow the audit division to be adequately monitored.

To help the FEC overcome the problems it identified, Arthur Andersen made a number of recommendations. First, the firm recommended that the FEC use limited audit procedures that would allow the commission to verify to the maximum extent possible that political committees were materially complying with the act rather than attempt to verify each transaction of every political committee. In order to do so effectively, said the Andersen study, the FEC would have to establish valid risk criteria so that the commission's limited audit resources could be concentrated on identified risk areas. The Andersen review also recommended that the FEC establish thresholds that would allow it to bypass the minor omissions and errors that occur in any campaign and concentrate on important problems. The study called for the categorization of audit reports to be eliminated and replaced with audit findings letters that indicate the scope and findings of the audit to the audited committee. According to the firm's recommendation, the committee would be given a reasonable time to respond, after which the findings letter and the manner in which issues were resolved would be released as the final audit report. In cases in which there are no material noncompliance issues, the study said, a simple letter should be issued by the FEC to that effect.

The Andersen review also recommended that audit reports be separated from matters under review (MUR), or potential compliance actions against committees, so that the reports themselves no longer be held up, as they had been in the past, until the MUR was resolved. The resolution of the specific MUR would be made public later. In addition, Andersen recommended that the FEC commissioners confine their review of FEC audits to those with unusual findings rather than attempt to review all reports, as it had been doing. Strict deadlines should be established and maintained for each phase of the audit process, the study said, to reduce the elapsed time of audits from the present average of thirty-three weeks to no more than eight to ten weeks. Establishment of a simple bookkeeping system for small, part-time campaign committees also would be helpful, the study maintained, to help ensure accurate disclosure reports and thus facilitate FEC audits. The Andersen review recommended that prior to a presidential committee's first request for matching funds, the FEC audit division make a review to ensure that the committee has adequate systems to safeguard and control public funds.

Finally, the Andersen study recommended that the FEC retain some form of its random audit program ("to validate the criteria used to identify risk or probability of noncompliance"),[41] develop a recruiting program and a training program to obtain and maintain a qualified auditing staff, and establish a small, part-time advisory committee to advise the FEC commissioners on policy matters only.

API reviewed the Andersen study and found "no significant partisan or other bias."[42] The API study also made a number of recommendations, some in addition to those made by Arthur Andersen. Like the Andersen study, API recommended that prior to the general election the FEC conduct audits of the preconvention records of the major presidential candidates running in the general election. The results of those audits, API said, should be made public before the November election. API also recommended that the FEC commissioners "be selected on the basis of expertise rather than partisanship."[43]

On September 20 the FEC commissioners and staff met to consider a management plan drawn up to implement the recommendations. One commissioner reportedly praised the recommendations but observed they had been made before.[44] Another pointed out that although the Andersen report concentrated on discretionary audits of PACs and House and Senate candidate campaign committees, the FEC's major concern for 1980 had to be the mandatory audits of the presidential campaigns.[45] The head of the commission's audit division expressed misgivings about the tight schedule proposed in the management plan. The plan was subsequently withdrawn so it could be reconsidered and give greater emphasis to presidential-campaign audits.

On November 1, the FEC approved new audit procedures for the 1980 presidential campaigns. Audits for both prenomination and general-election campaigns would take no more than six months to complete. Prenomination audit results, however, would not be made public prior to the general election for fear of releasing incomplete and possibly inaccurate information and for fear of not meeting an announced deadline. Specific time periods would be allotted for each step in the audit process, and the results of the whole audit would be included in a final audit-findings letter. In addition, in order to eliminate sources of delay, the FEC decided not to prolong more than one month efforts to determine the corporate status of business contributors; to restrict to one month the period during which a committee may respond to the FEC's findings prior to their publication, except in "certain unusual cases"; not to hold up publication of audit findings when the audit leads to an investigation by the FEC's office of general counsel but to publish the findings without any discussion of the specific matter being investigated; and not to attempt to specify in the final audit letter the degree of compliance with the law indicated by the audit.

1980 Presidential-Campaign Audits

Although the FEC completed its 1980 presidential nomination and general-election campaign audits of publicly funded committees far more quickly than it had completed similar audits of 1976 campaigns, only five of the ten 1980 prenomination-campaign audits were released prior to 1981. The audit of Sen. Edward M. Kennedy's prenomination campaign was the last to be released, in late September 1981, some thirteen months after Kennedy had withdrawn from the race. The audits of the three publicly funded general-election campaigns were released in 1981: the Carter audit in August, the Anderson audit in October, and the Reagan audit in December. Despite the considerable improvement in the amount of time it took to complete the audits, critics of FEC audit policy and procedures still found cause for complaint. In April 1981, lawyers representing nine of the campaign committees of 1980 Democratic and Republican presidential contenders and the national political parties sent joint letters to the commission and to Congress attacking the FEC's audit methods. In addition, both the Kennedy for President Committee and the Reagan-Bush Committee filed suit against the FEC over the agency's exercise of its audit authority.

FEC Appointments

Prior to the Supreme Court's *Buckley* decision, which required that all six FEC commissioners be appointed by the president, four of the agency's commissioners were designated by congressional leaders. Despite the 1976 Court ruling, President Gerald Ford continued to make his appointments with congressional wishes clearly in mind.[46] Congressional leaders fully expected Jimmy Carter to continue the practice. When Carter assumed the presidency in January 1977, the terms of two commissioners, Democrat Neil Staebler and Republican William Springer, were scheduled to expire on April 30, 1977, and the terms of two others, Democrat Thomas Harris and Republican Vernon Thomson, were scheduled to expire on April 30, 1979. Controversy surrounding Carter's attempts to fill the first two vacancies indicated he was less willing than his predecessor to yield to the wishes of Congress.

The controversy over Carter's first two nominees is described in the previous volume in this series.[47] His nomination of Republican Samuel D. Zagoria was withdrawn following strong objections by Republican party leaders, and his Democratic nominee, John W. McGarry, twice failed to receive Senate confirmation. Nevertheless, on October 25, 1978, President Carter made a recess appointment, replacing Neil Staebler with McGarry.

When the Ninety-sixth Congress opened, the matter of McGarry's confirmation by the Senate had to be considered once again. Carter's nomination of Max L. Friedersdorf for the Republican seat made McGarry's confirmation more likely, for it indicated the Republicans had won their objective, sought in the struggle over the Zagoria nomination, of influencing appointments to the FEC. Friedersdorf had a long history of Republican party involvement. After working as an assistant to former Congressman

Richard Roudebush (R-Ind.) from 1971 to 1974, he was special assistant and then deputy assistant for congressional affairs to President Nixon. He continued as deputy assistant under President Ford until 1975, when he became the president's assistant for legislative affairs. In January 1977 Friedersdorf became staff director of the Senate Republican Policy Committee, a position in which he earned praise from congressional Republicans.

Due in large part to Friedersdorf's popularity with party leaders, confirmation of the pair of FEC nominees moved swiftly through the Senate. When President Carter again submitted the appointments, the Senate Rules Committee unanimously voted to send the nominations to the Senate floor for confirmation balloting. Two weeks later, on February 21, 1979, the Senate confirmed both appointments by voice vote without objection. Both terms were scheduled to expire April 30, 1983.

Reiche and Harris Appointments

The controversy over Carter's first two FEC appointments ended just in time for the president to begin consideration of filling the two vacancies that would occur on April 30, 1979, when the terms of commissioners Thomas E. Harris and Vernon W. Thomson would expire. On May 1, 1979, Carter renominated Harris for a six-year term to the FEC and nominated Frank P. Reiche to replace Thomson. Reiche, a lawyer in private practice, who also had served as unpaid chairman of the New Jersey Election Law Enforcement Commission (ELEC) since its inception in 1973, had been among several Republicans on a list of acceptable appointees to fill a Republican vacancy on the FEC submitted to the president by Baker and Rhodes. Despite Reiche's solid party credentials, his nomination also met with opposition, especially from the conservative wing of the Republican party.

On May 9, the Senate Rules Committee held hearings on the Harris and Reiche nominations. Committee members questioned Harris about a number of problems the FEC had experienced during his term with the agency, including delays in completing the 1976 presidential audits. Questions addressed to Reiche focused on a possible conflict of interest between the FEC and his law firm and former clients. Reiche also was questioned on his attitudes about public financing of congressional campaigns. He responded that although he was not philosophically opposed to that system, his experiences with public financing of gubernatorial races in New Jersey indicated there would be a number of logistical problems in its application to the more varied congressional races.

Even before the Senate Rules Committee met to discuss the nominations of Harris and Reiche, opponents of Reiche's nomination took the offensive.

Despite Reiche's cautious testimony before the committee regarding public financing, the conservative publication *Human Events* described Reiche as "an enthusiastic supporter of taxpayer campaign financing and of strict contribution limits" and said his appointment would be "particularly dangerous."[48]

Former Nixon administration Treasury Secretary William Simon, a New Jersey resident, urged Republican congressmen to oppose Reiche's nomination. In a letter to Republican officials, Simon wrote that Reiche did not represent traditional Republican views and maintained that during Reiche's tenure as chairman, the New Jersey ELEC had shown "a consistent pattern of more government, more regulation, more limits, and more penalties."[49] Simon also wrote to more than a thousand New Jersey Republicans asking them to join him in opposing Reiche's appointment to the FEC. He wrote that Reiche would "bring a proven record of opposition to traditional Republican views to this critically important agency."[50] Simon encouraged recipients of his letter to write Baker, Rhodes, and Bill Brock, Republican National Committee chairman, expressing their opposition to Reiche.

On June 6 and 14, the Senate Rules Committee met and discussed the Harris and Reiche nominations; on June 14, the committee voted nine to zero to report both nominations favorably to the Senate. In a supplemental view concerning Reiche's nomination, Sen. Mark Hatfield (R-Ore.), ranking minority member of the committee, expressed his confidence that Reiche's nomination was a "step toward the restoration of much needed public confidence in the Federal Election Commission."[51] Hatfield said that Reiche's "experience with election law on the state level may prove particularly valuable in suggesting new approaches on the federal level," and he maintained that the nominee's "experience, public and party service, personal qualifications, and objectivity make him a superior nomination."[52]

Despite Hatfield's glowing recommendation and the unanimous approval of the Senate Rules Committee, conservatives continued to oppose Reiche's nomination. Sen. Gordon Humphrey (R-N.H.) exercised his right to place a hold on the nomination by which he was assured he would receive twenty-four hours notice before the nomination was brought to the floor. Humphrey's move was a clear signal that there would be some debate once the nomination was called up.

No hold, however, was placed on the nomination of Thomas Harris. Despite previous Senate practice of considering the nominees together in order to avoid partisan wrangling, the Senate approved Harris's nomination separately. Late in the night of June 19, the Senate leadership found it had no further business on the agenda, and it was suggested that uncontested nominations be taken up. Harris, whose name was on the list, was then quietly approved for an additional term as an FEC commissioner. The action reportedly infuriated Sen. Claiborne Pell (D-R.I.), chairman of the Rules Committee, who had not been consulted.[53] But it was not expected to endanger Reiche's nomination.

Conservative opposition to Reiche delayed consideration of his nomination for more than a month. Sen. Humphrey asked that the matter not be taken up, maintaining that a majority of Republican senators opposed it. On July 25, however, the Senate did consider the nomination.

Sen. Hatfield began the discussion by offering a strong recommendation in favor of Reiche's appointment. He reviewed the nominee's background and experience and met head-on the objection that Reiche's views on public financing of congressional campaigns should disqualify him from consideration. "As one who has spent many hours on this same floor arguing against taxpayer financing," said Hatfield, "and several more hours in Rules Committee sessions examining FEC regulatory problems, I want to assure my colleagues that I have confidence in Frank Reiche's views."[54]

Sen. Humphrey took the floor and began a filibuster to block Reiche's appointment. He renewed complaints that Reiche did not entirely reject the concept of public financing of congressional elections, in accordance with the position of the Republican National Committee; that Reiche's record as chairman of the New Jersey commission indicated that he favored expanding the power of regulatory commissions; and that Reiche would not be sufficiently partisan as a Republican appointee to the FEC. Humphrey and colleagues who took his side in the debate also used the opportunity to express their dissatisfaction with the FEC. Humphrey was joined in his filibuster by Sens. Jesse Helms, Orrin Hatch (R-Utah), Paul Laxalt (R-Nev.), James McClure (R-Idaho), and Robert Dole (R-Kan.).

After seven hours, the filibuster ended with an agreement to vote on a motion to recommit Reiche's nomination to committee. If passed, the motion would have killed the nomination for the session. The motion, however, failed, seventy to twenty-eight. The Senate then voted, seventy-three to twenty-five, to confirm the New Jersey Republican's nomination. On July 31, Frank Reiche was sworn into office as an FEC commissioner. He became the tenth commissioner since the FEC's establishment in 1975 and the first to have had election-campaign regulation experience prior to his appointment.

Friedersdorf's Resignation

The change of administrations following the 1980 elections did not alter the politics of FEC appointments. Although party labels were reversed, Congress and the White House continued to vie for influence in the appointment of FEC commissioners. In December 1980 Max Friedersdorf resigned from his FEC position to become President-elect Reagan's chief liaison with Congress and later head of the White House Office of Congressional Affairs. To replace Friedersdorf on the commission, President Carter made a recess appointment of former commissioner Vernon Thomson to fill the remainder of Friedersdorf's term. Carter also sent Thomson's nomination to the Senate for approval of a full term. Although no complaints were expressed, Thomson's nomination to a full term was taken off the Senate agenda after Reagan assumed office. Since two other seats on the commission were scheduled to expire on April 30, 1981, those of Democrat Robert Tiernan and Republican Joan Aikens, Reagan would have the opportunity to appoint half of the commission members within a few months of taking office.

Expressions of interest by Reagan in the possibility of limiting or even abolishing the FEC made while he was still a candidate generated concern among commission supporters. The president had an opportunity to do "great harm or . . . great service" to the FEC, stated 1981 commission vice-chairman Frank Reiche, who encouraged a departure from "partisan politics as usual" in the appointment process.[55]

Reiche also cited a recent Common Cause study complaining of the partisan politics in FEC appointments. What Common Cause objected to, however, was not what Reiche probably had in mind. Common Cause advocated a nonpartisan rather than a bipartisan structure for the commission. Reiche seemed more upset with the efforts of conservative Republicans to undermine the power of the FEC with appointments who oppose government regulation of the election campaign process. Indeed three staunchly conservative appointments by Reagan had the potential to turn the commission into a far different agency.

All three commissioners whose terms were up for consideration, including Vernon Thomson, indicated that they were interested in reappointment. Aikens had received early assurances from the administration that she would be reappointed, but new terms for Thomson and Tiernan were considered less likely. In fact Tiernan's reappointment never was seriously considered. In order to influence Reagan's choice, congressional Democrats decided not to recommend the outspoken Tiernan and to push for more likely prospects. J. Martin Jepsen, a former aide to both Sen. Harrison Williams (D-N.J.) and former senator Harold Hughes (D-Iowa) seemed to be a prime candidate. He was recommended by Senate minority leader Robert Byrd, minority whip Alan Cranston, and Democratic Conference secretary Daniel Inouye.

But there was a split in the Democratic leadership. House Speaker O'Neill submitted a recommendation for former Congressman Al Baldus (D-Wis.). The House leader blamed the split on a lack of communication between Senate Democrats and himself, causing both to arrive at their selections independently. Neither Byrd nor O'Neill, however, would compromise; Byrd would not accept Baldus, and O'Neill would not accept Jepsen. Shortly thereafter O'Neill withdrew his recommendation for Baldus but continued to reject Jepsen.

Sen. Wendell Ford (D-Ky.) then put together a list of Democratic suggestions for the post and forwarded it to the White House. All of the names on the list were rejected by the administration, and Senate Democrats were unable to agree on other suitable candidates. Subsequently rumors arose that the White House was going to nominate Lyndon Olson, Jr., a conservative Texas Democrat who was not on any of the earlier lists submitted by congressional Democratic leaders. The rumored nomination was reported to be a reward to the conservative southern Democrats who jumped party lines to support the administration's budget and tax-cut proposals.[56] News of Olson's pending appointment was first leaked by official sources in order to test the Democratic reaction. When it became known that the Texan had accepted $4,568 in contributions from NCPAC for a 1978 House campaign, the Democratic reaction was predictably negative. NCPAC's practice of targeting prominent Democratic officeholders for defeat in the 1978 and 1980 elections did nothing to help Olson's prospects. In a letter to President Reagan, Olson withdrew himself from consideration in order to avoid potentially embarrassing questions about NCPAC's support.[57]

Democratic Recommendations

At this point the Democrats regrouped. Speaker O'Neill and Sen. Byrd sent a joint letter to the White House stating that by October 23, they would submit a list of people competent to serve on the FEC. A list of six names was submitted on time. Those on the list were Patricia Knox, a Democratic activist from Detroit; former representative Edward Pattison (D-N.Y.); Danny McDonald, a former member of the Tulsa Board of Elections; Gloria Schaffer, a former Connecticut secretary of state; Richard Sloan, administrative assistant to Sen. Howard Metzenbaum (D-Ohio); and Janet Watlington, assistant director for government affairs at ACTION. The list was signed by both Byrd and O'Neill and other influential House and Senate Democrats. The letter reminded Reagan that when Democrats controlled the White House, Republicans in Congress were allowed to propose nominees for GOP vacancies at the FEC.[58]

The White House bowed to the Democratic pressure and nominated Tulsa Democrat Danny Lee McDonald to replace Robert Tiernan. As general administrator of the Oklahoma Corporation Commission, McDonald administered ten state regulatory divisions. He had previously been on the Tulsa County Election Board and had performed some research for the FEC as a member of the commission's advisory panel to the National Clearinghouse on Election Administration. Initially Reagan gave McDonald a recess appointment, but later the Oklahoman's appointment was confirmed by the Senate after perfunctory hearings.

After appointing McDonald to replace Tiernan, Reagan had yet to fill Friedersdorf's seat, temporarily held by Vernon Thomson, and Aikens's seat. From the beginning Aikens, a former public relations executive and Pennsylvania Republican activist, expected reappointment for another six-year term due to expire in 1987. She had been a member of the FEC since its inception and for the most part had remained respected by Republicans for her party loyalty. Aikens had significant support on Capitol Hill, and White House aides privately confirmed her reappointment expectations. The White House and congressional Republicans also agreed on their second Republican nomination: Lee Ann Elliot, a Chicago Republican who had served for sixteen years as associate executive director of the American Medical Association's Political Action Committee (AMPAC).

Elliot Controversy

Elliot's nomination made liberals within and outside Congress uncomfortable, both because of her work with AMPAC and her support for corporate PACs. Under federal law, all PACs are limited to a $5,000 contribution per candidate per election. AMPAC itself met those limits, but medical societies not directly affiliated with the AMA organized their own PACs in virtually every state. A confidential FEC report disclosed that in the 1976 and 1978 elections, the joint contributions of national and state medical PACs exceeded the $5,000 limit on 206 occasions.[59] Since those contributions would be legal only if they were made by truly independent political committees, the commission initiated a probe into the case. In a hearing before the commission, Elliot denied charges of wrongdoing. She testified that communications between the AMA and state medical associations on contributing to congressional elections were infrequent. She admitted there were some joint activities but no "comprehensive and equivalent program."[60] The FEC report was not so certain, calling Elliot's statements "self-serving and undocumentable" and contrary "to the circumstantial evidence we have otherwise obtained."[61] In July 1981 the commission concluded its probe by reprimanding AMPAC and forty-seven of its affiliated PACs, but the memories of Elliot's politics lingered on.

Elliot's stance on PACs also caused some concern. In 1980 she published an article encouraging the formation and organization of PACs as an effective means to increase political participation.[62] Further, her long-time involvement with AMPAC, coupled with her more-recent efforts to direct a PAC for a Chicago-based accounting firm, led to misgivings among many of the agency's proponents. Those who viewed with apprehension the fact that the growth of corporate PACs had outstripped the growth of labor PACs by almost fifteen to one from 1974 to 1980 were especially wary of appointing a corporate PAC representative to the commission.

Despite the controversy surrounding Elliot, she was well received by the president. In fact Reagan unexpectedly reversed the terms for which Aikens and Elliot anticipated appointment. The full six-year term Aikens expected went to Elliot, and Aikens was named to complete the two years remaining on Max Friedersdorf's term. News of the reversal surprised observers, including Aikens, who read about it in a newspaper. She reportedly asked an aide to find out if the newspaper had made a mistake. It had not. A White House official confirmed the story and told Aikens to "take it or leave it."[63] Although disappointed, she decided to accept the shorter term.

To enable the FEC appointees to operate pending Senate confirmation, all three were given recess appointments by the president on December 17, 1981. On January 25, President Reagan formally submitted the names of Danny Lee McDonald, Joan D. Aikens, and Lee Ann Elliot to the Senate for confirmation with terms to expire on April 30, 1987, 1983, and 1987, respectively. Following hearings, all three were confirmed by the Senate.

FEC Annual Reports

Despite the criticisms leveled at the FEC, the agency has not been devoid of accomplishments. A sympathetic view of the commission's activities may be found in the reports it publishes annually, summarizing the problems and issues the agency faced and how it resolved them. The reports also contain information on the structure and operations of the agency, biographical data on the commissioners, and recommendations for legislative action. During the period that this book examines, the commission published four such reports, for the years 1978, 1979, 1980, and 1981.[64]

Election-Law Litigation

During the period extending from the 1976 general election until well into 1982, a large number of lawsuits raised significant election law issues. Some suits were brought against the FEC; others were filed by the agency; still others did not involve the agency at all but served to test the limits of federal election law. Many of the suits are summarized here, but others are treated elsewhere in this book where the issues they raise are important to the subjects discussed or to the narrative.[65]

Unincorporated Committee Contribution Limits

During an April 1979 investigation of the California Medical Association (CMA), an unincorporated committee, and the California Medical PAC (CALPAC), its PAC, the FEC found probable cause to believe that the CMA had violated the FECA by making contributions exceeding $5,000 to CALPAC, which CALPAC accepted. At issue were direct contributions by the CMA to the committee, as well as in-kind contributions in the form of administrative and support services. The commission contended that the value of these contributions amounted to approximately $97,000 in 1976, $104,000 in 1977, and $136,000 in 1978.[66] Anticipating an FEC enforcement action as a result of the finding, the two groups filed suit against the FEC on May 7, 1979, in the U.S. Circuit Court of Appeals for the Ninth Circuit.[67]

The medical groups argued that the $5,000 ceiling imposed by 2 U.S.C. 441(a)(1)(C) on contributions to multicandidate political committees by "persons," including unincorporated associations, unfairly infringed upon their First Amendment rights of free speech and association by restricting the CMA's ability to engage in political speech through its PAC. The CMA also argued that the money, materials, and services it gave to CALPAC were intended to be used in the same way in which corporate and union treasury money can be used to administer a PAC. The medical association reasoned that if the law did not give it the right to make the same kind of expenditures permitted to corporations and labor organizations by 2 U.S.C. 441(b)(2)(C), then the law was in violation of the Constitution's freedom-of-association and equal-protection clauses. The case was heard before the court of appeals sitting en banc because a provision of the FECA requires that all questions concerning the constitutionality of the act be heard by such a court.

On May 23, 1980, the court of appeals ruled in a five-to-four decision that the CMA may not contribute more than $5,000 a year to CALPAC and rejected all of the constitutional claims asserted by the CMA. The court found that the contribution limit was necessary to prevent corruption and the appearance of corruption in federal political campaigns, one of the main provisions of the FECA. The court noted that the CMA, CALPAC, and its members were permitted to make contributions and expenditures in connection with federal elections as long as the per-candidate and per-committee contribution limits were respected. In addition, the CMA, an unincorporated association, did not fall under the expenditure limitations applicable to corporations and labor unions and was free to spend unlimited amounts in independent expenditures to promote its political views. The court found that the act did not abridge Fifth Amendment rights by discriminating against the political activities of unincorporated associations since the election law actually regulates unincorporated associations under an entirely different statutory scheme than applies to corporations and labor unions.

The CMA appealed the decision to the U.S. Supreme Court and reiterated the arguments the appeals court had rejected. On October 6, 1980, the Supreme Court agreed to consider the CMA's constitutional challenge to the FECA's limit on contributions by unincorporated committees to PACs.[68]

On June 26, 1981, the Supreme Court decided in a five-to-four ruling that Congress did not violate any constitutional principles when it enacted the $5,000 per year limit on the amount an individual or unincorporated association may contribute to any one PAC. In reaching its conclusion, the Court relied on the 1976 *Buckley* decision that validated the constitutionality of the contribution limits. The Court also held that Congress could establish different rules for unincorporated associations, labor unions, and corporations without violating the equal-protection clause because they are different entities with different structures and purposes and therefore require different forms of regulation in order to protect the integrity of the political process.

Contribution Limits and Independent Expenditures

On December 17, 1979, a liberal-conservative coalition of individuals and groups announced its intention to file a series of lawsuits asking the courts to find key parts of the FECA unconstitutional.[69] Specifically, the coalition planned to challenge limits on contributions to groups making independent expenditures, limits on contributions to challenging candidates and minority parties, and the annual $25,000 overall individual contribution limit. The group also planned to challenge the postal-rate subsidy that had been given to the Democratic and Republican parties but denied to minor parties and independent candidates. In a formal statement issued when the intended suits were announced, the coalition members noted that although they often disagreed with each other on major political issues and candidates, they believed that the FECA reduced "the amount of debate, information and ideas available to the voting public."[70] The statement was signed by five people—James Buckley, Gordon Humphrey, Eugene McCarthy, Stewart Mott, and Rhonda Stahlman—and by seven organizations—the Citizens Party, the Committee for a Constitutional Presidency, the Conservative Victory Fund, the Libertarian party, NCPAC, the Ripon Society, and Young Americans for Freedom.

The first lawsuit was filed on the day of the announcement in the U.S. District Court for the District of Columbia. Stewart Mott, NCPAC, and Rhonda Stahlman, a member of the board of directors of NCPAC, asked the court to strike down all limits on contributions to persons or groups making independent expenditures.[71] The plaintiffs contended that by regulating the amount of money that may be contributed to groups making independent expenditures, the FEC had ignored the Supreme Court's 1976 *Buckley* ruling that direct restraints on independent political activity are unconstitutional.

The issue raised by Stewart Mott was accentuated by his desire to join with television producer Norman Lear in a jointly funded independent promotion of John Anderson's presidential campaign. But Mott was concerned that their cooperation would lead the FEC to consider them a political committee subject to all legal restrictions governing such committees, including the contribution restriction that would limit the amount of money each individual could pool to $1,000 if they supported only one candidate, or $5,000 if they supported several candidates. The issue raised by Stahlman arose from her desire to donate more than $5,000 to NCPAC to support its independent-expenditure campaigns without having the contribution counted toward the law's overall $25,000 annual limit on contributions. Mott, Stahlman, and NCPAC contended that the restrictions on the amounts of money individuals may pool for joint independent expenditures and the limits on the amounts of money established multicandidate committees may accept from individuals for their independent ventures violated the contributors' rights to freedom of speech and association.

On June 30, 1980, U.S. District Judge Barrington D. Parker dismissed the suit brought by Mott, Stahlman, and NCPAC. Judge Parker dismissed Mott's complaint because he had not first sought an advisory opinion from the FEC asking whether the activity he wished to take together with Norman Lear would require them to register as a political committee.[72] At the time Mott filed suit, he had no legal authority to request an advisory opinion; only political committees, candidates, and federal officeholders were entitled to seek advisory opinions. Eligibility was changed to include any individual by the 1979 amendments but not until three weeks after Mott filed suit. Parker believed that Mott should have waited and sought relief through proper channels before entering the courts. Parker also dismissed Stahlman's and NCPAC's claim that since individuals are free to make unlimited independent expenditures on their own, they also should be free to make unlimited contributions to a committee making independent expenditures. He concluded that the constitutionality of the FECA limitations on contributions had been upheld in *Buckley* and that Congress had intended those limits to apply to committees making independent expenditures.[73]

In September 1981 NCPAC and Stahlman appealed the district court's dismissal of their claim.[74] In their brief to the U.S. Court of Appeals for the District of Columbia, they reiterated their contention that the laws limiting individual contributions to multicandidate committees making independent expenditures to $5,000 per year and counting such contributions toward the $25,000 ceiling on annual contributions by individuals violated their constitutional guarantees of free speech and association. The appellants also asked that the district court's decision not to certify the constitutional questions raised in the suit to the appeals court sitting en banc be held in error.

On December 8, 1981, the appeals court upheld the district court's decision. The appeals court determined that the 1981 Supreme Court decision, *California Medical Association* v. *FEC*, in which the contribution limits to political committees were ruled constitutional, also applied to NCPAC. The appeals court decided that since NCPAC not only made independent expenditures but also contributed to candidates, as did CALPAC, the *CALPAC* decision was applicable. The court further concluded that the challenged provision did not violate the appellants' First Amendment rights because it was an appropriate way by which Congress could seek to protect the integrity of the contribution restrictions upheld in *Buckley*. The appeals court also ruled that the provision did not violate the appellants' equal protection rights under the Fifth Amendment. Since no substantial constitutional questions remained, certification to an en banc court of appeals was not required. For the same reason, the appeals court issued no opinion with its decision.

Contribution Limits in Ballot Measure Campaigns

In December 1981, the U.S. Supreme Court struck down a Berkeley, California, municipal ordinance that limited to $250 the amount an individual or corporation was permitted to contribute to a committee supporting or opposing a ballot measure.[75] The case arose during a 1977 local referendum in Berkeley when the Citizens Against Rent Control (CARC), a California PAC, accepted nine contributions in excess of $250. Those illegal contributions totaled $18,600, in addition to which CARC raised $90,000 in contributions of $250 or less.[76] The money was used in a successful effort to defeat a measure imposing rent control on city apartments. When CARC was fined $18,600 by the Berkeley Fair Campaign Practices Commission under the ordinance limiting contributions, the committee, along with the Berkeley Board of Realtors and several property owners, filed suit against the city of Berkeley.

CARC argued that the ordinance unconstitutionally infringed on the rights of free speech and association. The CARC brief maintained that speaking out in contemporary society requires money and that any limit on the amount one may contribute to a committee formed to make its collective voice heard "limits the quality of public debate and diminishes the flow of information to the citizenry."[77]

Lawyers for the city of Berkeley argued that the law protected the rights of free speech and association while broadening the base of support for ballot-issue campaigns. By limiting the amount an individual or corporation was permitted to contribute to a committee supporting or opposing a ballot measure, the city maintained, each individual's allowable contribution was made more important in public debate of political issues. The restriction on speech represented by the contribution limit was minor, said the city, and was necessary to protect the integrity of the electoral process. Finally, the city emphasized that although the ordinance limited the money that individuals and corporations could give to committees organized to promote or defeat ballot issues, such committees could spend unlimited amounts to support or oppose ballot measures, and corporations and individuals could still make unlimited independent expenditures.

After the California Superior Court and the California Court of Appeals invalidated the ordinance as unconstitutional, the case was heard by the California Supreme Court. In August 1980 the court upheld the ordinance by a four-to-three decision. The California court pointed out that under the Berkeley law, individuals and corporations were free to do anything except make large contributions to a committee organized to support or defeat a ballot measure. The court ruled that large contributions to local ballot measure campaigns were a threat to the electoral system and the purpose of the initiative process.[78]

The decision was appealed to the U.S. Supreme Court, and on December 14, 1981, by an eight-to-one margin, the Court overturned the California Supreme Court's decision. The U.S. Supreme Court ruled that restrictions on ballot campaign contributions violated First Amendment rights by imposing a direct restraint on freedom of expression and political dialogue. In the majority opinion delivered by Chief Justice Warren Burger, the Court declared that a law limiting individuals who wish to join together to support or oppose a ballot measure but not limiting individuals acting alone is "clearly a restraint of the rights of association."[79] Such a law, he said, significantly restrains the freedom of expression "of groups and those individuals who wish to express their views through committees."[80] The chief justice also reasoned that there is much less justification for limiting contributions to committees working on ballot measures than for limiting contributions to candidate committees or to political committees that contribute to candidates. Limits on contributions to candidates and to committees contributing to candidates were upheld because unlimited contributions were thought to have the potential of corrupting officeholders, he said, whereas in a referendum campaign, there is no one to corrupt.

The ruling will have extensive repercussions because a number of state and local governments have imposed similar restrictions on contributions to referendum campaigns. Also, although the case involved only ballot measures, not candidates, the Supreme Court's ruling undoubtedly will be used to challenge limits on federal-campaign contributions.

Labor-Union PAC Contributions

On November 21, 1978, Henry Walther, membership-services director of the National Right to Work Committee (NRWC), filed suit in the U.S. District Court for the District of Columbia charging that the FEC was remiss in dismissing a series of complaints that he and the NRWC had filed with the commission alleging excessive contributions by the AFL-CIO to forty-five federal candidates.[81] Walther and the NRWC had complained that the AFL-CIO and its affiliated unions had violated the $5,000 limit on contributions by a multicandidate committee to congressional candidates. Each member union of the federation claimed an independent status for the purpose of making campaign contributions with each union subject to separate contribution limits. The NRWC maintained that all of the AFL-CIO affiliates should be treated as a single group subject to a single contribution limit. The FEC dismissed the forty-five complaints, ruling that it was permissible for a candidate to accept $5,000 from the AFL-CIO plus $5,000 from each of the federation's 106 member unions. To buttress its decision, the commission cited statements made in congressional debate and reports by congressional committees as evidence that Congress clearly intended to allow such contributions.

In their suit, Walther and the NRWC charged that when candidates or their campaigns accepted from both the labor federation's COPE and one or more of the PACs established by the AFL-CIO member unions contributions that in the aggregate amounted to more than $5,000, they knowingly accepted contributions in violation of the FECA contribution limit. Walther argued that COPE and the AFL-CIO member PACs were controlled by the same persons and therefore were affiliated and subject to one contribution limit under the law. U.S. District Judge Charles R. Richey rejected a motion by the FEC to dismiss the complaint and ruled that the commission erred in basing its rejection of the right-to-work group's challenge on what the FEC understood to be congressional intent. Judge Richey held that the question of whether candidates could receive funds from more than one PAC had to be decided by a finding of facts regarding whether the PACs in question were under common control. If they were under common control, the judge said, the union contributions would have to be lumped together to determine whether a candidate for the House or Senate had illegally received more than the limit of $5,000 from any single source.

On June 15, 1979, the district court granted summary judgment to the FEC. The court found that Walther's complaints contained serious shortcomings and determined that the commission's decision not to investigate them was eminently reasonable. On August 3, 1979, the same court dismissed seventeen cases—which had been consolidated with *Henry Walther*

v. *FEC*—brought by Walther against the candidates and committees whom he had named in the complaints filed with the commission.

Corporate PACs Solicitation Procedures

In 1971 the FECA sanctioned direct and open participation by labor and corporate organizations wanting to play a prominent role in partisan politics by allowing them to use treasury funds to set up, administer, and raise funds for PACs that would collect voluntary contributions from members and stockholders to be used to influence federal elections. The 1974 FECA amendments encouraged the development of corporate PACs by allowing corporations and unions with federal contracts to create and maintain PACs. Previously federal contractors had been barred from making direct or indirect contributions to federal-election campaigns. A 1975 FEC advisory opinion permitting corporations to use money from voluntary employee contributions to their PACs to influence federal elections further stimulated corporate PAC growth. From 1972 to the 1977-1978 election cycle, the number of corporate PACs increased from 89 to 812.

On October 10, 1979, the International Association of Machinists and Aerospace Workers (IAM) filed a complaint with the FEC claiming that the creation and proliferation of corporate PACs violated the tradition of preventing corporations from becoming directly involved in federal elections.[82] The IAM complaint was based on the union's analysis of financial-disclosure reports of ten of the nation's largest corporate PACs—those of Dart Industries, Eaton Corporation, General Motors, General Electric, International Paper, Standard Oil, Union Camp, Union Oil, United Technologies, and Winn-Dixie. For comparison purposes, the IAM also studied a smaller PAC, that of Grumman Corporation. The complaint requested that the FEC find solicitation practices of corporate PACs coercive and thus in violation of the FECA. The complaint also argued that portions of the FECA relating to corporate PACs should be held unconstitutional.[83]

The IAM concluded from their study that the solicitation techniques of corporate PACs were pregnant with coercion for four major reasons. First, said the union, the corporations concentrated their PAC donation requests on midlevel managerial employees, who were particularly vulnerable because their advancement depended on maintaining the good will of the employer. Second, the IAM maintained, the employees who were solicited to contribute to a company's PAC were not actually free to refuse the request because neither the identities of those who refused to contribute nor the amounts of individual contributions were kept private. Third, employees had no control over how their contributions were distributed by their PAC. The union claimed that the corporate committees ignored the personal interests of donors by spending money on congressional races in states outside those in which the money was raised. Moreover, the union complained, employees were not permitted to earmark their contributions, which limited the "free and voluntary" character of the donation. And finally, said the union, employees rarely declined to contribute, and the amounts of the contributions were inordinately high. As proof of this claim, the union offered evidence that middle-level managerial and professional employees gave between $116 and $338 each to the top ten corporate PACs in 1978 as compared with a national average political donation of $16. The IAM also noted that the response to corporate solicitations was 70 percent or higher compared with 3 percent for the general public.[84]

The IAM complaint alleged that by allowing corporations to engage in unrestricted solicitation of their managerial employees, the law gave corporations an enormous financial advantage over unions because of the power corporations exert over their managerial employees. Finally the IAM asserted that the First Amendment rights of stockholders were violated when corporations used the stockholders' assets to support a PAC.

In December 1979 the FEC unanimously rejected the IAM's complaint, which in essence demanded that the FEC outlaw all corporate PACs. Following the recommendation of its Office of General Counsel (OGC), the commission found no reason to believe that the ten major corporations had violated the FECA. The OGC stated that generous contributions from midlevel managerial and professional employees to their corporations' PACs was not sufficient evidence to demonstrate coercion and that the amount of the average contribution such employees made was not unreasonable when the size of their salaries was taken into account. The OGC also dismissed the allegation that the FECA gives corporations an unfair advantage over unions.

In February 1980 the IAM filed suit in the U.S. District Court for the District of Columbia arguing that the FEC's dismissal of its complaint was unjustifiable.[85] The union argued for overturning the FEC's dismissal on two separate grounds. First, the suit alleged that the corporate PACs utilized coercive fund-raising techniques contrary to law. Second, the union charged that the fund-raising practices were not only illegal but unconstitutional as well, violating the freedom-of-expression and equal-protection clauses of the Constitution. Judge Barrington D. Parker rejected the union's complaint that solicitation practices of corporate PACs were inherently coercive, and thus violated 2 U.S.C. 441(b)(3), and stated that the FEC had not abused its discretionary powers when it dismissed the complaint. But Judge Parker did agree that the IAM and corporate stockholders had sufficient standing to challenge the constitutionality of the FECA for themselves and for affected employees. The district court ordered the IAM to undertake an extensive investigation of the PAC operations of four of the corporations—

Dart, Eaton, United Technologies, and Winn-Dixie—in order to establish a factual record for certification of constitutional questions to the appellate court. The purpose of the investigation was to gather evidence to support the union's contention that the methods used by the corporations to generate PAC contributions violated constitutional rights.

The IAM pursued the investigation, but the union was not willing to drop its challenge regarding the legality of the corporate PACs' fund raising. Consequently the union initiated a two-track approach against the corporate PACs. On June 3, 1981, after examining the results of the IAM's investigation, Judge Parker certified the constitutional questions raised by the union for an en banc review by the appeals court. In its brief to the court of appeals, the IAM asked the court to invalidate provisions of the FECA that permit the existence of corporate-sponsored PACs on grounds that they unconstitutionally infringe upon the First Amendment rights of employees.[86] The union also appealed to the same court Judge Parker's decision to uphold the FEC's dismissal of its original complaint.

The appeal of the district court decision to uphold the FEC was resolved first. On August 20, 1981, the Appeals Court for the District of Columbia upheld, without issuing an opinion, the lower court's ruling that there had been no violation of law. The IAM appealed that decision to the U.S. Supreme Court, and in November 1981 the high court ruled that the corporations named by IAM had not acted illegally in soliciting contributions from eligible employees.

On April 6, 1982, the U.S. Court of Appeals also rejected the constitutional challenges to 2 U.S.C. 441b(3) that IAM had brought in its suit.[87] The appeals court ruled that Congress had justifiably attempted to shape the election law's solicitation procedures to take account of differences in organizational structure between corporations and labor unions. The court also found that the relatively high rate and amount of contributions from career employees to their corporation's PACs was not necessarily evidence of their having been coerced but could have been motivated by the employees' desire to further what they perceived as their own or their corporations' best interests. Finally the court found that since stockholders are free to withdraw at any time their investment in a corporation, their free-speech rights were not violated when the corporation used corporate assets to establish and administer a PAC.

Nonstock Corporation Solicitation Rights

Although the FECA prohibits contributions and expenditures by corporations in connection with a federal election, the act does allow corporations with capital stock to use treasury funds to solicit contributions for their PACs from among the corporations' stockholders, administrative and executive personnel, and their families. Corporations without stock may use treasury funds to solicit corporation members. The FECA does not allow corporations of either type to solicit nonmembers or the general public.

Shortly after World War II, the National Right to Work Committee (NRWC) was incorporated in Virginia to oppose membership in labor unions as a condition of employment. The organization created a political-action arm, the Employees Rights Campaign Committee (ERCC), to provide support for conservative candidates and others sharing its conservative viewpoint. Virginia law required the NRWC to state whether it had members. To prevent possible harassment of persons named on a membership list, the NRWC declared that it would not have members.[88]

In 1976 the ERCC requested an advisory opinion from the FEC regarding the legality of a fund-raising campaign it intended to undertake during the 1976 election. Shortly thereafter, however, the Supreme Court's *Buckley* decision prevented the FEC from issuing advisory opinions until after it was reconstituted. During that time, the NRWC began to solicit funds from its supporters for the ERCC. ERCC notified the FEC on August 31, 1976, that it wished to review its request for an advisory opinion, and on October 4, 1976, the FEC told ERCC that more information on NRWC membership would be required before an opinion could be issued. The additional information was not submitted, and the FEC declined to issue the requested opinion.

On October 20, 1976, the National Committee for an Effective Congress (NCEC), a liberal political-action organization, filed a complaint with the FEC charging the NRWC and its political-action affiliate with violating FECA fund-raising restrictions. Acting on the NCEC complaint, the FEC investigated the solicitation procedure of NRWC and ERCC and found reasonable cause to believe that the organizations had violated the solicitation restrictions of the FECA by seeking funds from nonmembers. On May 9, 1977, the FEC proposed a conciliation agreement, stipulating that NRWC admit to violating the act, pay a $5,000 civil penalty, and amend its articles of incorporation to become a membership organization. NRWC agreed to amend its articles of incorporation but refused to pay the fine. It also requested a clear definition of membership requirements under the act. On August 3, 1977, the commission rejected the committee's proposal, insisting that no further soliciting could take place without both a change in the articles of incorporation and payment of the $5,000 fine.

On October 20, 1977, the NRWC and ERCC, upon receiving notice that the FEC intended to file a civil action against them, filed their own suit against the FEC in the U.S. District Court for the Eastern District of Virginia.[89] Their suit challenged the constitutionality of 2 U.S.C. 441b(b)(4) (A) and (C) that limits nonstock corporations to soliciting their own members.

They claimed the provision violated their First Amendment right of free speech and their Fifth Amendment rights to due process and equal protection of the law. In addition, the NRWC and ERCC argued that since the FEC had refused to provide a definition of the term *member*, no compliance standards had been established. The groups asked for a permanent injunction against FEC enforcement of that provision of the act. In its motion to dismiss the suit, the FEC maintained that NRWC's articles of incorporation foreclosed it from being a membership corporation and that consequently its solicitation of supporters could be interpreted only as "directed at the general public, which is exactly what Congress intended to prohibit."[90] The FEC argued further that if NRWC's position was accepted by the court, any corporation could argue that it must be allowed to solicit any member of the general public it believed to be a supporter of its goals.

On December 21, 1977, the FEC filed a separate suit against NRWC arguing that the organization did not qualify as a membership organization under the provisions of the FECA.[91] According to the FEC suit, in 1976 NRWC and ERCC conducted several mass mailings in which they solicited approximately 276,000 persons, raising more than $77,616 for ERCC. The NRWC claimed that the persons solicited had previously responded to NRWC fund-raising appeals either by making contributions or by answering questionnaires. Each person who responded to those solicitations, whether or not he or she made a contribution, was listed by NRWC as a member. The FEC alleged that the committee violated the law because both NRWC's bylaws and the articles of incorporation it had filed with the state of Virginia declared that NRWC had no members. Furthermore, the FEC argued that the term *member* denotes a relationship to a nonstock corporation such as shareholders have to stock corporations. The persons listed as members by the NRWC had no such relationship to the group. The commission asked the court to enjoin ERCC from further solicitations of this nature and to order it to return all past contributions solicited unlawfully. The FEC also argued that NRWC should be forced to disclose the names of its members so that determination could be made as to the nature of its membership.

In response, NRWC and ERCC argued that the restrictions on solicitations by nonstock corporations were unconstitutionally vague. Election law limits solicitation to an organization's members. The NRWC claimed, however, that what constitutes membership was inadequately defined and that the FEC unreasonably declined to clarify the law upon the organization's request for an advisory opinion on the issue. The FEC refused to offer an opinion until the NRWC submitted a list of members. The NRWC defined its membership as all those who demonstrated some form of voluntary involvement with the group's activities, amounting to nearly 1 million members, and claimed only those persons were solicited. The committee maintained it kept its membership list confidential because of fears of possible harassment. The NRWC defended its articles of incorporation, which claim the group has no members, as a technicality designed to protect its membership. The state of Virginia, where the articles were filed, would have required public disclosure of the list otherwise. Finally, NRWC argued that the FECA's restrictions on the classes of persons a corporation may solicit, whether a stock or nonstock corporation, was an unconstitutional abridgement of First Amendment freedoms.

In February 1978 the cases were consolidated for argument before the U.S. District Court for the District of Columbia.[92] On August 19, 1978, U.S. District Judge Barrington D. Parker denied the FEC request that the NRWC disclose the names of its members, concluding that such disclosure would violate constitutional rights of freedom of association. On April 24, Judge Parker ruled that NRWC had illegally solicited contributions from persons who were not members of the organization. According to Parker, the term *member* "denoted a formal relationship in which a person . . . has a special right and obligation vis-à-vis an organization."[93] The persons solicited by NRWC, he ruled, had no such rights or obligations regarding the committee, and in fact, he said, there was extensive evidence that NRWC did not consider its contributors to be members; the NRWC's articles of incorporation specifically stated the committee would have no members. According to the ruling, the group's declaration in its articles that it had no members indicated NRWC's solicitation was a knowing and willful violation of the act. NRWC, noted the court, deliberately organized itself in such a fashion to avoid compliance with the requirements of a membership corporation. Further, the court determined that the NRWC concealed its no-membership status from the FEC when the group requested an advisory opinion on its right to solicit. The court also upheld the constitutionality of the portion of the FECA that limits corporations and labor organizations to soliciting certain restricted classes of individuals. The NRWC was ordered to refund the $77,616 in campaign contributions it had solicited by mail in 1976 and to pay a $10,000 fine for deliberate violation of the FECA.

The NRWC and ERCC appealed the decision to the U.S. Circuit Court of Appeals for the District of Columbia, which overturned the lower court's decision on September 4, 1981, ruling that the interpretation of 2 U.S.C. 441b(b)(4)(C) by the lower court and the FEC infringed on the First Amendment right of association.[94] Judge Homer Thornberry noted that the FECA does not provide a definition of *member* and that the FEC's regulations provide organizations wide latitude in determining their own membership standards. Thornberry believed that the district court's opinion had relied too heavily on the NRWC's own Virginia charter. He wrote that the appeals court saw no justification to apply a state-law standard to the case. State

definitions of members in nonstock corporations for purposes of state corporate or tax laws, wrote Thornberry, were unlikely to take account of "the
important First Amendment considerations at the heart of any controversy" involving the FECA.[95] Moreover, Judge Thornberry wrote,
the court failed to see how the interests of the FECA in eliminating corruption and the appearance of corruption in federal elections were served by
limiting the NRWC's solicitation activities since, unlike employees of corporations and members of labor unions, the persons solicited by the NRWC
"clearly are not subject to coercion."[96] Judge Thornberry was satisfied that
the NRWC's operation ensured that only those individuals who shared the
organization's political philosophy were solicited.

    While the NRWC was attempting unsuccessfully to receive compensa-
tion from the government for its legal expenses under the Equal Access to
Justice Act,[97] the FEC appealed Judge Thornberry's decision to the U.S.
Supreme Court. More than one year later, the high court reversed Thornberry's ruling, and reiterated that the individuals solicited by the NRWC
were not attached sufficiently to the operations or administration of the
organization to qualify as members. The court did not offer a definition of
member. In the opinion by Justice Rehnquist, the court acknowledged that
the restriction on corporate solicitation rights may infringe on First Amendment freedoms, but such infringement is outweighed by the government interest in preventing the accumulation of huge corporate political war chests,
and in protecting the rights of individuals who contribute money to a corporation or labor union for purposes other than supporting a particular
candidate. The court, however, did not resolve the FEC's penalty demands
upon the NRWC.

Trade-Association Solicitation Rights

Under federal-election law, although there is no limitation on the number of
times trade associations may solicit their noncorporate members, they may
solicit the shareholders and executive and administrative personnel of
member corporations and the families of such persons only after they have
obtained prior written permission of the corporations. Such permission
must be obtained annually. And although a corporation might belong to
several trade associations, it is allowed to permit such solicitation by only
one association in any calendar year.

    In April 1977 those provisions of the FECA were challenged by two
trade associations, the National Lumber and Building Dealers Association
and the National Restaurant Association, and the separate segregated funds
of three trade associations, the American Bakers Association (BreadPAC),
the Restaurateurs PAC, and the Lumber Dealers PAC (LUDPAC). The

legal challenge, directed by lawyers from the National Chamber Litigation Center, an organization affiliated with the U.S. Chamber of Commerce, was filed with the U.S. District Court for the Northern District of Illinois.[98]

The five groups contended that the FECA restrictions infringed upon their First Amendment rights of free speech and association and their Fifth Amendment right to equal treatment under the law. They asked the court to suspend enforcement of the restrictions on the way trade associations can solicit money or, alternately, to certify constitutional questions to the appeals court. In September 1977 the district court ruled that the plaintiffs lacked standing under an FECA provision that allows only the national committee of a political party, individuals eligible to vote in presidential elections, and the FEC to seek expedited review of the constitutionality of any provision of the law.[99] On October 6, 1977, the court also rejected the plaintiffs' motion for a preliminary injunction against enforcement of the solicitation restriction on trade associations.

On January 12, 1979, however, the U.S. Court of Appeals overturned the lower court's decision in response to a temporary appeal filed by Bread-PAC and the four other plaintiffs. The appeals court ruled that BreadPAC and the other groups did have standing to bring suit under the expedited-review procedure. The district court was then ordered to make further fact-finding efforts and to certify the constitutional questions that would then be sent to the appeals court for its decision.

In its brief to the appellate court, the plaintiffs argued that the FECA provisions requiring a trade association to obtain approval from a corporate member before it solicited the corporation's stockholders and administrative and executive personnel violated the association's right of freedom of association. The plaintiffs also argued that by imposing such limitations on trade associations and not on union, corporate, and independent PACs, the law violated its Fifth Amendment guarantee of equal protection. Finally, the trade association argued that the law's definitions of *solicitation* and *trade association* were vague and overly broad, thereby leaving the fundamental right to engage in free speech and association dependent on FEC judgment and interpretation.

On December 5, 1980, the U.S. Court of Appeals in Chicago rejected the BreadPAC challenge in a five-to-three decision ruling that the provision at issue served a compelling state interest to eliminate political corruption.[100] The court found that the requirement that a trade association receive prior approval from its corporate members before soliciting placed no prior restraint on the free flow of political information and opinion by trade associations. Since trade associations are unrestricted in soliciting individuals to become members and then to contribute both to the associations and their PACs, the court reasoned that the requirement of prior approval before soliciting corporate members does not impair freedom of association for such organizations. The court also dismissed the equal-protection challenge on the grounds that disparate treatment of trade associations, corporations, and labor unions was justified by the difference in their organizational structure and constituencies. Finally, the court found that the statute was not unconstitutionally vague in its definitions of *solicitation* and *trade association*.[101]

The five-year legal battle came to an end in March 1982 when the U.S. Supreme Court unanimously ruled that the plaintiffs lacked standing under federal election law to bring suit.

Corporate Contributions and Expenditures: I

In early 1980, while Sen. Edward Kennedy was a candidate for the Democratic presidential nomination, Phillips Publishing, Inc., sent a mailing to regular and potential subscribers soliciting subscriptions to its biweekly conservative newsletter, the *Pink Sheet on the Left*, and seeking donations to help place the newsletter in college libraries. The mailing included on a single page a subscription form and a "Teddy Kennedy Opinion Poll" that could be completed and returned to the newsletter's publishers. The poll asked questions such as, "Do you think Teddy Kennedy is a threat to the survival of America?" The mailing strongly emphasized the *Pink Sheet's* opposition to the campaign and philosophy of Sen. Kennedy.

In March 1980 the Kennedy for President Committee filed a complaint accusing the publishing company of making illegal corporate expenditures advocating Kennedy's defeat.[102] Under the FECA, "Any news story, commentary or editorial distributed through the facilities of any broadcasting station, newspaper, magazine or other periodical publication" is exempt from the law's spending restrictions "unless [the] facilities are owned by a political party, political committee or candidate."[103] But the Kennedy for President Committee contended that the exemption did not extend to advertising and suggested that if the mailing of anti-Kennedy materials to potential subscribers was paid for with corporate funds, then the mailing could be considered an illegal corporate expenditure to defeat a clearly identified candidate for federal office. The complaint added that if the mailing was not paid for with corporate funds, the newsletter should be required to register as a political committee and make periodic disclosure reports of its activities. Phillips Publishing responded by stating that the *Pink Sheet* was a periodical and was not controlled by any party, candidate, or committee; therefore promotional material it distributed was exempt from FEC regulation.

Acting on the Kennedy committee complaint, the FEC found "reason to believe" that the subscription mailing may have violated federal campaign laws requiring political committees to register with the FEC and to report political expenditures. The FEC concluded that the issue had to be investigated further in order to determine whether the publishing company's claim that the promotional mailing constituted an exempted news activity was true. In pursuing its investigation, the FEC asked the company officials to provide information on who financed the promotional mailing, how proceeds were used, how many letters were mailed, and how much was spent.

Phillips Publishing refused to comply with the FEC's formal orders to answer the inquiries. The publisher of the *Pink Sheet*, Thomas L. Phillips, contended that the newsletter was protected by First Amendment guarantees.[104] Lawyers for the newsletter also claimed that the FEC was trying to gain information of no relevance to its investigation, such as the names and addresses of members of the editorial staff and the location and numbers of the company's bank accounts. When Phillips Publishing refused to provide the information the FEC requested, the commission filed suit in the U.S. District Court for the District of Columbia on April 8, 1981, seeking a subpoena enforcement order.

On July 16, 1981, U.S. District Judge Thomas A. Flannery denied the FEC request to enforce its subpoenas for information from the newsletter's publisher and editor and also ordered the FEC to stop its investigation of the complaint. The judge ruled that the newsletter, as well as letters soliciting subscriptions, were exempted by federal law from FEC regulation.[105] Flannery said the FEC request to enforce the subpoenas was based on conjecture that a violation might have occurred and that this was not sufficient grounds for an FEC investigation into highly sensitive areas of freedom of speech and press.

The FEC initially appealed the decision, but on October 21, 1981, the commission changed its mind and filed a motion to withdraw the appeal "in the interest of judicial economy," although it continued to believe that "the district court's decision was erroneous."[106] On October 30, 1981, the U.S. Court of Appeals for the District of Columbia granted the FEC's motion to withdraw its appeal.[107]

Corporate Contributions and Expenditures: II

In February 1980, just two weeks prior to the New Hampshire primary, the *Reader's Digest* published an article entitled, "Chappaquiddick: The Still Unanswered Questions," which was highly critical of Democratic presidential candidate Sen. Edward Kennedy. In addition to publishing the article, the magazine commissioned and paid for the production of a computer reenactment of the 1969 automobile accident in which Sen. Kennedy had driven off a bridge on the island of Chappaquiddick, and his passenger,

Mary Jo Kopechne, was killed. The magazine hired experts to research the tidal flows in the area on the night of the accident. It publicized and promoted the article by making videotapes of the computer reenactment available to television networks and stations. Both the story and the tapes received national attention, and in at least one instance, part of the tape was broadcast by one of the major commercial television networks.[108]

In August 1980 an Oregon woman complained to the FEC that the promotional activities of the *Reader's Digest* had gone beyond the normal "reporting and commentary" functions of a news agency that are exempt from federal campaign laws.[109] She claimed that the magazine had stepped into an advocacy role when it ordered the studies and when it used the videotape to promote its article. In essence, her complaint alleged that the magazine publishing company had violated the provision of the FECA that prohibits corporations from expending funds to influence a federal election.

The complaint prompted the FEC to open a secret investigation of the Reader's Digest Association (RDA) in December 1980 to determine if the magazine publishing company had violated the election law's prohibition on corporate expenditures in federal-election campaigns. The FEC questioned not the magazine's decision to research and publish the article but the expenditures made by the RDA to publicize the article. A majority of FEC members concluded from the investigation that there was "reason to believe" that the expenditures represented an illegal use of corporate funds.

In order to examine the promotional expenditures made by the magazine publishing company, the FEC drew up fifteen questions for the RDA to answer. The questions were designed to help the FEC determine if the publicity was intended to increase sales of the February 1980 issue or to undermine Kennedy's bid for his party's presidential nomination. Citing the First Amendment guarantee of freedom of the press, the RDA refused to answer any questions regarding the article or its promotion. It then filed suit in the U.S. District Court for the Southern District of New York arguing that responding to the FEC's investigation would violate its right to speak freely and comment on newsworthy events and requesting that the investigation be halted.[110] The magazine asked the court to issue a temporary restraining order and a preliminary injunction to prevent the FEC from demanding answers to its questions and information about the videotapes, as well as the tapes themselves. The FEC responded that the RDA's suit was premature since the commission had not even made a ruling; it had only found reason to believe a violation may have occurred, a very early stage in an FEC investigation. The commission claimed it was simply trying to determine whether the complaint warranted more serious inquiry.[111]

On March 19, 1981, U.S. District Judge Pierre Leval denied the RDA's request for an injunction and restraining order to halt the FEC investigation and granted the FEC the right to pursue a limited investigation of the RDA.

The purpose of the investigation, according to the judge, had to be to determine if the RDA was acting as a press entity or in its corporate capacity when it distributed the tapes. Judge Leval ruled that unless the FEC could determine that press exemption did not apply to the *Reader's Digest*'s distribution of the tapes, the FEC would not be permitted to pursue any substantial investigation. He also ruled that the RDA was not compelled to provide the information the FEC sought.

In the ensuing investigation, the commission did not uncover any evidence to suggest that the distribution was outside the scope of the RDA's functions as a publisher. The agency therefore found no probable cause to believe the RDA had violated the FECA and recommended that the complaint be dismissed. On October 30, 1981, the U.S. District Court for the Southern District of New York ordered the dismissal of the suit.

Corporate Contributions and Expenditures: III

On May 26, 1981, the FEC filed suit in the U.S. District Court for the District of Columbia, charging the National Rifle Association (NRA) and its lobbying organization, the Institute for Legislative Action (ILA), with violating a provision of the FECA that prohibits corporations from making contributions and expenditures in connection with a federal election.[112] The FEC accused the two groups, both of which are corporations, of improperly advancing $37,126 to NRA's multicandidate PAC, the Political Victory Fund (PVF), during the 1978 and 1980 campaigns. Of the $37,126 advanced to the PVF, $13,610 allegedly was spent in contributions to the Reagan prenomination campaign, $3,269 in efforts to defeat Sen. Edward Kennedy in his bid for the Democratic presidential nomination, and additional funds on behalf of or against fifteen congressional candidates.[113] The PVF later reimbursed the money.

Before filing suit, the FEC attempted to obtain a voluntary conciliation agreement from the NRA, which would have required an admission of guilt and assessment of a relatively small civil penalty. When the NRA refused to agree, the FEC filed its suit, asking the district court to assess a penalty of either $5,000 or 100 percent of the violation against both the NRA and the two affiliates. The FEC also asked the court to rule the advances illegal and to issue an injunction against any such advances in the future.[114]

The NRA did not acquiesce to the conciliation agreement because it maintained the expenditures were administrative in nature. Federal election law does allow corporations to pay administrative costs of their PACs. In a letter to the FEC, PVF treasurer James J. Featherstone maintained that the fund utilized credit arrangements set up by the NRA and ILA to pay for travel, mailing and other services. He said the fund reimbursed the NRA and ILA "to ensure that no corporate funds are used in connection with a federal election."[115]

Corporate Contributions and Expenditures: IV

On August 5, 1981, the Athens Lumber Company, a family-owned business located in Athens, Georgia, filed suit in the U.S. District Court for the Middle District of Georgia mounting a direct challenge to the nation's oldest surviving law on the subject of campaign finance, the 1907 Tillman Act, which has since been codified as part of the FECA.[116] The suit specifically challenged section 441b(a) of the U.S. Code, which states that it is illegal for any national bank, corporation, or labor organization to make a contribution or expenditure in connection with a federal election. The Athens Lumber Company claimed this provision violated the company's First and Fifth Amendment rights.

Central to the Athens Lumber argument was the claim that the company's business was directly affected by the decisions of federal officeholders, by the general economic conditions of the United States, and by a large number of federal statutes, regulations, and policies. As examples of such factors the company cited high interest rates, resulting from governmental borrowing and governmental monetary policies, which made it impossible for many individuals and businesses to borrow funds with which to finance new construction, and environmental programs, which contributed to the shortage and increased costs of lumber materials.

These arguments had provided the impetus for the shareholders of Athens Lumber Company, all members of the same family, to draw up and unanimously endorse a resolution authorizing the company to spend up to $10,000 in corporate funds for political purposes. The resolution stated that the funds could be used to advocate the election or defeat of specifically identified candidates for election to federal office. The company was well aware that the particulars of the resolution violated the federal campaign law prohibiting corporate contributions and expenditures in federal-election campaigns, but its shareholders were determined to exercise what they considered their First and Fifth Amendment rights.[117]

The company resolved to assist and promote the election to federal office of those persons whom Athens Lumber believed were best qualified to serve the interests of the people of the United States. It proposed to accomplish its purpose by making direct contributions to federal candidates, making independent expenditures on behalf of federal candidates, and distributing political endorsements with customer billings. The company believed its efforts would promote its business and the welfare of its shareholders, customers, and suppliers.

Before taking any of its proposed actions, Athens Lumber filed its lawsuit in order to obtain declaratory judgment from the court that the company's proposed contributions and expenditures would not violate the election law. The company also wanted the court to rule that the provision was unconstitutional, null, and void. Athens claimed that section 441b(a) unconstitutionally suppressed the ability of corporations, national banks, and unions to communicate with and influence the electorate and in that way magnified "the political influence of natural persons or other organizations" that were not restricted by the provision.[118]

In December 1981, while Athens was awaiting the district court's decision whether to certify the constitutional questions raised to the en banc court of appeals, Common Cause and the IAM filed separate intervenor motions with the federal district judge. Both groups wanted to help defend the prohibition on direct corporate contributions to candidates for federal office. The IAM maintained that the union had a "distinct and special interest and a tremendous economic stake in the outcome of this litigation, for corporations and unions are natural and traditional opponents in both the economic and political arena."[119] The IAM claimed that an invalidation of the ban on corporate and labor-union contributions to candidates would destroy the delicate balance Congress sought to create when it sanctioned rules enabling corporations and labor unions to establish PACs to collect voluntary funds for disbursement to federal candidates. Common Cause claimed it had a direct interest in the outcome of the litigation because of its purpose to promote members' interest in civic betterment on a nonpartisan basis, particularly in campaign finance reform.

In its filing to intervene, the IAM alleged that if Athens Lumber was successful in its suit, American corporations would be able to use "their vast treasuries" for direct contributions to candidates and for independent expenditures on their behalf.[120] Common Cause maintained that without section 441b(a), corporations would flood federal election campaigns with millions of dollars, carrying the potential for corruption of the electoral process. Common Cause also asked to participate as a friend of the court if its intervenor motion was dismissed.

On January 19, 1982, U.S. District Court Judge Wilbur D. Owens denied the groups' separate intervenor motions and also refused to accept Common Cause as a friend of the court. Judge Owens wrote that the FEC could "more than adequately represent the interest of these organizations and their members" in making sure the action was effectively defended.[121] The FEC had opposed the interventions, arguing that the union had no standing to represent a public interest but only its own interest in maximizing its political influence, and that the Common Cause intervention would produce unwarranted delays while only duplicating the government agency's own efforts to defend the law.[122]

On February 9, 1982, Judge Owens dismissed the Athens Lumber Company's suit on procedural grounds, stating that federal courts are not testing grounds for hypothetical situations. He said that a concrete dispute did not exist between the company and the FEC, and that the justiciable level of controversy that must exist for the court to have jurisdiction over the complaint was totally lacking. The lumber company had not made contributions to federal candidates; it had merely stated its desire to do so. Moreover, he ruled, the company lacked standing under federal law to seek a review of the law under an expedited procedure.[123]

Athens Lumber Company immediately filed an appeal to a three-judge federal panel. On October 22, 1982, the federal appeals court reversed the lower court's decision and ruled that the company may challenge the FECA. Circuit Judge James C. Hill ruled that John P. Bondurant, the president of the company, could take the case before a twelve-judge en banc appeals court under the expedited-review provision of the act. The court determined that Bondurant, as an individual eligible to vote, fell within one of three categories of groups granted the expedited review. (The other categories are the FEC and national political parties.) The case is expected to be heard before the twelve-judge appeals court in 1983.

Public Funding and Spending Limits

The 1974 FECA amendments gave major-party presidential nominees the option of receiving a flat sum of money from the Presidential Election Campaign Fund to conduct their campaigns ($20 million plus a cost-of-living increase) on the condition that they not accept or spend funds from any other source or raise funds privately. On June 16, 1978, the Republican National Committee (RNC) and the Ripon Society of New York, a liberal GOP organization, filed suit in U.S. District Court for the Southern District of New York charging that it was unconstitutional to require presidential candidates who accept public funding for their general-election campaigns to adhere to a spending ceiling.[124] The RNC did not challenge the use of public funds, which had been upheld in the Supreme Court's 1976 *Buckley* decision, but rather the spending limit attached to the receipt of public funds and the ban on acceptance of contributions from individuals and political committees.

The GOP challenge was based primarily on the part of the *Buckley* finding that determined that, contrary to the First Amendment, limits on campaign spending substantially and directly restricted "the ability of candidates, citizens and associations to engage in protected political expressions."[125] The *Buckley* Court also ruled, however, that Congress could condition acceptance of public funds on an agreement by the candidate to abide by specific spending limits. In addition, defenders of the system in effect for the 1976 election, including the Carter administration, the FEC, and Common Cause, argued that Congress clearly had intended that public financing of general-election campaigns to be a substitute for private fund raising and not a supplement to it.

RNC chairman Bill Brock contended that the spending limit was an unconstitutional condition on the receipt of public funds.[126] He claimed that the limit violated the First Amendment rights of free speech and association and the Fifth Amendment right of due process by restricting the amount a candidate could spend while engaging in political speech, by limiting the amount a candidate's supporters could spend in grass-roots activity, and by preventing a candidate's supporters from contributing financially to his or her campaign.

But the Republican plaintiffs' principal claim was that the spending limit imposed as a condition of accepting public funds gives an incument president an enormous advantage over a challenger. They maintained that in exercising office, an incumbent engages in activities that influence the outcome of the election but that are not affected by the spending limit. An incumbent president, they said, also is able to attract media attention simply by conducting the nation's business. In addition, the Republicans contended, an incumbent's programs are based on research and expertise provided by executive branch staff at no cost to the incumbent's reelection campaign.

The Republicans further contended that the factor that helped Jimmy Carter, the challenger, defeat incumbent President Gerald Ford in 1976, though both contestants accepted public funds, was the support given to Carter by organized labor. According to the Republicans, the terms of the FECA give special privileges to organized labor. Specifically labor has the right to spend unlimited amounts of general treasury funds on political communications to union members and their families. In 1976, unions spent about $11 million on such communications for Jimmy Carter, whereas corporations spent only a fraction of that amount for President Ford.[127] The crux of the RNC's argument was that since the Democrats would have the support of organized labor in 1980 as well as the advantages of incumbency—presuming President Carter was renominated—the election law unfairly disadvantaged their candidate. Essentially the Republicans wanted to maintain federal subsidies at the level specified in the FECA but also allow both parties to spend all they could raise in small contributions in addition to that amount. In that way, they hoped to collect the funds they claimed they would need to offset whatever labor gave to the Democrats, as well as the advantages of incumbency.

The FEC filed a motion to dismiss the suit, arguing that the constitutional objections the RNC raised had been rejected by the Supreme Court in *Buckley*. In addition, the FEC argued, the RNC's suit was not a ripe controversy. Nevertheless, on November 30, 1978, the district court denied the FEC motion to dismiss and also granted permission to convene a three-judge district court to hear the case.

The U.S. District Court for the Southern District of New York and the U.S. Court of Appeals for the Second Circuit heard the suit concurrently.

On October 12, 1979, the three-judge district court dismissed all of the causes of action presented by the RNC. In February 1980 the court of appeals made the actual ruling, upholding the constitutionality of the spending limit.[128] The ten judges of the appellate court ruled unanimously that presidential candidates who accept federal funds to finance their campaigns are required to observe the regulations imposed by Congress that prohibit them from raising or spending private money for their campaigns.

The appeals court, speaking for the lower court as well, found that the FECA promotes rather than injures First Amendment freedoms. Public funding aids rather than inhibits freedom of speech, said the court, because it frees candidates from the burden of fund raising, allowing them to concentrate on communicating their stands on public issues and freeing them from dependence on large private contributions. In addition, the court ruled that since the law allows a candidate's supporters to express support by donations of personal services and through independent expenditures, the law respects First Amendment rights. The court also found that contrary to the plaintiff's argument, the current system did not favor an incumbent since President Ford, the incumbent in 1976, was defeated. Furthermore, the court stated that the advantages the FECA granted to unions to spend unlimited amounts on political communications with their members were balanced with those granted to corporations, since corporations are permitted to engage in similar activities directed at their executive and administrative personnel and their stockholders. The appeals court decision noted that organized labor support of Democratic candidates is not automatic and that President Carter was not especially popular with organized labor.

Hoping to test the public-funding provision of the FECA more thoroughly, the RNC appealed the decision to the Supreme Court. On April 14, 1980, the Court upheld the court of appeals, confirming the constitutionality of the expenditure limits imposed by the FECA on nominees who accept public funding.[129]

Party Committee Spending Authority

Under 2 U.S.C. 441a(d)(3), the national committee of a political party and the separate state committee of the party are each granted the authority to spend up to a specified amount of money in connection with the general-election campaign of the party's Senate candidate in the state—the greater of two cents multiplied by the state's voting age population or $20,000 (plus a cost-of-living increase). A separate provision, 2 U.S.C. 441a(h), permits each party's national senatorial campaign committee and national-party committee to contribute a total of $17,500 to a candidate for the party's

Senate nomination or to the party's Senate nominee during the year in which the election is held.

By developing a number of effective fund-raising techniques, the RNC had been able to raise more money than it could lawfully spend under the FECA in connection with the election of its 1980 Senate candidates. On the other hand, many Republican state-party committees had been relatively unsuccessful at fund raising. Relying on an FEC regulation that permits unlimited transfers of funds between committees of the same party,[130] the Republicans developed an arrangement to use both the RNC's excess funds and the state committees' unused spending limits.[131] A surrogate arrangement known as an agency agreement was established when the RNC and several state committees appointed the National Republican Senatorial Committee (NRSC) as their agent in making expenditures in connection with the Senate contests. As a result of the agency agreement, the national-party committees were able to increase their spending authority by more than $2 million.

On May 9, 1980, the Democratic Senatorial Campaign Committee (DSCC) filed a complaint with the FEC protesting this agency agreement. FEC regulations specifically permit a national political party to transfer its spending authority to another agent, but the Democrats claimed that allowing state committees to do the same violated the purpose of the provision giving state committees independent spending authority. The DSCC argued that state-party committees should not be allowed to transfer their spending rights because they were granted by Congress "as an incentive to party development and participation at the state and local level."[132]

On July 11, 1980, the commission unanimously rejected the DSCC's complaint. The FEC Office of General Counsel maintained that the distinction the Democrats attempted to draw between national and state committees was artificial and that there was no reason to believe that the NRSC had violated the act. On July 30, 1980 the Democrats filed suit with the U.S. District Court for the District of Columbia. In their court challenge, they once again questioned the legality of the agency agreement between the NRSC and the state parties. They asked the court to declare that the FEC's dismissal of its complaint had been contrary to the law. On August 29, 1980, the district court upheld the FEC's ruling that the practice is allowable under campaign law and stated that it must sustain all commission decisions that are not shown to be arbitrary or capricious.

On September 3, 1980, the DSCC appealed the district court decision to the District of Columbia's Circuit Court of Appeals. On October 9, 1980, in a two-to-one decision, the appeals court reversed the lower court's ruling and declared that the FEC's decision was contrary to the law.[133] The court concluded that the "plain language of 441a(d)(3) precludes" the agency agreements between state committees and the NRSC. In making the decision, the court said that the issue was not over a discretionary exercise of commission power but rather an interpretation of a federal statute, and therefore little or no deference was due to the commission. The appeals court held that the permission granted to national-party committees to assign their authority to make campaign expenditures does not extend to state-party committees. As a result, the three-judge court ruled that the NRSC had been spending money in violation of the federal election laws and thus invalidated the arrangements in which Republican state committees assigned to the national senatorial committee their authority to spend money in connection with Senate campaigns.

The NRSC immediately petitioned for a twenty-one-day deferral of the decision and an en banc review by the circuit's eleven judges. Unable to gain a rehearing of the case at the appellate court, the NRSC obtained a temporary stay of the court's enforcement order from Chief Justice Warren Burger. In asking the chief justice to delay the lower court's order, the NRSC said the appeals court decision had cast a political cloud over those Republican senatorial candidates who, "acting in good faith reliance on a unanimous decision by the FEC" that the agency agreement was lawful, had accepted funds from the NRSC.[134]

On March 2, 1981, the Supreme Court agreed to review the case in order to determine if state-party committees can delegate to national-party committees the authority to make federal-campaign expenditures. The case also gave the Supreme Court the opportunity to decide how much deference the federal courts should pay to the FEC in its day-to-day administration of the election laws. On November 10, 1981, the Supreme Court ruled unanimously that the NRSC could make expenditures on behalf of state parties that allow them to act as their surrogates.[135] Justice Byron White, writing for the Court, agreed that the language of 441a(d)(3) did not permit the NRSC to make expenditures in its own right. Nevertheless, he wrote, it did not follow that the NRSC could not act as an agent of a committee that is specifically authorized to make expenditures. He found nothing in the statute to suggest that a state committee could not designate another committee "to act in its behalf for the purposes of 441a(d)(3)."[136] Justice White said the appeals court should have deferred to the FEC's conclusion, which he said was correct in stating that nothing in the law prevented such agency agreements.

Political Use of Government Funds

On December 28, 1979, a group of supporters of Sen. Edward Kennedy's bid for the Democratic presidential nomination filed suit in the U.S. District Court for the District of Columbia accusing seven members of President Carter's cabinet and seven aides of improperly using their government positions and public funds to promote President Carter's reelection campaign.[137] The principal plaintiff in the suit was William Winpisinger, president of the IAM, and he was joined by Kennedy supporters in Iowa, New Hampshire, and the District of Columbia. The defendants included secretary of the cabinet Jack Watson, White House chief of staff Hamilton Jordan, and presidential press secretary Jody Powell.

The plaintiffs made three major allegations of illegal activity. First, they claimed public money had been spent to pay the salaries and travel expenses of administration officials while they undertook what were in essence campaign missions. In support of this allegation, they cited White House instructions to cabinet members to arrange their schedules in order that official appearances and campaign appearances coincided, so all or part of the travel expenses could be paid by the federal government. Second, the suit alleged that presidential appointees had been threatened with dismissal if they supported a candidate other than President Carter. Third, the plaintiffs alleged that federal grants and loans were awarded in return for the political support of state and local officials and for other political reasons. The suit supported this allegation by citing the cases of Mayor Jane Byrne of Chicago, who they said had been threatened with reprisals after supporting Sen. Kennedy, and Mayor Coleman Young of Detroit, who they said had been favored with federal grants after having come out in support of President Carter.[138] The plaintiffs argued that the alleged conduct of Carter subordinates threatened the integrity of the democratic system and debased the election of the nation's highest public official. They claimed the alleged actions put efforts to solicit contributions and support for Sen. Kennedy at an unfair disadvantage.

Allegations such as these made in the suit have been common throughout the history of presidential campaigns, but this suit appears to be the first in which members of a president's own party alleged such major violations.[139] The plaintiffs sought to halt the future misuse of funds, to prevent the use of government funds for political purposes, and to prevent administration officials from campaigning for the president. It also asked that the Carter-Mondale Presidential Committee be required to reimburse the federal government for salaries and expenses paid to public officials while they were doing campaign work. The attorney for the plaintiffs, Joseph L. Rauh, requested the federal district court judge to expedite the discovery phase of the lawsuit so that the misuse of funds could be stopped before the primary season began.[140]

On February 7, 1980, U.S. District Judge June L. Green dismissed the suit, ruling that the plaintiffs lacked standing because they failed to show that a "distinct and palpable" injury had been suffered and that the alleged actions of the Carter committee were in fact the cause of the injury for which they sought relief.[141] The judge agreed that Kennedy's supporters had experienced difficulty in persuading others to support him, but she said the difficulty might be due to other factors surrounding the coming election and not the alleged abuses.

The Kennedy supporters appealed the decision to the U.S. Court of Appeals for the District of Columbia. On April 10, 1980, the appeals court upheld the lower court decision and cited "prudential considerations" as an additional ground for dismissal.[142] The court stated that to grant the relief requested would have required the court to intrude pervasively in the executive branch of the federal government. Said the court, "The judiciary is not to act as a management overseer of the executive branch."[143] The Kennedy supporters appealed the decision to the U.S. Supreme Court, which on April 28, 1980, rejected the appeal without comment.

Congressional Franking Privilege

For nearly two hundred years, members of Congress have had the statutory authority to use the U.S. mails for official business free of charge, but the term *official business* never has been precisely defined. Some uses of the frank by congressional officeholders have led to complaints that officeholders have abused and exploited the franking privilege in a way that gives them an unfair advantage over their challengers in election campaigns. In October 1973 Common Cause filed suit against the postmaster general and the secretary of the treasury to prevent what it termed abuses of the frank.[144] The lobbying organization charged that the two executive agencies had acted unlawfully in failing to prevent unconstitutional and illegal use of the frank by members of Congress. In particular Common Cause charged that the franking privilege provides an unconstitutional subsidy to incumbents in their reelection campaigns.

The Common Cause suit met with considerable resistance as first the House and then the Senate attempted to block court efforts to obtain documents regarding the use of the frank. In the meantime both Houses of Congress considered franking legislation that would place greater restrictions on the use of the privilege, but none was enacted.[145] Finally, in September 1982, nearly nine years after Common Cause filed its suit, a three-judge district court panel ruled unanimously that members of Congress were entitled to the franking privilege under certain circumstances even though it might give them an advantage over their opponents in election campaigns. Although they acknowledged there might be cases in which an incumbent's use of the frank creates an imbalance in the campaign process, the judges found they had not been presented with evidence that the impact of the use of the privilege should lead them to redraft regulations regarding its use. Common Cause appealed the panel's ruling to the U.S.

Supreme Court, which accepted the case and was expected to rule on it in 1983.

Notes

1. For a description of events surrounding the establishment and subsequent restructuring of the FEC, as well as its first three years of operation, see Herbert E. Alexander, *Financing the 1976 Election* (Washington, D.C.: Congressional Quarterly Press, 1979), pp. 13-38, 59-163.

2. James Shoener, "Federal Election Commission," in Charles L. Heatherly, ed., *Mandate for Leadership* (Washington, D.C.: Heritage Foundation, 1981), pp. 745-750.

3. "Justice Department and FEC Agree on How Each Will Handle Violations," *Campaign Practices Reports,* February 20, 1978, p. 103.

4. Thomas B. Curtis, "Reflections on Voluntary Compliance under the Federal Election Campaign Act," *Case Western Reserve Law Review* 29 (1979):8.

5. Orlando Potter, "The Disposition of Compliance Cases and Penalties Incurred in the Enforcement of the Federal Election Campaign Act: An Analysis of Persuasion and Punitive Action," *Campaigns & Elections* 3 (1982):8.

6. See Carol F. Lee, "The Federal Election Commission, the First Amendment Rights and Due Process," *Yale Law Journal* 89 (May 1980):1199-1224.

7. "ABA Task Force Suggests Changes in FEC Enforcement," *Political Finance/Lobby Reporter,* March 24, 1982, p. 75.

8. Martin Tolchin, "Senate Debating Bill to Curb Regulatory Agencies," *New York Times,* May 23, 1982.

9. "The National Nit-Picker?" *Washington Post,* June 27, 1981.

10. "Plenty Is Wrong at the FEC," *Washington Post,* May 11, 1979.

11. Fred Barbash, "Criticism of the FEC Spreading as '80 Campaign Nears," *Washington Post,* April 30, 1979.

12. "Republican Senators Seek FEC Fund Cut," *Washington Post,* June 18, 1981.

13. Lee, "Federal Election Commission," pp. 1223-1224.

14. Theodore S. Arrington, "Some Paradoxes of Campaign Finance Reform," *Commonsense* (Fall 1979):56-72.

15. David Lambro, "The Best and Worst Government Agencies," *Washingtonian* (May 1981):23.

16. Quoted in Larry Light, "Reform-spawned Agency Stirs Discontent," *Congressional Quarterly Weekly Report*, April 19, 1980, p. 1026.

17. Quoted in Barbash, "Criticism of the FEC Spreading."

18. U.S. Congress, House Administration Committee, *An Analysis of the Impact of the Federal Election Campaign Act, 1972-78,* from the Institute of Politics, John F. Kennedy School of Government, Harvard University (Washington, D.C.: Government Printing Office, 1979), p. 17.

19. Quoted in Larry Light, "Deadlocks on the Election Commission," *Congressional Quarterly Weekly Report,* April 19, 1980, p. 1023.

20. Ibid.

21. Barbash, "Criticism of the FEC Spreading."

22. Ibid.

23. T.R. Reid, "Right to Work Group Begins Bid to Oust FEC's Harris," *Washington Post,* April 21, 1979.

24. Light, "Reform-spawned Agency," p. 1025.

25. Ibid.

26. Shoener, "Federal Election Commission," p. 749.

27. Light, "Reform-spawned Agency," pp. 1024-1025.

28. Quoted in Rhodes Cook, "The CLITRIM Incident," *Congressional Quarterly Weekly Report,* April 19, 1980, p. 1021.

29. Frank P. Reiche, chairman of the FEC, to the Honorable Charles McC. Mathias, chairman, Committee on Rules and Administration, U.S. Senate, February 1, 1982.

30. Quoted in Phil Gailey, "Election Unit's Task: Udall and Lance Cases," *New York Times,* February 17, 1982.

31. Cook, "CLITRIM Incident," p. 1021.

32. John Warren McGarry, chairman of the FEC, to the Honorable Edward Roybal, chairman of the General Government Committee on Appropriations, House of Representatives, October 9, 1981.

33. "Don't Weaken the FEC," *Dallas Times Herald,* April 9, 1982.

34. "Frenzel Introduces GOP Bill to Overhaul Election Law," *Political Finance/Lobby Reporter,* June 2, 1982, pp. 145-146.

35. "Mathias Sees Little Support for Killing Election Commission," *Campaign Practices Reports,* December 7, 1981, pp. 1-2.

36. Quoted in George Lardner, Jr., "The Assault on Watergate Reforms," *Washington Post,* June 5, 1981.

37. 2 U.S.C. 438(a)(8).

38. For a summary of the controversies raised by FEC audit policy during and after the 1976 elections, see Alexander, *Financing the 1976 Election,* pp. 91-100.

39. Arthur Andersen & Co., "Review of the Political Campaign Auditing Process" (September 1979).

40. Ibid., p. 2.

41. Ibid., p. 6.

42. Accountants for the Public Interest, untitled study of the Federal Election Commission's Audit Process (September 1979). See the letter of September 7, 1979, to Robert Tiernan, chairman of the FEC, from API, which is included in the study.

43. Ibid., p. 5.

44. *Campaign Practices Reports,* October 1, 1979, p. 1.

45. Ibid.

46. David S. Broder, "Politicizing the Election Commission," *Washington Post,* November 16, 1977.

47. For a description of the controversy raised by President Carter's first two nominees to the FEC, see Alexander, *Financing the 1976 Election,* pp. 141-147.

48. "Baker's FEC Choice Angers Conservatives," *Human Events,* May 26, 1979.

49. Cited by Allen F. Yoder, "Simon 'Unmasks' a Republican," *Record* (Hackensack, N.J.), June 7, 1979.

50. Letter of William Simon, June 9, 1979.

51. U.S. Congress, Senate, Rules Committee. *Nominations of Thomas Everett Harris and Frank P. Reiche to Be Members of the Federal Election Commission,* Executive Report 96-2, June 14, 1979, p. 15.

52. Ibid., p. 16.

53. *Campaign Practices Reports,* June 25, 1979, p. 1.

54. Congressional Record, 96th Cong., 1st sess., 1979, vol. 125, S10500.

55. Quoted in "FEC Slots: Commissioner Tells President to Fill Vacancies without Regard to Politics," *Political Finance/Lobby Reporter,* April 15, 1981, p. 87.

56. "Texan Reported Reagan Choice for FEC Post," *Washington Post,* August 29, 1981.

57. "Texan Withdraws Candidacy," *Political Finance/Lobby Reporter,* October 14, 1981, p. 258.

58. "Democrats to Reagan: Pick from Our List," *Political Finance/Lobby Reporter,* October 28, 1981, pp. 278-279.

59. Cited by Jack Anderson, "Ex-AMA Fox Eyes the FEC's Chicken Coop," *Washington Post,* November 7, 1981.

60. Quoted in ibid.

61. Ibid.

62. Lee Ann Elliot, "Political Action Committees—Precincts of the '80s," *Arizona Law Review* 22 (1980):539-554.

63. "Reports of Short-Term Catch Mrs. Aikens by Surprise," *Political Finance/Lobby Reporter,* July 1, 1981, p. 168.

64. See FEC, *Annual Report 1978* (Washington, D.C.: Office of Pub-

lications, 1979); FEC, *Annual Report 1979* (Washington, D.C.: Office of Publications, 1980); FEC, *Annual Report 1980* (Washington, D.C.: Office of Publications, 1981); FEC, *Annual Report 1981* (Washington, D.C.: Office of Publications, 1982).

65. Chapter 2 includes a summary of *FEC* v. *Hall-Tyner,* in which the exemption from FECA disclosure provisions granted by the *Buckley* Court in certain circumstances to minor political parties was at issue. Five suits are summarized in chapter 5: *CBS, ABC, and NBC* v. *Federal Communication Commission,* which raised the issue of federal candidates' right of access to broadcast time; *FEC* v. *Machinists Non-Partisan Political League and Citizens for Democratic Alternatives,* in which FEC jurisdiction regarding draft committees was at issue; *Carter/Mondale Presidential Committee* v. *FEC* and *Kennedy for President* v. *FEC,* both of which raised questions about certain FEC audit-related procedures; and *Citizens for LaRouche* v. *FEC,* which raised questions regarding FEC investigatory powers. Chapter 6 includes a summary of *Democratic Party of the United States* v. *LaFollette,* in which the right of national political parties to determine how their party nominees are chosen was at issue. Five suits are summarized in chapter 7; *Carter-Mondale Reelection Committee* v. *FEC, Common Cause* v. *Harrison Schmitt,* and *FEC* v. *Americans for Change,* all of which raised questions regarding independent expenditures in publicly funded presidential campaigns; *Reagan-Bush Committee* v. *FEC,* which raised questions about the FEC's audit authority and procedures; and *John Anderson* v. *FEC,* actually two separate suits in which public funding for independent presidential candidates and coordinated expenditures by independent candidate committees were at issue. Chapter 8 includes a summary of *First National Bank of Boston* v. *Bellotti,* in which corporate political rights were at issue.

66. Jim Mann, "$5,000 Limit on Political Gifts Upheld," *Los Angeles Times,* June 27, 1981.

67. *California Medical Association, et al.* v. *Federal Election Commission,* 641 F.2d 619 (9th Cir. 1980).

68. *California Medical Association, et al.* v. *Federal Election Commission,* 449 U.S. 817 (1981).

69. "Left/Right Coalition Sues FEC," *Open Politics Report* (January-February 1980):1.

70. Quoted in "Left/Right Coalition Launches New Legal Assault on Campaign Act," press release, Office of former Senator Eugene J. McCarthy, December 17, 1979, p. 4.

71. *Stewart Mott, et al.* v. *Federal Election Commission,* 494 F. Supp. 131 (D.C. Cir. 1980).

72. Ed Zuckerman, "Mott, NCPAC Suit Thrown Out, Appeal Hinted," *Political Finance/Lobby Reporter,* July 16, 1980, p. 2.

73. "Liberal/Conservative Suit against FEC Rebuffed," *Campaign Practices Reports,* July 7, 1980, p. 5.

74. *National Conservative Political Action Committee and Rhonda Stahlman, et al.* v. *Federal Election Commission,* 626 F.2d 953 (D.C. Cir. 1981).

75. *Citizens Against Rent Control* v. *The City of Berkeley,* 102 S.Ct. 434 (1981).

76. Jim Mann, "Justices Stirke Down Limit on Donations to Local Ballot Drives," *Los Angeles Times,* December 15, 1981.

77. Quoted in "What Price Public Debate? Supreme Court Will Decide," *Campaign Practices Reports,* October 26, 1981, p. 5.

78. "Supreme Court to Hear Argument on Berkeley, California, Contribution Limits," *Election Administration Reports,* March 19, 1981, p. 5.

79. Quoted in "High Court Rejects Limits on Donations to Referendum Drives," *IMPACT* (January 1982):1.

80. Quoted in Fred Barbash, "Court Strikes Down Contribution Limits in Referendum," *Washington Post,* December 15, 1981.

81. *Henry Walther, et al.* v. *Federal Election Commission,* 468 F. Supp. 1235 (D.C. Cir. 1979).

82. *Complaint against Operation of Corporate Political Action Committees, before the FEC* (Washington, D.C., October 10, 1979).

83. Ed Zuckerman, "Machinists Suit: Labor Union Wins License to Hunt Out Coercion in Corporate PACs," *Political Finance/Lobby Reporter,* February 11, 1981, p. 31.

84. Warren Weaver, Jr., "Coercing of Political Gifts Alleged in Union-Corporation Court Test," *New York Times,* June 21, 1980, p. 9.

85. *International Association of Machinists and Aerospace Workers, et al.* v. *Federal Election Commission,* No. 80-354 (D.D.C. 1980).

86. *International Association of Machinists and Aerospace Workers, et al.* v. *Federal Election Commission,* No. 81-1044 (D.C. Cir. 1981).

87. *International Association of Machinists and Aerospace Workers, et al.* v. *Federal Election Commission,* 678 F. 2d 1092 (D.C. Cir. 1982).

88. "Right to Work Committee Challenges Federal Election Act's Constitutionality," *Campaign Practices Reports,* October 31, 1977, p. 6.

89. *National Right to Work Committee, Inc., et al.* v. *Federal Election Commission, et al.,* No. 77-786A (E.D. Va., October 20, 1977).

90. "NRWC v. FEC," *FEC Record* (March 1978):6-7.

91. *Federal Election Commission* v. *National Right to Work Committee, Inc., et al.,* No. 77-2175 (D.D.C. December 21, 1977).

92. *Federal Election Commission* v. *National Right to Work Committee, Inc., et al. and National Right to Work Committee, Inc., et al.* v. *Federal Election Commission, et al.,* 501 F. Supp. 422 (D.C. Cir. 1980).

93. "Court Finds Right to Work Committee Guilty of 'Knowingly' Violating FECA," *Campaign Practices Reports,* April 28, 1980, p. 2.

94. *National Right to Work Committee, Inc., et al.* v. *Federal Election Commission, et al. and Federal Election Commission* v. *National Right to Work Committee, Inc., et al.,* 665 F.2d 371 (D.C. Cir. 1981).

95. Quoted in Ed Zuckerman, "National Right to Work Committee Can Solicit Members for PAC Funds," *Political Finance/Lobby Reporter,* September 16, 1981, p. 238.

96. Quoted in "Court Questions FECA Provisions," *Campaign Practices Reports,* September 14, 1981, p. 5.

97. "National Right to Work Committee Asks Recovery of Legal Costs in FEC Case," *Political Finance/Lobby Reporter,* October 14, 1981, p. 261.

98. *BreadPAC, et al.* v. *Federal Election Commission,* 635 F.2d 621 (7th Cir. 1977).

99. "BreadPAC v. FEC," *FEC Record* (May 1981):6.

100. *BreadPAC, et al.* v. *Federal Election Commission,* 591 F.2d 29 (7th Cir. 1980).

101. "BreadPAC v. FEC," *FEC Record* (May 1981).

102. *Federal Election Commission* v. *Phillips Publishing, Inc.,* 517 F. Supp. 1308 (D.C. Cir. 1980).

103. 2 U.S.C. 431(9)(B)(i).

104. "FEC Takes 'Pink Sheet' to Court: Publisher Claims Press Exemption," *Campaign Practices Reports,* April 27, 1981, p. 2.

105. George Brandon, "Court Orders Bureaucrats to Leave Press Alone," *Editor and Publisher,* August 8, 1981, p. 18.

106. "FEC Withdraws Appeal of Phillips Publishing, Inc. Suit," *FEC Record* (December 1981):6.

107. *Federal Election Commission* v. *Phillips Publishing, Inc.,* No. 81-2015 (D.C. Cir., October 30, 1981).

108. Joseph H. Cooper, "Election Commission, Editorial Campaigns Are Not Your Province," *New York Times,* February 15, 1981.

109. Julia Malone, "Election Watchdog Biting into U.S. Press Freedom?" *Christian Science Monitor,* February 17, 1981, p. 8.

110. *The Reader's Digest Association, Inc.* v. *Federal Election Commission,* 81 Civ. 596 (S.D.N.Y. 1981).

111. "Reader's Digest Association, Inc., v. FEC," *FEC Record* (May 1981):5.

112. *Federal Election Commission* v. *National Rifle Association, et al.,* No. 81-1218 (D.D.C. 26 May 1981).

113. "Election Panel Sues Rifle Association on Contributions," *Los Angeles Times,* May 5, 1981.

114. "FEC v. National Rifle Association of America," *FEC Record* (May 1981):7.

115. Quoted in "FEC Sues Rifle Association over Use of Corporate Funds," *Campaign Practices Reports,* June 8, 1981, p. 7.

116. *Athens Lumber Co., Inc., and John P. Bondurant* v. *Federal Election Commission and William F. Smith,* 531 F. Supp. 756 (M.D. Ga. 1981).

117. Ed Zuckerman, "Suit Challenges 75-Year-Old Ban on Corporate Political Gifts," *Political Finance/Lobby Reporter,* January 20, 1982, p. 9.

118. Ibid.

119. *Athens Lumber Co.* v. *FEC.,* p. 4.

120. "Machinists, Common Cause File in Athens Lumber Suit," *Campaign Practices Reports,* January 18, 1982, p. 3.

121. "Athens Lumber Judge Denies Union, Common Cause Motions," *Campaign Practices Reports,* February 1, 1982, p. 7.

122. Ed Zuckerman, "Judge Denies Intervention in Athens Lumber Case," *Political Finance/Lobby Reporter,* February 3, 1982, p. 24.

123. Ed Zuckerman, "Athens Lumber Files Appeal after Case Is Dismissed on Procedural Grounds," *Political Finance/Lobby Reporter,* February 17, 1982, p. 32.

124. *Republican National Committee, et al.* v. *Federal Election Commission,* 461 F. Supp. 570 (S.D. N.Y. 1978).

125. Quoted in "Republican's Suit Argues Spending Limit Unconstitutional in Presidential Race," *Campaign Practices Reports,* June 26, 1978, p. 4.

126. "Appeals Court Dismisses Republican Suit on FECA Funding of Presidential Election," *Campaign Practices Reports,* February 18, 1980.

127. "RNC et al., v. FEC," *FEC Record* (February 1979).

128. *Republican National Committee, et al.* v. *Federal Election Commission,* 616 F.2d 1 (2d Cir. 1980).

129. *Republican National Committee, et al.* v. *Federal Election Commission,* 487 F. Supp. 280 (1980).

130. 11 CFR 102.6(a).

131. "FEC Rejects Democrats' Attempts to Limit GOP Spending on Senate Races," *Campaign Practices Reports,* August 18, 1980, p. 4.

132. Quoted in Ed Zuckerman, "GOP Senatorial Spending Plans Upset by Appeals Court Ruling," *Political Finance/Lobby Reporter,* October 15, 1980, p. 7.

133. *Democratic Senatorial Campaign Committee* v. *Federal Election Commission,* No. 80-1903 (D.D.C., August 28, 1980).

134. *Democratic Senatorial Campaign Committee* v. *Federal Election Commission,* 660 F. 2d 773 (D.C. Cir. 1980).

135. *Federal Election Commission* v. *Democratic Senatorial Campaign Committee and National Republican Senatorial Committee* v. *Democratic Senatorial Campaign Committee,* 102 S.Ct. 38 (1981).

136. Quoted in Fred Barbash, "Court Upholds GOP Campaign Financing Device," *Washington Post,* November 11, 1981.

137. *Winpisinger* v. *Watson,* 86 F.R.D. 77 (D.D.C. 1980).

138. David E. Rosenbaum, "Kennedy Supporters Sue Carter Aides on Fund Use," *New York Times,* December 29, 1979.

139. Morton Mintz, "Carter Camp Effort to 'Buy' Renomination Charged in Suit," *Washington Post,* December 29, 1979.

140. Rosenbaum, "Kennedy Supporters."

141. "Judge Dismisses Suit of Kennedy Backers on 'Abuses' of Carter Administration," *Campaign Practices Reports,* February 18, 1980, p. 4.

142. *Winpisinger* v. *Watson,* 628 F.2d 133 (D.C. Cir. 1980).

143. Quoted in "Appeals Court Also Denies Kennedy Suit against Carter Administration 'Abuses,' " *Campaign Practices Reports,* April 14, 1980, p. 2.

144. *Common Cause, et al.* v. *Bolger,* 512 F. Supp. 26 (D.C. Cir. 1982).

145. For a detailed description of the Common Cause suit and congressional response to it, see Alexander, *Financing the 1976 Election,* pp. 771-777.

4 Spending in the 1980 Elections

More than $1 billion was spent on elective and party politics in the United States during the 1979-1980 election cycle. The spending covered a huge amount of political activity. In addition to candidates running for federal offices—the presidency, the vice-presidency, and seats in the houses of Congress—hundreds of thousands of candidates were nominated and elected to a wide variety of offices throughout the nation. Further, costly bond and other issues were on the ballot in many states. And the political parties, probably the most extensive organizations in the nation, required funding to carry out their activities.

The cost of politics is, relatively, not high. One billion dollars is a mere fraction of 1 percent of the amounts spent by federal, state, county, and municipal governments. It is roughly equivalent to the legal fees and related costs of the recent IBM and AT&T antitrust suits. It is less than the estimated amount spent on gambling connected with the 1981 Super Bowl and less than the combined annual advertising budgets of Procter & Gamble and Sears, Roebuck & Co., the nation's leading advertisers.

Money is essential to elective politics. Political campaigning consists largely of communications—their preparation, production, and delivery. And political communication, competing as it must for the attention of an electorate whose members often are more interested in sports, entertainment, other media events, or leisure-time activities, is costly. Communication costs—expenditures for television, radio, print media, and mass mailing—have taken a quantum leap in the last two decades, and consequently so has all political spending: from $175 million in the 1960 elections to $540 million in 1976 and $1.2 billion in 1980. Comparative spending figures from 1952, the first presidential election for which total political costs were calculated, through 1980, follow: 1952, $140 million; 1956,.$155 million; 1960, $175 million; 1964, $200 million; 1968, $300 million; 1972, $425 million; 1976, $540 million; and 1980, $1.203 billion.[1]

Political spending in 1980 (table 4-1) fell into seven major areas (all figures rounded off):

1. $275 million to elect the president, including prenomination campaigns dating from 1977, plus third-party and independent-candidate campaigns. Spending by the national-party and convention committees on behalf of presidential candidates is included in this category.

Table 4-1
The Campaign Spending Dollar in 1980
(millions)

Presidential (including conventions and minor parties)	$ 275
Congressional	239
National party	55
Nonparty (mostly PACs) (noncandidate spending, including party and PAC operations, exempt spending, direct-mail, and congressional independent expenditures)	95
State and local party (federal related) (nonpresidential; includes congressional and voter-turnout campaigns)	34
State (nonfederal) (statewide and legislative)	265
Local (nonfederal)	200
Ballot issues	40
Total	$1,203

Source: Citizens' Research Foundation.

Note: Most figures include the 1979-1980 election cycle, but most of the expenditures were made in 1980. Figures are adjusted for transfer of funds, loans, refunds, and so forth to avoid duplication. For example, party and nonparty or PAC contributions to candidates are included in the presidential and congressional totals, but in addition, national-party and nonparty costs (including party and PAC administration, operations, direct mail, and independent expenditures) are now so high that they merit a separate category. State- and local-party spending for the presidential campaigns, under the 1979 amendments to the FECA, are included in the figure of $275 million to elect the president. State- and local-party spending is federal related, such as for congressional campaigns, but nonpresidential is listed separately. State and local nonfederal spending refers to spending connected with gubernatorial, state legislative, county, and municipal campaigns. The figure for spending on ballot issues in 1980 is derived from Steven D. Lydenberg, *Bankrolling Ballots, Update 1980: The Role of Business in Financing Ballot Question Campaigns* (New York: Council on Economic Priorities, 1981). Other figures are from FEC and CRF compilations.

2. $239 million to nominate candidates and elect a Congress, including party and interest-group contributions to the candidates.

3. In addition, at the national level, noncandidate spending by the national parties totaled $55 million, and noncandidate spending by PACs totaled $71 million. This direct spending consisted mainly of administrative costs, direct-mail expenditures, and congressional independent expenditures. Adding in $24 million in communication costs and exempt spending brings the total to $95 million.

4. Federal-related state- and local-party spending reached $34 million. This category includes congressional-related activities such as voter-registration and get-out-the-vote drives but not state- and local-party spending on behalf of the presidential campaigns ($19 million), which is included in the presidential total.

5. $265 million to nominate candidates and elect governors and other statewide officials and state legislators.
6. $200 million to nominate candidates and elect to office scores of thousands of county and local public officials.
7. $40 million to wage campaigns relative to state and local ballot issues and amendments to state constitutions and county and municipal charters.

The detail at all levels in this national compilation reveals more about political finance in the 1979-1980 election cycle than had been available in previous presidential-election years. As more data become available at the state and local levels and regarding ballot issues, the more accurate can be the national estimate of total political costs. In view of the concern of many persons about the rising costs of politics, the public-policy implications of accurate and realistic data are readily apparent.

Federal-Election Campaign Spending

At the federal level, the 1980 elections marked a significant leap in reported political spending. Since the FECA and its 1974, 1976, and 1979 amendments have been in effect, political spending has been more meticulously reported than in prior years. Disclosure at the federal level, including disclosure of senatorial and congressional campaign receipts and expenditures, has been a successful feature of the FECA. Two important elements in the escalation in reported political spending are inflation and the fact that the FECA requires more persons and committees spending money to file reports with the FECA. A 35 percent increase occurred in the consumer price index (CPI) from 1976 to 1980. In such basic components of political spending as media advertising and public-opinion polling, the increments greatly exceeded the rise in the CPI.

For the second time, public funds were used to pay some of the necessary costs of the presidential campaigns. The federal funding and the prohibition of private contributions for the presidential general election made considerable private and interest-group money available for other political uses, and some of it, predictably, was funneled into the congressional campaigns, and some into state and local campaigns. The number of political committees filing at the federal level continued to proliferate —7,228 compared with 6,220 in 1976.

The hotly contested struggle for the presidential nomination in the Republican party was an additional factor accounting for increased political costs; more than $70 million was spent before Reagan was nominated (table 4-2). Moreover, a highly competitive contest for the presidential nomination in the Democratic party occurred when the incumbent president was

Table 4-2
Republican Presidential Prenomination Expenditures, 1979-1980

Qualifying for Matching Funds	Adjusted Disbursements	Independent Expenditures For	Communication Costs For	Other	Total Disbursement For
Candidate					
Anderson	$ 6,520,000	$ 196,000	$ 0	$ 0	$ 6,716,000[d]
Baker	7,070,000	1,000	2,000	4,000[a]	7,077,000
Bush	16,710,000	0	0	0	16,710,000[c]
Crane	5,220,000	0	0	0	5,220,000
Dole	1,390,000	0	0	0	1,390,000
Reagan	19,820,000	1,644,000	0	111,000[a]	21,575,000
Not qualifying					
Connally	12,620,000	288,000	0	0	12,908,000
Fernandez	250,000	0	0	0	250,000
Stassen	120,000	0	0	0	120,000
Totals[b]	$69,720,000	$2,129,000	$2,000	$115,000	$71,966,000[c,d]

Total candidate committee prenomination expenditures $69,720,000

Total prenomination-related spending $71,985,000

Source: Citizen's Research Foundation, based on various FEC compilations.

[a]Unauthorized delegates.

[b]Minor discrepancies due to rounding.

[c]An additional $17,000 in independent expenditures were reported against Bush.

[d]An additional $2,000 in communication costs were reported against Anderson.

challenged (table 4-3). In the general election, numerous forms of spending outside the control of the candidates, and spending by a significant independent candidate, contributed to costs well beyond the inflation factor.

Offsetting factors that contributed to an escalation in political spending were those tending to reduce spending: the effective contribution limits, the expenditure limitations applicable in the presidential campaigns, the prohibition of private contributions in the presidential general election, and, according to some perceptions, the inhibiting or chilling effects of the FECA and the FEC.

Presidential Spending

In the 1976 presidential campaigns, Democratic candidates outspent Republican candidates by nearly $10 million. A sharp reversal occurred in 1980. The Republican contests for nomination, with a large field of contenders, consumed $70.6 million, twice the amount spent by the Democrats, $35.7 million.[2] Tables 4-2 and 4-3 detail the primary-campaign expenditures for the Republican and Democratic campaigns, respectively. The tables include not only expenditures made by the candidates' campaign committees but also spending on behalf of and against the candidates, including independent expenditures and communication costs for and against and expenditures by unauthorized delegates and draft committees. In general-election campaigns, with federal funding and expenditure limits in force, spending would have been nearly in balance, except for the edge the Republicans had over the Democrats in national-, state-, and local-party spending, and in the nonlimited spending, which included independent expenditures. Only in the category of expenditures that could be coordinated with the candidates' campaign committees did the Democrats outspend the Republicans. The Reagan campaign cost $64.3 million compared with $53.9 million spent on the Carter campaign.

Total presidential campaign spending for the years 1968 to 1980 is shown in table 4-4. These figures cover the costs of prenomination and general-election campaigns, as well as the cost of running the national nominating conventions. For all years, minor-party and independent candidate spending is included, but 1976 and 1980 amounts include independent expenditures and communication costs as well, for both positive and negative activities.

Table 4-5 presents the percentages of total presidential spending by party for presidential campaigns since 1956, including both prenomination and general-election campaigns.

Data on the expenditures of national-level committees primarily concerned with the presidential general election are available since 1912. The

Table 4-3
Democratic Presidential Prenomination Expenditures, 1979-1980

Candidate	Adjusted Disbursements	Independent Expenditures For	Communication Costs For	Other	Disbursement For	Expenditures Against	Communication Costs Against	Total Disbursements Against
Brown	$ 2,650,000	$ 0	$ 23,000	$ 0	$ 2,673,000	$ 0	$ 0	$ 0
Carter	18,520,000	18,000	165,000	24,000[a]	18,727,000	34,000	80,000	114,000
Kennedy	12,270,000	56,000	443,000	538,000[b]	13,307,000	488,000	155,000	643,000
LaRouche	2,150,000	0	0	0	2,150,000	0	0	0
Totals[c]	$35,590,000	$74,000	$631,000	$562,000	$36,858,000	$522,000	$235,000	$757,000

Total candidate committee prenomination spending $35,590,000

Total prenomination-related spending $37,615,000

Source: Citizens' Research Foundation, based on various FEC compilations.

[a]Unauthorized delegates.
[b]Principally draft committees.
[c]Minor discrepancies due to rounding.

Table 4-4
Presidential-Campaign Spending, 1968-1980
(millions)

	1968	1972	1976	1980
Republican	$45.0	$ 69.3	$ 74.5	$152.1
Democratic	37.0	67.3	83.2	98.0
Other	9.0	1.2	2.0	24.9
Total	$91.0	$137.8	$159.7	$275.0

Source: Citizens' Research Foundation.

figures in table 4-6 include spending by presidential candidates and national-party committees. Although there were some unusual years, presidential spending has tended to follow an exponential curve from 1912 on, with aberrations in 1928 and 1972 when spending escalated by more than 100 percent. The lid imposed by expenditure limits in federally funded campaigns notwithstanding, 1980 fits into the historical pattern.

Breakdowns of the components of the $275 million spent to elect the president and vice-president in 1980 are detailed in the three following chapters on the prenomination campaigns, the conventions and the general election campaigns. Table 4-7 offers an overview that illustrates the financial complexity of modern presidential campaigns.

Table 4-5
Ratio of National-Level Direct Spending in Presidential Prenomination and General Elections, 1956-1980

	1956	1960	1964	1968[a]	1972	1976[b]	1980[c]
Republicans	59	49	63	55 (65)	67	52	56
Democrats	41	51	37	29 (35)	33	47	35
Other	0	0	0	16	0	1	9

Source: Derived from Heard, *Costs*. p. 20, and 1956 General Election Campaigns Report to the Senate Committee on Rules and Administration. Subcommittee on Privileges and Elections, 85th Cong., 1st sess. (1957), exhibit 4, p. 41. Deficits in 1956 are listed in this report as bills unpaid as of November 30, 1956. Heard's figures for Republicans and Democrats are for the full calendar year 1956, but labor figures are for January 1-November 30, 1956. Heard's ratio has been revised to include deficits. Figures for subsequent years appear in the earlier books of this series.

Note: Direct spending means figures adjusted for transfer of funds.

[a]Figures in parentheses are for Republican-Democrat ratio when other (mainly George Wallace) spending is excluded.

[b]Including presidential-related spending by the national committees and the convention committees.

[c]State- and local-party spending on behalf of the presidential candidates has been removed in order to maintain comparability with other years.

Table 4-6
Direct Campaign Expenditures by Presidential and National-Party Committees, General Elections, 1912-1980
(millions)

1912	$ 2.9[a]
1916	4.7
1920	6.9
1924	5.4[a]
1928	11.6
1932	5.1
1936	14.1
1940	6.2
1944	5.0
1948	6.2[a]
1952	11.6
1956	12.9
1960	19.9
1964	24.8
1968	44.2[a]
1972	103.7
1976	88.7
1980	142.9[a]

Source: Citizens' Research Foundation.

Note: Data for 1912-1944 include transfers to states. Total for 1948 includes only the direct expenditures of the national-party committees. For 1952-1968, data do not include transfers to states but do include the national senatorial and congressional committees of both parties. For 1972, for comparative purposes, data do not include state- and local-level information, except for the presidential candidates. The Nixon component includes all spending for his reelection. For 1976, amounts decreased due to public financing and expenditure limitations.

[a]Totals include minor-party and independent-candidate spending.

Presidential-Election Campaign Fund

The U.S. Treasury contributed almost $30 million to the 1980 presidential prenomination campaigns of ten candidates (four Democratic and six Republican) who qualified and almost $63 million to the general-election campaigns of Carter and Reagan ($29.4 million each) and Anderson ($4.2 million). In the general election, each major-party candidate was eligible to receive $29.4 million, compared with $21.8 million in 1976. The federal funding was increased to take account of a 35 percent rise in the CPI in the intervening period. The Anderson allotment was based on his receiving 6.5 percent of the vote; a 5 percent showing was required to qualify for the postelection grant. In addition, $8.8 million in public funds was allocated to the two major parties to hold their nominating conventions, although the parties spent only about $8.1 million and returned the remainder to the U.S. Treasury.

Table 4-7
Costs of Electing the President, 1980
(millions)

Prenomination		
Spending by candidates	$106.3[a]	
Independent expenditures	2.8	
Draft Kennedy	.5	
Delegate spending (unauthorized by candidates)	.1	
Communication costs	.9	
Vice-presidential candidates	.3	
Minor parties	1.2	
Subtotal		$112.1
Conventions (including host committees)		
Republicans	$ 5.1	
Democrats	4.2	
Subtotal		$ 9.3
General Election		
Spending by candidates[b]	$ 78.8	
Compliance	3.0	
Parties	27.5	
Republican National Committee media	4.5	
Independent expenditures	10.6	
Communications costs	1.7	
Labor, corporate, and associations	16.8	
Subtotal		$142.9
Miscellaneous out-of-pocket expenses		10.7
Grand Total		$275.0

Source: Citizens' Research Foundation.
[a]Includes compliance costs.
[b]Includes minor-party and independent candidates.

In all, the Presidential Election Campaign Fund paid out $100,597,136 in 1980, or about 37 percent of the total spent to elect the president (table 4-8).[3] These government funds came from the voluntary $1 checkoff on federal income-tax forms. The checkoff dollars are earmarked for the Presidential Election Campaign Fund, with the annual increments aggregating over each four-year cycle. After the 1980 payouts were made, approximately $69 million remained in the fund, to be carried over to the 1984 elections, along with such additional funds as accrue.

Presidential-Party Spending

In the wake of Watergate-related investigations, whose revelations of political and financial misconduct at the highest levels of national responsi-

Table 4-8
Payouts from the Presidential Election Campaign Fund

Prenomination matching funds		
Democrats		
Brown	$ 874,199	
Carter	5,027,854	
Kennedy	4,134,815	
LaRouche	525,174	
Total	$10,562,042	
Republicans		
Anderson	$ 2,276,324	
Baker	2,530,968	
Bush	5,676,556	
Crane	1,899,632	
Dole	442,857	
Reagan	6,340,223	
Total	$19,166,560	
Total Prenomination		$ 29,728,601
Nominating conventions		
Democratic	$ 3,684,335	
Republican	4,400,241	
Total conventions		$ 8,084,576
General-election funding		
Anderson	$ 4,242,304	
Carter	29,352,768	
Reagan	29,188,887	
Total general election		$ 62,783,959
Grand total		$100,597,136

Source: FEC, "Public Financing 1980 Presidential Election," press release, March 2, 1982.
Note: Totals subject to revision since some repayments are still being sought or are being contested.

bility brought the Republican party to its lowest ebb in recent history, the RNC set about to rebuild the party's fortunes. Over the years, it has meticulously constructed a highly sophisticated fund-raising apparatus that has allowed the party committee to provide the money and services party candidates have needed to help them return to competitive status in national election campaigns. The Democratic National Committee's (DNC) concerted efforts in the post-1980 election period to follow the RNC's lead serve as a measure of the Republican committee's success. Broadly based party support of the kind provided by the RNC is certain to increase in the future.

Since the parties' national committees generally represent the interests of their presidential wings, spending by the committees can be included in an extended analysis of related costs involved in conducting presidential campaigns. Tables 4-9 and 4-10 provide such breakdowns for both the Republican and Democratic presidential campaigns in 1980. The tables, which incorporate both the prenomination and general-election periods,

Table 4-9
Total Spending on Behalf of Republican Presidential Candidates in 1980 Campaigns
(millions)

Reagan		
Prenomination (including compliance costs)		$ 20.7
General election		
candidate committee	$29.2	
national committee (RNC)	4.5	
		$ 33.7
Compliance costs (general election)		1.5
Transition planning		.5
Total spending controlled by candidate		$ 56.4
General-election spending in support of Reagan-Bush		
State and local party	$15.0	
Labor; corporate and association	3.0	
Total coordinated spending		$ 18.0
Unauthorized delegates, independent expenditures and communication costs, primary and general election		12.9
Total Reagan		$ 87.3
Other Republican candidates		
Prenomination candidate committees	$49.9	
Unauthorized delegates, independent expenditures and communication costs	1.4	
Total other candidates		$ 51.3
RNC and affiliates		$ 48.5
Republican National Convention		
RNC convention committee	$ 4.4	
Host committee	.7	
		$ 5.1
Republican total		$192.2

Source: Citizens' Research Foundation.

Table 4-10
Total Spending on Behalf of Democratic Presidential Candidates in 1980 Campaigns
(millions)

Carter		
Prenomination (including compliance costs)		$ 18.5
Debts		.6
General election		
candidate committee	$29.4	
national committee (DNC)	4.0	
		$ 33.4
Compliance costs (general election)		1.5
Total spending controlled by candidate		$ 54.0
General-election spending in support of		
Carter-Mondale		
State and local party	$ 4.0	
Labor, registration, and get-out-the-vote	15.0	
Total coordinated spending		$ 19.0
Unauthorized delegates, independent		
expenditures and communication costs,		
primary and general election		1.7
Total Carter		$ 74.7
Other Democratic candidates		
Prenomination candidate committees	$17.2	
Draft committees, unauthorized delegates,		
independent expenditures, and communica-		
tion costs	1.7	
Total other candidates		$ 18.9
DNC and affiliates		$ 10.0
DNC convention committee	$ 3.7	
Host committee	.5	
		$ 4.2
Democratic total		$107.8

Source: Citizens' Research Foundation.

cover all spending by and on behalf of the candidates of the two parties, including national-party convention costs, coordinated national-party expenditures on behalf of each party's general-election candidate, and administrative and fund-raising costs for the two national-party committees and their affiliated committees. A comparison of the two tables shows that the Republicans far outspent the Democrats, by $192.2 million to $107.8

million. Greater party spending by the Republicans accounts for a substantial portion of that difference, with the remainder explained by independent expenditures, coordinated expenditures, and the larger number of Republicans contesting the presidential nomination.

Independent and Third-Party Candidates

Spending in 1980 on behalf of independent and third-party candidates increased dramatically from the 1976 presidential election. With the independent candidacy of John Anderson, independent and third-party expenditures rose from $2 million in 1976 to approximately $20 million in 1980. Third-party expenditures alone nearly tripled their 1976 total.

In historical perspective, the funds expended by independent and third-party candidates in 1980 represent a historic breakthrough. Until 1980, George Wallace had mounted the most-expensive campaign outside the two-party system. Wallace's campaign spending totaled approximately $7 million in 1968. Prior to that, only a few third-party candidates in this century had spent considerable sums. Records of receipts of national committees show $1.1 million spent for Henry Wallace's effort in 1948.[4] Theodore Roosevelt's Progressive party spent only $665,420 in 1912, followed in 1924 by the $236,963 in campaign expenditures of Robert LaFollette's Progressive party.[5]

John Anderson's National Unity Campaign was by far the most significant of the 1980 third-force candidacies. Having received more than 5 percent of the total vote, Anderson became the first independent candidate ever to qualify for public funding. The $4,242,304 in public funds, however, could not be awarded until after the election results verified Anderson's qualifications, placing the National Unity Campaign at a disadvantage in comparison with the major-party campaigns. Although Anderson spent $14.4 million in the campaign, nearly half of his costs related to fund raising, legal fees, and petition drives to get on state ballots. After the additional costs of personnel, operations, and travel, only about $2.3 million remained for media advertising.

Besides Anderson's campaign, there were nineteen minor-party candidates appearing on some or all of the state ballots. The Libertarian party and the Citizen's party accounted for the greatest share of the $5.8 million spent by all third parties in 1980. Somewhat surprisingly, the Communist party, which had produced the best-financed party campaign in 1976, did not fare as well in 1980.

The Libertarian party, led by Edward Clark, the party's presidential candidate, was the best organized and best financed of the minor parties. Gaining access to the ballot in all fifty states and the District of Columbia, the Libertarians found significant support in the mountain states and Alaska, receiving almost 12 percent of the vote in the latter. Much of the success of the Libertarians could be attributed to the financial support offered by Clark's running mate, David Koch of New York City. Promising more than $500,000 to the campaign effort for the second slot on the ticket, Koch's personal contribution helped enable the Libertarians to spend $3,320,678, a healthy stride ahead of their $400,000 budget in 1976. Koch's actual contributions to the campaign amounted to more than $1 million.

The Citizen's party, under the leadership of Barry Commoner, ranked next, with expenditures amounting to $1,140,171. The selection of vice-presidential candidate LaDonna Harris, the wife of former Senator Fred Harris of Oklahoma and a well-known activist herself, helped draw support from some of the "new-time" populists. Commoner and Harris organized forty-two Citizen's party committees, gaining access to the ballots of thirty-six states and the District of Columbia.

The Socialist Workers party, running Andrew Pulley as their presidential candidate, outspent Gus Hall's Communist party. The Socialist Workers spent a total of $526,000 compared with the Communist party's expenditures of $316,275. Although neither group achieved a nationwide ballot position, the Socialist Workers did register forty-six operational committees throughout the East and Midwest.

The next notable campaign in terms of finance was that of the Socialist party USA. Its presidential nominee, David McReynolds, placed a distant fourth, spending slightly more than $39,000.

The remaining third-force candidates include representatives of a host of minor parties ideologically ranging from the extreme right to the extreme left. They include American Independent, Conservative, Constitution, Freedom, Labor, National Referendum, Peace and Freedom, People's Capitalist, People's National, U.S. Congress, U.S. Labor, and Workers World. These other minor parties accounted for an aggregate total of only $228,000 in presidential campaign expenditures. Altogether, these third-force campaigns spent $20.2 million, representing a significant 7.3 percent of total presidential expenditures, an increase from 1.3 percent in 1976.

Congressional Spending

During the 1980 election cycle, U.S. House and Senate candidates spent a record $239 million, an increase of 21 percent over the 1978 congressional elections and $114 million more than in the 1976 congressional elections, an increase of 90 percent.[6]

The impact of inflation and the fact that 379 more candidates ran in this election than in 1978 were major factors in the growth in spending. A record

2,288 candidates were entered at some stage of the primary- and general-election campaigns.

As in previous elections, incumbents spent more than challengers, $103.6 million to $91 million, but the margin narrowed substantially compared with prior years. Open-seat candidates spent $44.4 million and primary losers $47.4 million. Democratic and Republican candidates were almost equal in their spending, with the Democrats spending $121.4 million and the Republicans $116 million. Because of the disparity in the number of candidates between the House (1,944) and the Senate (344), the House candidates spent considerably more—$136 million to $103 million—but again the margin compared with previous years narrowed significantly. Total congressional spending for the years 1972 to 1980 is shown in table 4-11.

Senate

Senatorial candidates spent $103 million in the 1980 elections, of which $74.9 million (73 percent) was disbursed by general-election candidates.[7] Democratic general-election candidates outspent their Republican counterparts by $39.9 million to $35 million, a switch from the 1978 senatorial elections when the Republicans spent $38 million compared with $27 million by the Democrats. More Democratic seats were at stake, however, and more were lost, despite a Democratic advantage in spending. In the 1976 election cycle, spending for Senate campaigns totaled $46 million; hence the 1980 total represents an increase of 124 percent. Of the $102,940,000 spent by candidates for the Senate in general-election and primary campaigns, Democrats spent $53.6 million, Republicans $48.9 million, and all other candidates $439,000.

Table 4-12 summarizes all senatorial campaign-related expenditures. This includes Republican, Democratic, third-party, and independent candidate spending for primary- and general-election campaigns. The table also

Table 4-11
Congressional Campaign Expenditures, 1972-1980
(millions)

Year	Total	Senate	House
1972	$ 66.4	$ 26.4	$ 40.0
1974	73.9	28.9	45.0
1976	125.5	46.3	79.2
1978	197.3	86.7	110.6
1980	238.9	102.9	136.0

Source: Citizens' Research Foundation and various FEC compilations.

Table 4-12
Senate Campaign Expenditures, 1979-1980

By candidates		
Democratic general-election candidates[a]	$39,900,000	
Republican general-election candidates[a]	35,000,000	
Other: Primary losers and third-party candidates	28,000,000	
Total, candidate spending		$102,900,000
By party senatorial committees[b]		
Democratic Senatorial Campaign Committee	$ 1,618,000	
Other Democratic party-identified senatorial committees	0	
National Republican Senatorial Committee	21,211,000	
Other Republican party-identified senatorial committees	705,000	
Total, senatorial committees		$ 23,534,000
Independent expenditures and communication costs in behalf of senatorial candidates		$ 2,046,000
Total, senatorial spending		$128,480,000

Source: FEC, press releases, "FEC Releases Final Figures on 1979-1980 Major Political Party Activity," February 21, 1982, and "FEC Releases Final Statistics on 1979-1980 Congressional Races," March 7, 1982.

[a]Total spending, including primary-campaign costs, for candidates in general election; the FEC does not make separate primary spending figures available.

[b]Direct spending only, transfers to candidates not included.

covers candidate and related party committees spending, adjusted to show party contributions to candidates that result in candidate spending. But just as the national-party committees are considered to represent the interests of the presidential wing of the party, so the party senatorial campaign committees represent the interests of the parties' individual senatorial-campaign committees. Hence this analysis includes the administrative and fund-raising costs of the party senatorial committees, as well as such spending by party-identified senatorial committees. Also included are related independent expenditures and communication costs. Analyzed in this manner, the total senatorial costs rise to more than $128 million.

House

A record 1,944 contestants sought seats in the House of Representatives in the primaries and general election. They raised $144 million and spent $136 million in these races. Spending by party was almost equal: $67.8 million by the Democrats and $67.1 million by the Republicans. Third-party and in-dependent candidates spent an additional $1.1 million. General-election candidates spent $116.9 of the $136 million total, an amount that includes their primary expenditures as well. PACs contributed $36 million to these contestants and only $2 million to primary losers. Democratic and Repub-lican spending was virtually equal in the general election also: $57.2 million to $58.6 million. Primary losers spent a record $19.1 million.

Table 4-13 summarizes all House campaign-related expenditures. This includes Republican, Democratic, third-party, and independent candidate spending for primary- and general-election campaigns. The table also covers candidate and related party-committee spending, adjusted to show party contributions to candidates as part of the candidates' spending once the money is received. Just as the senatorial campaign committees are con-sidered to represent the interests of the senatorial wing of the party, so the party congressional campaign committees represent the interests of the par-ties' House members. Hence this analysis includes the administrative and

Table 4-13
House Campaign Expenditures, 1979-1980

By candidates		
Democratic general-election candidates[a]	$57,200,000	
Republican general-election candidates[a]	58,600,000	
Other: Primary losers and third-party candidates	20,200,000	
Total, candidate spending		$136,000,000
By party congressional committees[b]		
Democratic Congressional Campaign Committee	$ 2,037,000	
Other Democratic party-identified congressional committees	1,488,000	
National Republican Congressional Committee	26,095,000	
Other Republican party-identified congressional committees	2,674,000	
Total, congressional committees		$ 32,294,000
Independent expenditures and communication costs in behalf of congressional candidates		$ 1,623,000
Total, house spending		$169,917,000

Source: FEC, press releases, "FEC Releases Final Figures on 1979-1980 Major Political Party Activity," February 21, 1982, and "FEC Releases Final Statistics on 1979-1980 Congressional Races," March 7, 1982.

[a]Total spending, including primary-campaign costs for candidates in general election; separate primary spending figures not available.

[b]Direct spending only, transfers to candidates not included (data counted as part of candidate expenditures).

fund-raising costs of the party congressional committees, as well as such spending by party-identified congressional committees. Also included are related independent expenditures and communication costs. Analyzed in this manner, the total House election costs rise to $169.9 million.

Table 4-14 summarizes 1980 Senate- and House-related spending. The components include general-election candidate spending identified by party

Table 4-14
Senate- and House-Related Spending by Candidates in 1980: Summary

Democratic		
Senate		
Candidate (general election)[a]	$39,900,000	
Democratic Senatorial Campaign Committee and other partisan-identified committees[b]	1,618,000	
House		
Candidate (general election)[a]	$57,200,000	
Democratic Congressional Campaign Committee	2,037,000	
and other partisan-identified committees[b]	1,488,000	
Total, Democratic candidates		$102,243,000
Republican		
Senate		
Candidate (general election)[a]	$35,000,000	
National Republican Senatorial Campaign Committee	21,211,000	
and other partisan-identified committees[b]	705,000	
House		
Candidate (general election)[a]	58,600,000	
National Republican Congressional Committee	26,095,000	
and other partisan-identified committees[b]	2,674,000	
Total, Republican candidates		$144,285,000
Independent expenditures and communication costs		
Senate	$ 2,046,000	
House	1,623,000	
Total, independent expenditures		$ 3,669,000
Other candidates: independents, primary losers and third-party candidates		
Senate	$28,000,000	
House	20,200,000	
Total, other candidates		$ 48,200,000
Total, congressional-related spending		$298,397,000

Source: Citizens' Research Foundation.
[a]Total spending, including primaries. Primary losers compiled as a unit, without computation by party.
[b]Direct spending, not including transfers of funds.

(Democratic-Republican) and by Senate or House; other party-identified direct spending (the national congressional and senatorial committees of both parties), plus other committees listed in table 4-15; primary loser and third-party spending; and independent expenditures and communication costs on behalf of congressional candidates.

Almost $300 million was spent in the congressional campaigns. Elements of this total are covered separately in party totals and amounts for

Table 4-15
Total Spending and Direct Spending, by Miscellaneous Partisan-Identified Congressional Committees

Democratic	*Total Spending*	*Direct Spending*
Democratic		
House		
Majority House Committee	$ 213,000	$ 96,000
DSG Campaign Fund	83,000	75,000
Democratic Candidates' Fund (O'Neill Fund)	49,000	35,000
Total, House	$ 345,000	$ 206,000
Senate and House		
Democratic Congressional Dinner Committee	$2,603,000	$ 871,000
Democraic House and Senate Council	791,000	777,000
Total, joint	$3,394,000	$1,648,000
Total, Democratic	$3,739,000	$1,854,000
Republican		
House		
Republican Majority of the House PAC	$ 148,000	$ 42,000
Whip's Fund for a Republican Majority	7,000	5,000
Total, House	$ 155,000	$ 47,000
Senate		
Republican Senate Majority Fund	$ 379,000	$ 218,000
Senate Defense and Economic Policy PAC (John Tower PAC)	52,000	51,000
Total, Senate	$ 431,000	$ 269,000
Senate and House		
1979-1980 Republican Senate House Dinners	$1,536,000	$382,000
Republican Congressional Boosters Club	704,000	226,000
Gerald R. Ford New Leadership Committee	248,000	220,000
New Republic Victory Fund	248,000	217,000
Total, joint	$2,736,000	$1,045,000
Total, Republican	$3,322,000	$1,361,000

Source: Citizens' Research Foundation.

independent expenditures and communication costs in other tables, however; hence this figure is not as widely used as the $238.9 million figure for campaign spending in 1980 as compiled by the FEC.

New Spending Categories

The FECA established certain new categories of political spending, defined as follows:

> Independent expenditures: Expenditures made on behalf of or opposing a clearly identified candidate but not in cooperation, consultation, or concert with the candidate or any authorized committee or agent of the candidate. Total reported: $16,084,000.[8]

> Unauthorized delegate spending: Expenditures by or on behalf of delegates receiving no financial or authorized support from presidential candidates; these expenditures are not counted against the candidate spending limits. Total reported: $144,071.

> Communication costs: Expenditures for partisan communications by corporations, labor, and membership organizations to their respective stockholders, executive, and administrative personnel and their families or members and their families, the costs of which are to be reported to the FEC when they exceed $2,000 per election. Total reported: $3,972,000.[9]

> Exempt spending: Legal and accounting costs incurred by political committees and candidates to ensure FECA compliance; the value of such services, however, is not exempt from reporting requirements.[10]

It is difficult to arrive at a meaningful estimate of two major components of exempt spending. First, although candidates and committees are required to report their exempt spending for legal and accounting services, the reporting methodology varies widely, making an informed estimate impossible; only FEC audits of every reporting unit could establish precise figures. Whenever discrete figures have been reported, as from campaigns in which expenditures limitations apply, they have been included in the totals. Legal and accounting costs reported by congressional-campaign committees and in political-party filings also are included in the totals. Second, labor and corporate PAC exempt spending is another unknown factor since it is not required to be disclosed. On the basis of what is known and taking into consideration historical patterns, total exempt spending in these categories clearly must have exceeded $30 million. When combined with reported exempt spending, the total for federal races equals $50.2 million. The component of this total spent on presidential candidates is shown in table 4-16.

Democratic and Republican Political Committee Receipts and Expenditures

In January 1982, the FEC released its four-volume *1979-1980 Reports on Financial Activity: Party and Non-Party Political Committees* for the 1980 campaigns.[11] Some 585 party-related political committees filed reports with the FEC.

The party report divides the committees into six categories according to their function within the party and the type of candidates they generally

Table 4-16
Summary of Presidential Independent Expenditures, Communication Costs, Unauthorized Delegates, Draft Committees, and Exempt Spending, 1980

	Independent Expenditures	Communication Costs	Other
Democratic independent expenditures			
Carter			
For	$ 46,000		
Against	246,000		
Other Democratic candidates			
For	77,000		
Against	491,000		
Communication costs, all Democratic candidates		$2,258,000	
Unauthorized delegates and draft committees, all Democratic candidates			$567,000
Republican independent expenditures			
Reagan			
For	12,246,000		
Against	48,000		
Other Republican candidates			
For	291,000		
Against	17,000		
Communication costs, all Republican candidates		321,000	
Unauthorized delegates supporting Reagan			111,000

Source: Citizens' Research Foundation, from various FEC compilations.

support. The committees include standing and ad hoc committees, as follows:

1.   The national committees, normally identified with the presidential campaigns.
2.   The senatorial and congressional committees that assist in the election of party candidates for the Senate and the House of Representatives.
3.   The Association of State Chairs, a Democratic committee only.
4.   Other national committees that are party-identified or auxiliary committees.
5.   The convention committees, including the host-city committees.
6.   State and local committees—that is, the central committees of the parties at the state, county, and municipal levels.

The report shows, by party and by type of committee, the figures for total receipts and expenditures as reported (gross) and as adjusted (net). The report provides a dollar breakdown of contributions and the number of contributions when available. Also provided are figures for cash on hand, outstanding debts and final balances.

Those who compiled the report stress the importance of examining both the gross and the net figures. The gross figures represent the total amounts reported by each of the committees. The net figures were derived by subtracting from these totals any repaid loans, refunded contributions, rebated expenditures, and redeemed Treasury notes and certificates of deposit. Also subtracted were transfers of funds received from related committees and earmarked contributions that would be reported as a receipt by another committee or candidate. Large amounts of money passed from party committee to party committee in the form of loans, transfers, and in-kind contributions and the difference between the reported and adjusted totals is substantial. The purpose of adjusting the figures to derive net amounts is to avoid double-counting.

The Republicans raised more money and spent more in every category than did the Democrats. Essentially the Republicans have outdistanced the Democrats in both ability and willingness to assist candidates for federal office and to apply national-party expertise to help develop stronger financial bases for the state parties.

A large number of party committees, operating at the state and local levels, filed reports with the FEC. As the new regulations allow, most but not all state central committees filed only federal election-segregated account reports. Some state central committees established separate federal accounts, but others reported all federal and state transactions. Some reported fund-raising events for the national party and transferred out most of the funds to national-level committees. Hence the bases for the compilations presented here differ.

The involvement of district, county, and municipal committees in federal campaigns is difficult to assess and impossible to apportion among presidential, senatorial, and congressional categories. Accordingly, there is no rationale by which to break down presidential and congressional components beyond those noted elsewhere. A compilation of state- and local-party spending, based on FEC reports, is shown in table 4-17. The five-to-two ratio of Republican versus Democratic direct party spending, after transfers of funds are subtracted, as reported to the FEC, probably would hold true even if all state- and local-party spending, federal and nonfederal, were reported.

When party reports at all levels are tallied, they indicate $170.5 million was spent by Republicans as compared with $35 million by Democrats, almost a five-to-one difference (table 4-18). The table figures represent adjusted disbursements for the years 1979-1980.

One stark illustration of the major party differences may be derived from the audited reports of the RNC and the DNC for 1979 and 1980. During the election cycle, the RNC and the DNC received similar amounts from major contributors and fund-raising events: $9,975,000 for the RNC and $9,492,185 for the DNC. During the same cycle, however, the RNC received $40,226,300 from responses to mail and telephone solicitations; whereas the DNC received $4,150,522 from responses to direct-mail appeals. Although the parties use different terminologies to describe categories of revenue, which makes direct comparisons difficult, the major difference between the two national party committees is obvious. In direct-mail receipts, the RNC leads the DNC by a ten-to-one margin.

Spending by Interest Groups

The January 1982 FEC compilation also contains data for PAC activity in the 1980 campaigns.[12] Some 2,551 PACs filed reports with the FEC.

Table 4-17
State- and Local-Party Spending, 1979-1980

	Democrats	*Republicans*
State central committees	$ 6,176,900	$25,127,300
Association of State Chairpersons	2,371,000	0
Other party-related committees	167,500	4,396,700
Local committees	1,986,000	4,300,000
Total, state and local	10,701,400	33,824,000
Less transfers	2,000,000	8,000,000
Direct spending	$ 9,000,000	$26,000,000

Source: Citizens' Research Foundation from various FEC compilations.

Table 4-18
Party-Committee Adjusted Disbursements, 1979-1980

Committee	Democrats	Republicans
National committees	$15,150,984	$ 75,821,719
Senatorial	1,618,162	21,211,482
Congressional	2,828,184	34,970,731
Association of state chairs	2,451,017	0
Other national	350,186	765,735
Party conventions	3,830,314	5,315,000
State and local	8,754,177	32,545,199
Totals	$34,983,024	$170,629,866

Source: Citizens' Research Foundation from various FEC compilations.

In the interest-group category are the PACs of corporations, labor unions, trade associations, cooperatives, professional groups, health-related groups, and agriculture and dairy interests. Ideological and single-issue committees also are part of this broad nonparty category. Registered PAC growth has been extensive (table 4-19). Three categories—nonconnected, cooperative, and corporation without stock—were so designated by the FEC in 1978 and hence do not appear in the earlier tabulations.

Of the 2,551 PACs registered with the FEC as of December 31, 1980, not all reported financial activity. Of those that did, 22 raised more than $1 million, and 223 raised more than $100,000. On the other hand, 417 were virtually inactive, with another 152 reporting receipts of less than $1,000. Some were newly organized groups testing the waters in 1980 and may proceed with more vigor in future elections.

The financial impact of PAC activity also demonstrated notable growth from the period 1972-1980, as evidenced from the data in table 4-20.

The FEC data show that PACs began the election cycle with almost $22 million cash on hand and spent $131.2 million between January 1, 1979,

Table 4-19
Growth of PACs, 1974-1981

Category	1974	1976	1978	1980	1981
Corporate	89	433	784	1,204	1,327
Labor	201	224	217	297	318
Trade, membership, and health	318	489	451	574	608
Nonconnected			165	378	539
Cooperative			12	42	41
Corporation without stock			24	56	68
Total	608	1,146	1,653	2,551	2,901

Source: Citizens' Research Foundation from various FEC compilations.

Table 4-20
Financial Activity of PACs, 1972-1980

Election Cycle[a]	Adjusted Receipts[b]	Adjusted Expenditures[b]	Contributions to Congressional Candidates
1972	n.a.	$ 19,168,000	$ 8,500,000[c]
1974	n.a.	25,000,000[d]	12,526,586
1976	$ 54,045,588	52,894,630	22,571,912
1978	79,956,291	77,412,860	35,187,215
1980	137,728,528	131,153,184	55,217,291

Source: Joseph E. Cantor, *Political Action Committees: Their Evolution and Growth and Their Implications for the Political System* (Washington, D.C.: Congressional Research Service, May 7, 1982), p. 67.

[a]The periods covered by the election cycles vary. Data for 1972 are relatively limited for the period prior to April 7, 1972, the effective date for disclosure under the FECA of 1971. Until then, campaign finance disclosure was governed by the Federal Corrupt Practices Act of 1925, under which much activity went unreported. 1974 data cover September 1, 1973, to December 31, 1976. 1978 data cover January 1, 1977, to February 22, 1980. 1980 data cover January 1, 1979, to December 31, 1980.

[b]Excludes monies transferred between affiliated committees; data thus are more representative of levels of financial activity.

[c]Excludes contributions to candidates defeated in primaries.

[d]Estimated.

and December 31, 1980. PAC contributions to all candidates represented about 45 percent of all PAC spending. PACs—principally ideological and single-issue committees—also spent $14.2 million on independent expenditures to promote or defeat certain candidates. Nearly $4 million was spent on internal communications as reported mainly by labor organizations.

In the 1980 elections, PACs contributed $20 million more to congressional candidates than they did in 1978, an increase of 67 percent, and about $32.6 million (144 percent) more than in 1976. As in prior years, more was contributed to House candidates (65 percent) than to Senate (32 percent) or presidential (3 percent) candidates. Incumbents received a greater share than did challengers or open-seat candidates, and Democrats received more than Republicans, although the spread between the parties narrowed in 1980 to less than 5 percentage points, with the Democrats receiving 52.2 percent of the total PAC contribution, and the Republicans 47.6 percent.[13]

Some classifications of PAC by the FEC are straightforward; others are not or are subject to reclassification. In the first grouping are corporate and labor PACs whose affiliates are readily identified in their statements of registration with the FEC; the FEC reports isolate these categories accordingly. Corporations without stock are largely savings-and-loan associations and mutual-savings banks.

Many trade-, health-, agriculture-, and dairy-related PACs, however, might easily be assigned to more than one group. For example, the National

Cotton Council might be included among trade association or agricultural groups. In table 4-21, which attempts to make more-definitive selections than the FEC classifications, it is included among rural-related groups. Numerous similar examples could be offered.

Some PAC names are misleading. For example, the Western Enterprise PAC was funded by Nevada hotel interests. A group of PACs that the FEC classified as nonconnected committees—Intermountain, Louisiana, three in Texas and Tri-state (Ohio, Indiana and Illinois)— actually had ties to the oil drilling and/or oil-service industries. Their combined spending approached $1 million. These, and similar committees in other industries, are included in table 4-21 in the reclassified trade and professional association category.

A significant number of committees were not identified as party-related so the FEC assigned them to nonparty status. Actually, the CRF found many to be party-related. Some are candidates' personal PACs, and others

Table 4-21
PAC Spending by Major Categories

Labor unions	$25,100,000[a]	
Corporations	31,418,000	
Corporations without stock	1,265,000	
Trade and professional associations	18,300,000[b]	
Health related	7,950,000	
Rural related	4,464,000	
Ideological[e]	38,613,000[c]	
Unassigned[f]	1,665,000	
Total		$128,775,000[d]
Committees reclassified into the national party-related category	$ 1,667,000	
35 excluded committees, such as state and local party, nonfederal candidates, 1978 election, for or against named candidates	$ 708,000	
Total		$ 2,375,000
Grand total		$131,150,000

Source: Citizens' Research Foundation.

[a]Labor unions spent an additional $3 million on internal communications.

[b]Associations spent an additional $159,000 on internal communications.

[c]NRA spent an additional $804,000 on internal communications.

[d]Not including communication costs as listed in notes a-c.

[e]Slightly overstated because transfers between the (mostly conservative) PACs were not factored in. The transfer total is only marginally significant.

[f]Derived from the FEC total of $131 million less the named categories. The CRF health total has been adjusted according to non-FEC information.

engage in purely partisan activity at the congressional level. A partial listing of such national-level groups will clarify their purposes. Some Republican-related committees are the Gerald R. Ford New Leadership Committee, the New Republican Victory Fund, the Republican Majority of the House PAC, and the Republican Senate Majority Fund. Democratic-related committees include the Democratic Candidates Fund (also known as the O'Neill Fund), the Democratic Convention 1980 Fund, the Democratic Study Group, and the Majority Congress Committee. A tally indicates that approximately $2.4 million spent by these committees properly should be identified as party-related.

The ideological and issue PACs represent slightly more than 15 percent of all such committees, but their spending constituted about 30 percent of all PAC spending. In 1972, such groups spent only $2.6 million, and in 1976 $12 million. In 1980 their spending rose dramatically to $39 million. Probably only the business-related PACs achieved greater visibility than did the ideological groupings.[14] Some of the ideological and issue PAC activities, such as independent expenditures, negative campaigning, and "hit lists," aroused considerable controversy. Legal challenges were made and restrictive legislation proposed. These PACs may well be the cutting edge of politics in the 1980s.

Ideologically conservative PACs far outdistanced liberal PACs, as measured by receipts, expenditures, and contributions to candidates.[15] Much less is known about some of the other issue or ideological categories. A CRF-classified listing of ideological PACs and their 1980 expenditure totals follows:

Conservative	$27,275,000
Liberal	2,050,000
Women and family	3,758,000
Guns and gun control	2,777,000
Environmental	747,000
Defense	413,000
Ethnic	220,000
Other single issue	200,000
Miscellaneous	1,173,000
Total	$38,613,000

Direct Spending by PACs

In compiling aggregates of political spending, PAC contributions to candidates must be excluded from the overall spending total since those funds have already been counted in the presidential and congressional totals. PAC independent expenditures also have been factored into other classifications. In table 4-22, these two categories of spending are deducted from the adjusted disbursement total. The items that stand out are those relating to the nonconnected (largely ideological) category; only 14 percent of these funds went directly to candidates, whereas 86 percent was spent by the PACs themselves.

This can be attributed to two factors: nonconnected groups have enormous fund-raising costs because they do not have a sponsoring organization and they rely primarily on expensive mail solicitations; and for the most part, they have made deliberate decisions to operate outside the traditional political system and conduct their own independent-expenditure or parallel campaigns on an issue-oriented basis. Thus taking all PACs together, as shown in table 4-22, $71 million represents direct spending. Subtracting $14

Table 4-22
PACs: Administration and Fund Raising

	Disbursements	Contributions to Candidates	Direct Spending
Corporations[a]	$ 32,683,000	$22,263,000 (68%)	$10,420,000 (32%)
Labor	25,100,000	14,213,000 (57%)	10,887,000 (43%)
Nonconnected organization[b]	38,613,000	5,218,000 (14%)	33,395,000 (86%)
Other[c]	34,754,000	18,496,000 (53%)	16,258,000 (47%)
Totals	$131,150,000	$60,190,000[d](46%)	$70,960,000 (54%)
Less: independent expenditures by PACs			(14,100,000)[e]
PAC administration and fund raising			$56,869,000
Communication costs and exempt costs			24,000,000
			$80,860,000

Source: Citizens' Research Foundation.

[a]Includes corporations without stock.

[b]Largely ideological.

[c]Trade-health-rural.

[d]Includes all contributions, including primary losers and presidential candidates.

[e]Some additional fund-raising costs may be found within the independent-expenditures category because direct-mail costs are apportioned when candidates (for or against) are mentioned in the solicitation letters.

million in independent expenditures leaves almost $57 million that can be attributed to administrative expenses. For the ideological groups, direct-mail or fund-raising costs, which were very high, are subsumed under administrative expenses.

Corporation, union, and trade association PACs are permitted by law to use treasury funds for fund-raising purposes, as well as for the costs of establishing and administering their PACs. The ideological committees not connected to sponsoring organizations cannot do so. Moreover, the corporate and union PACs are not required to report their administrative costs unless they come from voluntary funds rather than treasury funds, and only a few do so. If these amounts, estimated at $30 million, are added to $4 million reported in communication costs, which are not PAC expenses but those of PAC sponsors, then total direct spending would be even greater than that stated for the nonparty category.

Notes

1. For 1952-1976, Herbert E. Alexander, *Financing the 1976 Election* (Washington, D.C.: Congressional Quarterly Press, 1979), pp. 165-166, derived in part from Alexander Heard, *The Costs of Democracy* (Chapel Hill, N.C.: University of North Carolina Press, 1960), pp. 7-8. For the most part, trend data throughout this chapter are derived from these books.

2. This section is derived in part from FEC, "FEC Releases Final Report on 1980 Presidential Primary Activity," press release, November 15, 1981; FEC, *FEC Reports on Financial Activity, 1979-1980: Presidential Pre-Nomination Campaigns* (Washington, D.C.: FEC, October 1981).

3. The total payout actually was larger, but various candidates and committees were required to repay certain funds; nevertheless the campaigns had use of some larger amounts of money during the campaigns. The FEC continues to seek certain other repayments at this writing, so final payout figures may differ.

4. Heard, *Costs,* p. 54.

5. Louise Overacker, *Money in Elections* (New York: Macmillan, 1932), p. 79.

6. This section is derived in part from FEC, "FEC Releases Final Statistics on 1979-80 Congressional Races," press release, March 7, 1982; FEC, *FEC Reports on Financial Activity, 1979-1980: U.S. House and Senate Campaigns* (Washington, D.C.: FEC, January 1982).

7. As used by the FEC, spending by a general-election candidate means total spending, primary and general election combined, by a candidate running in the general election. This formulation omits primary losers.

8. FEC, "FEC Study Shows Independent Expenditures Top $16 Million," press release, November 29, 1981; FEC, *FEC Index of Independent Expenditures, 1979-80* (Washington, D.C.: FEC, November 1981).

9. FEC, press release, October 5, 1981; FEC, *FEC Index of Communications Costs, 1979-1980* (Washington, D.C.: FEC, September 1981).

10. Exempt spending refers to the costs of establishing and administering PACs, as well as fund-raising costs, for corporate, labor, and trade-association PACs. These costs may be paid from treasury or institutional monies and need not be voluntarily contributed; PAC money for direct political spending must come from voluntary contributions.

11. This section is derived in part from FEC, *FEC Reports on Financial Activity, 1979-1980: Party and Non-Party Political Committees* (Washington, D.C.: FEC, January 1982), vols. 1-4.

13. In comparison the Democratic percentages were 68 in 1974, 66 in 1976, and 54 in 1978. See Gary C. Jacobson, "Money in the 1980 Congressional Elections" (paper delivered at Midwest Political Science Association, Milwaukee, Wisconsin, April 30, 1982), table 4, p. 4.

14. Treating corporate PACs as a unit should not be taken as an implication that the corporate sector is monolithic in its giving. Other researchers and journalists have broken the corporate PAC sector into various parts. Perhaps the most extensive work of this type was undertaken by Marvin I. Weinberger and David U. Greevy, who divided the 1,204 corporate PACs on file with the FEC as of December 21, 1980, into the ninety-nine categories of the Standard Industrial Classification Index. Another comprehensive work of this type was done by Edward Roeder, who divided all PACs registered with the FEC as of May 1982 into twenty-six broad categories and several hundred subcategories. See Marvin I. Weinberger and David U. Greevy, *The PAC Directory* (Cambridge, Mass.: Ballinger Co., 1982), p. III-1, and Edward Roeder, *PACs Americana* (Washington, D.C.: Sunshine Services Corp., 1982), p. 689. BIPAC and Common Cause have both made similar categorizations of corporate PACs, albeit on a more limited basis. See "Business PAC Activity in the 1980 Election: A Study of PACs Sponsored by Fortune 500 Companies," *BIPAC Politikit,* (November 1981), pp. 34-43, and Common Cause, *A Common Cause Guide to Money Power and Politics in the 97th Congress* (Washington, D.C.: Common Cause, 1981). Finally, various journalistic reports have identified various lobbies in the business sector, often linking contributions from the PACs representing a particular industry to key members of Congress or to committees considering legislation that affects the industry. See, for example, Mark Green and Jack Newfield, "Who Owns Congress: A Guide to Indentured Politicians," *Village Voice,* April 21, 1980; Edward Roeder, "18 Finance Panel Members Got $300,000 from Chemical Industry," *Washington Post,* November 17, 1980; Morton Mintz, "Election

'80 Was Record Year for PACs, Especially Those on Right,'' *Washington Post*, January 27, 1981; and Bill Paul, "Money and Politics in the Railroad Industry," *Modern Railroads* (July 1982):49.

15. See chapters 8 and 9 and for further examples: Jane Stone, "Have Calumny, Will Travel," *Nation,* October 10, 1981, p. 344; Mintz, "Election '80 Was Record Year"; Maxwell Glen and James K. Poplin, "Liberal PACs Learning It Won't Be Easy to Stem the Conservation Tide," *National Journal,* March 20, 1982, p. 500; and Jeremy Gaunt, "Money Flows to the Right in 1982 Campaign," *Congressional Quarterly Weekly Report,* February 27, 1982, p. 482.

5 The Prenomination Campaigns

The 1974 and 1976 FECA amendments, which regulated the fund raising and spending of the 1976 presidential prenomination-campaign committees, for the most part remained intact for the 1980 campaigns. Although the 1979 FECA amendments somewhat eased the reporting requirements of the law, they did not alter the law's contribution or spending limit provisions or its provisions regarding federal matching funds.

Under the FECA, candidates for the 1980 presidential nomination who accepted public matching funds were permitted to spend no more than $14,720,000, plus 20 percent—$2,944,000—for fund raising. In addition the 1974 FECA amendments limited candidate spending in each state to the greater of $200,000 or sixteen cents per eligible voter, plus a cost-of-living increase. Candidates who did not accept public funding were not bound by the overall or the individual state limits. Payments made by the candidates for legal and accounting services to comply with the campaign law were exempted from the law's spending limits, but candidates were required to report such payments.

All candidates were bound by the contribution limits stipulated in the FECA. No candidate was permitted to accept more than $1,000 from an individual contributor or $5,000 from a multicandidate committee. Candidates who accepted public funding were allowed to contribute no more than $50,000 to their own campaigns. That limit also included the candidates' families.

As in 1976, to qualify for public matching funds available under the FECA, candidates were required to raise $5,000 in private contributions of $250 or less in each of twenty states. The federal government matched each contribution to qualified candidates up to $250, although the federal subsidies could not exceed $7,360,000, half of the $14,720,000 prenomination campaign spending limit. According to the law, the FEC could not pay out matching funds until January 1, 1980.

The Impact of the FECA

The spending and contribution limits of the FECA had a significant impact on the conduct of the 1980 presidential prenomination campaigns. According to a number of campaign participants, those limits often had a negative effect on the campaigns, indicating to them the desirability of further changes in the law.[1]

The Overall Spending Limit

The national spending limit of $17.7 million ($14.7 million plus the 20 percent fund-raising overage) for candidates accepting federal matching funds required candidates whose campaigns had a realistic chance to remain in the race for the long term to plan carefully when to spend the money they had available.[2] For example, they could spend heavily early in the campaign, hoping to gain enough momentum to help propel them in the campaign's later stages when they would have to spend less in order to remain within the spending limit. Or they could pick and choose where they spent money early, saving enough for heavier spending later in the campaign when the majority of primaries in the most populous states were held.

The Reagan campaign invested large sums early in the prenomination contest. Through March 31, 1980, when only eleven of the thirty-six Republican primary contests had been held, the candidate's committee reported having spent a little more than $11 million, 75 percent of the $14.7 million subject to limitation. The committee was forced to cut its monthly staff payroll in half[3] and to tighten financial control over the campaign.[4]

The Bush campaign, on the other hand, carefully husbanded its funds. Through March 31, the campaign committee reported having spent $9.7 million of the $14.7 million limit, making it possible to spend $1.3 million more than the Reagan campaign for the remaining presidential primaries. In fact, Bush outspent Reagan by as much as five to one in primaries in Pennsylvania, Michigan, and Texas. Bush won in Pennsylvania and Michigan and did better than anticipated in Texas, but the recognition and support Reagan had established early in the prenomination campaign were sufficient to carry him to the nomination.

In the Democratic prenomination contest, the Carter campaign approached the overall spending limit more rapidly than the Kennedy campaign. Through March 31, the Carter campaign committee reported having spent a little more than $9 million of the $14.7 million limit compared with a similar reported expenditure of $6.9 million by the Kennedy campaign. At that time in the contest, Kennedy was drawing even with Carter in fund raising,[5] putting pressure on the incumbent to spend carefully in the later primaries lest he have insufficient funds for a highly competitive convention, where the cost of staff, communications, and entertainment, as well as expenditures for preliminary battles in the platform, rules, and credentials committees, would count against his prenomination spending limit. Although Kennedy did carry the contest to the convention, Carter already had won more than enough delegates to assure him of the nomination.

None of the candidates for the presidential nomination initially reported exceeding the national spending limit. An FEC audit of the Reagan for President Committee, however, concluded that the committee had exceeded the limit by some $77,000 and recommended that amount be repaid by the committee to the U.S. Treasury.[6] As of December 31, 1980, the Carter campaign reported having spent $13.8 million of the $14.7 million subject to limitation.[7]

Throughout the prenomination-campaign period, candidates and campaign finance officers complained that the overall spending limit was set too low. The 1974 FECA amendments established a limit of $10 million to be adjusted according to annual increases in the CPI. Some of the items campaigns must buy did increase in cost compared with 1976 at approximately the rate of inflation. For example, just before the January 1980 Iowa caucuses, a full-page advertisement in the Sunday edition of the *Des Moines Register and Tribune* cost $7,173, 37 percent more than in 1976.[8] During the same period, however, the cost of television advertising doubled. One minute of advertising over a major network that cost about $50,000 in 1976 cost about $100,000 in 1980.[9] "The cost of running for office has almost doubled in four years," said one campaign fund raiser, who noted that the cost of gas had increased by about 100 percent and the cost of television advertising in some markets by as much as 80 percent.[10]

Faced with increased costs and what they perceived as a low spending limit, many campaigns sacrificed grass-roots campaigning and the paraphernalia that goes with it, such as buttons and brochures, and put substantial amounts of money into television advertising, which they considered indispensable (see table 5-1). The Bush, Carter, and Reagan campaigns reported spending $3 million or more on television advertising, and the Connally and Kennedy campaigns spent almost $2 million in this way. Also, campaigns organized their activities to draw maximum media attention so the candidates' messages would be transmitted to the public at no direct cost to the candidates. According to one campaign operative, campaigns had to "somehow beguile or trap the media" into doing what they could not do themselves.[11]

State Limits

Like the overall spending limit, the spending limits established by the FECA for the individual states called for strategic prenomination-campaign decisions, particularly in the early primary contests, and were the subject of criticism by candidates and campaign committees. Candidates, of course, felt the need to do well in the early prenomination contests, which customarily are assigned more importance by the news media than the number of

Table 5-1
Media Expenditures of Selected 1980 Presidential Prenomination Candidates

Candidate		Media	Production
Bush	Air time	$3,750,000	730,500
	Print	388,300	
Kennedy		1,017,250	805,100
Connally		1,900,000[a]	na
Carter		3,562,700	652,350
Reagan		3,000,000[a]	na
Brown		345,500	45,000
Baker	Television	670,000	
	Radio	160,000	281,500
	Newspapers	58,000	
Anderson		1,274,570[a]	na
Total		$16,126,320[b]	$2,514,450[b]

Source: Citizens' Research Foundation.

[a]Not broken down to indicate production costs. In some cases, production costs are subsumed in the media figure; in others, consultant fees are not isolatable.

[b]Amount uncertain because production costs were not ascertained in three cases.

delegates at stake would otherwise warrant. This need to do well early was reinforced by the election law under which a candidate who draws less than 10 percent of the vote in two consecutive primaries becomes ineligible for matching funds thirty days after the second primary and can be restored to eligibility only by winning 20 percent of the vote in a later primary. The spending limits in the states, however, are determined by demographics rather than the political importance of a state's prenomination contest. The low spending ceiling of $294,000 in New Hampshire, for example, forced the candidates to budget tightly.

Often the national-campaign organizations maintained control of expenditures in each state. Before the FECA, complained one campaign veteran, "We had some [local] control over the format and content. Now it's all run from Washington."[12]

Campaigns also resorted to a variety of subterfuges in an attempt to get around the state spending limits. Campaign staff members sometimes stayed overnight in a state bordering on the primary state so the cost of accommodations could be counted against the other state's limit. Remarked one campaign official in the midst of the first state primary contest of the season, "The motels on the New Hampshire border are going to do quite a business."[13] Primary-campaign flights were arranged to pass through cities outside the primary state, making them interstate trips, which, unlike intrastate trips, do not fall under the primary state's spending limit. A fundraising element was included with as many primary campaign events as possible so at least some of the cost of the events could be allocated to the 20 percent fund-raising overage. Similarly, funds were solicited in all mailings within a state so the mailing costs could be allocated to exempt fund raising rather than count against the state's spending limit. Primary-state campaign staff members sometimes were placed on the national-campaign committee staffs so at least a portion of their salaries could be excluded from the primary state's limit. Prior to the New Hampshire primary, some campaigns purchased television time in cities such as Boston, whose media markets include parts of New Hampshire, so television costs could be charged to the Massachusetts limit.

One candidate, John Connally, chose to reject public funding in order to avoid the individual state limits in the early primaries. He explained that he wanted the flexibility of using available resources "in the states where we need them most."[14] Before he decided to accept matching funds, Ronald Reagan said he preferred to forgo them "and at least be able to control our own strategy."[15] Reagan complained that campaigning had become a "government-regulated industry," preventing candidates from emphasizing efforts in one place rather than another.[16]

Although a number of candidates initially reported having spent close to the legal limit in early prenomination contests, such as those in Iowa and New Hampshire, none reported having exceeded any of the state spending limits. FEC audits, however, concluded that the Reagan, Carter, Kennedy, and LaRouche campaigns had exceeded individual state limits, and the agency required those campaigns to repay stipulated amounts to the U.S. Treasury.

Contribution Limits

Unlike the overall and state expenditure limits, which are indexed to take account of increases in the CPI, the contribution limits established by the 1974 FECA amendments—$1,000 per individual and $5,000 per multicandidate committee—are not indexed. Inflation has made the $1,000 individual limit, which some observers considered too low when it was enacted, even more restrictive. A $1,000 contribution in April 1980 was worth only about $641 when compared with the buying power of $1,000 when the limit went into effect.

Like the expenditure limits, the contribution limits often determined prenomination-campaign strategy and occasioned the criticism of campaigners. By prohibiting candidates from quickly gathering seed money for their campaigns from a handful of wealthy contributors, the contribution limits gave an advantage to well-known politicians who had already achieved significant name recognition and forced lesser-known candidates to begin the public side of their campaigns earlier than ever. In August 1978, two years before his party's nominating convention, Rep. Philip M. Crane (R-Ill.) formally declared his candidacy. By June 1979 he had been joined by six other major announced candidates for president. Only the best-known politicians, such as President Carter, Ronald Reagan, Sen. Howard Baker and Sen. Edward Kennedy, were able to put off their formal announcements until late 1979. Even so, Carter, Reagan, and Baker found it necessary to set up exploratory committees long prior to their announcements in order to do organizational and fund-raising groundwork.

In 1980, as in 1976, the individual contribution limit did achieve its intended effect of eliminating large contributions by wealthy contributors to favored candidates. The limit also altered fund-raising patterns. The role once filled by large contributors was now filled by well-connected individuals who could persuade a large number of persons to contribute the $1,000 maximum amount to the candidates for whom the fund raisers labored. "Blessed are the gatherers," said one such elite solicitor, who noted that "the guy who'll go out and raise $100,000" is much more valuable to a campaign than one who would give a single $1,000 contribution.[17]

Candidates also were forced to rely more often on costly direct-mail solicitations—in many instances the most effective way of reaching large numbers of small contributors—and on the direct-mail specialists who have emerged as important forces in political campaigns since the enactment of the 1974 FECA amendments. Entertainers, whose services were volunteered and hence not subject to the $1,000 limitation, were enlisted to hold benefit concerts for candidates. The Kennedy campaign called on singer and actress Barbra Streisand; the Brown campaign, rock star Linda Ronstadt; the Reagan campaign, Frank Sinatra; and the Carter campaign, country music singer Willie Nelson. It was observed that top entertainers became in many ways "the fat cats of the new era."[18] Artists, whose time, efforts, and talent on behalf of candidates were exempt from the contribution limit, were prevailed upon by the Kennedy campaign to donate artwork to be used at raffles and as door prizes at other campaign fund-raising events and to be offered as inducements to potential contributors.[19] The first $250 of each contribution raised by any of these methods—personal solicitation by well-connected fund raisers, direct-mail solicitation, benefit concerts, and artwork-aided solicitation—was matched by the same amount from public funds.

The contribution and expenditure limits of the FECA may have functioned as a two-edged sword regarding the potential candidacy of former President Gerald Ford. In March 1980 there was considerable speculation that Ford might announce his candidacy. By that time, Republican front-runner Ronald Reagan had already spent a substantial portion of the amount he was permitted under the national spending limit. He undoubtedly would have been financially hard pressed to counter a well-financed challenge by Ford in the remaining primaries. At the same time, the $1,000 individual contribution limit would have made it difficult for Ford to raise sufficient funds to mount an effective challenge, and so he chose not to join the competition.

In several ways, then, the contribution and spending limits served to reduce the flexibility and spontaneity of campaigns. Those limits also were partly responsible for the development and use of three methods of circumventing the limits: independent expenditures, draft committees, and presidential PACs. Each subject merits elaboration.

Independent Expenditures

In 1976, in the case of *Buckley* v. *Valeo*, the U.S. Supreme Court overturned a provision of the 1974 FECA amendments that limited to $1,000 per calendar year campaign spending by individuals "relative to a clearly identified candidate . . . advocating the election or defeat of such candidate."[20] The Court ruled that individuals and groups could spend unlimited amounts on communications advocating the election or defeat of a clearly identified candidate provided the expenditures are made without consultation or collaboration with the candidates or their campaigns. Following the ruling, the 1976 FECA amendments imposed no limitations on independent expenditures on behalf of or in opposition to federal candidates. According to subsequent FEC rulings, however, individual donations to independent committees are restricted to $5,000 per individual to each multicandidate committee and $1,000 per individual to each single-candidate committee. Also, any contributions to committees making independent expenditures are counted against the contributor's $25,000 overall limit to all federal campaigns in an election cycle.

In 1976 independent expenditures played a role of little importance in the prenomination or general-election campaigns, in part, no doubt, because of a lack of familiarity with the new election laws by those who might be inclined to make such expenditures. In 1980 the importance of independent expenditures increased significantly as a means of allowing individuals and groups to circumvent the contribution limits and to supplement candidate spending in early primary states with low spending ceilings or in later primary states when the candidate approached the national spending limit. In the 1975-1976 election cycle, an estimated $792,953 was spent independently by individuals and political committees for or against presidential and congressional candidates.[21] During the 1980 presidential prenomination campaigns, independent expenditures advocating or opposing the election of clearly identified candidates reported to the FEC totaled $2,743,497.[22]

Ostensibly Ronald Reagan was the major beneficiary of independent spending during the prenomination period; $1,643,468 was reported as spent independently on his behalf. Other candidates on behalf of whom independent expenditures were reported were John Connally, $288,032; John Anderson, $196,354; Edward Kennedy, $56,197; and Jimmy Carter, $18,096. In addition, $522,602 was reported as independent expenditures opposing various candidates.

Several political committees spent substantial amounts independently to further Reagan's candidacy. For example, the Fund for a Conservative Majority reported spending more than $880,000 on Reagan's behalf. Included among its pro-Reagan expenditures was some $60,000 spent in New Hampshire—at a time when Reagan was approaching the state's spending limit—on radio and newspaper advertising, mailing campaign literature, and busing pro-Reagan volunteers to campaign stops. The fund also reported spending some $80,000 on pro-Reagan radio and newspaper advertisements and direct mail in the Texas primary when the Reagan campaign was approaching the overall spending limit for the prenomination campaign. Kenneth F. Boehm, treasurer of the PAC, asserted that members of his group scrupulously avoided all contact with Reagan campaign aides to preserve the independence of the PAC's expenditures. According to Boehm, news reports of the Reagan campaign gave the PAC sufficient information about the campaign's strategy to allow the group to make its expenditures effectively.[23]

Other political committees that made large, pro-Reagan independent expenditures were the Congressional Club, an organization based in Raleigh, North Carolina, and funded initially by money left over from North Carolina Republican Sen. Jesse Helms's 1978 Senate campaign, which reported spending $473,000; and NCPAC, which reported spending $188,000. NCPAC also reported spending about $261,000 against Sen. Edward M. Kennedy and lesser amounts against President Carter and former President Ford, and the NRA reported spending $206,000 against Kennedy.

Not all of the money reported by these political committees as independent expenditures for or against candidates was used to fund activities such as newspaper or broadcast advertising to support or oppose candidates. In fact, a substantial portion of the expenditures were made for fund-raising purposes, particularly for direct-mail costs. Fund-raising letters that mentioned the names of particular candidates supported or opposed by the fund-raising group were listed as independent expenditures for or against those candidates, even if the letters were sent to individuals already predisposed to voting for or against the candidates. For example, even if a letter sent to Reagan supporters by a group making independent expenditures succeeded in raising a large amount of money for the group and adding new names to its contributor file, its costs still were counted as an independent expenditure to promote Reagan's candidacy.

Large independent expenditures on behalf of presidential prenomination candidates also were reported by several individuals. Texas industrialist and real-estate investor Cecil R. Haden reported spending $184,000 on behalf of John Connally and $32,000 on behalf of Ronald Reagan. Philanthropist Stewart R. Mott reported independent expenditures of $110,000 during the prenomination campaign, $90,000 on behalf of John Anderson and $20,000 on behalf of Edward Kennedy. Television producer Norman Lear spent $106,000 on Anderson's behalf. Theo N. Law reported spending $66,000 on John Connally's behalf, and former Texas state legislator Henry C. Grover reported spending $29,000, also on Connally's behalf.

Although significant amounts of money were reported as independent expenditures made during the prenomination campaign, even greater amounts were reported for the general-election campaign, particularly on behalf of the Republican party candidate, Ronald Reagan. The constitutionality of those expenditures was challenged in court.

Draft Committees

Early in 1979 a number of liberal Democrats began expressing openly their disenchantment with President Carter's performance in office. Newspaper advertisements published in the *Los Angeles Times*[24] and the *New York Times*[25] and financed by groups calling themselves Democrats for Change 1980 and the National Committee for a Democratic Alternative called upon Democrats to seek another candidate for 1980. Although no alternative candidate actually was endorsed, some members of the sponsoring groups let it be known they would support a candidacy by Sen. Edward Kennedy.

In time anti-Carter sentiment, which also took the form of "dump Carter" movements organized in individual states, began to focus even more clearly on Sen. Kennedy as an alternative candidate to President Carter.[26] On May 21 five Democratic congressmen announced they were organizing an effort to draft Kennedy as the party's nominee for president.[27] According to a Gallup Poll, 58 percent of Democrats polled said they would vote for Kennedy, and 31 percent said they would vote for Carter.[28] By June the percentage of those polled favoring Kennedy had increased to 62 percent and Carter's support had decreased to 24 percent.[29] As public opinion increasingly favored Kennedy, congressional pressure on the senator to announce his candidacy mounted.

By mid-August, committees to draft Kennedy had been organized in eighteen states in which Democratic primaries were scheduled. Kennedy disavowed any activities by such committees, which allowed them to qualify as unauthorized committees. The prospects of the committees were helped considerably by an August 16 FEC advisory opinion in response to a request from the Florida for Kennedy Committee.[30] The ruling held that the committee was permitted to accept individual donations of up to $5,000, $4,000 more than the $1,000 limit on contributions to the campaigns of those who had registered with the FEC as candidates for federal office, as President Carter had. The advisory ruling also held that the group was allowed to spend unlimited amounts of money seeking to draft a candidate and that such expenditures would not count against individual state spending limits should the draftee later declare candidacy. The FEC commissioners reportedly were unhappy with the ruling but maintained that the law gave them no choice but to give special treatment to campaign groups working independently without authorization by the potential candidate. In a related ruling issued less than a month later, the commission made clear that although draft-Kennedy groups in the same situation as the Florida for Kennedy committee were exempt from certain campaign law fund-raising and spending limits, such groups nonetheless were bound by the law's registering and reporting requirements.[31] Finally, in September 1980, long after the various draft-Kennedy committees had ceased to exist, the FEC issued another advisory opinion ruling that contributions made in 1979 to draft-Kennedy committees did not count against an individual's $25,000 annual contribution limit for 1980 because the committees were not authorized by Kennedy and because the contributions were not designated for a candidate as defined by the law.[32]

Some activity regarding draft-Kennedy committees became the subject of a lawsuit that was not decided until well after the 1980 general election. Between May 1979 and November 7, 1979, when Kennedy formally announced his candidacy, the Machinists Non-Partisan Political League (MNPL), the political arm of the IAM, contributed $26,720 to draft-Kennedy committees in eight states. In October 1979 the Carter campaign committee filed a complaint with the FEC contending that the draft-Kennedy groups were political committees according to the FECA, were affiliated with each other, and thus were allowed to accept jointly no more than $5,000 from any single donor. The complaint alleged that the draft committees and the IAM PAC knowingly violated the law's contribution limits.

Shortly thereafter the FEC found "reason to believe" the allegations were correct and issued a subpoena to MNPL and to Citizens for Democratic Alternatives, a group aided by MNPL, which played an important role in the formation of various draft committees. The FEC subpoena called upon the two groups to produce extensive information about the creation and financing of the committees. The MNPL insisted it had been engaged only in pre-candidacy activities over which the law had given the FEC no jurisdiction. But in January 1980 a U.S. district court upheld the FEC's position, enforcing the subpoena. The MNPL appealed that holding, and in May 1981 a three-judge U.S. court of appeals panel overturned the district court's decision.

The appeals court described the FEC subpoena demands as sweeping in their scope and maintained that release of the information required by the subpoena carried with it "a real potential for chilling the free exercise of political speech and association."[33] The court ruled that draft groups do not qualify as political committees under the Supreme Court's *Buckley* decision and that therefore the FEC lacked jurisdiction in the case.

In June 1981, the Democratic Senatorial Campaign Committee and the Democratic Congressional Campaign Committee filed a rehearing petition with the appeals court, maintaining that the court's decision posed a threat to the FEC's enforcement of the FECA. The decision, according to the committees, would lead to the creation of two distinct types of political committees: one for registered candidates, which would be subject to the law's contribution and spending limits, and the other for noncandidates, which would not be bound by the same limits. In addition, the FEC decided to seek a Supreme Court review of the appeals court decision and to ask Congress to revise the law. The appeals court denied the rehearing petition filed by the two Democratic committees, and in October 1981 the Supreme Court refused to review the case, thereby letting the appeals court ruling stand.

By the time Kennedy declared his candidacy on November 7, 1979, more than seventy draft committees had been organized in thirty-eight states.[34] According to reports filed with the FEC, receipts for all of the draft-Kennedy committees totaled $554,721 and expenditures totaled $543,453. The Florida for Kennedy Committee alone raised $266,172 and spent $264,345, about 48 percent of the total money raised and spent by the draft committees. New Hampshire Democrats for Change raised $81,491 and spent $80,044, and the Committee for Alternatives to Democratic Presidential Candidates, based in Iowa, raised $38,641 and spent $36,965. These three draft committees together accounted for about 70 percent of all the money raised and spent by the draft committees. Their efforts were directed, respectively, at three of the earliest prenomination events: the Florida Democratic party's presidential straw vote, the New Hampshire primary, and the Iowa caucuses.

A small number of individuals made relatively large contributions to more than one draft committee. According to FEC filings, for example, Mark Dayton, of the family that owns the Dayton-Hudson stores, contributed $5,000 each to New Hampshire Democrats for Change and to the Florida for Kennedy Committee and $2,000 to Minnesotans for a Democratic Alternative. Alida Dayton, his wife, contributed $5,000 each to the New Hampshire and Florida committees. Other contributors of more than $5,000 to draft-Kennedy committees included Joyce and Ted Ashley, Miles Rubin, and Stanley Sheinbaum.

Presidential PACs

In 1966 Richard Nixon prepared the way for his 1968 presidential nomination campaign by barnstorming the country on behalf of Republican candidates. The political IOUs he collected provided a foundation for his successful bid for the Republican nomination.

In the wake of the Republican defeat at the polls in 1976, several Republican hopefuls, with their eyes on 1980, adopted Nixon's strategy. Those potential candidates, however, added a new element to Nixon's barnstorming. In addition to crisscrossing the country on behalf of other Republicans, they made direct or in-kind contributions—more than $800,000 worth by December 31, 1978—to a variety of federal, state, and local candidates and party organizations. The vehicles through which they raised and contributed funds were PACs, which until then had been used largely by corporations, labor unions, trade associations, membership groups, and ideological groups to bring their support to bear on the political process.

In January 1977, the first of these PACs, Citizens for the Republic (CFTR), was formed, ostensibly to support the election of conservative Republican candidates. The group replaced the Citizens for Reagan Committee, which had conducted fund raising and strategy planning for the former California governor in his unsuccessful bid for the 1976 presidential nomination. CFTR was founded with a starting balance in excess of $1 million that the Citizens for Reagan Committee had raised from private sources and had received in federal matching funds during the 1976 prenomination campaign. An FEC audit completed in 1977 determined that of the $1,616,461 in surplus funds with which Citizens for Reagan ended the campaign, $580,857 represented matching funds that were repayable to the U.S. Treasury.[35] In November 1977, the Reagan committee repaid that amount to the Treasury, but by that time the funds had already helped provide CFTR with seed money to mount its own fund-raising drive.

According to reports filed with the FEC through December 31, 1978, CFTR spent $4.5 million during the 1977-1978 election cycle, almost $590,000 of it in direct or in-kind contributions to candidates and party organizations at the federal, state, and local levels.[36] CFTR maintained a full-time staff that eventually reached nearly thirty and executed most of its fund raising through direct mail, initially using a mailing list of more than 100,000 names that had been developed during Reagan's 1976 prenomination campaign.

In February 1977, CFTR began to publish a bimonthly newsletter; by December 1978 its circulation, which included contributors and the media, approached 40,000. Feature articles written by Reagan focused on a variety of conservative issues. Among CFTR's other activities were regional seminars, including political workshops, and speaking tours for Reagan.

By the end of 1978, the committee had distributed funds and services to 234 candidates for the House, 25 Senate candidates, 19 candidates for governor, 122 candidates for other offices ranging from lieutenant governor of California to clerk of Clinton County, Missouri, and candidates for several state Republican party chairmanships. In the process of raising funds, CFTR developed a mailing list of more than 300,000 contributors who would be good prospects for fund-raising appeals by a Reagan presidential committee.

Other Republican presidential hopefuls were quick to see the advantages of Reagan's strategy. By early 1978, three of them—George Bush, Sen. Robert Dole of Kansas, and John Connally—had established PACs of their own. Bush's Fund for Limited Government and Dole's Campaign America served primarily to arrange speaking engagements and fund-raising appearances for the two potential candidates. Both Bush and Dole relied primarily on their personal contacts with business leaders to raise the funds for their PACs. The PAC money permitted them to travel extensively, often to states holding primaries early in 1980, and to speak at Republican events and fund raisers. Their PACs were small operations compared with Reagan's CFTR—each had a staff of five or fewer—and they made relatively few direct contributions to candidates. According to reports filed with the FEC through December 31, 1978, Bush's Fund for Limited Government had expenditures of $228,321, of which $48,051 was spent in direct or in-kind contributions to candidates and party organizations at federal, state, and local levels.[37] Reports to the FEC for the same period indicated that Dole's Campaign America made expenditures of $197,399, contributing $11,954 to candidates and party organizations.[38]

John Connally's PAC—the John Connally Citizens Forum—had broader objectives than the PACs of Bush and Dole. It, too, served as a speaker's bureau for its sponsor, who maintained a heavy speaking and fund-raising appearance schedule. But Connally also intended his PAC, like Reagan's, to be an important source of campaign funds for Republican candidates and party organizations. The Connally PAC turned optimistically to direct mail to raise money. After going through about sixty-five mailing lists, however, the committee ended up some $250,000 short of the $1 million it planned to raise.[39] Nevertheless Connally was able to develop a list of proven contributors who could be approached to help finance his expected prenomination campaign. And his PAC did manage to contribute to candidates and party organizations $133,940 of the $718,884 it raised.[40]

No doubt the four PACs were helpful to the candidates who received direct or in-kind contributions from them. But they also were helpful to the prospective presidential candidates who sponsored them. According to the contribution limits of the 1974 FECA, the PACs were allowed to contribute as much as $5,000 per election to a House or Senate candidate. If the PAC sponsors had contributed as individuals or if their committees had not qualified as PACs under the law, they would have been limited to a contribution of $1,000 per candidate per election. In addition, a supporter of one of the potential presidential candidates could contribute a total of only $1,000 to that potential candidate but could contribute as much as $5,000 to the potential candidate's PAC. Finally the PACs allowed each of the four presidential hopefuls to raise and spend money without having it count against the overall and individual state spending limits that would apply to each candidate for the nomination who accepted federal matching funds. In sum, the PACs allowed their sponsors to gain the favor and support of federal, state, and local candidates and of state- and local-party organizations through contributions to those candidates and organizations, and they allowed the sponsors to travel extensively throughout the country, attracting media attention and increasing their name recognition among party activists and the electorate in general.

Among the four PACs, only Reagan's CFTR was intended to remain in operation. In fact, according to reports filed by CFTR for activity through August 31, 1980, during the 1979-1980 election cycle, the committee spent nearly $2 million, some $106,000 of it in direct or in-kind contributions to candidates and political committees. During the first six months of 1981, CFTR raised nearly $577,000 and spent $468,000.[41] The Bush, Connally, and Dole PACs closed down prior to their sponsors' announcements of candidacy or formation of exploratory committees preparatory to their candidacies.

Rep. Philip Crane of Illinois, the first Republican to announce his presidential candidacy, and former President Gerald Ford also campaigned actively for Republican candidates in 1978. Neither Crane nor Ford, however, formed a PAC to raise and spend funds, although Ford converted his 1976 campaign committee to a multicandidate committee that could donate surplus campaign funds to other candidates. Ford's committee did give $46,500 to forty-six House and Senate candidates.[42] Senate majority leader Howard Baker, who later became a presidential candidate, and House minority leader John Rhodes formed the Congressional Leadership Committee late in 1977 to help them campaign for other Republicans in 1978. George Bush was the honorary chairman of the committee.

Candidate Receipts and Expenditures

Despite the strictures of the FECA's spending and contribution limits, a significant amount of money was raised and spent by candidates for their parties' presidential nominations. As table 5-2 indicates, as of December 31, 1980, the sixteen presidential candidates whose financial activity exceeded

Table 5-2
1980 Prenomination-Campaign Receipts and Expenditures, by Candidate
(millions)

Candidate[a]	Receipts[b]	Individual Contributions	PAC Contributions	Matching Funds[c]	Disbursements[b]
Brown-D	$ 2.65	$ 1.71	$ .04	$ .89	$ 2.65
Carter-D	18.55	12.93	.46	5.05	18.52
Kennedy-D	12.29	7.75	.23	3.86	12.27
LaRouche-D[d]	2.14	1.55	.008	.53	2.15
Anderson-R	6.63	3.91	.02	2.68	6.52
Baker-R	7.14	4.20	.13	2.64	7.07
Bush-R	16.71	10.87	.13	5.72	16.71
Connally-R	12.72	11.64	.205	0	12.62
Crane-R	5.24	3.47	.002	1.75	5.22
Dole-R	1.43	.90	.045	.45	1.39
Fernandez-R	.25	.19	.002	0	.25
Reagan-R	21.39	13.76	.285	7.29	19.82
Stassen-R	.11	.006	0	0	.12
Clark-L	1.09	.57	0	0	1.02
Huncher-L	.15	.01	0	0	.10
Pulley-SW	.13	.10	0	0	.12
Totals	108.62	73.57	1.56	30.86	106.55

Source: FEC, news release, November 15, 1981.

Note: Each candidate listed reported financial activity in excess of $100,000; covers financial activity through December 31, 1980.

[a] Listed alphabetically, according to party affiliation; D = Democrat; R = Republican; L = Libertarian; SW = Socialist Workers.

[b] Adjusted to take into account transfers from or to affiliated committees, loan repayments, contribution refunds, and refunds or rebates to the campaigns.

[c] Figures are taken from the total reported by the campaigns through December 31, 1980.

[d] Although Lyndon LaRouche was the U.S. Labor party candidate for the presidency, he ran as a Democrat in Democratic primaries.

$100,000 raised $108.6 million and spent $106.6 million. In 1976 the seven-
teen presidential prenomination candidates who reported expenditures of
more than $100,000 spent only $67.2 million.[43] The 1980 prenomination-
campaign expenditures represent a 58 percent increase over the corresponding 1976 figure, whereas the rise in the CPI for the four-year period was
about 37 percent.

The relatively high expenditures for the 1980 prenomination campaigns
may be credited to several factors: early announcements and thus early campaigning by a number of out-party candidates; a greatly increased number
of primaries plus a number of other costly prenomination contests such as
caucuses and straw polls in which candidates felt obliged to participate; a
strong challenge to an incumbent president by a member of his own party;
and a relatively large field of out-party candidates capable of raising large
amounts of money. Further, some of the costs of campaigning had sky-
rocketed since 1976. According to some estimates, the costs of items and
services campaigns have to buy, such as television advertising and air travel,
increased by 50 to 70 percent and more.[44]

The largest percentage of the candidates' total receipts—67.8 percent—
came from individual contributions, which amounted to $73.6 million for
the sixteen candidates. PAC contributions, which are focused primarily on
congressional campaigns, came to $1.6 million, only 1.4 percent of the
primary-campaign receipts.

As in 1976, federal matching funds in 1980 provided an important
source of income for most of the major-party candidates. Eleven of those
candidates achieved the fund-raising threshold to qualify them to receive
matching funds, including John Connally, who declined to accept public
funding. As of December 31, 1980, the ten candidates who did accept public
funding had been certified to receive $30.9 million in matching funds, 32.7
percent of their total receipts and 28.5 percent of the total receipts of all sixteen candidates spending $100,000 or more. Matching funds certified in
1981 and 1982 for eligible candidates seeking to retire their prenomination
campaign debts and repayments required for various reasons by the FEC
alter those figures somewhat. Table 5-3 summarizes matching-fund activity
through April 15, 1981.

The maximum amount any candidate could receive in matching funds
was $7.4 million, one-half the national spending limit of $14.7 million.
Ironically only Ronald Reagan, who was certified to receive $7.3 million in
public funds, came close to the maximum (see table 5-3). Although Reagan
accepted public funds for his 1976 prenomination campaign, late in 1979 he
voiced opposition to public funding saying he preferred to see candidates
raising their own campaign funds.[45] After researching the pros and cons of
matching funds, however, the campaign staff concluded that their candidate could not run successfully in the large number of primaries scheduled

Table 5-3
Summary of Matching-Fund Activity for 1980 Presidential Prenomination Candidates as of April 15, 1981

Candidate	Number of Submissions	Amount Requested	Number of Contributions	Number of Resubmissions	Amount Certified by FEC	Maximum Entitlement Remaining
Anderson	7	$ 2,895,484	80,744	0	$ 2,680,347	0
Baker	14	2,699,562	67,490	0	2,635,043	0
Brown	15	996,153	16,273	3	892,249	0
Bush	12	6,373,497	86,612	0	5,716,247	0
Carter	28	5,490,096	63,423	3	5,117,854	$589,089
Crane	17	2,140,551	69,695	1	1,898,838	0
Dole	5	467,117	3,752	1	446,226	0
Kennedy	29	4,447,034	81,678	4	4,130,452	882,824
LaRouche	15	592,982	10,663	13	526,253	0
Reagan	10	8,254,771	213,747	0	7,294,462	0
Totals	152	$34,357,247	694,077	25	$31,337,971	

Source: *FEC Annual Report, 1980*, appendix 8, p. 65

if he had to rely solely on funds from private sources. The Reagan campaign submitted for certification for matching funds approximately 214,000 contributions, representing by far the most impressive number of individual contributors. The average contribution was $38. Nearly 89 percent of the campaign's submissions were certified. The Bush campaign was certified to receive about $5.7 million in matching funds, having submitted for certification nearly 87,000 contributions averaging $74. The Carter campaign qualified to receive about $5.1 million in public funds after submitting for certification some 63,000 contributions averaging $87. The Kennedy campaign was certified to receive about $4.1 million in matching funds; the campaign submitted for certification about 82,000 contributions averaging $55.

In 1976, the federal matching funds provided eligible but little-known outsiders the opportunity to compete effectively in the primary campaigns. Lacking access to traditional sources of large Democratic contributions, Jimmy Carter, without public funding, probably would have lost out early in the primary season to those candidates, such as Sen. Henry M. Jackson, who enjoyed such access. But the combination of contribution limits, which decreased the advantage large contributors could provide, and matching funds, which increased the value of small contributions, had an equalizing effect. Public funding allowed a Washington outsider, a regional candidate, to break into the field and establish his candidacy.

In 1980 the public money similarly helped candidates such as George Bush and John Anderson, who were not well known and who did not have the ready access to large amounts of private money enjoyed by some of their competitors. The public money helped Bush establish himself as front-runner Ronald Reagan's major competitor and to stay the course of the primaries and caucuses. Public funds also helped Anderson become an influential factor in some early Republican primaries and, more significant, to start building the name recognition and national organization he needed to mount his independent candidacy for the presidency.[46] In these cases, the FECA opened up the electoral process to some candidates who otherwise might not have been influential in that process.

All candidates, of course, raise funds, whether from public or private sources, so they may use that money to persuade voters to select them from among all those competing for office. But it is difficult to determine how effectively campaign money is spent. In 1980 the winners of the two major-party nominations were the candidates who spent the most money overall: Ronald Reagan, who reported spending $19.8 million, $3.1 million more than his nearest rival, George Bush, and Jimmy Carter, who reported spending $18.5 million, $6.2 million more than his nearest competitor, Edward Kennedy. In addition in both the Republican and Democratic prenomination contests, in approximately two-thirds of the cases the winner reported having allocated more money to the individual state than did his closest competitor. State-by-state figures are deceiving, however. In the absence of definitive and operable interpretations of FEC regulations, each campaign developed its own way of allocating expenditures to the states. Since the campaigns did not have sufficient funds to approach the limit in most states, there was little incentive for them to report highly accurate state-by-state figures. Further, FEC regulations exempt some large expenses, such as the cost of interstate travel and costs "directly relating to the national headquarters," from allocation to individual states, although such expenditures might aid the campaign effort in particular states.

In fact, the expenditure of money is only one factor in the complex equation leading to electoral success. Other factors, some under the candidates' control and some not, also are important, including the time a candidate has available to campaign; his or her ability to communicate with audiences both directly and through the media, particularly television; the issues the electorate perceives to be at stake in a campaign; the occurrence of national or international crises; and the advantages of incumbency. No candidate for the presidential nomination may hope to achieve success without large expenditures of money, but neither may candidates reasonably hope to win the nomination simply by outspending their rivals.

Compliance

As in 1976, candidates who accepted public matching funds were required to supply the FEC with substantial documentation to prove their campaigns had remained within the spending limits stipulated in the FECA. All candidates, regardless of whether they accepted matching funds, were required to file regular reports with the FEC to prove their campaigns had complied with the law's contribution limits and to fulfill the law's requirements regarding disclosure of contributions and expenditures. Efforts to comply with the law imposed additional expenses on the campaigns. Lawyers and accountants who could lead candidates through the complexities of election-campaign laws and devise systems to keep track of campaign receipts and expenditures were as prominent in the campaigns as political operatives.

Late in December 1979 it was estimated that Reagan national headquarters in Los Angeles employed sixty full-time staff members to comply with the reporting requirements of the FECA.[47] In March 1980 it was reported that fifteen staff members at the Carter-Mondale headquarters in Washington were working full time to prepare reports for the FEC.[48] Carter campaign officials reported spending $1,907,509 on compliance, about 10 percent of its reported expenditures of $18.5 million. The Baker campaign reported exempt legal-activity expenditures of $56,269 and accounting costs

of $1,060,912 for a total of $1,117,181. That figure represents 15.5 percent
of the campaign's reported expenditures of $7.1 million.

Some campaign officials were sufficiently frustrated by the FEC's oversight of campaign-compliance procedures that they voiced their complaints in
a well-publicized criticism of the FEC and its audit process. In a joint letter to
FEC chairman John W. McGarry dated April 30, 1981, attorneys for nine
1980 presidential campaigns and for the Republican and Democratic national
committees complained that campaign regulations had become a "hyper-
technical exercise the standards for which, it would appear from preliminary
reports, can only be understood long after the campaign is ended."[49]

Accusing the commission of being insensitive "to the realities of the
presidential campaign process and the First Amendment expression which is
at the heart of every political campaign," the Campaign Counsel Group, as
it called itself, complained in particular that the commission staff often
substituted its judgment for that of campaign committees, which had acted
in good faith in attempting to comply with the law. In many cases, the
group maintained, the commission staff made retroactive determinations
that committees had violated the law even though the committees had taken
"reasonable" approaches to the issues under discussion. Such retroactive
rulemaking, said the group, often came in the area of state spending limitations. The complaint alleged that although campaigns, following FEC regulations, made efforts to allocate costs reasonably among various states, in
the audit process the commission staff often overrode those determinations
and substituted determinations of its own regarding allocation to states of
such items as national staff salaries, media costs, and interstate phone calls.
In this reallocation process, some campaigns, said the letter, were pushed
over state spending limits and then penalized by a fine equal to the alleged
overspending.

The Campaign Counsel Group registered four additional complaints
about the FEC audit process: lack of standard auditing procedures, denial
of access to information bearing on audit issues, lack of an FEC hearing,
and excessive length of the audit process. The group's letter petitioned the
FEC to postpone for thirty days the publication of presidential campaign
audits while correcting what the group perceived as serious problems in the
prenomination-campaign audit process.

This remarkable agreement among campaign representatives brought a
negative response from the FEC, which defended the commission's procedures and pointed to a bookkeeping manual published by the commission as
a guide for those to be audited.[50] The commission's response omitted reference to two 1979 studies of its audit policies and procedures commissioned
by the agency.[51] Both reviewed the audit process in depth, and both made
recommendations for change. The FEC then revised its audit policies but
presumably not to the satisfaction of the Campaign Counsel Group.

Candidate Debates

The FECA as administered by the FEC also had an impact on one method candidates had to make their views public: the candidate debate or forum. A 1976 FEC policy statement prohibited corporations and labor unions from contributing to the funding of the 1976 presidential debates sponsored by the League of Women Voters (LWV). The FEC based its policy on federal law barring corporations and unions from making contributions "in connection with" a federal election. In February 1977 the league filed suit and claimed that the FEC ruling prevented the organization from raising sufficient funds to pay for the debates. When an FEC motion that the court dismiss the LWV suit was rejected, the commission called a hearing on the matter. In testimony given in September 1977, the LWV argued that the ruling had a "chilling effect" on the organization's efforts to raise money to pay for the debates and that as a result the league was forced to draw $92,000 from reserves and the operating budget of its Education Fund to help pay the $325,000 debate costs. League president Ruth Clusen said organizations would be reluctant to sponsor future debates unless the ruling was overturned.

After hearing this and other testimony, in December 1977 the FEC approved a proposed regulation allowing corporations and labor unions to donate funds to certain nonprofit groups to pay for the costs of sponsoring candidate debates. The contributions would be restricted to those nonprofit organizations, such as the LWV, that were exempt from federal taxation, that had a history of neither supporting nor endorsing candidates or political parties, and that would administer the debates. Once the proposed regulation was approved, the suit was dismissed as moot.

The proposed regulation, however, never was submitted to Congress, but it was included in a series of proposed amendments to the FECA. The bill was adopted by the House Administration Committee in March 1978, but it failed in the Senate.

In June 1979 the commission sent to Congress new proposed regulations governing the financing, sponsorship, and structure of debates among presidential candidates and candidates for other federal offices. The 1979 proposal regarding debate financing and sponsorship was the same as that proposed in late 1977. Unions and corporations would be permitted to use treasury funds to contribute to the sponsorship of nonpartisan debates as long as the debate sponsor was a tax-exempt, nonprofit organization with a history of neither supporting nor endorsing candidates or political parties. The commission reasoned that funds contributed or spent to sponsor debates were not contributions or expenditures under the law because the debates were designed to educate voters rather than influence elections. In addition, the regulations included specific directives for the manner in which debates had to be structured to qualify as nonpartisan debates. For example, for debates during a presidential primary election, debate sponsors were given three options for deciding which candidates would be included in a debate: inviting all candidates seeking party nomination for the same office who were qualified to appear on a state primary-election ballot in the region in which the debate was to be held, as well as each recognized and active candidate in any caucus or convention state within the region; inviting all candidates for the same office nominated by all parties of the same type, that is, major, minor, or new; or inviting only those candidates seeking the nomination of a particular party in the region where the debate was to be held, for example, the Republican party. In that case the debate sponsor also would be required to invite all candidates of any other party of the same type to a similarly restricted debate. The third option would be available only when each party of the same type had at least two candidates seeking nomination to the same office. ·

The proposed regulation soon encountered stiff opposition, particularly from the broadcast industry whose representatives argued that the regulations would prohibit commercial radio and television stations from conducting candidate debates. Industry spokespersons advised the FEC to "observe its jurisdictional boundaries" and cautioned the agency not to pursue regulations that might discourage broadcasters from conducting political debates.[52] CBS also singled out for criticism the proposed regulation that would prevent a debate among one major party's primary election candidates if the other major party had an uncontested primary election. Although the FEC maintained that the proposed regulations were not intended to prohibit broadcasters from presenting or covering debates and attempted several times to rewrite the regulations, the opposition continued. The Federal Communications Commission (FCC) urged Congress to reject the FEC proposals on the grounds that they would impede the broadcast industry's efforts to inform the electorate during federal-election campaigns.[53]

On September 18 the Senate vetoed the FEC regulations. A month later the FEC solicited public comment on debate funding and sponsorship, as well as on FEC authority regarding debates in an effort to develop new rules that would overcome the objections raised previously. As the 1980 primary season drew closer, the need for clarity regarding candidate debates became greater, a point Ruth Hinerfeld of the LWV underscored for the FEC commissioners. According to Hinerfeld, the league needed $800,000 to carry out its plans to sponsor a series of candidate forums in which several candidates would be invited to explain their positions and respond to questions.[54] To raise the money, she said, the league had to begin fund raising immediately and needed an FEC policy statement assuring corporations and labor unions that it was lawful for them to contribute.

Representatives of the broadcast industry, on the other hand, told the FEC it should refrain from issuing any regulations regarding the production or arrangement of federal-candidate debates. "To do otherwise," said a National Association of Broadcasters spokesperson, "would chill and restrict the free flow of ideas."[55] Among groups offering comments, only the National Citizens Committee for Broadcasting, an organization chaired by consumer advocate Ralph Nader, urged the FEC to propose extensive regulations, including regulation of the television networks, to ensure fair, nonpartisan debates.

Despite the need of potential debate sponsors for prompt action regarding debate funding, the FEC extended the deadline for submitted written testimony on the matter until November 20, 1979. Once the testimony was received, the commission would have to draft and submit new regulations, which, in the normal course of events, would not become effective until thirty legislative days had passed. In the meantime, the *Des Moines Register and Tribune* announced that it would hold a debate for Republican presidential contenders on January 5 and for President Carter and Sen. Kennedy on January 7. The newspaper's executive editor, James Gannon, defended the plans, maintaining that staging a political debate was "a legitimate function of the press and . . . not a contribution to a political campaign."[56]

Finally, early in December, the FEC drafted new regulations on federal-candidate debate sponsorship and funding and later that month voted by a five-to-one margin to send them to Congress. The new regulations exempted from the law's definitions of contribution and expenditure any funds spent by certain nonprofit organizations and bona-fide new media corporations to stage nonpartisan candidate debates. They allowed nonprofit organizations that do not endorse, support, or oppose political candidates or parties to stage such debates. They also permitted bona-fide news media to stage nonpartisan candidate debates. The regulations specified only that a debate include at least two candidates and not promote or advance one over the other. The rest of the structure was left to the discretion of the staging organization. Finally, the regulations permitted corporations and labor unions to contribute funds to nonprofit, nonpartisan organizations staging candidate debates. Although news media staging nonpartisan candidate debates were not allowed to receive such contributions, broadcasters were permitted to accept regular commercial advertising and underwriting by corporations and labor unions to finance the broadcast of debates.

For a time the fate of the regulations remained uncertain. Two broadcasters' groups, the National Association of Broadcasters and the Radio and Television News Directors Association, agreed with FEC commissioner Max Friedersdorf, the only commissioner to vote against the proposed regulations, that by establishing the new rules the commission was asserting jurisdiction where it had none. The broadcasters' organizations urged Congress to veto the regulations, arguing that news organizations already had the right to stage candidate debates and that the new rules would limit the exercise of that right. The two groups did recommend that Congress leave intact the proposed regulation allowing nonprofit groups to receive corporate and labor union contributions to finance candidate debates.

During the thirty-day legislative period in which Congress had an opportunity to veto the proposed regulations, the FEC took an action that jeopardized the passage of the new rules. When the *Nashua Telegraph*, a New Hampshire newspaper, announced its intention to stage a Republican debate between Ronald Reagan and George Bush, Republican candidates Howard Baker and Robert Dole filed a complaint with the FEC charging that such a restricted debate would be illegal. The commission ruled that the debate as planned would violate FEC rules because it would, in effect, be a partisan debate, and news organizations, said the FEC, were allowed under the proposed rules to sponsor only nonpartisan debates. Broadcasters opposed to the FEC action and to the proposed regulations argued that the decision to invite a particular number of candidates to a debate was a matter of journalistic discretion.

Despite misgivings based in part on the FEC's handling of the *Nashua Telegraph* case, Congress decided to let the debate regulations go into effect. By the time they did so in mid-March, however, valuable fund-raising time already had been lost by the LWV. The league was unable to raise from private contributions the entire $37,500 needed to finance a Republican candidates' forum in New Hampshire prior to that state's primary and consequently had to dip into its Education Fund to make up the difference.[57] The delay in passage of the regulations also jeopardized the funding of additional candidate forums the league had planned for Illinois, Texas, and California.

The Impact of Electoral and Party Reform

The campaign finance law's impact on the prenomination campaigns often was reinforced by electoral and party reforms regarding the selection of delegates to choose the parties' nominees and by candidates' efforts to influence those initiatives. Twelve years earlier, in 1968, there were only fifteen primaries in which less than 40 percent of the party convention delegates were chosen. Due in large part to the antibossism movement in the Democratic party following the tumultuous 1968 Democratic convention, the number of primaries was gradually increased in an effort to diminish the influence of the party hierarchy and make the choice of the party more responsive to the electorate. In 1972, twenty-three states conducted presidential primaries; in 1976 the number had increased to thirty. In 1980, thirty-five states, Puerto Rico, and the District of Columbia held presidential primary elections. Seventy-six percent of the Republican delegates and 71 percent of the Democratic delegates were elected in primaries or were chosen by a separate process that was bound to reflect the primary results.[58] The delegates generally were bound by state law or party rules for at least one ballot to the candidates they were elected to support.

Like public financing, continued emphasis on selection of delegates through primary elections further diminished the power of party leaders and, theoretically at least, made the selection of the nominee reflect the will of the electorate. It also gave lesser-known candidates opportunities to advance their candidacies, which they would not have had under the previous system. But the primary system had its drawbacks. Because of the large number of primary state contests and the large percentage of delegates chosen through them, candidates had little choice other than to run widely. No longer could a candidate follow the formula used by John Kennedy, who ran in only four contested primaries in 1960. Consequently candidates found they had to resort to methods of campaigning that would allow them to reach the largest number of potential voters in the least amount of time. Most often that meant television advertising and arranging campaign schedules and events to attract television and other media coverage. Before the primaries began, one newspaper editorialist observed that some candidates would "end up spending more time in television studios than chatting with live voters."[59] Running in a large number of widely scattered primary states and relying in good measure on television campaigning meant more expensive prenomination campaigns. (See table 5-1 for a summary of candidates' television costs.) According to some observers, it also meant citizens were given little opportunity to discover and evaluate the real qualities of the candidates they were considering.

Winner-Take-All

Party rules regarding the manner in which delegates were allocated to candidates in primary states also had a significant impact on electoral outcomes. About two-thirds of the Republican primary state delegates were elected according to a winner-take-all system at either statewide or district levels or a combination of the two. In the remaining primary states, delegates were allocated to candidates to reflect their primary vote. The system favored Ronald Reagan in the crowded Republican field. For example, in four early winner-take-all contests in South Carolina, Florida, Georgia, and Wisconsin, Reagan won more than 60 percent of the vote only in Georgia. But he won 146 of the 152 delegates at stake in the four primaries.[60] Further, in early primaries in which he did not receive the highest number of votes,

Massachusetts and Connecticut, Reagan benefited from the proportional-representation system, receiving about one-third of the delegates in each state.[61] Through the first fourteen primaries, George Bush and John Anderson combined received nearly as many primary votes as Reagan but only about one-third as many delegates.[62]

Long before the primary season began, efforts were underway to eliminate the winner-take-all system in Reagan's home state of California where 168 delegates—17 percent of the total needed to secure the nomination—would be at stake. Only in California and Puerto Rico had the Republican party scheduled a primary in which all of the delegates would be awarded to the candidate with the highest statewide vote. The efforts, however, were unsuccessful. Reagan partisans won an intraparty skirmish over the matter first in the California Senate and then in California Republican Party Central Committee proceedings. A subsequent campaign by proponents of proportional allocation of delegates to qualify an initiative for the June 1980 ballot that would eliminate the winner-take-all system failed, despite support from former President Gerald Ford and total expenditures of $625,000.[63] By the time the California primary was held, all of Ronald Reagan's Republican opponents had conceded him the nomination. Reagan won the primary election overwhelmingly, receiving 80 percent of the vote and all 168 delegates.

Proportional Allocation

For the 1980 primaries, the Democratic party virtually eliminated the winner-take-all system of allocating delegates. Instead, delegates were allocated to candidates in each state in proportion to their popular support, as long as the candidates received a minimum percentage of the vote, set by each state party between 15 and 25 percent. Only Illinois and West Virginia were allowed to hold loophole primaries: modified winner-take-all systems in which delegates were elected from congressional districts and without proportional representation. The proportional-representation system encouraged the candidates to seek delegates even in states where their opponents were thought to enjoy a significant advantage. The run-everywhere strategy, however, put an added drain on campaign treasuries already burdened with rising campaign costs and an increasingly restrictive overall expenditure limitation.

President Jimmy Carter was the prinicipal beneficiary of the Democratic party's delegate-allocation system. For example, through the first fourteen primaries, Carter won 54 percent of the popular vote and 63 percent of the primary state delegates.[64] Included in Carter's delegate total were 165 delegates he won in Illinois, the only winner-take-all primary among the first fourteen. If the Illinois delegates had been divided proportionally Edward Kennedy's popular vote total would have entitled him to some fifty delegates rather than the fourteen he received.[65]

Caucuses

Although the emphasis in delegate hunting in recent years has shifted from caucus states to primary states, about one-fourth of the 1980 convention delegates were selected by the caucus method. Because of the significant number of delegates at stake in these caucuses and because a number of caucuses were held early in the season, some caucus states received considerable attention from the candidates. In Iowa, for example, where caucus victories in 1976 gave Jimmy Carter helpful exposure and momentum, five candidates—Carter, Kennedy, Baker, Bush, and Reagan—reported spending close to the maximum allowed, attracting considerable media attention and increasing the voter turnout fivefold on the Republican side and threefold on the Democratic side. George Bush, the Republican winner, began campaigning in Iowa a full year before the January 21 precinct caucuses. Other candidates were not far behind in trying to establish the grass-roots organizations they would need to identify and line up supporters and get them out on caucus night.

Although Texas and Michigan on the Democratic side dropped their primaries in favor of caucuses, the future of the caucus method remains uncertain.[66] Voter turnout is lower in caucus states than in primary states, and election results are more susceptible to the influence of party leaders. Caucus advocates maintain that caucuses serve to strengthen political parties. According to one caucus advocate, caucuses "get people more involved in party organization and issues. Voting in primaries takes no commitment."[67]

Early Jockeying

In addition to active campaigning far in advance of scheduled primary and caucus contests during the year prior to the elections, candidates and potential candidates expended considerable energy and money trying to influence party rules and primary laws in states where they had not yet been written and to arrange the primary schedule to show off their strengths and minimize their weaknesses. The most-noteworthy—and expensive—of the pre-primary skirmishes among candidates to gain favorable position early were the straw polls conducted by both the Republican and Democratic state parties in Florida at the November state party conventions. The polls were intended by party officials to attract media attention to the state and to energize rank-and-file party members. Given Jimmy Carter's success in a 1975 Iowa poll that brought him national attention, many candidates felt obliged to participate in the Florida polls, and the media felt obliged to cover them.

Most of the delegates to the Republican state convention were chosen by lottery at GOP county caucuses held from mid-August through mid-September. Twenty percent of each county's delegates were chosen by a specially appointed committee. About half of the delegates to the Democratic state convention were chosen by voters at county caucuses on October 13. The delegate candidates were not identified on the ballot by presidential preference. The remaining delegates were chosen by state party officials thought to be friendly to President Carter.

Although the state convention delegate-selection processes were confusing—RNC chairman Bill Brock called the Republican process "the great Florida crapshoot"—and although the results of the November straw votes would have no direct bearing on Florida's March 11 primary elections, several candidates and potential candidates spent large sums, or had large sums spent on their behalf, in efforts to demonstrate early momentum.[68] Reagan forces spent $300,000 in Florida in 1979, with most of the money earmarked to win the straw vote. John Connally's campaign spent $250,000 in an unsuccessful attempt to outpoll Reagan.[69] Carter forces spent an estimated $250,000 mobilizing for the October 13 county caucuses.[70] That expenditure, which offset a similar expenditure by draft-Kennedy forces, enabled Carter to come out ahead in the caucuses and in the nonbinding state convention vote.[71]

Other presidential straw polls included a Massachusetts presidential-preference conference in late October 1979, sponsored by the Republican state chairman, a straw poll at a GOP conference in Maine on November 3, and a nonbinding preference poll at the California Democratic state party's platform convention on January 20, 1980. The polls commanded varying degrees of the candidates' energy, and money spent by their campaigns to influence their outcomes was credited against the expenditure limits of the states in which they were held.

The Republicans

In August 1978, nearly two years before the Republican nominating convention, Rep. Philip M. Crane of Illinois became the first major candidate to declare his candidacy for the 1980 presidential nomination. With his early announcement, Crane continued a trend toward increasingly early formal entry into the presidential prenomination contest by little-known, out-party candidates seeking name recognition and a head start in fund raising and campaign staff organization.

In time, Crane was joined by six other Republicans who remained in serious contention at least through the early stages of the primary season: Rep. John Anderson of Illinois, Sen. Howard Baker of Tennessee, George Bush, John Connally, Sen. Robert Dole of Kansas, and Ronald Reagan. In addition two other Republican officeholders, Sen. Lowell Weicker of Connecticut and Sen. Larry Pressler of South Dakota, made brief forays into the Republican prenomination contest. Businessman Benjamin Fernandez and perennial candidate Harold Stassen also made runs for the Republican nomination, but they never were influential factors in the race. Finally, in March 1980 a national Draft Ford Committee was formed to persuade former President Gerald Ford to run again, but Ford, after considerable press speculation, declined to do so.

Reagan

Although Ronald Reagan did not announce his candidacy until November 13, 1979, his strong challenge to President Ford in the 1976 prenomination contest and his continuing activity on behalf of Republican candidates and organizations in his position as chairman of Citizens for the Republic made him the front-runner from the start of the campaign. Initial campaign strategy called for Reagan to enter all of the prenomination contests but to remain above the fray by ignoring his Republican rivals and focusing criticism on the record of President Jimmy Carter. That strategy was abandoned after Reagan lost the first major prenomination contest, the January 21 Iowa caucuses, to George Bush. Reagan had campaigned sparingly in Iowa—reportedly spending less than forty hours in the state in three months—and had declined to participate in public debates and joint appearances with the other Republican candidates, whereas Bush had begun campaigning in the state early in 1979 and had spent long hours developing a campaign organization and cultivating potential caucus participants.[72]

The Reagan campaign regained momentum with a February 26 primary victory in New Hampshire, after which the candidate dismissed his campaign director, John Sears, who had devised the initial strategy, as well as two Sears associates, Jim Lake, who had served as press secretary, and Charles Black, who had served as national political director. Sears was replaced by lawyer William J. Casey, a former head of the Securities and Exchange Commission. Edwin Meese III, who had been the former California governor's chief of staff and a cabinet member, continued to serve as chief policy adviser to Reagan and a principal strategist of the Reagan campaign.

Despite having spent close to two-thirds of the overall spending limit by the time of the New Hampshire primary, Reagan continued to enjoy success at the polls. Primary losses in Massachusetts, Connecticut, Pennsylvania, and Michigan were only temporary setbacks on the road to the nomination. By the conclusion of the primary season, all of his challengers had withdrawn from the race, and the candidate had captured more than enough convention delegates to win the nomination on the first ballot. By the time the convention closed, the Reagan campaign had spent $19.8 million, making it the most expensive of the prenomination campaigns.

Fund Raising: The Reagan for President Committee registered with the FEC on February 28, 1979, and by the end of the year reported total receipts of $7.2 million. The committee drew support from Reagan's large and loyal political following and had a ready-made base upon which to construct its fund-raising operation: the mailing lists developed by Reagan's PAC, Citizens for the Republic. In fact, direct mail accounted for a substantial portion of the campaign's receipts, both in 1979 and throughout the prenomination period. For example, during its first full quarter of campaign fund raising, from March through June 1979, the committee reported receipts of $894,000, more than half of it coming in response to direct-mail appeals.[73] Those mailings, however, cost the campaign more than $200,000.[74] Through late April 1980, about 45 to 50 percent of Reagan's campaign funds, according to committee treasurer Angela (Bay) Buchanan, had come from direct-mail drives with average contributions between $18 and $33.[75] Reagan's success with direct mail, which can be an effective way of appealing to a large number of small donors, also is reflected in the number of individual contributions under $250 that his committee submitted for federal matching funds: 213,103, about 89 percent of which were certified. George Bush submitted the next largest number of individual contributions for certification: 86,612.

Reagan's success in raising money from small contributors, often through direct mail, was complemented by larger contributions, particularly from his home state. For example, through late April 1980 more than one-third of the contributions the Reagan campaign received in amounts of $200 or more came from his California base.[76] Reagan's contributor list included a number of entertainment figures he knew from his earlier career as a screen actor, including Johnny Carson, Art Linkletter, Bob Hope, and Frank Sinatra, as well as a large number of small businessmen and professionals around the country. The Reagan campaign also drew on the candidate's Hollywood connections to raise funds on his behalf. For example, the campaign reportedly grossed $400,000 in November 1979 from concerts that starred Sinatra, Dean Martin, and singer Wayne Newton and that were held in Boston and Texas.[77] The campaign employed television appeals and fund-raising dinners to raise campaign money. The dinners met with mixed success. One held in New York at the time of Reagan's announcement only broke even. A $1,000-per-person dinner held in Detroit in mid-May 1980, however, reportedly raised more than $300,000.[78]

Although Reagan's total 1979 receipts of $7.2 million were second only to the $9.2 million reported by John Connally's campaign for the same period, the campaign did experience some fund-raising difficulties. According to its 1979 year-end report to the FEC, the committee had cash on hand of about $555,000 but debts of almost $1.5 million, the largest reported indebtedness of any other campaign. The campaign's costs were high, and funds were raised at a substantially slower pace than some campaign strategists had hoped. For example, by September 1979 campaign planners hoped to have raised about $4 million; the actual figure by that time, however, was less than $2 million.

In late August 1979, long-time Reagan adviser Lyn Nofziger, who had served as deputy director for finance on the committee, resigned his position amid reports of conflict regarding management of the campaign's finances and efforts to moderate the candidate's public stands on issues. At the time of his resignation, Nofziger noted simply, "I just figured it was time for me to move on."[79] According to later reports, however, Nofziger was forced out by Reagan's campaign director, John Sears, who maintained that Nofziger had acted "unilaterally and without authority" in running up such substantial fund-raising expenses that the campaign was likely to exceed the overall spending limit.[80] Sears leveled the same charges against another Reagan aide, Michael Deaver, who replaced Nofziger and then was himself forced out of the campaign in November 1979. Before September 1979, Sears maintained, Reagan knew full well that the campaign was not raising very much money and that the money being raised was at a tremendous cost. Sears said the candidate realized he had to "get the budget in hand" if, upon accepting public funds, the campaign was to stay within the spending limit.[81] There also were other reports that Nofziger had not been notably successful in raising funds and that he was criticized by some campaign aides for arranging to have some of the direct-mail drives carried out by Integrated Communications Systems, a Santa Monica, California, firm of which he was part owner.[82]

Nofziger denied having mismanaged the Reagan campaign finances.[83] When asked in mid-September 1979 to explain the inability of the Reagan campaign to meet its fund-raising goals, Nofziger cited two factors: not having a declared candidate and strong competition from John Connally for contributions from business people.[84]

An additional factor in the dispute between Nofziger and Sears was the latter's handling of Reagan, particularly what Nofziger maintained were attempts to "repackage" Reagan to appeal to more midde-of-the-road voters.

Other conservative supporters of the candidate also were concerned about the perceived effort to moderate Reagan's public image and particularly about its effect on fund raising. If Reagan turned away from his conservative values, said one Reagan backer, "a lot of the allies he has had [would] just become neutral."[85]

About three months after Sears himself was forced out of the campaign following the New Hampshire primary, Nofziger and Deaver rejoined the campaign, Nofziger to handle media relations and Deaver to share in developing campaign strategy.

Campaign fund raising began to improve after Reagan announced his candidacy on November 13, 1979. During the fourth quarter of 1979, the candidate's committee reported individual contributions of about $3.4 million. In January 1980 individual contributions amounted to almost $1 million, and in February the amount was almost $900,000. In addition, despite often-voiced philosophical objections to the use of taxpayer funds to help finance presidential campaigns, Reagan chose to accept federal matching grants. By the time his campaign had ended, it had been certified to receive almost $7.3 million in matching funds, far outstripping other qualified candidates' campaigns and demonstrating its appeal to a relatively large number of small contributors. Early in 1980 the campaign made use of an agreement with the Riggs National Bank in Washington, D.C., to lend it money to be used for operating funds with the loans to be repaid when the campaign received federal matching funds. In January the campaign reported borrowing $2.8 million and in February $1.4 million. As Reagan's nomination became more probable, his fund-raising results increased accordingly. In March, April, and May, his campaign reported total contributions of about $1.6 million, $1.8 million, and $1.7 million, respectively. The campaign's need to take out loans to meet operating expenses decreased correspondingly, and outstanding loans were paid off.

Despite its fund-raising successes, the campaign did experience some cash-flow problems. Ten days before Florida's March 11 primary, the campaign was faced with $1.5 million in unpaid bills. The telephone company reportedly threatened to disconnect the campaign's telephones in the state, and a travel agency said Reagan would be stranded in Iowa if bills were not paid.[86] The campaign found the funds to pay its outstanding bills, however, and Reagan won handily in Florida, gaining about 57 percent of the popular vote and all fifty-one convention delegates.

The financial difficulties the campaign experienced during the primary season actually were due less to an inability to raise needed funds than to the danger of exceeding the overall spending limit that applied to candidates who accepted public funds—the very problem departed campaign director John Sears had predicted. Although efforts to remain below the limit required extensive cutbacks in campaign staff, media advertising, and candidate travel, the Reagan campaign had developed sufficient momentum through early and impressive primary victories to carry the candidate through the remainder of the campaign.

By late March, Reagan had built up such a commanding lead over the other two GOP contenders who remained in the running, George Bush and John Anderson, that he felt free to concentrate his attack on President Jimmy Carter, who was well on the way to his party's nomination. By mid-May, his remaining opponent, George Bush, was short of funds and of delegates committed to his nomination. Reagan, having received the endorsement of the major Republican candidates who had withdrawn from the race, began in earnest to plan his general-election campaign, putting in place the staff and issues panels that would advise him in the fall. By the time the primary season had ended, Reagan had won twenty-nine of the thirty-three primaries in which he had competed—he skipped only the Puerto Rico and District of Columbia contests—and had garnered about 60 percent of the popular vote.

The Reagan campaign reported adjusted receipts of $21.4 million. Contributions from individuals accounted for $13.8 million, matching funds for $7.3 million, and PAC contributions for an additional $285,000. Of the $13.8 million in individual contributions, unitemized contributions accounted for nearly $6.5 million, almost 47 percent. Prior to January 8, 1980, all contributions from individuals exceeding $100 had to be itemized—identified according to the name and address of the contributor, his or her place of business and employer's name, and the amount and date of the contribution. The 1979 FECA amendments, which went into effect on January 8, raised the reporting threshold to $200. The relatively large dollar amount and the percentage of total contributions represented by unitemized contributions indicate Reagan's appeal to a comparatively large number of small contributors. Itemized contributions of $1 to $499 accounted for about $1.7 million, 12.3 percent of Reagan's total receipts from individual contributions. Contributions of $500 to $749 accounted for about $1.5 million, 10.7 percent of the total, and contributions of $750 and up accounted for about $4.2 million, 30.4 percent of the total.[87] Reagan received a significant percentage of his larger contributions from his home state. According to FEC compilations, Reagan received 31 percent of his itemized contributions of $500 and up from California; those contributions totaled almost $1.8 million. In that same category of giving, Texas was the next most generous state for Reagan, supplying his campaign with about $586,000, almost 10.3 percent of his donations of $500 and up. New York and Florida supplied an additional $395,000 and $325,000, respectively, in that category of donations.

Reagan received the bulk of his PAC money only after his prenomination campaign victory was assured. He received about $12,600 in 1979, about $14,600 during January and February 1980, about $100,000 during March and April 1980, and about $158,000 thereafter. Among PACs that contributed $5,000, the maximum allowed, were Build PAC, connected with the National Association of Home Builders; the National Good Government Fund, connected with the Houston law firm of Vinson, Elkins, Searls, Connally & Smith; El Paso Co. PAC; and the Bluebonnet Fund, associated with the Houston law firm of Baker and Botts. Corporate PACs accounted for almost 78 percent of Reagan's contributions from political action committees; trade, membership, and health PACs for about 11 percent; and nonconnected PACs for about 5 percent.

Reagan also benefited from $1.6 million in expenditures made independently on his behalf by a number of political committees. The Fund for a Conservative Majority (FCM) reported spending almost $884,000 on Reagan's behalf. Although a significant portion of those expenditures were made for fund-raising costs, according to FCM spokespersons, funds also were spent on campaign activities at critical moments of the campaign. For example, when Reagan was approaching New Hampshire's $294,400 spending limit, the FCM reportedly spent about $60,000 on pro-Reagan media advertising, campaign literature, and volunteer activity in targeted wards. In addition the Life Amendment PAC claimed to have bused antiabortion supporters into New Hampshire to operate phone banks, drop literature, and make personal contacts supporting Reagan.[88] And in the May 3 Texas primary, when Reagan was fast approaching the overall spending limit, the FCM spent $80,000 on pro-Reagan advertising and activity.

Costs: Not only did the Reagan for President Committee raise more money than any other prenomination-campaign committee; it also spent more money than any other committee, $19.82 million in all. The high rate of spending, much of it early in the campaign, caused the committee serious problems as the campaign entered the heart of the primary season. Fund-raising costs were high. By early September 1979, the Reagan organization, which would include some 370 persons at its peak size, already had more than 100 persons on its payroll.[89] Campaign strategists had decided it was important for the campaign to maintain a presence in as many states as possible in order to prevent any setbacks that the media might interpret as a loss of momentum on the part of the front-runner. Campaign receipts at that time were said to be about $300,000 a month, but they were exceeded by expenses of about $500,000 a month.[90]

Like other candidates, Reagan was forced to spend money early in the jockeying for position that now marks the political year preceding the primary and caucus contests. The straw vote taken at Florida's November 17 Republican presidential-preference convention and the caucuses leading up to it were the focus of some $300,000 the Reagan campaign spent in Florida alone in 1979.[91] Fearful of being embarrassed in the national media by a poor showing in an important state and prompted by John Connally's reported expenditures of $250,000 to influence the outcome of the straw vote, the campaign mounted a heavy advertising, telephone, and direct-mail campaign. Although Reagan had initially dismissed the Florida convention as "utterly irrelevant," he later publicized widely the fact that he bested Connally in the straw vote.[92]

Although the fast-approaching expenditure limit prevented Reagan from using his television skills to full advantage in the later stages of the campaign, media costs nevertheless represented a significant expenditure category for the campaign committee. The Reagan for President Committee spent an estimated $2.8 million to $3.2 million on radio and television advertising. Some $400,000 of that was spent to televise Reagan's formal announcement of his candidacy on November 13, 1979. The candidate's committee had sought to purchase half an hour of prime time from each of the three major commercial television networks to broadcast the announcement, but the networks refused—as they refused similar requests from the Connally and Carter campaigns—maintaining it was too early for television politicking. CBS offered the candidates two five-minute spots, one during prime time and the other during the day, which Reagan and Connally grudgingly accepted. According to one television specialist, the networks were reluctant to sell time to the candidates because they were competing fiercely for popularity ratings and were engaged in "the delicate autumnal process of inculcating regular viewing habits in the audience."[93] In addition, such a sale probably would have represented a significant loss of revenue for the networks. According to one report, commercial spots aired during the popular half-hour prime time television show "M*A*S*H" would have brought in $900,000 in November 1979, whereas a presidential-campaign committee would have paid about $180,000 for a similar half-hour of prime broadcast time.[94]

Although the Reagan committee bought the five-minute slots offered by CBS, it felt that televising the candidate's announcement was sufficiently important that it created its own network of about ninety stations, which covered the nation's fifty largest metropolitan areas and many of its smaller ones. The announcement, a thirty-minute speech, was taped on the afternoon of November 13 and broadcast over the makeshift network at 7:30 P.M. the same day.

Early in January 1980, committee treasurer Bay Buchanan warned that heavy spending was creating some serious problems for the campaign.[95] Nevertheless campaign strategy rather than finances appeared to dictate relatively low media spending by the Reagan campaign in preparation for the first important prenomination contest, the January 21 Iowa caucuses. With the exception of half an hour of television time purchased for live cov-

erage on seven local stations of a speech Reagan delivered at a rally in Des
Moines on January 19, the campaign limited its broadcast media advertising
to radio.[96] One estimate of Reagan's total media expenditures in Iowa was
$80,000[97] out of $466,000 in expenditures allocated to the state by the committee on reports filed with the FEC.[98] In explaining why relatively little
money had been budgeted for media advertising, Reagan press coordinator
Richard Lobb said that unlike his opponents, Reagan had no name or identification problem. Campaign efforts, he said, were focused on making sure
"people go out on the night of the caucus and vote."[99]

Despite Reagan's limited use of the broadcast media in Iowa, his campaign did succeed in winning a ruling from the FCC that was a boon to all
media campaigners in that state's prenomination contest. At the request of
the Reagan for President Committee, the FCC issued a ruling that called for
the state's broadcasting stations to sell candidates broadcast time at no
more than the lowest unit charge, the rate they offered their best customers.
In 1971 the Congress had amended the Communications Act of 1934 to require that forty-five days preceding the date of a primary election (and sixty
days preceding the date of a general or special election) stations may charge
a political candidate no more than the lowest unit charge for the same class
and amount of time for the same period. In other words stations had to
treat candidates in a manner comparable to their most favored commercial
customers. The January 1980 ruling requested by the Reagan committee extended the 1971 ruling to include the Iowa caucuses, which the FCC declared "an integral part of a primary election."[100] According to Ruth Jones,
media consultant and time buyer for the Reagan campaign, the FCC ruling
saved the campaign 20 to 45 percent in Iowa.[101]

Reagan did not take advantage of the most significant event offering
free media exposure in the state prior to the caucuses, a televised debate
sponsored by the *Des Moines Register*. His unwillingness to participate
reflected campaign director John Sears' belief that the candidate had little
to gain and everything to lose from public exposure. In fact Sears reportedly
told one newsman, "It wouldn't do any good to have [Reagan] going to cof-
fees and shaking hands like the others. People will get the idea he's an ordinary man like the rest of us."[102] The six candidates who did accept the invitation to debate took turns criticizing Reagan for his absence. The
criticism, and Reagan's limited campaigning in the state, took their toll.
When the caucus results were tabulated, George Bush had collected 33 percent of the vote to Reagan's 27 percent. Although only thirty-seven
delegates were at stake in Iowa and only a small portion of the nation's electorate—about 115,000 voters—took part, Bush's victory represented a
major upset. The Iowa caucuses were the first formal contest in the
presidential race, and, as the media pointed out, it was in Iowa that Jimmy
Carter was propelled to the forefront in 1976.

The caucus results also signaled a change in Reagan prenomination-campaign strategy. Up to that time, said Reagan strategist and pollster Richard B. Wirthlin, Reagan had been "very much aloof. He was giving cameo appearances, he wasn't staying in any state long enough to make an impact. His advantage was frittered away by the refusal to debate [in Iowa], which was received unkindly by Iowa Republicans."[103] Everyone, including John Sears, acknowledged that a different strategy was required.

With Wirthlin's surveys showing Bush leading in New Hampshire, the next important prenomination contest and the first primary in which both Reagan and Bush were on the ballot, Reagan abandoned his earlier style and tactics and took to the campaign trail in earnest. At one point he spent twenty-one days in a row on the road, mostly in New Hampshire, but also in South Carolina and Florida, whose primaries were to follow the February 26 New Hampshire contest within a space of two weeks. He also decided to meet his opponents in debate, a decision that, according to most observers, helped him regain the advantage. On February 20, seven Republican candidates met in debate in Manchester, New Hampshire. Although neither Reagan nor Bush performed particularly well as far as the press was concerned, Wirthlin's postdebate poll showed Reagan had improved his standing significantly.

A second debate, which took place three days later in Nashua, New Hampshire, solidified Reagan's standing. Representatives of the Reagan and Bush campaigns agreed to meet in a face-to-face debate to be sponsored by the *Nashua Telegraph*. The week of the debate, however, the FEC ruled that the newspaper would violate election-law regulations if it went ahead with its plans. According to the FEC, since only two candidates were to participate, the Reagan-Bush encounter would be a partisan debate—in effect an illegal contribution by the newspaper to the two candidates. When Hugh Gregg, Bush's campaign manager in New Hampshire, subsequently refused to pay any of the expenses, the Reagan campaign agreed to pay the entire $3,500 that the debate would cost. Then, unknown to Bush, John Sears invited other Republican candidates to take part in the debate. When Bush discovered that fact only upon arriving for the debate on the evening of February 23, he refused to meet with the other candidates and said it was up to the *Nashua Telegraph* to decide who should participate. When debate moderator Jon Breen, the editor of the newspaper, announced to the audience that the other candidates present—Howard Baker, Robert Dole, John Anderson, and Philip Crane—would not be allowed to take part, Reagan protested the decision was unfair and maintained that since he was paying the debate costs, he should have the right to include other candidates. And when the four candidates mounted the stage to the applause of the audience, Bush refused to acknowledge their presence. The four then walked off to press conferences in which they criticized Bush roundly. In the debate that followed, Reagan, by all accounts, bested his shaken rival and helped clinch victory in New Hampshire.

Reagan won approximately 50 percent of the vote cast in the New Hampshire primary, more than twice as much as Bush, his nearest competitor. Although Bush would experience a few primary victories before the prenomination campaign concluded, he never seemed to recover from his overwhelming defeat in New Hampshire.

On the afternoon of the primary, Reagan handed John Sears, Charles Black, and James Lake press releases in which their resignations from the campaign were announced. The dismissal of these political operatives, which otherwise might have been interpreted by the press as a sign of disarray in the campaign, was consequently subordinated to Reagan's primary victory.

Although Reagan came in third to Bush and Anderson in the March 4 Massachusetts primary and narrowly bested Anderson in the Vermont primary on the same day, his largest problem for the remainder of the primary season was the overall spending limit imposed on candidates who had accepted matching funds. By the time of the New Hampshire primary, the Reagan campaign had spent about two-thirds of the $14.7 million it was allowed to spend over the course of the entire prenomination campaign. In addition, the campaign disclosed that it was at that time $600,000 in debt.[104] An important part of new campaign director William Casey's responsibility was to help the campaign get a grip on its spending. Casey started immediately. On March 6, two days before the South Carolina primary, Casey cancelled the campaign's chartered jet, stranding reporters and some staff members but saving the campaign thousands of dollars. The candidate stumped the state in a small private jet and by bus. The cutback apparently did not harm Reagan who turned back a determined challenge by John Connally, winning 54 percent of the vote and all twenty-five of the state's national convention delegates. Reagan followed that performance with a string of impressive victories in the March 11 primaries in Alabama, Georgia, and Florida. In Florida the campaign mounted its last major media campaign, spending some $400,000.[105]

In time the campaign staff was reduced by about one-third the number it had reached in January 1980, and the payroll was cut in half. Still Reagan continued to pile up victories. He won the Illinois primary on March 18, putting a damper on the hopes of second-place finisher John Anderson who counted on a strong showing in his home state to move his campaign forward. Reagan lost the Connecticut primary to Bush on March 25 but decisively won the more-important New York primary on the same day.

On April 1 the front-runner won both the Kansas and Wisconsin primaries, effectively knocking John Anderson, who campaigned heavily in Wisconsin, out of the Republican prenomination contest. Despite these electoral victories, Reagan's shaky financial position made him vulnerable to well-financed campaigns in the remaining primaries, a number of which were to be held in delegate-rich states. In fact in the April 22 primary in Pennsylvania, for which the Bush campaign reported allocating about $1.4 million compared with the Reagan campaign's $250,000, Bush defeated Reagan by almost 10 percentage points of the total vote. In Texas, where Bush outspent Reagan by a margin of about three-to-one, Bush did far better than anticipated, making significant inroads into the front-runner's support. And in Michigan, where Bush outspent his rival by about two-to-one, he won by about 25 percentage points.

Nevertheless, the lead Reagan had built up in the early primaries and caucuses and his natural strength in many of the later primary and caucus states were more than enough to see him through. The eighteen delegates he won in Oregon on May 20, the same day as the Michigan primary, put him over the top according to most delegate counters. His sweep of the remaining primary and caucus contests only served to confirm the choice Republican voters had already made.

According to the FEC final report on 1979-1980 prenomination-campaign financial activity through December 31, 1980, the gross disbursements of the Reagan for President Committee amounted to $26 million. When that figure is adjusted to take into account loan repayments, compliance funds, contribution refunds, and other refunds and rebates, the adjusted disbursement total amounts to $19.8 million. Information supplied by the Reagan for President Committee as part of its 1980 year-end report permits the following breakdown into broad categories of the gross disbursement figure reported to the FEC:

Operating expenditures	$15,568,893.95
Fund-raising costs (20 percent)	2,944,000.00
Legal and accounting costs	1,002,934.79
Matching-fund repayments	954,238.13
Transition-fund transfer	250,000.00
Compliance-fund transfer (for general election)	345,000.00
Loans paid	5,513,300.00
Contributions refunded	167,162.67
Transfers out	1,205.00
Total	$26,746,734.54

Although no further breakdown is possible on the basis of the information supplied, some of the costs may be specified more precisely on the basis of information from other sources. Regarding reported operating expenditures of about $15.5 million, broadcast media costs, as noted, amounted to $2.8 million to $3.2 million. About $230,000 was spent on survey research and an additional $23,000 on media research, particularly for the purchase of television time on cable networks to assess the impact of advertisements in small test markets. Other large categories of expenditure were staff salaries, consultant fees, and candidate travel. Although the staff payroll was halved in March 1980 and travel costs were reduced substantially, the campaign had spent lavishly in both categories early in the season. In addition a 1980 year-end report by the Reagan-Bush committee, the Republican candidate's general-election committee, regarding the financial activity of the Reagan-Bush Compliance Fund indicates that the Reagan for President Committee transferred $345,000 from its prenomination-campaign surplus to the general-election-campaign compliance fund.

Some additional information about Reagan committee expenditures may be gleaned from the report of the FEC audit division on the committee. For example, according to the report, on October 1, 1979, the committee retained the services of a media consultant who received a fee of $3,500 per week in lieu of the standard 15 percent agency commission on all time and space placed. Using committee worksheets and documentation, the auditors arrived at a breakdown of categories of expenses that the committee indicated were classifiable as exempt fund-raising costs, that is, costs subject to the 20 percent fund-raising exemption. The largest categories were direct-mail services (about $1.5 million), fund-raising events and associated costs ($633,000), and salaries, consulting fees, and associated costs ($538,000). Other categories, including the allocable portions of national headquarters' expenses, tour travel expenses, and states' mailing expenses, brought the total of classifiable exempt fund-raising costs to $3,505,914. The committee, however, reported a lesser amount—$3,322,829—as exempt fund-raising, legal, and accounting expenditures. When the auditors, who used the committee's figure, took into account $2,576 reported as refunds of fund-raising expenses, they determined that the committee's fund-raising expenses had exceeded the $2,944,000 fund-raising expense exemption allowed by $376,252 and recommended that amount be reclassified as operating expenses chargeable to the committee's overall spending limit.

The FEC audit also indicates that the Reagan for President Committee reported in December 1980 having transferred $250,000 to the Presidential Transition Fund. Of this amount, some $165,000 represented contributions to the committee dated after July 16, 1980, the date of Reagan's nomination. This transfer, characterized as permissible by the auditors, saved the committee from having to refund the contributions or otherwise dispose of them under the law.

The audit of the Reagan for President Committee determined that the committee had exceeded the $14.7 million overall spending limit by $77,387 and recommended that amount be repaid by the committee to the U.S. Treasury. The audit also determined that the committee had exceeded the spending limit in New Hampshire by $137,737 and recommended repayment of that amount. The committee had reported spending $280,748 in the state, less than the $294,400 limit. But the auditors found allocation errors regarding media expenses, salary and consulting fees, travel expenses, and vendor payments amounting to $151,773, putting the committee more than $137,000 over the state spending limit. Finally, the auditors determined that the committee had concluded the campaign with a surplus of approximately $3 million and was required to return to the Treasury a total of $952,880 in unused federal funds. The committee disputed the auditors' calculation of its surplus and made a payment of $754,045, which it determined was the portion of its surplus made up of federal funds. That figure, combined with two earlier repayments of $179,293 and $20,901, the committee made for excess matching funds received, totaled $954,238.

Bush

George Bush, who eventually became Reagan's chief prenomination competitor, had no natural constituency. Although he was a long-time Texas resident, he was born and raised in Connecticut and attended eastern schools. His political credentials were impressive. After a successful career in the oil business, he served two terms as a congressman from Houston, then as ambassador to the United Nations, envoy to China, RNC chairman, and director of the Central Intelligence Agency. Only one of those positions, however, was an elective office, and in none of them had Bush succeeded in becoming well known to the general public.

Because of his lack of name recognition, Bush started his drive for the nomination early. In the fall of 1977, he and James Baker III, who was to become his campaign manager, laid plans for formation of the Fund for Limited Government, a PAC that would serve as a vehicle for Bush's presidential ambitions.

Bush formed his exploratory campaign committee in January 1979 and formally declared his candidacy the following May. Throughout 1979 the candidate worked to raise funds and to establish the campaign organization he would need to overtake the acknowledged favorite, Reagan. In Iowa his spadework paid off. Bush bested Reagan by six percentage points in the January 21 Iowa caucuses, which propelled him to the forefront of the campaign, but he was unable to sustain his momentum. In his first head-to-head primary-election contest with Reagan five weeks later in New Hampshire, Bush lost overwhelmingly. He was a victim of his own lackluster performance in debate as well as of Reagan's vigorous campaigning in a state many of whose Republicans already were partial to the conservative Reagan philosophy.

Bush had planned to contest every primary and caucus, a plan he carried out until lack of funds and of electoral success forced him to withdraw from the campaign on May 26. Along the way he won six primaries—those in Massachusetts, Connecticut, Pennsylvania, and Michigan, in which he defeated Reagan, and those in Puerto Rico and the District of Columbia, which Reagan did not contest—and to come out ahead in the Republican party caucuses in Iowa and Maine. His dogged campaign against significant odds earned him the second highest number of convention delegates among Republican candidates and recorded the second highest expenditure total among those candidates: $16.7 million when adjusted for loan repayments, compliance funds, contribution refunds, and other refunds and rebates.

Fund Raising: The George Bush for President Committee registered with the FEC on January 5, 1979. The committee had one chairman throughout the duration of the campaign, James Baker, who also served as Bush's campaign director, and three treasurers: Robert Visser, who served from January 5 until April 5, 1979; Thomas Roberts, who served from April 5, 1979, until June 30, 1980; and W. Garrett Boyd, who served from July 1, 1980, through completion of the FEC audit of the campaign.

By the end of 1979, the committee reported receipts of $4,455,097 and expenditures of $4,379,790. The campaign's total receipts were third highest among Republicans for that period and fourth highest overall. Only Connally, Reagan, and Carter reported having received more money in 1979.

The campaign's fund-raising approach was a mix of personal solicitation, fund-raising dinners and events, and direct mail. According to Timothy L. Roper, vice-president of National Direct Mail Services, which provided the Bush campaign with fund-raising advice and services, Robert Odell, NDMS president, had advised the campaign to establish just such a mix.[106] Odell's strategy called for 40 percent of campaign funds to come from fund-raising events, 35 percent from direct mail, 20 percent through "traditional state efforts through the work of appointed state chairmen and committees," and 5 percent to come in spontaneously or through any of the other three fund-raising channels.[107]

The campaign relied on each of the fund-raising efforts recommended. A preannouncement dinner in Washington reportedly netted the campaign $70,000.[108] The direct-mail efforts generally shunned the mass-mailing approach sometimes successful for candidates with clear ideological positions and concentrated on small mailings of highly personalized letters to carefully selected lists. A wide variety of such lists were used, including lists of Yale and Andover graduates and Houston oil and gas producers. Among the most-successful lists were Bush's own Christmas-card list of some 3,000 friends and acquaintances and his personal political file of nearly 25,000 names, many of them gathered as he toured the country under the auspices of the Fund for Limited Government.[109] A mailing to the Christmas-card list reportedly returned nearly $400,000.[110] One mass mailing by the Bush campaign proved to be notably successful. On instructions from the campaign's political director, David Keene, prior to the Iowa caucuses the campaign staff put together lists of nearly 1.5 million registered voters from Massachusetts, New Hampshire, Florida, Alabama, Vermont, Illinois, and other states. Two letters were composed, one touting victory, the other a strong second-place finish, and each was ready to be printed and mailed as soon as the Iowa results were in. The victory message was sent out in a telegram format primarily as political advertising, but a fund-raising reply form was included to help the campaign recoup some of the $200,000 cost. The mailing brought in $220,000—when matching funds are considered, it returned $350,000 gross to the campaign—and added 10,000 names to the campaign's donor file.[111]

Early in the campaign, Bush was heavily dependent on contributions from individuals connected with the oil and the banking industries. For the first three months of 1979, the campaign reported receipts of $663,000. Of that amount, at least $50,000 came from persons in the oil industry and an additional $40,000 from individuals involved in banking and securities operations.[112] Among Bush's early large contributors were Henry Ford II, Peter Stroh, of Stroh's brewing company, and George Weyerhauser of the timber corporation bearing his name.[113] By year's end, according to one report, individuals identified in FEC filings as "business executive," "corporate officer," "investor," or "oil producer," accounted for 3,691 of the 9,300 itemized contributors to the campaign and about $1.1 million of the campaign's receipts.[114] The average contribution of those individuals was $437.[115] Among such donors from the American business community, in addition, were Chase Manhattan Bank board chairman David Rockefeller, Amerada Hess Corporation chairman Leon Hess, and Hunt Oil Company chief executive officer Ray L. Hunt, all of whom gave the maximum $1,000.[116] Bush also drew contributions from CIA figures. William Colby, Bush's predecessor at the agency, gave $1,000; former CIA director Richard Helms, $200; and former deputy director Ray S. Cline, $450.[117]

Bush's fund-raising success during 1979 enabled him to qualify for $891,091 in federal matching funds with his first submission to the FEC in early January 1980. But it was his somewhat unexpected victory in the January 21 Iowa caucuses that led to the most significant augmentation of his campaign treasury. In January, the Bush campaign reported having raised about $1.1 million.[118] A fund-raising dinner held in Chicago about a week and a half after the Iowa caucuses reportedly brought in about $250,000 from 1,500 persons.[119] In February, propelled by the candidate's Iowa victory, the campaign took in $2.4 million from individuals.[120]

But just as electoral success led to fund-raising success, the failure to achieve notable results at the polls had an adverse effect on raising money. After his overwhelming loss to Reagan in New Hampshire on February 26, Bush managed to win just two of the primaries held during March, the contests in Massachusetts and Connecticut, whereas Reagan swept the seven remaining primaries. Individual contributions to the Bush campaign in March fell to less than $1 million.[121] The campaign was forced to take out a $2.8 million loan from a Houston bank but managed to repay $1.8 million by the end of the month.[122]

For most of the remainder of the campaign, money continued to flow into the Bush campaign treasury, though at a much slower rate than in the period following the Iowa victory. This steady but unspectacular fund raising, combined with federal matching funds, allowed Bush to remain in the race almost until the final primaries. According to one report in mid-May, about $150,000 a week continued to come in, although by that time Reagan had built up a commanding lead.[123] Bush counted on a significant victory in the May 20 Michigan primary to provide the momentum he would need to raise the $500,000 his staff thought necessary to contest the June 3 California primary. Bush won handily in Michigan, but Reagan's victory in Oregon's primary on the same day appeared to put Reagan over the top in delegates needed for the nomination. On May 23 Bush withdrew from the California primary. "I don't see the dollars," he said. "And the numbers are extremely tough without California."[124] On May 26, Bush withdrew from the race, ending his two-year quest. Because of a widespread perception that the campaign was over, he said, "It has become increasingly difficult to raise the funds needed."[125] At the time of his withdrawal, Bush estimated his campaign was about $300,000 in debt.[126]

The Bush campaign reported adjusted receipts of $16.7 million of which contributions from individuals accounted for $10.9 million. The campaign also received matching funds in the amount of $5.7 million and PAC contributions of $130,000. Of the $10.9 million in individual contributions, about $3.2 million, some 29 percent, came from unitemized contributions. Itemized contributions of $1 to $499 accounted for about $3 million, about 28 percent of Bush's total receipts from individual contributions. Contributions of $500 to $749 accounted for about $2 million, or 18 percent, and contributions of $750 and up accounted for an additional $2.7 million, about 25 percent of the total. Texas was the biggest source of Bush's itemized contributions of $500 and up, supplying the campaign with almost $913,000, about 19 percent of his donations in that category. New York supplied about $747,000, almost 16 percent of his donations of $500 and up. Illinois and California supplied about $368,000 and $345,000, respectively.

The Bush campaign received $5.7 million in matching funds, 34 percent of its total adjusted receipts. The campaign submitted 86,612 contributions to be certified for matching—the second highest total submitted by any candidate in 1980—and almost 90 percent of the submissions were certified.

The greatest influx of PAC contributions to the Bush campaign came during the first two months of 1980 when Bush moved to the forefront of the prenomination race. During that period, the campaign received $41,275 in PAC contributions. The campaign had received $26,216 from PACs prior to July 1, 1979, and $25,954 from July 1 to December 31, 1979. PAC receipts fell to $25,555 during the two months following his distant second-place finish in New Hampshire and several primary losses thereafter. From May 1, when Reagan's lead appeared almost insurmountable, the campaign took in only $8,775 in PAC contributions. More than 92 percent of Bush's total of $130,035 in PAC contributions came from committees connected with corporations. Among the campaign's PAC donors were Zapata PAC, connected with an oil company the candidate co-founded, which gave $500; the Bluebonnet Fund, associated with the Houston law firm of Baker and Botts, which gave the maximum $5,000; and the National Good Government Fund, connected with another Houston law firm, Vinson, Elkins, Searls, Connally & Smith, which gave $2,500. Although Bush did not benefit from any reported independent expenditures on his behalf, more than $17,000 was spent independently to oppose his candidacy.

Costs: During 1979 the Bush campaign spent all but $75,000 of the $4.5 million it raised. Only about $2.7 million of its expenditures, however, was subject to the overall spending limit. In comparison the Reagan campaign had already spent nearly $5.5 million that was subject to limitation. Further, at the end of 1979 the Bush campaign reported no debts, whereas the Reagan campaign reported debts of $1,475,378 against cash on hand of $554,574. Although the Reagan campaign proved able to raise more money than the Bush campaign, the careful budgeting that characterized the latter campaign helped Bush stay in the race longer than any other Republican candidate but Reagan and even to spend the funds he needed late in the race to win important primaries and keep his nomination hopes alive.

Like other Republican candidates, Bush expended funds on preelection-year jockeying for position. For example, in the fourth quarter of 1979, when the Florida Republican party's presidential straw vote was taken, the Bush campaign reported expenditures allocable to the state of about $90,000. Organizational efforts in key states also led to significant expenditures. For example, by April 1979 the Bush campaign had appointed a full-time campaign director for Iowa to supervise the laborious process of identifying potential supporters and gaining their commitment to the candidate. At that time, too, Bush and his family began traveling regularly to the state.

Political advertising accounted for a significant portion of the campaign's 1979 expenditures, to be expected of any candidate seeking to improve his name recognition. The campaign spent $35,000 on radio and television in Iowa and $8,000 on full-page newspaper advertisements simply to increase recognition of Bush and, according to campaign political director Keene, "to build morale for the troops."[127] By fall 1979, Bush had won a series of five consecutive straw polls in the state. In late September and early October 1979—about five months before the New England primaries—the campaign spent $67,150 on television in Massachusetts, Maine, and New Hampshire, $37,300 on radio in those states and in Vermont, and $40,000 on direct mail.[128] The television advertisements included sixty- and thirty-second spots drawn from a Bush speech before a live audience in San Antonio, Texas, and sixty-second radio commercials. "We wanted to get in early, before other commercials were aired, to get attention," explained Keene.[129] By late December 1979 it was reported that the campaign had spent about $190,000 on television and radio advertising, most of it in New England.[130] Many of the advertisements, prepared by Robert Goodman of Baltimore, sought to emphasize Bush's experience: "George Bush, a President we won't have to train," said the advertisements.

In Iowa, the Bush campaign reported spending more than $462,000; the state spending limit was $489,882. Of that amount it is estimated that some $80,000 was spent by the campaign on broadcast advertising.[131] Two other Republican candidates, Howard Baker and Reagan, reported even greater spending in the state. In the end, it was Bush's superior organization and tireless campaigning, combined with Reagan's neglect of Iowa and his refusal to join his opponents in a Republican forum sponsored by the *Des Moines Register* on January 5, that determined the outcome. Bush won 33 percent of the vote cast by about 115,000 Iowans who participated in the Republican caucuses, six points more than Reagan and 19 percent better than Baker.

The somewhat unexpected victory suddenly cast Bush in the role of campaign front-runner, a position for which he was unprepared. Later James Baker said that the campaign committee expected Bush to finish second in the race and be free of the front-runner's burden until the New Hampshire primary six weeks later, a preferable outcome. "We didn't have the long-term base that Reagan has out there," Baker said.[132] After the Iowa victory, advice that the candidate identify with specific issues rather than continue to speak only in the general terms was rejected. "The thought was, why change something that was working," explained Baker.[133]

For the next five to six weeks, the campaign attempted to ride the momentum generated by the candidate's win in Iowa. The campaign reported spending nearly $265,000 in New Hampshire, about $30,000 less than the state's limit. Much of that was spent on media advertising, with advertisements trying to capitalize on the fact that Bush had spent more time campaigning in the state than most of his opponents. The Bush campaign also spent a significant amount—one estimate was $150,000—on television advertising on Boston television stations whose signals reach into southern New Hampshire.[134] Nevertheless Bush was unable to maintain his post-Iowa momentum. His performance was mediocre in a February 20 debate with six other candidates, including Reagan, in Manchester, New Hampshire, and awkward, at best, in his head-to-head debate with Reagan three days later in Nashua. By ignoring his other Republican rivals, whom Reagan had asked to join in the debate but who had not been officially invited by the debate sponsor, the *Nashua Telegraph*, Bush appeared callous and unable to adapt. When the New Hampshire results were in, it was clear that Reagan had reclaimed his constituency and his position as front-runner. Bush, who lost the popular vote by a two-to-one margin and picked up only five of the state's twenty-two delegates, was forced to start over in his quest for the nomination. If any encouraging news came out of his Granite State defeat, it was that the Reagan campaign was in debt and had already spent about two-thirds of the legal maximum, with thirty-three primaries remaining in which the two candidates were slated to contest with each other. Further, the New Hampshire outcome dealt serious blows to other Republican candidates, particularly to Sen. Robert Dole, who received only 608 votes, and Rep. Philip Crane, who received only 2,628 votes, but also to Sen. Howard Baker, who spent heavily in the state but finished a distant third. If other candidates were to fall by the wayside, Bush would remain as the only alternative to Reagan.

The New England-born former U.N. ambassador did rebound somewhat in the March 4 Massachusetts primary, winning 31 percent of the vote and fourteen delegates. But the edge was taken off this victory by several factors: Reagan himself won 29 percent of the Massachusetts vote and thirteen convention delegates—one fewer than Bush—and also was victorious in the Vermont primary, held the same day, with 31 percent of the popular vote. Perhaps even more harmful to Bush's campaign was the fact that Rep. John Anderson finished a close second in both races, winning 31 percent of the Massachusetts vote and 30 percent of the Vermont vote. The press tended to emphasize Anderson's surprising results, depriving Bush of useful publicity. Further, the emergence of Anderson meant that Bush might lose important votes to the Illinois congressman in later races. Bush did take some satisfaction, however, in the withdrawal of Sen. Baker from the race following the March 4 primaries and from the strong financial position he still held in comparison with Reagan and Anderson. According to political director Keene, the candidate had his biggest fund-raising day ever the day before the March 4 primaries, bringing in $120,000.[135]

Unfortunately for Bush, the next four primaries were held in the South where polls showed Reagan was particularly strong and where Bush had no significant following. On March 8 Reagan overwhelmed John Connally and

Bush in the South Carolina primary, leading to Connally's withdrawal from the race. Bush finished a distant third, winning only 15 percent of the popular vote and no convention delegates. He went down to similar defeats by Reagan in the March 11 primaries in Alabama, Florida, and Georgia, despite reported expenditures of $444,000 in Alabama compared with Reagan's $180,000, and $1.3 million in Florida compared with Reagan's $1.2 million. In Georgia Reagan had a reported spending advantage of $260,000 to about $20,000 for Bush.

In the March 18 Illinois primary, John Anderson once again deprived Bush of an opportunity to slow Reagan's increasing momentum. Anderson won 37 percent of the vote in his home state to Reagan's 48 percent, not enough to give Anderson the impetus he sought but far better than Bush's third-place finish with 11 percent of the vote. Still, Bush campaign officials did not lose heart. According to campaign director Baker, the campaign had spent only 61 percent of the $14.7 million permissible under the FECA, which meant substantial sums could be spent on the twenty-seven remaining primary contests in which the vast majority of convention delegates would be chosen.[136]

Bush did win the primary in Connecticut, where he had family ties, a week later, but he overwhelmingly lost the presidential-preference vote in New York to Reagan on the same day. The candidate had to wait almost a month before his next primary victory. That victory came in Pennsylvania where Bush concentrated fourteen days of campaigning prior to the primary date and spent $1.4 million. Reagan, who by this time was seriously hampered by the overall spending limit, spent about $250,000 on his Pennsylvania campaign. Among Bush expenditures were payments to produce and place a series of four thirty-minute commercials showing Bush in "town meetings" that were aired on Philadelphia television.[137] Bush defeated the front-runner by nine percentage points of the popular vote, but Reagan collected more than half of Pennsylvania's eighty-three delegates in a separate delegate-selection procedure.

Despite this temporary reprieve, Bush soon returned to his second-place position. Among the remaining primaries he contested, he finished better than expected in Texas, where he outspent Reagan by a reported $695,000 to $216,000 and won more than 47 percent of the vote. He also won the District of Columbia, which Reagan did not contest, and the Michigan primary, where a two-to-one spending advantage and the active support of popular Michigan governor William Milliken proved too much for Reagan.

When it became apparent after the May 20 Oregon primary that Reagan probably had won enough convention delegate votes to claim the nomination and that the Bush campaign could not raise sufficient funds to contest the winner-take-all California primary on June 3, Bush, after some hesitation and equivocation, withdrew from the campaign. He made clear he would ask his more than two hundred convention delegates to cast their votes for Reagan on the first ballot.

According to the FEC final report on 1979-1980 prenomination-campaign financial activity through December 31, 1980, the gross disbursements of the George Bush for President Committee amounted to $22.2 million. When adjusted to take account of loan repayments, contribution refunds, and other refunds and rebates, the disbursement total amounts to $16.7 million. Information provided by committee officials covering financial activity through November 24, 1980, allows expenditures to be broken down into several functional categories. Although the total—$22 million—does not agree with the total listed in the later FEC report—$22.2 million—it is sufficiently close that the breakdown accurately specifies how the campaign spent its funds.

Payroll	$ 1,445,976
Consulting fees	273,678
Outside contractors	805,157
Media production	730,592
Media time	3,747,159
Media space	388,307
Travel	1,977,408
Direct mail	3,069,601
Telephone	1,088,600
Data processing	174,976
Events	703,785
Printing	478,804
Loan repayments	4,467,315
Interest on loans	21,632
Office supplies	237,135
Rent	326,121
Furniture and equipment	156,370
State expenses (advances)	132,814
Miscellaneous	93,847
Return of unacceptable contributions	111,293
Phone banks	67,362
Campaign materials	573,224
Equipment rental	230,568
Cost of resale items	17,171
Taxes and insurance	663,316
Total	$21,982,211

Among the most significant expenditures reported are $4.9 million for media production and media space and time buys; $3.1 million for direct mail; and $2.5 million for staff payroll, consulting fees, and payments to outside contractors, including $246,539 paid to Market Opinion Research to do polling for the Bush campaign in both 1979 and 1980. According to committee officials, expenditures reported for direct mail and for events may be combined to indicate total fund-raising costs of about $3.8 million. Other notable expenditures include nearly $2 million for travel, more than $1 million for telephones, and $950,000 for rental of office space, purchase of office supplies, and purchase or rental of furniture and equipment. Bush committee spokespersons indicated that the campaign's debt of approximately $300,000 at the time of the candidate's withdrawal could be considered paid off before the convention if matching funds due at that time are taken into account. Finally, although the information provided by the Bush campaign does not indicate how much the campaign spent on fund raising and legal and accounting expenses exempt from the overall prenomination-campaign spending limit, the FEC final report indicates that $3.2 million was spent for those purposes.

An FEC audit of the George Bush for President Committee released on February 4, 1981, and covering financial activity through June 30, 1980, determined that although some funds were not properly allocated to various states, no state expenditure limitation had been exceeded.[138] Similarly the audit determined that despite some overallocations to exempt legal and accounting and fund-raising categories, the overall expenditure limitation had not been exceeded. The audit found that the committee had failed to itemize refunds and rebates totaling $35,364 and to disclose intermediaries for thirty-four contributions totaling $3,959. In each case, the committee filed an amendment to comply with the requirements of the FECA, and no further action was taken. Finally, the audit determined that the committee had received excess payments for its final two matching-fund submissions in the amount of $39,691. The committee voluntarily repaid that amount, and no further action was required.

Anderson

On June 8, 1979, Rep. John Anderson of Illinois became the eighth Republican to declare his candidacy for the presidential nomination. The ten-term congressman from Rockford, Illinois, about eighty-five miles northwest of Chicago, had let it be known he was exploring the possibility of a presidential bid as early as August 1978 when he reportedly met with fifteen long-time financial backers and received promises of sufficient money to undertake a "serious exploration" of his national support.[139] Although he had risen through the Republican congressional ranks to become chairman of the House Republican Conference, the third-ranking position in the House GOP leadership, Anderson was not well known to the voting public. If his campaign was to be successful, he had to attract the attention and then the support of the electorate.

The congressman, generally known as a conservative on fiscal matters and a liberal on social issues, quickly staked out positions and adopted a style that set him apart from his Republican competitors and captured the attention of the media. He endorsed a life-style of sacrifice and decreased consumption. He confronted hostile audiences, such as New Hampshire gun owners opposed to his stand on licensing firearms. He supported the Panama Canal treaties, extension of time to permit the ratification of the Equal Rights Amendment, and the embargo on shipments of grain to the Soviet Union in response to the Soviet invasion of Afghanistan. Although he did not contest the Iowa caucuses, his outspoken participation in the *Des Moines Register*-sponsored Republican forum in early January helped earn him 4 percent of the vote and the first inkling of national attention. In New Hampshire five weeks later, he finished fourth, receiving 9.8 percent of the vote and falling two hundred votes short of winning his first two convention delegates. Nevertheless he attracted significant media coverage. A week later he won almost 31 percent of the vote in Massachusetts, where he finished second to George Bush, and 29 percent of the vote in Vermont, where he finished second to Ronald Reagan. His strong finishes took the gloss off Bush's Massachusetts victory and gained even greater media attention for Anderson.

Anderson did not mount serious campaigns in any of the next four primaries, all held in the South, choosing instead to concentrate his attention on the March 18 primary in his home state. After a debate in which candidates Bush, Crane, and Reagan all questioned Anderson's Republicanism, the candidate finished second to front-runner Reagan, winning 36.7 percent of the vote. Shortly after the Illinois primary, the possibility of Anderson's withdrawing from the GOP race and mounting an independent candidacy for the presidency began to be raised in the media. Subsequently, third-place finishes in Connecticut, Kansas, and Wisconsin made clear that the Illinois congressman could not reasonably hope to overtake Reagan. On April 24, Anderson announced he was abandoning his race for the Republican presidential nomination and would seek the presidency as an independent candidate. During his nine-and-a-half month quest for the nomination, his campaign spent $6.5 million.

Fund Raising: Anderson's lack of name recognition may be reflected in the relatively slow progress of his campaign fund raising during 1979. From the time of his announcement early in June until September 30, for example, the campaign reported having raised only $287,449, by far the lowest total among the seven Republicans who had any reasonable chance of remaining in contention for the nomination. By December 31, his campaign reported receipts of $505,991, still the lowest total among major contenders. Of that amount, the campaign had spent more than $476,000 and reported cash on hand of about $30,000. According to one report, however, Anderson was not lacking in influential supporters. A list of his large contributors in 1979 was said to include David Rockefeller, Chase Manhattan Bank chairman; his brother, Laurence Rockefeller; John Hay Whitney, chairman of the International Herald Tribune; Andrew Heiskell, chairman of Time, Inc.; William W. Scranton, former Pennsylvania governor and presidential candidate; and Robert O. Anderson, chairman of Atlantic Richfield Co.[140]

During the first month of 1980, Anderson's fund-raising fortunes did not improve appreciably. His campaign reported receipts for January 1980 of $153,504. His total receipts by the end of the month were only about half the total of Sen. Robert Dole, who reported the next lowest amount, and they paled in comparison with the more than $12 million Ronald Reagan's campaign had raised by that time. As his name recognition increased, however, his campaign treasury grew. In February he raised some $426,000 from individuals, and in March, following his surprising results in New England primaries, that figure rose to more than $2 million in individual contributions, more than any other candidate raised from individuals during that month.[141] These private donations were matched by federal subsidies, which further helped Anderson's financial position. On April 9, 1980, the FEC certified $974,220 in matching funds for the Anderson campaign, compared with the $1.2 million the candidate had received previously.[142]

Direct-mail solicitation of funds, which was an important source of campaign income, was conducted for the Anderson campaign by the Virginia-based firm of Craver, Mathews, Smith and Company. The firm had sent one test letter for Anderson in August 1979, but the 1 percent rate of return did not warrant continuing the effort.[143] After Anderson's performance in the Republican debate held in Iowa early in January, however, Tom Mathews decided it was time to try again. On February 3, the firm sent out a test mailing of 48,000 pieces. The issue-oriented letter emphasized Anderson's unconventional stands on a variety of issues and presented him as a "dark horse" but "an honest man with sound experience."[144] The letter received a good rate of return of 5 percent and an average contribution of $32.[145]

Early in March campaign manager Michael MacLeod said the campaign was averaging an unusually high $4.30 return for each dollar it spent on direct mail.[146] In mid-April Tom Mathews noted that Anderson had attracted nearly 80,000 contributors, with contributions averaging $30.[147] According to Mathews, Anderson's disappointing results in the April 1 primary in Wisconsin would not seriously affect the campaign's fund raising. "The people giving are not affected by these primaries," he said, maintaining they did not care if Anderson won or lost as a Republican candidate.[148] Shortly after Anderson announced his independent candidacy, Roger Craver compared Anderson's direct-mail fund-raising success with that of Common Cause ten years earlier. He noted that it took Common Cause twenty weeks to build a list of 100,000 supporters. Said Craver, "Anderson will reach the 100,000 mark this week, within 10 weeks of direct mail soliciting."[149]

Anderson also received financial support from individuals identified with liberal causes. Philanthropist Stewart Mott, who had been the major contributor to George McGovern's 1972 presidential campaign, staged a fund-raising party for Anderson at his New York penthouse,[150] and liberal Democrat Stanley Sheinbaum organized an Anderson fund raiser in Beverly Hills attended by more than three hundred persons.[151] Actor Paul Newman volunteered to make fund-raising commercials for the candidate.[152] And television producer Norman Lear took out newspaper advertisements touting the Anderson candidacy.[153]

Anderson's new-found affluence brought about changes in the campaign's style. Chartered buses and planes replaced cabs and commercial flights as growing numbers of reporters and television crews were assigned to follow the candidate. Secret-service agents were acquired, largely to provide crowd control. Staff members worked around the clock to open mail-in contributions and count receipts. Nevertheless Anderson was unsuccessful at the polls. After campaigning for almost ten months and actively contesting six primaries without winning a victory, on April 24 the candidate withdrew from the GOP race and announced he would run as an independent candidate for the presidency. On May 8 the Anderson committee filed with the FEC a statement of its financial position that indicated a substantial surplus. At the time the committee returned to the treasury $323,573, the amount of the surplus the committee estimated was made up of unused matching funds.[154] An FEC audit later determined the committee's surplus at the time of Anderson's withdrawal was $988,125 and that the total amount of excess matching funds it had received was $401,779. The audit also determined that a total of $1,918 in matching funds had been paid to the committee for contributions that had not been backed with sufficient funds. Thus the total amount of matching fund payments the committee was required to repay the Treasury was $403,698.

The Anderson campaign reported adjusted receipts of $6.6 million. Of that amount, $3.9 million came from individual contributions and $2.7 million from federal matching funds. Anderson received only about $25,000 from PACs. Of the $3.9 million Anderson received from individuals, unitemized contributions accounted for $2.6 million, almost 67 percent of the total. His campaign, then, was heavily dependent on a relatively large number of small contributors. Itemized contributions of $1

to $499 accounted for $783,057, about 20 percent of total receipts from individuals. Contributions of $500 to $749 brought in $220,710, about 5.7
percent of the total, and contributions of $750 and up accounted for
$297,430, about 7.6 percent of the total. The candidate received almost 27
percent of his contributions of $500 and up from his home state of Illinois;
those contributions totaled $139,580. Contributors of $500 and up from
New York gave $124,130, almost 24 percent of the total receipts in that
category, and contributors of $500 and up from California gave $58,763,
about 11 percent of that total.

Public matching funds of $2.68 million accounted for more than 40 per-
cent of the campaign's receipts. The campaign submitted 80,744 contributions for certification—the third highest total among Republicans after
Reagan and Bush—and more than 92 percent of those submissions were certified. The average contribution submitted was $36, the lowest average for
any candidate, further indicating the campaign's dependence on small contributors.

Of the $24,495 Anderson received in PAC contributions, about $17,500
was contributed in 1979. Among PAC contributors to the campaign were
the National Abortion Rights Action League, which gave the maximum
$5,000. NOW PAC, affiliated with the National Organization for Women,
also gave $5,000, and Friends of Family Planning gave $1,000. Trade,
membership, and health PACs accounted for about 52 percent of the total
PAC contributions to the campaign, corporate PACs for about 35 percent,
and nonconnected PACs for about 8 percent.

Anderson also had $196,355 spent independently on behalf of his
Republican campaign. Stewart Mott spent $90,000 on Anderson's behalf,
and television producer Norman Lear spent $106,000. Both paid for
newspaper advertisements supporting Anderson's candidacy. For example,
Lear spent a reported $16,000 on full-page pro-Anderson advertisements in
the *Boston Globe* on March 2 and 3, just before the Massachusetts
primary.[155] He placed similar advertisements backing Anderson in other
Massachusetts newspapers. Mott placed a two-page advertisement in the
New York Times on March 23, one page encouraging voters to vote for and
contribute to Anderson and the other encouraging them to vote for and support Kennedy. The advertisement called the two the "best candidates in
each major party." Mott also paid for pro-Anderson thirty- and sixty-
second radio spots in Illinois, Connecticut, and Wisconsin on behalf of
Anderson.

Costs: The Anderson campaign's modest fund-raising results in 1979 did
not allow it to spend heavily in the preelection year. For example, although
some candidates spent hundreds of thousands of dollars to influence the
outcome of the Republican straw vote in Florida in November 1979, Ander-

son reported his total Florida spending for 1979 and 1980 combined to be only $500. And although it could be reported by early November 1979 that a number of candidates had already done a significant amount of media advertising, by that same time Anderson had not yet made any commitment for media advisers.[156] Of Anderson's total receipts of $505,991 for 1979, the candidate reported expenditures of $476,422.

In the early part of 1980, Anderson campaign spending, like its fund raising, remained relatively low. For example the campaign reported total expenditures of only $1,233 for Iowa, largely to pay the costs of two appearances by the candidate in the state.[157] In one of those appearances, the January 5 Republican forum, he furthered his reputation for outspokenness by supporting the embargo of grain to the Soviet Union as part of the nation's response to the Soviet invasion of Afghanistan. Although that position was highly unpopular among Iowa grain farmers, Anderson managed to gain national attention and to win 4 percent of the vote cast in the January 21 Republican caucuses.

The campaign's increasingly successful fund-raising efforts during February 1980 are reflected in increased spending. For the February 26 New Hampshire primary, the campaign reported expenditures of $246,570, fourth highest among the Republican contestants. Anderson finished fourth in the race, winning 9.8 percent of the vote. Since according to state law a candidate had to win 10 percent of the vote to win any convention delegates, Anderson asked for a recount. In the recount, however, the candidate actually lost 25 votes, leaving him 201 short of the delegate cutoff point.[158]

According to one report, prior to the New Hampshire primary, Anderson had contracted for about $200,000 in television advertising in Boston.[159] Although the advertisements would reach voters in southern New Hampshire, the costs were allocable to the Massachusetts state spending limit, which was $1,001,667 compared with the New Hampshire limit of $294,400. The Anderson advertisements sought to set him apart from the other candidates on a host of specific issues—energy, women's rights, tax cuts—and to portray him as a person who spoke his mind and offered no easy solution to the nation's problems.

Anderson's strong second-place finishes in Massachusetts and Vermont in primaries on March 4 made him a force to be reckoned with in the prenomination race. In Massachusetts, where he was narrowly defeated by George Bush, Anderson reported spending $438,177, considerably less than both Bush and Reagan. In Vermont, where Reagan bested him by only a percentage point of the popular vote, he reported spending only $41,889, half of Bush's reported expenditures and one-third of Reagan's. Not only did Anderson boost his own chances by far exceeding low initial expectations for him in the two states, he also dealt a serious blow to rival George Bush. "We got a bad break from Anderson emerging," said Bush campaign manager James Baker. "Just at the point we had gotten to be the alternative to Reagan, along came Anderson. The media hype was perfect for him—right before the primary in his home state."[160]

Anderson did not compete in the four southern primaries that followed the New England contests, but instead attempted to use his second-place finishes in Vermont and Massachusetts to propel him to success in his home state Illinois primary March 18. At one point shortly before the primary, with the help of favorable newspaper coverage, television advertisements heralding "the Anderson difference," and total reported spending of $652,293, Anderson actually was the favorite to win.[161]

A Republican debate on March 13 in Chicago may have contributed to Anderson's eventual primary loss. All three of the candidate's rivals, George Bush, Philip Crane, and Ronald Reagan, suggested he might be more comfortable outside the GOP fold. Crane went so far as to tell Anderson, "You're in the wrong party."[162] Anderson did not take kindly to their suggestions. When the primary votes were tabulated, Reagan was the clear winner, with 48.4 percent of the vote to Anderson's 36.7 percent. Bush finished a distant third with 11 percent.

Disappointed with the Illinois results, Anderson turned his attention to the April 1 open primary in Wisconsin where he counted on crossover votes from Democrats to boost his chances. Despite vigorous campaigning and reported expenditures of $484,128—second only to expenditures of $574,471 by the Bush campaign—Anderson finished third, winning 28 percent of the vote to approximately 40 percent for Reagan and 30 percent for Bush.

Although reports of the possibility of a third-party or independent candidacy by Anderson had been on the increase in the press since the candidate's Illinois primary loss, the candidate still talked of continuing the Republican campaign. In fact front-runner Reagan's home state of California appeared to be Anderson's next big target. There he hoped to persuade sympathetic Democrats to reregister as Republicans by the May 3 legal deadline so they could vote for him in the state's June 3 winner-take-all primary. During his campaign trip to California, however, Anderson took time to reevaluate his chances and concluded there was no realistic possibility he could win the Republican nomination. On April 24 he announced he was withdrawing from the Republican race and beginning a quest as an independent candidate for the presidency.

According to the FEC final report on 1979-1980 prenomination-campaign financial activity through December 31, 1980, the Anderson for President Committee's net disbursements amounted to $7.2 million. When that figure is adjusted to take into account loan repayments, contribution refunds, and other refunds and rebates, the disbursement total amounts to $6.5 million. With information provided by the Anderson committee, the committee's expenditures through April 24, 1980, may be broken down into functional categories. Although the report accounts for only $4.7 million of the committee's expenditures, it does serve to indicate the campaign's major costs:

Wages	$ 532,441.37
Supplies	92,127.89
Telephone	229,482.35
Rent	182,198.24
Postage	161,881.52
Travel	438,215.55
Printing	262,114.31
Fund raising	1,075,956.28
Advertising	1,274,569.28
Utilities	5,431.42
Miscellaneous	228,225.89
Consulting	59,177.19
Computer	100,881.24
Taxes	71,270.09
Total	$4,708,973.33

Two of the categories of expenditure, fund raising and advertising, accounted for $2,350,226, 50 percent of the expenditure total reported. Other significant categories of expenditure were wages and consulting fees, which combined accounted for $586,618; travel, which accounted for $438,215; and telephone, which accounted for $229,482. In addition, a report provided by the National Unity Campaign for John Anderson, Anderson's independent presidential-campaign committee, covering activity through June 31, 1981, indicates the Anderson for President Committee transferred $713,000 to the National Unity Campaign.

An FEC audit of the Anderson for President Committee determined that overdrafts in the committee's direct-mail account between April 28, 1980, and May 30, 1980, amounted to $13,037. According to FEC regulations, an overdraft is to be considered an illegal contribution by a bank or institution unless it is made on an account subject to automatic overdraft protection or unless the overdraft is subject to a definite interest rate, which is usual and customary, and there is a definite repayment schedule. None of these conditions appeared to apply to the Anderson committee overdrafts. The committee explained that the overdrafts were the result of bookkeeping errors and had not been uncovered earlier because of coordination problems between committee offices in Illinois and Washington, D.C. After the committee repaid the overdrafts, as well as a charge for use of the overdrawn funds, no further action was required.

The audit determined that the committee had failed to disclose a number of deposits and that it had failed to document properly expenditures totaling $63,205. In both cases the committee subsequently provided the information required by law, and no further action was needed. Finally, the audit determined that $401,780 represented the amount of the committee's surplus as of April 24, 1980, made up of federal matching funds. The committee repaid that sum to the U.S. Treasury.

Connally

Like Republican rival George Bush, John Connally could boast an impressive list of political credentials. He had served as secretary of the Navy under President John Kennedy, had been elected three times as Democratic governor of Texas, and had served as secretary of the treasury under President Richard Nixon. Unlike Bush, Connally enjoyed significant name recognition. A Gallup Poll reported in August 1979 indicated he had higher name recognition than any potential Republican contender except Ronald Reagan and former President Gerald Ford.[163] Unfortunately for Connally, a substantial percentage of those who recognized his name had an unfavorable impression of him. Some considered him a wheeler-dealer. Others were still suspicious of him because of his indictment on the charge of taking a $10,000 bribe from milk producers while treasury secretary in return for lobbying in favor of higher milk price supports, even though Connally had subsequently been acquitted. Still others mistrusted him because of his switch from the Democratic to the Republican party in 1973. Further it had been some eleven years since Connally had last run for office, and he had no built-in campaign organization.

Connally began early to try to overcome negative impressions on the part of voters and to build support for his candidacy. Throughout 1978, he toured the United States in his capacity of chairman of the John Connally Citizens Forum, speaking before Republican party groups, and raising money to fund his extensive travel and speaking engagements and to assist party organizations and candidates. In January 1979 he formally declared his candidacy and set out to raise the funds he would need to overtake Ronald Reagan whom public-opinion polls showed to be the favorite among potential Republican voters. A decision was made early by campaign strategists to focus on communicating with large audiences rather than on grass-roots organizing. "We could generate major coverage and major crowds," explained Eddie Mahe, who served as Connally's campaign director until January 1980. "To use John Connally in someone's kitchen didn't make any sense when he could be speaking to 2,000 people in a convention center."[164]

Throughout 1979 Connally enjoyed extraordinary fund-raising success. The $9.2 million he raised surpassed by $2 million the total raised by Reagan, the next most successful fund raiser. But the Connally campaign spent money almost as quickly as it came in, much of it on staff salaries, travel, and expensive media advertising. In addition, the campaign refused to accept public matching funds, allowing it to ignore campaign spending limits but making it entirely dependent on private contributions.

The first real test of the campaign's strategy and measure of the effect of its heavy spending came in the January 21 Iowa caucuses. Connally finished a poor fourth with 10 percent of the vote. He fared even worse in the three New England primaries in late February and early March, failing to win even 2 percent of the vote in any of the contests. With time running out, Connally chose to stake his chances on the results of the March 8 South Carolina primary. Despite vigorous campaigning, substantial spending, and the wholehearted support of the state's senior senator, Strom Thurmond, Connally finished a distant second, winning 29.6 percent of the vote to Reagan's 54.7 percent. The next day Connally officially withdrew from the race. His campaign cost $12.6 million and succeeded in winning only one convention delegate as a result of the February 2 Arkansas caucus.

Fund Raising: From the time John Connally declared his candidacy in January 1979 until January 1980, the Connally campaign committee had little difficulty raising funds. During the first quarter of 1979, the campaign reported receipts of $1.2 million. Of that amount about $130,000 was reported to have been contributed by some 200 persons identified as executives in the oil and gas industry.[165] Among contributors were executives of some of the nation's largest corporations, including Lockheed, Armco Steel, Mobil Oil, Standard Oil, and Pepsico.[166] Although business executives were well represented among campaign donors, Winton M. Blount, Connally's campaign chairman, said at the time that the campaign had "a broad spectrum of support."[167] Said Blount, "The average contribution—with over 10,000 people contributing—was $133."[168]

By September 30, 1979, the Connally campaign reported having raised $4.3 million, more than any other candidate. By December 31 receipts had reached almost $9.2 million. At that time the candidate's campaign reported indebtedness of about $150,000 but cash on hand of more than $950,000.

Most of the campaign's fund raising was accomplished by personal solicitation, often by well-placed corporate fund raisers or by fund-raising events. Among the events, there were some ticketed dinners, such as three held in California—in Fresno, San Francisco, and Los Angeles—in late October 1979, which grossed about $1 million.[169] But most often funds were raised at events by making an appeal at the end of Connally appearances before selected groups.

In August 1979 conservative direct-mail expert Richard Viguerie, who had been working for Republican candidate Philip Crane, switched to John Connally. At the time Viguerie's addition to the Connally staff, reportedly as a volunteer, was heralded by campaign chairman Blount as "a tremendous plus."[170] Viguerie, however, was handicapped by a late start. To be successful, direct mail, especially mass mailings, require considerable lead time, perhaps as much as a year more than Viguerie had available. Viguerie did arrange mailings to about seventy-five test lists and found that business lists, Republican-contributor lists, and Texas lists were particularly successful. But direct mail never proved to be a high-priority fund-raising method in the Connally campaign.

By December 1979 Connally felt secure enough to refuse federal matching funds, becoming the first major candidate to do so since the matching-fund system was first used in the 1976 election. The candidate, who maintained he had always been opposed philosophically to publicly funded campaigns, had a more pragmatic reason for declining the funds.[171] He was convinced the only way he could overtake Ronald Reagan was to outspend him in key states, something he would not be able to do if he was bound by the individual state spending limits applied to each candidate who accepted the matching funds. Also influential in Connally's decision was the refusal of the national television networks to sell the candidate broadcast time in October and November when he needed to increase his recognition around the country and drum up national support. In making the decision to forgo public funds, Connally was counting on continuing fund-raising success and hoping voters would not conclude he was trying to buy the nomination, a possibility rival Republican John Anderson encouraged when he called Connally's strategy a throwback to an era when big money bought elections.[172]

In January 1980 the campaign's fund raising began to falter. The campaign reported receipts of about $850,000 for the month but expenditures of about $1.4 million. Connally's poor fourth-place finish in Iowa did little to encourage increased giving. The campaign's staff of 140 was cut in half. Management of the campaign was transferred from Eddie Mahe to Charles Keating, a Cincinnati industrialist with a reputation for budget cutting. Diane Waltman, a professional fund raiser, resigned from the campaign, in part because of her disagreement with the decision to forgo matching funds.

Early in February Connally borrowed $500,000 on a thirty-day personal note from the Houston National Bank.[173] A campaign spokesman explained the money was needed to meet deadlines to pay for television time in southern primary campaigns and that Connally hoped to make the money back from a mid-February nationally televised fund-raising appeal tied to a nationwide chain of fund-raising parties.[174] The telecast did air as scheduled, reportedly in twenty-one major media markets in the country at a cost of $160,000.[175] According to press reports, the effort raised $1.5 million, but two-thirds of that was understood to be in pledges rather than cash.[176] A later report from a former campaign staff person, however, indicated that the televised appeal at best broke even, and may actually have lost money, and that far fewer than the hoped-for 5,000 house parties actually were held. In addition the effort was not organized to bring in receipts quickly even though the campaign needed a rapid influx of cash.

In February Connally closed down campaign offices in all states but those holding primaries during the following four weeks and took much of his staff off salary. His son, John Connally III, took over the direction of the campaign from Charles Keating. Connally put his hopes on a strong showing in South Carolina's March 8 primary. "My campaign starts in South Carolina," he said about two weeks before the primary.[177] In fact his campaign ended there. After finishing a distant second to Reagan and failing to win a single convention delegate, Connally returned to Texas to reassess his campaign. On March 9, he announced his withdrawal from the race.

Although Connally was not bound by the law's spending limits, he was bound by its reporting requirements. According to reports filed with the FEC, the Connally campaign had adjusted receipts of $12.7 million, of which $11.6 million came from individual contributions and $205,000 from PACS. Other political committees, a category that includes joint fund-raising committees such as that established to aid Connally and other defeated Republican candidates, accounted for $172,704, and other income for $174,961. In addition FEC reports indicate that the candidate had lent the campaign $578,883, of which only $50,000 had been repaid by December 31, 1980.

Of the $11.6 million in individual contributions, unitemized contributions accounted for about $2.4 million, a little more than 20 percent of the total. Itemized contributions of $1 to $499 accounted for about $2.7 million, almost 23 percent of the total. Contributions of $500 to $749 accounted for $1.6 million, about 13 percent of the total, and contributions of $750 and up accounted for $5.2 million, about 44 percent of the total.[178] No other Republican candidate received more money from the $750 and up category of contributions than Connally, nor was any other Republican candidate as dependent on this category of giving.

According to internal worksheets provided by the Connally for President Committee, the campaign had established fund-raising quotas for each state, ranging from a low of $30,000 in several states, including Maine, Utah, and Rhode Island, to a high of $5 million in Texas. A state-by-state breakdown of receipts dated February 13, 1980, indicates that the quotas were met or exceeded only in two states: New Hampshire, whose $30,000 quota was exceeded by almost 116 percent, and Wyoming, whose $30,000 quota was exceeded by almost 9 percent. In all other states, fund-raising results fell short, sometimes far short, of goals. For example, by mid-

February the campaign had achieved only 55 percent of its $2 million goal in California, 26 percent of its $1.3 million goal in Illinois, and 36 percent of its $650,000 goal in Michigan. The campaign did achieve 83 percent of its ambitious $5 million goal in Texas. The same mid-February breakdown of receipts indicated that by that time, 53,900 donors had contributed to the campaign.

An FEC breakdown of individual contributions of $500 and up indicates that Texas was by far the most generous state for Connally in that category of giving; 3,487 Texas donors gave $2.8 million, almost 41 percent of the campaign's total contributions in that category. California was the next most generous state, supplying the campaign with $825,805, almost 12 percent of Connally's donations of $500 and up. Florida and New York supplied an additional $391,583 and $377,725, respectively, in that category of donations.

In 1979 Connally received more than $170,000 of the $205,000 he received from PACs. Almost 87 percent of his PAC contributions came from committees associated with corporations and about 6 percent came from trade, membership, and health PACs. Among PACs contributing $5,000 were the National Good Government Fund, connected with the Houston law firm of Vinson, Elkins, Searls, Connally & Smith, of which the candidate was a senior partner; the Bluebonnet Fund, associated with another large Houston law firm, Baker and Botts; and the El Paso Co. PAC.

More than $288,000 was reported to the FEC as independent expenditures made on behalf of Connally's candidacy. Three individuals accounted for almost the entire amount: Texas industrialist and real estate investor Cecil R. Haden spent $184,000 on behalf of Connally, Theo N. Law spent $66,000, and former Texas state legislator Henry C. Grover spent $29,000. Grover's expenditure funded pro-Connally newspaper advertisements in Iowa prior to the Republican caucuses in that state.[179]

Costs: The Connally for President Committee not only raised more money than any other candidate's committee during 1979, it also spent more money. By December 31, the committee reported expenditures of $8.2 million, about $1.1 million more than the Reagan for President Committee, and debts of more than $150,000. Staff salaries and consultant fees, travel, and media advertising accounted for a significant portion of the campaign's 1979 costs. For example, by April 1979 the campaign already had aired a series of five-minute programs in secondary markets in a variety of states at a cost of less than $25,000.[180] In the late summer the campaign spent $35,000 on television and $12,000 on radio to influence the results of the Republican state party presidential straw vote in Florida in November 1979.[181] Those expenditures were part of an estimated $250,000 spent by the campaign in that Florida effort, which netted only a poor second-place finish to Reagan.[182]

The Connally campaign reportedly sought to buy substantial amounts of national network time during the final months of 1979: five five-minute spots, half an hour of prime time, fifteen minutes on Thanksgiving Day, and "comparable time within 72 hours of any 'major program' on behalf of Ronald Reagan."[183] This attempt was in keeping with the campaign's decision to direct its appeal to mass audiences and to compensate for the campaign's lack of local organization. The networks, however, refused Connally's request, as they did requests by President Jimmy Carter and Ronald Reagan to buy time in late 1979, maintaining that the public was not yet ready for political campaigning. CBS offered the candidates two five-minute spots each; Connally and Reagan both accepted. Connally's first five-minute spot, which aired early in November, reportedly cost about $31,000.[184] By late December 1979 it was reported that Connally had spent $250,000 on radio and television advertising, including the network spots and spots broadcast in the individual states.[185]

In an effort to compensate for its inability to purchase the national network broadcast time it sought, the campaign purchased full-page advertisements in regional major magazines in January and early February. Campaign strategist Eddie Mahe later regretted the decision, noting that spending the same amount on television advertisements at that time "undoubtedly would have had more impact."[186]

The Connally campaign continued to spend significant amounts for television advertising in local markets. Television advertisements in Iowa prior to the January 21 caucuses portrayed Connally as a rancher familiar with the problems of agriculture and as a family man. One report of the cost of his commercials on television stations around the state was $119,000.[187] Despite such expenditures, Connally finished no better than fourth in caucus results. This poor finish, coupled with low standings in New Hampshire polls and faltering fund raising, led the candidate to husband his resources for primaries in which he felt he had a better chance of success, such as the March 8 South Carolina primary.

The centerpiece of Connally's South Carolina campaign was a television blitz aimed at helping the candidate overtake Reagan and Bush. By February 22, the campaign had spent about $80,000 for advertisements on eight of the state's twelve television stations and had plans to spend more before the primary date.[188] Connally himself spent seventeen days in the state, often in the company of the state's influential senior senator, Strom Thurmond. In order to help fund the South Carolina campaign, on February 19 Connally took his staff off salary temporarily, saving an estimated $95,000 a week.[189] The candidate's efforts, however, went for nought; Reagan defeated him by about 25 percentage points of the popular vote and won all twenty-five of the state's convention delegates. The day after the primary, Connally withdrew from the Republican presidential race, a victim of Reagan's popularity and, perhaps, his own committee's profligate spending early in the campaign. Said Ben Barnes, the campaign's fund-raising manager in the latter stages of the campaign, "There was no financial management in the early days of the campaign."[190]

When the campaign came to a close, Connally's debt was estimated at about $2.1 million.[191] Included in that amount was the half-million dollar loan the candidate made to his own campaign so it could repay the bank loan the campaign had taken out to pay for its February 14 fund-raising telethon. Other reported campaign debts included $234,000 to the Richard A. Viguerie Company for direct-mail services, $180,000 to advertising firms in Washington and in Austin, Texas, and $21,000 to a resort in Fairfield Bay, Arkansas, where in early January Connally had wooed delegates to the Arkansas state convention.[192] There he won his only delegate to the GOP national convention.

According to the FEC final report on 1979-1980 prenomination-campaign financial activity through December 31, 1980, the net disbursements of the Connally campaign were $13.7 million. When that figure is adjusted to take into account loan repayments, contribution refunds, and refunds and rebates, the adjusted disbursement total amounts to $12.6 million. Information provided by the Connally for President Committee allows committee expenditures of $12.5 million through March 31, 1980, to be broken down into broad functional categories. According to a committee spokesperson, additional expenditures of $1 million to $1.3 million were made after that time, but the breakdown was not maintained. Although the total expenditure figure provided by the committee report differs from the net disbursement figure in the FEC final report, the two figures are sufficiently close so that the committee breakdown accurately indicates how the campaign spent its funds:

Personnel costs	$ 1,800,000
Consultants and outside services	1,700,000
Rents and occupancy	430,000
Communications	630,000
Postage and supplies	905,000
Media	1,900,000
Travel and related	1,800,000
Furniture and fixtures	160,000
Deposits	230,000
Advances to states	1,110,000
Phone banks	640,000
Legal and compliance	275,000
Refunds and loan repayments	680,000
Other	197,000
Total	$12,457,000

Among the campaign's major costs were personnel, consultants, and outside services, which combined cost the campaign about $3.5 million; media, which cost $1.9 million; and travel and related expenses, which cost $1.8 million. Other significant expenditures were $905,000 for postage and supplies, $640,000 for phone banks, and $630,000 for communications.

Baker

Although Tennessee senator Howard Baker did not announce his candidacy for the Republican presidential nomination until November 1, 1979, the possibility of a race for the presidency apparently was included in Baker's political planning much earlier. In September 1977 it was reported that Baker had considered following a path similar to that taken some years earlier by Jimmy Carter by not running for reelection to the Senate in 1978 and spending the following two years campaigning fulltime for the nomination.[193] But Baker decided his position as Senate minority leader would provide a better springboard for a presidential bid, and he sought and won a third term as senator, despite having cast an unpopular vote in favor of the controversial Panama Canal Treaty. By late 1978 Baker had made his decision to seek the nomination and to use his leadership position to gain national exposure that would favor his candidacy.

For the first seven months of 1979, however, Baker's campaigning was limited to what he could accomplish as a self-described "weekend warrior," who had to tend to his Senate leadership duties during the week. He had wanted to make his opposition to President Carter's Strategic Arms Limitation Treaty (SALT II), his campaign centerpiece, but eventually he found voters were far more interested in other matters, such as inflation and the rising cost of energy. When he finally announced his candidacy in November 1979, most of his major Republican rivals had a significant advantage in organization and in exposure as candidates, as well as in fund raising.

In the first major prenomination contest, the January 21 Iowa caucuses, Baker finished a distant third, winning only 10 percent of the vote. He finished second to George Bush in a two-man race in Puerto Rico's February 17 primary, winning 37 percent of the popular vote but none of the commonwealth's fourteen convention delegates. In New Hampshire's February 26 primary, he finished third again with only about 13 percent of the vote and two delegates. Baker dropped to a fourth-place finish in the Massachusetts and Vermont primaries held on March 4. On the following day, he withdrew from the race. By the time the books were closed on his campaign, $7.1 million had been spent.

Fund Raising: Despite the candidate's relatively late start in serious campaigning for the nomination and his even later formal announcement of candidacy, the Baker committee achieved some creditable fund-raising results during 1979. At year's end, the committee reported receipts of $3.1 million with cash on hand of nearly $140,000. But the campaign also reported indebtedness of $1 million. Direct-mail solicitation accounted for the greatest percentage of the campaign's income, in both 1979 and 1980. A variety of special events and personal solicitation of funds by finance committee members in various states also were important sources of campaign receipts, with telephone solicitation, PAC donations, and other fund-raising methods supplying the remainder of the Baker committee money.

The first direct-mail packages for Baker were designed and written in December 1978, shortly before the Baker Search Committee registered with the FEC on January 31, 1979. The first mailing, sent to 15,000 previous donors to Baker campaigns, announced the Tennessee senator's intention to consider the possibility of seeking the presidential nomination. That mailing reportedly raised $250,000 at a cost of $10,000. Three additional prospect mailings followed, including one to set up a national advisory board for the prospective candidate and a telegram encouraging donors to contribute to Baker so he could continue his work against ratification of SALT II. Subsequently four to eight mailings were sent to persons on the donor list developed from the previous mailings, with a mailing sent out every thirty-five to forty days.

About 40,000 individuals responded to direct-mail appeals from Baker, contributing about $1.4 million. The average contribution was about $36. Another report put direct-mail receipts as high as $1.7 million. Tennessee residents were Baker's natural constituency; they responded generously to direct-mail appeals from the candidate's committee, as well as to other fund-raising methods.

Internal working papers provided by the committee indicate Baker's most successful months for raising private contributions were November and December 1979, shortly after his announcement, when he raised about $500,000 and $550,000, respectively. January receipts from private contributions dipped slightly to about $430,000, and despite a disappointing third-place finish in the Iowa caucuses late in January, February receipts from private sources were about $480,000. When Baker failed to make strong showings in any of the New England primaries in late February and early March, however, donations dropped significantly. At the time of Baker's withdrawal from the presidential race on March 5, his campaign debt was estimated to be more than $1 million.[194] By mid-May, despite continued fund raising following Baker's withdrawal, the debt was still about $850,000.

FEC reports covering financial activity through December 31, 1980, indicate the Baker campaign had receipts of $7.2 million. Contributions from individuals accounted for $4.2 million, matching funds for $2.6 million, and PAC donations for $130,000. Contributions from other committees accounted for an additional $170,000. Unitemized contributions of $1.6 million accounted for about 38 percent of Baker's total private contributions. Itemized contributions of $1 to $499 brought in $1.2 million, about 28 percent of the total; contributions of $500 to $749 accounted for $598,000, about 14 percent of the total; contributions of $750 and up brought in $870,000, about 20 percent of the total private contributions to the campaign. More than 41 percent of Baker's individual contributions of $500 and up came from his home state of Tennessee, which supplied the campaign with $608,504 in that category of giving. New York supplied $178,110 in donations of $500 and up, and California supplied $123,601 in such donations.

The Baker campaign was certified to receive $2.6 million in federal matching funds. The campaign submitted 67,490 contributions for certification, more than 97 percent of which were certified. Those contributions submitted averaged $40.

During 1979 Baker received more than $48,000 of his total PAC contributions of $130,000. He received an additional $30,000 in January and February 1980. His PAC total dropped to about $6,500 in March and April, the period immediately after his withdrawal. But Baker, who retained his influential Senate position, received almost $45,000 in PAC contributions from May 1, 1980, on, to help him retire his campaign debt. No significant independent expenditures for or against Baker were reported.

Costs: As with most other major contenders for the Republican nomination, Baker's principal expenditures were made for media advertising, staff salaries, and travel. The campaign also spent a substantial portion of its total disbursements on fund raising, particularly the direct-mail fund raising. At its peak the Baker committee had about 130 persons on its payroll, including consultants, and most of them were assigned to work in primary and caucus states.

Political consultants Douglas Bailey and John Deardourff handled the Baker campaign's media strategy and advertising. Although Baker reportedly tried for some time to secure their services, he was able to do so only in November 1979, when the consultants had some assurance that former President Gerald Ford would not enter the race. In the first week of January 1980, the campaign sponsored advertisements showing the candidate at the Watergate hearings in which Sen. Baker played a notable role. Those advertisements were pulled, however, when public reaction made it apparent that many Republican voters preferred not to be reminded of the affair. More successful were advertisements showing Baker in a relaxed setting talking about why he wanted to be president or featuring the candidate speaking out on specific issues of importance to the region in which the advertisements were broadcast, such as federal revenue sharing, a popular issue in New Hampshire.

Baker's most widely noted television advertisement was a five-minute program that showed the candidate shouting down an Iranian student in an appearance before a student audience at the University of Iowa. This and other Baker advertisements were shown frequently to Iowa viewers prior to the January 21 Republican caucuses. Despite heavy media spending in the state—an estimated $100,000 of the $480,000 the campaign allocated to Iowa—Baker finished a distant third in the caucus voting.[195]

In Puerto Rico's February 17 primary, essentially a two-man race with George Bush, Baker finished second with only 37 percent of the vote despite having outspent Bush by a margin of $154,000 to $150,000. In New Hampshire a week and a half later, Baker finished third in the voting; he reported spending $269,000, more than the figure reported for Bush, who finished ahead of him, but less than that reported for winner Reagan. Baker's reported spending for the March 4 Massachusetts and Vermont primaries, the final two races he contested, was about $276,000 and $50,000, respectively, both figures far below the state limits. On March 5, four months after he declared his candidacy and after committing ninety days to full-time campaigning, Baker announced he was withdrawing from the race.

FEC reports through December 31, 1980, indicate net disbursements of $9.1 million for the Baker committee. When that figure is adjusted to take account of loan repayments and various refunds and rebates, the disbursement total amounts to $7.1 million. Information provided by the Baker committee permits the following breakdown of committee expenditures through mid-August 1980. Although the total disbursements reported by the committee at that time exceed the later FEC adjusted disbursement figure, the committee breakdown does indicate approximately how much the Baker campaign spent in major categories of activity:

Political activity (including primary and convention states)	$2,455,158.06
Candidate services (including travel, housing, and staff)	677,765.98
Nonexempt legal activity	3,376.66
Exempt legal activity	56,269.24
Accounting	1,060,912.67
Media production	281,542.62
Television time buys	669,152.73
Radio	160,068.26
Newspapers	58,484.55
Direct-mail fund raising	1,497,261.76
Other fund raising	685,072.13
Consulting fees	169,424.76
Total	$7,774,192.48

The category of political activity accounts for about $2.5 million of the campaign's total costs. Among other notable campaign expenditures are fund raising, $2.2 million; media advertising, $1.2 million; accounting, $1.1 million—a surprising 14 percent of the overall total—and candidate services, $677,766. According to the FEC final prenomination-campaign report, the Baker Committee had exempt fund-raising, legal, and accounting expenses of $3.7 million.

Baker ended his campaign more than $1 million in debt. About a third of that amount reportedly was owed to a Tennessee bank from which the candidate's campaign had received a loan, and about the same amount was owed to media consultants Bailey and Deardourff.[196] The campaign retired the debt through a direct-mail solicitation program and joint fund-raising ventures with other Republican candidates.

An FEC audit of the Baker Committee released on December 18, 1980, and covering the committee's financial activity through March 31, 1980, noted that the committee had responded to an audit staff recommendation following the earlier threshhold audit of the Baker Committee that the gross, rather than merely the net, pay of field personnel be allocated to the appropriate states.[197] No further action was recommended regarding this matter. The audit also determined that the committee's reported cash balance as of March 31, 1980, was overstated by $17,356 due to a number of reporting and accounting errors. The committee amended its report to correct the overstatement, and no further action was taken. Finally, the audit determined that as of August 25, 1980, the committee had net outstanding campaign obligations of $271,163. That amount took into account $50,000 the committee estimated it would receive from the Republican Presidential Unity Committee, a joint fund-raising committee established to help retire the prenomination-campaign debts of a number of Republican candidates. Based on that outstanding debt, the committee received matching funds of $114,516. In an addendum to the final audit report of the committee released on April 20, 1981, it was determined that the actual net proceeds from the joint fund-raising committee due to the Baker Committee totaled $252,821.[198] The committee's net outstanding campaign obligations were recalculated accordingly, and it was determined that the committee had received excess matching payments of $104,074. The committee refunded that amount, and no further action was recommended.

Other Candidates

Several other candidates entered the race for the Republican presidential nomination, but none achieved significant electoral results. On August 2, 1978, Rep. Philip Crane of Illinois became the first major candidate of either party to declare his candidacy for the presidential nomination.

Despite his early start, the six-term congressman never was a serious factor in the outcome of any of the primary elections or other important prenomination contests. On April 17, 1980, after eighteen months of campaigning, Crane withdrew from the race and threw his support to Ronald Reagan. According to FEC reports of financial activity through December 31, 1980, the Crane for President Committee had adjusted receipts of $5.2 million, including $3.5 million from individual contributions and $1.8 million in matching funds. Later the committee received an additional $150,000 in matching funds. FEC reports for activity through the same period indicate that the Crane committee had gross disbursements of $5.4 million and adjusted disbursements of $5.2 million. The FEC audit found that as of April 3, 1980, the committee's outstanding campaign obligations were $532,120, much owed to Richard Viguerie for early mailings.

Sen. Robert Dole of Kansas announced his candidacy on May 14, 1979. Despite groundwork laid through his activities with Campaign America and the name recognition he had established in 1976 as President Gerald Ford's running mate, Dole's campaign never caught on. On March 15 he announced his withdrawal from the Republican race. According to FEC reports for financial activity through December 31, 1980, the Dole for President Committee had adjusted receipts of $1.4 million, including $900,000 in individual contributions and $450,000 in matching funds. Net disbursements by the Dole committee amounted to $1.5 million and adjusted disbursements to $1.4 million. The FEC audit determined that as of March 27, 1980, the campaign's outstanding obligations were $60,391, and that by June 30, 1980, the campaign had received sufficient private contributions and matching funds to retire all of its debts.

Benjamin Fernandez, owner of a management-consulting firm in Southern California and party activist among Hispanic voters, ran an eighteen-month-long campaign for the Republican nomination before bowing out on June 3, 1980. According to FEC reports of financial activity through December 31, 1980, Fernandez raised about $250,000 to conduct his campaign, including more than $190,000 in private contributions and about $35,000 in loans. He ended his effort more than $148,000 in debt. He did not qualify for matching funds.

In 1980 Harold Stassen, former governor of Minnesota and cabinet-level officer in the Eisenhower administration, made his seventh unsuccessful bid for the presidential nomination. FEC reports indicate Stassen had adjusted receipts of about $110,000; only about $6,000 came from private contributions, whereas Stassen contributed more than $24,000 to his own campaign and lent his campaign an additional $74,500. Adjusted disbursements by the campaign amounted to about $120,000, and, as of December 31, 1980, the campaign reported indebtedness of about $44,000.

Second-term Sen. Lowell Weicker of Connecticut declared his candidacy for the Republican nomination on March 12, 1979. Only two months after he had declared, Weicker became the first announced candidate to withdraw from the race. He maintained that his decision was based on results of a poll that showed him running well behind former President Ford and Ronald Reagan, neither of whom had declared candidacy, and that indicated a decline in job-performance ratings as a senator and in levels of commitment by Republicans, Democrats, and independents. Weicker maintained that he had had no trouble raising campaign funds and gaining backers, but campaign aides reportedly said privately that funding was a problem.[199]

On September 25, 1979, Sen. Larry Pressler of South Dakota announced his candidacy for the Republican presidential nomination. His announcement came as something of a surprise given his relative youth—thirty-seven years—and the relatively short time he had served in national elective office: four years in the House of Representatives and only eight months in the Senate. Pressler's candidacy never aroused widespread enthusiasm or support. On January 8, 1980, after less than four months of campaigning, Pressler withdrew from the race citing the difficulty he had in raising money and the fact that he had just been excluded from the *Des Moines Register*-sponsored debate among Republican candidates held about two weeks prior to the state's caucuses.

Finally, for a substantial portion of the prenomination period, speculation that former President Gerald Ford would enter the Republican nomination race cropped up frequently in the media. The speculation was fueled in equal parts by Ford's own actions and by those of his supporters. For example, in mid-1978 Ford hired a political aide to help him coordinate his political campaign activities. Shortly afterward he converted his 1976 campaign committee into a multicandidate committee that would enable him to distribute the approximately $220,000 remaining in the fund[200] to other Republican candidates who might be helpful to him if he decided to enter the 1980 race. In addition, in September 1978 a small group of Republicans in New Hampshire formed a draft movement to put Ford's name on the state's Republican primary ballot. Later that year a nationwide Gallup Poll of rank-and-file Republicans gave Ford a six-point edge over Reagan. Throughout this period, Ford maintained that he had no plans to be a candidate for the nomination, but he did not eliminate the possibility.

Late in 1979 Ford appeared to be changing his mind and reportedly told political associates he might consider a race if he thought he had a reasonable chance of winning and would not have to take on a long and exhausting campaign.[201] Mixed signals by Ford regarding his intentions probably kept some Ford supporters from backing other moderate candidates and complicated an already crowded field. Early in March 1980 a group of Ford supporters, headed by former Secretary of the Air Force Thomas C. Reed and including former Ambassador Leonard Firestone and financier Max Fisher, announced they were forming a national Draft Ford Committee to encourage Ford to run. By that time front-runner Ronald Reagan had spent more than two-thirds of the national spending limit; some Ford partisans thought the former president would be able to raise sufficient funds to outspend Reagan in many of the remaining primaries, making it difficult for him to continue his string of election victories. After meeting with political advisers, however, Ford announced on March 15 that he would not be a candidate for the Republican nomination. Influential in his decision was the fact that he would not have been able to compete for more than 800 of the GOP's 1,994 convention delegates and that he had a reasonable chance to win support of only about 600 of those who remained, not enough to win a first-ballot victory at the convention. Also influential was the fact that public support by moderate Republican officeholders for a Ford candidacy never materialized.

Campaign Debt Reduction

With the exception of John Anderson, all of Ronald Reagan's major Republican rivals ended their prenomination campaigns in debt. According to one report, as of mid-May 1980, the Connally campaign's deficit was close to $1.5 million; the Baker campaign had a deficit of $890,582; the Crane campaign reported a deficit of $398,056; and the Dole campaign estimated its deficit at $113,000.[202] That same report quoted George Bush's campaign manager James Baker estimating the Bush campaign deficit at less than $200,000,[203] but a later report said the campaign deficit was about $300,000.[204] The Fernandez campaign concluded with a debt of about $148,000.[205]

When the primary campaign ended, most of those losing Republican candidates banded together with Ronald Reagan to help pay off the losers' campaign debts. Former candidates Baker, Connally, Dole, Crane, and Fernandez joined Reagan as hosts of a series of fund-raising events, one a reception sponsored by the 1980 United Republican Committee and held on June 16, and three others—a dinner, a reception, and a luncheon—sponsored by the 1980 Republican Presidential Unity Committee and held on June 13, 20, and 27, 1980. Both committees registered with the FEC on May 16, 1980, and both listed J. Stanley Huckaby as treasurer. Huckaby formerly had served as treasurer of the Baker committee. Although the Bush campaign did not seek a share in the proceeds of these fund-raising events, preferring instead to pay off its debt with funds raised through direct-mail solicitations, Bush supported the efforts and lent his name to some of the events.

The first of the events, a $500-a-plate dinner attended by 1,100 persons in Beverly Hills on June 13, brought in $550,000.[206] A substantial portion of the net proceeds from that dinner funded a thirty-minute television show drawn from the dinner, which was aired on CBS on June 21 and served as a fund-raising appeal whose proceeds were divided among the various candidates. According to one report, it cost between $150,000 and $180,000 to produce the television appeal, $123,000 to buy air time for it, and $65,000 to pay for advertisements encouraging viewers to watch it.[207] The formula for dividing the proceeds of the television appeal and the subsequent events held in New York, Chicago, and Houston, was 43 percent for both Connally and Baker, 4.5 percent each for Crane and Dole, 4 percent for Fernandez, and 1 percent for Reagan. In addition winning candidate Reagan benefited from the exposure he received, particularly on television, and from the endorsements of those whom he had defeated. Although joint fund-raising events, which are specifically provided for in the FECA, had often been held in the past, this series of events was unique in its efforts to promote a single candidate at very little cost to the candidate's campaign.

According to an FEC audit of financial activity through December 31, 1980, the 1980 Republican Presidential Unity Committee, which sponsored three of the events and the television appeal, reported receipts of $1,395,883, expenditures of $950,033, and cash on hand of $445,849.[208] An FEC audit of the 1980 United Republican Committee for the same period showed the committee had receipts of $132,751, expenditures of $129,848, and cash on hand of $2,903.[209]

FEC audits of some of the candidates involved in the joint fund-raising events provide information about how some of the proceeds were distributed. An audit of the Dole for President Committee through June 30, 1980, reported that the Dole campaign received $12,491 as its share of proceeds from the June 16, 1980, reception sponsored by the 1980 United Republican Committee.[210] The audit also reported that funds from the 1980 Republican Presidential Unity Committee were to be disbursed only to the extent necessary to satisfy the debts of participating candidates. Although the actual disbursement had not been made at the time of the Dole campaign audit, the audit staff reported that the unity committee's net proceeds as of June 30, 1980, were $264,028 and that Dole would require only $3,361, considerably less than the 4.5 percent of the proceeds he had agreed to, in order to satisfy his remaining debts.[211]

An audit of the Crane for President Committee through October 23, 1980, reported that the Crane campaign received $12,926 as its share of the proceeds from the June 16, 1980, reception sponsored by the 1980 United Republican Committee.[212] The audit also reported that as of September 30,

1980, the net proceeds of the 1980 Republican Presidential Unity Committee were $732,227 and that the Crane committee's agreed-upon 4.5 percent share came to $32,950.[213] Finally an addendum to the final FEC report on the Baker Committee released on April 20, 1981, reported that as of August 25, 1980, the net proceeds of the 1980 Republican Presidential Unity Committee's joint fund-raising efforts that were due to the Baker Committee amounted to $252,821.[214]

With the exception of John Connally, who had declined public funds, and Benjamin Fernandez, who failed to qualify for them, the candidates who participated in these joint fund-raising events were able to apply for federal matching grants for the qualifying contributions they received as their share of the proceeds from the joint efforts. The proceeds were distributed in such a way that no contributor to the joint efforts violated the FECA's $1,000 contribution limit per candidate and in a way that maximized the amount of funds available from federal matching grants.

Losing candidates also used a variety of other approaches to pay off their campaign debts. Like George Bush, Howard Baker turned to direct mail. Stephen Winchell & Associates, a Washington, D.C., direct-mail firm, conducted a debt-retirement campaign for Baker that included three house file mailings and two prospect mailings. One of the mailings, sent on behalf of the Presidential Unity Committee, went to 26,000 persons who had contributed $250 and up to the campaigns of Reagan, Connally, Baker, Crane, and/or Dole. It brought in $268,000 from 3,000 contributors at a cost of $26,000; Baker's share was based on the number of names his campaign had contributed to the mailing. Another mailing was sent out over President Ford's signature to 572,000 persons. Some 15,000 contributors responded with $264,000 in donations. In all Winchell & Associates raised $886,393 to retire Baker's debt, including proceeds from Baker's share of the Presidential Unity Committee mailing, at a cost of $300,800. In addition a sizable portion of the gross money raised qualified for matching public funds. By July 16, 1980, it was reported that Baker had paid off his campaign debt, which one campaign official said had once reached $1.3 million.[215]

John Connally retired a small portion of his substantial campaign debt by selling furniture, equipment, and office supplies from his campaign headquarters. For example, the National Republican Congressional Committee reportedly bought six typewriters from the Connally campaign for $600 apiece.[216]

Connally also contemplated a novel approach to debt reduction. His campaign arranged with a number of artists to exchange their work for payment of the artists' materials. The campaign would then sell the artwork donated and use the proceeds to reduce Connally's debt. The FEC previously had ruled that artists who give their works to political committees are making donations of their personal services rather than financial contributions. The commission also ruled, however, that the purchasers of artwork from political committees are bound by the election law's $1,000 individual contribution limit. In order to get around that ruling, the Connally committee wanted to sell the artwork through an art dealer without advertising the sale as a means of raising funds for Connally. In that way the committee hoped the sale would be considered a sale of assets, which, like disposal of left-over campaign materials, is not covered by the law's contribution limits. But the FEC ruled that because the money would be put to a political use, the purchases of the artwork would still be bound by the $1,000 contribution limit.[217] According to the commission, the full purchase price, rather than the profit to the committee, would constitute the amount of the purchaser's contribution, just as the full purchase price of a ticket to a fund-raising dinner is counted as a contribution by each individual ticket purchaser. Further, the Internal Revenue Service (IRS), in a private letter ruling, said a political committee would be subject to a 46 percent corporate tax rate on income from artwork sold through an art gallery. According to the IRS, the only political income exempt from taxation is that which comes from a political event and not from what can be considered ordinary trade or business.[218]

A June 1982 news report put Connally's outstanding debt at $1.6 million, including more than $500,000 the candidate had loaned to his own campaign.[219] In July 1982 it was reported that one of the Connally committee's creditors, an Arlington, Virginia, printing firm, filed suit against the former candidate, two of his aides, and the committee for about $29,000 in printing costs.[220] At that time one of the aides mentioned in the suit noted that the committee was making pro-rata payments to creditors and said it would be a "long time" before the debt was eliminated.[221]

The Democrats

In the 1976 presidential prenomination period, an incumbent president met with a strong challenge from a member of his own party. The unusual character of this phenomenon, however, was tempered by the the fact that the incumbent, Gerald Ford, had never been elected to the presidency but had assumed the office in 1974 after the resignation of Richard Nixon. Neither had Ford been elected to the vice-presidency from which he had moved up to the chief executive's office; rather he had been appointed by Nixon to complete the term of Spiro Agnew who had resigned under pressure in 1973. By the time the 1976 presidential campaigns were getting underway, Ford had been in office a relatively short period of time and did not enjoy the usual advantages of incumbency.

In the 1980 presidential prenomination campaign, an incumbent president once again met with a strong challenge from a member of his own party.

But this time the incumbent, Jimmy Carter, had been elected to the office and had occupied it for nearly three years by the time his major challenger, Massachusetts Sen. Edward Kennedy, formally announced his candidacy. Carter also was challenged by California Gov. Edmund G. Brown, Jr., whose last-minute campaign in 1976 had stirred considerable excitement among the electorate and brought Brown five primary victories. Lyndon LaRouche, U.S. Labor party founder, and Cliff Finch, former Mississippi governor, also ran as candidates for the Democratic nomination, but neither was a factor in the outcome of any of the prenomination contests.

Carter

Despite low standing in public-opinion polls throughout most of 1979, there never was any serious doubt that President Jimmy Carter would seek renomination, no matter who chose to run against him in the Democratic primary and caucus contests. And although campaign strategy called for Carter to remain a noncandidate as long as possible, relying on the tools at an incumbent's disposal to gain favor among opinion leaders and the electorate, there were indications that when the time came, the president would campaign actively and directly for the nomination. On November 6, prior to his formal announcement, he had even agreed to debate his Democratic opponents, with a first meeting scheduled to take place in Iowa early in January.

Events outside the control of the Carter administration intervened to alter whatever campaign strategies had been devised. On November 4, the U.S. embassy and its personnel in the Iranian capital of Tehran were seized. On December 27 Soviet troops invaded Afghanistan. These two international crises served to rally support around the incumbent. Carter's standing in the polls improved markedly, and on December 28 the president announced he was withdrawing from the scheduled debate and would not campaign outside the White House in order to give the crises his undivided attention.

Carter's decision to withdraw from direct campaigning became an issue throughout the prenomination contest, but it apparently did not hurt his chances for reelection. In the first major prenomination contest, the January 21 Iowa caucuses, Carter overwhelmed his rival by a 59 to 31 percent margin of the popular vote. He followed that with a convincing win in the influential New Hampshire primary on February 26. Kennedy rebounded, as expected, by winning his home-state primary in Massachusetts on March 4, but Carter took some of the gloss off that victory by crushing his opponent in Vermont's primary on the same day. The president then put together a string of victories in southern primaries, where he was expected to do well, followed by a win in Illinois, which some thought would knock Kennedy out of the race. The challenger, however, won both the New York and Connecticut primaries on March 25 and signaled his intention to stay in the race despite increasing odds against him.

The first two months of the primary season established a pattern for the remainder of the contest: Carter's victories were punctuated by enough Kennedy victories to keep the challenger in the race and to escalate the cost of the Democratic prenomination campaigns. Kennedy finished with a flourish, winning five of the eight primaries held on June 3, including two of the three largest states contested. But Carter won enough delegates on that final primary day to assure him of a first-ballot nomination at the Democratic convention. In all Carter won 51 percent of all Democratic votes cast to Kennedy's 38 percent; he won twenty-four of the thirty-four primaries he contested and twenty of the twenty-five state and territorial caucuses.

Despite Carter's seemingly insurmountable lead in delegates pledged to his candidacy, Kennedy continued to contest for the nomination, hoping to engineer a convention rules change that would allow delegates to vote for the candidate of their choice at the time of the convention. Although the challenger did succeed in influencing the content of the Democratic party platform, his last-ditch effort to wrest the nomination from the incumbent failed. After Kennedy's withdrawal on the first night of the party's convention, President Carter won renomination on the first ballot. His long and hard-fought campaign cost $18.5 million, the most expensive Democratic campaign and the second most expensive among all contestants in 1980.

Fund Raising: The Carter-Mondale Presidential Committee registered with the FEC on March 16, 1979. Evan Dobelle, a 1976 campaign aide who subsequently served as Democratic party treasurer, was tapped as campaign committee chairman and campaign coordinator, and John Dalton, who had been serving as president of the Government National Mortgage Association, became campaign treasurer. In August Dobelle was moved to the campaign's fund-raising arm and was replaced by Tim Kraft, who had been in charge of political affairs at the White House. And in December Dobelle was replaced as committee chairman by Robert Strauss, a long-time party activist who had served in a variety of positions in the Carter administration. Dalton was replaced as committee treasurer by S. Lee Kling, who served from mid-November 1979 through the FEC audit of the campaign.

The Carter committee's initial fund-raising strategy called for the campaign to raise all of the private funds it would need for the 1980 campaign by the end of 1979. The objective, said Dobelle, was to raise as much money as possible before the primaries and caucuses so the committee would not have "to spend [its] political time trying to raise funds in February or

March."[222] Although the goal was unrealistic, the committee got off to a good start. Within two weeks of registering with the FEC, the committee announced it had raised sufficient funds in the proper amounts to qualify for federal matching grants. Most of the $304,000 raised during those first two weeks came in response to personal appeals to contributors. Among early donors, oil- and gas-company executives gave at least $18,000, and nine executives of the Northwest Pipeline Co., operator of the Alaska oil pipeline, gave about $2,500.[223] In a short time, the Carter committee added fund-raising dinners, and these two methods—personal solicitation and fund-raising dinners—became the mainstays of the committee's money-raising efforts. For example, a $500-a-plate fund raiser on Sen. Kennedy's home ground in Boston on June 20 netted the campaign $75,000.[224]

By the end of June, the Carter committee reported receipts of $1,545,700 and expenditures of only $598,350.[225] The committee's receipts were second highest among all presidential-campaign committees reporting—exceeded only by the $2.2 million collected by John Connally's campaign—and its cash surplus of $947,350 was greater than that of any other committee. More than $65,000 of the committee's receipts came from PACs, including $5,000 each from PACs associated with Coca-Cola Co., the Trust Company of Georgia, and Grumman.[226] Among contributors of $1,000 to the Carter campaign by this time were Dwayne O. Andreas, chairman of a large grain company; Washington lawyer and Democratic party veteran Clark Clifford; elder statesman Averell Harriman; Israel Cohen, president of Giant Food; and John Cowles, Jr., chairman of the *Minneapolis Star and Tribune*.[227]

In the third quarter of 1979, Carter committee fund raising slowed considerably. The Carter presidency appeared to be in disarray. Carter's Camp David domestic summit in July, which led to the firing of three cabinet secretaries, did little to inspire confidence in his administration. Much of the Jewish community, usually a major source of financial support for Democratic presidential campaigns, was disturbed by aspects of the administration's Mideast policy. Many labor unions, generally cool toward Carter, were awaiting the results of the burgeoning draft-Kennedy movement. Direct-mail solicitations enjoyed only limited success. In fact, of the more than $13 million in private contributions the Carter campaign eventually raised, only about $800,000 was contributed in response to direct-mail appeals, at a cost of about 26 percent. According to one report, sales of tickets to a $1,000-a-plate June 25 Carter fund-raising dinner in Washington met with considerable resistance, and the dinner achieved a net profit of $174,214 "only after prodigious effort."[228] By the end of September 1979, the committee reported receipts of $2,422,720—only about $900,000 more than reported three months earlier—expenditures of $1,535,956, and a cash balance of $886,764.[229]

Carter fund raising picked up considerably during the final quarter of 1979, though not enough to allow the campaign to reach its original ambitious goal. According to campaign aides, Carter's victory in the mid-October Florida caucuses leading up to the state Democratic party's presidential straw vote gave the as-yet-unannounced candidate a fund-raising boost. Democratic contributors, said fund raiser Dobelle, were "looking for some kind of signal the President was viable as a candidate."[230] Florida, he said, was it. And Carter's December 4 announcement of candidacy and the fund-raising events surrounding it substantially increased the campaign treasury, even though Carter himself, maintaining he would forgo political activity until the American hostages held in Tehran were released, did not take part in the fund-raising tour originally planned to kick off his reelection campaign.

The most successful month for the fund-raising dinners the campaign was so dependent on was December 1979. A series of eleven such dinners, held during a four-day period from December 4 through December 7 in various localities such as Washington, New York, Chicago, and Atlanta and attended by Vice-President Walter Mondale, the candidate's wife Rosalynn, campaign chairman Strauss, or other committee and administration officials, brought in about $2.4 million. By mid-May 1980, ten more large fund-raising dinners held in other locations around the country would bring in an additional $1.6 million. According to reports filed with the FEC by the Carter committee, by December 31, 1979, the campaign had receipts of $5,751,581, almost $2 million more in receipts than the Kennedy campaign, whose fund raising began only during the final quarter of the year. Further the Carter campaign reported cash on hand of $911,000 and no indebtedness, whereas the Kennedy campaign reported cash on hand of $418,832 and debts of $905,973.

Throughout the 1980 primaries and caucuses, the Carter campaign maintained its financial advantage over the rival Kennedy campaign. Carter forces were more successful in raising funds, particularly from larger donors, and the Kennedy campaign suffered financially from extravagant spending early in the prenomination season. Since the President maintained his resolve to stay in the White House as long as the crises in Iran and Afghanistan were not concluded, the campaign depended heavily on Carter surrogates as the main attractions at fund-raising events. Rosalynn Carter, Vice-President Mondale, and campaign chairman Strauss were the candidate's chief stand-ins. Strauss was particularly productive, both because of his fund-raising skills and because he could travel rather inexpensively, without the large entourage that accompanied the first lady, the vice-president and, certainly, the president himself. One Midwest swing by Strauss in January reportedly netted the campaign $500,000 in contributions, and a February trip to California with Rosalynn Carter brought in an

additional $700,000.[231] A two-day swing by Strauss through Florida, in-
cluding eight fund-raising events in seven cities, reportedly brought in
$500,000.[232] Strauss himself was said to maintain he could produce $100,000
a day on fund-raising tours at an average expense of $6,000 to $7,000,
which went largely for the cost of his transportation in a small chartered
jet.[233] He also estimated that his efforts generated a substantial amount of
free television coverage for the campaign: $150,000 to $200,000 worth on
the Florida tour alone.[234] In addition the campaign drew some funds from
benefit concerts. Two concerts, one held in Atlanta and featuring country
music star Willie Nelson and the other held in Washington, D.C., and
featuring Waylon Jennings, brought in $130,000 and $100,000, respectively.

The campaign drew contributions from less high-powered events. For
example, the "Tupperware circuit," a round of 6,000 sessions of coffee,
doughnuts, and campaign promotion held in various localities around the
country generated funds from the grass roots. By late March, with only half
of the hostesses of such gatherings reporting, the parties had already brought
in more than $350,000.[235]

In January, bolstered by the president's rise in the polls as Americans
rallied around their leader and benefiting from Kennedy's stumbling per-
formances in broadcast interviews and on the campaign trail, the Carter
campaign took in almost $2.8 million, including $1.8 million in federal
matching funds. The total exceeded Kennedy campaign receipts for the
same period by more than $500,000. Carter's impressive victory over Ken-
nedy in the January 21 Iowa caucuses probably was reflected in the campaign's fund-raising results. For the month of February, the campaign reported private contributions of more than $2 million, more than twice the
Kennedy total. Although the monthly gap between the two campaigns narrowed somewhat over the next four months, the Carter campaign maintained
its fund-raising lead. It also spent more than the Kennedy campaign, which
posed a potential problem as the campaign progressed. By the beginning of
April, it was estimated that if the campaign continued to spend at the rate it
had established, by the end of May it would have only about $600,000 left
under the overall spending limit. This would leave relatively little money to
contest the eight primaries scheduled for June 3 and, if necessary, to wage a
nomination battle at the party's convention in mid-August.[236] By May 1,
however, the campaign had about $4.1 million in spending leeway,[237] with
Carter enjoying an imposing lead in the delegate count. Some members of
the campaign staff began to turn their attention to the general-election campaign, but there was considerable concern that Sen. Kennedy's insistence on
remaining in the race and the possibility he would carry his fight all the way
to the convention would drain the Carter campaign treasury and divert the
campaign staff's energies from preparing for the fall campaign. Further,

the resumption of presidential travel later in May would put added pressures on campaign funds. Right up to the end, the Carter campaign fundraising apparatus was forced to sustain its efforts, with all of the money it raised going to fund the president's protracted battle for the nomination.

During May, Carter swept all of the scheduled primaries except the one held in the District of Columbia. The delegates he picked up along the way brought him so close to the number he needed to win the nomination that it was not necessary for his campaign committee to invest large sums in an effort to seek victory in all of the contests scheduled for June 3. Instead the campaign concentrated its attention on the Ohio primary, which Carter won, along with primaries in West Virginia and Montana. Those victories gave Carter more than the 1,666 delegates he needed for the nomination. Nevertheless Kennedy carried on, forcing the Carter campaign to raise funds to finance a delegate-tracking system to keep delegates loyal to the president through the convention's first ballot. These efforts were successful but costly, both in money spent and in the time diverted from the fall campaign against Reagan and Anderson. When the Carter prenomination campaign finally came to a close, it reported a debt of about $600,000.

The Carter campaign reported adjusted receipts of $18.6 million through December 31, 1980. Contributions from individuals accounted for $12.9 million, matching funds for $5.1 million (additional matching funds would be added to match contributions to Carter's debt retirement program), and PAC contributions of $460,000. Of the $12.9 million in individual contributions, unitemized contributions accounted for only about $1.9 million, just under 15 percent of the total. Itemized contributions of $1 to $499 accounted for $2.3 million, about 17 percent of Carter's individual contribution total. Contributions of $500 to $749 also accounted for almost $2.3 million, and contributions of $750 and up accounted for about $6.5 million, more than 50 percent of the total. No other presidential campaign was as dependent on larger contributors as the Carter campaign.

Of the more than 11,000 contributors of $500 and up to the Carter campaign, those from Florida accounted for a little more than $1 million, about 11.7 percent of the total contributed in that category. New York contributors of $500 and up supplied the campaign with more than $970,000, about 11 percent of the total in that category of giving, and California donors in the same category supplied more than $910,000, about 10.3 percent of the total. Carter's home state of Georgia supplied an additional $506,000 in such contributions.

Those same states also were the leading sources overall in Carter campaign contributions from individuals. According to the Carter committee, as of September 26, 1980, Florida was the leading source of campaign funds; 5,486 contributions brought more than $1.3 million to the campaign.

California was next, with 6,426 contributions totaling $1.2 million, followed by New York with 4,546 contributions totaling $1.8 million, and Georgia, with 9,834 contributions totaling $1 million.

As of February 1982, the Carter campaign had received $5.1 million in federal matching funds. The campaign submitted 63,423 contributions for certification; about 93 percent of the submissions were certified. The average contribution submitted was $87, higher than that submitted by all other candidates' campaigns except that of Sen. Robert Dole.

The incumbent's campaign drew $460,651 in contributions from PACs, $175,000 more than given to Ronald Reagan, whose campaign had the second highest PAC contribution total. Still, Carter's PAC contributions represented only about 3.4 percent of his private contribution total and about 2.4 percent of his total adjusted receipts. Fifty percent of the PAC money given to the Carter campaign was contributed during 1979. The most contributed during any two-month period of 1980 was $87,250 given to the campaign during January and February of that year. The campaign received more than 56 percent of its PAC contributions from corporate PACs, more than 17 percent from labor PACs, and about 17 percent from trade, membership, and health PACs. Among PACs giving the maximum $5,000 contribution to the Carter campaign in addition to those already noted were PACs associated with the Houston law firm of Baker and Botts, the National Association of Home Builders, the Florida Power & Light Company, the Amalgamated Clothing Workers, the Communications Workers of America, and the United Steelworkers.

President Carter benefited from a little more than $18,000 in independent expenditures supporting his candidacy, but he also had a little more than $34,000 in such expenditures made against his candidacy, including more than $8,000 spent by NCPAC. More significant than independent expenditures for or against the Carter candidacy were communication costs incurred by organizations supporting or opposing Carter. Such costs are incurred by corporate, labor, or membership organizations to pay for partisan political communications with their stockholders, executive and administrative personnel or members, and their families. During the prenomination campaign, President Carter benefited from more than $165,000 spent on such communications favoring his candidacy and had almost $80,000 spent on such communications opposing his candidacy. Five of the eleven labor organizations reporting internal communications on behalf of Carter were education-related groups, including the NEA. Those groups spent more than $55,000 on pro-Carter internal communications. The Communications Workers of America reported the largest single amount for pro-Carter communication costs: $50,646. The American Federation of State, County and Local Employees accounted for the entire $79,860 reported as communication costs opposing Carter.

In addition to spending $45,454 on internal communications favoring Carter's candidacy, the NEA, grateful for the president's successful advocacy of the Department of Education, provided Carter with support in other important forms. For example, in Iowa the NEA's 31,000-member state chapter, aided by six professionals from the organization's national headquarters, put twenty-six of its staff members in the field full time and operated 6,700 telephones in an effort to turn out pro-Carter voters in the January 21 caucuses.[238] The NEA's political director, Ken Melley, estimated that the 1.8 million-member union spent approximately $500,000 in salaries and expenses for the forty to fifty staff members involved full time or part time in state primary and caucus contests in support of Carter,[239] and acknowledged that state chapters might have spent as much.[240] In addition hundreds of local teacher-volunteers reportedly spent after-school hours in pro-Carter organizational and get-out-the-vote activities.

Another group that provided useful support for Carter, though not on the scale of that provided by the NEA, were chiropractors grateful to the president for including a provision in his national-health-insurance proposal making chiropractors eligible for Medicare reimbursement without requiring that physicians first refer patients for chiropractic services. When the president's position became clear early in January 1980, chiropractic groups informed their members in Iowa where they claim to have influenced some 15,000 votes on behalf of Carter in the January 21 caucuses.[241] In New Hampshire chiropractors sent letters to many of their 40,000 patients around the state urging them to "thank Jimmy Carter by voting for his re-election as President of the United States."[242] In addition, in January 1980 the National Chiropractic Political Action Committee donated $1,000 to the Carter campaign—the group's first contribution to a presidential candidate.[243]

The Carter campaign used skillfully the political advantages that come with incumbency, despite early avowals by campaign aides that incumbency would not be a great advantage in the campaign. Early in April 1979, then coordinator Evan Dobelle said there would be no telephones, meetings, or memorandums in the White House relating to the campaign.[244] Nevertheless by the time the campaign concluded, it was clear the president had used the powers of his office to benefit his renomination effort. White House pressure and influence succeeded in encouraging state officials to arrange at least a portion of the primary and caucus schedule to favor the president. And several invitations to perform at the White House during Carter's term probably helped persuade singer Willie Nelson to conduct a benefit concert for the candidate.

During 1979, prior to his self-imposed confinement in the White House, the president reportedly visited twenty-four states, eighteen of which would hold presidential primaries in 1980.[245] Despite allegations by RNC chairman William Brock that some of Carter's trips were "overtly political,"[246] and a

complaint filed with the FEC by the IAM that the Carter reelection committee should be required to pay a fair percentage of travel costs when campaigning was involved, White House and Democratic party officials insisted
that the trips were nonpolitical and maintained that the DNC or local-party
organizations paid for that portion of any trip that may have been devoted
to such activities as party fund raising. None of the Carter trips was financed
by the re-election committee. A 1975 FEC advisory opinion ruled in effect
that a president's campaign does not begin until January 1 of an election
year and that travel prior to that time would be presumed to be presidential
rather than political.

Taxpayer-financed travel by President Carter late in the campaign also
became a campaign issue. On May 9 Carter spoke before the World Affairs
Council and held a town meeting in Philadelphia, his first appearances outside Washington in six months. Since the trip was billed by White House
aides as nonpolitical, the cost was borne by taxpayers and not by the
Carter campaign. Aides explained that both appearances had been scheduled
for early November 1979 but were postponed because of the Iranian crisis.
They also pointed out that the trip could have no impact on the delegate-
selection process in Pennsylvania, which had already been completed. But
Kennedy campaign officials maintained that the trip had been arranged to
influence the upcoming June 3 New Jersey primary, pointing out that parts
of New Jersey are in the Philadelphia media market. In fact, according to
one report, the president's visit received saturation coverage on Philadelphia television and radio stations, which blanket the southern half of New
Jersey.[247]

Further, the president had available a large number of well-known and
influential surrogate campaigners, and his reliance on them was undeniable
during his six-month White House isolation. The fund-raising efforts of the
candidate's wife, his vice-president, and his campaign chairman have been
noted; the cost of their travel and other expenses were paid for by the Carter
reelection campaign. Other surrogates made both official and political appearances on Carter's behalf; both presumably benefited the Carter
renomination effort, but only the costs of those efforts deemed political
were borne by the campaign. For example, prior to the Florida presidential-
preference caucuses, eleven administration officials reportedly traveled to
the state; travel for six of them was considered official and the cost was paid
for by taxpayers, who also paid a portion of the expenses of three of the
others.[248] In December 1979 Secretary of Agriculture Robert Bergland
hosted hearings on the issue of preserving the family farm in nine states, six
of which were scheduled for presidential primaries early in 1980.[249] In
January 1980, thirty members of the White House staff used vacation time
or unpaid leaves to bolster the efforts of thirty-five paid campaign aides
working for Carter in Iowa.[250] Some Carter surrogates made no attempt to

conceal the political ramifications of their activities. Secretary of Transportation Neil Goldschmidt acknowledged he was part of the "political arm" of the cabinet,[251] and even threatened to retaliate against Mayor Jane Byrne of Chicago for having endorsed Sen. Kennedy by denying $135 million in discretionary funds to her city.[252] Secretary of Housing and Urban Development Moon Landrieu encouraged every cabinet member "to become more politically sensitive."[253] Other high officials in positions long thought beyond the scope of partisan political practices allowed themselves to be used to further Carter's renomination campaign. Thus Deputy Secretary of State Warren Christopher and CIA Director Stansfield Turner appeared in discussions with President Carter in television advertisements designed to help Carter exploit national-security issues.

Carter also demonstrated that he knew how to exercise the command of the media at a president's disposal. On the day before the Iowa caucuses, he appeared on NBC's "Meet the Press," having accepted a long-standing invitation from the program's producers despite having withdrawn from a scheduled television debate with his Democratic caucus opponents less than a month earlier. Four days before the New Hampshire primary, he called a prime-time news conference, and he repeated the strategy four days before the Illinois primary. And at 7:20 A.M. on the day of the Wisconsin primary, he held a widely reported press conference in the Oval office in which he declared that the latest move in Iran regarding the fate of the hostages was "a positive step." The president also used his position to influence the flow of news coming out of the White House, often by holding background-information sessions for members of the press with a tacit agreement that in return for information the reporters would not reveal the source of their stories. This allowed the president to make his stance on issues known to selected newspersons and usually to gain favorable publicity.[254]

Carter adroitly used discretionary funds at his disposal to plant seeds of support for his renomination or to nurture support where it had already taken root. In the week before the Florida presidential-preference caucuses, for example, the administration announced a number of federally funded projects, including two in Miami, a new Job Corps center and a tourism project in the Cuban community.[255] On January 10, 1980, the Department of Housing and Urban Development announced urban development action grants to cities in several states with upcoming primaries: $5.5 million to two cities in Massachusetts, $2.8 million to three cities in Alabama, $17 million to two cities in Illinois, and $13.5 million to three cities in New York.[256] Shortly before the New Hampshire primary, Mrs. Carter toured the American Skate factory in Berlin, New Hampshire, and announced a Commerce Department loan guarantee of $1.5 million to the company.[257] Sen. Kennedy had toured the same factory the previous day but had no such largesse to dispense.

Finally, the president cultivated support by inviting influential citizens to the White House for briefings. Many of those took place during the president's period of White House confinement. For example, more than 150 New Yorkers were briefed two weeks before the New York primary.[258] Groups of Floridians were briefed during the month prior to the presidential-preference caucuses, and New Englanders received similar treatment shortly before primaries in New Hampshire, Maine, and Massachusetts.[259] And although confined to the White House, the president managed to stay in touch with a number of potential voters through use of the telephone. Before the Iowa caucuses, for example, he reportedly made more than three hundred calls to Iowa residents and gained useful publicity in the process.[260]

Costs: During the first three quarters of 1979, the Carter committee's reported expenditures were relatively low. As the incumbent, Carter did not have to spend heavily in order to increase his name recognition. Late in August, however, the committee realized that it would have to increase its fund-raising efforts sharply and hold spending to a minimum if it was going to enter the election year on competitive financial grounds. Although Sen. Kennedy continued to decline announcing his candidacy, the growing draft-Kennedy movement and Kennedy's own less-than-Shermanesque declarations that he had no intention of seeking the nomination suggested that the Carter committee should prepare to wage a costly prenomination campaign.

One exception was made to the committee's decision to hold the line on spending. Carter strategists agreed to invest heavily to win the Florida caucuses in October and the presidential straw vote a month later. Although the outcome of the vote would have no direct bearing on the state's primary election on March 11, the strategists determined that Carter could not afford a defeat at the hands of draft-Kennedy forces in the state. The committee budgeted nearly $300,000 for its effort to prevent what could have been a damaging preprimary loss.[261] White House aides and Carter family members were dispatched to the state to bolster the efforts of twenty-five full-time campaign staff members.[262] Influential Floridians were invited to the White House for briefings. These efforts paid off in Carter victories both in the caucuses and the straw votes. Because Kennedy's cause was advanced by a draft committee without the official backing of the Massachusetts senator, however, it did not serve as an accurate gauge of the relative strength of the two men. A true test of strength, Kennedy noted, would be the Iowa caucuses.

The campaign also planned to make a significant expenditure for half an hour of national network television time early in December for the president's announcement of candidacy for renomination. When the campaign attempted in mid-October to purchase the time, however, the networks rejected the request, as they had rejected similar requests by the campaigns of John Connally and Ronald Reagan. One network's vice-president for legal affairs explained that the decision was based largely on the network's "sense of whether the public [was] ready for political campaigning."[263]

On October 29 the Carter committee filed a complaint with the FCC. The refusal by the networks to sell the time requested, said the complaint, effectively denied Carter "reasonable access" to the public "via our only national, commercial television network system."[264] In response the networks defended their decisions, maintaining it was too soon to begin selling such time to presidential candidates and that sales of such time to all of the presidential candidates represented a potential disruption of network programming schedules. In a November 20 ruling, the FCC sided with the Carter committee. By a vote of four to three, commission members ruled the networks had violated the reasonable-access provisions of the Communications Act of 1934 and told the networks to advise them within four days regarding how they would comply with the law.

All three networks asked the FCC to reconsider its findings, but the commission turned back the appeals. The networks then filed papers in federal court seeking a review of the FCC order and a stay until the issue was resolved. On November 29 a temporary stay was granted. Although the Carter committee maintained its interest in the proceedings, the continuing crisis in Iran caused it to deemphasize the president's formal declaration of candidacy; the committee purchased five minutes of prime time from CBS to broadcast the announcement on December 4. In mid-December the committee purchased thirty minutes of prime time from ABC for a January 6 broadcast beginning at 7 P.M. EST. At that time, the committee aired the half-hour program on the president's administration that had been planned for broadcast a month earlier. The cost of producing the program was reported to be $200,000;[265] air time reportedly cost an additional $130,000.[266]

Despite its purchase of the time, the Carter committee filed a brief supporting the FCC in the suit brought by the networks, as did a number of other parties, including the National Citizens Committee for Broadcasting and Americans for Democratic Action. In mid-March 1980, in the midst of the primary campaign, the federal court upheld the FCC. The court ruled unanimously that federal candidates have an "affirmative right" of access to air time. After the court rejected a subsequent request by the networks for a rehearing of the case, the networks appealed to the U.S. Supreme Court where they argued that the FCC requirement violated their First Amendment rights by interfering with their editorial discretion regarding what goes on the air. In a decision handed down in July 1981, however, the

Court held in favor of the FCC, ruling that the First Amendment rights of candidates to present their views and of voters to obtain information outweigh the constitutional rights of broadcasters.

By December 31, 1979, according to reports filed with the FEC, the Carter committee had spent $4.8 million, about $2.9 million of it subject to the overall spending limitation. The unamended quarterly reports filed by the committee throughout 1979 indicate that staff salaries, consulting fees, and travel other than airline travel were among the committee's major expenditure categories. Throughout the election year, the president, confined by his own choice to the White House, depended heavily on surrogate campaigners and on media advertising, especially television advertising, as well as news coverage of his press conferences and other White House activities, to deliver his message to voters. As in 1976, in 1980 Gerald Rafshoon took charge of Carter's media advertising. Carter's pollster, Patrick Caddell, had concluded that the president's personal traits were his greatest strength, whereas Kennedy's personal characteristics were his greatest weakness. Rafshoon's advertisements sought to build on those conclusions, initially by emphasizing such distinctions between the two candidates without mentioning Kennedy by name. Later in the campaign he produced advertisements that openly questioned Kennedy's character.

In Iowa, television advertisements, many of which were drawn from the documentary on the president that finally was aired on January 6, portrayed Carter not only as a man ready and willing to make difficult decisions but also as a warm human being and a devoted father. One estimate of the cost of the advertisements was $50,000 to $60,000.[267] When the caucus votes were tallied, the results indicated that Carter, benefiting from an outpouring of support in a time of crisis and from questions raised about his opponent's character, had come out ahead by a 59 to 31 percent margin of the votes cast. Carter's results were particularly impressive in view of the curb his administration had recently imposed on grain sales to the Soviet Union in reprisal for its invasion of Afghanistan, a move unpopular with Iowa farmers.

The incumbent continued his winning ways in New Hampshire's bellwether primary on February 26. In New Hampshire the Carter campaign's television advertisements continued to portray him as a decisive leader and a family man. The campaign's radio advertisements, however, were pointed in their criticism of Sen. Kennedy, portraying him as a big spender and an ineffective leader. The Carter committee originally allocated $283,686 to New Hampshire in its reports to the FEC, but here the FEC audit determined that the committee had exceeded the spending limit, this time by more than $24,000. Carter's margin over Kennedy in New Hampshire was about 47 to 37 percent, with Gov. Brown picking up close to 10 percent of the vote.

As expected, Carter was soundly defeated by Kennedy a week later in the senator's home state of Massachusetts, where the reported spending by both candidates was about the same; but in Vermont, where a nonbinding primary was held on the same day, Carter defeated his opponent by an even greater margin. According to information filed with the FEC by the two candidates' campaigns, Carter outspent Kennedy in Vermont by a margin of more than two to one.

Although the Carter campaign always appeared to be in better financial shape than the Kennedy campaign, it did experience a variety of difficulties. Early in March, campaign directors encouraged employees to go off the payroll and work for the campaign on a freelance basis so the campaign would not have to pay taxes. Despite such difficulties, Carter strengthened his lead in March by sweeping three southern primaries on March 11, including the primary in his home state of Georgia by a popular-vote margin of ten to one, and by winning a narrow victory over his opponent in Puerto Rico's March 17 primary. On the following day he delivered a crushing blow to Kennedy's chances by defeating him in Illinois, the first significant showdown in a large industrial state, by a 65 to 30 percent margin of the popular vote, winning 163 delegates to Kennedy's 16. In Illinois Carter outspent his rival by a margin of five to one. With an impressive string of victories behind him, Carter hoped to knock his opponent out of the race by defeating him in New York's March 25 primary. Public-opinion polls showed him well ahead of his rival, but his campaign staff took no chances and poured almost $1.2 million into the New York campaign, more than double the total for the financially strapped Kennedy campaign. According to one preelection estimate, the campaign would spend $750,000 on broadcast advertising during the three weeks preceding the primary.[268] Despite the polls and despite the prodigious spending, Kennedy came out on top by a 59 to 41 percent margin of the popular vote. Kennedy also won in Connecticut's primary the same day by a margin of about 47 to 42 percent. The New York results were partially due to a negative reaction by Jewish voters to an embarrassing turnabout by the Carter administration on a United Nations vote regarding Israeli settlements in occupied West Bank territory in the Middle East. The vote also manifested a general anti-Carter feeling that apparently had little to do with Kennedy.

New York and Connecticut made clear that Kennedy was going to stay in the race, and that made Wisconsin's April 1 primary all the more important. Caddell's polls showed Carter in the lead but indicated his handling of the hostage crisis in Iran posed a problem among some potential voters. The campaign had placed twenty-three paid staff members in the state months earlier and supplemented their efforts with those of White House volunteers. In all, the campaign reported spending $214,816 in the state, more than four times the amount reported by the Kennedy campaign. As if to leave nothing to chance, the president called an early-morning press conference on the day of the primary to announce what he called a "positive step" in resolving the hostage crisis. His optimism proved unfounded, but he won in Wisconsin by almost 26 percentage points and in the Kansas primary on the same day by a similar margin.

Still Kennedy continued his campaign, and Carter's advisers looked ahead to the next major primary contest, to be held in Pennsylvania on April 22. Caddell's polls indicated that result in Pennsylvania might be similar to those in New York: Voters might express their anti-Carter feelings by voting for his opponent. Complicating the issue was the fact that the Carter campaign was approaching the overall spending limit, with a large number of important primaries yet to be held. Campaign manager Tim Kraft argued against increasing expenditures in Pennsylvania in order to ensure that there would be sufficient funds for the months ahead.[269] But media adviser Rafshoon insisted the anti-Carter sentiment could be overcome if sufficient funds were spent on a new media plan designed to turn the protest vote around. Rafshoon won the argument and set about to film new commercials showing individual citizens questioning Kennedy's personal character. The commercials were aired during the final week of the primary campaign and according to campaign aides were instrumental in holding Kennedy to a narrow victory and in assuring Carter half of the state's 185 delegates. FEC reports indicate Carter outspent Kennedy in Pennsylvania by a margin of more than three to one. About $400,000 of the Carter campaign's budget of more than $700,000 reportedly was devoted to media advertising.[270] Carter's victory on the same day in the Missouri caucus, where he won sixty delegates to Kennedy's ten, also served to neutralize his opponent's showing in Pennsylvania.

After a narrow loss to Kennedy in Michigan's caucuses at the end of April, May was Carter's month. He won every primary on the schedule except the one held in the District of Columbia, even though the campaign was forced to hold down spending in states such as Maryland in order to conserve funds for big-state primaries on June 3. His victories put him close to the delegate total he would need to assure him of a first-ballot win at the Democratic convention. They also allowed his financially strapped campaign to focus its energies and spending on Ohio to nail down the renomination rather than diffuse its time and money over the eight primaries scheduled for June 3. Carter campaigned personally in Ohio, his first avowedly political activity outside Washington in six months. The strategy worked. Although the challenger won five of the eight primaries, Carter won three and gained enough delegates in all eight races to give him more than he needed for renomination.

Nevertheless Kennedy vowed to continue his fight for the nomination, claiming that much of Carter's delegate support was soft and subject to being won over. The challenger's determination not to concede forced the Carter campaign to assemble a delegate-tracking operation: twenty to thirty campaign workers and fifty volunteers who would stay in touch with Carter delegates until the convention.[271] This effort, along with those to quell open-convention movements building up around other alternative candidates, required additional expenditures by the Carter committee and diverted it from preparing for the general-election campaign against Reagan and Anderson. In May, when it became clear that Kennedy would not bow out of the race, one Carter aide observed that if the campaign lost the next two months of lead time in campaign organization for the general election, "we could lose the whole thing."[272]

The FEC final report for Carter committee financial activity through December 31, 1980, indicates the committee had net disbursements of $18.5 million. Information provided by the Carter-Mondale Presidential Committee allows the committee's expenditures as of November 15, 1980, to be broken down by cost centers. Expenditures for each cost center listed include fund raising and compliance costs. Although the total expenditure figure does not correspond exactly with the later adjusted disbursement figure reported to the FEC, it is sufficiently close that the breakdown may be accepted as an accurate indication of how the campaign spent its funds:

Chairman	$ 321,524
Field	690,708
Administration	1,833,714
Treasurer	189,383
Finance	1,041,488
Contribution refunds	71,530
Legal	177,112
Fund raising	2,355,085
Scheduling and advance	1,318,883
Press	114,578
Media	3,883,811
Computer services	190,093
Labor	145,317
Campaign manager	502,864
Research	50,580
VIP	820,784
Polling	645,790
Convention	445,044
States and regions	3,984,494
Total	$18,782,782

According to the breakdown, the Carter-Mondale campaign spent more than $3.8 million on media advertising, $645,790 on polling, and $445,044 on convention expenses. The committee allocated $2,355,085 to the fund-raising cost center but indicated that figure includes $86,981 in operating expenditures and $53,751 in compliance costs. Thus the actual fund-raising costs incurred by this cost center amount to $2,214,353. The figures allocated to most of the other cost centers, as well as most of the states and regions, however, include additional fund-raising costs totaling $121,983. Further, the Carter committee allocated $648,237 of the campaign's overhead to fund raising. Total fund-raising costs of the campaign according to information provided were $2,984,573. The figures allocated to most of the headquarters cost centers and the states and regions include compliance costs; these totaled $1,502,361. The committee allocated $405,148 of the campaign's overhead to compliance, bringing total compliance costs to $1,907,509. Finally, according to the FEC final prenomination-campaign report for financial activity through December 31, 1980, the Carter committee had cash on hand of $31,727 but debts totaling $661,647.

An FEC audit of the Carter-Mondale Presidential Committee released on January 21, 1981, covering committee financial activity through August 31, 1980, as well as some additional activity through September 30, 1980, initially determined that the committee had exceeded the spending limits in three states: in Iowa by $53,477, in Maine by $35,781, and in New Hampshire by $34,177.[273] Among areas in which the audit staff found that improper allocations had been made by the committee were media expenses, travel-expense reimbursements, miscellaneous-vendor payments, interstate travel connected with the use of Air Force Two by Vice-President Mondale and Mrs. Carter, and long-distance telephone calls from the states in question to locations outside those states. The audit staff also found the committee had outstanding debts in each of the states that had not been reported. The auditors rejected the committee's argument that a portion of the excessive spending should be excused because the committee had made a good-faith effort to determine each state's spending limit prior to FEC publication of such limits and that by following its own determination early in the campaign, it had been led to spend more than was ultimately permitted. The audit staff recommended that $123,435—the total of excess expenditures in the three states—be repaid to the U.S. Treasury.

The committee rejected some of the auditors' conclusions, including the determination that the worth of long-distance calls made to the committee's national headquarters from the states in question should count against state limits. In June 1981 the FEC reconsidered its decision on this matter, and on August 14, 1981, the committee submitted documentation to the FEC regarding $23,944 worth of such calls. The auditors subsequently recommended that the amount of excess state expenditures originally determined be reduced by $23,944, as well as by smaller adjustments made for miscellaneous expenses, to $98,292 and recommended that amount be repaid to the U.S. Treasury.[274]

The audit staff determined that the committee had received three contributions in excess of the legal limit from registered committees that were not qualified as multicandidate committees and recommended that the excess portions of the contributions totaling $5,000 be refunded. The auditors found that the committee had failed to itemize properly a number of earmarked contributions, of transfers from other committees, and of expenditures. In each case the committee amended its reports, and no further action was recommended.

Finally the audit staff determined that as of September 28, 1980, the committee's net outstanding campaign obligations were $756,589 and that no matching-fund payments in excess of the candidate's entitlement had been made. But the auditors also found that the committee had spent $5,947 for general-election campaign-related expenses prior to Carter's nomination and $21,183 in such expenses between the time of his nomination and September 28. The audit staff recommended that the latter figure be deducted from the candidate's remaining matching-fund entitlement and that $5,947 be repaid to the Treasury. Similarly the audit staff found that the committee had paid $60 in parking tickets prior to Carter's nomination and $195 after the nomination. It determined both were nonqualified campaign expenses and recommended the $195 be deducted from the candidate's remaining entitlement and the $60 be repaid to the Treasury.

In an audit-related matter, the Carter-Mondale committee wanted to establish a special fund to pay the costs of litigation and postelection compliance with the campaign law. An FEC ruling, however, made clear that any money collected for compliance matters would be subject to the law's reporting and contribution limit provisions.[275] Under the ruling the Carter committee could establish a separate legal fund to pay for private litigation costs, and the fund would be free from FECA restrictions, but any funds collected or disbursed in the process of complying with FEC enforcement actions or audits would be subject to the law.

In another audit-related matter, the FEC determined that the committee had received $5,000 from the Prince George's County Medical Political Action Committee, which was not registered with the commission. Although the Carter committee returned the money, it was fined $250. The PAC, which subsequently registered with the FEC, was fined $2,000.

In July 1982 the Carter-Mondale Presidential Committee asked an appeals court to review FEC audit findings. The petition for review alleged that the commission had failed to give the committee a hearing during the audit process, had unjustifiably refused to accept the committee's good-faith effort to stay within what it estimated the state expenditure limits would be, and had not reduced the committee's repayment obligation even though campaign debts in the states in which the auditors found excess spending had been reduced. The committee also maintained that the FEC should be required to compute the committee's repayment only on the basis of public funds held by the committee and not on the basis of private and public funds combined.

Kennedy

On November 7, 1979, after months of speculation that he would enter the Democratic race, Edward M. Kennedy, three-term senator from Massachusetts, formally announced his candidacy. In each presidential election year since the assassination of his brother Robert in 1968, Kennedy had been mentioned prominently as a Democratic contender. Although questions repeatedly had been raised regarding Kennedy's responsibility in a 1969 automobile accident at Chappaquiddick Island off the Massachusetts coast, which resulted in the death of Mary Jo Kopechne, a former campaign aide to Sen. Robert Kennedy, his role in that incident did not dim enthusiasm in some quarters for Kennedy's candidacy. At the Democrats' midterm conference in Memphis in December 1978, Kennedy had fanned the fires of enthusiasm with a stirring speech in which he declared that sometimes the party must sail against the winds. As the next presidential election approached, the Massachusetts senator gradually increased the distance between himself and the Democratic incumbent.

Several developments suggested that 1980 might be Kennedy's year. President Carter's popularity had plunged dramatically, and public-opinion polls through much of 1979 gave Kennedy a commanding lead over the incumbent. Draft-Kennedy movements, which sprang up around the country, suggested the senator enjoyed significant grass-roots support. And ten years had passed since the tragedy of Chappaquiddick—enough time, some thought, for the event to be buried sufficiently deep in the public consciousness that it would pose no serious obstacle to a Kennedy campaign for the nomination.

Kennedy's campaign started late, and although it enjoyed remarkable fund-raising success initially, it quickly found itself in financial difficulty. The campaign spent heavily, even extravagantly, at the very beginning and made little effort to budget carefully for the long months ahead. More important, the seizure of American embassy personnel in Iran early in November and the subsequent Soviet invasion of Afghanistan rallied public opinion around the incumbent president and prevented Kennedy from getting the public hearing he sought for the domestic economic proposals upon which he built his campaign.

Kennedy's initial hope of knocking Carter out of the race evaporated early with the president's overwhelming victory in Iowa's January 21 caucuses and his convincing win in New Hampshire's February 26 primary. Beset with serious financial problems and shaken by defeats at the polls, it was Kennedy's turn to consider withdrawing from the race. Instead he settled in for what would be one of the most grueling prenomination campaigns in recent history, stretching out over thirty-four primaries and twenty-five state and territorial caucuses and on into the Democratic convention itself. Along the way Kennedy won enough victories—for example in primaries in Massachusetts, New York, Pennsylvania, and California—to persuade him to stay in the race.

When the primary season ended, Kennedy had won only ten of the thirty-four Democratic primaries and five of twenty-five caucuses; his opponent had gained considerably more than the number of delegates he needed to win the party convention's nomination. Nevertheless, Kennedy, hoping the president's delegates would grow disillusioned with him, or at least that he would have an opportunity to shape the Democratic party's platform, pressed on with his campaign. He finally withdrew from the race on the first night of the convention only when it became apparent he would have no opportunity to shake Carter's delegates loose. His unsuccessful effort cost $12.3 million.

Fund Raising: The Kennedy for President Committee registered with the FEC on October 29, 1979, the latest registration date for the campaign committee of any other major candidate for the 1980 nomination. Kennedy's late start in both fund raising and grass-roots organizing hurt the campaign during the primary season, but initially there were few outward indications the campaign would have difficulty raising the funds it needed. Within four days of having registered with the FEC, the Kennedy committee announced it had raised $225,000, more than enough to qualify for federal matching funds.[276] A series of cocktail parties and dinners held around the country immediately after Kennedy's announcement and featuring the candidate added to the campaign treasury. Two trips he made to California in December helped bring the campaign $500,000.[277] The campaign enjoyed its most successful week for fund raising from December 10 to 17, when $1.9 million was raised through a series of fund-raising events. Morris Dees, considered one of the most expert direct-mail fund raisers in politics, had joined the campaign late in October, boding well for the campaign's finances. But heavy initial spending prevented the campaign from building up any cash reserves, and a public response of support for the president for his actions in the hostage crisis in Iran robbed Kennedy of the popular advantage he had held over his opponent. According to a mid-October Gallup Poll, Kennedy led Carter by a two-to-one margin among Democrats; by early December Carter had taken a 48 to 40 percent lead.[278]

As the public rallied around Carter in the face of a foreign crisis, Kennedy had increasing difficulty in raising the funds he needed for his campaign. Further, his own early performance on the campaign trail did little to aid the efforts of his staff to raise money. A CBS News interview with the candidate aired on national television a few days before his announcement damaged Kennedy's chances. Appearing hesitant and inarticulate, he offered no clear reason for seeking the presidency and no compelling explanation of his behavior in the Chappaquiddick tragedy. In early campaign appearances, he often offered vague and sometimes stumbling responses to questions. In time he polished his campaign style, but the specter of Chappaquiddick haunted him throughout the campaign, and he rarely was able to divert public and press attention from Iran, and later Afghanistan, to the domestic economic issues he raised in his campaign appearances.

By December 31, 1979, the Kennedy committee reported receipts of $3,893,272 and expenditures of $3,474,439. It also reported indebtedness of $905,973 stemming from a loan the committee had received from the Chemical Bank of New York. On November 15 the bank had agreed to lend the committee up to $1 million at an interest rate of half a point above the prime rate for commercial loans of ninety-day securities.[279] As collateral the committee provided the matching funds that would be due the candidate after January 1 and certified to the bank that it had already received more than enough matchable contributions to qualify for federal funding. The committee also was required to take out an insurance policy on Kennedy's life and health in excess of $1 million and to name the bank as the beneficiary.

For January 1980 the committee reported receipts of $2.2 million, including private contributions and public matching funds. That total was about $500,000 less than Carter campaign receipts for the same period, and Kennedy campaign expenditures for January were reported to be about $2.3 million, about $500,000 greater than the corresponding figure for his opponent's campaign. At the end of the month Kennedy was in debt about $658,000, and his poor showing in Iowa, where he lost the January 21 caucuses by a 59 to 31 percent margin, made it even more difficult to close the financial gap between him and his opponent.

The campaign's difficult financial position caused it to redouble its fund-raising efforts, as well as to cut costs and to seek to counteract some of the advantages enjoyed by the incumbent. Thus on the day of the Iowa caucuses, the campaign's costly chartered jet was grounded. In addition Kennedy supporters filed a sweeping lawsuit accusing the president of using government money and abusing government power to further his campaign. The suit, which alleged Carter had used government employees, including cabinet members and White House aides, to campaign for him at government expense and had used the promise of government jobs and grants to compel support for his candidacy, was unsuccessful. So was an attempt by the Kennedy campaign to seek a ruling from the FCC granting the candidate equal time to respond to "distorted and inaccurate statements" it alleged Carter had made about Kennedy in a nationally televised news conference on February 13.[280]

In New Hampshire's February 26 primary, Carter defeated Kennedy by a 47 to 37 percent margin of the vote; Kennedy had to wait until the March 4 primary in his own state of Massachusetts for his first primary-campaign victory. But even as he was winning at home, he was suffering a loss in the neighboring state of Vermont. Kennedy lost four more—in Alabama, Florida, and Georgia, where he expected the President to do well, and in Illinois, where he thought he would do well—before he won again, in New York and Connecticut on March 25. The string of early campaign losses, interrupted only by his home-state victory, forced the campaign to reduce the salaries of several staff members and to release others in order to put more money into a media advertising campaign.[281] These economy measures led some staff members, including finance chairman Martin Katz, to resign for personal financial reasons and others to scale back their involvement in the campaign.[282] The campaign also was forced to obtain a $100,000 loan from the Chemical Bank of New York, using as collateral a portrait of Kennedy painted by Andy Warhol.[283] An additional loan of $240,000 was obtained from the District of Columbia National Bank.[284] Collateral for that loan was a limited edition of three hundred Jamie Wyeth lithographs of Kennedy appraised at $800 each.[285]

The campaign began to use artwork in additional ways to raise funds. At first, individual artists donated their works to the campaign to be used as door prizes to attract people to Kennedy fund-raisers. At one such event one hundred supporters contributed $500 each at a reception held at Kennedy's home. The door prize, an original watercolor by Andrew Wyeth appraised at more than $30,000, was won by three persons who put up $170 each and thus received an enormous return on their investment.[286] Wyeth's efforts brought in $50,000 or more at fund-raising events where his works were used as door prizes.[287] According to federal law, the only part of Wyeth's contributions that counted toward the individual contribution limit was the cost of materials the artist used to create his works. Under the law the artist's time and effort is considered volunteer activity that is not counted as a contribution.

This artistic fund-raising effort was so successful it was subsequently refined and made more systematic. Through contacts cultivated by Miles Rubin, a wealthy Kennedy backer, a number of prominent artists, including Warhol and Wyeth, Robert Rauschenberg, Leon Polk Smith, and Jack Youngerman, were invited to contribute original works to the campaign. Most of the artists were recruited by Artists' Rights Today, a New York lobby for artists' interests in such areas as tax law. Many of the artists approached were drawn to Kennedy because of his outspoken liberal views and because he had advocated federal tax assistance for artists. The original works contributed were printed by a silk-screen process or by lithography in editions of forty-five to three hundred. The prints were then appraised and offered to the public for a suggested contribution determined by the appraised values, which ranged from $225 to $1,500. In an illustrated brochure published by the campaign explaining the "Artists for Kennedy" program, potential contributors were reminded of the $1,000 individual contribution limit. When a contributor made a donation for the appraised value of a print held by a bank as part of the collateral for a loan, the contributor's name and address were sent along with the contribution to the bank. The bank then instructed the gallery holding the print to mail it to the contributor, and the proceeds were used to defray the loan. If the prints were held by the campaign committee and no bank loan was involved, the committee had the print mailed to the contributor and used the proceeds for campaign funding.

Contributors who participated in the program helped the Kennedy campaign with their donations and in return received a work of art that probably was worth more than their contributions and that certainly would appreciate in value with the passage of time. According to one campaign official, by January 1981, various uses of donated artwork had brought in about $250,000 to $300,000, and sale of the works through art galleries continued to generate funds.

Kennedy's financial difficulties early in the primary season when he was losing at the polls caused the campaign to alter its fund-raising approach in other ways. From March on, the campaign, which had drawn a sizable portion of its initial funds from large donors and high-priced fund-raising events, was forced to raise funds from the grass roots. Overall the campaign held more than 195 fund-raising events, not including the events of December 10 to 17. After March, $2.3 million was raised through small fund raisers, the largest of which brought in $35,000 but whose average yield was $7,000. Most of these small fund raisers were held in primary states, with Kennedy attending about 85 percent of them and other members of the Kennedy family the rest. In all, fund-raising events brought the campaign $4.2 million.

Despite the presence of direct-mail specialist Morris Dees on the campaign's fund-raising staff, most of Kennedy's contributors came from sources other than direct mail. According to one report, an initial mailing of one million pieces brought in 15,000 contributions averaging $32.[288] Although the net profit from the mailing was $200,000,[289] the 1.5 percent response rate did not indicate direct mail would play a significant role in the fund-raising campaign. Explained Dees in December 1979, "Kennedy isn't thought of as their advocate by the liberal, donating section of the country.''[290] Direct mail was used in the Kennedy campaign, however, to resolicit donors once they made their initial contributions. Among Kennedy mailings, a package that included copies of an address Kennedy gave at Georgetown University six days after his Iowa loss, in which the candidate discarded the vagueness that characterized earlier attempts to articulate his positions, brought in two dollars for every dollar spent.[291] A mailing offering a commemorative medallion to donors of $50 or more yielded an average contribution of about $35.[292] When Dees agreed to work for the Kennedy campaign, he arranged that a special bank account be set up for deposit of direct-mail receipts and that the monies deposited be used first to pay bills incurred by the direct-mail operation and to finance further mailings. What was left was given to the campaign.

Kennedy's victories in New York and Connecticut on March 25 gave the candidate and his campaign new life, but hoped-for momentum from these victories never developed; the senator went down to defeat by substantial margins in the April 1 primaries in Kansas and Wisconsin and in the April 5 primary in Louisiana. Still the campaign went forward, fueled by its bank loans and by money raised through the efforts of its fund-raising staff and of the candidate himself. The efforts paid off in Pennsylvania where Kennedy narrowly defeated Carter on April 22, and in Michigan, where the Massachusetts senator won an equally narrow victory in the state's April 26 caucuses.

Although Carter held a commanding lead over his opponent in the delegate count by this time, Carter continued to raise more money, but the gap was narrowing, and Carter was coming close to the overall spending limit with twenty primaries and several caucuses still to be contested. May proved disastrous for the Kennedy campaign. Carter won victories in every state and territory holding a prenomination contest except the District of Columbia. By the end of the month, the president had not won enough delegate votes to ensure renomination, but he was close enough to the total needed to make it practically impossible for Kennedy to defeat him. Kennedy enjoyed June 3, when he won five of the eight primaries scheduled. But the delegates Carter won in the same contests were more than enough for the nomination.

Kennedy chose to ignore the delegate count and carry his fight for the nomination to the convention floor. He succeeded in winning some major party-platform victories but was unable to wrest Carter's delegates from him. On August 11, the first night of the convention, he announced his withdrawal from the race. The Kennedy campaign helped finance its postprimary battle for the nomination in a novel way. In June the campaign sent out a "Convention Sweepstakes" mailing offering ten winners free rooms at the Waldorf Astoria Hotel and unlimited convention passes.

Although FEC regulations prohibit the matching of contributions "in the form of a purchase price paid for a chance to participate in a raffle, lottery or similar drawing for valuable prizes," the campaign filed for matching funds on the contributions it received from the solicitation.[293] Initially the FEC's audit division held back about $62,000 in matching funds pending the commission's decision on the legitimacy of the sweepstakes. Ultimately the commission concluded that the contributions were matchable, noting that the entry blanks did not require contributions in particular amounts and even allowed individuals to enter without making a contribution. In fact the campaign informed the FEC that one-third of the entrants and three of the ten winners did not make contributions.[294]

The Kennedy for President Committee reported adjusted receipts of $12.3 million through December 31, 1980. Contributions from individuals accounted for $7.7 million, matching funds for $3.9 million, and PAC contributions for $230,000. Of the $7.8 million in individual contributions, unitemized contributions accounted for $2.8 million, about 36 percent of the total. Itemized contributions of $1 to $499 accounted for $1.8 million, almost 23 percent of the total. Contributions of $500 to $749 accounted for $816,000, more than 10 percent of the total, and contributions of $750 and up brought in about $2.4 million, about 31 percent of the total. California, Massachusetts, and New York were the states most generous to Kennedy in contributions of $500 and up. Californians contributing such amounts gave $531,000 to the campaign, 16.4 percent of the total in that category. Massachusetts residents gave almost $500,000 in such gifts, 15.5 percent of the total. New Yorkers gave $483,000 in gifts of $500 and up, 15 percent of the total.

To the matching funds of $3.9 million certified for the Kennedy committee through December 31, 1980, may be added matching-fund payments of $270,000 received through February 1982. This matching-fund total of $4.1 million represents about 32 percent of the campaign's total adjusted receipts. The campaign submitted more than 81,000 contributions to be certified for matching, about 92 percent of which were certified by the FEC.

Almost 70 percent of the $232,374 in PAC contributions the Kennedy committee received by December 31, 1980, came from PACs associated with labor unions. Corporate PACs accounted for more than 16 percent of the total and trade, membership, and health PACs for more than 8 percent. Kennedy received more than $55,000 in PAC contributions in 1979 and more than $100,000 after July 31, 1980.[295] Much of the latter amount came from labor union PACs after the Democratic convention to help the campaign retire its substantial debt, which amounted to more than $1 million. Among PACs contributing the maximum $5,000 to Kennedy were the American Federation of Teachers Committee on Political Education, the Bricklayers, Masons and Plasterers Union PAC, and the Machinists and

Aerospace Workers PAC. In addition, HCI PAC, which is associated with Handgun Control Inc., contributed $1,000 to the Kennedy campaign.

Kennedy benefited from $56,197 in independent expenditures made on his behalf, including $20,000 spent by Stewart Mott for a pro-Kennedy newspaper advertisement in the March 23 edition of the *New York Times.* But far more, $487,688, was spent independently to oppose Kennedy's candidacy, including $260,507 spent by NCPAC and $205,905 spent by the NRA. Independent expenditures against Kennedy accounted for the lion's share of the $538,978 spent in independent expenditures against all candidates for the 1980 presidential nomination. In addition, the National Rifle Association Institute for Legislative Action spent $155,500 in internal communications to its members opposing the Kennedy candidacy. That figure, however, was surpassed by the $443,077 spent on such communication costs in favor of Kennedy. Six labor organizations provided that support, with the American Federation of State, County and Municipal Employees reporting the largest such expenditure: $228,132. Labor unions also provided volunteer workers for the Kennedy campaign, including United Auto Worker support in most of the major states.

Costs: The Kennedy campaign anticipated receipts of $3 million by the end of 1979 and $6 million by mid-February 1980.[296] By December 31, 1979, its reported receipts were almost $3.9 million, and by January 31, 1980, receipts had risen to more than $6.1 million. But the Kennedy committee spent money even more quickly than it came in from contributions and from matching funds. By mid-December the campaign staff numbered three hundred persons, some of whom worked at national headquarters, a renovated Cadillac dealership in Washington, D.C., and others in the campaign's twenty-five field offices around the country.[297] A number of top officials were paid at an annual rate of $42,000 to $50,000, including deputy campaign chairman and former Iowa senator Dick Clark, who received the top salary of $50,000, and finance chairman Martin Katz, speechwriter Richard Carey Parker, political strategist Carl Wagner, as well as Peter Edleman, Mark Schneider, Robert Bates, Joanne Howes, and Ronald Brown.[298] Campaign chairman and manager Stephen Smith, Kennedy's brother-in-law, took no salary, nor did other members of Kennedy's family or former Wisconsin governor Patrick Lucey.

Candidate travel also was a major expense. The campaign chartered a Boeing 727 and spent an estimated $40,000[299] to refit the interior to include forty-two first-class seats for reporters, tourist-class seats for Secret Service and campaign staff, and an executive suite for the candidate, which included an elaborate stereo tape system[300] and a device to permit a telephone to be plugged into the interior at each campaign stop.[301] When in use, the plane reportedly cost $10,000 a day, plus several thousand dollars in charges for each takeoff and landing.[302] When not flying, the plane still cost the campaign $5,000 a day.[303] Over the objections of finance chairman Katz, the plane sat on the ground for one ten-day period at Christmas while the candidate vacationed in Palm Beach, Florida. Campaign chairman Smith and Kennedy apparently considered the plane to be an important symbol of a nationwide election effort; in addition, there was reluctance to give it up before the January 21 Iowa caucuses for fear doing so would be interpreted as a sign of political weakness. Although members of the media who flew on the chartered jet were charged 225 percent of first-class fare—the standard charge was 150 percent of a first-class commercial airline ticket for the same trip—the Kennedy plane reportedly operated at a net loss of about $250,000 in November and December alone.[304]

The rate of reimbursement charged media representatives for flights on the Kennedy charter became an issue when some news organizations and publications, such as Associated Press and *Newsweek* magazine, cut back on the number of trips their representatives made with the candidate on the chartered jet. Others asked the campaign to explain the high charges, which covered not only the flight but meals served in flight and a share of ground facilities such as buses, press rooms in hotels, typewriters, and telephones. A one-day round trip with the candidate from Washington, D.C., to Waterloo, Iowa, for example, cost each media representative $698, compared with $310 it would have cost for a first-class ticket on a commercial airliner and $258 for a tourist-class ticket.[305] A longer Kennedy trip in December to Chicago, Miami, Washington, Boston, New York, Denver, San Francisco, Los Angeles, and St. Louis cost $3,685 per media representative.[306] Kennedy campaign officials acknowledged that flying on the candidate's chartered jet was costly but pointed out that the plane had been designed to carry ninety-six passengers but had been reconfigured to carry seventy-three, with a more comfortable seat arrangement for media personnel; thus the per-person cost of operating the plane was higher than it would have been without the reconfiguration. Figures indicated the media had been paying about 70 percent of the cost of the jet but had been occupying only about 57 percent of the seats. Finance chairman Katz explained this was due partly to the fact that the charge to the Secret Service, whose agents occupied thirteen tourist-class seats, was based on the comparable tourist-class fare.[307] "We're not making money on this operation," said Katz. "We're losing, obviously."[308] The objections that news organizations made to the amounts they were charged by the Kennedy campaign became moot, however, when the campaign grounded its charter on January 21.

The costs of paying salaries and funding travel for the candidate and the sixteen to twenty aides who generally accompanied him, as well as substantial costs for fund raising, telephone, and advertising during 1979, outstripped the campaign's ability to raise funds from private sources.[309] It ended the year more than $650,000 in debt, having borrowed close to a million dollars to cover costs associated with Kennedy's announcement. Campaign officials explained the heavy spending as a matter of strategy. "Running against an incumbent president," said Martin Katz interpreting the thinking of campaign strategists, "we had to have a national campaign."[310] Katz also explained the high salaries as a matter of loyalty to many former Kennedy Senate aides who left high-paying jobs in private business to join the campaign.

The costs that dominated Kennedy campaign spending in 1979 continued to do so for the first three weeks of 1980. To these were added the costs for media advertising focusing on the January 21 Iowa caucuses. The campaign felt compelled to spend more than it anticipated on media advertising in Iowa to make up for the free media exposure it lost when President Carter withdrew from the debate with Kennedy that had been scheduled for January 5. The campaign reportedly spent about $20,000 on television advertising geared to the Iowa contests, including a half-hour program in six markets devoted in part to criticizing Carter for withdrawing from the debate, a five-minute program showing the candidate discussing issues with local residents in an American Legion Hall, and some thirty- and sixty-second spots. The advertisements were produced by Charles Guggenheim, Kennedy's media adviser at that time.[311] The campaign also aired a number of sixty-second radio advertisements bluntly criticizing the president. Those media costs represented only a small portion of the total amount allocated to Iowa, an amount in dispute between the campaign committee and the FEC audit division. According to the postnomination audit by the FEC, the committee allocated $380,792 to Iowa, but the audit staff added to that additional expenditures of $255,664, putting the campaign well over Iowa's $489,882 spending limit.[312] In spite of heavy spending, Kennedy lost by what was considered an astonishing margin: he won only 31 percent of the popular vote and only about a third of the state's convention delegates.

Kennedy's prospects looked dim. The campaign was in debt, and the candidate's poor showing in Iowa would do little to encourage further contributions. The chartered jet was grounded. The payroll was pared back. And strategy was altered. No longer would Kennedy attempt to tone down his liberal rhetoric in an effort to broaden his appeal. In a speech delivered at Georgetown University in Washington, D.C., only a week after the Iowa elections, Kennedy offered specific proposals that set him apart from Carter and put him firmly in the liberal political camp once again. The speech served to revive Kennedy's own spirit and that of his supporters. It also had more concrete results. During the two weeks following the speech, $400,000 was added to the campaign treasury.[313]

It was clear the Kennedy campaign could no longer afford the expensive nationwide effort it had originally planned. Most of the resources available were funneled into New Hampshire and Massachusetts in the hope the candidate's native New England would be more receptive to his appeal for support. According to one estimate, about $225,000 was budgeted for television and radio commercials in New England.[314] In one thirty-minute paid political broadcast, Kennedy sought to meet the Chappaquiddick issue head-on. The candidate explained that his account of the tragedy is "the only truth I can tell because that is the way it happened," and he asked to be judged by basic American standards of fairness.[315] Despite heavy spending in New Hampshire—considerably more than the limit, according to FEC auditors—the primary voters preferred President Carter by a 49 to 38 percent margin. In his home state of Massachusetts, where his campaign's reported expenditures of about $307,000 nearly matched the Carter campaign's reported allocation of $310,000, Kennedy, as expected, fared much better, receiving 65 percent of the vote and seventy-seven of the state's delegates. In the vote in neighboring Vermont on the same day, however, Carter was the winner by an even more overwhelming margin.

Plagued by continuing financial difficulties and acknowledging his opponent's strength in his native South, Kennedy did not campaign extensively in any of the southern states holding primaries on March 11. Instead he focused his attention and resources on the Illinois primary scheduled for March 18. Carter won easily, as expected, in Alabama, Georgia, and Florida, where he outspent Kennedy by substantial margins, and added a narrow primary victory in Puerto Rico, where Kennedy's reported expenditures of almost $190,000 far surpassed the $20,000 total for the Carter campaign. In the meantime, the Kennedy campaign took half of its advance and scheduling staff—at least fifteen persons—off payroll and made similar cuts elsewhere among the campaign staff.[316] Salaries were reduced, forcing some staff members to leave the campaign and others to work for it only part time. Savings from the reductions, as well as proceeds from bank loans, were channeled into media advertising in Illinois. The campaign spent almost $200,000 on media advertising to influence the primary outcome, the greater portion of its total expenditures in the state.[317] But there, too, Carter prevailed, outspending Kennedy by a five to one margin and winning 165 delegates to Kennedy's 14.

New York and Connecticut held primaries a week after Illinois, but Kennedy's organization had little money to put into last-minute advertising. What preelection week advertising it could manage drew the attention of viewers to a recent United Nations vote in which the U.S. ambassador had voted first in favor of condemning Israeli settlements in occupied Arab territory and then renounced the vote in an embarrasing turnabout. New York and Connecticut voters, some apparently upset over the vote and others generally dissatisfied with Carter and hoping to send him a message, gave

Kennedy two of his campaign victories. The margins of victory, including a 59 to 41 percent margin in New York, were substantial enough to breathe new life into Kennedy's campaign. Whatever sense of euphoria filled the Kennedy campaign organization after the double victory, however, dissipated in light of Kennedy's double loss in Wisconsin and Kansas on April 1. Kennedy had originally hoped to do well in Wisconsin, a state with a notable liberal tradition. But he was competing for the liberal vote in the state's open primary with John Anderson and Gov. Edmund G. Brown, Jr., making a last-ditch effort in the state. His precarious financial position did not permit his campaign to mount a media advertising campaign or to flood the state with campaign workers; the campaign's state coordinator operated with a staff of only four persons.[318] On top of all that, there was the primary morning announcement by Carter that a "positive step" had been taken by the Iranian government in the hostage crisis, an announcement made with "suspicious haste," according to one Kennedy aide.[319] Whatever the reason, Kennedy went down to defeat, winning only 30 percent of the vote to Carter's 56 percent.

Kennedy looked beyond the April 5 primary in Louisiana, which he expected to, and did, lose, to the April 22 primary in Pennsylvania. Although his campaign was outspent in the state by a reported margin of more than three to one, Kennedy did mount a major effort, which included fourteen days of campaigning by the candidate and television advertisements featuring Carroll O'Connor, television's Archie Bunker, predicting a depression under Carter and vouching for Kennedy's trustworthiness. This effort was rewarded with a narrow victory, but Carter's overwhelming win in the Missouri caucuses on the same day gave him a net delegate gain for the day of almost fifty delegates. Kennedy's slender margin of victory in Michigan's April 26 caucuses did nothing to trim the gap between the two candidates. Nevertheless Kennedy forged on. New television advertising produced by New York filmmaker David Sawyer, who had replaced Charles Guggenheim just before the New York primary, focused on Kennedy's Senate record and his perception of the presidential role. One five-minute prime-time advertisement broadcast late in April on ABC cost $18,334; another such five-minute advertisement early in May on NBC cost about $26,000.[320] Additional advertisements were broadcast in local markets where primary elections were scheduled during May and June. On the stump Kennedy continued to berate his opponent for remaining in the White House and repeated his challenge to Carter to debate.

Despite these efforts and despite the fact that the Carter campaign was drawing close to the legal spending limit, of all the primary contests held during May, Kennedy could salvage a victory only in the District of Columbia. By month's end Carter's delegate lead was insurmountable. On June 3, he could afford to focus his attention on the limited objective of winning the delegates he needed to nail down renomination instead of actively contesting all eight primaries. His campaign chose the Ohio primary as the most likely contest in which to pick up the votes he needed. The Kennedy campaign's television advertising encouraged the voters to keep the contest alive and the convention open by rejecting Carter and voting for the Massachusetts senator. Kennedy himself described the June 3 primaries as a "referendum on whether Democrats want a fair debate and a free choice" and offered to release his delegates if Carter were to meet him in debate prior to the convention.[321]

The Kennedy campaign, hampered by a shortage of money, focused its spending in California and New Jersey, where it outspent the Carter campaign, according to FEC reports, whereas the Carter campaign spent more heavily in Ohio. Kennedy's California expenditures included a $195,000 television advertising campaign,[322] and in New Jersey his campaign staffed twenty-two field offices around the state and used volunteer phone banks to reach an estimated 150,000 voters.[323] Kennedy did win five of the eight primaries on June 3—those in California, New Jersey, New Mexico, Rhode Island, and South Dakota—but his opponent won three primaries and more than enough delegate votes to give him a clear convention majority.

Kennedy refused to yield. "Today Democrats from coast to coast," he said, "have decided that this campaign must go on."[324] Kennedy campaign operatives established a network to remain in touch with convention delegates. The campaign closed its field offices in the June 3 primary states but expanded its national staff to include a group assigned to develop strategy for the convention. Kennedy operatives and supporters waged vigorous battles in platform and rules committee hearings, seeking to include planks favored by the candidate and rules changes favoring his candidacy. By the first day of the convention, however, it became apparent that the campaign had exhausted its avenues for wresting the nomination from President Carter. Kennedy withdrew at last, conceding the nomination to Carter.

According to the FEC final report on 1979-1980 prenomination-campaign financial activity through December 31, 1980, the Kennedy for President Committee reported net disbursements of $16.7 million and adjusted disbursements of $12.3 million. Information provided by the committee allows its expenditures to be broken down into functional categories. Although the total expenditure figure in the committee's report differs slightly from the adjusted disbursement figure in the FEC report, the two totals are sufficiently close that the committee breakdown may be accepted as an accurate indication of how the committee spent its funds:

Salaries and personal services	$ 2,189,164
Consulting	124,751
Food and lodging	846,085
Airline travel	679,695
Airline charter	1,227,385
Travel reimbursement for auto and train	521,364
Office equipment, rent, and supplies	899,500
General media	959,531
Media production	805,100
Media miscellaneous	57,725
Polling	160,250
Telephone	1,667,395
Printing, mail, and reproduction	1,500,417
Interest	56,182
Campaign miscellaneous	444,728
Convention expenses	41,747
Get-out-the-vote	1,595
Compliance, legal, accounting, and fund raising	122,865
Total	$12,305,479

The largest category of expenditure for the Kennedy campaign was travel, which accounted for a total of $2,428,444, including $1,227,385 in airline charter costs. Salaries and consulting fees combined accounted for $2,313,915, and media expenditures came to $1,822,356. Other large expenditures were $1,664,225 for telephone charges, $1,500,417 for printing, mail, and reproduction, and $899,500 for office and equipment rental and supplies. According to the committee report, exempt fund raising, compliance, legal, and accounting costs, which were incurred in nearly every category of expenditure reported, came to $1,316,147, including $122,865 in specifically designated compliance costs. Although the committee report lists convention expenses as $41,747, that figure represents only expenses specifically designated as such. A committee spokesperson later estimated total convention costs for the Kennedy campaign as at least $150,000, including $40,000 for convention headquarters and almost $30,000 to set up an art gallery at the Waldorf Astoria at which works donated to the campaign by a variety of artists were offered as inducements to contributors. Finally, it is worth noting an additional expense incurred by the campaign. Even when campaign funds were low, a doctor and a nurse were paid to accompany the candidate full time in case he was subject to the type of attack that had felled his two brothers.[325]

The FEC audit of the Kennedy for President Committee was the source of disputes between the commission and the committee that lasted well beyond the release of the audit on September 28, 1981.[326]. The audit found a number of errors that the committee was able to correct by filing amended reports or otherwise complying with commission requests. Those errors included failure to report certain expenditures, misstating some reported financial activity, failure to provide a number of bank records, failure to report some contributions from political committees, accepting excessive contributions from registered political committees, failure to report some outstanding debts, and holding questionable contributions for an excessive length of time.

The most-controversial finding of the audit report was its determination that the committee had exceeded the spending limits in New Hampshire and Iowa by $238,000. To totals for each state from monthly state allocation reports maintained by the committee, which reflected amounts allocated to the states from national operating accounts and state and scheduling accounts, the audit staff first added expenditures made from various other state accounts that had not been allocated. To this total for each state were added a number of expenditures the audit staff maintained the committee should have included in its report but did not. These expenditures included payments made from the committee's national operating accounts during March and April, after the elections had taken place, which the committee did not include in the state allocation reports; payments for purchase of certain radio, television, and newspaper advertising; payroll expenses for field and advance personnel in the states; payments for per-diem and expense reimbursements; outstanding debts in the two states; and a variety of vendor payments.

In its response to the audit findings, the committee provided documentation indicating the per-diem and expense reimbursements were not allocable to Iowa or New Hampshire. The committee also explained how it determined, with the assistance of two accounting firms, whether expenses were allocable to particular states. According to the committee response, state coordinators in four sample states were interviewed to determine how much time individual employees working in those states were spending on exempt compliance and fund-raising activities. The percentages determined were applied to overhead costs and to field staff salaries, and the totals were not included in the allocations the committee attributed to the two states. The audit division, however, found the information provided by the committee inadequate and requested further documentation verifying the accuracy and reasonableness of the committee's fund-raising and compliance allocations.

The committee also explained that it had isolated all types of interstate travel and communications and considered expenses for such activities exempt from allocation to individual states according to FEC regulations. Consequently those expenses were not included in the allocations the committee attributed to the two states. In the meantime the FEC clarified its policy regarding allocation of telephone charges to individual states. According to that policy, long-distance calls made from a state to national headquarters were not required to be allocated to the states. The audit division requested that all affected presidential-candidate committees' state allocation schedules be amended in light of the commission's determination, along with supporting documentation. When such an amendment was not forthcoming from the Kennedy committee, the audit staff declined to adjust the totals allocable to the two states in question for interstate telephone calls the committee claimed were exempt from the state limits. The auditors adjusted the totals for the interstate travel and delivery charges for which adequate documentation had been provided.

The Kennedy committee also submitted new media-expense allocation figures for the two states based on a new allocation formula. The audit staff did not object to the new formula but found it had not been applied to all of the media buys and refunds that would be affected by it. The auditors again requested additional documentation. Finally, the committee maintained that many of the expenditures that had been allocated by the audit staff to the two states were for services provided to the national press for which media representatives had reimbursed the campaign. But the audit found that the committee had not provided sufficient information regarding services it rendered to the national press or regarding the amounts of money billed to and received from the press for reimbursements. It also declined to accept the committee's position that the salaries of advance persons who devoted all or part of their time to the national press should not be allocated to the states to which they were assigned.

Once adjustments had been made in initial audit findings in response to the documentation and explanations provided by the committee, the audit determined that the committee had exceeded the Iowa spending limit by $146,575 and the New Hampshire spending limit by $91,451. It also found that the committee had made payments totaling $141 for parking tickets. The audit recommended that the committee repay the Treasury $238,167.

The audit also determined that as of November 28, 1980, the Kennedy for President Committee's net outstanding campaign obligations totaled $1,134,566, including estimated wind-down costs of $149,700 to cover committee operations through May 15, 1981. That determination, however, did not take into account the valuation of art prints held by the committee as a capital asset of the committee. The audit staff's initial attempts to discover what prints were on hand on the date of the candidate's ineligibility and what their value was yielded from the committee only the information that as of August 15, 1980, the committee had 6,904 prints on hand. The committee cited difficulties in determining the value of those prints, including the fact that an independent appraisal would cost at least $10,000, and maintained that the prints should not be treated as capital assets since they could not be readily converted to cash or used to settle debts. In a decision made in mid-September 1981, the FEC determined that individual pieces of artwork valued at more than $500 are capital assets that reduce the committee's net outstanding campaign obligations and that the appraised value shown on the committee's original fund-raising brochure, "Artists for Kennedy," would be used to determine the value of the works held by the committee as of August 13, 1980.

The audit division gave the Kennedy committee thirty days from its receipt of the audit report to provide documentation that would indicate the repayments the auditors recommended were not required. On October 21, 1981, the committee filed a complaint against the FEC in the District of Columbia U.S. District Court, alleging that the commission had violated the Sunshine Act by considering the final audit report in closed session. In addition William Oldaker, the committee's legal counsel, sought and received a two-week extension of the deadline to allow the committee to gather the material needed. Oldaker complained that in attempting to regulate state presidential-primary spending limits, the commission was "venturing out into an area where there are no standards."[327] On November 9, 1981, the committee provided the FEC with a step-by-step response to the commission's final audit report and with letters, work papers, bills, and other documentation it maintained would support its case.

On December 21, 1981, the district court resolved the claims brought by the Kennedy committee in its suit by issuing a consent order requiring the FEC to make available to the committee and to the public portions of the transcript involving the commission's consideration of the final Kennedy audit report, as well as documents pertaining to those meetings. The court's order also explained how any disputes over which portions of the transcript were released were to be resolved.

In a matter unrelated to those issues, the agency fined the committee $4,000 for violations by one of its authorized committees, Kennedy for President/Puerto Rico. Among the violations were failure to disclose the existence of a checking account, to report receipt of certain contributions, to disclose the names of some contributors of more than $200, and paying out money received before it had been deposited.

Brown

In 1976 Gov. Edmund G. Brown, Jr., of California was catapulted into national prominence when he mounted a belated challenge to front-running

Democratic presidential contender Jimmy Carter and defeated him in five of the six primaries he entered. Despite his failure to keep Carter from gaining the nomination, the California governor's presidential ambitions did not diminish. Throughout the next three years—including 1978 when he easily won reelection to a second term as governor—Brown did little to discourage reports in the press of his presidential aspirations. Those reports became more frequent in 1979 when President Carter's popularity plummeted and some Democratic voters began to look for alternatives. Top aides to Brown encouraged him as early as April 1979 to announce his bid soon, if that is what he intended, so necessary organizational and fund-raising work could begin. Brown, however, waited until the end of July to signal his intentions by establishing an exploratory campaign committee, which made him eligible to solicit contributions for a presidential campaign. The committee set as its fund-raising objective $10 million to $11 million and planned on an additional $4 million in matching funds.[328] Brown's fund-raising organization, however, fell far short of its goals, and his campaign never lived up to the promise of his 1976 showing.

Brown finally began campaigning in earnest in October, when he spent half of the month on out-of-state election efforts in which he set forth his campaign themes, including a call for a balanced budget, gradual elimination of nuclear-power plants, and expanded space exploration. His campaign's fund-raising efforts, however, were encountering difficulties due at least in part to signs pointing to a Kennedy candidacy and to the candidate's own low standing in public-opinion polls. As of September 30, 1979, the campaign had raised only about $260,000, much of it from California, and had not yet qualified for matching funds. And as the candidate stepped up his campaigning, his committee reportedly was spending at a rate of $100,000 a week.[329]

On November 8, Brown formally announced his candidacy amid efforts to improve his financial prospects through solicitation of donations from California state employees, fund-raising dinners, and benefit concerts. A $250-a-plate dinner in Beverly Hills before the announcement netted $152,000,[330] and a dinner in San Francisco brought in an additional $135,000.[331] Fund-raising concerts featuring the rock band Chicago in Los Angeles and Brown's rock star friend, Linda Ronstadt, in San Diego and Las Vegas brought in additional funds. Ronstadt also hosted a reception for Brown at her Malibu home in December, which brought in $35,000.[332] By the end of the year the Brown committee reported receipts of $1,367,380 and cash on hand of $223,538.

Brown needed some positive exposure to the voters and preferably a good showing in one of the early primary and caucus season contests to give impetus to his campaign's fund raising. But neither possibility developed. Although he had planned to deemphasize Iowa, Brown spent more time and money in the state than his campaign committee had planned in order to be invited to the *Des Moines Register*-sponsored January 5 debate with Carter and Kennedy. But Carter's withdrawal and Kennedy's subsequent refusal to debate Brown alone deprived the California governor of the national television exposure he sought. Brown received less than 1 percent of the popular vote in the January 21 Iowa caucuses, the predictable result of his limited campaigning and his committee's inability, or unwillingness, to buy television advertising in the state. The candidate hoped for better results in the February 10 Maine caucuses, though he set up an organization in the state only at the end of January. Despite vigorous, though concentrated, campaigning in the state by Brown and a number of surrogates, including his parents, Brown finished a distant third, receiving 12.1 percent of the preference vote cast by caucus participants. He finished third again in New Hampshire's February 26 primary where he won only 9.6 percent of the vote.

Although Brown did not withdraw from the contest at that point, he did withdraw from active competition in all of the March primaries to concentrate on the April 1 Wisconsin primary. During March, however, several staff members, including campaign manager Tom Quinn, left the underfunded campaign. Many of them had been working without pay since early February, and many had encouraged Brown to abandon the race.[333] Brown did receive help for his last-ditch effort in Wisconsin from volunteers organized by Marshall Ganz, a United Farm Workers organizer on loan to the campaign. And he did mount a major media effort in the form of a thirty-minute statewide "television extravaganza" produced for the candidate by Hollywood producer Francis Ford Coppola at a cost of $150,000, according to one estimate,[334] and broadcast on March 28 at a cost of about $35,000 for air time.[335] The production was beset with technical problems and probably did little to help Brown's chances of a good showing. He ran a distant third once again, receiving only 12.4 percent of the vote and his only delegate of the campaign. Brown withdrew from the race the night of the primary without endorsing either of his rivals; his campaign debt was estimated to be about $600,000,[336] including a $150,000 loan from the American City Bank in Los Angeles.[337]

According to the FEC final report on 1979-1980 prenomination-campaign financial activity through December 31, 1980, the Brown for President Committee had adjusted receipts of $2.7 million, about $1.7 million from individual contributions, $890,000 from matching funds, and $40,000 from PACs. A sizable portion of Brown's contributions came from his home state of California. For example, 91 percent of Brown's contributions of $500 and up were contributed by Californians, for a total of $706,197. Among California donors were more than 180 state employees, among whom at least 15 contributed $1,000, the legal limit.[338] Other contributors included Edgar M. Bronfman, chairman of Seagrams & Sons, the whisky distillers; Hugh Hefner, publisher of *Playboy* magazine; Vidal Sassoon, president of a Beverly Hills-based hair-products company; and entertainer Johnny Carson.[339]

The FEC report also indicated that the Brown for President Committee made adjustment disbursements of $2.7 million, including $30,330 allocated to Iowa, $113,872 to Maine, $115,774 to New Hampshire, $154,413 to Massachusetts, and $461,362 to Wisconsin. Of the total disbursements, $572,880 was allocated to exempt fund-raising, legal, and accounting costs. According to figures provided by the committee, $339,129 was spent on broadcast media, $293,419 on television costs, and the rest on radio costs in Maine, New Hampshire, and Wisconsin.

The FEC audit of the Brown for President Committee found that the committee had improperly reported advances to field personnel and had provided inadequate information regarding voluntary expenses for fund raising allowed under the 1979 FECA amendments.[340] These errors were corrected by the committee in amended reports, and no further action was taken. The audit staff also determined that as of April 3, 1980, the committee's net outstanding campaign obligations amounted to $442,506 and that contributions and interest income, as well as matching-fund contributions received since that date, had put the committee in a cash-surplus position. The auditors determined the surplus of $19,774 represented matching funds received over and above what was needed to satisfy the committee's obligations and recommended that amount be repaid to the Treasury. The committee subsequently submitted documentation supporting additional qualified campaign expenditures not considered by the audit staff, as well as greater winding-down costs than the audit staff had estimated. The auditors then found that the committee was entitled to all of the matching funds it had received and that it had a remaining entitlement of $2,690.

Finally the FEC audit determined that the committee had failed to document expenditures for $52,261 in campaign expenses and recommended the committee repay that amount to the Treasury. The committee subsequently documented $34,210 of those expenditures to the audit division's satisfaction, leaving $18,050 to be repaid by the committee.

In a subsequent finding, the FEC auditors discovered that fourteen Brown committee staff persons had deposited campaign funds in their personal accounts and had later paid campaign expenses from the accounts. The commission fined the Brown committee $1,500 for violating the provision of the federal election law that prohibits mixing campaign and personal funds.

LaRouche

The campaign of Lyndon LaRouche for the Democratic presidential nomination was more notable for the bizarre behavior of campaign operatives and of the candidate than for its effect on electoral outcomes. LaRouche, who had run for president in 1976 on the U.S. Labor party ticket, signaled his intention to repeat as his party's candidate in 1980 when his committee registered with the FEC on January 29, 1979. On November 9, 1979, however, the committee amended its statement of organization to indicate the candidate would seek the Democratic party's nomination for the presidency. The ease with which LaRouche was able to join the Democratic race, though he had no ties to the Democratic party, at the very least testifies to the vagueness of party labels and to a lack of controls over participation in party primaries.

Prior to the New Hampshire primary, documents were discovered in a room in a Concord, New Hampshire, YMCA that had been occupied by a LaRouche campaigner that indicated a number of New Hampshire public officials had been targeted by the campaign for harassing telephone calls.[341] Several officials reported having received such calls after having had confrontations with LaRouche campaigners over leafleting or voter registration. LaRouche himself reportedly admitted that campaign workers impersonated reporters and others to obtain information about his opponents.[342] Such tactics did little to help his standing with voters in New Hampshire, where he received only a little more than 2,000 votes in the February 26 primary. LaRouche's election results were no better in other primary contests in which he was on the ballot.

According to the FEC final report on 1979-1980 prenomination-campaign financial activity through December 31, 1980, the LaRouche campaign had adjusted receipts of $2.1 million, including $1.6 million in individual contributions and $530,000 in matching funds. According to the same report, the campaign's adjusted disbursements totaled $2.2 million. The FEC audit of LaRouche's campaign committee determined the committee had exceeded the New Hampshire spending limit by $73,660 and had received $36,958 in federal matching funds after it had collected enough money in private contributions to retire the campaign's debt.[343] Additional audit findings required further repayments for matching funds received for checks drawn on insufficient funds, for loans received, and for contributions refunded, bringing the total to be repaid by the committee to the Treasury of $111,698. A court challenge to the audit findings by the committee failed.

After the audit was completed, the FEC launched several additional investigations of the LaRouche committee, reportedly questioning contributors to the committee in an attempt to verify its eligibility for matching funds. The committee subsequently went to court and argued that the FEC investigations had a chilling effect on the political process and amounted to harassment of the committee and abuse of the commission's authority.[344] On March 11, 1982, Judge Charles Brieant of the U.S. District Court for the Southern District of New York ruled that the FEC had violated the First Amendment rights of Citizens for LaRouche and temporarily prohibited the commission from opening new investigations of the committee until current investigations were completed.[345]

In September 1982, after a review of additional campaign records of the LaRouche committee, the FEC revised its repayment demand. The commission concluded that the committee had exceeded the New Hampshire spending limit by $36,586 and that it was not entitled to $18,085 in winding-down costs it had claimed and ordered the committee to refund $54,671. The commission also continued to seek greater disclosure of the campaign's contributors.

Campaign Debt Reduction

Soon after the prenomination campaign concluded, it appeared that the two major Democratic contenders would join forces, as their Republican counterparts had, to help each other reduce their substantial campaign debts. The Carter committee's debt reached a high of $650,000, of which about $330,000 was owed to committee media adviser Gerald Rafshoon, whereas the rest was incurred in fund-raising efforts. The Kennedy committee's debt reached as high as $2.2 million, including bills of $600,000 received in August 1980, many of them to pay convention costs. In return for Senator Kennedy's help in the general-election campaign, President Carter agreed to participate in a series of joint fund-raising events to help reduce both candidates' debts. A separate committee, the Carter-Kennedy Unity Dinner Committee, was established, and three dinners were scheduled: one in Washington, one in Los Angeles, and one in New York. Only one of the dinners was held, the one in Washington, and according to a Kennedy campaign spokesperson, Kennedy received $279,000 from this event, $230,000 from individuals, and $49,000 from PACs. Carter reportedly received none of the proceeds because the agreement stipulated that Carter would pay the costs—which were said to be about $60,000—but would share only in proceeds above $500,000. A Carter campaign representative said the FEC subsequently disapproved the arrangement and ordered the Kennedy campaign to pay the Carter campaign $40,000.

Fund-raising events held after the general-election campaign to reduce the Carter prenomination-campaign debt met with only limited success. A concert held in Atlanta yielded no profit. A fund-raising dinner in September 1981, also in Atlanta, netted $33,500, of which $9,000 was allocated for campaign-debt reduction; $3,350 to the Carter general-election campaign-compliance fund; $3,600 to pay for penalties imposed on the campaign by the FEC; and $17,950 to pay for various litigation costs. As of late January 1982, the campaign's debt stood at $637,000.

In addition to the $279,000 his campaign received from the single unity dinner, by August 1981 Kennedy had received $133,000 from fund-raising events held in California, New York, and Chicago; about $50,000 from PACs; $160,000 in response to direct-mail appeals; $50,000 from the sale of artwork; $300,000 from returns of deposits and refunds to the campaign; and $650,000 in matching funds. The use of artwork to offset some of Kennedy's indebtedness became an issue late in 1980. The Kennedy committee asked the FEC if it could use the artwork to satisfy some of its debts. The commission, however, could not arrive at a clear-cut opinion about whether the campaign law's $1,000 contribution limit would apply to transactions in which the committee paid its debts with art, leaving the committee free to make its own decisions.[346] By the end of January 1982 the campaign's debt stood at $270,000, and the Kennedy committee was in the process of settling with a number of creditors, exchanging a percentage of each payment due in return for cancellation of the debt. The percentage of each settlement was determined by the size of the debt. The committee established three classes of creditors—small, medium, and large—and generally offered the same percentage to creditors in each class. In that way the committee hoped to avoid questions about whether the settlements were made in good faith.[347]

In mid-1982 a Washington, D.C., stationer filed a lawsuit against Kennedy and his deputy campaign manager for nonpayment of a $24,000 debt the Kennedy campaign owed him for supplies. Campaign committee lawyers argued that allowing such suits would have a chilling effect on First Amendment rights of political expression, but the plaintiff contended that Kennedy and his aide were liable because the Kennedy for President Committee had failed to incorporate and thus had not provided him with any automatic forewarning of limited liability.

Gov. Edmund G. Brown, Jr., paid off his $600,000 campaign debt through proceeds from a number of private fund-raising events.

Notes

1. See, for example, Herbert E. Alexander and Brian A. Haggerty, *The Federal Election Campaign Act after a Decade of Political Reform* (Los Angeles: Citizens' Research Foundation, 1981), a report of a conference held in Washington, D.C., in April 1981. A number of participants criticized the spending and contribution limit provisions of the law and offered specific suggestions for change. An appendix to the book contains a statement signed by a number of 1976 and 1980 presidential-campaign finance officers objecting to those provisions and calling for specific changes. That statement was based on proceedings of an earlier Citizens' Research Foundation conference held in Washington in December 1980.

Several other books provide useful information and analysis regarding the course of the 1980 presidential campaigns, including: Jack W. Germond and Jules Witcover, *Blue Smoke and Mirrors* (New York: Viking Press, 1981); Jonathan Moore, ed., *The Campaign for President: 1980 in Retrospect* (Cambridge, Mass.: Ballinger Publishing Co., 1981); Gerald M. Pomper, ed., *The Election of 1980* (Chatham, N.J.: Chatham House Publishers, 1981); Austin Ranney, ed., *The American Elections of 1980* (Washington, D.C.: American Enterprise Institute, 1981); Ellis Sandoz and Cecil V. Crabb, Jr., *A Tide of Discontent: The 1980 Elections and Their Meaning* (Washington, D.C.: Congressional Quarterly Press, 1981); and Theodore H. White, *America in Search of Itself: The Making of the President, 1956-1980* (New York: Harper & Row, 1982).

2. Figures cited throughout this chapter for net candidate committee disbursements may exceed the national spending limit because they include money spent on such items as compliance and press reimbursements, which do not count toward the limit.

3. Christopher Buchanan, "Candidates Must Adjust to Spending Lid," *Congressional Quarterly Weekly Report*, May 10, 1980, p. 1244.

4. "Candidates Spend Their Budgets Away," *Business Week*, March 17, 1980, p. 27.

5. See Warren Weaver, Jr., "Carter Campaign Approaching Its Spending Limits," *New York Times*, April 22, 1980.

6. FEC, *Report of the Audit Division on Reagan for President* (Washington, D.C., February 2, 1981).

7. FEC, *FEC Reports on Financial Activity, 1979-1980: Final Report, Presidential Prenomination Campaigns* (Washington, D.C., October 1981), p. 8.

8. *Voter Alert: Election 1980* (Los Angeles: University of Southern California Center for the Study of Private Enterprise, August 1980), p. 4.

9. Ibid.

10. Ben Barnes quoted in "Penny-Pinching Politics," *Time*, March 3, 1980, p. 18.

11. Richard G. Stearns quoted in Howard Rosenberg, "Media's Political Message," *Los Angeles Times*, June 6, 1980.

12. John P. Kenny quoted in William J. Lanouette, "On Tuesday, the Candidates Will Learn How Their Campaigns Played in Peoria," *National Journal*, March 15, 1980, p. 439.

13. Cited by Fred Barbash, "FEC Moves to Close Campaign Spending Loophole," *Washington Post*, September 1, 1979.

14. Quoted in Allan J. Mayer et al., "The Political Money Game," *Newsweek*, December 24, 1979, p. 31.

15. Quoted in Richard Bergholz, "Reagan Criticizes Federal Campaign Funding Laws," *Los Angeles Times*, December 14, 1979.

16. Quoted in Mayer, "Political Money Game," p. 31.

17. Robert Mosbacher quoted in Maxwell Glen, "Despite Tight Campaign Spending Laws, Former 'Fat Cats' Have a Role to Play," *National Journal*, February 9, 1980, p. 230.

18. Earl C. Gottschalk, Jr., "Presidential Candidates Beseech Rock Groups and Other Stars to Give Fund-Raising Concerts," *Wall Street Journal*, January 29, 1980.

19. T.R. Reid, "The Artful Dodge," *Washington Post*, July 21, 1980.

20. *Buckley* v. *Valeo*, 424 U.S. 1 (1976).

21. See Larry Light, "Surge in Independent Campaign Spending," *Congressional Quarterly Weekly Report*, June 14, 1980, p. 1635; see also Joseph E. Cantor, "The Evolution of and Issues Surrounding Independent Expenditures" (Washington, D.C.: Congressional Research Service, May 5, 1982), pp. 20-21.

22. FEC, *Final Report, Presidential Prenomination Campaigns*, p. 8.

23. "Independent Expenditures Suddenly Become Hottest Item in Campaign Financing," *Campaign Practices Reports*, July 7, 1980, p. 10.

24. "We're Sorry, President Carter," advertisement, *Los Angeles Times*, March 2, 1979.

25. "Democrats Who Are Disappointed in President Carter," advertisement, *New York Times*, May 6, 1979.

26. See, for example, George B. Merry, "N.H. Party to Smile for Carter," *Christian Science Monitor*, April 24, 1979.

27. Steven V. Roberts, "5 Congressmen Join to 'Dump' President," *New York Times*, May 22, 1979.

28. Cited by Jeanine Kasindorf, "Waiting for Teddy," *New West*, August 13, 1979, p. 65.

29. Ibid.

30. FEC, advisory opinion 1979-40, "Financial Activities of Unauthorized Committees"; see FEC, *Annual Report 1979* (Washington, D.C.: Office of Publications, 1980), pp. 78-79.

31. See *Campaign Practices Reports*, September 17, 1979, p. 10.

32. FEC, advisory opinion, 1980-81, "Application of 1980 Annual Limit to Individual's 1979 Contributions to Draft Committees"; see *Federal Election Commission Record* (October 1980):4.

33. Cited by Ed Zuckerman, "FEC's 'Draft Kennedy' Subpoenas Invalidated by U.S. Appeals Court," *Political Finance/Lobby Reporter*, May 27, 1981, p. 133.

34. "Draft Kennedy Inquiry," *Congressional Quarterly Weekly Report*, May 10, 1980, p. 1254.

35. FEC, *Report of the Audit Division on the Citizens for Reagan* (Washington, D.C., April 13, 1978).

36. Since federal election law does not require itemization of all expenses on behalf of nonfederal candidates, such as travel costs for fundraising appearances, the actual amount expended on campaign activity is not reflected in the contribution figures.

37. Rhodes Cook, "GOP Presidential Hopefuls Give Plenty to Party Candidates in 1978," *Congressional Quarterly Weekly Report*, February 17, 1979, p. 309.

38. Ibid.

39. Ibid.

40. Ibid.

41. Ed Zuckerman, "PACs Collect $30.5 Million During First Half of 1981," *Political Finance/Lobby Reporter,* September 9, 1981, p. 231.

42. Ibid., p. 308.

43. According to an FEC news release of November 15, 1981, the fifteen candidates who qualified for matching funds in 1976 reported disbursements of $66.9 million. In addition, Sen. Robert Byrd (D-W. Va.) reported spending $148,264, and then Sen. Walter Mondale reported spending $137,138. See Herbert E. Alexander, *Financing the 1976 Election* (Washington, D.C.: Congressional Quarterly Press, 1979), p. 169.

44. See, for example, Adam Clymer, "Inflation and a Limit on Contributions Strain Presidential Hopefuls' Budgets," *New York Times* February 4, 1980; see also "Inflation Runs Wild on the Campaign Trail," *U.S. News & World Report*, March 31, 1980, pp. 33-34; and Maxwell Glen, "It's More Expensive to Run for President as Inflation Takes to the Campaign Trails," *National Journal,* February 23, 1980, pp. 311-313.

45. See Bergholz, "Reagan Criticizes Federal Campaign Funding Laws."

46. See Joel Goldstein, "Impact of Federal Financing on the Electoral Process" (paper prepared for presentation to the 1981 Kentucky Political Science Association annual meeting, February 27-28, 1981, Bowling Green, Kentucky).

47. Mayer, "Political Money Game," p. 32.

48. "Penny-Pinching Politics," p. 18.

49. Edward L. Weidenfeld, Timothy G. Smith, et al., letter from the Campaign Counsel Group to John McGarry, chairman of the FEC, April 30, 1981; see also "Campaign Lawyers Join in Asking FEC to Remedy Audit Problems," *Campaign Practices Reports*, May 11, 1981, p. 2, and "FEC Auditors Called Insensitive, Arbitrary by Campaign Lawyers," *Political Finance/Lobby Reporter*, May 13, 1981, p. 120.

50. John W. McGarry, Frank P. Reiche, et al., letter to the Campaign Counsel Group, May 14, 1981; see also "FEC Defends Audit Process, Takes Criticisms' Under Advisement,' " *Campaign Practices Reports*, May

25, 1981, p. 4; and "FEC Offers No Apology for Presidential Audits," *Political Finance/Lobby Reporter*, May 20, 1981, p. 127.

51. FEC, "Review of the Political Campaign Auditing Process" by Arthur Andersen & Co., (mimeographed, September 1979). See also FEC, untitled study of the FEC's Audit Process by Accountants in the Public Interest (mimeographed, September 1979).

52. "Broadcast Industry Protests FEC Proposal to Restrict Sponsorship of Debates," *Campaign Practices Reports*, August 20, 1979, p. 5.

53. Merrill Brown, "FCC Says FEC Rule Would Bar Most Political Debates on TV," *Washington Star*, September 11, 1979.

54. "FEC Seems Anxious to Repair Damage Done to Debates," *Broadcasting*, October 29, 1979, p. 70.

55. Ibid.

56. Cited by John R. Finnegan, "A Contribution to Understanding," *St. Paul Sunday Pioneer Press*, November 25, 1979.

57. Warren Weaver, Jr., "Financial Support Problem Imperils Campaign Debates," *New York Times*, February 20, 1980.

58. Rhodes Cook, "Attention Shifts to First Presidential Primaries," *Congressional Quarterly Weekly Report*, February 2, 1980, p. 281.

59. "Media Politicking," *Washington Post*, January 2, 1980.

60. Rhodes Cook, "Carter, Reagan Complete First Phase of Preference Primaries Far Ahead of Their 1976 Pace," *Congressional Quarterly Weekly Report*, April 19, 1980, p. 1003.

61. Ibid.

62. Ibid.

63. Lou Cannon, "California May Abolish GOP 'Winner-Take-All' Primary," *Washington Post*, January 3, 1980.

64. Cook, "Carter, Reagan Complete First Phase," p. 1003.

65. Ibid.

66. Both states held nonbinding preference primaries.

67. Elaine Karmarck quoted in Richard J. Cattani, "Campaign '80—Vote Hunt Starts in Iowa," *Christian Science Monitor*, January 18, 1980.

68. Cited by Rhodes Cook, "Straw Presidential Polls Gain Early Notice," *Congressional Quarterly Weekly Report*, November 3, 1979, p. 2473.

69. Ibid.

70. Ibid.

71. Ibid.

72. See Lou Cannon and William Peterson, "GOP," in Richard Harwood, ed., *The Pursuit of the Presidency 1980* (New York: Berkeley Books, 1980), p. 125.

73. "Reagan Raises $1.4 Million in Campaign Funds," *Washington Post*, July 26, 1979.

74. Ibid.

75. E.J. Dionne, "Small Donors Gave Reagan Primary Aid," *New York Times*, July 2, 1980.

76. Ibid.

77. Gottschalk, "Presidential Candidates Beseech Rock Groups."

78. Richard Bergholz, "Reagan Eludes Specifics as He Meets Michigan Auto Workers," *Los Angeles Times*, May 15, 1980.

79. Cited by Richard Bergholz, "High-Ranking Aide in Reagan Camp Quits," *Los Angeles Times*, August 28, 1979.

80. Paul Houston and Carol Blue, "Reagan Fired Them, 3 Top Aides Say," *Los Angeles Times*, February 19, 1980.

81. Ibid.

82. See Robert Scheer, "California Cronies Have Reagan's Ear," *Los Angeles Times,* June 26, 1980.

83. Houston and Blue, "Reagan Fired Them."

84. Robert Lindsey, "Reagan Campaign Said to Be in Debt as Donations Lag," *New York Times,* September 6, 1979.

85. Peter Voss cited by ibid.

86. Cited by Margaret Piton, "The Buck Starts Here," *Working Woman* (October 1981):72.

87. The Reagan campaign reported contribution refunds, miscellaneous loans, and loan repayments of $168,813, which accounts for the difference between the campaign's adjusted individual contribution total of $13.8 million and the total of itemized and unitemized contributions.

88. See "Interest Group Analysis of the New Hampshire Primary," *Political Action Report,* March 15, 1980, p. 9.

89. See Lindsey, "Reagan Campaign Said to Be in Debt."

90. Ibid.

91. Rhodes Cook, "Fund Raising Doubles since Four Years Ago," *Congressional Quarterly Weekly Report,* February 23, 1980, p. 569.

92. Cited by Carey McWilliams, "Second Thoughts," *Nation,* December 15, 1979, p. 615.

93. Les Brown, "Networks Opposing Political Ads Now," *New York Times,* October 14, 1979.

94. See "TV Politics," *Time,* November 12, 1979, p. 76.

95. Cannon and Peterson, "GOP," p. 151.

96. One source indicates the half-hour purchase cost the campaign $8,000. See "Candidates Are Off and Running, Media in Tow," *Broadcasting,* January 14, 1980, p. 217. Another source indicates it cost $50,000. See Bernard Weinraub, "Political Commercials Fill Iowans' Eyes and Ears," *New York Times,* January 19, 1980.

97. "Candidates Spending a Total of $2.8 Million in Iowa Caucuses, 10 Times the '76 Level," *New York Times,* January 21, 1980.

98. The FEC audit of the Reagan prenomination campaign noted allocation errors by the Reagan committee for the state of Iowa but indicated the state spending limit of about $490,000 had not been exceeded. FEC, *Report of the Audit Division on Reagan for President.*

99. Cited by Bernard Weinraub, "Advertisements in Iowa Offer Preview of How Image Makers Intend to Cast Candidates," *New York Times,* January 7, 1980.

100. "To the FCC, Iowa Caucus Is a Primary," *Washington Post,* January 15, 1980.

101. Susan Thero, "Politicians Get an Even Break on Advertising Rates," *National Journal,* March 1, 1980, p. 346.

102. Cited by Cannon and Peterson, "GOP," p. 123.

103. Cited by ibid., p. 127.

104. Richard Bergholz, "N.H. Winners, Losers Plotting Next Moves," *Los Angeles Times,* February 28, 1980.

105. Robert G. Kaiser, "TV Ads: An Aid," *Washington Post,* May 12, 1980.

106. "More on Direct Mail" (letter of Timothy L. Roper), *Campaigns and Elections* (Spring 1981):44.

107. Ibid.

108. Betty Beale, "Bush Comes on Strong at Fundraising Dinner," *Washington Star,* April 25, 1979.

109. "More on Direct Mail," p. 45.

110. Ibid.

111. Ibid.

112. T.R. Reid and Fred Barbash, "GOP Presidential Hopefuls Have Produced $4 Million," *Washington Post,* April 12, 1979.

113. Ibid.

114. Peter C. Stuart, "Big Business Is Bullish About GOP's George Bush, *Christian Science Monitor,* February 21, 1980.

115. Ibid.

116. Ibid.

117. Ibid.

118. Patrick Riordan, "Ahead in Polls, Ahead in Funds: It's Carter, 2-1," *Philadelphia Inquirer,* February 3, 1980.

119. Ibid.

120. Buchanan, "Candidates Must Adjust," p. 1244.

121. Ibid.

122. Ibid.

123. T.R. Reid, "Money Is Still Pouring in for Perceived Also-Rans," *Washington Post,* May 17, 1980.

124. Cited by Ellen Hume, "Bush Withdraws from California Race—No Money," *Los Angeles Times,* May 23, 1980.

125. Cited by Ellen Hume, "Bush Ends His 2-Year Quest for Presidency," *Los Angeles Times,* May 27, 1980.

126. Ibid.

127. Cited by "The Candidates: Getting Their Acts Together," *Broadcasting,* November 5, 1979, p. 38.

128. Ibid.

129. Cited by ibid.

130. Bernard Weinraub, "Candidates Opening Drives in New England," *New York Times,* December 20, 1979.

131. "Candidates Spending a Total of $2.8 Million."

132. Cited by Hume, "Bush Ends Quest."

133. Cited by Ellen Hume, "Lack of Political Nerve Blamed for Bush's Eclipse," *Los Angeles Times,* March 20, 1980.

134. Robert G. Kaiser, "The John, Jerry, Howard, George, Teddy and Jimmy Show," *Washington Post,* February 10, 1980.

135. Ellen Hume, "Bush Happy with Narrow Primary Victory," *Los Angeles Times,* March 6, 1980.

136. Cited by Hume, "Lack of Political Nerve."

137. Kaiser, "TV Ads."

138. FEC, *Report of the Audit Division on George Bush for President* (Washington, D.C., February 4, 1981).

139. David S. Broder, "Anderson of Illinois Entering 1980 Race," *Washington Post,* August 8, 1980.

140. Laurence H. Shoup, "Who's Behind John Anderson?" *Inquiry,* August 4, 18, 1980, p. 14.

141. Buchanan, "Candidates Must Adjust," p. 1247.

142. "Anderson Gets $974,220 in Federal Election Funds," *Los Angeles Times,* April 10, 1980.

143. Dan Balz, "Anderson," in Harwood, *Pursuit of the Presidency,* pp. 223, 225.

144. Ibid., p. 227.

145. Ibid., p. 225.

146. "Financial Support Growing for Once-Strapped Anderson," *Los Angeles Times,* March 11, 1980.

147. Ronald J. Ostrow, "Anderson's Campaign a Happening," *Los Angeles Times,* April 13, 1980.

148. Ibid.

149. Cited by *Christian Science Monitor,* April 28, 1980.

150. Charles T. Powers, "Anderson Drive Rolls On in Comic Page Confusion," *Los Angeles Times,* March 3, 1980.

151. Balz, "Anderson," p. 222.

152. Ibid.

153. Ibid.

154. FEC, *Report of the Audit Division on the Anderson for President Committee* (Washington, D.C., December 18, 1980).

155. Powers, "Anderson Drive Rolls On."

156. "The Candidates: Getting Their Acts Together," p. 36.

157. "Candidates Spending a Total of $2.8 Million."

158. "Anderson Short in New Hampshire Recount," *Los Angeles Times,* March 15, 1980.

159. Kaiser, "The John , Jerry, Howard."

160. Cited by Cannon and Peterson, "GOP," p. 144.

161. Bob Secter "Anderson Receives a Wild Reception," *Los Angeles Times,* March 16, 1980.

162. Cannon and Peterson, "GOP," p. 149.

163. Robert Shogan, "Connally Takes Aim at Big Reagan Lead," *Los Angeles Times,* August 12, 1979.

164. Cited by Cannon and Peterson, "GOP," p. 135.

165. Reid and Barbash, "GOP Presidential Hopefuls."

166. Ibid.

167. Ibid.

168. Ibid.

169. Richard Bergholz, "Connally Backers Set $1 Million State Goal," *Los Angeles Times,* October 28, 1979.

170. Bill Peterson, "Viguerie Leaves Crane, Enters Connally's Camp," *Washington Post,* August 3, 1979.

171. Mayer, "Political Money Game," p. 31.

172. Cited by ibid.

173. Adam Clymer, "Connally Is Scrambling to Keep Troubled Presidential Bid Afloat," *New York Times,* February 7, 1980.

174. Ibid.

175. Bill Peterson, "Connally Turns to a Telethon in S.C. Drive," *Washington Post*, February 15, 1980.

176. See Warren Weaver, Jr., "Carter Far Ahead of Kennedy in Campaign Funds," *New York Times*, February 22, 1980, and Richard E. Meyer, "Ada Mills in Connally's Bag—for $10 Million," *Los Angeles Times*, March 7, 1980.

177. Cited by Robert Shogan, "Reagan Overwhelms Bush, Connally in South Carolina," *Los Angeles Times*, March 29, 1980.

178. The Connally campaign reported $151,947 in contribution refunds, miscellaneous loans, and loan repayments. This figure accounts for the difference between the campaign's adjusted individual contribution total of $11.6 million and the total of unitemized and itemized contributions.

179. "Carter Errors Lead to Crisis, GOP Is Told," *Washington Post*, January 16, 1980.

180. "The Candidates: Getting Their Acts Together," p. 38.

181. Ibid.

182. Cook, "Straw Presidential Polls," p. 2473.

183. "Carter Says He's Ready for Prime Time in December, But Networks Disagree," *Campaign Practices Reports*, November 12, 1979, p. 3.

184. "TV Politics," p. 76.

185. Weinraub, "Candidates Opening Drives."

186. Cited by Meyer, "Ada Mills."

187. "Candidates Are Off and Running," p. 27.

188. William J. Lanouette, "You Can't Be Elected with TV Alone, But You Can't Win without It Either," *National Journal*, March 1, 1980, p. 344.

189. Ibid.

190. Cited by "Candidates Spend Their Budgets Away," p. 26.

191. Buchanan, "Candidates Must Adjust," p. 1244.

192. Ibid., p. 1247.

193. Adam Clymer, "Baker Wary on National Race But Talks Up National Issues," *New York Times*, September 3, 1977.

194. Buchanan, "Candidates Must Adjust," p. 1247.

195. "Candidates Off and Running," p. 28.

196. Buchanan, "Candidates Must Adjust," p. 1247.

197. FEC, *Post-Primary Report of the Audit Division on the Baker Committee* (Washington, D.C., December 18, 1980).

198. FEC, *Addendum to the Final Audit Report on the Baker Committee* (Washington, D.C., April 20, 1981).

199. Diane Henry, "Weicker Pulls Out of GOP Race; Won't Back Any Other Candidate," *New York Times*, May 17, 1979.

200. Adam Clymer, "Ford Revises '76 Campaign Group to Let Others Use Surplus Funds," *New York Times*, July 12, 1978.

201. See Adam Clymer, "Ford Weighs a Low-Key Drive for GOP Nomination," *New York Times*, October 1, 1979.

202. Richard Bergholz, "Reagan and GOP Losers Band Together to Pay Off Campaign Debts—for 'Unity,'" *Los Angeles Times*, May 29, 1980.

203. Ibid.

204. "Reagan and Former Rivals Pooling Fund-Raising Lists," *New York Times*, June 10, 1980.

205. See, for example, Frank del Olmo, "Also-Ran to Vote, Concede," *Los Angeles Times*, June 3, 1980.

206. "6 Losing Candidates Vow Fealty to Reagan at Republican Unity Dinner," *New York Times*, June 15, 1980.

207. Ibid.

208. FEC, *Report of the Audit Division on 1980 Republican Presidential Unity Committee* (Washington, D.C., February 26, 1981), p. 1.

209. FEC, *Report of the Audit Division on the 1980 United Republican Committee* (Washington, D.C., January 27, 1981), p. 1.

210. FEC, *Report of the Audit Division on the Dole for President Committee*, p. 6.

211. Ibid., pp. 6, 7.

212. FEC, *Report of the Audit Division on Crane for President Committee*, p. 7.

213. Ibid.

214. FEC, *Addendum to Final Audit Report on the Baker Committee*, p. 2.

215. "Baker Pays Off Campaign Debt of $1.3 Million," *Los Angeles Times*, July 16, 1980.

216. Buchanan, "Candidates Must Adjust," p. 1247.

217. "Connally Plan to Sell Art Works Limited to $1,000 by FEC," *Campaign Practices Reports*, May 26, 1980, p. 708.

218. "Connally Artists Return to Drawing Boards," *Political Finance/Lobby Reporter*, May 28, 1980, p. 4.

219. See Edward T. Pound, "Presidential Campaign Debts Linger As '80 Losers Can't Find New Funds," *Wall Street Journal*, June 2, 1982.

220. "Arlington Printer Sues Connally Campaign," *Washington Post*, July 1, 1982.

221. Ibid.

222. Cited by Adam Clymer, "Carter Re-election Unit Has Raised Enough to Obtain Matching Funds," *New York Times*, April 4, 1979.

223. Reid and Barbash, "GOP Presidential Hopefuls."

224. Stacy Joina, "Mass. Political 'Big Guns' Tentatively Back Carter's Re-election," *Washington Post*, June 30, 1979.

225. Robert Pear, "Carter Campaign Panel Has Raised $1.5 Million for 1980," *Washington Star*, July 12, 1979.

226. Ibid.

227. Ibid.

228. Rowland Evans and Robert Novak, "Carter's Dwindling Campaign War Chest," *Washington Post*, September 29, 1979.

229. FEC, *Threshold Audit Report of the Audit Division on the Carter/Mondale Presidential Committee, Inc.* (Washington, D.C., July 10, 1980).

230. Cited by Bill Boyarsky, "Carter Campaign Donations Rise after Florida Victory, Aide Says," *Los Angeles Times*, October 18, 1979.

231. Morton Kondracke, "The Fundraising Tally," *New Republic*, February 23, 1980, p. 12.

232. Warren Weaver, Jr., "Strauss Is Emerging as Star Attraction in Carter Fund-Raising Drive," *New York Times*, March 2, 1980.

233. Ibid.

234. Ibid.

235. Eleanor Randolph, "Carter Campaign Aides Find Plus in His Absence," *Los Angeles Times*, March 30, 1980.

236. Weaver, "Carter Campaign Approaching."

237. "Spending Limits Loom as Carter and Reagan Approach Nomination," *New York Times*, May 22, 1980.

238. Francis X. Clines, "Iowa Democratic Caucus: Union vs. Union," *New York Times*, January 15, 1980.

239. David S. Broder, "Teacher's Union: Vital Bloc for Carter," *Washington Post*, July 2, 1980.

240. Jerome Cramer, "Teachers Jump into National Politics," *Executive Educator* (November 1980):21.

241. Timothy B. Clark, "Carter and the Chiropractors—The Tale of a Political Deal," *National Journal*, February 16, 1980, p. 272.

242. Ibid., p. 270.

243. Ibid.

244. Cited by Clymer, "Carter Re-election Unit Has Raised Enough."

245. Peter C. Stuart, "Carter Wields 'Perks' of Office," *Christian Science Monitor*, December 10, 1979.

246. Cited by Martin Tolchin, "Brock Calls Carter Trips Political; White House Says They're Presidential," *New York Times*, August 7, 1979.

247. Martin Schram, "The Carter Bandwagon: A Little Slow in Starting," *Washington Post*, May 10, 1980.

248. Stuart, "Carter Wields 'Perks' of Office."

249. Ibid.

250. Steven R. Weisman, "30 Carter Aides Campaign for Him in Iowa," *New York Times*, January 16, 1980.

251. Cited by Stuart, "Carter Wields 'Perks' of Office."

252. "Carter Gets TV Time; Ford Gives Republicans a Hint," *New York Times*, November 25, 1979.

253. Cited by Stuart, "Carter Wields 'Perks' of Office."

254. See Dom Bonafede, "A Valuable Presidential Tool," *National Journal*, February 2, 1980, p. 197.

255. Stuart, "Carter Wields 'Perks' of Office."

256. Sara Terry, "Carter Timing of Urban Grants Called Shrewd, But Not Unfair," *Christian Science Monitor*, March 4, 1980.

257. Randolph, "Carter Campaign Aides Find Plus."

258. Ibid.

259. Ibid.

260. Ibid.

261. *Baron Report*, September 14, 1979, p. 3.

262. Ibid.

263. Howard Monderer of NBC quoted in Brown, "Networks Opposing Political Ads Now."

264. "Carter Group Complains on TV Time for Speech," *New York Times*, October 30, 1979.

265. Terence Smith, "F.C.C., 4-3, Upholds the President in Bid for Prime Time on Television," *New York Times*, November 21, 1979.

266. "Candidates Are Off and Running," p. 27.

267. Ibid., p. 29.

268. "Carter and Kennedy Ads Go Their Separate Ways," *New York Times*, March 19, 1980.

269. Martin Schramm, "Carter," in Harwood, *Pursuit of the Presidency 1980*, p. 115.

270. Robert Shogan, "Kennedy Leads, Bush Wins in Pennsylvania," *Los Angeles Times*, April 23, 1980.

271. Terence Smith, "Confident Carter Aides Shifting Focus to General Election," *New York Times*, May 7, 1980.

272. Tim Finchem quoted in ibid.

273. FEC, *Report of the Audit Division on the Carter/Mondale Presidential Committee, Inc.* (Washington, D.C., January 21, 1981).

274. FEC, *Memorandum Re: Carter/Mondale Presidential Committee, Inc., Telephone Allocation* (Washington, D.C., November 9, 1981).

275. FEC, advisory opinion 1981-16.

276. "Kennedy Panel Meets Criterion in Record Time," *Los Angeles Times*, November 2, 1979.

277. Michele Willens, "Brand on the Eastern Primaries: Bankrolled in California," *California Journal*, February 1980, p. 58.

278. "Carter Pulls Ahead of Kennedy in Poll," *Washington Star*, December 12, 1979.

279. "FEC Says $1 Million Loan to Kennedy Was in 'Ordinary Course of Business,'" *Campaign Practices Reports*, June 23, 1980, p. 4.

280. "Kennedy Asks FCC Order to Give Him Free TV Time," *Los Angeles Times*, February 28, 1980.

281. Martin Schramm, "Kennedy Unfunded," *Washington Post*, March 14, 1980.

282. Ibid.

283. Ibid.

284. Karen Feld, "Special Event Fundraisers," *Campaigns and Elections* (Spring 1981):31.

285. Ibid.

286. Reid, "Artful Dodge."

287. Feld, "Special Event Fundraisers," p. 30.

288. Kondracke, "The Fundraising Tally," p. 13.

289. Ibid.

290. Cited by Richard J. Cattani, "Democratic Left Doesn't Open Wallet for Kennedy," *Christian Science Monitor*, December 17, 1979.

291. "Direct Mail Fundraising Roundtable: The Pros Speak," *Campaigns and Elections* (Fall 1980):28.

292. Ibid., p. 40.

293. 11 CFR 9034.3(h).

294. "Kennedy's Convention Sweepstakes' Contest Ruled Not Violating Matching Fund Rules," *Campaign Practices Reports*, August 4, 1980, p. 7.

295. Included in the $100,000 figure is an undisclosed amount in PAC contributions that were not dated.

296. Kondracke, "Fundraising Tally," p. 12.

297. Ibid.

298. Martin Schramm, "Kennedy's Decision to Stay in the Race," *Washington Post*, February 5, 1980.

299. Ibid.

300. Eleanor Randolph and Ronald J. Ostrow, "Maze of Campaign Laws Forces New Campaign Strategy," *Los Angeles Times*, January 28, 1980.

301. Schramm, "Kennedy's Decision."

302. Ibid.

303. Ibid.

304. Ibid.

305. "Cost of Covering Kennedy Upsets Media," *Washington Post*, December 20, 1979.

306. "AP Cuts Trips with Kennedy as Too Costly," *Los Angeles Times*, December 20, 1979.

307. "Cost of Covering Kennedy."

308. B. Drummond Ayres, Jr., "Kennedy Plane Too Expensive, Editors Assert," *New York Times*, December 20, 1979.

309. Kondracke, "Fundraising Tally," p. 12.

310. Cited by ibid.

311. "Candidates Are Off and Running," p. 28.

312. FEC, *Report of the Audit Division on the Kennedy for President Committee*, p. 26.

313. Kondracke, "Fundraising Tally," p. 13.

314. Bernard Weinraub, "Kennedy Campaign Alters Advertising," *New York Times*, January 31, 1980.

315. Cited by ibid.

316. Schramm, "Kennedy Unfunded."

317. Ibid.

318. David S. Broder, "An 'Unnatural Hush' Falls over Wisconsin Primary," *Washington Post*, March 30, 1980.

319. Eleanor Randolph, "Kennedy Blames Wisconsin Loss on Carter Iran Report," *Los Angeles Times*, April 3, 1980.

320. Bernard Weinraub, "Kennedy TV Campaign Will Stress Positive Image," *New York Times*, April 25, 1980.

321. Cited by Robert Shogan, "Kennedy to Free Delegates If Carter Agrees to Debate," *Los Angeles Times*, May 30, 1980.

322. Richard E. Meyer, "Kennedy TV Campaign for State Put at $195,000, Carter's at $150,000," *Los Angeles Times*, May 29, 1980.

323. Robert Shogan, "NJ Seen as Best Kennedy Chance," *Los Angeles Times*, June 2, 1980.

324. Cited by Jack W. Germond and Jules Witcover, "Carter Gets His Needed Total," *Washington Star*, June 4, 1980.

325. T.R. Reid, "Kennedy," in Harwood, *Pursuit of the Presidency 1980*, p. 81.

326. FEC, *Report of the Audit Division on the Kennedy for President Committee* (Washington, D.C., September 28, 1981).

327. Cited by "Kennedy Attorney Claims FEC Tried to Regulate through Audit," *Campaign Practices Reports*, October 26, 1981, p. 8.

328. W.B. Rood, "Brown Files Papers to Seek Presidency," *Los Angeles Times*, July 21, 1979. See also Anthony Lewis, "The Brown Appeal," *New York Times*, August 30, 1979.

329. Richard Bergholz, "Support for Brown Lagging as He Arrives in Chicago," *Los Angeles Times*, October 8, 1979.

330. Larry Stammer, "Brown to Move Headquarters of Drive to Boston," *Los Angeles Times*, November 7, 1979.

331. Larry Stammer, "Brown Raises $155,000 in S.F., Criticizes Carter," *Los Angeles Times*, November 14, 1979.

332. Carol Blue, "180 State Aides Gave to Brown Presidential Campaign," *Los Angeles Times*, May 9, 1980.

333. William Endicott and Doug Shuit, "Brown Seeks Go-Getter to Shore Up Sagging Drive," *Los Angeles Times*, March 1, 1980.

334. Tim Onosko, "Media Madness," *Village Voice*, April 21, 1980.

335. William Endicott, "Brown Goes Hollywood in Wisconsin," *Los Angeles Times*, March 29, 1980.

336. Nancy Skelton, "Chip Carter Woos Gov. Brown's Chief Money-Raiser, Offers to Help on Debt," *Los Angeles Times*, May 6, 1980.

337. Blue, "180 State Aides."

338. Ibid.

339. Ibid.

340. FEC, *Report of the Audit Division on Brown for President* (Washington, D.C., December 16, 1980).

341. "Alleged LaRouche 'Target List' Found," *Los Angeles Times*, February 2, 1980.

342. Ibid.

343. FEC, *Report of the Audit Division on the Citizens for LaRouche* (Washington, D.C., April 15, 1981).

344. "FEC Abused Powers, Says Federal Judge," *Campaign Practices Reports*, March 20, 1982, p. 4.

345. "U.S. Judge Orders Moratorium on FEC's Probes of LaRouche," *Political Finance/Lobby Reporter*, March 24, 1982, p. 77.

346. "Kennedy Artwork Stymies Agency," *Political Finance/Lobby Reporter*, January 14, 1981, p. 5.

347. Pound, "Presidential Campaign Debt Linger."

6 Financing the Conventions

The Republican party held its national convention in Detroit in mid-July, and the Democratic party held its convention in New York a month later. In each case, convention delegates ratified the choice for party nominee that voters had previously made in primary elections and state party caucuses. Both Ronald Reagan and Jimmy Carter went to their respective conventions with more than enough delegates to assure their nominations. Only the process of choosing a vice-presidential nominee, which included an unprecedented and ultimately unsuccessful effort to get a former president to join the ticket in the second spot, added an element of drama to the Republican convention. And only Sen. Edward Kennedy's determined refusal to concede defeat provided an initial aura of suspense regarding the outcome of the Democratic convention. But after a Kennedy-supported effort to overturn the rule requiring all delegates to vote on the first ballot for the candidate whom they were elected to support was defeated on the first evening of the convention, the result of the Democratic convention was as much a forgone conclusion as that of its Republican counterpart.

The Regulatory Context

As in 1976, in 1980 the two major political parties received federal grants to finance their conventions. Under the 1974 FECA amendments, the parties were eligible to receive from the presidential checkoff fund grants of $2 million each, to be adjusted according to rises in the CPI. The 1979 FECA amendments raised the basic grant to $3 million. When indexed to take account of the rise in the cost of living since January 1, 1975, the effective date of the 1974 law, the federal subsidy amounted to $4,416,000 for each party to finance its convention.

For their 1976 conventions, the parties received their federal grants in installments. Each party received an initial payment of not more than 30 percent of the full entitlement, with subsequent payments based on projected expenses and drawn on a quarterly schedule. Both parties disliked this arrangement, maintaining that their spending was made inefficient by the quarterly schedule and that convention officials were spending an inordinate amount of time soothing creditors because money was not available to pay bills as needed. For the 1980 conventions, the federal subsidy was paid out to each party as requested. The Democratic party drew large amounts early, a reflection of its poor financial position compared with that of the Republican party.

The federal grant, which is used to pay for such convention-related expenses as salaries and professional fees, platform hearings prior to the convention, convention security services, printing, telephone, travel, and convention staff food and lodging, replaced in large measure the previous mode of convention financing whereby host cities and local businesses furnished cash and services to party conventions and national corporations bought advertising space in convention program books, legitimately claiming the sometimes considerable cost as a business expense, which qualified as an income-tax deduction. Under the law, none of the grant money may be used to defray the expenses of any candidates for the presidential nomination or of delegates participating in the convention.

A June 1975 advisory opinion permitted certain types of contributions to convention-arrangements committees and expenditures on their behalf in addition to the federal subsidy. The FEC ruled that state and local governments where the conventions are held could provide certain services and facilities, such as convention halls, transportation, and security assistance, the cost of which would not count against the parties' expenditure limits. The FEC also permitted the parties to accept such items as free hotel rooms and conference facilities in return for booking a certain number of room reservations, as long as other conventions of similar size and duration receive similar benefits. In addition, the commission allowed host committees and civic associations working to attract or assist the political conventions to accept contributions from local businesses and from national corporations with local operations as long as the contributions were made "in the reasonable expectation of a commensurate return during the life of the convention"[1] and the profits went primarily to the local outlets when the contributions came from national corporations. These FEC opinions remained in force for the 1980 national nominating conventions.

Convention Site Selection

The FEC advisory opinion sanctioning certain spending in order to attract a political convention assured that the parties would continue to engage in the complex process of encouraging and weighing bids from potential convention host cities and committees. The lure of considerable delegate and convention visitor spending—estimates of the amount spent by convention goers in Kansas City and New York in 1976 approached $10 million in each city—and of the possibility of drumming up additional convention business through positive media reports of the host city ensured that potential convention cities would continue to join in the bidding process. The FEC ruling permitted federal funds to be spent by both parties in the operations of their respective site-selection committees. The Democrats, for example, who broke down the costs of the bidding process from other convention expenses, spent $6,021 in federal funds selecting a convention site.

Seven cities—Detroit, Minneapolis-St. Paul, Dallas, New Orleans, Kansas City, Miami Beach, and New York—wined and dined the Republican party site committee and offered packages of enticements designed to attract the Republican National Convention. New Orleans offered its huge Superdome as a convention site, an abundance of hotel rooms close to the facility, and the added attraction of what Rep. David Treen (R-La.) called the best restaurants in North America, "if not in the entire world."[2] Democratic Gov. Bob Graham reportedly said he would ask the state legislature to appropriate up to $7 million to help finance Miami Beach's bid for the convention. New York assured the Republicans of the same hospitality it had offered the Democratic National Convention in 1976 and, as it did then, included a promise from organized labor that the convention would not be disrupted by labor disputes.

In the end, Detroit's bid was accepted by the Republicans. Among the factors in the industrial city's favor was its offer of more convention space than any other contender, which the city promised to make available to the party as long in advance of the July 14, 1980, convention opening date as the party desired. In contrast, the convention facility offered by Dallas was considered too small, and it was not available for use in mid-July, the party's first choice for the time of its convention. The New Orleans Superdome was considered too large, even though the city promised to spend $350,000 for a curtain to subdivide the space and make it more suitable for conducting convention business. And the bids of three cities—Kansas City, New Orleans, and Miami Beach—were hampered because their states had failed to ratify the Equal Rights Amendment, which for years had been supported in the Republican convention platforms. Ironically, at its 1980 convention, the Republican party withdrew its traditional support for the ERA.

Also in Detroit's favor was party chairman William Brock's conviction that meeting in Detroit, a traditional Democratic labor stronghold whose population in 1980 was about 55 percent black, would serve the party's efforts to reach out to the urban community, to union members, and to minority groups. Brock's support apparently was influential in overcoming the objections of some party leaders that Detroit was a depressing city with little to offer convention delegates.

Five cities—Minneapolis-St. Paul, Dallas, Philadelphia, Detroit, and New York—made bids to host the Democratic National Convention. Although President Carter was said to have preferred a southern city as a convention site, several potential southern sites, such as Atlanta and New Orleans were eliminated because Democratic party rules forbade holding a convention in any state that had not ratified the ERA. Minneapolis-St. Paul dropped out of the bidding because it could not offer the convention facility space or hotel rooms—20,000 first-class rooms within twenty minutes' driving time of the convention center—required by the party's site committee. Other requirements listed by the committee for potential convention sites reportedly included free use of a convention center for several weeks, construction and decorations in the convention hall, free transportation for delegates from their hotels to the center for convention functions, and office space for convention staff.[3]

Dallas dropped out of the competition after having made the most unusual, and controversial, bid for the convention. Dallas representatives, who said their city council prohibited using municipal funds to finance the convention, pledged to raise $3 million from the private sector to pay Democratic expenses, including use of the Dallas Convention Center, construction and decorations in the convention hall, electrical power and janitorial services, and liability and security coverage.[4] Questions arose about the ability of the Dallas host committee to raise that amount, as well as about the legality of the committee's proposal to finance the convention through private contributions. According to FEC guidelines, private contributions to such efforts must come from local sources—the host committee emphasized statewide sources in its presentation[5]—and local retail companies making contributions may donate sums only in proportion to what they reasonably anticipate recovering from convention-generated business. Democratic site-selection committee members did not think it would be possible to obtain a timely ruling from the FEC on the legality of the Dallas proposal.

The three cities remaining made similar offers of free services, such as rent-free use of convention space, a free transportation system for delegates, alteration and decoration of the convention hall, and whatever police overtime would be required. Philadelphia sweetened its offer of approximately $7 million in free goods and services, along with a pledge by local union leaders of uninterrupted service and support for the Democratic nominee,[6] with a pledge of $1 million "in cold, hard cash."[7] Detroit, which had offered a $3.1 million package, including a $300,000 contribution,[8] then pledged that its business community would match the cash contribution of any competing city.[9] At the time the offers of cash were made, it was not clear whether FEC regulations would allow them or would require that such contributions be made in goods and services instead.

When the time came for a decision, New York, which had not made an offer of a cash contribution, received the nod. Included in New York's convention-enticement package was $4.5 million to rent and renovate Madison Square Garden,[10] $2 million for police salaries,[11] and additional money for delegate transportation, office rental, security, and other services. New York also was able to offer the 20,000 first-class hotel rooms required by the site-selection committee, including 2,000 suites for use by high-level politicians and party officials.[12] Both Detroit and Philadelphia would have had to house some delegates at a considerable distance from their convention centers or to put them up in college dormitories. In addition the Philadelphia convention center's ceiling was only twenty-eight feet high—it "would make the convention look squashed on television," said site-selection chairman Don Fowler[13]—and some concern was voiced by selection committee members that the convention staff would not have sufficient time to set up so soon after the Republican convention in Detroit.

Additional factors in New York's favor were positive memories of the 1976 Democratic convention held there and of the security the city's police force provided, and possibly the assurance of support by high-ranking city Democratic officials for a major fund-raising dinner to be held in the city.[14] One member of the selection committee maintained, however, that "the fund-raiser can in no way be a condition precedent for getting the convention."[15]

Host Cities and Committees

The process of successfully selling their cities to the Republican and Democratic parties as convention sites was only the beginning for Detroit and New York city officials and host committees. To accommodate the estimated 20,000 persons expected to converge on Detroit for the Republican convention, by January 1979, a full year and a half before the Republican gathering, the city had already contracted for 14,200 hotel and motel rooms and had arranged with six area colleges an option to use an additional 5,000 dormitory rooms. Since some of the delegates would have to be housed in Windsor, Ontario, across the Detroit River in Canada, a separate Canadian Host Committee for the 1980 Republican National Convention was set up in accord with U.S. and Canadian regulations prohibiting Detroiters and Windsorites from working directly with each other on arrangements for a political convention. And when the Radisson Cadillac, one of the city's four major downtown hotels, threatened to fail, some fifty major Detroit-based corporations stepped in and promised to raise $1 million to bail the hotel out so it could remain open for the convention.[16] The hotel had promised 875 rooms for convention use, about one-third of the gathering's downtown hotel space.[17]

The city spent an estimated $2 million in private and public money sprucing up the city in anticipation of the convention.[18] Derelict buildings were demolished or boarded up, and attention was focused on the city's new

$367 million Renaissance Center, a gleaming glass-and-steel hotel and office complex that served as Republican convention headquarters, and on the newly built 20,000-seat Joe Louis Arena, the actual convention site, and the adjacent Cobo Hall, the second-largest convention hall in the nation, which would serve as a media headquarters.

To ease the burden of providing convention security, Detroit received a grant of $3.5 million from the federal Law Enforcement Assistance Administration (LEAA). The city, however, reportedly did not use all of its grant and returned more than $300,000 to the government.[19]

Detroit's civic host committee, headed by Thomas Murphy, chairman of General Motors Corporation, spearheaded a drive to welcome Republican delegates and alternates, some 4,000 in all, as well as the 8,000 reporters and broadcast technicians who were expected to attend the convention. The host committee worked with the RNC on hotel assignments, delegate transportation, food supplies, and security. A host committee call for volunteers in the spring of 1980 drew 3,600 responses almost immediately, more than the committee needed.[20] Volunteers blew up the 25,000 balloons that rained down upon the heads of delegates at peak convention moments, staffed information booths on the esplanade between convention headquarters and the convention arena, and delivered daily events calendars to each state delegation at their hotels. One team of volunteers prepared and delivered 4,540 welcome bags to convention delegates and alternates. An FEC advisory opinion ruled that a local business might donate the bags, inscribed with the convention's name on one side and the company's name on the other, because their value was nominal and they were provided for bona-fide advertising purposes in the ordinary course of business.[21]

The host committee organized an opening regatta to welcome convention visitors, sponsored a citywide party to celebrate the gathering, and arranged daily events to entertain delegates during their free time. A preconvention party sponsored for members of the press by the committee reportedly was budgeted at $40,000 to cover the cost of food from sixty area restaurants, musical entertainment, and quantities of beer, wine, and spirits.[22]

According to an FEC audit report covering financial activity through September 30, 1980, the civic host committee raised nearly $719,000 in contributions to fund its activities; by September 30, 1980, all but $60,000 of this had been spent.[23] In addition the committee received a favorable ruling from the FEC allowing it to transfer funds from its general account, made up of money donated by individuals and local businesses for use in promoting the city and its commerce, to an account used to defray qualified convention expenses.[24] The latter account, which had not been opened until the committee decided it would undertake to help the RNC cover some convention expenses, was inadequate for that purpose. The host committee explained to the FEC that the money in the general account it would use to make up the difference had come from local retailers who had agreed it could be used for convention expenses.

Both Detroit city officials and GOP leaders were pleased with the result of their joint efforts. City officials were persuaded the convention gave the city a needed public-relations boost and expressed confidence that it had generated between $30 million and $40 million for the city's economy.[25] Said Republican leader Brock, "The taxis worked, the elevators worked, the police worked—in fact, I have not heard one single complaint from a delegate."[26]

New York City officials also made sure their city was cleaned up in good time to welcome the 20,000 to 25,000 delegates, alternates, newspersons, and party and government officials expected for the mid-August Democratic National Convention. Potholes were filled, overgrown grass cut, streets swept, and trash hauled away. To make sure the convention arrangements were carried out according to the specifications of party leaders, the city spent an estimated $4.8 million,[27] including a reported $2 million to rent Madison Square Garden, which the city took over on June 30, a full six weeks before the convention started; $2 million for construction in the arena in preparation for the gathering and for postconvention removal of the construction; $200,000 for insurance; $139,000 for transportation; $100,000 for telephone costs; and additional funds to house convention staff persons.[28]

Like Detroit, New York was offered $3.5 million in federal funds from the LEAA to help cover the costs of convention security. Some 3,000 city police officers were assigned to convention security duty within and outside the convention hall.[29] City officials had estimated that $3.25 million of the LEAA grant would be used to pay overtime for officers assigned to convention security[30] and that total security costs would exceed the federal reimbursement.[31] Unlike Detroit, New York drew the entire amount made available by the LEAA.

The New York civic host committee, headed by Preston Robert Tisch, operated on a $400,000 budget and carried out a program similar to that of its Detroit counterpart.[32] Preconvention parties were held for New Yorkers who would serve the delegates: police officers, taxi and bus drivers, and sanitation workers. On their arrival in New York, delegates were met at the airport by volunteers who showered them with complimentary trinkets donated by local retailers, hotels, museums, and labor unions. The host committee arranged reservations for theater, sporting-event and museum-exhibit tickets, which the delegates had to pay for themselves, and hosted a variety of free events for the delegates' entertainment, including a buffet dinner and seats at a New York Yankees-Baltimore Orioles baseball game.[33] The FEC ruled that the New York Yankees Baseball Club might donate 1,000 tickets to the host committee to help the committee welcome the delegates to the city.[34] The tickets were not counted as an impermissible corporate contribution by the baseball club, nor did they count against the Democratic party's convention spending limit.

The most-expensive event sponsored by the host committee for convention guests was a preconvention evening affair at the New York City Music Hall, including drinks, a box dinner, and a show tracing one hundred years of Broadway entertainment. "That's costing us more than anything else," said Cissie Aidinoff, the committee's executive director. "But that's the big event. That's New York."[35]

Both city and host committee officials believed the cost of their combined efforts was worthwhile; it was estimated that the convention would generate some $30 million in income for New Yorkers and that it would give a boost to the city's tourism, its second-largest industry.[36]

Delegate Apportionment, Selection, and Allocation

Although votes at each party's national convention on the matter of the presidential and vice-presidential nominations as well as on matters regarding party platform, rules, and credentials are cast by elected and appointed delegates, the manner of apportioning, selecting, and allocating those delegates differs between the two parties. The delegate-apportionment system adopted at the 1972 Republican National Convention for its convention in 1976 largely remained in force at the 1980 convention. Under this system, each of the fifty states received six delegates at large plus three delegates for each congressional district. In addition, the states were awarded bonus delegates at large if they delivered their 1976 presidential electoral votes to the Republican nominee. Each state that did so was awarded four and one-half delegates at large plus the number of delegates equal to 60 percent of the electoral votes from the state, rounded upward to the nearest whole number. Bonus delegates at large also were awarded if states elected various other Republican candidates in 1976 and 1978, with a maximum number of bonus delegates stipulated for each category of Republican victory. For example, each state electing a Republican senator in 1976 received an additional delegate at large, up to a maximum of two such delegates for Republican senatorial victories. In all, 1,994 delegates and an equal number of alternates representing the fifty states, the District of Columbia, Guam, Puerto Rico, and the Virgin Islands were allowed for the 1980 Republican Convention.[37]

Under the delegate-apportionment system adopted by the Democratic party, approximately half of the delegates allocated to each state were determined according to the state's electoral votes and half according to the state's share of the Democratic popular vote for president in the last three presidential elections. Further, the size of each state's delegation at the 1980 convention was increased by 10 percent over 1976 to allow party and elected officials to be included. Party rules require that 75 percent of each state's delegation be chosen at the congressional district level or lower. In all 3,383 delegates and 2,053 alternates representing the fifty states and the District of Columbia, Puerto Rico, Guam, the Virgin Islands, and Democrats Abroad were allowed for the 1980 Democratic convention.[38] Actually, since Democratic delegations from the smallest states are permitted to have fractional votes to enlarge their numbers, the total number of delegates exceeded the total number of full votes. One-hundred fifty-nine partial-vote delegates cast 107 votes.[109]

In November 1979 a call was issued by the RNC for selection of delegates to the party's 1980 nominating convention. Delegates were permitted to be selected from that time until twenty-five days before the convention opened. Seventy-six percent of the Republican delegates were elected in primaries or were chosen by a separate process that was bound to reflect the primary results.[40] About two-thirds of the Republican primary state delegates were selected according to a winner-take-all system in which all at-large delegates were awarded to the candidate with the highest number of votes state-wide, or in which all at-large delegates in a district were accorded to the candidate who received the highest number of votes in the district. Although Republican rules suggested that state delegations be split evenly between men and women, they did not require such a division. About 29 percent of the 1980 convention delegates were women,[41] and about 60 percent were white males.[42] The rules established no goals, timetables, or plans regarding affirmative action to ensure selection of delegates representing women's and minority groups. Party rules in 1976 had required delegates bound to a specific candidate by state law in primary states to vote for that candidate no matter what their personal presidential preferences were. This so-called justice resolution, which had been backed by supporters of President Ford at the 1976 convention who were worried some Ford delegates might vote for Ronald Reagan in defiance of state laws binding them to Ford, was deleted by party delegates to the 1980 convention.

Although Democratic party rules specified that delegate selection was to take place between the second Tuesday in March and June 23, exceptions were made for Iowa, Maine, New Hampshire, Minnesota, and Massachusetts to begin the process earlier. Seventy-one percent of the Democratic delegates were elected in primaries or were bound to reflect primary results.[43] For the 1980 Democratic race, the party virtually eliminated the winner-take-all method of delegate selection. Delegates were allocated to each candidate in proportion to the percentage of popular votes they received, as long as the candidates received a minimum percentage of the vote, to be set by each state party, generally between 15 and 25 percent.

Loophole primaries, modified winner-take-all systems in which delegates were elected from congressional districts and without proportional representation, were allowed in only two states, Illinois and West Virginia. Delegates from these states constituted only 9 percent of Democratic delegates elected from primary states and only 6 percent of all convention delegates.

A party rule adopted in December 1978 required that state delegations be divided evenly between men and women. Nevertheless the DNC granted Illinois an exemption from this rule after deciding the state party had made a good-faith effort to comply with it.[44] In addition party rules required each state to adopt and implement an affirmative-action plan to ensure adequate representation of youth and various minority groups. A 1979 FEC advisory opinion ruled that reporting obligations governing national nominating conventions did not apply to funds received and expenditures made by the New Jersey State Democratic Committee to implement such a program.[45] The commission noted that since such contributions and expenditures are not made in order to influence the election of any person to federal office or to influence the results of a primary, they are not subject to the limitations of the FECA, and payment of such costs need not be made out of the state committee's federal account. The commission also noted, however, that since such expenses are incurred in connection with the federal-election process, they may not be paid from prohibited contributions: from funds donated by foreign nationals, from labor union or corporation treasury funds, or from funds from national banks. Finally, party rules bound delegates for one ballot to the candidate they were elected to support, unless the candidate released them in writing. This delegate binding rule received a determined but unsuccessful challenge in the party rules committee deliberations prior to the convention and at the convention itself.

Delegate-Candidate Spending

In a 1980 advisory opinion, the FEC outlined how the FECA would apply to certain spending by delegate candidates.[46] The opinion made clear that since delegate candidates do not seek federal office, money they spend to advocate their own selection is neither subject to the act's limitations nor is it reportable. Contributions to delegate candidates, however, are chargeable to the donor's individual $25,000 annual contribution limits, and contributions may not be received from prohibited sources. Spending by delegate candidates for campaign materials such as bumper strips and yard signs used in connection with volunteer activity and advocating the delegate candidate's selection, as well as referring to a specific presidential candidate, is neither limited nor reportable under the federal law. But spending by delegate candidates for public media advertising, such as television broadcasts, print advertising, and direct mail, which both advocates the delegate candidate's selection and refers to a presidential candidate, is counted as a reportable independent expenditure if it advocates the presidential candidate's election and is not made in consultation with the candidate or his authorized agents or committees; or as an in-kind contribution if made in consultation with the presidential candidate's campaign. In the latter case, that portion of the expenditure that may be allocated to the presidential candidate is chargeable to that candidate's expenditure limits. Finally, according to the opinion, delegate slates become political committees if they spend more than $1,000 during a calendar year. As political committees, delegate slates are subject to the reporting requirements and contribution and spending limits of the law. They also are subject to the requirements for individual delegate candidates regarding expenditures for public media advocating the selection of a delegate candidate and referring to a presidential candidate. The FEC did develop regulations governing contributions to and expenditures by convention delegates, but these did not become effective until August 7, 1980, too late to have a significant influence on the 1980 conventions.

Spending by presidential candidates to influence delegate selection in any state counted against that candidate's spending limits. Spending by state- and local-party committees to cover the administrative costs of caucuses or conventions was not considered reportable under the federal law.

Since much of the delegate candidate spending was not reportable, information about such expenditures, drawn largely from journalistic reports, is unverifiable. For example, a slate of delegate candidates supporting Sen. Edward Kennedy in the Eighteenth Congressional District on Manhattan's East Side and headed by historian Arthur Schlesinger, Jr., reportedly spent up to $1,000 on its campaign.[47] On the Republican side in the same district, a local Republican leader maintained he lost in his bid for a delegate's seat at the convention because of a campaign, including telephone banks and letters, that outspent his side $100,000 to $6,000.[48]

Specific information about presidential candidate spending to influence delegate selection also is sketchy. The Carter-Mondale campaign, for example, reportedly set aside $4,000 for mailings, literature, and rentals in connection with a series of seventeen seminars across New York State on how to become a delegate to the Democratic National Convention.[49] Also in New York, where two caucuses were held after the state's March 25 binding presidential primary in each congressional district to choose delegates pledged to support Sen. Kennedy and President Carter, the Democratic State Committee spent a reported $12,000 for printing ballots and explanatory literature and up to $800 for rent for each caucus site.[50]

The Republican Convention

Unlike in 1976, when incumbent President Ford had to fight off the challenge of Ronald Reagan for the Republican nomination, in 1980 the Republican National Convention took place in an atmosphere of unity. Reagan came to the convention with more than enough delegate votes to lock up the nomination, as well as with pledges of support from his vanquished Republican rivals. He was nominated on the first ballot, receiving 97 percent of the total votes cast. The only suspense at the convention was provided by speculation over Reagan's choice of a running mate. The suspense was heightened on the third day of the convention by a flurry of sometimes contradictory reports that aides to Reagan and former President Ford were carrying on discussions that might lead to Ford's accepting the second spot on the 1980 ticket. The discussions broke down late in the evening, and Reagan, in an unprecedented move, went to the convention arena to end the rampant speculation about a possible Ford vice-presidency and to announce his choice of George Bush as his running mate. Despite some reports that North Carolina Sen. Jessee Helms would allow his name to be placed in nomination in opposition to Bush and despite an organized effort by supporters of New York Rep. Jack Kemp early in the convention to boost him for the second spot, Bush received 1,832 votes in the first vice-presidential roll call, with Helms finishing a distant second with 54 votes and Kemp third with 42 votes. Neither Helms nor Kemp was formally nominated for the position.

Helms had indicated vice-presidential aspirations as early as the February 26 New Hampshire primary when he was the only GOP candidate to be listed for the office. The Jesse for Vice-President committee waged a serious campaign on his behalf, spending $219,401 for the unsuccessful bid. The campaign on behalf of Jack Kemp was considerably less extensive. An independent group of Kemp supporters, Republicans for Victory in '80, spent $56,700 preparing such items as 4,000 Reagan-Kemp posters, 600 Reagan-Kemp straw hats, 5,000 Jack-Kemp-for-Vice-President brochures, and 2,000 copies of Kemp's book, *American Renaissance*, for distribution during the convention.[51] Although Kemp disavowed the support of the group as well as any intentions to seek the vice-presidential nomination, the group held daily press briefings, hosted a reception for delegates and alternates, and orchestrated a convention floor demonstration on behalf of the New York congressman.[52]

Potential sources of disharmony at the convention had been eliminated by the work of the platform, rules, and credentials committees, which met prior to the convention, or by the inability of opponents of those committees' decisions to muster sufficient support to reopen discussion on the convention floor. As might be expected of a document drawn up by a 106-member committee chosen by the individual state delegations, who were overwhelmingly committed to Reagan, the party platform was basically consistent with the nominee's stated views. It called for tax cuts and less government regulation and criticized the Carter administration, particularly on matters of foreign policy. For the first time since 1940, the platform did not include a plank supporting ratification of the Equal Rights Amendment. Although Reagan opposed ratification, he recommended that the platform espouse no position on the issue, and the platform committee agreed. The plank regarding women's rights instead affirmed the "party's historic commitment to equal rights and equality for women" and noted that ratification of the amendment is in the hands of state legislatures. Party moderates who sought to reaffirm traditional Republican support for the ERA were unable to gather enough votes for a minority report on the plank, and efforts in several state caucuses to line up a majority of delegations in favor of suspending the rules to debate the issue before the full convention failed.

Some moderates also were upset with a platform plank calling on a Reagan administration to appoint federal judges who "respect traditional family values and the sanctity of innocent human life." A plank supporting a constitutional amendment "to restore protection of the right to life for unborn children" also aroused controversy. But on these planks, too, opponents failed to win enough votes to warrant a minority report, and there was no discussion on the convention floor. On the matter of election reform, the platform opposed "national postcard voter registration schemes" as open to fraud and expressed preference for state and party determination of the presidential nominating process to enactment of a uniform national primary, which "would only add to the already high costs of, and excessive federal intrusion into, presidential primary campaigns." The platform called for repeal of "restrictive campaign spending limits that tend to create obstacles to local grassroots participation in federal elections" and opposed public financing of congressional campaigns as a tax subsidy for incumbent members of Congress.

Like the party platform, the report of the Republican convention's rules committee was adopted by the full convention without debate and by a voice vote. In deliberations that took place just before the convention opened, the rules committee made some significant changes in the party's comparatively small body of rules. Committee members voted to delete the justice resolution by which party rules had been used to reinforce state laws requiring delegates to vote at the convention for the candidate to whom they were pledged. Opponents of the resolution argued successfully that states, and not national conventions, had the duty to enforce state laws.[53] The committee also changed the term of office of the RNC chairman from four years to two years and specified that the election of the chairman be held in odd-numbered rather than even-numbered years, thus freeing that election from the pressures of presidential politics. The immediate effect of this change was to give the current RNC chairman, Bill Brock, who had been reelected July 8 despite some initial opposition from Reagan partisans, a six-month term. Brock subsequently was given a cabinet-level appointment as the Reagan administration's international trade representative and was succeeded in the chairman's post by Richard Richards.

An additional new rule prohibited the RNC from contributing to a candidate in a contested primary race unless the committee first received the written consent of the Republican state chairman and of the state's two other national committee members. In 1978 the RNC had contributed funds to moderate Republican Maurice Van Nostrand's unsuccessful U.S. Senate primary race against conservative Roger Jepsen, who went on to win the general election. Conservatives wanted to make sure that did not occur again.

Efforts to change the party's method of allocating delegates to the individual states were voted down by the rules committee, but the committee did authorize a study to consider proposals to increase delegate representation from the populous states and to overhaul the presidential primary system. Also voted down was a proposal to increase the number of delegates from Puerto Rico, although Puerto Rico was promised that if it were granted statehood by 1984, it would be allocated as many delegates as states of similar size.

Only two credentials disputes arose prior to the convention, and these were settled easily by the convention's credentials committee. The credentials of the three delegates from Kentucky's Second District were challenged by other local political figures on the grounds that nominations for the delegate positions had not been permitted from the floor. Instead a nominating committee had put up a slate of candidates for the state convention's approval. The challenge was overturned by the credentials committee, which ruled that under national-party rules, the challengers should have appealed first to the Kentucky state convention. Both sides in the dispute backed Reagan for the presidential nomination.

The second dispute arose over a challenge led by two Reagan supporters regarding the credentials of the thirteen delegates whom John Anderson won in the March 4 Massachusetts primary. The challengers argued that all thirteen should be replaced by uncommitted delegates since Anderson withdrew from the Republican race on April 24, before the May 3 congressional district caucuses and the May 13 state committee meeting at which the delegates actually were selected. The credentials committee voted to bump two of the Anderson delegates in favor of two Reagan supporters who previously had backed Anderson but had been dumped by the state Anderson committee because of their pro-Reagan leanings.

Receipts reported by the arrangements committee of the RNC to conduct convention business came to $4,517,451.76,[54] of which $4,416,000 was granted to the committee from federal funds allocated under the FECA. An FEC audit, which reviewed the committee financial activity through March 4, 1981, determined that the unspent portion of the committee's federal entitlement allocation came to $15,758.85 and recommended that that amount be repaid to the U.S. Treasury.

Actual expenditures of federal funds at the convention amounted to $4,390,090.10, leaving a surplus of $25,909.90 (table 6-1). The difference of about $10,000 between the surplus and the funds returned to the U.S. Treasury was set aside as a qualified convention expense to assist in mailing the official proceedings and to reimburse the accountant for the final statement of expenditures.

Table 6-1
1980 Republican National Convention Expenditures

Subsistence (food and housing)	$ 528,256.24
Transportation	217,037.88
Salaries	425,115.41
Professional services	376,318.00
Legal services	160,117.44
Agency charges	481,713.54
Computer services	18,853.95
Printing (not including official proceedings)	177,291.98
Construction	696,702.65
Meetings and conferences	134,966.61
Rent expenses	19,537.59
Music and films	244,644.90
Telephone	180,466.71
Furniture and office equipment	383,500.07
Convention supplies	151,616.23
Utilities	40,481.37
Insurance	39,266.00
Lease car expense	3,735.00
Miscellaneous, Contingency	55,468.53
Printing of official proceedings	55,000.00
Total	$4,390,090.10
Federal grant	$4,416,000.00
Total expenditures	4,390,090.10
	$ 25,909.90
Returned to federal government	$ 15,758.85
Cash on hand	$ 10,151.05[a]

Source: Information provided by the RNC.
[a]Used to assist in mailing the official proceedings and to reimburse accountant for final report.

Other qualified convention expenditures of federal funds can be broken down into a number of categories. The costs of such basic necessities as food, housing, and transportation for those involved in the administration of the convention came to about $750,000. Supplies necessary for convention operations, including utilities, telephone services, furniture, and office equipment, and other miscellaneous supplies ranging from balloons to paper, added another $750,000 to the bill. Various professional, legal, and service charges amounted to well over $1 million of federally funded expenses. The largest single-item expenditure of $696,702.65 was the construction cost of making the facilities suitable for convention purposes.

The Democratic Convention

In contrast to its Republican counterpart, the Democratic National Convention took place in an atmosphere marked by the same tension and infighting that had characterized the primary and caucus contests between President Carter and Sen. Edward Kennedy. Although Carter came to the convention with some 300 more delegates than he needed for the nomination, Kennedy was determined not to give up without a fight. Kennedy's strategy was to seek a change in the party rules requiring delegates to vote on the first ballot for the candidate whom they were elected to support. Kennedy supporters were defeated on the proposal first in rules committee deliberations and then in a roll-call vote of the full convention. Kennedy subsequently withdrew from the race, conceding victory to his opponent. Despite his withdrawal, most of his supporters voted for him on the presidential nomination roll call, with the result that President Carter was renominated with only 64 percent of the total vote, a relatively small percentage for an incumbent. Vice-President Walter Mondale was renominated by acclamation before the roll call was completed.

The controversies between the two Democratic presidential candidates were particularly evident in the deliberations of the rules and platform committees and in convention floor debate over their decisions. In 1978 the DNC had approved a recommendation of the party's rules review panel, known as the Winograd Commission after its chairman, Michigan party chief Morley Winograd, that all national convention delegates be bound to vote for the presidential candidate they were elected to support for at least the first convention ballot, unless that candidate released them in writing. Delegates who violated the rule would be subject to being replaced by delegates of the presidential candidate's choice. The committee also voted to accept a formula by which delegations would be required to reflect fairly the preferences of presidential primary and caucus voters. At the same time, however, the party charter held that no delegate might be forced "to vote contrary to his conscience and preference." The rules by which the national convention was to be conducted were subject to the deliberation and decision of the convention itself. Kennedy supporters sought to appeal to the convention rules committee, and if necessary to the full convention, to reject the proposed delegate-binding rule and to allow delegates to vote according to their own preferences. If successful, they hoped to persuade enough Carter delegates, freed from the binding rule, to switch their votes to Kennedy and give him victory on the presidential nomination roll call.

Kennedy partisans argued before the party rules committee, which met more than a month prior to the convention, that the binding rule would deprive delegates of any choice or discretion and would make the candidate rather than the delegate the boss of the convention. Carter supporters argued that to reject the rule would amount to breaking faith with the voters who selected the delegates during the presidential nominating process. When it came to a vote, the rules committee—made up of Carter and Kennedy supporters in proportion to the number of delegates pledged to each candidate—decided by an 87.25 to 65.5 margin to accept the delegate binding rule. Although Kennedy lost that battle, his side did receive enough votes to file a minority report on the issue, allowing them to bring the matter before the full convention. Both sides prepared for the floor fight through extensive contact with delegates by letter, telephone, and personal meetings. On the weekend before the convention, Kennedy announced his delegates were free to vote their consciences on all convention issues. On the first night of the convention, the issue was debated before a nationwide prime-time television audience in much the same terms as it had been debated before the rules committee, and with similar results. Carter delegates defeated the minority report by a 546-vote margin; the final vote closely paralleled the final delegate count for the two candidates. Shortly after the vote, Kennedy announced his withdrawal from the race, removing the last obstacle to Carter's renomination.

Kennedy forces had filed four other minority rules reports disputing Carter efforts to streamline convention proceedings, but these were withdrawn in return for Carter concessions. The most significant concession was an agreement by Carter forces to accept a platform accountability rule that would require presidential candidates to state in writing any objections they have to particular planks in the party's platform. Kennedy strategists reasoned that if they were able to gain approval for a number of platform planks opposed by Carter, this rule, proposed before Kennedy's withdrawal as a candidate, would put Carter in the politically embarrassing position of having to disavow portions of the party's platform and would thereby strengthen Kennedy's hand.

On other rules matters, the rules committee approved a charter amendment to prohibit sexual preference from barring an individual from participation in the party but rejected a proposal to include homosexuals in the party's affirmative-action outreach program. The committee also rejected a Kennedy-backed proposal to end the exemption given to Iowa, New Hampshire, Maine, Massachusetts, and Minnesota, which had allowed them to begin their delegate-selection process before the opening date officially set by the party. In 1980 Carter had defeated Kennedy in all those states but Massachusetts. Finally the committee agreed there would be a midterm party conference to be held in December 1982, and it instructed the national committee to reconsider the length of the delegate-selection process. Only two minority reports on these matters came before the full convention, and the most significant of these, calling for a thorough review of the entire presidential-selection process, was approved instead of the more limited study called for by the minority of the rules committee.

The drafting of the Democratic party platform also manifested the ideological and political divisions separating the Carter and Kennedy camps at the convention. The drafting process was marked throughout by considerable negotiations between representatives of the two candidates, which led to much alteration of draft proposals but gave Kennedy supporters little satisfaction on matters they considered most important, particularly their call for wage and price controls, for a $12 billion program to alleviate unemployment, and for national health insurance. Prior to the convention, Carter forces suffered only one setback, that at the instigation of defecting Carter delegates who led a successful effort to have included a proposed plank supporting orderly retirement of nuclear plants as alternative fuels become available. A second challenge to a Carter position by a Carter delegate, which would have deleted all references in the platform favoring the MX missile, was narrowly defeated by a 76.5 to 69 margin.

When the platform committee hearings concluded, twenty-three minority positions had received the requisite 25 percent support of the committee membership to be brought to the full convention as minority reports. Eighteen of the minority reports had been filed by Kennedy partisans, representing the Massachusetts senator's determination to carry his differences with the President to the convention floor. Preconvention negotiations with Carter representatives narrowed Kennedy-backed minority planks to thirteen. Two of the remaining minority reports were originated by organized feminists on the platform committee; one called for the party to withhold support from any candidate not supporting the ERA, and the other supported use of Medicare funds for abortions and opposed "involuntary or uninformed sterilization."

The first day of full convention debate over the platform did not go well for the Carter side. The Kennedy-backed proposal for a national health-insurance program was defeated, but by a narrower margin than Carter's supposed delegate support indicated. Then the Kennedy report calling for a jobs policy that would make creating jobs the "single highest domestic priority" was approved by a 1,790.6 to 1,392.8 margin. The two minority reports initiated by women's groups and backed by Kennedy also were approved: the pro-ERA report on a voice vote and the abortion-funding report by a substantial margin in a telephone roll call.

Debate on opposing planks regarding the economy took place by mutual agreement on the second evening of the convention. The final scheduled speaker was Sen. Kennedy, whose half-hour address electrified the convention audience, many of them fervent Kennedy supporters. Moved by his eloquence and fired by a subsequent forty-minute demonstration, the delegates went on to approve by voice vote three of the four major economic planks backed by Kennedy: a plank calling for a $12 billion jobs program, a plank pledging to take no actions that would "significantly increase unemployment," and a plank opposing high interest rates and unemployment as a means of combatting inflation. The Kennedy plank calling for an immediate wage and price freeze, however, was defeated, also by a voice vote. The outcome of the vote on each of these issues had been determined by telephone negotiations between the two camps mediated by the convention chairman, Speaker of the House O'Neill. Once an agreement had been reached, the votes were mere formalities. On the following day Carter forces regained a measure of control over the convention and fared considerably better in the platform report deliberations. Kennedy planks calling for repeal of special tax breaks for oil companies, opposing taxes and fees aimed at reducing oil consumption, and requiring oil companies to be federally chartered were defeated by voice vote, although other Kennedy planks pledging support for development of renewable energy sources, calling for a ban on acquisition of coal and solar energy firms by oil companies, and giving states and Indian tribes the power to reject nuclear-waste-disposal sites they believe are unsafe were approved, also by voice vote. The full convention subsequently rejected a minority plank opposing deployment of the MX missile system, as well as a minority plank calling for a freeze on testing and deployment of all nuclear weapons and delivery systems.

Once the platform had been adopted, Carter was required by the new platform accountability rule to submit in writing to the convention delegates a pledge of his support of the platform and an explanation of any specific objections to it. Although it had been agreed that such a statement would be submitted two hours before the nominating speeches were scheduled to begin, the Carter camp was unable to meet the deadline, and the president's response was distributed only after the nominating speeches had started. The carefully worded statement avoided direct comment on the language of some planks Carter had opposed, such as the ERA plank barring Democratic party support to candidates who do not back the amendment, and accepted only the "intent" of other planks, such as the $12 billion job-creation plank, without committing the president to a specific level of support. The statement concluded with a call to unity among party members.

On many matters—economic issues, health care, women's rights—the Democratic party platform differed significantly from the Republican platform approved a month earlier. The matter of election reform represents another point of difference. Unlike its Republican counterpart, the Democratic platform called for public funding of congressional campaigns and simplified procedures for voter registration. It also supported lowering the contribution limits for PACs, closing the loophole that allows independent expenditures in presidential-election campaigns, and increasing opportunities for participation in party and government offices by low- and moderate-income citizens.

Unlike the platform and rules committee reports to the Democratic convention, the credentials committee report did not provide any cause for dispute among partisans of Carter and Kennedy. The Kennedy side had filed a minority report challenging the credentials of six Virginia delegates pledged to Carter but withdrew the challenge prior to the convention during the course of preconvention negotiations with Carter representatives. A committee report free of controversy was adopted by voice vote on the first day of the convention. Several other minority reports were filed by Kennedy forces, but since those concern the 1984 national convention, they were not scheduled to be considered until the 1982 midterm convention.

To conduct its convention business, the Democratic National Convention Committee raised $4,480,138.43; of that total $4,416,000 was federal subsidy. Qualified expenditures of the federal entitlement amounted to $3,712,071.53, leaving an unspent portion of $703,928.47 to be returned to the U.S. Treasury (table 6-2).

The Democrats spent considerably less than the Republicans on their convention. Not only did the Democrats spend less of their federal allotment than did the Republicans, but the Democrats raised only about half of the nonfederal convention funds garnered by the Republicans. Considering that federal funds were available, the Democratic committee apparently wanted its convention to be a frugal event.

The qualified convention expenditure of housing and transportation for those involved in the administration of the convention came to a relatively small $150,000. But the costs of other convention operations were substantial. Rental of the New York office and convention hall totaled $850,000, and the process of ticketing and credentialing added $145,000 more. Salaries for convention officers, administrators, and legal services amounted to nearly $500,000. And these salaries did not include the $428,000 expenditure for the salaries and operations of assorted standing and advisory committees, such as the arrangements, platform, rules, and credentials committees. The commission that investigated compliance matters with federal

Table 6-2
1980 Democratic National Convention Income and Expenditures

Income	
Federal grant	$4,416,000.00
Expenditures	
Executive	
Convention officers	59,066.15
Convention manager	172,254.38
Administration/	
comptroller/legal	147,672.64
Convention secretary	116,608.81
Convention operations	
New York office	490,097.14
Convention hall	360,242.19
Housing	79,417.70
Transportation	90,142.26
Tickets and credentialing	136,239.52
Communications	145,116.28
Telephone	211,144.51
Security	330,970.38
Unallocated	443,691.66
Convention committees	
Site-selection committee	6,021.58
Arrangements committee	75,077.35
Platform committee	160,703.83
Rules committee	45,685.74
Credentials committee	60,751.52
Compliance review	
commission	79,985.40
Miscellaneous	
Convention program	105,438.34
Convention souvenirs	22,091.06
Hospitality, VIP	33,877.27
Film	312,354.60
Unallocated	7,429.72
Total Expenditures	$3,712,071.53

Source: Information provided by the DNC.

Note: Expenditures through June 30, 1981. A communication from the DNC in March 1982 indicates that the adjusted expenditure total was $3,683,187.03 and that the DNC returned $731,665.10 to the U.S. Treasury.

campaign laws was included in the committee total. Other miscellaneous expenses of programs, souvenirs, and entertainment came to about $480,000.

The Democratic convention served as a focal point for Democratic party fund raising. Party contributors of $2,500 or more received VIP treatment at the convention, including seats at the convention, special tickets admitting them to a VIP cocktail lounge, and opportunities to join the convention delegates on the floor during convention sessions.[55] The cost of the lounge was prorated between the Democratic Finance Council and the convention committee. By the time the convention opened, it was reported that 197 persons had contributed the $2,500 required for the special convention treatment, adding some $500,000 to the party treasury.[56] Political committees reportedly were asked to contribute $3,500 to receive the convention VIP treatment.[57]

Additional funds were spent in conjunction with the Democratic National Convention to fuel the efforts of a group initially called Democrats for an Open Convention. As early as the beginning of 1980, several prominent Democrats, led by Arnold Picker, a former film-industry executive who was named Edmund Muskie's 1972 campaign finance director, S. Harrison (Sonny) Dogole, a Philadelphia businessman who had raised funds for Sen. Henry Jackson's 1976 presidential campaign, and Paul Ziffren, a Los Angeles lawyer and former Democratic national committeeman, laid the groundwork for a campaign to leave open the possibility that a candidate other than President Carter and Senator Kennedy could receive the party's nomination at its national convention. While the primary and caucus fights between the two major contenders were being waged, funds to support the group's efforts were being raised, largely by telephone solicitation. Early in July, it was reported that the group would organize and go public and that prominent Washington lawyer Edward Bennett Williams would be sought as the group's head.[58] Although the individuals said to be involved in the effort included some Kennedy supporters, it was speculated that the most-active members favored a candidacy of Muskie or Jackson or, perhaps, Vice-President Walter Mondale. Late in July a group of junior Democratic congressmen, including supporters of both Carter and Kennedy, announced organization of the Committee to Continue an Open Convention;[59] it was this group that benefited from the fund-raising efforts of Picker and his colleagues and which attorney Williams agreed to head. At the time the formation of the committee was announced, a congressional leader said the group had about $200,000 in pledges to finance its lobbying activities among convention delegates.[60] Despite verbal support for an open convention from some prominent Democrats, such as Gov. Hugh Carey of New York, who was said to have had presidential aspirations of his own,[61] and Senate majority leader Robert Byrd of West Virginia, and from several union leaders, the committee's efforts to free convention delegates from the binding rule, like those of supporters of Kennedy, were unsuccessful.

According to the committee's year-end 1980 report to the FEC, $108,981.39 was raised in contributions from individuals and PACs, and $51,746.35 was spent on committee operations. An additional $999 was listed as contributions to federal candidates and other political committees. A leading figure in the group noted some weeks after the convention that surplus funds would be returned to contributors on a prorated basis. By the end of 1980, $40,192.80 was reported as returns of contributions to individuals and

$5,500 as refunds to other political committees. Before termination of the committee in 1981, however, the remainder of approximately $10,000, minus limited operating expenses, had been contributed to various federal campaign committees, including Norm Dicks for Congress and People for Jackson.

Additional Convention-Related Spending

In addition to the spending by host cities and committees, by political parties, and by political committees seeking to influence convention outcomes, a number of other sources spent money for a variety of convention-related expenses.

The major candidates for the presidential nomination incurred significant convention expenses for staff, housing, communications, and delegate lobbying, particularly Carter and Kennedy who carried their expensive primary battle into the convention itself. For example, the Carter-Mondale prenomination campaign report revealed that $388,741 was spent on convention-related expenses, expenses that counted toward the campaign's overall prenomination spending limit.

Security provided for the conventions by host-city police forces and by ushers and private security personnel hired by the two political parties was supplemented by Secret Service agents responsible for protecting the candidates,[62] and indirectly by the Federal Bureau of Investigation.[63] The LEAA provided separate grants of $3.5 million to each host city to pay for the city police forces.[64] The total costs of security at the conventions, however, including those forces hired by the parties and FBI, must have been significantly greater than indicated by the LEAA grants.

Spending by the mass media to cover the conventions far exceeded all other convention-related expenditures, and spending on television coverage accounted for the lion's share of those costs. As one Republican convention organizer put it, "The whole idea is to make the event into a TV production instead of a convention."[65] The cost of these media extravaganzas to the major networks alone has been estimated as high as $45 million.[66] Each network reportedly moved 650 to 750 employees to the GOP convention in Detroit and built extensive broadcast facilities for on- and off-camera personnel.[67] The broadcast booths in Detroit's Joe Louis Arena alone were said to have used enough lumber to build three large homes.[68] Network coverage of the conventions was supplemented by increased live, local station coverage at an additional expense.[69] The conventions were covered extensively by the print media. An estimated 4,000 newspaper and magazine staff members were included among the 8,000 media personnel on hand for the Detroit convention.[70] The Associated Press and United Press International reportedly sent 160 persons to the GOP gathering and spent $250,000 each.[71] The *Washington Post* was represented by thirty-five staff members at a cost of $60,000.[72] The *New York Times* was reported to have rented five houses in the exclusive Detroit suburb of Grosse Pointe for about $2,000 each for one week.[73]

No figures are available regarding the amounts spent by convention delegates for their own transportation expenses or for lodging, meals, and other expenses in the convention cities, since federal law does not require such expenditures to be reported. According to one report, many GOP convention delegates expected to spend $1,000 or more on such items.[74] Profiles of the Republican delegates suggested that many of them had attained income levels that would allow for such spending. According to a CBS News Poll, the delegates' median family income was $47,000.[75] Spending by delegates and alternates, as well as by members of the press and convention guests, is one of the most significant factors encouraging prospective host cities to bid for the national political conventions.

Although the FEC does not require disclosure of delegate spending at the convention, it did issue some advisory opinions regarding the sources of funds for such spending. In one advisory opinion, it held that a congressman might use campaign funds to pay his expenses to the convention and left it to him to determine whether he should report his expenses as an expenditure to further his election or as a nonpolitical disbursement.[76] In another opinion, it held that the NEA was not permitted to use general treasury funds to pay the travel and living expenses of members attending the national convention as delegates.[77] Although only twenty-two NEA members were delegates or alternates to the Republican convention, 464 served as delegates or alternates at the Democratic convention, all but 29 of those delegates supporting President Carter.[78] NEA delegates and alternates raised money for their convention expenses in a variety of ways, including raffles, bake sales, and, in Iowa, through $400 grants from the state association's PAC.[79] The national association's PAC also offered loans of $250 plus a 20 percent reimbursement for NEA delegates' airfares.[80]

The 1974 FECA amendments had already closed off another possible source of funds for delegate expenses by stating that public funds could not be used "to defray the expenses of any candidate or delegate." The FEC interpreted this clause to mean that any party payments for delegate expenses would be deducted from the public subsidy and counted against the convention spending limit.

Future Reform

Both the Republican and Democratic national conventions took action to alter the process by which presidential candidates are nominated. The decisions to appoint or instruct committees to study the entire presidential-selection process represent a response to widespread dissatisfaction with the length and cost of the process operative during the 1979-1980 election cycle. The right of the national political parties to determine how their party nominees are to be chosen was given some support by a 1975 Supreme Court decision holding that the interests of the state must be compelling in order to overrule eligibility requirements set by the party in the selection of delegates. In this case, state interests were not sufficiently compelling to overrule the party's First Amendment rights of free association.[81] The national committees received added support by another Supreme Court ruling, handed down in late February 1981 in the case of the *Democratic Party of the United States v. LaFollette*.[82] In that decision the Court held that the state interest in preserving the integrity of the electoral process by providing secrecy regarding a voter's party affiliation also was not sufficiently compelling to warrant interference with the national-party requirement of a closed primary.

Since 1903 the state of Wisconsin has held open primaries in which citizens are allowed to cross party lines and vote in the primary for any candidate. State law requires convention delegates to vote, at least on the first ballot, for the candidate to whom they are pledged, but Democratic party rules hold that only those willing to identify themselves publicly as Democrats may participate in the delegate-selection process. In 1979 state officials sought a court ruling to require the national party to recognize the state's open primary and succeeded in getting a favorable ruling from the Wisconsin Supreme Court. The Democratic convention did seat the Wisconsin delegates, but the party appealed the Wisconsin court's decision to the U.S. Supreme Court, where it won a reversal. Justice Potter Stewart wrote for the majority that neither a state nor a court may constitutionally substitute its own judgment for that of a political party in determining the makeup of the state's delegation to the party national convention. The party's choice of method, wrote Stewart, "is protected by the constitution."[83]

The Court's decision in the Wisconsin open-primary case may have offered the parties the latitude many reformers have thought the parties needed to determine when primaries should be conducted, whether they should be statewide or regional, whether delegate selection should return to the caucus system, and so on. The role of the federal and state governments as opposed to the national political parties in structuring the presidential-selection process has not been fully clarified. Still, the recent decisions have opened the road for a reform movement to be led by the national parties.

Minor-Party Conventions

Under the FECA a minor party is eligible for a partial convention subsidy if the candidate of such a party received more than 5 percent of the vote in the previous presidential election. In accordance with the 1976 presidential election results, no minor party qualified for public funds in 1980.

Minor parties that did hold nominating conventions funded them in a variety of ways. For example, the Libertarian party, which chose corporate attorney Ed Clark as its nominee at its September 1979 convention in Los Angeles, reportedly paid its convention costs of $250,000 through registration fees, banquet ticket sales, and $35,000 from the party treasury.[84] The newly formed Citizens' party held a three-day convention in Cleveland in mid-April 1980 and chose ecologist Barry Commoner as its presidential nominee and native American activist LaDonna Harris as his vice-presidential running mate. In fact the choice of the presidential ticket by the convention's approximately 275 delegates representing thirty states had to be ratified by a mail ballot of the party's members. The party reportedly paid its convention costs of about $35,000 by drawing money from the party treasury and supplementing it with funds raised from a $25 registration fee charged to convention delegates and observers.[85] Delegates to the Socialist Workers party convention, held at Oberlin College in Ohio in the winter of 1979, chose Andrew Pulley as their standard-bearer. The delegates reportedly paid their own ways to the convention and stayed in college dormitories. In addition they contributed $15 each to pay for rental of meeting rooms and general overhead.[86]

Notes

1. FEC, advisory opinion 1975-1, "Convention Financing," June 24, 1975; *Federal Register*, July 15, 1975, p. 26660.
2. Quoted in "New Orleans Solicits GOP for Deep South Convention," *Washington Post*, October 24, 1978.
3. Adam Clymer, "New York Appears Leading Choice for 1980 Democratic Convention," *New York Times*, June 18, 1979.
4. John Geddie, "Convention Chances Hinge on Cash," *Dallas Morning News*, May 12, 1979.
5. Ibid.
6. Gregory Jaynes, " 'Funny' Philadelphia in Serious Plea to Democrats," *New York Times*, June 8, 1979.
7. William J. Mitchell and Remer Tyson, "Dems Still Consider 4 Cities," *Detroit Free Press*, May 12, 1979.
8. Jaynes, " 'Funny' Philadelphia."
9. Mitchell and Tyson, "Dems Still Consider."
10. Steven R. Weisman, "Party Conventions Mean More Than Just Politics," *New York Times*, June 24, 1979.
11. Frank Lynn, "Hotel Rooms Rather Than Politics Main Factor in Democrats' Choice," *New York Times*, June 29, 1979.

12. Ibid.

13. Quoted in Bill Peterson and Lee Lescaze, "Democrats Pick New York for 1980 Convention," *Washington Post*, June 29, 1979.

14. Clymer, "New York Appears."

15. Ibid.

16. "Detroit Hopes to Rescue Hotel for G.O.P. Gathering," *New York Times*, January 16, 1980.

17. Ibid.

18. "A Spirited GOP Gears Up for Its Big Show," *U.S. News and World Report*, July 14, 1980, p. 28.

19. Mary Meehan, memorandum, July 31, 1980.

20. Lucia Mouat, "Volunteer Workers Show Detroit Really Does Love a Good [Political] Party," *Christian Science Monitor*, July 15, 1980.

21. FEC, advisory opinion 1980-53, "Donation of Promotion Items to Host Committee of National Conventions," June 17, 1980; see *FEC Record* (August 1980):6.

22. Blaine Harden, "Convention!" *Washington Post Magazine*, July 13, 1980, p. 17.

23. FEC, "Report of the Audit Division of the Civic Host Committee for the 1980 Republican National Convention" May 13, 1981 (mimeographed), p. 1.

24. "Host Committee May Transfer Funds to Pay GOP Convention Expenses, FEC Says," *Campaign Practices Reports*, November 24, 1980, p. 7.

25. "Detroit Officials Are Elated At Boost from Convention," *Washington Post*, July 20, 1980.

26. Quoted in ibid.

27. Clyde Heberman, "City Girds for Democrats's Arrival with Flurry of Final Preparations," *New York Times*, August 6, 1980.

28. "Convention Equation: More Apples, Less Reading Matter," *New York Times*, August 3, 1980.

29. Selwyn Raab, "Dogs and Horses to Help in Protecting Convention," *New York Times*, August 2, 1980.

30. Ward Morehouse III, "Convention Security Will Test NYC Task Force," *Christian Science Monitor*, June 17, 1980.

31. Raab, "Dogs and Horses to Help."

32. "Convention Equation."

33. Maurice Carroll, "City Plans a Lively Time for Democrats in August," *New York Times*, June 27, 1980.

34. FEC, advisory opinion, 1980-21, "Baseball Tickets"; see *FEC Record* (June 1980):5.

35. Quoted in Carroll, "City Plans a Lively Time."

36. "Convention Equation."

37. See RNC, *Delegate Selection Procedures for the 1980 Republican National Convention* (Washington, D.C.: February 1980); see also RNC, *Rules Adopted by the 1976 Republican National Convention* (Kansas City, Mo.: Lowell Press, August 1976); Joseph E. Cantor, *The Presidential Nominating Conventions of 1980* (Washington, Conn.: Center for Information on America, 1980), p. 6.

38. See Cantor, *Presidential Nominating Conventions.*

39. Paul T. David, "The National Conventions of 1980" (mimeographed), p. 3.

40. Rhodes Cook, "Attention Shifts to First Presidential Primaries," *Congressional Quarterly Weekly Report*, February 2, 1980, p. 281.

41. David, "National Nominating Conventions of 1980," p. 4.

42. "GOP's Turn in the Spotlight," *U.S. News and World Report*, July 21, 1980, p. 15.

43. Cook, "Attention Shifts," p. 281.

44. Leslie Bennetts, "Women Leaders Optimistic over Equal Division of Convention Delegates," *New York Times*, January 2, 1980.

45. FEC, advisory opinion 1979-7, "Delegate Selection"; see also *FEC Record* (June 1979):5.

46. FEC, advisory opinion 1980-5, "Delegate Selection"; see also *FEC Record* (May 1980):2.

47. Frank Lynn, "New York's Democrats Caucus for Delegates," *New York Times*, April 27, 1980.

48. Maurice Carroll, "Albano Beaten as Delegate, Faces Fight for Post on State Committee," *New York Times*, April 6, 1980.

49. Frank Lynn, "Few Attend Democrats' Sessions for Would-be Delegates," *New York Times*, March 3, 1980.

50. Lynn, "New York's Democrats."

51. Martin Tolchin, "Kemp's Friends Push Him as Vice-Presidential Choice," *New York Times*, July 12, 1980.

52. Tom Morgenthau, "Republican of the Future?" *Newsweek*, July 28, 1980.

53. In 1980 only eighteen states, whose allocation of 765 delegates—38 percent of the total—clearly bound GOP delegates by state primary law, and an additional three states, whose allocation represented 5.5 percent of the total, had primary laws that might be interpreted to bind the delegates. See Richard J. Cattani, "Will Party Conventions 'Unbind' Delegates?" *Christian Science Monitor*, March 7, 1980.

54. FEC, "Report of the Audit Division on the Arrangements Committee of the Republican National Committee for the 1980 Republican National Convention" April 9, 1981 (mimeographed).

55. William J. Eaton, "Democrats Give Donors Best Seats," *Los Angeles Times*, August 10, 1980.

56. Ibid.

57. Ibid.

58. Robert Shogan, "Democratic Group to Work to Nominate Someone Other Than Carter, Kennedy," *Los Angeles Times*, July 3, 1980.

59. Robert Shogan, "Party Insurgents Formally Open Drive to Dump Carter," *Los Angeles Times*, July 29, 1980.

60. Ibid.

61. Joyce Purnick, "Carey Is Said to Regret the Campaign That Wasn't," *New York Times*, August 5, 1980.

62. See, for example, Raab, "Dogs and Horses to Help."

63. See Morehouse, "Convention Security."

64. Mary Meehan, "How the Donkey and the Elephant Turned into Pigs," *Inquiry Magazine*, July 7, & 21, 1980, p. 13.

65. Kenneth Reitz, quoted in Adam Clymer, "Republicans Are Bouyed by Survey on Party's Image," *New York Times*, July 7, 1980.

66. Howard Rosenberg, "Is Convention Coverage TV Arms Race?" *Los Angeles Times*, August 5, 1980. For other estimates, see Harden, "Conventions!" which estimated the networks would spend $7 million to $10 million each on the GOP convention; "GOP's Turn in the Spotlight," estimated the networks would spend more than $15 million on the GOP convention.

67. Harden, "Convention!" p. 15.

68. Ibid.

69. See Francis X. Clines, "About Politics," *New York Times*, June 20, 1980.

70. "GOP's Turn," p. 14.

71. Harden, "Convention!" p. 16.

72. Ibid.

73. Ibid., p. 15.

74. "GOP's Turn," p. 15.

75. Cited by Adam Clymer, "The Conservatives' Message," *New York Times*, July 16, 1980.

76. FEC, advisory opinion 1980-29; see *FEC Record* (June 1980):7.

77. FEC, advisory opinion 1980-64, "Labor Organization's Payment of Members' Delegate Expenses"; see *FEC Record* (August 1980):7.

78. Harrison Donnelly, "Teacher Organization United behind Carter—For a Price," *Congressional Quarterly Weekly Report*, August 9, 1980, pp. 2277-2278.

79. James Cramer, "How Teachers Paid Their Way to Democratic Convention," *Executive Educator* (November 1980):22.

80. Ibid.

81. *Cousins* v. *Wigoda*, 419 U.S. 477 (1975). For a summary of the 1972 Democratic convention dispute settled by this ruling, see Herbert E.

Alexander, *Financing the 1972 Election* (Lexington, Mass.: Lexington Books, D.C. Heath and Company, 1976), pp. 261-262.

82. *Democratic Party of the United States* v. *LaFollette*, 49 U.S.L.W. 4178, 4183 n31 (U.S. 1981).

83. Cited by Jim Mann, "States May Not Tell Parties How to Select Presidential Nominees, High Court Rules," *Los Angeles Times*, February 26, 1981.

84. Meehan, "How the Donkey and the Elephant," p. 15.

85. Ibid.

86. Ibid., p. 14.

7 General-Election Campaigns

The general election of 1980 marked the second time in American history that public funds were provided for major-party candidates to conduct their election campaigns. Although both major-party candidates accepted the federal grants and thus were not permitted to accept any private contributions to further their campaigns, viewed from the point of view of money spent to influence the outcome of the general election, three different but parallel campaigns actually were conducted, either by the candidates or on their behalf.

The first campaign, in which spending was legally limited and mostly subsidized by the U.S. Treasury, was within the control of the major-party nominees and their campaign organizations. This campaign was financed primarily by public funds. Under the 1974 FECA amendments, each candidate received from the Presidential Election Campaign Fund a grant of $20 million increased by the cost-of-living adjustment calculated by the Department of Labor using 1974 as the base year. That increase brought the total grant in 1980 to $29.4 million. This public funding was supplemented by funds raised privately by each of the major national parties for spending on behalf of its presidential ticket. According to the 1974 FECA amendments, the national-party spending limit is based on the voting-age population of the nation as certified by the secretary of commerce. In 1980 that limit equaled $4.64 million. Thus approximately $34 million could be spent in this campaign under the direction of each major-party nominee's campaign organization.

The second campaign, in which spending was provided for but not limited under the law, was in part under the direct control of the candidates and their organizations and in part outside their control. Those funds spent in this campaign that were outside candidate control, however, could be coordinated with spending by the candidates, although that did not always happen. This campaign was partially financed by funds raised by each candidate's campaign organization from private contributions to pay the candidates' legal and accounting costs of complying with the stipulations of the law. This second campaign also was financed in part by funds raised by state- and local-party committees, which were allowed under the 1979 FECA amendments to spend unlimited amounts on volunteer-oriented activity on behalf of the parties' presidential tickets and by money raised under the auspices of the parties' national committees and the presidential campaigns from sources outside federal restraints—from individuals, unions, and corporations willing to have their contributions channeled to those states where such contributions were permitted and could be used by state- and local-party committees to fund such activities as volunteer-oriented voter-registration and -turnout drives. Spending allowed under the 1979 amendments was coordinated by the national-party committees in consulta- tion with the candidates' organizations. Finally, this campaign was financed in part by additional funds spent on behalf of the candidates by labor unions, corporations, trade associations, and membership groups on par- tisan communications with their own constituencies and on nominally non- partisan activities directed to the general public. Such spending could be coordinated with the candidates' organizations, although efforts at coor- dination were not always successful. Further, during 1980 the FEC was criticized for not giving precise guidance regarding various coordinated ac- tivities, party and nonparty, and for not defining affiliated committees and determining whether their activities were an influence on the election.

The third campaign, in which spending also was provided for but not limited under the law, was funded by independent expenditures. According to the Supreme Court's *Buckley* ruling in 1976, individuals and groups are allowed to spend unlimited amounts for or against candidates, provided the expenditures are made without consultation or collaboration with can- didates or their campaigns. The widespread use of independent expen- ditures in 1980, primarily on behalf of the challenger, Ronald Reagan, was highly controversial and was the subject of various complaints and suits.

These three parallel campaigns were supplemented by less direct, more subtle efforts to influence the electoral outcome. Each of these efforts either cost their sponsors money or provided the candidates with benefits whose financial value, though difficult to calculate, is substantial. They include an expensive Republican party-sponsored media campaign designed ostensibly to benefit all Republican candidates; nominally nonpartisan organized group activities focusing on issues closely related to the campaigns; and a number of uses of incumbency to benefit the occupant of the White House, Presi- dent Jimmy Carter.

In addition to expenditures made in the course of the three parallel cam- paigns, substantial funds were spent in 1980 on the independent campaign of John Anderson and on various minor-party campaigns for the presidency. These expenditures also contributed to making the 1980 presidential elec- tions the most expensive in the nation's history—$275 million in all (see table 4-7).

Reagan

To conduct his general-election campaign, Republican candidate Ronald Reagan benefited from a patchwork of funds amounting to about $64 million (see table 7-1). Although this total gave Reagan an overall spending advantage in comparison with his opponent, President Jimmy Carter theoretically was able to coordinate as much spending on his behalf while also enjoying the advantages of incumbency.

Sources of Funds

On July 24, 1980, despite a request by President Carter's campaign committee that the FEC deny a federal grant to the Reagan campaign on the grounds that so-called independent expenditures being made on Reagan's behalf actually were spent in cooperation or consultation with the candidate or his staff, the FEC approved payment of $29.4 million in federal funds to the Reagan-Bush Committee. In 1976, both publicly funded candidates chose to leave their money with the federal Treasury and draw against it as needed. In 1980 the Reagan campaign took the entire grant all at once and invested cash that was not needed immediately in U.S. Treasury bills. The bills matured each Thursday, and the portion that was not needed to pay campaign debts or deposits was then invested in new bills.[1] Although the campaign had to pay federal and state income taxes on the interest received and return the rest to the Treasury, the investments did generate money that could be used during the campaign and in that way helped ease cash-flow problems caused in part by the large deposits the campaign was required to make to obtain such needed items as telephone service and air travel. When money left over from those deposits was refunded at the conclusion of the campaign, it could be used to pay the Treasury the interest the campaign had earned on its investments of public funds.

Table 7-1
Major-Candidate Sources of Funds, 1980 General Election
(millions)

	Sources of Funds	Reagan	Carter
Limited campaign:	Federal grant	$29.44	$29.44
candidate-controlled	National party	4.6	4.0
Unlimited campaigns	State and local party	15.0	4.0
Candidate may	Labor[a]	1.5	15.0
coordinate	Corporate, association[a]	1.5	0
	Compliance	1.5	1.5
Independent of candidate	Independent expenditures[b]	10.6	.03
Total		$64.14	$53.97

Source: Citizens' Research Foundation.

[a]Components of these amounts include internal communications costs (both those reported, in excess of $2,000, as required by law, and those unreported, of $2,000 or less), registration and voter-turnout drives, overhead, and related costs.

[b]Does not include amounts spent independently against Carter ($209,781) or Reagan ($47,868).

RNC Fund Raising: The RNC had no difficulty raising the $4.6 million it was allowed to spend on behalf of its candidate. According to the 1976 FECA amendments, national-party committees are permitted to raise the money from private sources with a limit of $20,000 on individual contributions during a calendar year. Under the leadership of Bill Brock, who took over as RNC chairman in January 1977, the committee stepped up its fund-raising activities, depending on direct-mail solicitations to raise most of its money. By year's end, the RNC had added 100,000 names to its contributor file, which now included 350,000 names, and netted $7.3 million.[2] In 1978, 510,000 donors gave the committee $10.1 million after fund-raising costs had been paid.[3] A 1978 law allowing national-party committees to mail at the nonprofit rate of 3.1 cents rather than the commercial bulk rate of 8.4 cents allowed the RNC to expand its direct-mail program. In that year, the committee mailed 18 million fund-raising letters and netted $12 million from 550,000 contributors.[4]

In 1980 the RNC reported having raised $36.36 million in donations from small donors responding to direct-mail appeals and telephone solicitations; from major donors; from individuals participating in special events staged by the committee; and in contributions from PACs and other multicandidate committees. Table 7-2 summarizes the amounts given in each category and the percentage of the total represented by each category. That 73 percent of the total was given by small donors (those contributing under $500) is largely a measure of the committee's success with direct-mail fund raising. If gross income from promotional direct mail and from fund-raising events held jointly with some state- and local-party committees is included, the total amount raised by the RNC in 1980 is $46.5 million. Although promotional mailings to recruit new contributors generally are

Table 7-2
Republican National Committee Fund Raising, 1980

Sources of Income	Amount (millions)	Percent of Total
Small donors (under $500), direct mail, and telephone	$26.48	73
Major donors	7.73	21
Special events	1.82	5
PACs and other multi-candidate committees	.33	1
Total	$36.36	100

Source: Information provided by the RNC.

Note: Gross income from professional direct mail and from joint fund-raising events held in individual states not included.

viewed as a break-even activity, in 1980 the RNC grossed $7 million from such mailings and netted $1.3 million while adding approximately 400,000 new names to its contributor files.

During 1980 approximately 812,000 individual contributors made a total of 1.2 million contributions to the RNC. The average contribution among those responding to direct-mail and telephone solicitations was $25, and the average contribution overall, including gifts from major donors, was $38. The cost of fund raising, excluding costs of promotional mailings and events held with state- and local-party committees, was 19.6 percent of the total raised.

In order to ensure that the national-party committee would have available the full $4.6 million it was allowed to spend on behalf of its presidential ticket, the RNC set aside the first $5,000 of each contribution of $10,000 or more it received during the 1979-1980 election cycle.[5] In 1980 alone there were 865 such contributors, called Eagles, although some of those were individuals who had contributed $10,000 or more to state Republican committees. In addition to the $4.6 million it was allowed to spend as coordinated party expenditures (expenditures on behalf of Reagan-Bush), the RNC used a substantial portion of the funds it raised to pay for activities in support of the entire Republican ticket, which was beneficial to the party's presidential and vice-presidential candidates.

Additional Funds: The federal grant of $29.4 million and the aggressive fund raising of the RNC ensured that $34 million was available to the Reagan-Bush Committee to spend as it wished on its general-election campaign. That amount, however, represents only a portion of the funds available for the Republican general-election campaign. The Reagan-Bush Committee also raised $2.1 million for its compliance fund,[6] including $345,000 transferred from the Reagan for President Committee, the candidate's prenomination-campaign committee. Only about $1.5 million of it was available during the campaign; the rest was raised to help with postcampaign compliance costs. The compliance money was raised even though the campaign deemphasized the compliance fund and encouraged potential donors to give instead to state and local Republican party committees to spend on behalf of the ticket.

The Reagan-Bush Committee and the RNC went to great lengths to make sure state- and local-party committees were able to take full advantage of the provisions of the 1979 FECA amendments that were designed to encourage the grass-roots political activity that was missing from the 1976 general-election campaigns. The RNC sent legal memoranda to all state-party chairmen summarizing what state- and local-party committees were permitted to do for the presidential ticket. The Reagan campaign not only encouraged potential contributors to its compliance fund to give instead to state- and local-party committees; the candidates also took part in fund-raising events intended to fill state- and local-party committee coffers. For example, a fund-raising event held in Texas in mid-September, attended by Reagan, George Bush, and a host of other party luminaries, raised $2.7 million for use against the Democratic ticket in the state.[7] It is difficult to determine precisely how much money was available to state- and local-party committees for spending to benefit the Republican presidential ticket. Not all of the money spent by state committees for that purpose came from the committees' federal accounts, and thus not all of it was subject to federal reporting. According to one account, in addition to money actually raised by state- and local-party committees for spending on the presidential ticket, the Republican party, under the auspices of its national committee, raised some $9 million from individuals and corporations, which then was chan-neled into those states where such contributions to party committees were permitted and where spending for voter-identification and -turnout drives would have the greatest benefit.[8] When money raised for the presidential ticket by state and local parties is combined with the money raised nationally and channeled to individual states, the total spent by state- and local-party committees on behalf of Reagan-Bush reaches $15 million.

Additional funds in support of the Republican ticket were spent by some labor unions, including the International Brotherhood of Teamsters, and a few corporations. Further, the NRA reported spending $64,524 on pro-Reagan communications directed to its members. All such labor, corporate, and membership group spending on behalf of Reagan-Bush, which could be, but was not necessarily, coordinated with the Reagan campaign organi-zation, amounted to about $3 million.

Independent Expenditures: In addition to benefiting from funds directly under the control of his campaign and from money spent on his behalf by state- and local-party committees that coordinated their spending with the campaign committee, as well as from some spending by labor, corporate, and membership groups, Ronald Reagan attracted substantial independent expenditures on his behalf, made possible by Supreme Court decision in the case of *Buckley* v. *Valeo*. The apparent effectiveness of independent expen-ditures on behalf of Reagan during the prenomination period and the con-viction that contributors to Reagan's prenomination campaign would seek outlets to further his general-election campaign encouraged several groups to begin organizing independent-expenditure campaigns even before Reagan had been formally nominated. Despite Reagan's own disavowal of such efforts, and despite RNC chairman Bill Brock's professed discomfort with them, by mid-July five such groups had announced plans to make in-dependent expenditures on Reagan's behalf. Three of the groups had been in existence and had proven direct mail fund-raising ability: NCPAC, the

Fund for a Conservative Majority, and the Congressional Club. Two other groups were formed expressly to advance Reagan's candidacy: Americans for Change, headed by Sen. Harrison Schmitt (R-N.M.), and Americans for an Effective Presidency, organized by Peter Flanigan, managing director of Dillon Reed & Co., a New York investment firm. Both included prominent Republicans among their founders and steering committee members.

Early in the general-election campaign, exaggerated estimates suggested independent committees would raise $50 million to $70 million to help Reagan.[10] Financial expectations were lowered, however, when it became apparent that groups seeking to make independent expenditures had to compete against each other for available dollars and that the newly organized committees lacked the ongoing fund-raising capability of permanent committees. For example, at the national level, the RNC, the National Republican Senatorial Committee, and the National Republican Congressional Committee combined grossed about $112.3 million in 1979-1980.[11] It was unrealistic to expect that independent support for Reagan could approximate in a few months what the long-established national Republican committees, with their proven lists of contributors and their regular appeals, had achieved over the years. In addition, lawsuits brought by the Carter-Mondale Committee, Common Cause, and the FEC questioning the legality of such expenditures and the independence of the committees proposing to make them, chilled some early independent activity and diverted some of the committees' funds to legal battles. Nevertheless some $10.6 million was reported as independent expenditures on behalf of Ronald Reagan during the general-election period.

Expenditures

Reagan campaign financial strategy sought to make the most of all of the various funds at the campaign's disposal, whether the funds were controlled directly by the campaign organization or by other organizations but could be coordinated with the campaign. The campaign's overall election strategy determined when and where the various funds were to be spent. According to Richard Wirthlin, the campaign's chief pollster and strategist, the campaign organization decided to put its available resources into relatively few states in an effort to maximize its chances of winning the necessary 270 electoral votes.[12] Specifically, that strategy entailed protecting Reagan's western base, including California, targeting the industrialized states surrounding the Great Lakes, and making inroads into Carter's southern base, focusing particularly on states bracketing the South, such as Texas, Florida, and Virginia. In addition the campaign organization decided that the election outcome probably would be determined in the final ten to twenty days. Consequently the Reagan organization allocated its resources so that the full force of its persuasive influence could be exercised during that period. For example, the campaign committee spent $6 million on media advertising during the final ten days of the campaign.[13]

In order to ensure that as much as possible of the $29.4 million it received in federal funds was spent without exceeding that limit, the Reagan-Bush Committee took several precautions.[14] Spending reports were checked daily and special attention was given to possible keypunch errors regarding how and where funds were spent. Computer printouts of campaign spending were available weekly early in the campaign and daily or every other day during the campaign's final month. In addition provision was made for the possibility of declaring all campaign employees volunteers on October 30, the campaign's final payday. This strategem, which could have saved the campaign as much as $1 million, never had to be used.[15] Tight cost controls were maintained over campaign spending, and sufficient cost-control specialists were hired with committee compliance funds to tabulate spending manually if a campaign computer broke down in the closing days.

Campaign strategy called for money from public funds to be spent primarily on media advertising, candidate travel, and campaign committee headquarters' expenses. The RNC funds were to be spent in part on organizing and supervising state- and local-party activities on behalf of the presidential ticket. The state and local parties in turn were to bear the costs of purchasing such volunteer paraphernalia as bumper stickers, brochures, yard signs, and so on, and of conducting voter-registration and -turnout drives on behalf of Reagan-Bush.

Media: The lion's share of the public funds received by the Reagan-Bush Committee was devoted to media advertising, particularly to television. To handle the committee's advertising, in June, Campaign '80 was set up as an independent entity by Dailey & Associates, a Los Angeles advertising agency, to operate during the Republican campaign. Agency president Peter H. Dailey, who had set up a similar organization that worked for President Nixon's reelection in 1972 and who served as a deputy director of the Reagan-Bush Committee, served as chairman and chief executive of Campaign '80. Richard T. O'Reilly, an advertising consultant, served as president of the agency for all but the first month of the short-lived organization. Other key personnel included John Overacre, creative director, and George S. Karalekas, who served as consultant on the media and did the network television buying. In all, Campaign '80 was staffed by twenty-nine persons, seven working in suburban Washington, D.C., and the remainder in New York City.[16]

According to the strategy adopted by the Reagan campaign organization, there was heavy advertising in twenty states, with the bulk of it concentrated in Michigan, Illinois, Ohio, Indiana, New Jersey, Florida, Texas, and Pennsylvania.[17] Nevertheless, because of the discounts available to the campaign for buying time in several major markets, some 45 percent of the campaign's media budget was spent on network television.

In its first phase, which began with a five-minute ABC network spot on August 28, the media campaign sought to project a positive image of the candidate.[18] Advertisements focused on Reagan's record as governor, his economic plans, and his desire for peace.

Once Reagan media advisers were satisfied they had established a positive base for their candidate, they aired a second series of advertisements intended to convey the message that Reagan's opponent, Jimmy Carter, was a failure as a leader and administrator.

Campaign '80 aired forty to fifty commercials that focused on the candidate or on his opponent's record and about twenty-five surrogate commercials, with former President Ford or Betty Ford, Nancy Reagan, or various governors.[19] In addition the in-house advertising agency produced three full-page newspaper advertisements, advertisements for the ethnic media, and a variety of radio spots.[20] Some of the television commercials produced by Campaign '80 never were used, they had been prepared to respond to what Reagan advisers were calling the October surprise, referring to the possibility that the American hostages held in Iran might be released shortly before the election, thus perhaps boosting Carter's chances. The advertisements reportedly "expressed great relief" about the hostages' return but "asked about the policy that let it happen in the first place."[21]

Many of the campaign's advertisements, particularly those focusing on the candidate, were criticized as being dull and unimaginative. Most often Reagan was shown against a traditional backdrop talking directly to the television cameras. Campaign strategist Wirthlin acknowledged that they "were about as exciting as milk and bread."[22] But the straightforward approach was adopted for good reason. "Early in the campaign," said Wirthlin, "our research suggested that voters were not impressed with slick, paid political advertising. Rather, they wanted to see the candidate addressing them directly, describing what he would do if elected."[23] Other campaign aides reportedly suggested that the straightforward approach was dictated by the fact that Reagan's actor image made flashy camera work counterproductive.[24]

As in the prenomination campaign, the cost of television advertising was high. Network charges could range from $26,000 for a five-minute spot at 10:55 p.m. to $94,000 for a thirty-second spot adjoining a top-rated, weekday prime-time show, and $144,000 for a thirty-second spot during a popular Sunday evening prime-time show.[25] A sixty-second spot on the opening night of NBC's miniseries, "Shogun," cost the Reagan campaign $75,000.[26]

In all the Reagan campaign spent $16.8 million on media advertising and production, including about $10.8 million on television time, $1.5

million on radio time, $2.2 million on newspaper and magazine space, and
$2.3 million on production costs. Table 7-3 provides a breakdown of the
Reagan committee's time and space buying. Because the agency was an in-
house organization, it did not charge the committee the 15 percent fee
customarily charged by advertising agencies for their services to cover their
overhead plus profit. The difference between the gross and net figures in the
table is that 15 percent; thus the table provides a measure of how much the in-
house agency actually saved the campaign organization. The table also provides a breakdown of the creative tactics the agency used and of the targets for
the campaign's advertising. Not included in the table are $2.25 million in pro-
duction costs incurred by the agency: the actual incremental costs to produce,
edit, dub, and otherwise prepare the spot commercials and longer programs.

The Reagan campaign also tried to make use of free television time. On
September 21 Reagan debated independent candidate John Anderson in a
televised broadcast carried nationwide on prime time by NBC and CBS.
President Carter had refused to join in debates with his opponents unless
the first included only himself and Reagan. Reagan advisers gambled that
their candidate would make a good showing against Anderson and that the
electorate would think poorly of Carter for having rejected the invitation to
debate. They realized that although Reagan could not command media attention the way the incumbent could, participation in a televised debate, at
no cost to his campaign, probably would give him more exposure than he
could possibly buy. Richard Wirthlin maintains Reagan's participation in
the debate helped reinforce some of the campaign's key objectives, including increasing Reagan's credibility and giving him an opportunity to
reassure viewers he was neither dangerous nor irresponsible.

Reagan also participated in a one-on-one debate with Carter shortly
before the election. The decision to do so reportedly was made after considerable discussion among campaign officials, some of whom felt Reagan
had taken a sufficiently large lead among potential voters that he could win
the election without running the risks posed by an event beyond his control.
Despite such misgivings, postdebate surveys conducted by the Reagan team
showed that although Carter scored well technically, "every attitudinal
measure . . . pointed to a smashing Reagan success."[27]

Like so many other campaigns in the age of visual politics, the Reagan
campaign organized many of its activities to invite coverage on the evening
news. Crowd events, such as noon rallies or strolls through ethnic
neighborhoods, were scheduled to allow time for films to be edited for slots
on the national news. The campaign sought free air time to reply to
statements President Carter made at the opening of a nationally broadcast
news conference on September 18 regarding progress that he maintained his
administration had achieved on domestic and international fronts. The networks, however, rejected the request, characterizing the news conference as
a legitimate news event exempt from the so-called equal-time regulations.[28]

Table 7-3
Reagan-Bush Committee Media Expenditures
(thousands)

	Total Expenditures[a]			Creative Tactics	Target Universe
	Gross	*Net*	*Percent*		
Television					
Network	$ 7,581	$ 6,444	44.3	70%—30's/25% "Fives"/5%—30 Min	National[b]
Spot	5,158	4,384	30.2	90%—30's/ 5% "Fives"/5%—30 Min	Twenty-five key states[c]
Subtotal	12,739	10,828	74.5		
Radio					
Network	344	292	2.0	98%—60's/ 2% "Fives"	National
Spot	1,417	1,204	8.3	100%—60's	Twenty-five key states[c]
Subtotal	1,761	1,496	10.3		
Subtotal broadcast	14,500	12,324	84.8		
Print					
National magazines	265	225	1.5	Spread, black and white (fast close newsweeklies)	National
Local newspapers	2,345	1,992	13.7	Full-page black and white	Fifteen key states[c]
Subtotal print	2,610	2,217	15.2		
Grand total	$17,110	$14,541	100.0		

Source: Information provided by Campaign '80.

Note: Does not include $2.25 million in production costs.

[a]Net figures, which represent those actually paid by the committee, exclude the customary 15 percent advertising agency fee.

[b]Includes national cable systems and superstations.

[c]Includes special-interest and ethnic activity (Black, Spanish, major European voter blocs, as well as campaigns targeted at senior citizens, farmers, and various professional and trade groups).

Other Expenditures: Among other Reagan-Bush Committee expenditures for which figures are available are expenditures for survey research costs. The committee paid $1,038,299 to Decision Making Information (DMI), headed by pollster Richard Wirthlin, and other polling organizations for survey research. The bulk of those funds—$1,012,999—was used to pay the costs to the committee of conducting two to four surveys in each of seventeen states and eight national surveys and of tracking closely developments in eleven states during the final two-and-a-half to three weeks of the campaign. The remaining $25,300 was spent on focus-group interviews. The campaign tried to measure the effectiveness of its television commercials by showing videotapes of them to groups of citizens and soliciting their responses. An additional $300,000 was paid by the committee to DMI for strategizing and modeling.

Candidate travel accounted for a substantial portion of Reagan committee spending. Where the candidate traveled was determined by the campaign's geographical strategy. In mid-September it was reported that 40 percent of Reagan's scheduled campaign time (forty-nine days of travel and twenty-five major appearances) was to be devoted to five states considered pivotal to his election campaign: Ohio, Illinois, Pennsylvania, Texas, and Florida.[29] Other important categories of Reagan campaign expenditures paid for largely out of the $29.4 million federal grant were staff salaries and consultant fees and headquarters overhead.

RNC Spending: Of the $4.6 million the RNC had available to spend as coordinated party expenditures—expenditures on behalf of its presidential ticket—the committee actually spent $4.5 million. Most of that sum was spent to supplement the Reagan-Bush Committee's own expenditures for the items and services campaigns need to purchase. Information provided by the RNC allows the national-party committee's expenditures on behalf of Reagan-Bush to be broken down into the following broad categories:

Transportation	$1,030,000
Polling	564,000
Advertising	1,125,000
Direct mail, postage, mailing services	808,000
Media	314,000
Printing	37,000
Telephone	236,000
Professional services	262,000
Youth for Reagan Program (allocable portion)	53,000
Campaign '80 (allocable portion)	27,000
Campaign materials	27,000
Miscellaneous	41,000
Total	$4,524,000

Although the breakdown indicates that spending for transportation amounted to about $1 million, the RNC actually paid out almost $1.8 million in campaign-related travel costs. The difference between the two figures—about $750,000—represents a portion of the reimbursements received from the news media, the Secret Service, and the campaign organization's own compliance fund for their shares in those travel costs. Although the RNC had paid the travel costs from the $4.6 million it was allowed to spend on behalf of Reagan-Bush, all of the reimbursements due on those expenditures originally were paid to the Reagan-Bush Committee. This arrangement became a matter of dispute between the Republican organization and the FEC.

After audit staff fieldwork and the customary exit interiew with FEC auditors, the Reagan-Bush Committee amended its 1980 year-end report to attribute $748,163 in campaign-tour related reimbursements to the RNC.[30]

The RNC also devoted a substantial portion of its coordinated party expenditures to advertising. Of the $1.1 million it reported spending in this category, $1 million was spent on newspaper advertising, a little less than half what the Reagan-Bush Committee itself spent on print advertising during the campaign (see table 7-3).

Other large categories of national-party committee expenditures on behalf of Reagan-Bush were $808,000 for direct mail, postage, and mailing services; $564,000 for polling, including $550,000 to DMI, which also provided polling services to the Reagan-Bush Committee; $314,000 for media, at least $245,000 of which was spent on media buys; $262,000 for professional services; and $236,000 in telephone charges.

The $4.5 million the RNC spent in coordinated party expenditures represents only a small portion of the national-party committee's total disbursements for 1980. According to the RNC treasurer's year-end report, the committee paid out $39,926,700 during the election year. About $16.2 million was spent on party operations. An additional $14.5 million was spent on candidate, state, and party support, and $7.7 million was spent on fund raising.

One of the RNC's primary responsibilities in the general-election campaign was to oversee Commitment '80, a program intended to mobilize thousands of Reagan volunteers in a massive pro-Reagan voter-turnout drive. Although RNC figures show that only $27,000 of the money it spent on Commitment '80 was considered allocable to the $4.6 million it could spend on coordinated party expenditures, the national-party committee spent $1 million of nonallocable funds on the program.[31] On September 6 groups of Republican activists, ranging in size from 135 to 175 persons, gathered at 486 locations around the country to watch a message from Reagan and other party leaders on a television cassette.[32] The message urged them to invite groups of their friends to their homes a week later to view a half-hour commercial broadcast by CBS and featuring the Republican candidate. About 800,000 persons were said to have responded to that invitation.[33] Those persons were asked to participate in a door-to-door and telephone canvassing campaign on October 4 to identify Republican voters and then to follow up by seeking to turn out the Republican vote a month later. The use of the unpaid volunteers did not count against the expenditure limit imposed by the law on the Reagan-Bush Committee and the RNC.

It is difficult to measure the success of Commitment '80. Although the program reportedly reached some 800,000 volunteers, how many of them actually went out into their neighborhoods is unknown. Party officials in some states, such as Pennsylvania, reported a good response on October 4, but elsewhere, such as in Florida, the day's events were postponed because of organizational problems.[34]

The RNC also found other ways to spend money to benefit the party's presidential ticket without the expenditures counting against the national committee's coordinated party expenditure limit. In January 1980, after extensive testing in the summer and fall of 1979, the Republican party embarked on a program to justify Republicanism. The centerpiece of the program was a media campaign to encourage viewers to "vote Republican for a change." Through June 1980, the Republicans spent $5.3 million on a television advertising program to improve their image. The program met with such success that additional funds were committed to carry it through the general-election season. By year's end the RNC, in cooperation with the Republican House and Senate campaign committees, had spent $9.5 million on the program.[35]

According to a Republican party official, the program was not intended to advocate the election of specific candidates but "to further the cause of the party generally."[36] Nevertheless, although the advertisements in the program barely mentioned Reagan, by publicizing "the Republican team," stressing Reagan's main issues, and airing where they would help the Reagan campaign most, they clearly served his campaign.[37]

The RNC also reportedly budgeted $1 million for voter registration.[38] Although such efforts were directed primarily at helping candidates for state and local offices, since they emphasized registration of Republican voters, they undoubtedly benefited the party's presidential candidates.

State- and Local-Party Committees: Not only did the Reagan-Bush Committee and the RNC seek to take advantage of the 1979 FECA amendments by providing state- and local-party committees with substantial fund-raising assistance, they also sought to maximize state- and local-party spending on behalf of the presidential ticket. Under the 1979 amendments, political-party committees at the state and local levels are allowed to spend unlimited amounts of money for the party's presidential nominee as long as the spending is related to volunteer activity. The law permitted widespread dissemination of such volunteer paraphernalia as banners, buttons, bumper stickers, handbills, brochures, posters, leaflets, yard signs, and party tabloids. It also allowed state and local parties to spend unlimited amounts on volunteer-operated voter-registration and -turnout drives, including the use of phone banks.

The Reagan campaign organization counted on the state- and local-party committees to undertake such volunteer-oriented activities and on the national-party committee to organize state and local efforts so that the principal campaign committee's allotment of $29.4 million could be used primarily for media and candidate travel. According to one report, twelve to eighteen RNC staff members worked on local contests and voter-identification and -turnout drives in the states throughout the campaign.[39] It is difficult to determine how much state- and local-party committees spent, under the supervision of the national-party committee, on behalf of Reagan-Bush. The RNC in consultation with the Reagan-Bush campaign channeled about $9 million from individuals and corporations into various states to pay for state- and local-party volunteer activities on behalf of the presidential ticket. When added to the funds state- and local-party committees spent on such activities from money they had raised from their own sources, the total spent by all state and local Republican party committees on behalf of the presidential ticket amounts to about $15 million.

Some information about state- and local-party committee spending and activities on behalf of Reagan-Bush is available from news reports. Early in October, Texas Republicans planned to use funds raised for the state party at a Republican gala in mid-September to pay for a program in which 30,000 volunteers operated phone banks in thirty-nine cities for sixty-six hours a week until election day.[40] The same report described a more-modest effort in New York's Nassau County to operate 300 phones during the last ten days of the campaign soliciting support for Reagan.[41] A report early in November 1980 noted that Florida's Republican party had budgeted $10,000 to $16,000 to fund its participation in Commitment '80,[42] that Pennsylvania's GOP had budgeted $250,000 for voter identification and turnout,[43] and that the Illinois state GOP had budgeted about $100,000 for Commitment '80 door-to-door canvasses and an additional $250,000 for phone banks.[44] And in mid-September, in response to Carter campaign claims of a major effort in California, Reagan's California campaign chairman indicated that $1.5 million would be raised entirely within California by the party organization to pay for staffing and voter-turnout efforts.[45]

National-, state-, and local-party efforts on behalf of Reagan-Bush were critical to the success of the Republican presidential campaign. Such efforts, made possible in large part by the 1979 FECA amendments, also

were of great benefit to the party as a whole. National- and state-party committees found it necessary to work together, and, as RNC chairman Brock
pointed out, the presidential campaign was forced to work with the party
structure.[46] On the Republican side, at least, the new campaign laws served
their intended purpose of strengthening the political parties.

Compliance Costs: The one purpose for which the major-party presidential
campaigns were allowed to accept private contributions and to exceed the
$29.4 million spending limit was for legal and accounting costs related to
compliance with the FECA. These contributions are subject to the campaign law's $1,000 individual contribution limit. According to a report pro-
vided by the Reagan-Bush Compliance Fund, by December 31, 1980, the
fund had received almost $1.2 milion in such contributions. Transfers from
PACs and from the Reagan for President Committee, the candidate's
prenomination-campaign committee, as well as interest earned on money
contributed to the compliance fund, brought total receipts to almost $1.6
million. The same report indicates expenditures from the compliance fund
totaling $993,890, including $942,606 listed as operating expenditures.

The 1980 year-end report supplied by the Reagan-Bush Compliance
Fund was prepared early in 1981 and could not take into account the significant wind-down expenses the fund incurred during 1981 prior to release of
the FEC audit report issued in December of that year or the expenses of
litigation with the FEC over the audit. That accounts for the difference between receipts and expenditures indicated in the fund's 1980 year-end report
and the figures reported in the FEC audit report indicating the compliance
fund received $2,110,857 and spent $1,512,152.

Expenditures made from the compliance fund paid the salaries of cost-
control specialists and seven campaign staff lawyers for their work in making sure the campaign organization complied with the FECA. The staff
lawyers' work was reviewed weekly by two additional lawyers who did contract legal work for the campaign.

Group Spending: Customarily Republican party presidential candidates do
not receive substantial support from labor unions and their PACs, and 1980
was no exception. Some unions, however, did endorse Ronald Reagan and
spent money to advance his campaign. Early in October the executive board
of the 2.3 million-member International Brotherhood of Teamsters endorsed Reagan, the first major union to do so. The union had remained
neutral in the 1976 contest between candidates Jimmy Carter and President
Gerald Ford. Shortly afterward, the National Maritime Union of America,
with 50,000 members, endorsed Reagan despite earlier anti-Reagan
statements in the union newspaper. These and other unions that favored
Reagan probably spent about $1.5 million on behalf of the Republican can-

didate. Corporate interests generally supported the Reagan-Bush ticket, but their expenditures on behalf of the ticket did not approach labor expenditures on behalf of the Democratic candidates. In all, corporations and trade associations probably spent about $1.5 million on pro-Reagan communications to employees, stockholders, members and their families.

The NRA, a membership group strongly opposed to gun-control legislation, reported spending $64,524 on pro-Reagan "internal communications" with its members. The NRA also reported spending $45,609 on internal communications opposing President Carter in the 1980 general election.

Independent Expenditures: Litigation: Soon after plans were announced for substantial independent spending on behalf of Reagan-Bush, opponents of the independent expenditure committees responded with a variety of legal measures to prevent the committees from achieving their political goals. On July 2, 1980, the Carter-Mondale Reelection Committee and the DNC jointly filed a complaint with the FEC alleging that five self-styled independent committees—NCPAC, the Fund for a Conservative Majority, the Congressional Club, Americans for Change, and Americans for an Effective Presidency—actually were working in concert with the Reagan campaign. The complaint did not cite examples of specific contacts between the Reagan campaign and the five committees but pointed instead to the overlapping relationships many of the leaders of these organizations had with each other and with the Reagan campaign organization and the Republican party.[47]

The complaint by the Democratic candidates' campaign organization and the party's national committee asked the FEC to withhold from the Reagan-Bush Committee the $29.4 million in public funds available to major-party presidential candidates. The Democratic committees based their request on a provision in the federal election law that required major-party presidential candidates applying for federal funding to certify to the election commission that they will not accept private contributions to their campaigns. According to the complaint, the expenditures proposed on behalf of Reagan-Bush by the five groups listed actually were being made or would be made in cooperation or consultation with Reagan or his staff and therefore should be counted as contributions rather than independent expenditures.[48]

The Democrats requested that the FEC begin an investigation within a week, so that after Reagan was formally nominated by the Republicans, the agency would be ready to refuse him federal funds if he asked for them. The FEC, however, refused to expedite the request. The day before the FEC was scheduled to act on Reagan's request for federal funds, the Carter-Mondale Committee filed suit in the Court of Appeals for the District of Columbia claiming the Reagan campaign had violated or would violate the law, and seeking a ruling blocking the FEC from approving the request. The court refused to grant the stay, and the FEC certified the Reagan campaign as eligible for the $29.4 million payment. The commissioners argued that once a major-party nominee satisfies the basic requirement of the law—a sworn statement in which the candidate agrees to cooperate with the commission's audit process, not to exceed the legal spending limit, and not to accept private contributions—the commission has no choice but to certify the candidate as eligible.

Although the appeals court refused to issue the stay sought by the Carter-Mondale Committee, it did order that a three-judge panel be set up to hear the committee's appeal of its decision. On September 12 the appeals-court panel dismissed the Carter-Mondale suit as "premature" in the light of the FEC's pending investigation of the matter and upheld the commission's decision to certify federal funds for the Reagan campaign.[49]

Soon after the Carter-Mondale Committee had filed its complaint with the FEC but before it turned to the appeals court to block certification of funds for Reagan-Bush, the Democratic presidential campaign committee sought to counteract pro-Reagan independent expenditures by another means. On July 18, 1980, the campaign committee mailed a letter to television stations around the country warning them of legal problems they might encounter if they broadcast political advertisements paid for by groups claiming to be independent supporters of Reagan.[50] The letter reiterated the Carter-Mondale position that the groups were not truly independent of the Reagan campaign and suggested that stations that broadcast the groups' commercials might be obligated to provide free time to representatives of opposing viewpoints under the fairness doctrine or to individuals attacked by the advertisements under FCC rules regarding personal attack or political use of broadcast time. Predictably, Sen. Harrison Schmitt, chairman of Americans for Change, one of the groups specifically identified in the Carter-Mondale letter, called the letter "blatant intimidation bordering on harassment."[51]

The letter to broadcasters apparently caused some stations to delay selling air time to independent committees until an FCC decision could be made, but some advertisements paid for by independent groups supporting Reagan were aired.[52] On September 4 the Carter-Mondale Committee asked the FCC for a declaratory ruling that it was entitled to free time under the fairness doctrine to respond to the broadcasts. On October 3, the commission unanimously ruled that broadcasts sponsored by independent groups supporting Reagan did not entitle the Carter-Mondale Committee to free air time. But the commission did rule that such broadcasts obligated radio and television stations to sell the Democratic campaign committee or any independent groups supporting the Democratic candidates equivalent time at equal rates. The Carter campaign organization appealed the FCC decision but later dropped its suit, reportedly to use the campaign's limited resources in other ways.[53]

The Carter-Mondale suits represent only one element of the litigation surrounding independent expenditures during the general-election campaigns, but they certainly represent the most political use of litigation in that regard. Such complaints and suits are costly diversions, in terms both of time and money, but in 1980 they were pursued, as a tactic derived from the complexities of the FECA, to achieve political goals and to generate publicity favorable to the complainant or unfavorable to the defendant.[54]

On July 1, 1980, Common Cause, a national citizens' lobbying organization, which had been influential in gaining passage of the FECA of 1971, brought suit in the U.S. District Court for the District of Columbia against Americans for Change, an independent committee that had been established specifically to make expenditures on behalf of Ronald Reagan's presidential campaign. The Common Cause suit not only alleged the organization's activities on behalf of Reagan were not independent, it maintained they were illegal. Like the Carter-Mondale suit, the Common Cause suit maintained that officers of the so-called independent groups actually maintained numerous ties with the Republican party and its national committee.

The Common Cause suit also argued that even if Americans for Change was found to be independent of the Reagan-Bush campaign organization, it was illegal. It based its argument on a provision of the Presidential Election Campaign Fund Act that prohibited organized political committees from spending more than $1,000 on behalf of a candidate who has become eligible to receive public funds. The specific provision, section 9012(f)(1) of the Internal Revenue Code, never was directly considered by the Supreme Court in *Buckley* and was left untouched when Congress rewrote the election law to conform to the Court's ruling.

On July 11, 1980, the FEC intervened in opposition to the Common Cause suit, maintaining it had exclusive jurisdiction over civil enforcement of violations alleged in the suit, and on July 15 the FEC filed its own suit against three of the groups which had announced plans for pro-Reagan independent expenditures: Americans for Change, Americans for an Effective Presidency, and the Fund for a Conservative Majority. Unlike the Carter-Mondale and the Common Cause suits, the FEC suit did not allege that the independent committees were acting in collusion with the Reagan-Bush Committee. The FEC suit did charge that proposed expenditures by the three independent committees would violate section 9012(f)(1) of the Presidential Election Campaign Fund Act and asked the court to uphold the validity of the law and allow the commission to pursue its own enforcement of it.

Following the filing of the FEC suit, a three-judge panel was convened to consider the Common Cause and the FEC suits on an expedited basis. On August 28 the panel rejected the challenges but delayed providing a written opinion of its legal reasoning. Common Cause immediately announced it would appeal to the Supreme Court, but the FEC refrained from comment pending the court's full opinion. Although the court's decision left unsettled for the moment the matter of the constitutionality of section 9012(f)(1), the three-judge panel dismissed the question about the independence of the committee named in the Common Cause suit, ruling that the FEC and not the court had jurisdiction over that matter. Subsequently the lobbying organization filed a complaint with the FEC charging that five groups— Americans for Change, Americans for an Effective Presidency, the Fund for a Conservative Majority, the Congressional Club, and NCPAC—were not independent of the Reagan campaign organization and that therefore they had violated federal election law by making expenditures on behalf of Reagan.

On September 30, the three-judge federal district court panel issued its written opinion on the Common Cause and FEC suits. The judges struck down section 9012(f)(1) of the Presidential Election Campaign Fund Act as an unconstitutional restriction on the First Amendment rights of individuals. Judge Malcolm Wilkey wrote that the free-speech rights protected under the *Buckley* decision extended beyond individuals and that political committees may not be denied the right to make independent expenditures "merely because they are *efficient* groupings of like-minded individuals."[55] Common Cause had already filed a motion of appeal at the Supreme Court, and the FEC filed its notice of appeal shortly after the appeals court handed down its opinion.

In February 1981, long after the 1980 general election had taken place, the Supreme Court agreed to review the appeals court decision. Both the FEC and Common Cause argued that the growth of independent committees could frustrate congressional efforts to limit the influence of large sums of money on presidential elections. In October 1981 the Court heard oral arguments in the case; Justice Sandra Day O'Connor, then in the first week of her first term, disqualified herself from the case, giving no reason for her decision. On January 19, 1982, the Court upheld the appeals court's decision of September 1980 by reaching a four-to-four deadlock on the case. As customary in such cases, no written opinion was handed down nor were the votes of the individual justices disclosed. Because there was no final ruling, it remains possible that another challenge to unlimited spending on behalf of presidential candidates could reach the Supreme Court from another circuit court.

Independent Spending: Although the courts ultimately ruled in favor of the independent committees, the litigation hampered the fund-raising efforts of at least some of the groups. Late in August, while the court of appeals heard arguments in the Common Cause and the FEC suits, Sen. Harrison Schmitt of Americans for Change said the lawsuits had "a chilling effect on contributions.''[56] When Schmitt first announced formation of his organiza-tion early in June 1980, he estimated that the committee could raise and spend $20 million to $30 million on behalf of Reagan.[57] He based his esti-mate on the amount that had been raised by Republican candidates during the prenomination season. At the time committee officials claimed $150,000 had already been raised toward their goal,[58] and they said additional funds would be raised by contacting wealthy donors who already had given to Republican presidential candidates and through direct mail using available donor lists. Money was to be spent on pro-Reagan television advertise-ments, surrogate speaking tours, and direct-mail promotions.

By the time of the Republican convention in mid-July, Schmitt was estimating his group would raise $18 million to help Reagan's campaign.[59] Litigation with the Carter-Mondale Reelection Committee, Common Cause, and the FEC, however, diverted committee officials from fund raising and may have made contributors hesitate about donating to the group. In addi-tion, the newly formed committee had no previous history of fund raising and found itself competing with other independent groups for available money. By September 1, estimates of the amount actually raised by Americans for Change ranged from $279,000[60] to $350,000.[61] The group's fund-raising goal was scaled down dramatically, and by mid-October it had abandoned its plans for pro-Reagan television advertisements.[62] Instead it concentrated on radio spots focusing primarily on industrial and border states where Carter was thought to be weak, such as Pennsylvania, Ohio, Texas, Virginia, and Indiana.[63]

Another group, Americans for an Effective Presidency, headed by a number of former Nixon-Ford appointees, also announced ambitious plans for raising and spending money on behalf of Reagan. Initial estimates ranged from $6 million to $15 million,[64] but within a short time, the group had halved its original goal.[65] By mid-September reports of the amount the group actually had raised ranged from $166,000[66] to a little more than $300,000.[67] By mid-October $1.2 million reportedly had been raised and $850,000 spent on behalf of the Republican candidate.[68] Some of the funds were used to pay for television advertising prepared by Bailey, Deardourff and Associates and broadcast in targeted states, including Ohio, Illinois, Texas, and Florida.[69]

Three other PACs that had announced their intentions to raise and spend money independently had more-modest fund-raising goals. These groups already had in place direct-mail fund-raising operations of proven achievement. The NCPAC announced a fund-raising goal of $500,000 to $2 million for its Ronald Reagan Victory Fund;[70] by mid-October it had raised and spent $981,000 on its pro-Reagan effort, including television adver-tisements broadcast in southern states such as Louisiana, Alabama, Mississippi, and Florida.[71] The Congressional Club initially reported it hoped to spend $500,000 on Americans for Reagan;[72] by mid-September it had raised $600,000[73] and had used some of its funds to pay for television commercials in North Carolina.[74] The Fund for a Conservative Majority initially announced plans to raise and spend $3 million to $10 million on Citizens for Reagan in '80;[75] by mid-October this group reportedly had raised about $3 million—a report that turned out to be exaggerated—and was using a portion of its funds on pro-Reagan and anti-Carter television and radio advertisements in four states: Connecticut, New York, Pennsylvania, and Florida.[76] The fund's target was said to be "blue-collar ethnic Catholic voters" in the first three states and Cuban voters in Florida.[77] One of its television commercials was rejected by CBS for its alleged poor taste.[78] The network subsequently refused to broadcast any political commercials paid for by independent committees.

Although the five committees that announced their intentions of making large independent expenditures on behalf of Reagan received the lion's share of publicity regarding such spending during the general-election campaign and actually accounted for most of the pro-Reagan independent expenditures, a number of other groups, as well as some individuals, also spent independently to further the Republican candidate's campaign. For example, Christians for Reagan, a PAC established by the Christian Voice Moral Government Fund, reported spending more than $400,000 on pro-Reagan mailings to fundamentalist Christians. This activity represents only one element of highly publicized efforts by fundamentalist Christian groups intended to benefit Reagan. Texas industrialist Cecil R. Haden spent more money on behalf of Reagan than any other individual: $381,151 during the general-election period. Haden reportedly paid for full-page newspaper advertisements in 283 newspapers.[79] Other individuals who spent substantial amounts on behalf of Reagan were Richard De Vos and Jay Van Andel, cofounders of Amway Corporation, who reported spending $70,575 and $68,433, respectively.

Although independent expenditures on behalf of Reagan did not approach the original estimates offered by some independent committees when the general-election campaigns were being organized, a substantial amount was spent independently to further his campaign: $10.6 million in all. The five committees that were the subject of the complaints and suits accounted for a major portion of those expenditures: Congressional Club, $4,127,952; NCPAC, $1,670,762; Americans for an Effective Presidency, $1,270,208; Fund for a Conservative Majority, $1,175,726; and Americans for Change, $711,856. It is worth noting, however, that a significant percentage of the pro-Reagan independent expenditures reported by those committees actually went to pay for fund-raising costs. This was particularly true of the committees that relied on direct mail to raise funds: NCPAC, the Congressional Club, and the Fund for a Conservative Majority. For example, according to one report, of the $4.6 million the Congressional

Club reported as independent expenditures on behalf of Reagan during the prenomination- and general-election campaigns, only $700,000 paid for television commercials and voter appeals. The rest—$3.9 million—was used to pay direct-mail fund-raising costs.[80] The same report estimated that only about $600,000 of the almost $2 million NCPAC reported as independent expenditures on behalf of Reagan in 1980 was used to influence voters.[81] David Keene, a political consultant who had been hired by NCPAC to manage a pro-Reagan media and mail campaign in southern states, acknowledged that the $1.4 million spent on fund-raising mail had little effect on Reagan's victory.[82] The letters, he said, had been sent to committed conservatives. According to federal election regulations, if a candidate's name is used in a fund-raising appeal being conducted ostensibly on the candidate's behalf, the expenditures for the appeal must be listed as aiding the candidate's cause, even if the principal beneficiary is the fund-raising committee or its direct-mail consultant. There was some independent spending against Reagan's candidacy, but it amounted to less than $50,000.

Other Spending: In addition to funds reported to the FEC as independent expenditures on behalf of Ronald Reagan, other money was spent by a variety of groups on activities intended to further Reagan's chances of being elected. The most highly publicized of these activities were conducted by a number of evangelical Christian groups in the fundamentalist tradition. Customarily, fundamentalist Christians have shunned partisan politics as irrelevant to their religious mission. Early in 1979, however, a number of fundamentalist leaders made known their intentions to become involved in the 1980 elections, through speaking out from the pulpit and at rallies on issues around which they thought the election campaigns should revolve, through distribution of newsletters and voting records of officeholders, and, in some cases, through the establishment of PACs originally intended to raise and donate money to favored candidates, as well as spend money on their behalf.

Some groups were especially well publicized. The Moral Majority was formed in June 1979 by the Rev. Jerry Falwell, an independent Baptist preacher and pastor of a church in Lynchburg, Virginia. Within a short time, the group claimed chapters in all fifty states, a newsletter mailing list of 400,000 persons, and a first-year budget of $1.2 million.[83] The purpose of the group was to establish "a moral climate in which it is easier for politicans to vote right than wrong."[84] The Moral Majority also established a separate PAC, but after a lackluster performance it was left dormant and then disbanded following the 1980 elections. The Christian Voice also was formed in 1979. Based in California, it claimed a membership of 190,000 by September 1980.[85] Like the Moral Majority, the Christian Voice established a PAC, Christians for Reagan. This PAC remained intact throughout the election campaigns and reported spending more than $400,000 in independent expenditures on behalf of Ronald Reagan. The Religious Roundtable, founded by Edward McAteer, a veteran marketing man for the Colgate-Palmolive Company, served as a coalition organization for a number of fundamentalist leaders, including Falwell, and prominent members of the New Right, such as Paul Weyrich of the Committee for the Survival of a Free Congress and Howard Philips of the Conservative Caucus.

Particularly important to organized fundamentalist political activity in 1980 was the electronic church, the television and radio stations over which many of the fundamentalist preachers broadcast their sermons and church services. Although the preachers could not use the airwaves to endorse specific candidates, they did make known their views on a wide variety of issues, such as opposition to abortion and the Equal Rights Amendment and support for prayer in public schools. Generally their positions agreed with those espoused by candidate Reagan. Among the most notable of the electronic preachers were Falwell, whose "Old Time Gospel Hour" reportedly was broadcast weekly over 327 television stations and 278 radio stations;[86] M.G. (Pat) Robertson, of Virginia Beach, Virginia, whose 700 Club was relayed daily to 150 television stations and 3,000 cable systems around the country;[87] and James Robison, of Fort Worth, Texas, cofounder with Ed McAteer of the Religious Roundtable, who broadcast his program over 100 television stations throughout the Southwest.[88] The preachers also used their electronic pulpits to appeal for funds for their ministries.

Although there is no evidence such funds were used to pay for the partisan political activities of lobbying groups or PACs formed under the auspices of what came to be called the New Christian Right, at least in the case of the Moral Majority, such fund raising was of direct and indirect benefit. Sophisticated mailing lists developed from responses to Rev. Falwell's appeals for funds to support his ministry were available for use by the Moral Majority, Inc.[89] And according to one report, funds raised by Falwell through televised appeals on his "Old Time Gospel Hour" were loaned interest free to the Moral Majority, which, despite reported receipts of $400,000 a month at the time, was said to be strapped for funds throughout the year.[90]

The activities of organized fundamentalist groups to influence the outcome of the 1980 elections varied. In addition to publishing its newsletter, the *Moral Majority Report*, and sponsoring speaking tours for Falwell around the country, the Moral Majority sought to register conservative Christian voters and to recruit and train candidates for political office, often at the local level. Although the organization did not publicly endorse any candidate, except through its short-lived PAC, there was little question about where its sympathies lay.

Although it reported more than $400,000 in independent expenditures on behalf of Ronald Reagan, a substantial portion of it doubtless spent on fund-raising appeals in which Reagan's name was mentioned, the Christian Voice was best known for its "Congressional Report Card," a report of senatorial and congressional voting records on "14 key moral issues," including not only such issues as prayer in public schools, abortion, and sex education but also spending controls and tax cuts, sanctions against Rhodesia, and unionization of public-school teachers.

Determining how much influence organized fundamentalist Christian groups had on the outcome of the 1980 presidential election is difficult. According to some of their leaders, their influence was great. "We know we were responsible for 2.5 million first-time voters in 1980," said Cal Thomas, the Moral Majority's vice-president of communications.[91] Thomas also maintained that the organization had been instrumental in getting millions of like-minded persons to vote in the 1980 elections. And Richard Viguerie, the conservative direct-mail specialist who provided fund-raising assistance to some of the groups, said, "We've just seen the tip of the iceberg of the Christian movement" in electoral politics.[92]

There were some indications, however, that the influence of the fundamentalist groups may have been overstated. In a postelection study, political scientist Seymour Martin Lipset and sociologist Earl Raab concluded that the efforts of such groups "had no measureable effect on the 1980 elections. Instead the available evidence appears to sustain a thesis that the electoral swing toward conservatism and the emergence of a political evangelical movement were parallel developments which may have been mutually reinforcing rather than related to one another as cause and effect."[93]

Reagan campaign strategists acknowledged some impact on the Reagan vote by the Moral Majority, "but not either in the breadth or depth as it's frequently described," said Richard Wirthlin.[94] The Reagan pollster and strategist added, "I think that they were critical in some of what we call the border Southern states—specifically North Carolina, possibly Kentucky, possibly Tennessee, perhaps Alabama, to a lesser extent maybe in Mississippi. But when you go beyond those regions the number in those groups was relatively small, and their ability to activate others or persuade others, especially Democrats to switch party or allegiance, was quite minimal."[95]

Determining how much money was spent by fundamentalist groups to influence the outcome of the elections also is difficult. In the midst of the general-election campaign, the Carter-Mondale Reelection Committee estimated that "television evangelist spending" for Reagan would be about $5 million, excluding the financial activity of conservative Christian PACs. Their estimate, however, was based largely on news reports regarding fundamentalist political activity. The financial information in those reports, which sometimes conflicted with each other, often was drawn from figures reported by the organiztions themselves. The Carter-Mondale Committee also estimated that an additional $2.5 million would be spent on activities that would benefit Reagan by "right-wing special-interest groups," including such groups as the American Security Council, the Institute of American Relations, and the Foreign Affairs Council, which sponsored and distributed anti-Carter films and mailings.

Audit Report

The report of the FEC audit division on the Reagan-Bush Committee showed the committee's total receipts were $32.5 million and its total expenditures $31.7 million.[96] The audit uncovered some minor violations by the committee, including the failure to disclose the amount and nature of certain debts and obligations, as well as transfers to and from an affiliated committee, which the campaign committee subsequently corrected in its first-quarter 1981 report. No further action was required. The audit also found that the committee had collected $465,040 in interest income from investment of the public funds it received. According to the audit staff, that income was subject to $213,918 in federal income tax and an unknown amount of state and local income tax. The FEC ordered that the value of the interest income, less the applicable taxes—approximately $251,122—be returned to the Treasury according to federal law. The committee complied with the FEC order.

In addition to those routine matters, the audit uncovered an arrangement between the Reagan-Bush Committee and the RNC that generated considerable controversy. The FEC began its audit in January 1981, completed its fieldwork in March, and delivered to the committee a copy of its interim audit report in mid-June. After reviewing the interim report for a month, the committee sought and received a two-week extension. When that period was completed, the committee sought an injunction from the U.S. district court barring the agency from releasing the audit or making any final decisions on its recommendations until the campaign committee had had an opportunity to present its side of the case. Although the auditors' findings had not yet been made public, in accordance with FEC regulations, papers filed with the committee's suit indicated the auditors were recommending the committee be required to repay the Treasury about $1.6 million for apparent violations of the law.[97]

In its suit, the committee claimed that the commission withheld information the committee needed to respond to the auditors' conclusions, refused to give the committee enough time to go through the documents related to the audit, and failed to grant the committee's request for an administrative hearing to discuss the audit. In its response to the suit, which it filed with the district court in September, the FEC maintained it was required by law to make public the results of audits it was obligated to conduct and pointed out that federal law also required the commission to protect the confidentiality of any investigations until they are finally resolved. The FEC legal brief pointed out that the commission had not yet reviewed its audit staff's preliminary report and that consequently the Reagan-Bush Committee's request for a preliminary injunction was premature. In fact, shortly afterward, the commission expressed dissatisfaction with the interim report and instructed commission auditors to do further work on the audit before drafting a final report.[98]

Arguments regarding a permanent injunction were scheduled to be heard on October 21, and the FEC was instructed to withhold public release of the audit until the matter was resolved. During the court proceedings, Reagan-Bush Committee lawyers maintained that the FEC had no authority to make public an audit report that discloses alleged violations of the law and that to do so would hamper its efforts to gain a fair hearing of its challenge to those findings. FEC lawyers countered that the commission had the duty to make a final audit that does not contain information about possible enforcement matters. The court found in favor of the FEC, ruling that if the commission were prevented from publishing the audit report, such information "that Congress has declared to be of important public interest never could be disclosed."[99] An attempt by the Reagan-Bush Committee to appeal the district court's decision was unsuccessful.

On December 11, 1981, the audit report was released by the FEC. The report revealed that a dispute regarding $1.1 million that the audit staff initially had recommended the Reagan-Bush Committee be required to repay had been resolved in commission proceedings in favor of the committee. According to the final audit report, during the course of the general-election campaign, the RNC had spent $1.6 million of its $4.6 million allowance on campaign-related tours. The Reagan-Bush Committee subsequently billed the news media, the Secret Service, and the Reagan-Bush Compliance Fund for their shares of campaign tour costs. The audit staff found that $1.1 million of the reimbursements the committee received was based on the RNC tour-related expenditures and took the position that such an arrangement was inconsistent with federal election law. According to the auditors, this transaction in effect increased the expenditure limit of the publicly funded Reagan-Bush campaign.

In its response, the committee maintained that the arrangement was in conformity with an agency relationship existing between the campaign committee and the RNC, although it could point to no specific agency agreement. The FEC, however, held that although the party national committee could coordinate its legally permitted expenditures with the candidate's campaign committee, such funds could not be contributed to the candidate or be given over to the control of his campaign organization. In other words the commission insisted that the two expenditure limits—the candidate organization's and the party committee's—could not be combined. Because the two committees did not exceed the combined limit, however, the commission did not recommend any action against the Reagan-Bush Committee. But it did require that amendments be made in the reports of the two committees to reclassify the reimbursements in question according to audit findings. The commission noted that in the future it would insist that the funds of candidate and party committees be kept separate and that each be responsible for making expenditures under its spending ceiling.

Carter

President Jimmy Carter, like his challenger, benefited from a patchwork of funds intended to advance his general-election campaign. The funds available to support the president amounted to about $54 million, almost $10 million less than the total amount available to support Ronald Reagan's candidacy (see table 7-1). Nevertheless Carter had the theoretical possibility of coordinating as much spending on his behalf as his challenger. He also had at his disposal the tools of incumbency: greater command of media attention, influential surrogates to speak on his behalf, and control over discretionary government spending. Although the value of incumbency cannot readily be translated into equivalent campaign expenditures, it is generally agreed to be considerable.

Sources of Funds

Like the Reagan-Bush Committee, the Carter-Mondale Reelection Committee received from the Presidential Election Campaign Fund a grant of $29.4 million to conduct its general-election campaign. Also like the Reagan committee, the president's campaign committee invested a portion of the federal grant in order to earn interest that would ease cash-flow problems. The Carter-Mondale Committee bought certificates of deposit at commercial banks[100] and also invested some money in a money-market fund. The interest earned partially offset some of the money the campaign was required to tie up in deposits needed for campaign services, including about $1 million deposited with American Telephone and Telegraph and $100,000 with Avis Rent A Car. The interest had to be paid to the U.S. Treasury at the conclusion of the campaign, after federal and state taxes on the income had been paid.

DNC Fund Raising: Despite showing improvement in its fund-raising results over the course of the four-year period from 1977 through 1980, when compared with the previous four-year period, Democratic party fund raising lagged far behind that of the Republican party. This financial disadvantage was demonstrated in the comparatively low level of support the Democratic party was able to offer its candidates, including its presidential and vice-presidential candidates. Although the national-party committee was allowed to spend $4.6 million in coordinated party expenditures, according to an analysis of DNC income and expenditures by the accounting firm Arthur Andersen & Co., which covered a four-year period through December 31, 1980, the national-party committee spent only $3.39 million on presidential-campaign support. The accounting firm's analysis, released on February 13, 1981, noted that subsequent to December 31, 1980, the DNC assumed and paid approximately $105,000 of expenses of the Carter-Mondale Reelection Committee, bringing the total to almost $3.5 million. The analysis also indicated that additional Carter-Mondale Committee expenses might be assumed by the DNC at a later date. DNC officials noted that total coordinated party expenditures for the 1980 general election probably would amount to about $4 million. The DNC funds combined with the public funds granted to the Carter-Mondale Committee brought to $33.4 million the amount of money within the control of the presidential-campaign organization.

Although the DNC's overall fund-raising results improved from 1977 to 1980 compared with previous results, the national party committee failed to build a broad base of small contributors, as the RNC had done, and grew increasingly dependent on large donors and fund-raising events. In 1976, 54 percent of the $7.3 million the DNC received in contributions came from major contributors and fund-raising events. In 1977, 55 percent of $5.2 million in contributions came from those sources. In 1978, 59 percent of the $5.1 million contributed to the DNC came from large gifts and various fund-raising events. In 1979 those sources accounted for 54 percent of the $3.7 million contributed to the national-party committee. Finally, in the general-election year, 61 percent of the $12.2 million contributed to the DNC was given by major donors or by individuals and groups responding to party fund-raising events. Table 7-4 summarizes DNC sources of revenue for the election year, indicating the amount received according to categories and the percentage of the total represented by each category. DNC 1980 revenues of $12.3 million represent only about one-third the $36.4 million raised by the RNC during 1980.

A memorandum from the DNC treasurer regarding party fund raising for the first eleven months of 1980 provides additional information about Democratic party contribution patterns.[101] According to the memorandum, the $2.44 million that had been contributed to the DNC through November 30 in response to direct-mail appeals came from 133,000 contributors, with an average of about $18 per contribution. That money was raised at a cost of twenty-eight cents per dollar. At the close of November the Democratic

Table 7-4
Democratic National Committee Revenues, 1980

Sources of Income	Amount (millions)	Percent of Total Revenues
Contributions		
Direct mail[a]	$ 2.48	20
Major contributors and fund-raising events[b]	7.47	61
Joint fund-raising contributions	.72	6
Contributions for payment of pre-1975 indebtedness	.36	3
Nonfederal contributions[c]	1.13	9
Old debt forgiveness	.11 ⎫	1
Other revenues	.03 ⎭	
Total	$12.30	100

Source: Information provided by the DNC.

[a]Contributions solicited from the general public by use of mailing lists.

[b]Contributions raised by individuals who agreed to solicit $10,000 or contribute a total of $5,000 per year. Contributions received in connection with fund-raising events, such as dinners, are applied to satisfy that commitment.

[c]Funds raised for expenditure in nonfederal races and, where appropriate under law, on state-party voter-registration, voter-identification, and voter-turnout drives.

National Finance Council had 475 active members who gave $5,000 or raised $10,000 during the year. From July 2 through October 24, 1980, the national-party committee engaged in a nationwide, function-related fund-raising program that involved more than seventy-five events. This program raised in excess of $5.9 million, although party officials were prevented by the protracted nomination process from starting the program until after July 1. And even when the matter of the nomination had been settled, party officials discovered their fund-raising events had to compete for the attention of potential donors with a variety of other Democratic fund raising, including events to raise money for the Carter-Mondale Compliance Fund and to pay off prenomination-campaign debts of the major candidates. President Carter spoke at a number of DNC-sponsored events, including a barbecue in Kentucky that brought in $200,000 and a reception in Dallas that attracted 126 couples at $5,000 per couple.[102] In both cases the proceeds of the fund raisers were to be divided between state organizations and the DNC.

Additional Funds: In addition to funds directly under the control of the Carter campaign organization to further the campaign, other funds were raised and spent for purposes directly related to the campaign. The Carter-Mondale Committee raised approximately $1.5 million to pay the costs it incurred in complying with FECA stipulations. This money was raised through fund-raising events, personal solicitation, and targeted direct-mail appeals. For example, a benefit concert held in Memphis, Tennessee, on October 9 and featuring singer Dionne Warwick raised about $41,000.[103] The Carter-Mondale Reelection Compliance Fund was to receive 70 percent of the proceeds and the Tennessee Democratic State Party 30 percent. One compliance-fund letter appeal to PACs asked for contributions of up to $5,000 to help the Carter campaign offset what the letter maintained was a tremendous Republican financial advantage.

The Carter-Mondale Reelection Committee tried to take advantage of the 1979 FECA amendments that allowed greater financial participation by state- and local-party committees in presidential general-election campaigns. In this area, however, the committee operated at a decided disadvantage. The national-party committee had not cultivated ties with existing state- and local-party committees to the degree the RNC had in recent years, nor had it been able to stimulate new local-party committee organizations designed to attract new party members. The presidential campaign organization's own state organizational efforts were hampered by Sen. Edward Kennedy's persistent refusal to concede the nomination to President Carter.

Like their Republican rivals, the Carter-Mondale Committee prepared legal manuals and guidelines for the presidential committee's state coordinators and for state-party chairpersons. These documents explained in detail the extent to which state- and local-party committees could spend money and provide volunteer assistance in support of the party's presidential ticket. In addition in mid-May the Carter-Mondale campaign reportedly began to undertake a state-parties project; by the middle of the next month, nine campaign operatives had been placed on the DNC payroll and were at work in nine key states, concentrating on party building.[104] The party's presidential and vice-presidential candidates and a variety of administration officials took part in fund-raising events designed at least in part to benefit state- and local-party committees, and other funds were raised by events such as the Dionne Warwick concert and a fund raiser in Houston that generated more than $100,000 for the Texas State party organization.[105]

Despite the 1979 amendments and the efforts of the DNC and the Carter-Mondale Committee made to help state- and local-party committees take advantage of them, state- and local-party organizations were able to spend only about $4 million on activities intended to benefit the presidential ticket. Of that amount about $1.3 million was raised at the national level from unions and individuals and channeled to state- and local-party committees in states that permitted such contributions,[106] and the remainder was raised by Democratic party state and local committees from their own sources.

In 1980 as in previous presidential general-election years, most labor unions backed the Carter-Mondale ticket, although many of them had supported Sen. Kennedy in the prenomination campaign. The AFL-CIO, the UAW, and other major unions endorsed the Democrats and after a slow and reluctant start mounted a considerable campaign on behalf of the incumbents. Labor unions are not required to report the greater part of their traditional expenditures in a presidential general-election campaign—for example, money spent on regularly published union newsletters, which might include articles advocating the election or defeat of a candidate, or money spent on nominally nonpartisan voter-registration and -turnout drives—but it is estimated that unions spent $15 million on communications and activities intended to benefit Carter-Mondale. Included in this figure are more than $1.3 million that unions reported spending on pro-Carter internal communications. Federal law requires communications costs to be reported to the FEC when they exceed $2,000.

Independent Expenditures: Although independent expenditures increased dramatically in the 1980 general election, President Carter did not benefit from the increase. In fact more money was spent independently to oppose the Carter candidacy than to support it. Only $27,773 was spent independently favoring Carter, and $209,781 was spent independently opposing him. The policy of the Carter-Mondale Committee was to discourage such expenditures. The labor spending on behalf of Carter, however, more than offset the $10.6 million spent independently on behalf of Carter's Republican challenger. Further, unlike individuals or committees making independent expenditures, labor leaders were free to consult Carter campaign officials and to coordinate their efforts for maximum benefit to the campaign.

Expenditures

The Carter campaign, like the rival Reagan campaign, sought to capitalize on the various funds that campaign law allowed it to draw upon for support. A manual prepared for campaign coordinators in the states, for example, described in some detail the kinds of expenditures state- and local-party committees could make on behalf of the presidential ticket as well as the benefits of such spending. "A state party's purchase of . . . campaign materials can allow Carter/Mondale to concentrate its funds on increased campaign funding of media, travel and other non-exempt expenditures in the state," read the manual. "And full coordination between the presidential campaign and the state or local party is permitted."[107] The manual also detailed permissible expenditures on behalf of the presidential ticket. A similar manual prepared for Democratic state party chairpersons noted that "the spending of the $29.4 million obviously is the core of the general election campaign.''[108] It explained that the campaign committee would concentrate the public funds ''on media, candidate travel, state coordinators, polling and other functions that only it logically can perform.''[109]

Unlike the Reagan campaign, however, the Carter campaign was not able to count on a high level of expenditures by state- and local-party committees. Further, labor spending on its behalf, though significant in dollar terms, came late in the campaign and sometimes without the wholehearted support of labor leaders. Consequently the campaign organization was forced to use some of its public grant to pay for services and items the Republicans could count on their local committees purchasing or funding. The campaign's flexibility was reduced, and strict controls had to be exercised over campaign committee spending.

In order to maximize their limited flexibility, Carter campaign officials prepared preliminary budgets and scheduled polls in key states whose results would help them determine whether budgeted expenditures actually should be made in full, or perhaps increased, or whether money should be moved elsewhere in the budget. Scheduling of polls took into account deadlines by which phone banks had to be ordered and deposits made with telephone companies. Officials tried to keep money in reserve for heavy spending during the last three weeks of the campaign. They were hampered in their efforts by the lead time needed for many of the campaign's activities. According to one report, for example, it required at least five days to arrange for a presidential trip if adequate press and volunteer preparation was to be made.[110] To ensure the best time slots on television required arrangements a month in advance and on radio two to three weeks in advance.[111]

Money became so tight at the end of the campaign that campaign officials, in an attempt to save money for television commercials, encouraged top administration officials to take advantage of a provision of the 1974 FECA amendments that would allow them to pay up to $1,000 in campaign travel expenses out of their own pockets.[112] The law also permitted them to assume the costs of living expenses incidental to any such volunteer activity on behalf of Carter-Mondale.

Media: The Carter campaign spent more than two-thirds of its public grant of $29.4 million and considerably more than half of the almost $34 million under its control during the general-election campaign on media advertising, particularly on television. As in 1976 and in the 1980 prenomination campaign, Carter's media advertisements were prepared and placed under the direction of Gerald Rafshoon, who worked in coordination with Carter pollster Patrick H. Caddell.

The initial Carter advertisements sought to portray the candidate as quiet, calm, and hard working—able to shoulder the heavy demands of the presidency. They often depicted him meeting with foreign heads of state,

conferring with top administration officials, working long into the night at
the White House. The first of the Carter advertisements were delivered to
the networks by Labor Day and broadcast on September 5.[113] By late
September, twenty-two advertisements had been produced, and Carter
commercials had been booked into network time every day until election
day.[114]

Once advertisements emphasizing Carter's positive qualities had made
their appeal to shaky supporters and undecided voters, a second series seeking to discredit Reagan were broadcast. One, aired on September 18—
earlier than planned due to a slip-up by campaign media advisers—showed
an empty Oval Office while a voice asked if a person with Ronald Reagan's
"fractured view of America" should occupy that office.[115] In the final
phase of the Carter media campaign, advertisements were directed to
wayward Democrats and were intended to leave potential voters with good
feelings about the candidate. Party luminaries, such as Edward Kennedy
and Rep. Morris Udall of Arizona, were shown praising the president, and
typical Democrats were depicted endorsing him and his aims.

Although Rafshoon maintained that he was not able to buy all the air
time he wanted,[116] the Carter campaign spent $15.8 million to purchase
television broadcast time, $4 million to $5 million of it in the closing days of
the campaign, according to pollster Caddell.[117] The campaign spent an additional $2.6 million to broadcast radio advertisements and $2.1 million more
on print advertising and media production costs. Among Carter radio
advertisements was a series of three nationwide broadcasts over the Mutual
Radio Network, each lasting twenty minutes and devoted to discussion of
issues such as economic policies. The first of the broadcasts cost the campaign $22,000.[118] Other Carter radio advertising sought to discredit indepen-
dent candidate John Anderson. The campaign did not invest heavily in print
advertising, although it did run advertisements in special-interest publications, such as those catering to farmer and ethnic groups.

The Carter campaign tried to make good use of free television time.
Here the president had an advantage over his opponents because as the incumbent, he attracted media attention by fulfilling the responsibilities of his
office, however politically motivated his activities as president might have
been. Thus in addition to free coverage on the national and local evening
news of his town meetings and election campaign rallies, Carter received
full network coverage of his news conference on September 18 and news
coverage of other activities, such as receiving foreign diplomats or heads of
state and signing important bills.[119]

Carter did turn down one significant opportunity for free television exposure when he refused to join Reagan and Anderson in a nationally televised

debate on September 21 and held out instead for a one-on-one debate with Reagan. In doing so the president took a calculated risk that whatever loss of esteem he might suffer in the eyes of the electorate would be less damaging than the loss of votes he might suffer if Anderson, who was thought to appeal to some of the same constituencies, was to make a strong showing in the same forum as the incumbent. Carter campaign officials also were convinced that in a one-on-one debate with Reagan, Carter's knowledge of government and grasp of facts, figures, and detail would give him an edge and that Anderson's presence would serve only to diffuse viewer judgments about the outcome and reduce the president's chances of scoring a clear victory.

Carter did agree to debate Reagan one-on-one late in the campaign, despite advice from some advisers, including Patrick Caddell, who argued that the experience of the 1976 campaign demonstrated that debates are always challengers' vehicles. According to Les Francis, DNC executive director, campaign officials made the decision to accept the League of Women Voters' invitation to a Reagan-Carter debate in order to draw contrasts on issues. "We had to get that contrast to get those undecideds to move back our way," said Francis. "We had to reemphasize the fact that Carter was a Democrat and there were strong distinctions on programs and policies between the two. We hadn't been able to do that in the campaign at that point, and the debate was a good way to do it."[120]

As Reagan and Anderson sought free air time to respond to what they called political remarks Carter made at his September 18 press conference, Carter attempted to get free air time to respond to pro-Reagan advertisements sponsored by independent political committees. But the FCC ruled against Carter, saying that imbalances caused by limits on federal campaign spending were beyond its jurisdiction.

Other Expenditures: After following the so-called Rose Garden strategy of staying close to the White House during the prenomination campaign, President Carter and his advisers made plans for considerable travel for the candidates and their representatives during the general-election campaign. The campaign initially budgeted $900,000 for presidential travel and an additional $900,000 for surrogate travel. Actual expenditures exceeded the total amount budgeted for both categories by almost $300,000, according to information provided by campaign officials through November 24, 1980. The campaign made a number of efforts to keep travel costs under control and to minimize associated accommodation costs. Whenever possible, the president avoided overnight trips, thus saving the cost of hotel accommodations for himself and his entourage. He sometimes chose to fly on a small Jetstar, which seated eight, instead of the customary Air Force One, a Boeing

707 that cost $4,530 an hour to operate compared with $1,533 an hour for the executive jet.[121] Aides traveling on campaign business were told to stay in private homes or to double up when hotel rooms were required.

The Carter-Mondale Committee travel itinerary for the five-day period from October 9 through 13 indicated visits to sixty-three locations throughout the nation—some of them such as New York City, Los Angeles, and Boston listed more than once—by the president, his running mate, their wives, and other relatives, and a variety of administration officials and other surrogates. During the final week of the campaign, the president visited twenty-six cities in fifteen states and traveled 15,000 miles in the air; he visited six key states and traveled 6,645 miles during the campaign's final twenty-four hours alone.[122] The final week of the campaign also proved busy for Carter surrogates, as thirty-two administration officials, from Cabinet secretaries to assistant departmental secretaries, were scheduled to visit twenty-six states, including all those where the race was rated as close.[123]

The campaign relied heavily on polls conducted by Patrick Caddell's Cambridge Survey Research. Poll results helped determine where campaign money should be spent and where other campaign resources could best be used. One million dollars was budgeted by campaign officials for polling costs, but according to one report, through October 15 Caddell already had collected more than $1.4 million for his services from the Carter-Mondale Committee.[124] When the campaign ended Caddell submitted a final bill for $400,000, but because the Carter-Mondale Committee had already spent up to its $29.4 million limit, the bill was sent to the DNC to be paid out of the $4.64 million the national-party committee was allowed to spend on behalf of the party's presidential ticket. The bill became a matter of some controversy when officials of the debt-ridden party balked at payment in the aftermath of the drubbing at the polls their candidates had received. They maintained, and Carter officials confirmed, that the DNC had no written contract with Caddell and had not commissioned certain surveys. But a Carter campaign aide said there had been an agreement that the campaign organization would pay all bills that had to be paid immediately and that the DNC would pay some bills that could be deferred.[125] Caddell was infuriated at the DNC response and maintained he had agreed to defer receiving some of the money due him so the committee would have cash available for last-minute campaign costs.[126]

Because the Carter campaign could not count on the national and state parties to operate telephone banks and other voter-turnout projects the way the Reagan campaign could, the campaign committee had to spend considerable sums on mobilizing Democratic voters. The committee budgeted $1.2 million for voter-turnout activities. The phone banks included in such activities accounted for a significant portion of the $1.8 million paid in telephone costs, according to the campaign's report through November 24, 1980. Other significant Carter campaign committee expenditures included $955,755 for payroll, $1,191,299 for consultants, and $1,985,124 for contracted services. A substantial amount of the polling costs were listed as contracted services expenses.

DNC Spending: Although the DNC originally thought it would be able to raise and spend the entire $4.6 million it was allowed on behalf of its presidential ticket, it managed to spend only about $4 million in such coordinated party expenditures. At least $600,000 of that amount was spent after the campaign had concluded and the DNC agreed to assume some of the obligations of the Carter-Mondale Committee, which had reached its legal spending limit. Media advertising accounted for a substantial portion of DNC spending on behalf of Carter-Mondale. For example, during a period of several days following October 20, the DNC Services Corporation, which carried out the national-party committee's business functions, reported assuming a total of $1.17 million in media expenses on behalf of the campaign committee.[127]

A portion of the DNC's coordinated party expenditures went to pay Patrick Caddell's Cambridge Survey Research for polls conducted on behalf of Carter-Mondale. A report published late in November 1980 based on information filed with the FEC covering the period through October 15 indicated that the DNC had paid Caddell's firm $711,000 for surveys in connection with the Carter campaign.[128] The DNC paid Caddell additional money to conduct a series of state surveys, ostensibly to benefit Democratic candidates for the House and the Senate. There were reports, however, that some of those surveys actually were conducted on Carter's behalf in key states but that their cost, $365,000, was charged to Democratic senatorial candidates.[129] Richard Conlon, executive director of the Democratic Study Group, which included many House Democrats, called the practice "a fraud."[130]

Similar charges were leveled regarding money expended by the DNC for voter-registration efforts. It was reported the national-party committee spent $537,000 for voter-registration efforts—about 90 percent of the total spent in that category according to an analysis of DNC spending by an outside accounting firm—in sixteen states where the presidential contest was thought to be close.[131] In most states that were written off by the presidential campaign committee, relatively little was spent on such efforts, even though Democratic candidates were vying for other offices.

According to an audit conducted by the Arthur Andersen & Co. accounting firm, during the 1980 election year, the DNC spent $11.4 million, including about $1.8 million on fund-raising expenses, $2 million on general

and administrative expenses, and $7.6 million on political projects and con-
stituency building. The audit figures, which were released on February 13,
1981, did not take into account an additional $600,000 the DNC spent after
the general election on behalf of the party's presidential ticket. That
amount brings to $8.2 million the total for spending on political projects
and constituency building.

Voter identification and turnout represented an important element in
the national-party committee's efforts at constituency building. The DNC
audit figures indicate that $1 million was spent on voter-registration and
-turnout activities and that an additional $428,000 was spent on targeting.
Political consultant Chris Brown directed a sophisticated precinct targeting
effort for the Democratic candidates by analyzing voting patterns in
175,000 precincts throughout the nation to find out where Democrats might
best conduct their voter-registration drives.[132] On the basis of Brown's data
and of polling results, as well as other criteria, including the percentage of
potential voters who belonged to minority populations and the ease with
which voters could be registered, the DNC focused its efforts on fifteen
states, among them New York, New Jersey, Ohio, Texas, Mississippi,
Alabama, and South Carolina.[133]

After the election was completed, the DNC was criticized by some
elected party leaders for focusing on the presidential election at the expense
of other Democratic candidates. Senate majority leader Robert C. Byrd
(D-W. Va.) said he was convinced that "too little help was given to
Democrats up for House and Senate seats."[134] Speaker of the House
Thomas P. O'Neill, Jr., also criticized the DNC for "poor" support of con-
gressional candidates and for being responsive only to "the whims of the
President and the presidential election."[135]

State- and Local-Party Committees: Despite the 1979 FECA amendments,
the Carter-Mondale Reelection Committee was not able to count on state-
and local-party committees for the kind of support the Reagan-Bush Committee received from Republican state- and local-party organizations. The
lengthy prenomination campaign hampered fund-raising activities on
behalf of the party committees.

The failure of state- and local-party committees to provide significant
support for Carter-Mondale, however, also was due to other factors, particularly the national-party leaders' inability to foster ties with state and
local committees and provide party-building assistance at local levels. One
postelection study, which included interviews with a wide variety of persons
active in the 1980 campaigns, quoted Carter-Mondale aides acknowledging
that the Democrats' "competence at the state and local level was
terrible."[136] According to the study, several of the Democrats interviewed
observed that intraparty divisions have always been a problem and noted

that "lack of enthusiasm or outright hostility on the part of state and local organizations toward the incumbent president in 1980 severely undercut party efforts across the board."[137]

As with the Republican committees, it is difficult to determine how much Democratic state and local parties spent to benefit the party's presidential ticket. One Democratic strategist reportedly estimated that Republican committees outspent Democratic committees by a ten-to-one margin in many states and that the inequality was greatest in states with large numbers of electoral votes.[138] In all, Democratic state- and local-party committees probably spent about $4 million on behalf of Carter-Mondale. That figure includes money spent on activities that directly supported the presidential ticket, and therefore was drawn from the committee's federal accounts and reported to the FEC, and on activities that indirectly supported the ticket's federal candidates, including the presidential and vice-presidential candidates.

News reports provide some information about spending by party organizations in particular states. In Texas Carter campaign and state-party voter-registration and -turnout drives reportedly cost between $250,000 and $500,000.[139] In late September 1980 it was reported that Texas Democratic organizations had already worked for six months to identify unregistered likely Democratic voters.[140] Once such voters were registered, the party stayed in touch, often through letters signed by local celebrities of the same ethnic origin as the registrant. In Florida during the campaign, a deputy chairman of the state Carter-Mondale Committee said state and local Democratic parties were "really taking the lead" in efforts to turn out the voters, particularly among the state's voting-age blacks.[141] A postelection report based on filings with the Virginia State Board of Elections said the state's Democrats spent nearly $52,000 on President Carter's losing campaign effort and described the figure as "a fraction of what state Republicans spent."[142]

Compliance Costs: The Carter-Mondale Reelection Committee, like the Reagan-Bush Committee, was allowed to accept contributions to defray the costs of ensuring compliance with the federal election laws. According to the FEC audit of the Carter campaign committee, during the course of the general-election campaign the compliance fund received $1.5 million and spent $939,701.[143] Those figures did not take into account subsequent contributions to the fund, expenditures for campaign winding-down costs, or some of the expenditures made out of the campaign's general-election accounts in individual states to pay for compliance-related activities.

Information provided by the Carter-Mondale Reelection Committee through November 24, 1980, allows compliance costs of $757,000 to be broken down into the following categories:

Payroll	$227,203
Consulting fees	47,597
Temporary employment	3,840
Contracted services	260,155
Fund-raising events	92,499
Political events	16,293
Occupancy	992
Postage and delivery	15,467
Telephone	31
Printing and reproduction	6,905
Stationery and supplies	17,783
Furniture and equipment	12,408
Travel	39,381
Petty cash	836
Media	9,365
Campaign materials	2,238
Contribution refunds	(1,000)
Interest and tax	4,995
Total costs	$756,988

A Carter committee aide later estimated that in addition, about $200,000 was spent on winding-down expenses, including costs incurred in relation to the FEC audit, and about $500,000 was spent out of general-election accounts in individual states for compliance-related activities, bringing total compliance costs to almost $1.5 million. The Carter committee made each state coordinator responsible for compliance in the state, including supervising the state campaign's bookkeepers and lawyers for compliance purposes. The national headquarters sent money to pay for compliance to each state coordinator— about 6 percent of the state campaign's costs—and indicated the money could be deposited in the state's general-election account to be subtracted out later to pay compliance-related bills. The amount subtracted out was about $500,000, and that figure was not available when the campaign organization prepared its report covering the period through November 24, 1980.

In 1976 the Carter campaign received in-kind contributions in the form of professional services provided by volunteer lawyers and accountants who assisted the campaign in complying with the FECA. In 1980 the Carter-Mondale Committee had no volunteer accountants and hired some controllers in some of the large states. There were, however, some local volunteer lawyers who assisted Carter campaign counsel Tim Smith.

Labor Spending: Many labor leaders felt ambivalent toward the Democratic presidential candidate. They were dismayed with the Carter administration's economic policies, which AFL-CIO President Lane Kirkland had called "destructive" and "backward" when the prenomination campaign was not yet completed,[144] but they were appalled by the propsect of having Ronald Reagan as president. Although many union leaders had backed Sen. Edward Kennedy during the prenomination-campaign race, the majority of them endorsed President Carter in the general-election campaign and eventually managed to mobilize their unions' resources in an effort to reelect him.

Early in September Carter picked up the endorsement of the board of the 13.6 million-member AFL-CIO. In urging the endorsement, union president Kirkland charged that Reagan's supporters were "among the most bitterly anti-union forces in America."[145] Despite such urging, at least two member unions—the 800,000-member IAM and the 1 million-member American Federation of State, County and Municipal Employees—refused to endorse the Democratic candidate. Later, however, Jerry Wurf, president of the government employees union, relented and helped throw the support of his union behind Carter.

Endorsement of Carter-Mondale was not quickly translated into enthusiastic efforts on behalf of the Democratic ticket. Said one political consultant to several unions, "The effort is there—but not the enthusiasm."[146] As the campaign drew closer to election day, however, the efforts of labor unions to reelect President Carter increased. The AFL-CIO and its affiliates distributed several million four-page newsletters alleging Reagan had opposed collective bargaining rights for teachers and farm workers when he was governor of California and that he was opposed to occupational health and safety provisions currently in the law.[147] The UAW distributed a six-page attack on Reagan positions to its members.[148] In all, labor distributed about 100 million pieces of literature denouncing Reagan, as well as John Anderson, and supporting Carter.[149]

According to AFL-CIO political director Alexander Barkan, labor unions also operated massive phone banks in every state urging members to vote for Carter even if they opposed his views on specific issues.[150] On October 28 national AFL-CIO leaders were scheduled to join state and local union officials on a closed-circuit satellite television conference in thirty cities in important industrial states to rally union support for the Democratic ticket and to kick off labor's final voter-turnout drive in those states.[151] Some examples of local-level union efforts on behalf of Carter are available. The Texas AFL-CIO used a computer to help identify unregistered union voters according to union locals and used fourteen phone banks to reach most of the state's registered union members before November 4.[152] About $125,000 was budgeted for this effort.[153] In Los Angeles, the Building Trades Council assigned 300 union business agents to register workers and get them to the polls.[154]

In 1976 organized labor probably spent about $11 million on behalf of the Carter-Mondale ticket.[155] In 1980, due at least in part to inflation, labor spending on behalf of Carter-Mondale reached about $15 million. The money was spent on internal communications with union members and their families, on voter-registration and -turnout drives, and on overhead and other costs. Included in the total is $1.3 million that forty organizations spent on reported communications costs. The AFL-CIO's COPE led the way with expenditures of $382,120, followed by the United Steelworkers of America, which spent $195,739; the NEA, which spent $133,034; and the United Auto Workers, which spent $119,278 on internal communications. The NRA reported spending $45,609 on internal communications opposing Carter.

Not only did labor expenditures on behalf of Carter-Mondale more than match independent expenditures on behalf of Reagan-Bush; the fact that labor spending could be and often was coordinated with the Carter-Mondale campaign made such spending more effective than independent spending. On the other hand, state- and local-party committee spending on behalf of Reagan-Bush, which matched pro-Carter labor spending, probably was more effective than labor spending because it was more successfully coordinated with the presidential campaign it supported, largely as a result of the efforts of the RNC.

Independent Spending: "The Carter-Mondale policy is actively to discourage . . . independent expenditures," read a legal manual for the Democratic campaign committee's coordinators in the states. "The law is tricky and the slightest evidence of cooperation or consent by anyone in our campaign may be sufficient to convert an ostensibly independent expenditure into a campaign expense—which means that we have to pay for it."[156] Whether because of the campaign committee's stated opposition to independent expenditures or because of a lack of interest on the part of independent spenders, President Carter attracted only $27,773 in independent spending on his behalf. Individuals and groups making independent expenditures opposing Carter's candidacy spent $209,781 on their efforts.

Incumbency: As in the prenomination campaign, in the general-election period Carter campaign aides stated that the president would not use the advantages of his office to further his candidacy. "The President does not intend to abuse the incumbency," read the campaign's legal manual for state coordinators. "This means that federal resources will not be donated to the campaign."[157] Early in September the White House issued guidelines for travel by administration officials during the general-election campaign.[158] It noted that cabinet officials and agency heads would be asked to assist in the reelection campaign and in other political activities, but it also sought to assure that appropriated money and government credit would not be used to fund campaign travel or appearances. According to the guidelines, payment for campaign-related travel was to come from the sponsoring political organizations—the Carter-Mondale Reelection Committee, the DNC, or other party committees and candidate organizations. When the Carter-Mondale Committee was paying the costs, any stop that involved more than incidental campaign activity was to be treated wholly as a campaign stop. Thus if a cabinet secretary flew to a particular city for an official event and a Carter-Mondale rally, and the campaign-related costs were being paid for by the campaign committee, the entire stop had to be treated as a campaign stop when calculating travel costs. If, however, the secretary made the trip to attend an official event and a Democratic party fund raiser and the costs were being paid by the DNC, the travel costs could be divided between the DNC and the government on an event-time basis. That meant the DNC would pay that percentage of travel costs represented by the percentage of DNC event time over the total event time at the stop.

The travel guidelines also cautioned administration officials regarding political comments at official events in order to forestall any legal challenge or public criticism. In addition, the guidelines noted that no government aircraft were permitted to be used for campaign stops on trips and that government ground transportation was not permitted to be used at any campaign stop. Administration officials other than White House personnel and those appointees confirmed by the Senate were reminded they were not permitted to engage in campaign or other political activity.

Despite the guidelines, Carter's Republican opponents maintained that Carter had, in fact, abused his powers as an incumbent in the presidential race. On September 11, the RNC filed twenty-nine Freedom of Information requests with government agencies demanding information regarding travel and public appearances by agency officials. Republican party chairman Bill Brock claimed the incumbent had demonstrated a clear and consistent pattern of abuse and cited reports in the press that indicated administration officials had been making political trips at taxpayer expense.[159] The Republicans' objection to allegedly political remarks at the beginning of the President's September 18 press conference has already been noted.

Actually there are some indications that the mantle of incumbency weighed heavily on the president. Some insiders ventured that Carter ran best as a challenger. "I worry when he's not the underdog," said one.[160] And White House counsel Lloyd Cutler observed that the best thing in Ronald Reagan's favor was that "he has been out of office for the last six years."[161]

Carter did take advantage of some of the tools of his office. He received nationwide television coverage for his September 18 press conference, and he was able to count on a large number of influential, well-known surrogates—his cabinet secretaries and other appointees—to attack Reagan's stands on various issues they were familiar with and to praise the administration's record. The administration also was able to time federal grants to benefit the president's reelection campaign. For example, late in October it was reported that five senior administration officials had recently traveled to five midwestern cities to announce grants and received extensive local publicity.[162] The city of Toledo, Ohio, received $3 million to help retrain skilled workers, and Cleveland received an increase of $2.7 million in such funds.[163] In Flint, Michigan, a $1.3 million crisis center was opened to help auto industry workers cope with alcohol and drug problems.[164] "It is political," acknowledged Cleveland's Republican Mayor George V. Voinovich, "but if Ronald Reagan were President, he'd be doing the same thing."[165]

Audit Report

On August 18, 1981, the FEC released the report of its audit of the Carter-Mondale Reelection Committee.[166] According to the report, based on a filing of the committee on February 26, 1981, the committee had receipts of $29,773,960 and expenditures of $29,208,250.

The report uncovered no major violations by the committee. Although the auditors noted that records and documentation were missing for some contributions and expenditures, that certain debts and obligations had not been properly itemized, and that some information was missing from FEC reports filed by the committee, the committee subsequently amended its report to the satisfaction of the audit staff, and no further action was required. The auditors also noted that the committee had earned $190,785 in interest on federal funds it had deposited in interest-bearing accounts. According to the report, the committee had paid $85,542 in taxes on that interest and estimated it would pay an additional $2,073 in the first two months of 1981. The audit staff calculated that the remaining $103,170 was repayable to the U.S. Treasury. After further field work was conducted in September 1981 and additional information was provided by the campaign committee, the amount repayable was reduced to $87,232.[167]

The FEC also asked the campaign committee to pay the Treasury $924 it had received as improper contributions, $800 of it in the form of a discount by a vendor who noted on his invoice that he intended it as a contribution to the campaign. Finally, the FEC required the committee to repay $1,270 for computer reprogramming and printing costs incurred by Carter's prenomination-campaign committee but paid by the general-election committee.

Anderson

John Anderson's independent candidacy for the presidency functioned as a lightning rod in what often was described as a volatile election campaign year. Anderson attracted support from independent voters who claimed no party affiliation, from Democrats disillusioned with Jimmy Carter's performance in office, and from moderate Republicans apprehensive over Ronald Reagan's professed conservatism. He also attracted strong opposition from a variety of quarters. The DNC made efforts to keep Anderson's name off the presidential ballot in as many states as possible, reportedly spending close to $200,000 to do so.[168] The Carter campaign suggested to banks, at least indirectly, that they might encounter legal problems if they loaned money to the Anderson campaign.[169] The Democratic campaign also tried to exclude Anderson from nationally televised debates and aired anti-Anderson television and radio advertisements.[170] Minor-party candidates, upset that Anderson was permitted to join in a nationally televised debate and they were not, and disturbed at the FEC's mid-campaign decision to declare Anderson eligible for retroactive federal funds if he received at least 5 percent of the popular vote, also were critical of the independent candidate.

Anderson's campaign was plagued throughout by fund-raising difficulties—unlike the major-party candidates he received no federal funds in advance of his campaign—and by the need to spend a substantial portion of available funds on legal battles. Indeed, the Anderson campaign was waged as much in the courtroom as on the campaign trail.

Sources of Funds

After Anderson declared his independent candidacy on April 24, he was able to transfer $713,000 in surplus funds from his prenomination-campaign organization to his National Unity Campaign. He also was able to build on the organizational network he had developed during the prenomination period, in part with the help of federal funds, and to appeal for additional contributions from individuals and groups who had supported his Republican campaign.[171] Since the general election is counted as a separate election from the primary election, Anderson was permitted to solicit additional funds from previous contributors, even those who had contributed the legal maximum to his prenomination campaign.

Despite these advantages, in comparison with major-party candidates, Anderson began his campaign with several handicaps. He received no federal grant in advance of his campaign. In fact, because he had declared himself an independent candidate rather than the candidate of a political

party, there was no provision in the law—as there was for third-party candidates—that would have allowed him to receive federal money retroactively, if he achieved a certain measure of electoral success. He was required to
fund his campaign entirely from private contributions raised according to
the FECA's $1,000 limit on individual contributions and $5,000 limit on
contributions from multicandidate committees. He was obligated to comply
with the disclosure requirements and contribution limits of the law, but
money raised to pay compliance-related legal and accounting costs was subject to the same set of limits. Thus potential contributors were not permitted
to donate $1,000 to further the campaign and an additional sum to help pay
compliance costs. He had no national- or state-party organizations working
on his behalf, spending money in addition to what his campaign organization could raise and spend, and providing volunteer services. And he was
confronted with the arduous task of collecting the required number of
signatures in each state to get his name on the ballot.

Fund raising was slow and fell short of expected, and needed, amounts.
In the two weeks following Anderson's announcement of candidacy as an
independent, the campaign reported receiving contributions of $500,000.[172]
But if the campaign was to raise the $12 million officials said they needed to
mount a competitive effort, the fund-raising pace would have to be doubled
quickly. That did not happen. The independent candidate's campaign drew
less in private contributions in May or June than the $2 million his
Republican prenomination-campaign organization had raised in March, its
last full month.[173] Anderson's controversial meeting with Edward Kennedy
late in July, after which he reportedly said he might reconsider his position
if President Carter did not secure the Democratic nomination, did nothing
to help his fund-raising efforts, as backers began to question the seriousness
of his candidacy.[174] Nor did the relative calm of the Democratic convention
serve his fund-raising purposes, since it did not yield the disgruntled
Democrats he hoped might flock to his campaign. During August, the
Anderson campaign took in slightly more than $1 million in individual con-
tributions, which represented an even lower weekly average than the campaign had experienced earlier.[175] Between April and August the campaign
reported raising slightly less than $7 million and being in debt about $1.2
million.[176] September, with its announcement of the League of Women
Voters' decision that Anderson would be allowed to participate in a
scheduled debate, was marked by an upturn in contributions to the campaign. During the first three weeks of September, the campaign raised an
average of $475,000 a week, up from the August weekly average of
$270,000 and the highest weekly average since the campaign had begun.[177]

An FEC decision early in September declaring Anderson eligible for
retroactive public funds if he received 5 percent or more of the vote on
November 4, and an additional FEC ruling early in October that bank loans

to the campaign secured by postelection public financing would not violate
federal law, appeared to give fund raising a boost. The campaign, however,
was unable to arrange the commercial loans it sought and turned instead to
the 200,000 persons who already had contributed to the campaign to appeal
for loans to finance final campaign efforts, including some radio and television advertising.[178] This appeal yielded about $1.8 million for use in the
campaign's closing days. Including money received from such loans and
$4.2 million received in postelection federal funds, the Anderson campaign
raised $17.1 million, about half what the major-party candidates had under
their control and a much smaller percentage of the totals those candidates
spent or had spent on their behalf.

Direct Mail: The Anderson campaign conducted most of its fund raising
through direct-mail appeals handled for the candidate by Craver, Mathews,
Smith & Co., of Arlington, Virginia, which also conducted Anderson's
prenomination-campaign direct-mail fund-raising drive. Tom Mathews, a
partner in the firm, also served as an Anderson press spokesman and
political adviser. The Anderson campaign began with a mailing list of nearly
100,000 persons who had contributed to the candidate's Republican
primary campaign.[179] A variety of existing mailing lists were tested in an effort to add new names to the contributor file, but the most responsive addi-
tions to the Anderson lists were the names of thousands of individuals
around the nation who signed Anderson ballot petitions in the various
states.[180]

The day before Anderson announced his independent candidacy, the
direct-mail firm sent out 2 million fund-raising appeals. By the third week
of May, it was reported that Anderson was receiving contributions at a rate
of $50,000 to $60,000 a day, primarily in response to direct-mail solicitations.[181] At the same time, a liberal-oriented mailing brought in about
$300,000 from 80,000 persons who had contributed to the Anderson
prenomination campaign and added 25,000 new names to the contributor
file.[182] Early in June the National Unity Campaign's direct-mail drive
received a boost from a federal court ruling that struck down a law that
allowed only the two major political parties special low postal rates.

The postal-rate subsidy had been enacted into law in 1978 with the intention of benefiting the major parties and their national and state committees. In the following year, however, when it had become apparent that the
letter of the law applied to all political parties, Congress acted to restrict the
subsidy to major parties. On behalf of several of the excluded parties as well
as independent candidate Anderson, the New York Civil Liberties Union
filed suit charging postal-rate discrimination. In June 1980 a federal district
court found the congressional limitations favoring the major parties were
unconstitutional. Under the ruling, the Anderson campaign, as well as a

variety of minor parties, also were allowed to mail at a rate of 3.1 cents per piece of third-class mail instead of the 8.4 cents per letter rate they had been paying. Some Anderson aides estimated the ruling could save the independent campaigns $344,000 in the mailing of 6.5 million appeals.[183]

The campaign's expectations turned out to be exaggerated. Although the court ruling clearly opened up the postal-subsidy program to the previously excluded political groups, Congress did not increase appropriations to accommodate them. In both fiscal years 1979 and 1980, revenues forgone remained roughly within the $4 million level of approprations that Congress was willing to allocate to the program. In 1978 all minor parties combined received only about $92,000 of that subsidy money for their mailings, and in 1980 those parties, together with Anderson's independent campaign, received a subsidy of about $119,000.

Through late July the direct-mail drive accounted for 75 percent of the independent campaign's receipts.[184] And when the campaign found it impossible to arrange the bank loans it sought to finance an intensive media campaign in October, direct-mail appeals were used to solicit small loans from previous contributors. Letters were mailed to the campaign's 200,000 contributors asking them to lend the campaign the difference between what they had already contributed and the $1,000 maximum individual contribution allowed by federal law.[185] The loans were to be repaid with interest from federal funds Anderson expected to receive after the election. The effort to secure loans from individuals brought $1.8 million to the campaign, much of it in small amounts.

Other Fund Raising: Although direct mail was the mainstay of the Anderson campaign's fund-raising efforts, the campaign did employ other fund-raising methods, including newspaper advertising; solicitations made in connection with personal appearances by the candidate, his running mate, Patrick Lucey, former Democratic governor of Wisconsin, and their relatives; and local grass-roots events. A number of folk and rock stars, including singer James Taylor, and the band Cheap Trick, three of whose members came from Anderson's home town of Rockford, Illinois, were enlisted to perform at fund-raising events.[186] A phone bank operation brought in $175,000 over the Labor Day weekend.[187] A luncheon for Anderson held in Los Angeles late in September and attended by thirty-six persons raised about $28,000 for his campaign. In mid-October the candidate received $50,000 from a fund-raising dinner in Beverly Hills hosted by two of his supporters, actor Ed Asner and University of California regent Stanley Sheinbaum.[188]

Anderson received only minimal support from PACs, which accounted for about $16,000 of the campaign's receipts. According to information provided by the National Unity Campaign, twenty PACs contibuted to the campaign, including the National Abortion Rights Action League PAC and the Liberal Party Federal PAC, both of which contributed the maximum $5,000. An additional $14,000 was received from PACs as earmarked contributions from individuals.

The Anderson campaign established the Arts for Anderson program, coordinated by Arthur Glimcher, head of Pace Galleries in New York.[189] Glimcher solicited a number of artists to create original artworks that were to be used as lottery prizes, with chances being sold at $1,000 each.[190] The FEC audit of the National Unity Campaign indicates, however, that because of problems posed by the receipt and disposition of the artwork, the gallery owner never transferred the artwork collected to the committee.[191] In addition the campaign created the National Finance Council, made up of affluent supporters who gave $1,000 each to the campaign and pledged to raise $10,000 more.[192] By mid-August, the council had nearly seventy members, including retailer Stanley Marcus, lawyer Albert Jenner, and philanthropist Stewart Mott.[193]

Mott's relationship with the Anderson campaign organization was a matter of some controversy. During the prenomination campaign, the liberal activist and heir to a General Motors fortune independently spent more than $90,000, mostly on newspaper advertising, to support Anderson's Republican candidacy. Early in April, he announced formation of a group to support an independent Anderson candidacy for the presidency and engaged an election-law expert to look into requirements Anderson would have to meet to get on the general-election ballots in various states.[194] Mott maintained he had not spoken with the candidate about this effort.[195] In May, after Anderson had announced his independent bid, Mott wrote two lengthy memos to the candidate and key staff persons making candid suggestions regarding the needs of the campaign and criticizing some campaign aides, particularly media adviser David Garth. In mid-June Anderson aides released a letter the candidate had sent to the FEC disavowing Mott's efforts. "However well-intentioned," he wrote, "Mr. Mott's efforts have proved disruptive."[196] But late in July the campaign announced it was restoring its ties with Mott, who would serve the National Unity Campaign as a fund raiser.[197] In October Mott sent additional memos to Anderson, which, among other things, noted that Mott Enterprises, a direct-mail advertising and fund-raising firm the philanthropist owned, had extended a $500,000 line of credit to the campaign and that $407,000 of the amount had been drawn down. That amount represented some costs of a September fund-raising appeal mailed to 1.3 million persons.[198] Mott said he got the idea to extend credit to the Anderson campaign from the 1976 Carter campaign in which Carter media adviser Gerald Rafshoon extended considerable credit to the campaign.[199] Mott expected to be repaid from postelection federal funds he was confident Anderson would receive.

Federal Funds: Under federal election law, eligible minor party or new-party presidential candidates who receive 5 percent or more of the total number of popular votes cast for the office of president are entitled to receive postelection federal grants. Any such grant is to equal an amount that bears the same ratio to the amount granted to the major-party candidates at the beginning of their election campaigns as the number of votes cast for the minor- or new-party candidate bears to the average number of votes cast for the major-party candidates. Thus, if the major-party candidates receive an average of 40 percent of the vote and a minor- or new-party candidate receives the remaining 20 percent, that candidate is entitled to one-half the federal grant the major-party candidates received. The law includes no reference to independent presidential candidates, those who seek the office without having been nominated by a political party.

In 1976 independent presidential candidate Eugene J. McCarthy asked the FEC to declare him eligible for the same retroactive subsidies the law provides for minor-party candidates. The commission rejected his appeal, by voting three to three along party lines. It was suggested at the time that the three Democratic members were influenced to vote against the request because they thought McCarthy might take votes away from Jimmy Carter.[200] McCarthy abandoned a subsequent court challenge to the commission's ruling after he failed to win the minimum 5 percent of the votes to qualify for federal funding.

In July 1980 Anderson and his supporters filed suit in federal court challenging the FEC ruling in the matter. Campaign strategists believed bankers would be more likely to loan the campaign money if they knew Anderson could qualify for postelection federal funds, which he could use to pay off the loans. When the court suggested relief might best be sought from the commission itself, the Anderson campaign filed the court papers with the FEC as an advisory opinion request. On September 4 the FEC ruled five to one to approve an advisory opinion proposed by the commission's legal staff, which concluded that although Anderson presented himself as a nonparty candidate, his campaign behaved like a political party.[201] Thus, said the proposal, like political-party candidates, Anderson should be considered eligible for retroactive public funding.

Anderson was delighted with the FEC ruling because he thought it would make him eligible to borrow money on the anticipated subsidy, which could then be used for television commercials.[202] Not everyone greeted the decision as favorably. Barry Commoner, the new Citizens party presidential candidate, called the ruling a distortion of the election and noted that, unlike Anderson's campaign, his party had gone to "great expense and effort" to meet the requirements to be recognized as a political party.[203]

The sense of euphoria that characterized the Anderson campaign following the FEC ruling evaporated quickly when it became apparent the hoped-for loans would not be forthcoming. Initially the commission refused to certify formally to the Treasury Department that Anderson would be eligible for a retroactive subsidy. The commissioners explained that such a certification would be premature since they had no assurance the candidate would achieve the threshold 5 percent showing. Banks, permitted by federal law to lend a campaign money only in the ordinary course of business and only when assured of repayment, consequently were unsure whether any loans they might give Anderson might be counted as contributions and therefore be ruled illegal. According to the Anderson campaign, this difficulty was exacerbated by a memorandum the Carter campaign circulated among some banks warning them of legal problems they might face if they loaned money to Anderson.[204] Carter campaign officials acknowledged the existence of a memorandum outlining the legal risks in lending to the Anderson campaign but maintained it was an internal research memo that was not circulated outside the Carter campaign or used to influence banks not to make such loans.[205]

In order to improve its prospects of receiving bank loans, the campaign turned once again to the FEC, asking the commissioners to rule that such laws would not violate federal campaign law. In a lengthy advisory opinion approved by a five-to-one vote on October 2, the commissioners concluded that bank loans to the National Unity Campaign "would not violate the requirements that bank loans be 'made on a basis which assures repayment.' "[206] Under the FEC ruling the total amount banks could loan Anderson would be keyed to Anderson's average standing in four public-opinion polls. The commissioners made clear they were making no recommendations to banks regarding the advisability of loaning money to Anderson.

The Anderson campaign even drafted a loan accord promising to obtain a $10 million disability policy for Anderson from Lloyd's of London, at a cost of $10,000 a month, and a $10 million life insurance policy to ensure prospective lenders that the loans would be paid off if the candidate became disabled or died prior to the election.[207] Nevertheless the campaign was unable to negotiate the loans it sought. In mid-October, when Anderson's standing in public-opinion polls had dropped from his 15 percent standing at the time the FEC ruled he would be eligible for public funds to about 8 percent, the campaign committee announced it was giving up on its efforts to secure bank loans.[208] Instead Anderson would rely on small loans from previous contributors, which the campaign had begun to solicit during the final week of September. The campaign succeeded in raising $1.8 million in such loans, considerably less than the $10 million it had hoped for from banks.

On the basis of his performance in the general election, in which he received almost 5.7 million votes—about 6.6 percent of the votes cast—Anderson received $4,242,304 in postelection federal funds. Initially the FEC calculated he should receive $4.21 million based on his unofficial vote total. The commission granted him $4.16 million, holding back 1 percent of the total calculated, pending official figures. When the official figures became available, the commission calculated the Anderson-Lucey campaign was eligible to receive an additional $77,398. The federal funds allowed the campaign to repay the loans it had received from individuals and to pay off some other campaign debts. Some lenders of small amounts refused the repayments.

Additional Litigation: The Anderson campaign turned to the courts and to the FEC in an additional attempt to open up new sources of funds for the general-election drive. Following the FEC's decision that the National Unity Campaign was the functional equivalent of a political party and that Anderson consequently was eligible for postelection federal funding if he received 5 percent or more of the popular vote, the campaign's counsel filed papers at the agency to create a new committee, called the National Unity Campaign 441a(d) Committee. The name was derived from a section of the FECA that allows national political-party committees to spend privately raised funds on their presidential candidates. In 1980 the parties were allowed to spend up to $4.6 million for this purpose. The campaign filed suit in the U.S. District Court in Maine, which had a relatively uncrowded calendar, seeking a ruling that the new committee had the same right as a national political-party committee to accept up to $20,000 yearly from individuals and $15,000 from multicandidate committees and to spend up to $4.6 million in coordinated party expenditures on behalf of Anderson. Under the current law, the plaintiffs argued, Anderson supporters were denied equal protection and their rights to free speech and association because they were permitted to contribute only a maximum of $1,000 to the candidate's campaign committee and were denied the possibility of contributing additional funds to a supporting committee to further his candidacy.

Both district and appeals courts refused to grant the National Unity Campaign 441a(d) Committee its request for a preliminary injunction, preventing the FEC from refusing to treat it as a national committee of a political party. Shortly before the election, the new committee filed an advisory opinion request with the FEC asking the commission to decide if the new committee could operate as a national-party committee under the FECA. On November 20, the commissioners voted unanimously that the committee did not qualify as a national committee, since it supported no other candidates than Anderson and Lucey.

Campaign Receipts: According to information provided by the National Unity Campaign covering the period from April 24, 1980, through June 30, 1981, the campaign had total revenues of $17.1 million, as follows:

Individual contributions	$9,760,000
In-kind contributions (from individuals)	111,000
PAC contributions	16,000
Bank loans	400,000
Loans from individuals	1,830,000
Federal funds	4,242,000
Transfer from Anderson for President Committee	713,000
Interest from bank deposits (before taxes)	59,000
Total	$17,130,000

Contributions accounted for the largest percentage of campaign funds, including $9.76 million from individuals, $111,000 in in-kind contributions, and $16,000 from PACs. Counted in with the $9.76 million total for individual contributions is approximately $440,000 that the campaign received in 1981, partly in response to a mailing sent to individual lenders asking for new contributions to help make up the campaign's deficit. A postelection federal grant provided the campaign with $4.2 million, and loans provided an additional $2.2 million, including $1.8 million from individuals and $400,000 from banks. In May the campaign received a bank loan of $100,000, in June an additional loan of $100,000, and in July a third loan of $200,000. Finally the campaign received $713,000 transferred from Anderson's prenomination campaign and $59,000 in interest on bank deposits.

No communications costs supporting Anderson's candidacy were reported to the FEC, but $60,003 was reported as communications costs opposing him, including $22,229 spent by the UAW and $9,076 by the United Mine Workers' Coal Miner's PAC. Only $3,084 was reported as independent expenditures in favor of Anderson and $2,635 as independent expenditures opposing him.

Expenditures

Just as Anderson had to rely on sources of funds quite different from those that financed his major-party opponents, he had to face some different campaign costs. Specifically, the Anderson campaign had to spend a substantial portion of its funds on gaining access to various state ballots and on raising campaign funds from private sources. In addition the campaign faced costs similar to those of the Reagan and Carter campaigns: campaign staff payroll, candidate travel, media advertising, compliance, and so on. Time and money spent on ballot access and fund raising drained campaign resources, making it impossible to mount a significant media advertising campaign and causing cutbacks in staff and travel as the campaign drew to its conclusion. According to campaign officials, the Anderson campaign spent $16.6 million, excluding some winding-down costs; $14.4 million represented net campaign operating expenditures.

Ballot Access: When John Anderson announced his independent candidacy on April 24, the deadline for filing petitions seeking to place a name on the state's presidential ballot already had passed in five states: Kentucky, Maine, Maryland, New Mexico, and Ohio. In addition, in other states Anderson faced a wide variety of restrictive laws that would have made it difficult for him to qualify for a ballot position. Five states—New York, West Virginia, Arizona, Nebraska, and Texas—had statutes prohibiting anyone who voted in a presidential primary election from signing a petition for a third-party or independent candidate. Other states, such as North Carolina, had "sore loser" statutes that prohibited a candidate whose name was on the state's presidential primary ballot from running as an independent in the general election. A Utah law required that each signature on a ballot petition be notarized. Laws in several other states required that petition circulators be registered voters in those states. And Michigan had no procedure by which an independent candidate could win a listing on the presidential ballot.

Where state laws made it impossible for Anderson to get on the ballot or appeared to pose unreasonable obstacles, campaign lawyers, directed by attorney Mitchell Rogovin, challenged the laws. This task was made more difficult and expensive because the laws varied from state to state and because both the Carter campaign and the DNC took steps to keep Anderson off the ballot, including providing legal advice to state Democratic committees working against ballot access for the independent candidate.[209] In states in which filing deadlines had passed, the campaign filed suits charging that the laws violated the Fourteenth Amendment of the Constitution, which guarantees equal protection under the law. The campaign received favorable rulings in all of the states, although an appeals court ruled against Anderson in Ohio. The appeals court's action, however, was too late to prevent Anderson's name from appearing on the state ballot. After the general election the U.S. Supreme Court agreed to hear Anderson's challenge of the Ohio law.[210]

The Anderson campaign eventually succeeded in having the candidate's name placed on the ballot in all fifty states and the District of Columbia, but the cost was substantial. According to campaign officials, $2 million was spent on ballot access for the candidate, including approximately $1.08 million for state petition drives, $100,000 for in-house salaries, $150,000 for administrative support at national headquarters, and $672,000 for legal costs.

Fund Raising, Staff, and Travel: Although direct-mail fund-raising appeals raised a far larger percentage of the Anderson campaign's funds than any other fund-raising method, such costs represented the largest category of expenditure by the campaign. About $3 million was spent on direct mail for postage and for design, printing, and related costs. The campaign spent an additional $400,000 on fund raising, including the costs associated with organizing fund-raising events and with designing and placing newpaper appeals.

The Anderson campaign staff included about 250 paid members at its greatest number.[211] In late August, when Anderson was experiencing a slow decline in his standing in public-opinion polls and his campaign's expenditures were outrunning its income, the campaign's management underwent major changes. David Garth, who had been serving as Anderson's media adviser, became the campaign's director as well. Campaign manager Michael MacLeod retained his title but moved over to the financial side of the campaign. Three other top campaign aides resigned, citing personal reasons: Edward Coyle, who had been deputy campaign manager; Francis Sheehan, who had been treasurer; and Michael Fernandez, who had served as chief scheduler. Press secretary Michael Rosenbaum also retained his title but was assigned to work out of the campaign's Washington headquarters, and Tom Mathews, a partner in the direct-mail firm engaged by Anderson, became the candidate's traveling press spokesman. Mitchell Rogovin remained as the campaign's general counsel.

Along with the shakeup in the campaign management came efforts to reduce campaign expenditures across the board. Staff members took cuts in salaries, and state field offices were put on a self-supporting basis.[212] A month later the staff was cut back to save money to be used for television commercials in the campaign's closing days.[213] In spite of reductions and cutbacks, the National Unity Campaign spent $1.71 million on personnel.

The campaign also spent $2 million on candidate travel. This expenditure category was among those subject to cutbacks in late August when the campaign was short of cash. One of David Garth's first acts in his position as campaign director was to cancel a whistle-stop train tour across six states, starting in the candidate's hometown of Rockford, Illinois. According to press secretary Rosenbaum, the trip would have cost about $250,000, including $85,000 for telephones.[214] Although the campaign would have recovered a portion of the total from reimbursements by news organizations, the trip was too expensive to undertake, said Rosenbaum.[215]

Media: The Anderson campaign's ballot-access problems and fund-raising difficulties did not leave much money to mount a television advertising campaign. The campaign's advertisements began to air earlier than those of either of the major-party candidates. Late in July and early in August, Anderson advertisements were broadcast in eight advertising media markets and on a national cable network.[216] The cost was $500,000, a portion of it recouped by responses to fund-raising appeals included in the advertisements.[217] In its first week, the television campaign returned $100,000 in cash and pledges.[218]

The next wave of Anderson commercials was not aired until late in the campaign, when individual loans from previous small contributors made it possible to mount a modest media drive that included fifteen- and thirty-minute advertisements on all three commercial networks the night before the general election.[219] The Anderson campaign spent about $2.3 million on media advertising, $1.6 million of it on buying broadcast time, $314,000 on consulting fees and expenses paid to Garth Associates, and $142,500 on producing television commercials of varying length, as well as some radio commercials. An additional $201,000 was spent on newspaper and related advertisements.

Because the Anderson campaign could not afford an extensive paid media drive, the candidate tried to get all of the free television and radio time and newspaper space he could obtain. The campaign arranged as many media interviews as possible, especially for local television stations, in an attempt to increase Anderson's name recognition and inform potential voters about his program. A decision by NBC to have Anderson appear as an unpaid guest commentator on the network's *Today* program during the mid-July RNC drew protests from Republican officials and from at least one third-party candidate. Anderson, who was traveling in Europe at the time of the convention, was interviewed by a network correspondent, and tapes of the interviews were telecast twice daily via satellite. The Anderson campaign attempted to get free air time for its candidate to respond to allegedly political remarks made by President Carter during the opening portion of the incumbent's September 18 news conference, which was broadcast by all three networks. The networks, however, characterized the conference as a legitimate news event not subject to the equal-opportunities requirement of the federal law.

The most significant free media coverage Anderson received was coverage of his participation in a nationally televised debate with

Republican candidate Reagan. When the League of Women Voters set up a tentative fall debate schedule, it had made no decision regarding participants, although Anderson and several third-party candidates had asked to take part. The league's decision on the matter was complicated by the fact that President Carter had announced as early as May that he would not participate with independent candidate Anderson in any debates. According to Anderson Carter's decision showed "contempt for the political process."[220] He and his aides felt strongly that his appearance in debate with the major-party candidates would help establish him as a legitimate candidate.

Early in August the league announced its criteria for issuing debate invitations. The major-party candidates would be invited automatically, but independent and third-party candidates would have to reach a 15 percent threshold of support as measured by a number of national public-opinion polls and be on enough state ballots to have a mathematical possibility of winning enough electoral votes to win the presidency. Libertarian party presidential candidate Ed Clark, who by this time had met ballot-access requirements in most states but did not rank high in the polls, called the criteria "narrowly partisan, exclusionary and a disservice to the American people."[221] Carter's position on presidential debates softened somewhat; he allowed for the possibility of a three-way debate but maintained that one debate should be set aside for Reagan and himself. This position quickly became a demand that the first presidential debate be conducted with only Reagan and Carter as participants. Reagan, on the other hand, declared he had no objection to a three-way debate that included Anderson.

The Anderson campaign focused its efforts on ensuring that the candidate would qualify for the league's debate invitation by the September 10 deadline, and the candidate himself acknowledged that if he failed to qualify, "it would be a serious blow."[222] When Anderson did meet the 15 percent threshold, the league issued its invitation, and President Carter promptly refused to participate. Both Reagan and Anderson criticized the president for his stand, but to no avail. The Citizens party filed charges with the FEC and with the IRS asking the IRS to review the league's tax-exempt status in view of its exclusion of minor-party candidates from the debates. The FEC rejected the complaint, and the new party's lack of funds prevented it from seeking judicial review of the commission's decision.

On September 21 the debate between Anderson and Reagan was held in Baltimore and broadcast nationwide by NBC and CBS. Although it is difficult to determine whether either candidate won the debate, Anderson's participation did gain him exposure to a huge nationwide audience at no direct cost to his campaign. One estimate placed the number of television viewers at 50 million to 55 million.[223] League efforts to stage a second debate, this one between Reagan and Carter, initially were unsuccessful.

Carter accepted, but Reagan, acting on advice that he was leading Carter in the polls, declined. In mid-October Reagan reversed his decision and agreed to meet Carter on October 28 in a league-sponsored debate that excluded Anderson. Although Anderson said it was "highly unfortunate that the League of Women Voters has knuckled under to the White House," he dismissed any idea of mounting a legal challenge to block the two-man debate.[224] On the night of the debate, he did appear in a counterdebate on the Cable News Network, which used time-delay devices to splice in Anderson responses to the debate positions of the two major candidates. It is impossible to determine what effect Anderson's exclusion from the second debate had on the chances of the candidate, who showed a slow but steady decline in popular support over the final two months of the campaign.

Campaign Expenditures: Information provided by the National Unity Campaign for John Anderson covering the period from April 24, 1980, to June 30, 1981, allows total campaign expenditures of $16.6 million to be broken down into the following categories:

Direct-mail fund raising	$ 3,000,000
Other fund raising	400,000
Ballot access	2,008,000
Other field expenditures	425,000
In-kind expenditures	111,000
Media	$2,294,000
Candidate travel	2,000,000
Personnel	1,711,000
Administration and compliance	1,007,000
Communications	773,000
Legal	320,000
Printing	306,000
Bank loan repayments	400,000
Individual loan repayments	1,830,000
Total	$16,585,000

When loan repayments of $2.2 million are subtracted from the expenditure total, the campaign's operating expenditures amount to $14.4 million. Fund-raising costs of $3.4 million and ballot-access costs of $2 million make up more than one-third of the campaign's net operating expenditures. Other significant costs have been noted. Media costs amounted to $2.3 million; candidate travel, $2 million; and personnel, $1.7 million.

Audit Report

On October 19, 1981, the FEC released its audit division's report on John Anderson's National Unity Campaign.[225] The auditors found the campaign had understated its receipts, failed to report or properly itemize certain expenditures, failed to disclose some in-kind contributions, had received what appeared to be anonymous cash contributions in excess of the legal limit, and failed to itemize properly some of the individual loans it received. The committee subsequently amended its report to the commission to provide the information required, and no further action was recommended. In addition the auditors concluded that the Anderson campaign was required to repay the U.S. Treasury $639,950. The smallest portion of that total— $183—was due for parking fines the campaign committee had paid and that the auditors determined were nonqualified campaign expenses. A larger amount—$58,665—was due for interest the auditors concluded the committee had earned on investment of federal funds. According to audit staff findings through September 30, 1981, the committee earned $108,553 on such investments and paid $49,888 in federal, state, and local taxes on the earnings, leaving the total noted to be repaid to the U.S. Treasury. The committee maintained that not all of the money it had invested was federal money.

The largest and most controversial amount the auditors concluded the committee should repay the Treasury was $581,102.17, which they determined the campaign had received from public funds in excess of its federal entitlement. The campaign had received $4,242,304 in federal funds determined by the percentage of the popular vote the candidate had received on November 4. Two months later the committee mailed repayment checks to approximately 18,340 of the 18,759 individuals who had lent the campaign money. Each check was written in the amount of the loan plus interest. The mailing included a solicitation signed by the candidate asking the recipients to return all or a portion of their repayment checks to the committee to help it repay the campaign's remaining debt. According to the audit report, through March 6, 1981, the committee received $225,861 in repayment checks endorsed by the lenders and deposited by the committee and $179,991 in personal checks from lenders. In addition $20,194 worth of checks were returned to the committee but were not deposited because they were not negotiable for a variety of reasons, and $14,456 represented loans forgiven by lenders in December 1980. The total amount of loans that were converted to contributions, then, was $440,502. According to the auditors, that amount was to be included in computing the committee's outstanding qualified campaign expenses in order to calculate how much federal money the campaign was entitled to. When that amount was included and other adjustments were made, such as excluding postelection fund-raising costs of $100,000 from the campaign's obligations for qualified campaign expenses, the auditors determined the committee had a surplus of $581,102.17. Since federal funds are to be granted only in the amount necessary to cover the candidate's qualified campaign expenses, the auditors concluded that amount should be repaid to the U.S. Treasury. The committee, however, maintained that since the loans from individuals were outstanding at the close of the expenditure report period, the subsequent conversion of some of those loans to contributions by some lenders did not alter the committee's debt for purposes of determining its outstanding campaign obligations and thus its federal entitlement. The committee also maintained that if the FEC rejected its argument, it retained the right to return the money in dispute to the individual contributors rather than pay the money into the Treasury. The audit staff rejected both committee positions, but as of March 1982, the Anderson campaign had repaid none of the $639,950 the audit staff stipulated as due the Treasury.

In a related matter, early in 1982 the Anderson campaign was fined $5,000 for depositing $21,541 in campaign funds in the personal accounts of four of its agents, fieldworkers in four different states.[226] The FECA prohibits mingling of campaign and personal funds.

Minor Parties

Minor- or third-party candidates running for president in 1980 shared many of the problems faced by independent candidate John Anderson. Unlike Anderson, a number of them were candidates of political parties whose national-party committees were eligible to receive contributions of up to $20,000 from individuals and $15,000 from multicandidate committees and to make coordinated party expenditures of up to $4.6 million on behalf of their presidential tickets. But like Anderson the minor-party candidates were hampered by many of the provisions of the FECA. Since none of the minor parties active in the 1980 general election had candidates who had received 5 percent or more of the vote in 1976, none of them was eligible to receive federal funds in advance of their campaigns. Consequently they were required to finance their campaigns entirely from private funds raised under the law's individual and multicandidate committee contribution limits and to use their funds to pay not only for campaign expenses but also for compliance with the law.

Also like Anderson, the minor-party candidates faced the daunting task of qualifying for the ballot in the individual states. Although most such candidates did not have to contend with early filing dates for ballot petitions as Anderson did, since they had been chosen by their respective parties well in advance of the state deadlines, because they were not as well financed or well known as Anderson, they had greater difficulty getting enough signatures on petitions in a number of states that had comparatively high requirements. California, the most-populous state in the union, required 101,297 valid signatures on a ballot petition before a candidate would be certified to appear on the state's ballot. Some states with much smaller populations required a proportionally higher number of signatures. Georgia required 57,539; Maryland, 55,517; and Oklahoma, 38,871. One observer calculated that a minor party would have to spend $750,000 and collect 1.2 million valid signatures in order to get on the ballot in all 50 states.[227]

Finally, Anderson himself posed an additional problem for at least some of the minor-party candidates who found themselves overshadowed by the better-known independent candidate. Both the Libertarian party and the newly formed Citizens party, for example, had hoped to make sufficiently strong showings to establish themselves as credible alternatives to the major parties, but with Anderson in the race, they received little media attention.

In 1980 minor-party candidates and their national-, state-, and local-party committees spent about $5.8 million on their presidential campaigns. (A breakdown of that total by political party is provided in chapter 4.)

Notes

1. William J. Lanouette, "Campaign Spending Irony," *National Journal*, October 4, 1980, p. 1656.

2. Timothy B. Clark, "The RNC Prospers, the DNC Struggles As They Face the 1980 Elections," *National Journal*, September 27, 1980, p. 1618.

3. Ibid.

4. Ibid.

5. Rhodes Cook, "National Committee Given Major Role in Fall Campaign," *Congressional Quarterly Weekly Report*, July 19, 1980, p. 2011.

6. FEC, *Report of the Audit Division on the Reagan-Bush Committee, the Reagan-Bush Compliance Fund and the Democrats for Reagan* (Washington, D.C., December 11, 1981), p. 2.

7. Ibid.

8. Elizabeth Drew, A Reporter at Large, "Politics and Money—II," *New Yorker*, December 13, 1983, p. 64.

9. See, for example, James M. Perry, "Reagan's Backers Plan to Spend Big for Him, and His Foes Cry Foul," *Wall Street Journal*, June 19, 1980. According to Reagan-Bush campaign manager William Casey, the campaign tried to divert funds from independent groups to state parties. See Jonathan Moore, ed., *The Campaign for President, 1980 in Retrospect* (Cambridge, Mass.: Ballinger Publishing Co., 1981), p. 234. See also, Lee May, "Brock Leery of Outside Funding," *Los Angeles Times*, July 1, 1980.

10. "Independent Expenditures Suddenly Become Hottest Item in Campaign Financing," *Campaign Practices Reports*, July 7, 1980, p. 8.

11. Amounts updated, but see Richard E. Cohen, "Democrats Take a Leaf from GOP Book With Early Campaign Financing Start," *National Journal*, May 23, 1981, p. 920.

12. See "Face Off: A Conversation with the Presidents' Pollsters, Patrick Caddell and Richard Wirthlin," *Public Opinion* (December 1980-January 1981):2-12. See also Richard Wirthlin, Vincent Breglio, and Richard Beal, "Campaign Chronicle," *Public Opinion* (March 1981):43-49.

13. "Face Off," p. 8.

14. See William J. Lanouette, "For the Presidential Candidates, $34 Million Is Not a Dime Too Much," *National Journal*, October 4, 1980, p. 1656.

15. Ibid.

16. Philip H. Dougherty, "Campaign Shop Ran Tight Ship," *New York Times*, November 18, 1980.

17. Ibid.

18. Campaign Notes, "First Reagan Ad of Fall Campaign Appears on TV," *Washington Post*, August 30, 1980.

19. Dougherty, "Campaign Shop Ran Tight Ship."

20. Ibid.

21. Ibid.

22. "Face Off," p. 10.

23. Wirthlin, Breglio, and Beal, "Campaign Chronicle," p. 47.

24. See Bernard Weinraub, "Carter and Reagan Go on Attack in Ads," *New York Times*, October 19, 1980.

25. Dom Bonafede, "Campaigning by TV—It's Expensive, But Does It Make Any Difference?" *National Journal*, October 11, 1980, p. 1704.

26. Ed Magnuson, "Taking Those Spot Shots," *Time*, September 29, 1980.

27. Wirthlin, Breglio, and Beal, "Campaign Chronicle," p. 49.

28. Warren Weaver, Jr., "Three TV Networks Turn Down Reagan," *Los Angeles Times*, September 20, 1980.

29. See Ed Magnuson, "The Mood of the Voter," *Time*, September 15, 1980, p. 11.

30. FEC, *Report of the Audit Division on the Reagan-Bush Committee*, p. 7.

31. *Financing Presidential Campaigns: An Examination of the Ongoing Effects of the Federal Election Campaign Laws upon the Conduct of Presidential Campaigns* (Cambridge: Institute of Politics, John F. Kennedy School of Government, Harvard University, January 1982), p. 6-12.

32. Clark, "RNC Prospers," p. 1620.

33. Ibid.

34. Steven V. Roberts, "GOP Goes Door to Door in a National Vote Drive," *New York Times*, October 5, 1980.

35. Moore, *Campaign for President*, p. 196.

36. Michael E. Baroody, cited by Bernard Weinraub, "GOP Buoyed by Response to Ads, Plans to Extend TV Campaign, *New York Times*, June 15, 1980.

37. See Michael J. Malbin, "The Republican Revival," *Fortune*, August 25, 1980, pp. 87-88.

38. Clark, "RNC Prospers," p. 1620.

39. *Financing Presidential Campaigns*, p. 5-48.

40. Adam Clymer, "From Lowly Grass Roots, Mighty Votes Are Grown," *New York Times*, October 5, 1980.

41. Ibid.

42. Michael J. Malbin, "How Many Go to the Polls Could Settle the Election," *National Journal*, November 1, 1980, p. 1841.

43. Ibid., p. 1842.

44. Ibid.

45. Kenneth Reich, "GOP Says Carter State Campaign Is 'Smoke-screen,'" *Los Angeles Times*, September 12, 1980.

46. See "GOP Success Aided by New Campaign Law Provisions," *Political Finance/Lobby Reporter*, December 17, 1980, p. 2.

47. "Carter Committee Asks FEC to Deny Federal Funds to Reagan Campaign," *Campaign Practices Reports*, July 17, 1980, p. 2.

48. "Court Throws Out Carter Campaign Suit to Block Public Funding for Reagan," *Campaign Practices Reports*, September 29, 1980, p. 5.

49. Ibid.

50. Timothy G. Smith, letter of the Carter-Mondale Presidential Committee, Inc., to Broadcasters, July 18, 1980.

51. "Carter Proponents Hint Legal Problems in TV Time Sold to Independent Committees," *Campaign Practices Reports*, August 4, 1980, p. 4.

52. "FCC Denies Carter Request for Free Time to Reply to Independent Groups' Broadcasts," *Campaign Practices Reports*, October 13, 1980, p. 5.

53. See "Carter Campaign Drops Suit for Free Equal Time," *Campaign Practices Reports*, October 27, 1980, p. 4.

54. See, for example, David M. Ifshin and Roger E. Warin, "Litigating the 1980 Presidential Election," *American University Law Review* 31 (1982):101.

55. Cited by "Fund Act Unconstitutionally Restricts Independent Spending, Court Says," *Campaign Practices Reports*, October 13, 1980, p. 5.

56. "Independent Expenditures: Court Hears Pro-Reagan Spending Cases," *Political Finance/Lobby Reporter*, August 27, 1980, p. 3.

57. See, for example, "Reagan Group Hopes to Raise $20 Million," *Los Angeles Times*, June 6, 1980; Bill Peterson, "Funds Loophole Exploited," *Washington Post*, June 6, 1980.

58. Ibid.

59. William J. Eaton, "Reagan's Campaign Starts—Unofficially," *Los Angeles Times*, July 16, 1980.

60. "Money Politic," *The Political Animal*, September 8, 1980, p. 2.

61. Maxwell Glen, "Free Spenders—The 'Other' Campaign for Reagan Chooses Its Targets," *National Journal*, September 13, 1980, p. 1513.

62. Larry Light, "Independent Reagan Groups Have Shaved Spending Plans," *Congressional Quarterly Weekly Report*, October 18, 1980, p. 3153.

63. Ibid.

64. See, for example, "Independent Expenditures Suddenly Become," p. 8; see also Perry, "Reagan's Backers Plan to Spend Big."

65. Bill Peterson, "GOP Fears Fund Loophole Will Lure 'Unguided Missiles,'" *Washington Post*, June 29, 1980.

66. Glen, "Free Spenders," p. 1513.

67. William J. Eaton, "Reagan Backers Pressed for Funds," *Los Angeles Times*, September 20, 1980.

68. Light, "Independent Reagan Groups," p. 3153.

69. Ibid.

70. See, for example, "Independent Expenditures Suddenly Become," p. 8.

71. Light, "Independent Reagan Groups," p. 3153.

72. "Independent Expenditures Suddenly Become," p. 8; see also Perry, "Reagan Backers Plan to Spend Big."

73. Glen, "Free Spenders," p. 1513.

74. Light, "Independent Reagan Groups," p. 3153.

75. "Independent Expenditures Suddenly Become," p. 8; see also Perry, "Reagan Backers Plan to Spend Big."

76. Light, "Independent Reagan Groups," p. 3153.

77. E.J. Dionne, Jr., "Independent Groups for Reagan Lagging in Fund-Raising Effort," *New York Times*, August 28, 1980.

78. Glen, "Free Spenders," p. 1515.

79. Rone Tempest, "Texan a Big Spender But No 'Soft Touch,'" *Los Angeles Times*, December 4, 1981.

80. Robert D. Shaw, "New Right Gave Candidates Little," *Miami Herald*, March 29, 1981.

81. Ibid.

82. Ibid.

83. Bill Keller, "Who's Who in the Christian Right," *Congressional Quarterly Weekly Report*, September 6, 1980, p. 2628.

84. Ronald Godwin, quoted in ibid.

85. Ibid.

86. Maxwell Glen, "The Electronic Ministers Listen to the Gospel According to the Candidates," *National Journal*, December 12, 1979, p. 2142.

87. "Preachers in Politics," *U.S. News & World Report*, September 24, 1979, p. 40.

88. Glen, "Electronic Ministers," p. 2142.

89. See ibid., pp. 2143-2145.

90. Allen J. Mayer et al., "A Tide of Born-Again Politics," *Newsweek*, September 15, 1980, p. 32.

91. Quoted in Dom Bonafede, "New Right Preaches a New Religion and Ronald Reagan Is Its Prophet," *National Journal*, May 2, 1981, p. 781.

92. Quoted in Gaylord Shaw, "'New Right' Leaders Bask in Their Success," *Los Angeles Times*, November 6, 1980.

93. Seymour Martin Lipset and Earl Raab, "The Election and the Evangelicals," *Commentary* (March 1981):30.

94. Quoted in Moore, *Campaign for President*, p. 193.

95. Ibid.

96. FEC, *Report of the Audit Division on the Reagan-Bush Committee*.

97. "Reagan Campaign Seeks Court Order to Intervene in FEC Audit Process," *Political Finance/Lobby Reporter*, August 19, 1981, p. 213.

98. "Commission Spurns Reagan Audit," *Political Finance/Lobby Reporter*, September 23, 1981, p. 247.

99. Cited by "Reagan/Bush Committee Fails to Bar Campaign Audit Release," *Campaign Practices Reports*, November 23, 1981, p. 2.

100. Lanouette, "Campaign Spending Irony," p. 1656.

101. Memorandum to Members of the Democratic National Committee from Peter G. Kelly, Treasurer, and Charles T. Manatt, NFC Chairman, December 31, 1980.

102. Don Irwin, "Carter Vows to Whip the Republicans," *Los Angeles Times*, July 22, 1980.

103. FEC, *Report of the Audit Division on the Tennessee Carter/Mondale Victory Fund Committee* (Washington, D.C., February 2, 1982), p. 1.

104. Jack W. Germond and Jules Witcover, "Carter is Using State Parties to Top Funds Limit," *Washington Star*, June 17, 1980.

105. Dan Balz, "Mexican Americans Gain in Texas Party," *Washington Post*, June 23, 1980.

106. Drew, "Money and Politics—II," p. 75.

107. Ibid., p. 14.

108. Carter-Mondale Reelection Committee, "Legal Guidelines for State Party Chairs" (mimeographed, August 1980), p. 4.

109. Ibid.

110. Lanouette, "For the Presidential Candidates," p. 1657.

111. Ibid.

112. Steven Dornfeld, "Carter Camp Asks Officials to Campaign at Own Expense," *St. Paul Pioneer Press*, October 29, 1980.

113. Ibid.

114. Magnuson, "Taking Those Spot Shots," p. 18.

115. Robert G. Kaiser, "Campaign Staffs Take Leash Off Mudslinging Ads," *Washington Post*, September 20, 1980.

116. Bonafede, "Campaigning by TV," p. 1704.

117. "Face Off," p. 63.

118. Edward Walsh, "Carter, in Radio Talk, Asserts His Plans Can Boost Economy," *Washington Post*, October 13, 1980.

119. See, for example, "Carter Again Leaves White House to Sign Politically Appealing Bill," *Los Angeles Times*, October 8, 1980.

120. Quoted in Moore, *Campaign for President*, p. 245.

121. Richard Bergholz, "Carter Cutting Back Campaign Travels, Saving Funds for Later," *Los Angeles Times*, September 9, 1980.

122. George J. Church, "Reagan Coast to Coast," *Time*, November 17, 1980, p. 23.

123. Peter C. Stuart, "Top Officials Crisscross US in Final Week of Campaign to Help Carter," *Christian Science Monitor*, October 27, 1980.

124. Edward Walsh, "When Carter Fell, So Did the Fortunes of Caddell, Rafshoon," *Washington Post*, November 25, 1980.

125. Curtis Wilkie, "A $400,000 Tab for Last Carter Polls," *Boston Globe*, November 21, 1980.

126. Dom Bonafede, "A $130 Million Spending Tab Is Proof—Presidential Politics is Big Business," *National Journal*, January 10, 1981, p. 52.

127. Bonafede, "$130 Million Spending Tab," p. 52.

128. Walsh, "When Carter Fell."

129. See, for example, David Rogers and Curtis Wilkie, "O'Neill Assails Party Panel," *Boston Globe*, November 22, 1980.

130. Ibid.

131. Ibid.

132. Clark, "RNC Prospers," p. 1621.

133. Ibid.

134. Quoted in Kathy Sawyer, "Byrd Faults Party Panel on Handling of Election," *Washington Post*, November 16, 1980.

135. Quoted in Rogers and Wilkie, "O'Neill Assails Party Panel."

136. *Financing Presidential Campaigns*, p. 5-48.

137. Ibid., pp. 5-48, 5-49.

138. Ibid., p. 5-48.

139. Malbin, "How Many Go to the Polls," p. 1840.

140. Clark, "RNC Prospers," p. 1621.

141. Malbin, "How Many Go to the Polls," p. 1841.

142. "Va. Democrats Spent $52,000 for President," *Washington Post*, December 12, 1980.

143. FEC, *Report of the Audit Division on the Carter-Mondale Reelection Committee, Inc.* (Washington, D.C., August 18, 1981).

144. Quoted in Philip Shabecoff, "Labor Uneasy over Carter," *New York Times*, April 30, 1980.

145. Quoted in Edward Walsh, "President Picks Up Endorsement of AFL-CIO," *Washington Post*, September 5, 1980.

146. Victor Kamber, cited by David S. Broder, "Carter and Labor," *Washington Post*, October 31, 1980.

147. Ed Townsend, "Union Leaders Working Hard to Keep Labor's Rank and File in Carter Camp," *Christian Science Monitor*, October 7, 1980.

148. Ibid.

149. Harry Bernstein, "Carter Gains as Labor Mounts Late But Massive Drive," *Los Angeles Times*, October 28, 1980.

150. Ibid.

151. Ibid.

152. Malbin, "How Many Go to the Polls," p. 1840.

153. Ibid.

154. Harry Bernstein, "Unions Can't Yet Promise Carter Enthusiasm," *Los Angeles Times*, September 23, 1980.

155. Michael J. Malbin, "Neither a Mountain nor a Molehill," *Regulation* (May-June 1979):43.

156. Carter-Mondale Reelection Committee, "Legal Manual for State CMRC Coordinators" (mimeographed, August 1980), p. 29.

157. Ibid., appendix, p. 5.

158. "Guidelines for Travel by Administration Officials during the General Election Campaign" (mimeographed, September 8, 1980).

159. "Brock Charges Illegal Use of Powers of the Presidency," *New York Times*, September 12, 1980.

160. Eleanor Randolph, "Role of Incumbent Hangs Heavily on the President," *Los Angeles Times*, September 28, 1980.

161. Ibid.

162. Steven Rattner, "Federal Santa Clauses Busy as Election Day Nears," *New York Times*, October 26, 1980.

163. Ibid.

164. Ibid.

165. Quoted in ibid.

166. FEC, *Report of the Audit Division on the Carter-Mondale Reelection Committee, Inc.*

167. FEC, *Addendum to the Final Audit Report of the Carter-Mondale Reelection Committee, Inc.* (Washington, D.C., February 10, 1982).

168. Initially it was reported that the DNC had budgeted $225,000 to keep Anderson off the ballots (see "Democratic Panel to Spend $225,000 in Effort to Keep Anderson Off Ballots," *Los Angeles Times*, June 5, 1980).

After reports that this strategy had been criticized even by some Democratic officeholders (see Eleanor Randolph, "Ghost and Democrats Try to Thwart Anderson Drive," *Los Angeles Times*, June 14, 1980), a decision apparently was made not to use large amounts of DNC funds to keep Anderson's name off the state ballots (see Godfrey Sperling, Jr., "Carter Dons Kid Gloves in Anti-Anderson Effort," *Christian Science Monitor*, June 19, 1980). But after the campaign, Les Francis, DNC executive director, was asked how much the national-party committee had spent to keep Anderson off the ballots. Reference was made to the $2 million the Anderson campaign reportedly spent on ballot access, and Francis said the DNC had spent "not a tenth of that" on the anti-Anderson effort (cited by Moore, *Campaign for President*, p. 202).

169. "Anderson Aides Blast Memo on Loan Risk," *Los Angeles Times*, September 19, 1980.

170. Jack Nelson, "Carter Accepts Dare, Wins Applause as He Campaigns in High Jobless Areas," *Los Angeles Times*, October 2, 1980. See also Hume, "Carter Hits a New Low."

171. For a discussion of how the FECA benefited Anderson's independent campaign, see Joel Goldstein, "Impact of Federal Financing on the Electoral Process: 1980" (paper prepared for presentation to the 1981 Kentucky Political Science Association Annual Meeting, February 27-28, 1981).

172. Roger Smith, "Anderson's Task: Convincing Voters, Contributors He Can Win," *Los Angeles Times*, May 10, 1980.

173. Rhodes Cook, "Money Woes Limit Anderson, Third Party Presidential Bids," *Congressional Quarterly Weekly Report*, August 16, 1980, p. 2375.

174. Bill Peterson, "Anderson Won't Withdraw If Kennedy Is Nominated," *Washington Post*, August 8, 1980.

175. E.J. Dionne, "Election Panel Says Fund-Raising for Anderson Slumped in August," *New York Times*, September 24, 1980.

176. Ibid.

177. Ibid.

178. Richard L. Maddox, "Anderson Campaign Seeks More from Contributors," *New York Times*, October 9, 1980.

179. Cook, "Money Woes Limit Anderson," p. 2376.

180. Ibid.

181. Roger Smith, "Anderson Hopes to Raise $50,000 on Visit to L.A.," *Los Angeles Times*, May 22, 1980.

182. Ibid.

183. "Anderson Wins Low Postal Rates," *Los Angeles Times*, June 7, 1980.

184. Cook, "Money Woes Limit Anderson," p. 2376.

185. Maddox, "Anderson Campaign Seeks More."

186. Dionne, "Election Panel Says Fund-Raising."

187. Dom Bonafede, "Anderson's Staying Power the Key as He Plays the Third Man Theme," *National Journal*, September 13, 1980, p. 1525.

188. William Endicott, "Despite Setbacks, Anderson Still Says He Can Win," *Los Angeles Times*, October 17, 1980.

189. Cook, "Money Woes Limit Anderson," p. 2377.

190. Ibid.

191. FEC, *Report of the Audit Division on the National Unity Campaign for John Anderson* (Washington, D.C., October 19, 1981), p. 15.

192. Cook, "Money Woes Limit Anderson," p. 2377.

193. Ibid.

194. "Millionaire Mott Aiding 'Independent Anderson,'" *Los Angeles Times*, April 9, 1980.

195. Ibid.

196. Cited by Eleanor Randolph, "Anderson Acts to Shed Backer as 'Disruptive' Force," *Los Angeles Times*, June 17, 1980.

197. Jean Merl, "Anderson Warns of Right-Wing Dictators," *Los Angeles Times*, July 25, 1980.

198. "Mott Extends Credit to Anderson Effort," *Detroit Free Press*, October 21, 1980.

199. Steven Dornfeld, "'Fat Cat' Finds Way to Fund Anderson," *St. Paul Pioneer Press/St. Paul Dispatch*, October 25, 1980.

200. "Election Subsidy Suit Could Alter Anderson Outlook," *New York Times*, July 9, 1980.

201. FEC, advisory opinion 1980-96.

202. Bill Peterson, "FEC Rules Anderson Eligible for Funds," *Washington Post*, September 5, 1980.

203. "FEC Rules Anderson Eligible for Post-Election Funding," *Campaign Practices Reports*, September 15, 1980.

204. "Anderson: Carter Memo Warns Banks of Loan Risk," *Christian Science Monitor*, September 24, 1980.

205. "Anderson Aides Blast Memo."

206. Quoted in "Anderson Finances," *Political Finance/Lobby Reporter*, October 8, 1980, p. 3.

207. "Anderson's Insurance," *Newsweek*, September 29, 1980.

208. Bill Peterson, "Anderson Campaign Alleging Sabotage, Gives Up Efforts to Borrow From Banks," *Washington Post*, October 16, 1980.

209. Randolph, "Ghosts and Democrats."

210. Robert Sangeorge, "Supreme Court to Hear Anderson's Challenge of Election Law," *Washington Post*, May 4, 1982.

211. Bonafede, "Anderson's Staying Power," p. 1525.

212. Bill Peterson, "Campaign Sagging, Cash Short, Anderson Shakes Up His Staff," *Washington Post*, August 29, 1980.

213. Endicott, "Despite Setbacks."

214. David Treadwell, "3 Top Aides Quit in Major Shakeup of Anderson Staff," *Los Angeles Times*, August 29, 1980.

215. Ibid.

216. Warren Weaver, Jr., "Anderson TV Drive Is Experiment in Merchandising Political Product," *New York Times*, August 8, 1980.

217. Ibid.

218. Ibid.

219. Warren Weaver, Jr., "Anderson Staff Is Ending Drive in Upbeat Mood," *New York Times*, November 3, 1980.

220. Quoted in Terence Smith, "President Won't Debate Anderson; Independent Hopes Called Fantasy," *New York Times*, May 28, 1980.

221. Quoted in "League Releases Criteria for Presidential Debates," *National Journal*, August 16, 1980, p. 1372.

222. Quoted in Richard E. Meyer, "Presidential Debates Pose a Dilemma for Anderson," *Los Angeles Times*, August 24, 1980.

223. Robert Shogan, "Who Won? 3 Candidates Gained, Lost in Debate," *Los Angeles Times*, September 23, 1980.

224. Quoted in Jack Nelson, "Reagan OKs One-on-One Carter Debate," *Los Angeles Times*, October 18, 1980.

225. FEC, *Report of the Audit Division on the National Unity Campaign for John Anderson.*

226. "FEC Fines Conservative PAC, Two Campaign Committees," *Campaign Practices Reports*, April 12, 1982, p. 8.

227. Peter Samuels, cited by Richard J. Walton, "The Two-Party Monopoly," *Nation*, August 30-September 6, 1980, p. 176.

8 Sources of Funds: Groups and Individuals

The ultimate impact of the FECA has been to diminish the importance of the wealthy individual contributor and to enhance that of the group contributor. These groups, known as PACs, are allowed to give up to $5,000 to federal candidates per election—$10,000 if the maximum is given for primary and general elections combined—as opposed to $1,000 per election for individuals.

PACs in the 1980 Election

In the 1979-1980 election cycle, PACs raised and spent more money and contributed more to federal candidates than in the 1975-1976 and 1977-1978 election cycles combined. By June 30, 1980, receipts for each PAC category, except labor, exceeded total receipts in those categories for the entire 1978 election.[1] Some 2,785 PACs were registered with the FEC during 1979-1980; of those, 2,155 contributed to federal candidates. The total number of PACs shrank to 2,551 by the end of 1980, however, as a number of them concluded their federal activities. In contrast, 1,146 PACs were registered in 1976 and 1,653 in 1978. The 1980 increases in both numbers of PACs and in their financial activity occurred in every category of PAC operation: ideological, issue, corporate, trade, labor, health, and membership.[2]

Although every PAC category experienced such growth during the years between 1976 and 1980, some grew more noticeably than others. At the end of 1980, there were 1,204 corporate, 297 labor, and 574 trade, membership, and health PACs compared with 433 corporate, 224 labor, and 489 trade, membership, and health PACs at the end of 1976.[3] In addition, some 378 nonconnected, 42 cooperative, and 56 corporation-without-stock PACs were registered with the FEC in 1980; prior to 1977, these PACs were classified under the trade, membership, and health heading.[4]

During the 1979-1980 election cycle, all PACs combined raised more than $137.7 million and spent approximately $131.2 million. Some 223 PACs raised $100,000 or more; of these, 22 raised more than $1 million. At the other end of the scale, 417 PACs raised less than $100 and 152 raised between $100 and $199 during the cycle.[5] Seventy-seven percent of all PACs made contributions to candidates, and 49 percent gave $10,000 or more.

Congressional candidates received $55.2 million from PACs (table 8-1); general-election candidates received $51.9 million during the cycle. Senate general-election candidates received 20.7 percent of their contributions from PACs; House general-election candidates received 28.9 percent.[6] According to one source, victorious House candidates in 1980 received 42.8 percent of their contributions from PACs.[7] Less than $2 million was contributed to presidential candidates. PAC money was almost evenly distributed between Democrats and Republicans in 1980: 52.2 percent went to Democrats, 47.6 percent went to Republicans, and 0.2 percent went to other candidates.[8] In 1976 Democrats were preferred to Republicans, 66 to 34 percent. The major shift appears to have occurred in 1978, when the Democratic share fell to 54 percent and the Republican share rose to 46 percent.[9] Despite the well-publicized efforts of some conservative, nonconnected PACs to unseat several liberal senators in 1980, PAC contributions in both 1978 and 1980 continued to favor incumbents, with challengers receiving only slightly more than one-third as much as incumbents and about one-fourth of all PAC contributions.[10] PACs appeared somewhat less interested in spending on open-seat races in 1980; 11 percent of total 1980 PAC contributions went to candidates in such races, compared with 19 percent in 1978.

In addition to contributions to candidates, PACs spent approximately $14 million on independent expenditures and $3.2 million on helping to retire candidates' previous election debts. Also, the sponsors of PACs—corporations, associations, and labor unions—are allowed to use treasury funds to make direct partisan communications to their executive and administrative employees and stockholders and their families, or to members and their families; nearly $4 million was spent on such communication costs in addition to PAC spending.[11]

The most significant surge in 1980 giving came from corporate PACs, which more than doubled their contributions, from $9.8 million in 1978 to $21.6 million in 1980.[12] In 1980, for the first time, corporate PACs gave more money to candidates than any other category of PAC; in fact, more than one-third of all PAC contributions came from corporate PACs.[13] In the meantime, labor PACs were increasing their numbers and expenditures much more slowly and were losing their historically strong position among the categories of PACs. According to a special report by the Democratic Study Group, labor receipts as of June 30, 1980, were up 30 percent over the same point in 1978, and corporate PAC receipts were up 121 percent over the same period.[14]

Of all PAC contributions, the portion given by labor has declined steadily from its high point of 50 percent in 1974 to 24 percent in 1980.[15] Although 1980 marked the first time corporate PACs raised and spent more money than labor PACs, according to Joseph E. Cantor, it is likely that

Table 8-1

Contributions to Candidates for Federal Office by Nonparty Political Committees, 1980 Elections

Committee Type	Number[a]	Candidate Contributions	Presidential	Senate	House	Incumbent	Challenger	Open Seat	Democrat	Republican	Other
Corporation	1,101	$21,560,863	$1,085,711	$7,731,966	$12,743,186	$12,277,452	$ 6,890,458	$2,392,953	$7,734,554	$13,793,260	$ 33,049
Labor	240	14,213,099	306,633	4,192,159	9,714,307	10,136,711	2,450,756	1,625,632	13,294,448	905,151	13,500
Nonconnected	243	5,217,705	106,936	1,927,306	3,183,463	1,659,535	2,633,222	924,948	1,553,740	3,618,714	45,251
Trade, member, health	490	16,988,685	250,156	4,635,748	12,102,781	11,060,222	3,906,245	2,022,218	7,498,981	9,454,628	35,076
Cooperative	31	1,507,164	42,200	396,437	1,068,527	1,219,476	113,290	174,398	966,461	540,703	0
Corporation without stock	50	702,180	41,879	253,193	407,108	477,115	153,740	71,325	364,794	335,786	1,600
Total	2,155	$60,189,696[b]	$1,833,515	$19,136,809	$39,219,372	$36,830,511	$16,147,711	$7,211,474	$31,412,978	$28,648,242	$128,476

Source: FEC, press release, February 21, 1982, p. 3.

[a]The number of committees recorded here reflects those active during the 1979-1980 electoral cycle and therefore does not include all such committees on file with the FEC.

[b]Includes contributions to presidential-primary campaigns and to candidates not up for election in 1980.

business-oriented PACs—the combination of corporate and trade association PACs—first outspent labor in 1976.[16]

Expenditures by nonconnected PACs, which include ideological, issue-oriented, and functional groups, increased at an even greater rate during the 1979-1980 election cycle than did those of corporate PACs; such PACs recorded a $21 million increase and doubled their spending over the two-year period.[17] In addition, the two most financially active PACs in the 1979-1980 cycle were nonconnected: the Congressional Club (founded by Sen. Jesse Helms, R-N.C.), which raised $7.9 million and spent $7.2 million, and NCPAC, which raised $7.6 million and spent $7.5 million.[18] In all, nonconnected PACs raised more money than any other category of PAC during the 1979-1980 cycle, amassing $40,067,137 in adjusted receipts. These PACs, however, ranked fourth in campaign contributions, in large part because of their generally high fund-raising and administrative costs and their use of independent-expenditure campaigns.[19] Trade, membership, and health and corporate PACs raised the next highest totals: $33,931,819 for trade, membership, and health PACs and $33,879,272 for corporate PACs. Labor slipped to fourth place at $25,677,031. Cooperative and corporation-without-stock PACs raised approximately $2.8 and $1.4 million, respectively.

Nonconnected PACs held seven of the top ten places among PACs when ranked according to receipts reported to the FEC for the 1979-1980 election cycle:

1. National Congressional Club (nonconnected), $7,873,974.
2. NCPAC (nonconnected), $7,648,540.
3. Fund for a Conservative Majority (nonconnected), $3,163,528.
4. Realtors Political Action Committee (National Association of Realtors), $2,739,879.
5. Citizens for the Republic (nonconnected), $2,357,684.
6. Americans for an Effective Presidency (nonconnected), $1,920,377.
7. UAW-V-CAP (United Auto Workers), $1,792,406.
8. AMPAC (American Medical Association), $1,728,392.
9. Committee for the Survival of a Free Congress (nonconnected), $1,647,556.
10. National Committee for an Effective Congress (NCEC) (nonconnected), $1,570,788.

The same ten PACs also ranked highest according to expenditures reported to the FEC for the cycle, although there are slight variations in the rank ordering. However, none of the nonconnected PACs among the top ten PACs measured by receipts and expenditures was ranked among the top ten PACs according to contributions to candidates:

1. Realtors Political Action Committee, $1,536,573.
2. UAW-V-CAP, $1,422,731.
3. AMPAC, $1,348,985.
4. Automobile and Truck Dealers Election Action Committee (National Automobile Dealers Association), $1,035,276.
5. Machinists Non-Partisan Political League (IAM), $847,708.
6. AFL-CIO COPE Political Contributions Committee (AFL-CIO), $776,577.
7. Committee for Thorough Agricultural Political Education (Associated Milk Producers), $738,289.
8. Seafarers Political Activity Donation (Seafarers International Union of North America), $685,248.
9. United Steelworkers of America Political Action Fund (United Steelworkers of America), $681,370.
10. National Association of Life Underwriters PAC (National Association of Life Underwriters), $652,112.

Predictably, this mushrooming of PAC activity has left its mark on campaign spending. Congressional spending in 1980 was double that in 1976 and up 23 percent over 1978. Increased PAC contributions of $19.9 million accounted for nearly half of the increase between 1978 and 1980.[20] Some 2,288 federal candidates, excluding presidential candidates, raised $248.8 million from all sources for primary and general elections in 1980. More than $1 billion was spent on elections at all levels in 1980, almost doubling the cost in 1976.[21] The boom in election spending also has reached the state and local levels.[22]

Corporate and Other Business-Related PACs

In 1979 political scientist Edwin M. Epstein predicted that in the 1980 election campaigns, "There could be over a thousand corporate PACs operating with aggregate receipts of $25-30 million and contributions of $15-18 million."[23] At the time many observers considered Epstein's views exaggerated. Reality, however, exceeded his prediction on each count. Some 1,204 corporate PACs were registered with the FEC by the end of 1980; these groups spent $31.4 million, and their contributions to congressional candidates alone amounted to $19.2 million.[24]

The growth of corporate PACs between 1976 and 1980 was remarkable. In 1976 corporate PACs accounted for only one-tenth of all PACs; in 1980 they represented half of the total.[25] By 1978 corporate PACs had drawn approximately even with labor PACs in amounts contributed to congressional candidates; in 1980 they surpassed their labor counterparts in this category by more than 50 percent.[26]

Corporate PACs represent only one category of business-related PACs. Most researchers also include trade association, corporation-without-stock, and cooperative PACs in the larger category. Others take an even broader view, including various health, legal, agricultural, membership, and some ideological PACs.[27] All of the PAC groupings mentioned here give most of their contributions, at least on the federal level, to Republicans, with the ideological PACs (a category roughly equivalent to the FEC's nonconnected groups) the most favorable to Republicans in their giving, followed by corporate and trade, membership and health PACs.[28]

These other business-related PACs also have contributed substantial amounts to federal candidates. In 1978, trade, membership, and health PACs contributed more than all labor PACs, and three of them alone—two trade groups and a doctors' group—contributed more than half as much to congressional candidates as all labor PACs combined.[29] In 1980 the trend continued, with trade, membership, and health PAC congressional contributions surpassing labor contributions by about 20 percent.[30] Although they gave less than 40 percent as much as labor did to candidates in 1980, nonconnected PACs also were important.[31] Seven of the ten PACs spending the most money in 1980 were nonconnected; eight nonconnected PACs topped $1 million each in expenditures.[32] In addition, some nonconnected PACs ran large independent expenditure campaigns, led by the National Congressional Club, which reported $4.6 million worth of pro-Reagan expenditures, and NCPAC, which reported $3.3 million in independent expenditures, including almost $1.1 million for a well-publicized negative campaign against six liberal Democratic senators.[33] The two remaining categories, corporations without stock and cooperatives, are, with a few exceptions, minor players. Cooperatives gave slightly more than $1.5 million; corporations without stock gave slightly more than $700,000.[34]

Potential for Growth

Although figures released by the FEC for the first eighteen months of the 1981-1982 election cycle indicate that the rate of PAC growth, including that of corporate PACs, may be slowing,[35] other evidence suggests that corporate PACs continue to have great potential for growth, both individually and in the aggregate. For example, Epstein found that as of September 1978, only about 22 percent of the 3,755 U.S. corporations with assets of $10 million or more had a PAC.[36] A post-1980 election study by Civic Service found that only 276 of the Fortune 500 companies had PACs that contributed to congressional candidates in 1980.[37] Marvin I. Weinberger and David U. Greevy found that 285 of the Fortune 500 companies and 357 of the first and second 500 (the top 1,000 companies) had formed PACs by the end of 1980.[38]

The greater potential lies in the growth of individual PACs. The FECA places no restrictions on the amount a PAC can raise or on the number of candidates to whom a PAC can contribute. Common Cause vice-president Fred Wertheimer noted that the National Automobile Dealers PAC went from $14,000 in contributions in 1974 to $1 million in 1978, and added, "So can AT&T, GM and the major oil companies."[39] Although total corporate PAC contributions in 1980 outstripped those of labor PACs, the average labor PAC continued to give more than the average corporate PAC.[40] In fact the relatively small amounts contributed by individual corporate PACs, as well as some decentralization in giving, tends to obscure the aggregate contribution total of these PACs. It also may encourage smaller business interests, whose contributions would be dwarfed if corporate PAC giving were higher on a per-candidate basis, to enter the PAC arena.[41]

Although corporate PACs do not raise as much money, on an individual basis, as do labor PACs, contributors to corporate PACs give more on the average and may be more responsive to solicitation requests. The Civic Service survey of Fortune 500 companies found that during the 1979-1980 election cycle, the average PAC contributor gave $161.37. Approximately one-third of those contributors gave between $51 and $100 and another third gave $101 to $250.[42] A 1978 Public Affairs Council survey found an average contribution of $108.34 for corporate PACs with a payroll-deduction option and $126.19 for corporations without a payroll deduction.[43] The Public Affairs Council survey also found a significant negative correlation between the number of persons solicited and the percentage of responses.[44] According to the Fortune 500 survey, during the 1979-1980 cycle, corporate PACs on the average solicited almost two-thirds (62.7 percent) of their eligible executive and managerial personnel and received contributions from 388 donors.[45] Although the FECA permits corporations twice a year to solicit nonexecutive, nonmanagerial employees (including union members), less than one corporate PAC in ten does so.[46] Corporate PACs solicit 13.9 percent of their total employees on the average.

Nor do corporate PACs often seek support from shareholders. The Fortune 500 survey found that about one-sixth of the corporations responding solicited shareholders. Of those corporations some 36 percent solicited 25 percent or less of their shareholders. Another 38.4 percent solicited 76 to 100 percent of shareholders. This split result also showed up in the percentage of solicited shareholders responding. Some 54 percent of the corporate PACs reported that 10 percent or fewer shareholders contributed, but another 20.5 percent said that more than three-quarters of the shareholders solicited gave to the corporate PAC.[47] More than half of the contributing shareholders gave between $11 and $50. Nearly half of the PACs responding said shareholders provided one-tenth or less of total PAC contributions, but another 20.6 percent said that more than three-quarters of their total contributions came from shareholders.[48]

Treasury Funds

Corporations, like labor unions, can finance out of general treasury funds the establishment, administration, and solicitation costs of their sponsored PACs.[49] In addition, if they belong to trade associations, corporations are allowed to help defray similar costs for association PACs.[50] These costs do not have to be reported to the FEC.

Having a wealthy corporate or union sponsor to foot this bill is no small advantage. Estimates of the costs borne by nonconnected PACs that rely heavily on direct-mail solicitation range as high as 90 percent of the total funds raised.[51] In 1976, an Atlantic-Richfield executive reported that the company paid $7 in administrative and fund-raising costs for every $5 raised.[52] Defraying such costs from the corporate treasury frees for political purposes the money raised from employees and stockholders. A Congressional Research Service study of the twenty PACs contributing the most to federal candidates in 1980, however, showed that all connected PACs, including corporate PACs, could have made considerably greater political expenditures if they had received more money from their sponsors.[53]

In seeking to make their voices heard, corporate PACs and their sponsors have an arsenal of options available: They may spend their funds directly for political education, for direct and indirect lobbying, for endorsement of candidates among their employees and shareholders (and their families), and for registration and get-out-the-vote drives. According to the Fortune 500 survey, however, most corporate PACs appear satisfied to keep their executives informed through annual reports and newsletters, although about one-quarter (24.3 percent) communicate through regular PAC meetings or seminars.[54] During election years, nearly half of the PACs responding published information on issues affecting the corporation. In addition, some 36.8 percent carried out registration efforts, 28.5 percent conducted get-out-the-vote drives, and 18 percent sponsored political-education programs. More than one-fourth of the PACs reported that they engaged in none of those activities.[55] Independent expenditures, a favorite tool of the nonconnected PACs, and internal communications, a device long used by labor PACs, are little used by corporate PACs or their sponsors. Only 3 percent reported independent expenditures, and only 3.7 percent reported internal communications.[56]

Corporate Apprehension

One reason for the narrow range of solicitation and for the relatively subdued sponsor activity of corporate PACs may be the apprehension of corporate executives that the public would respond negatively to a highly politicized business sector. This apprehension leads some corporations to forgo forming a PAC entirely. One such corporation is DuPont. A company spokesperson suggested that although the general public tolerates labor-sponsored PACs, it views corporate PACs with some suspicion. Thus DuPont decided not to form a PAC in order to avoid getting into "any kind of activity where the public perceives things with some doubts."[57] Many executives seem to fear that the public, in the wake of Watergate-related revelations of corporate misconduct, has developed the opinion that the business sector is monolithic and that it seeks to control the federal government through economic power for its own ends. William S. Sneath, chief executive officer of Union Carbide, fears that continued corporate PAC growth could "create an anti-business backlash of dangerous dimensions."[58] Some companies, such as AT&T, have encouraged each of their subsidiaries to form a PAC, thereby diverting attention from the corporate center of power.[59] Other companies take special precautions with their PACs, such as choosing as trustee of the PAC monies a bank that does not do other business with the corporation.[60] Another response came from the board of the Public Affairs Council, which adopted a formal code of ethics. According to Joseph J. Fanelli, president of the Business-Industry PAC (BIPAC), the code is written in such a way that, in the case of activities that might give the appearance of violating the law, it goes beyond what is legally required "to protect the company and the individual contributor from any hint of wrongdoing."[61] Finally some corporate executives promote their companies' PACs as a wellspring of democratic virtue.[62]

Although the corporate sector cannot be termed monolithic in regard to party giving, at least not in comparison with labor, several organizations play key roles in coordinating the corporate political agenda. BIPAC and the National Chamber Alliance for Political Action of the Chamber of Commerce of the U.S.A. are the leaders in disseminating research and information of interest to corporate PACs across the nation. The influence of these two groups is particularly strong on smaller corporate PACs that cannot afford to undertake research.[63] In addition, four trade association PACs have sprung up to coordinate the business voice: the National Association of Business PAC, the National Federation of Independent Businesses, the Congressional Small Business Campaign Committee, and the National Association of Association PACs.

Solicitation Methods

In handing corporations the right to solicit executive and administrative employees, the FEC in the SunPAC decision (advisory opinion 1975-23) recommended guidelines for corporate solicitation:

First, no superior should solicit a subordinate. Second, the solicitor should inform the solicited employee of the political purpose of the fund for which the contribution is solicited. Third, the solicitor should inform the employee of the employee's right to refuse to contribute without reprisal of any kind.[64]

In addition, federal law prohibits PACs from accepting contributions obtained through physical force, job discrimination, financial reprisals, or threats of such action.

Restrained by what Epstein calls the "fishbowl test" of public opinion,[65] corporate executives claim to "bend over backwards" to prevent coercion[66] and adhere to the FEC's recommended guidelines for solicitation. Yet there may be a subtle pressure on executives to contribute to the company PAC that is beyond even the best-intentioned corporate president's power to prevent. A Litton Industries employee noted that although it is not mandatory to contribute to the company's PAC, any eligible employee who does not contribute or contributes less than expected is "liable to be called in for a pep talk from the divisional president."[67]

Dart Industries (now Dart & Kraft Inc.) has frequently been cited as a company that pressures its executives to contribute. Justin Dart says his critics have mistaken salesmanship for coercion. Says Dart, "We try to make people give because it's in their self-interest, it's good for them."[68] For a while the DartPAC selling campaign included a face-to-face pitch from the president and lists of employee names and suggested contributions sent to division presidents. Those methods have since been abandoned.

Another factor in the discussion of alleged coercion of contributions from corporate employees is the role of payroll deductions as a means of raising corporate (and union) PAC funds. Corporations were given permission to provide for a voluntary payroll deduction for the company PAC in the SunPAC decision.[69] Corporations also must provide, at cost, a similar withholding procedure for the company's union PAC if the corporate PAC has one.[70] One critic of payroll withholding claims that "the amount levied can be easily tied to the size of the employee's salary" and that the method makes detecting phony bonuses and salary increases difficult.[71] Both corporate and union PACs generally regard payroll deduction as the most efficient method of raising contributions. According to the Fortune 500 survey, about seven in ten corporate PACs use a payroll withholding system.[72]

Trade associations may solicit the stockholders and administrative or executive personnel of member corporations, provided that a corporate member grants prior approval. In addition, no other associations are permitted to solicit those corporate employees during that calendar year.[73] The corporations are free to restrict the solicitation pool and the number of solicitations during the year. According to the Fortune 500 survey, nearly nine corporate PACs in ten bar trade associations from soliciting their employees.[74] Nor are the corporations any less possessive about their shareholders. One corporation executive said he would be surprised "if 3 percent of the companies are willing to let an association PAC work their shareholders."[75] Many corporations belong to several trade associations, with each association reflecting a different facet of the company and representing a different constituency within the company. This can make the choice of which association will be allowed to contribute an awkward one.[76] Therefore, successful associations often are not those with company members but those with individual members, such as realtors, or with professional members, such as doctors.

Spending Decisions

According to Richard E. Cohen, the sponsoring organization usually has broad authority to control the spending decisions of its PACs, and customarily a board of directors is established as the ultimate decision-making body of the PAC.[77] The Fortune 500 survey found that the contributions of two-thirds of corporate PACs are determined by such a board or committee. Some 11.6 percent of the survey respondents said that an employee committee made the decision, 9.8 percent reported that decisions were made jointly by their PAC committees and Washington staffs, and 7.7 percent said decisions were made jointly by their PAC committees and the sponsors' chief operating officers.[78] The day-to-day operations of the PAC generally are handled by a designated manager, who may serve only part time in that capacity and whose principal occupation might be that of governmental-affairs specialist of the connected organization.[79] The Fortune 500 survey also found that four-fifths of the connected firms make their method of candidate selection known to their employees and shareholders.[80] A survey by Smith and Harroff taken in 1979 concluded that a majority of corporate executive and administrative employees felt they needed more information concerning the workings of their companies' PACs.[81] Approximately one-fourth of the corporate PACs in the Fortune 500 survey allowed employees to earmark their contributions; about one-eighth raised more than 10 percent of their funds on an earmarked basis.[82]

Money and Access

Corporate PAC giving to key members of Congress, particularly committee chairmen, through contributions, honorariums, article fees, and other payments, has been closely examined by academicians, populists groups, and the media.[83] In this literature, the business sector often is accused of seeking access to moderate and conservative Democrats with secure seats or choice committee assignments while giving heavy support to Republican challengers against weak Democrats.[84]

The *Washington Post* reported in November 1980 that eighteen of twenty members of the Senate Finance Committee received more than $300,000 in contributions from chemical industry PACs.[85] At the time, the committee was considering legislation that would make chemical manufacturers liable for cleanup costs and damages resulting from hazardous waste dumps and toxic chemical spills. Fifteen of the eighteen received more than $5,000 each.[86] The *New York Times* noted that Rep. James Jones (D-Okla.) of the Ways and Means Committee received $43,218 in corporate PAC contributions in 1978, three times the total of the next-highest Oklahoma candidate.[87] The *Village Voice,* in an article headlined "Who Owns Congress: A Guide to Indentured Politicians," called Jones "Big Oil's slick rising star" and identified various "lobbies" within Congress, based on business-related PAC contributions.[88]

Among the consumer groups, Common Cause reported in 1978 that members of the House Interstate Commerce Committee, which in July of that year voted twenty-two to twenty-one to kill President Carter's hospital cost-containment legislation, received $101,259 in campaign contributions from PACs affiliated with the American Medical Association.[89] The report went on to state that the twenty-two congressmen who voted to kill the bill received $85,150, that thirty-five members of the committee received such contributions, and that opponents of the bill received contributions averaging more than four times higher than proponents.[90] Common Cause also accused AMPAC and other business-related PACs of hedging their bets by giving to both sides in the 1978 Texas senatorial contest between incumbent John Tower and Democratic challenger Bob Krueger.[91]

The newsletter *Political Action Report* rebutted the Common Cause assertion that various business-related PACs hedged their bets in the Texas senatorial race. The newsletter noted that some of the groups, including AMPAC, gave to both Senator Tower, the eventual Republican candidate, and Rep. Krueger, the Democratic candidate, during the primary season.[92] During the general election, PACs generally narrowed their support to one candidate. But in several cases, corporate PACs gave to both candidates during the general election, for various reasons. E-Systems, a corporation with six PACs—one at its Dallas headquarters and one each at five divisions throughout the country—lets each of its PACs select candidates for support independently. In another case, Harold P. Shawlee, director of Union Oil of California's Political Awareness Fund, explained why his group gave $2,000 to Tower and $1,000 to Krueger during the general election: "There are occasions when we get requests [from contributors] to support both candidates, which we do."[93]

Public Citizen, a group headed by consumer activist Ralph Nader, reported in October 1981 that twenty-four of the thirty-five members of the House Ways and Means Committee accepted $280,491 in contributions from corporate PACs during the first six months of 1981 while the committee was considering legislation that would cut corporate taxes by an estimated $500 billion over the next decade. The study concluded that the tax bill the president signed on August 13, 1981, "contained everything business ever dared to ask for, and more."[94]

The business community has reacted to these reports. In taking issue with the Public Citizen report on business PAC giving to the Ways and Means Committee, BIPAC replied that the tax-bill vote could more easily be explained by party affiliation: all committee Republicans voted for the measure; all but one of the committee Democrats voted against it.[95] Furthermore, BIPAC aired a complaint often made by the business community in relation to such studies: that the FEC's method of categorizing PACs puts professional groups—lawyers, engineers, accountants, architects, and others—plus banking and savings and loan institutions into the business category. BIPAC noted that these diverse groups actually have differing interests.[96]

Assessing the PAC Phenomenon

The PAC phenomenon is either a bane or a boon to the electoral system, and democracy in general, depending on who is making the assessment. Until the 1980 elections, the argument over the merits of corporate PACs generally followed party lines. Since then, however, there has been evidence that a number of Democrats are attempting to draw more business PAC funds. For example, House Democrats have established a task force to seek a bigger share of campaign contributions from business PACs. The primary purpose of the task force is to monitor PAC contributions to determine how much goes to Democrats and how much to Republicans.[97] Also, Rep. Andy Ireland (D-Fla.) reflected the receptiveness of many Democrats to business-related PACs, announcing in May 1982 that he would serve as treasurer of the new Congressional Small Business Campaign Committee. Ireland claimed that for too long Congress had paid only lip service to small business and that when it came time to make important decisions on tax and monetary policy, "small business lost out to other organized interests in the society."[98]

Corporate and business-related PAC proponents stress that contributions are made by employees, of their own free will, and that their aggregate political voice, meeting with other such voices in the political arena, form something close to the textbook ideal of pluralistic democracy. According to a spokesman for a major energy company, PACs are the only vehicle whereby management employees "can band together to effectively advocate the political position in which they believe."[99] Opponents believe that PAC power distorts the democratic system by enabling corporations, in effect, to make contributions to federal candidates, a practice outlawed in 1907. According to journalist and author Jack Bass, through corporate PACs, corporate managers can now do indirectly with voluntary contributions what the law prohibits them from doing directly with corporate treasury funds: "create political indebtedness through direct contributions to candidates."[100]

Labor PACs

Labor union PAC influence, which has played a large part in Democratic presidential victories since 1936, diminished in 1980, due to a combination of factors: a huge growth in the numbers and expenditures of corporate, trade-association, and nonconnected PACs; labor's own disillusionment over the policies of President Carter; its split over the candidacy of Sen. Edward M. Kennedy; the blue-collar appeal of Ronald Reagan; and the general conservative mood of the electorate.

Reporting labor's failure in 1980, however, is not the same as writing its political obituary. Labor continues to play a big role in the PAC picture, spending more than $25 million and contributing more than $13 million to congressional candidates in 1980.[101] In fact, six labor organizations each reported spending more than $1 million on direct and in-kind contributions to federal candidates during the 1979-80 election cycle: United Auto Workers, United Transportation Union, International Association of Machinists, AFL-CIO Committee on Political Education, Seafarers International Union, and the International Ladies Garment Workers Union.

In addition, labor organizations, which are allowed to make partisan communications to their members, spent about $3 million of union treasury money on such activities, plus many more millions on registration and get-out-the-vote drives.[102] Furthermore, labor (and business) can legally make partisan communications on behalf of candidates without having to report their costs to the FEC if the communication costs total less than $2,000 per election or if they are published in a newsletter or magazine whose basic purpose is not political. These activities, which aim directly at the nation's unionized work force, were estimated by Edwin Epstein to be worth more than $20 million in the 1978 congressional elections.[103] Yet they were not enough to tip the balance in 1980 when the Republicans, in addition to winning the presidency, captured the Senate for the first time since 1954 and gained thirty-four seats in the House.

Labor versus Business-Related PACs

One reason for labor's relative lack of influence in 1980 is found in the FEC figures for PAC receipts, expenditures, and contributions. During the 1979-1980 election cycle, labor organizations raised $25.7 million and spent $25.1 million. Expenditures were up 35 percent from 1978 and 43 percent from 1976. During the same four-year period, however, the figures on corporate PAC growth were far more dramatic. Corporate PAC expenditures were up 107 percent between 1978 and 1980 and 441 percent between 1976 and 1980. In other words, corporate PAC spending more than doubled in each cycle. Although labor's contributions to congressional candidates in 1980 were up 28 percent over 1978 and 60 percent over 1976, corporate contributions nearly doubled between 1978 and 1980.[104]

The picture becomes even more lopsided when labor PACs are matched against all business-related PACs.[105] Business-related PACs outspent labor PACs by 174 percent in 1980, up sharply from 1976 when business-related PAC expenditures exceeded labor's by only 18 percent. In 1978, business-related PACs spent nearly twice as much as their labor counterparts. In contributions to congressional candidates in 1980, business-related PACs outspent labor PACs by 132 percent. In 1976 the gap was only 22 percent. Part of the reason for business's ability to outspend labor is the greater number of business-related PACs. In 1980, there were an estimated 1,729 business-related PACs versus 297 labor PACs.[106]

Labor's declining share of total PAC activity has prompted AFL-CIO president Lane Kirkland to comment, "In terms of money . . . we can't begin to match what they [candidates] get from other sources."[107] Julius Uehlein, an official of the United Steelworkers, maintained that day after day labor's friends in government were voting against labor's interests. "I know they are being bought," he said. "Votes are not enough any more. We need money."[108]

Furthermore, the number of labor PACs and the amounts raised by such PACs are not expected to keep pace with the predicted growth in the business PAC sector. Joseph E. Cantor observes:

> Unlike in the corporate sector, the potential for increase in labor PACs is distinctly limited. Most of the large, politically active unions have operated PACs for many years. In contrast, most of the remaining unions are either too small or not sufficiently political or, as affiliates of national and international unions, are subject to the same single contribution limit as their parent bodies, thus reducing the incentives to establish PACs.[109]

However, because of their mass membership and internal means of communication, unions and their PACs have unique advantages, which, if utilized fully, could increase labor influence in 1984 and beyond.

Labor in the 1980 Election

In the general election, labor lined up almost unanimously behind President Carter, but at the same time it radiated a general lack of confidence in the president that seemed to reinforce similar widespread feelings in the electorate. Most labor leaders had few kind words for the president's performance in office. Labor supported Carter largely because it feared losing Democratic control of the Senate (twenty-four of the thirty-four seats up for election were held by Democrats), large losses in the House, and the prospect of a Reagan victory.

Labor's fear of Republican candidate Reagan—the clear front-runner for the nomination from the outset of the primary season—rested on several items. According to *Congressional Quarterly*, Reagan's support for the provision of the Taft-Hartley Act that allows states to pass right-to-work laws that prohibit union-shop contracts "fuels much of organized labor's opposition."[110] Also, a comment Reagan made on the campaign trail, which he later denied, that labor unions should be placed under antitrust legislation redoubled labor's efforts to oppose the former California governor.[111] Reagan also supported repeal of the Davis-Bacon Act, which requires government contractors to pay wage rates no lower than the construction rates generally prevailing in the area and opposed the minimum wage "as a matter of principle."[112]

It was against this backdrop that labor supported Democratic nominee Carter. AFL-CIO president Kirkland, who at one point had denounced President Carter's economic policies as "disgraceful," seemed to set the tone for labor in 1980. Kirkland said that although the labor movement was less than happy with President Carter, "we can generate a great deal of enthusiasm against Reagan, believe me."[113] The labor federation's political director Alexander Barkan clarified the point to the federation's affiliates: "Our real enemy is Ronald Reagan, and we will endorse President Carter."[114] When individual unions did endorse the president's reelection, however, they were noticeably lukewarm. For instance, the International Longshoremen's and Warehousemen's Union endorsed the president despite "many disagreements" with his administration. According to the statement of the executive board, Carter offered "a degree of concern for social and economic justice and restraint in foreign affairs" that surpassed the "reactionary" outlook of the Republican party.[115] But the endorsement concluded that the board wanted it understood that it was not giving the Carter administration or its programs and policies a blanket endorsement.

Moreover, late in the primary season, after Carter had virtually clinched his renomination, some labor leaders who had backed Sen. Kennedy earlier in the year threatened to withhold support unless the president adjusted his policies in the direction of what they considered the Democratic norm.

John T. Joyce, president of the Union of Bricklayers and Allied Craftsmen, told the media that either Carter would have to come around, perhaps by doing something to combat unemployment, or the union would have "to become convinced that Reagan would be as atavistic as he sounds."[116] Los Angeles AFL-CIO executive William Robertson warned that labor might not back the president if he ignored the liberal traditions of the Democratic party.[117]

Carter Administration Policies

Certainly much of labor's apprehension over the Carter administration stemmed from the president's policies. But the personal bond between the Democratic president and labor, which had existed in the Roosevelt, Truman, Kennedy, and Johnson administrations, was lacking. John F. Henning, head of the 1.7 million-member California AFL-CIO, said that President Carter made labor feel "like an unwanted stepchild" and spoke repeatedly about establishing a labor party.[118] William Winpisinger said the president treated labor "with contempt."[119] If Winpisinger's evaluation was correct, however, the contempt flowed in both directions; George Meany once called Carter "the worst president since Herbert Hoover."[120]

Clearly the majority of labor leaders in 1980 wished for a candidate other than Carter, preferred Kennedy by a wide margin, and would have supported him overwhelmingly if there were less political risk involved. This risk included antagonizing a sitting president and nominating instead a candidate who might be perceived as too liberal for the electorate at large, thus badly splitting the Democratic party and thereby enabling a relatively easy victory for Reagan and the right wing of the Republican party. According to the late Jerry Wurf, then president of the American Federation of State, County and Municipal Employees, the tragedy was that labor was acting on its fears instead of its hopes: "our fears of Reagan instead of our hopes for a candidate like Kennedy" for whom Wurf claimed labor could enthusiastically work.[121] Yet a number of unions gambled on the Kennedy candidacy. About twenty-five AFL-CIO-affiliated unions backed Kennedy in 1980; some twenty backed Carter.[122] AFL-CIO-affiliated unions supporting Kennedy by November 1979 included the International Association of Machinists, the International Union of Bricklayers and Allied Craftsmen, the International Chemical Workers, the Painters Union, the United Mine Workers, the United Rubber Workers, and the Treasury Workers Union.[123] Six large AFL-CIO unions, however, plus the National Education Association, were early backers of Carter: the International Ladies Garment Workers Union, the Amalgamated Clothing and Textile Workers Union, the Seafarers International Union, the Brotherhood of Railway and Airline

Clerks, the United Food and Commercial Workers, and the Communications Workers of America.[124]

Teamsters Union

Not all of the labor movement stayed with the Democratic party. Notably the 2.3-million member Teamsters Union, the country's largest, announced its support of Reagan in October 1980, following an August 27 meeting between Teamsters leaders and Reagan. According to Teamsters spokesman Duke Zeller, "The overriding consideration was that there is considerable rank-and-file support for Reagan."[125] Furthermore, Carter angered both labor and management in the trucking industry by pushing trucking deregulation. Specifically, the Teamsters became opposed to the Carter administration after both the Labor and Justice departments began investigations into allegations of fraud and mismanagement in the union's Central States Pension Fund. The union was neutral in 1976 and supported Richard Nixon in 1972. No major labor leaders supported the independent candidacy of John Anderson, and his rank-and-file support was minimal.

A large segment of labor rank and file, however, showed signs of warming to the traditional social values, tax-cutting rhetoric, and polished charm of Ronald Reagan. In June 1980 *Congressional Quarterly* quoted one labor leader as saying, "A groundswell of blue-collar support for Reagan is moving out there like crazy."[126] Union leaders reacted by increasing partisan communications opposing Reagan. The same tactic was used in 1968 when significant numbers of unionists were swayed by the right-wing populism of George Wallace's American Independent party candidacy. By July some unions were estimating that 35 percent of their members were supporting Reagan.

Based on results of a poll taken on election day, the AFL-CIO's COPE claimed that AFL-CIO members generally remained faithful to the Democratic party, with 58 percent of the federation's members casting their ballots for Carter, 17 percent better than his showing at large.[127] Said COPE leader Barkan, "Under very difficult circumstances, we held onto the loyalty of our members."[128] The poll also found that about 65 percent of union members voted compared with 52 percent overall.[129] But a poll of 12,782 persons taken by the *New York Times* and CBS showed that only 47 percent of those who identified themselves as union members voted for Carter and 44 percent for Reagan. In 1976, unionists voted for candidate Carter 59 to 39 percent over President Ford.[130] A later poll commissioned by CBS and the *New York Times* showed an erosion of support for the Democratic party in union households between 1977 and 1981.[131]

Rank-and-File Profile

One clue to the rank-and-file appeal of Reagan may be provided by Michael Harrington, chairman of the Democratic Socialist Organizing Committee. According to Harrington, on issues such as drugs, religion, family, and foreign affairs, many union members are social conservatives; the traditional Democratic hold on those persons is due largely to the party's economic stance. In 1980, however, the Democrats were perceived as failing with the economy, so the workers followed their conservative impulses and voted for Reagan.[132] Another clue comes from a confidential poll taken by the AFL-CIO in the summer of 1980. According to the poll, conducted by Opinion Research Survey, 60 percent of the federation's members did not think it made any difference which party occupied the White House or controlled Congress when it came to passing legislation restricting unions. Also, 72 percent of those polled opposed military cuts, 65 percent favored a constitutional amendment to balance the federal budget, 60 percent opposed the Panama Canal treaties, 51 percent opposed strict handgun control, and 44 percent opposed legalized abortion.[133] One postelection commentary described the end result in this way:

> Blue collar and rural white voters are the keys to realignment, as well as the ingredients of Reagan's 1980 victory. . . . The GOP was able to make breakthroughs among "lunch pail" Democrats by emphasizing popular anti-busing and anti-abortion positions and their own economic solutions. In every region of the country, Reagan carried blue collar and suburban and small urban industrial counties that Nixon in 1960 and 1968 and Ford in 1976 were unable to win.[134]

Finally, weak support for Carter at the polls translated into Republican gains at the congressional and state levels. Only 59.5 percent of the candidates supported by COPE won election in 1980, the lowest total since 1968.[135]

Checkoffs

Heavily outspent by corporate PACs in the 1980 election, labor has turned to payroll checkoffs as a primary means of soliciting contributions for its own PACs. States a policy resolution adopted by the AFL-CIO at its 1979 convention, "Only through such political checkoffs, can the AFL-CIO hope to keep its endorsed candidates competitive."[136]

The use of payroll checkoffs for union fund raising is not new; in selected industries, it has long been a means of collecting union dues. The AFL-CIO is now urging its connected unions in the private sector to negotiate contract provisions in which the employer agrees to have a set amount, authorized by individual employees, deducted regularly from their paychecks. In the public sector, unions are being encouraged to negotiate checkoffs or seek legislation to permit them.[137]

The FEC has insisted that such checkoffs must be completely voluntary. In a 1977 ruling, the FEC struck down the so-called reverse checkoff being used by the NEA. Under the NEA plan, teachers were required to submit to an automatic deduction that would be funneled into the fund, unless they filled out a form requesting a refund.[138] The FEC did not, however, challenge the labor organization's right to have a political checkoff option. The FEC also ruled against the checkoff plan of the International Union of Allied Novelty and Production Workers, AFL-CIO, whereby members were asked to earmark $1 of their monthly dues for the union PAC. Contributors to the PAC and noncontributors alike would pay the same amount in total union dues.[139] In ruling the practice an unlawful diversion of union funds, the FEC declared the contributions would not be truly voluntary, because, as dues, they would be payable to the union in any event.[140]

But unions have been largely successful in their drives to implement checkoff plans. The seminal case in this regard involved AT&T and the Communication Workers of America. After an FEC enforcement action, Matter Under Review 947, AT&T agreed to provide all union workers at all its affiliates with a payroll checkoff with contributions accruing to the unions. The FEC interpreted federal law to require companies that use a checkoff to collect funds for their own PACs to provide an identical method, at cost, for labor unions.[141] As of May 1980 labor checkoffs were in use at six of AT&T's subsidiaries,[142] with approximately 10 percent of the workers volunteering an average checkoff of $1 per month. That rate, applied to the entire company, would yield about $1 million every two years for the Communications Workers of America's Committee on Political Education.[143] Costs of such checkoff plans may be billed to the labor organization, or it may pay in advance.[144]

In addition, the FEC has ruled that the PAC of a union local may solicit members of another local of the same union. A local of the United Association of Pipefitters wished to solicit contributions for its PAC from members of other pipefitter locals employed within its jurisdiction. It also wished to solicit individuals who were not members of the union but who were employed on construction jobs, subject to bargaining agreements held by the local. These persons paid the local a weekly fee for a permit card entitling them to work on such jobs and were represented by the local while working on those jobs, although they paid no initiation fees or dues. The FEC noted that it had already allowed the PAC of a corporation that was a wholly owned subsidiary of another corporation to solicit the managerial personnel of other corporations also wholly owned by the parent corporation.[145]

Such checkoff plans have brought impressive results. Ernest Post, political director of the United Steelworkers, said in 1981 that his union's checkoff system, which lets members contribute 2 cents per workday or $5 per year, has been a success. During the first six months of 1981, the Steelworkers' PAC raised $157,901, a 74 percent increase over the corresponding period in 1979, when $90,590 was raised.[146]

Labor PACs look toward checkoffs as the means by which they can correct, or at least slow, the growing gap in money raised between labor- and business-related PACs. But checkoffs are not viewed as a final solution, as a *Memo from COPE* makes clear. The labor-federation newsletter maintained that until all federal-election campaigns are publicly financed, union members can back union-endorsed candidates adequately only "through the checkoff of political contributions by members on a broad scale."[147]

Independent Expenditures

The growth of independent expenditure committees and their influence in the 1980 elections have been the focus of much attention and controversy by the media, politicians, and academicians. During the 1979-1980 election cycle, 105 PACs and 33 individuals reported to the FEC independent expenditures totaling $16.1 million.

But concentrations of spending may be more important than the total expenditures. Some $13.7 million—85 percent—was spent on the presidential race, $11 million of which was spent during the general-election campaigns. Moreover, Ronald Reagan was the beneficiary of $10.6 million in independent spending advocating his election, whereas only $27,773 was spent independently on behalf of Jimmy Carter.

Independent spending also was heavily concentrated in senatorial races. Six candidates, all incumbent Democrats, were the targets of more than $1.2 million in independent spending advocating their defeat. Such negative independent expenditures accounted for 78 percent of the $1.7 million spent independently on the 1980 Senate races.[148]

The concentration of independent spending was even greater when considered from the point of view of the spenders. One analysis indicated that the nation's ten largest PACs accounted for 80 percent of all independent spending.[149] Another analysis reported that 81 percent of all independent expenditures in 1979-1980 were made by "ideologically conservative PACs."[150] And FEC figures indicate that just one such group—NCPAC—spent more than $1 million in attempting to defeat six incumbent senators.

The debate over independent expenditures goes beyond the matter of how much money was spent. The quality of such independent campaigning and the individuals and groups most likely to participate also have become issues. Independent-expenditure campaigns in 1980 became a hallmark of the New Right, a loose coalition of individuals and groups that situates itself to the right of the Republican party's conservative mainstream. According to one source, one of the reasons so many "right-wingers" chose to contribute to independent-expenditure committees in 1980 "was that they felt the Republican Party had become too moderate."[151] It came as no surprise that after the 1980 election, DNC chairman Charles T. Manatt called independent-expenditure groups "an evil influence" on the political system.[152] Such groups also have been criticized by Republicans, who appear to have benefited from independent expenditures in 1980. RNC chairman Richard Richards maintained that independent-expenditure groups "create all kinds of mischief."[153] Richards attempted, unsuccessfully, to reach an agreement with NCPAC whereby it would not independently campaign in areas where it was not wanted.[154]

Unlike the two major parties, which seek to accommodate conflicting claims in an effort to forge a broad coalition among party candidates, the independent-expenditure groups surfacing in 1980 tended to be more narrowly focused. The majority were interested either in swaying public and candidate opinion on a single issue (abortion and gun control are examples) or toward right-wing ideological positions on a handful of issues.

Independent-expenditure groups also are different in method from corporate and business-related PACs, which prefer to make direct contributions to candidates.[155] The motivation of many of the independent groups is summarized in a statement of a Christian Voice Moral Government Fund official following criticism by Charles Grassley (R-Iowa), a candidate favored by New Right groups: "We just wanted him in office, and if deriding us will help him, that's OK."[156]

Independent-Expenditure Rules

Although independent expenditures have always been allowed under election campaign law, they were not attractive before enactment of the FECA with its strict limits on individual giving. Under the 1925 Federal Corrupt Practices Act, which the FECA superseded, a contributor could give large sums of money directly to a candidate by parceling the money among multiple political committees working for the candidate. Nevertheless, large contributors did from time to time take the independent route. For example, in 1968 Stewart Mott spent $100,000 independently on newspaper advertisements to persuade Nelson Rockefeller, then governor of New York, to run for president. In 1972, Mott spent an additional $50,000 independently in criticizing President Richard Nixon for his Vietnam war record.[157]

Such expenditures have received increased attention since the FECA was enacted in 1971. The FECA defines an independent expenditure as "an expenditure by a person expressly advocating the election or defeat of a clearly identified candidate which is made without cooperation or consultation with any candidate, or any authorized committee or agency of such candidate, which is not made in concert with, or at the request of, any candidate, or any authorized committee or agent of such candidate."[158] If an expenditure is not truly independent—if coordination with candidates, their committees, or their agents is involved—it is considered an in-kind contribution and counted toward the law's contribution limits.

In its original form, the FECA made candidates responsible for independent expenditures and forbade the media from accepting political advertising without certification from the candidate; such spending was then counted toward the candidate's overall spending limit. (Under the 1971 legislation, federal candidates were limited to spending 10 cents per eligible voter, or $50,000 whichever was greater, for advertising time in the communications media.) In 1973, however, in the case of *American Civil Liberties Union* v. *Jennings*, the U.S. Supreme Court found the media-certification provision to be an unconstitutional exercise of prior restraint on freedom of speech.[159] Under the 1971 law, negative independent expenditures could elude candidate spending limits if the independent spender certified that the activity was not authorized, either directly or indirectly, by any federal candidate. Independent advertisements were to carry identification of the person or group making the expenditure.[160]

The 1974 FECA amendments imposed restrictions of another kind on independent expenditures by making them chargeable to the $1,000 limit on individual contributions to federal candidates. The House Administration Committee upheld this restriction on independent expenditures, maintaining that without such a limitation wealthy groups and individuals could spend large sums "and thus severely compromise the limitation on spending by the supported candidate himself."[161]

In 1976, in the case of *Buckley* v. *Valeo*, the Supreme Court disallowed this method of limitation. The Court held that the $1,000 limit on independent expenditures violated the First Amendment right of association because it "precluded most associations from effectively amplifying the voice of their adherents."[162] In a dissenting opinion, Justice Byron White said that unlimited independent spending would result in "transparent and widespread evasion of the contribution limits."[163]

The 1976 amendments attempted to limit campaign expenditures according to the court-established guidelines. The new rules retained the individual contribution limits established by the 1974 amendments and required full disclosure of independent expenditures exceeding $100. The latter provision sought to bring individuals and committees making independent expenditures up to the level of disclosure required of campaign committees.[164] Whereas individuals were allowed to give $5,000 to multicandidate committees, however, the 1976 amendments limited to $1,000 the amount an individual was permitted to give to a single-candidate independent-expenditure committee.[165]

Increased Independent Activity

Despite these legislative attempts to restrain independent activity, such expenditures increased markedly following the *Buckley* decision. According to a March 1977 FEC report, $454,128 was spent independently between January 1, 1975, and February 28, 1977. Of this, 73 percent was spent on presidential races, 13 percent on senatorial contests, and 14 percent on House contests. A differing estimate was made by *Congressional Quarterly*, which claimed $792,953 was spent independently in 1976 alone. This figure included independent spending by PACs; the FEC estimate included only individuals and groups not registered as PACs with the FEC. Furthermore, the *Congressional Quarterly* study employed a stricter definition of what constituted an independent expenditure.[166]

The FEC and *Congressional Quarterly* also released differing estimates of independent expenditures for the 1977-1978 election cycle. On November 3, 1978, the FEC reported that $104,901 had been spent independently between January 1, 1977, and October 10, 1978. Updated figures, released in July 1980 by the FEC, indicate that $317,647 was spent on independent expenditures during the full 1977-1978 cycle. Of this total, $242,683, or 76 percent, was spent in favor of candidates. *Congressional Quarterly*, however, reported that only $147,764 was spent independently during the cycle. The publication claimed that the FEC figure was inflated because its compilation included filers who had overly broad conceptions of what constituted an independent expenditure.[167]

The 1979 amendments to the FECA raised the reporting threshhold for individuals and groups (other than PACs) making independent expenditures from $100 to $250; persons and non-PAC groups making independent expenditures were required to report the identity of persons contributing more than $200. The period before a federal election during which expenditures of more than $1,000 were to be reported within twenty-four hours was lengthened from fifteen to twenty days.[168]

The rather unusual pair of Stewart Mott (also a plaintiff in the *Buckley* case) and NCPAC brought suit against the FEC in 1979, maintaining that contribution limitations on independent-expenditure committees violated rights of speech, press, and association guaranteed under the First Amendment. But on June 30, 1980, the limitations were upheld by U.S. District

Court Judge Barrington Parker who declared that "transfers of money to enable another to speak out are not entitled to the same deference as direct mail expenditures."[169]

Common Cause also brought suit against the FEC seeking enforcement of a largely ignored provision of the Internal Revenue Code that placed a limitation on the amount political committees (but not individuals) could spend independently. Although the FEC joined in fighting for the rule, on September 30, 1980, a three-judge panel of the District Court for the District of Columbia unanimously struck down the rule. Wrote circuit court Judge Malcolm Wilkey, "It is absolutely plain that the free speech rights protected under *Buckley* extend beyond individuals."[170] The ruling held, albeit tenuously, when on January 19, 1982, the Supreme Court, which had agreed to hear an appeal, deadlocked four-to-four on the issue, with Justice Sandra O'Connor abstaining.

Against this backdrop of legislative amendments to the FECA and court decisions regarding independent expenditures, a distinct ideological faction known as the New Right increasingly dominated the independent-expenditure area in the years following 1976.

The New Right

The rise of the New Right—a loosely knit coalition of politically conservative individuals, PACs, think tanks, and publications—has been well documented both in sympathetic[171] and in critical[172] accounts. Combining elements of the traditional conservatism of such opinion shapers as William F. Buckley, Jr., James J. Kilpatrick, and M. Stanton Evans; the anti-Communist political activism of 1964 presidential candidate Sen. Barry Goldwater; the free-market economics of Milton Friedman; and, more recently, the moral fervor of fundamentalist Christianity, the New Right has captured media attention and exercised political influence far beyond that enjoyed by any of its conservative antecedents. Alan Crawford, a conservative critic of the New Right, acknowledges that the leaders and organizations that compose the coalition "seek radical social and political change, and, unlike previous radicals of the Right, they have built a political and organizational network through which to further those aims."[173]

The New Right rose in large part because of dissatisfaction with the Republican party as the defender of political conservatism and moral orthodoxy. From the New Right viewpoint, the Republican mainstream is merely the moderate wing of the liberal establishment, reaching a consensus with the Democrats on numerous matters considered inimical to true conservatism: a secular national morality that condones abortion and prevents prayer in the public schools; detente with the Soviet Union; a Keynesian approach to economics; and support for most social-welfare programs, affirmative-action programs, and the Equal Rights Amendment. Therefore, says New Right activist Paul Weyrich, members of the New Right are "radicals who want to change the existing power structure. We are not conservatives in the sense that conservative means accepting the status quo."[174]

Because the New Right's agenda is so broad—to frame an alternative vision of American political and moral values and to implement that vision by gaining the seats of political power—its leaders have attempted to create a comprehensive infrastructure to promote their agenda at several levels. Operating at the broadest level are the large New Right PACs, the Moral Majority and like-minded evangelical groups, and the major New Right publications, all of which seek to publicize the coalition's social conservatism and to drum up support for candidates who favor it. At another level are the single-issue groups—antiabortion, antifeminist, antiunion, antitax, pro-family, pro-defense, pro-gun, and other issues—and their specialized newsletters, which focus attention on particular New Right concerns. At the policymaking level are New Right think tanks and foundations, which contract with conservative and right-wing thinkers to give New Right proposals intellectual underpinnings and to refute liberal arguments. At the governmental level, New Right officeholders may belong to any of several informal groups in which they work out positions and legislative strategies.

Direct Mail: New Right leaders believe the nation's major institutions—the federal government and bureaucracy, the media, the courts, academia, and even big business—are dangerously liberal and that, in their respective ways, they thwart the conservative impulses of most Americans. This repudiation of the bipartisan mainstream is, although to a lesser exent, reflected in anticorporate, as well as antigovernment, attitudes. According to Richard Viguerie, considered the nation's foremost direct-mail specialist for New Right candidates and causes, the movement needed to contact the grass roots through a medium that bypassed the liberal establishment. The answer was direct mail.

Led by Viguerie, a handful of political direct-mail consultants have helped alter fund-raising patterns for many candidates and political groups. Relying on computerized data banks, these consultants mail millions of letters yearly, and receive millions of dollars in return, creating a vast nationwide network of ideological givers. It is this ability of direct-mail to reach new givers who would otherwise be outside the political arena that has made direct mail the dominant advertising medium of the New Right.

More than anything else, the development of the computer has enabled direct mail to emerge as an effective mass medium. Computerization has permitted advertisers to break through the impersonalization of form letters and broadcast advertising. From information stored in computer banks, a direct-mail consultant can send out a million fund-raising letters, addressing each recipient by name, tailoring the body of the letter to each individual's political concerns and affiliations. A second factor in the emergence of political direct mail is the individual contribution limit imposed by the FECA, which effectively eliminated the possibility of relying on the large giver but placed a premium on fund raisers with access to large numbers of smaller contributors.

In direct mail, a successful operation often results when a candidate with a clear-cut ideology to the right or the left on the political spectrum asks for a contribution from persons with similar views. The pitch of the letter almost always is emotional; fear tactics and a sense of urgency often are used. Many direct-mail appeals probably would alienate large numbers of the public since their messages are directed to selected audiences with well-defined views. That these messages do not reach the wrong people is almost as important as making sure they reach the right people.

The evidence of direct-mail specialist Morris Dees suggests that direct-mail fund raising is most effective for candidates identified with sharply defined ideological views. In 1972 Dees and colleague Thomas Collins were remarkably successful in raising funds through mass-mail appeals for George McGovern; four years later when Dees raised funds through the mail for Jimmy Carter, the response was considerably less successful. And in 1980, Sen. Edward M. Kennedy proved too moderate for Dee's direct-mail effort. According to Dees, "Direct mail won't work for a centrist candidate."[175]

The power of direct mail was first realized in 1964 when Republican presidential nominee Barry Goldwater, abandoned by his party's moderate eastern wing, mailed 12 million appeals and received $4.7 million in return.[176] Goldwater received more than 221,000 contributions during the general-election period.[177] An additional $1 million was raised for the campaign by a direct-mail drive conducted on behalf of the Republican Sustaining Fund.[178]

Direct-Mail Costs: Because millions of pieces, costing twenty-five to thirty cents each, must be mailed to develop a nationwide contributor list sufficient to fund a presidential primary or senatorial campaign, the costs of direct mail are high.[179] This list-building process leaves some candidates with little to spend for their campaigns despite raising large amounts through the mail.

Much of the criticism regarding the great expense of mass-mail solicitations has been directed at the Viguerie Co.; some of Viguerie's allies in the

New Right agree that his services at times are prohibitively expensive. For example, the Committee for the Survival of a Free Congress (CSFC) dropped Viguerie as its direct-mail fund raiser. According to Elaine Hartman, who now does the mailings for CSFC, "Paul [Weyrich] . . . said if we couldn't raise funds at a reasonable cost, there would be no point in sitting here and collecting money."[180] Rep. Philip Crane found his campaign for the 1980 Republican presidential nomination consistently in debt to the Viguerie Co. during the early prenomination period when direct-mail bills exceeded receipts.[181] Crane eventually was charged more than $2 million for Viguerie Co. services against total campaign receipts of $3,481,000.[182] Viguerie also raised $310,000 for Roger Jepsen's Republican U.S. Senate nomination campaign in Iowa in 1978, making it the most expensive Senate primary campaign in the state's history. Viguerie's bill was $307,000.[183]

Critics of direct-mail fund raising also point to the small percentages of total funds raised that New Right groups contribute directly to candidates and to their practice of including direct-mail costs as part of their independent-expenditure campaigns.[184] In an analysis of the largest New Right PACs in 1980, one investigative journalist found that less than 6 percent of the $19 million raised by such groups actually went as contributions to candidates.[185] The two largest—the National Congressional Club and NCPAC—collected $12.3 million yet contributed less than $250,000 to candidates. They spent about $9.5 million on operating expenses and direct-mail fund raising.[186]

New Right Response: New Right leaders respond that the funds they raise finance candidate training schools, polls, and consultants, all of which show up on disclosure reports as operating expenses, not contributions. Furthermore, they maintain that the large amounts raised through direct mail have brought the New Right movement a great deal of publicity, and therefore credibility, as a political force. According to Viguerie, those who consider direct mail merely a fund-raising tool fail to recognize its other possibilities. "Raising money is only one of several purposes of direct mail advertising letters," he says. "A letter may ask you to vote for a candidate, volunteer for campaign work, circulate a petition among your neighbors, write letters and post cards to your senators and congressmen, urging them to pass or defeat legislation and also ask you for money to pay for the direct mail advertising campaign."[187] He adds that direct mail is the only form of political advertising that pays for itself. But critics counter that direct mail is virtually useless as political advertising because letters are sent to those persons who already are the most likely to be supporters of the mailer's candidate or cause. Says conservative direct-mail consultant Bruce Eberle, "When you're doing a fund-raising appeal, you're preaching to the converted."[188]

Direct-mail consultants also argue that direct mail offers nonestablishment candidates and groups a chance to build a grass-roots network of contributors and to demonstrate their fund-raising appeal. The most dramatic evidence of the way in which direct mail has helped open up the political process for some candidates may be the number of first-term senators identified with the New Right who had little or no political experience before taking office and who appeared to benefit from direct-mail-financed New Right activities: John Warner (R-Va.), Paula Hawkins (R-Fla.), John East (R-N.C.), Gordon Humphrey (R-N.H.), Orrin Hatch (R-Utah), Jeremiah Denton (R-Ala.), Harrison Schmitt (R-N.M.), and Don Nickles (R-Ok.). Often candidates and consultants benefit from an arrangement whereby the consultants give candidates or groups thousands of dollars in free credit in establishing a direct-mail program in exchange for an agreement to allow the direct mailer to use the names of new-found givers in other direct-mail campaigns. Through this list-sharing process, the Viguerie Co. has built up its substantial mailing list.

The FEC appeared to sanction high direct-mail costs in Advisory Opinion 1979-36, when it approved a contract between Working Names, a direct-mail firm, and Rep. Walter Fauntroy (D-D.C.) whereby the firm would pay start-up costs if the Fauntroy committee set aside 75 percent of the total receipts for monthly payments to Working Names. The contract stipulated that the firm could charge up to 75 percent of the total receipts unless the company decided during the testing period that the program was unfeasible. In that case the mailer could demand all of the receipts.

Sen. Mark Hatfield (R-Ore.) suggested during a 1979 meeting of the Senate Rules and Administration Committee that direct-mail abuses could be diminished if the FECA was amended to require more disclosure by "Viguerie-type operations." At the same hearing, Common Cause vice-president Fred Wertheimer said an investigation should be made of the credit transactions between fund raisers and candidates. "Direct mail is often like a banking activity—where certain customers are given credit, going beyond what anyone else would do."[189]

Congressional Independent Expenditures

Some 101 individuals and groups spent more than $2.3 million independently on House and Senate races during the 1979-1980 election cycle. Nearly $1.7 million was spent for or against 89 Senate candidates; $684,727 was spent for or against 321 House candidates (table 8-2). The figures for both houses of Congress represent huge increases over the 1977-1978 election cycle when $62,800 was spent independently on House races and $65,000 on Senate races.[190]

Independent spending in 1979-1980 congressional races heavily favored Republican candidates. Positive independent expenditures favored Republicans more than two-to-one in dollar terms, whereas negative expenditures against Democrats were more than twenty times greater than against Republicans. Negative independent spending—money spent to advocate a candidate's defeat—accounted for 78 percent of the independent spending in Senate races; in House races, negative spending accounted for only 12 percent of the total.

NCPAC

Negative independent expenditures are thought to have played an important role in the defeat of four liberal Democratic senators in 1980: John C. Culver of Iowa, Frank Church of Idaho, George McGovern of South Dakota, and Birch Bayh of Indiana. These defeats seem to have stunned many Democrats more than their party's loss of the presidency, and a great deal of attention was paid to such right-wing independent expenditure groups as NCPAC, which claims to have spent more than $1 million on its negative campaigns against six Democratic senators, including the four mentioned. Among the five most-active New Right PACs in 1980, NCPAC was the only one to spend independently on congressional races.[191]

The NCPAC method for large-scale participation in the political process is unique in the history of American political campaigns. Under its outspoken leader, John T. "Terry" Dolan, who has voiced antipathy toward both major political parties, NCPAC has sought to force Democratic and Republican candidates alike to adopt more conservative political views.[192] The threat to Democratic officeholders is obvious: NCPAC seeks out and opposes candidates it believes are too liberal. But more subtle is the effect of NCPAC and other New Right groups on Republicans. Michael J. Malbin has suggested that such groups as NCPAC often bring up issues even Republicans would rather not grapple with.[193] In fact, RNC chairman Richard Richards has said that the elimination of "extremist" groups, specifically NCPAC, would be in the best interests of his party and the political system.[194] Members of both parties claim that NCPAC and other influential New Right PACs are determining the national agenda to some extent.

Nevertheless, such groups must choose their targets carefully at the congressional level. According to Joseph E. Cantor, an analyst of American national government for the Congressional Research Service, "The significance of independent expenditures lies not so much in the nationwide statistics, however impressive their growth has been, as in the concentration of them in particular election contests."[195]

NCPAC's goals in 1980 appeared to be best achieved in small states.

Table 8-2
Independent Expenditures on House and Senate Races, 1979-1980 Election Cycle

Candidate Type	Democrats				Republicans				Others				Subtotals				Grand Total	
	For	#	Against	#	For	#	Against	#	For	#	Against	#	For	#	Against	#		#
House	$190,615	91	$ 38,023	32	$410,478	205	$45,132	6	$479	1	$ 0	0	$601,572	297	$ 83,155	38	$ 684,727	321
Senate	127,381	24	1,282,613	15	231,678	58	12,430	5	0	0	$ 0	0	359,059	82	1,295,043	20	1,654,102	89
Total	$317,996	115	$1,320,636	47	$642,156	263	$57,562	11	$479	1	$ 0	0	$960,631	379	$1,378,198	58	$2,338,829	410

Source: FEC, "FEC Study Shows Independent Expenditures Top $16 Million," press release, November 29, 1981, p. 4.

For example, although Birch Bayh, a targeted senator from the rather large state of Indiana (population 5.5 million, twelfth largest in the nation) did lose, targeted senators from other large states, such as Sen. Alan Cranston of California and Sen. Thomas F. Eagleton of Missouri, were reelected. NCPAC-targeted senators in Idaho (population 944,000), Iowa (population 2.9 million), and South Dakota (population 690,000) were defeated.

NCPAC draws its support from a computerized mailing list of known givers to right-wing causes, who often willingly contribute to the defeat of any liberal officeholder, even if they are not among the official's constituents. In 1980, columnist Jack Anderson noted that NCPAC had already spent $135,000 in its anti-McGovern campaign, although FEC officials indicated that NCPAC's list of contributors, filed with the agency, included no itemized receipts from South Dakota. This suggested to Anderson that little of the anti-McGovern money was coming from his constituents.[196]

According to Terry Dolan, the average NCPAC contributor is male, older than average, and often a resident of a sun belt state. His average contribution is $14. NCPAC also has a number of large contributors. The group's 161-member policy council is composed of persons who have given the organization $5,000, the legal annual maximum.[197]

Although it is credited with the most well-publicized use of independent expenditures, NCPAC was not the first to use the tactics in congressional campaigns. In 1972 Environmental Action started its "dirty dozen" campaign to publicize the alleged antienvironmental records of twelve congressmen. The organization gave up the practice after the 1976 campaign because, according to a spokesperson, "it became difficult to guarantee that our people were not strategizing with the campaign people."[198] Negative independent expenditures also are credited with helping to defeat Sen. Dick Clark (D-Iowa) in 1978. Antiabortion forces claim that leafleting of church parking lots the Sunday before the election helped unseat the pro-choice senator.[199]

Negative Campaign Strategy

NCPAC's method has been to attack early. Its 1980 target campaigns were underway by June 1979, some seventeen months before the election. According to Dolan, it is not possible to "create a new image" for a candidate "unless you begin early and repeat the message often enough."[200] Dolan believes that creating a negative image for a candidate is more effective than attempting to criticize his stands on particular issues. A targeted candidate faces negative radio commercials running as often as seventy-two times per day and as many as two hundred television commercials per week. Says Dolan, "By November, there will be people voting against [the targeted candidate] without remembering why."[201] Some NCPAC opponents are convinced that the group's tactics work. "It is almost like subliminal hypnosis," said one McGovern supporter.[202]

Even in a small state, a NCPAC-style negative campaign is expensive. Early in 1980, Dolan estimated that the Church, McGovern, and Culver campaigns would cost about $100,000 each, the Bayh campaign about $150,000, and the Cranston campaign about $350,000.[203] Actually NCPAC spent more than $600,000 combined against Church, McGovern, and Culver, some $142,000 against Bayh, almost $200,000 against Cranston, and just over $100,000 against a sixth targeted senator, Eagleton. Overall NCPAC was able to spend more than anticipated on its senatorial target campaigns because it cut back on negative independent expenditures opposing Sen. Edward M. Kennedy once it became obvious that he was not going to wrest the Democratic presidential nomination from Jimmy Carter.[204] Those observers who play down the effect of New Right groups on the 1980 election note that NCPAC's senatorial target campaigns, large as they were, represented no more than 8 percent of the total spending by the two major candidates in any of the campaigns.[205] Dolan, on the other hand, claims that NCPAC's negative campaigns stripped targeted senators of up to 20 percentage points at the polls.[206]

At the heart of the controversy that surrounds NCPAC are charges that its negative advertisements often exaggerate, distort, and mislead, and sometimes lie. The media have been particularly outspoken on this point. In editorials the *Washington Post* has claimed that "cynical" independent campaigns have enabled candidates to take the high road in their own campaigns "with full knowledge that lots of of help is on the way down below,"[207] and the *Detroit Free Press* has said that such campaigns "resort to mud-slinging, distortion and appeals to bigotry."[208]

Against McGovern, NCPAC ran television commercials attacking the senator as a globe trotter who was "touring Cuba with Fidel Castro while the energy crisis was brewing." In newspaper advertising, NCPAC charged McGovern with selling out both Taiwan and the United States. Against Bayh, NCPAC ran a thirty-second television commercial showing a cleaver slicing through a large balogna as a voice-over announces, "One very big piece of baloney" is Birch Bayh "telling us he's fighting inflation." Against Cranston, NCPAC used a commercial called the "rating game." A Mrs. Verna Smith of Sacramento was asked how she thought the National Taxpayers' Union rated her senator on protecting her dollar. When she enthusiastically replied, "100 percent!" an announcer declared "You lose!" Cranston's rating, he said, was actually a lowly 8 percent.[209]

NCPAC critics object particularly to the module format of the ads.[210] The McGovern globe-trotter advertisement was used with minor changes against Culver; the "baloney" advertisement was also used against

Cranston; and the same Mrs. Smith, now a resident of Indianapolis, played the "rating game" against Bayh.[211] NCPAC critics also like to point out a commercial run against Church that showed a Republican state legislator standing in front of an empty missile silo charging that "Senator Church has always opposed a strong national defense." The empty silo, however, formerly housed an early Titan missile, withdrawn from service when the more-sophisticated Minuteman missiles were deployed. Replied Dolan to charges that the commercial was filmed in front of the wrong silo, "We don't think that's important. What we want to do is talk about his [Church's] record."[212]

Although most of the postelection media analyses of the defeats of Senators McGovern, Church, Bayh, and Culver cited as a major factor the negative independent-expenditure campaigns, NCPAC's in particular, some observers have played down the impact of such campaigns on the election outcomes. According to a postelection report in the *Congressional Quarterly*, Republican officials as well as many of the candidates who defeated targeted liberal Democrats minimized the New Right's influence. Some even claimed that it hurt their campaigns. Among the factors they listed as decisive in their campaigns were fresh but experienced candidates, generous amounts of party support, a popular presidential candidate heading the ticket, and a "throw-out-the-bums" mood on the part of the electorate. In general they attributed whatever influence the New Right had to the great attention given to the coalition's efforts by the press.

Independent Fund Raising

Almost all observers agree that the large independent-expenditure groups are good at raising money, particularly by direct mail. But although the New Right groups appear to be channeling a mass of small contributions into large independent expenditure campaigns reflecting the contributors' political wishes, some evidence points toward such groups' actually spending most of their funds on building up their own mailing lists and plowing their contributions back into additional mailings. According to one account, NCPAC is estimated to have spent well over $3 million on direct-mail fund raising in 1979-1980.[213] In the senatorial target campaigns, a large percentage, possibly half, of the funds NCPAC reported as spent for negative communications actually were spent for fund raising. Among the mailings written off as political were solicitation requests to persons outside the states represented by the targeted senators who could not possibly have a direct effect on the vote.

According to the *FEC Index of Independent Expenditures*, NCPAC spent $773,645 in its target campaigns against McGovern, Bayh, Church, and Culver, or about 83 percent of the total negative expenditures made against the four candidates.[214] After NCPAC, the largest independent spender against the four targeted senators who were defeated was Americans for Life, Inc., which spent $92,468. Five other antiabortion groups spent a combined $5,999 in independent expenditures, making a total of $98,467 in independent expenditures by antiabortion groups against the four senators. In addition, these groups spent $23,854 in favor of the four victorious Republican opponents. NCPAC made only token expenditures for the four Republic challengers, spending $149 supporting Steve Symms (R-Idaho), $112 for James Abdnor (R-S.D.), $345 for Dan Quayle (R-Ind.), and $2,746 for Charles Grassley (R-Iowa).

Some $66,119 was spent independently supporting the four targeted senators, although $58,746 of that amount was spent independently in favor of John Culver by the League of Conservation Voters. One individual, Richard Dennis, made expenditures totaling $3,615 supporting the four targeted senators. His newspaper advertisements also chastized the New Right's negative campaign tactics.[215] Finally, although targets McGovern, Bayh, Culver, and Church were the focus of more than $800,000 in negative independent expenditures, their four challengers attracted nothing in negative independent expenditures.

Other Interest Groups

In addition to the New Right groups, substantial independent expenditures were made during the 1979-1980 election cycle by groups representing a variety of single interests. Some twenty-one antiabortion groups spent $256,500 independently on congressional races, splitting almost evenly between positive ($130,034) and negative ($126,466) expenditures. One pro-choice group, the National Abortion Rights Action League, made $2,934 in independent expenditures, all of it opposing the senatorial candidacy of James Buckley (R-Conn.).

The largest antiabortion group, Americans for Life, Inc., spent $115,585, most of it against the NCPAC-targeted senatorial candidates. The next-largest spenders were the Life Amendment Political Action Committee, which provided some of the most emotionally jolting independent expenditures of 1980,[216] and the Pro-Life Action Council. These groups spent $52,666 and $22,963, respectively.

Another single-interest group spending considerable sums independently to influence congressional races in 1980 was the gun lobby, led by the

NRA Political Victory Fund, which spent $218,393, all but $3,281 supporting candidates. The NRA was second only to AMPAC in independent spending supporting House candidates, making $116,855 in positive expenditures on behalf of fifty-two candidates, and $3,281 in negative expenditures against two candidates, John J. Buckley (R-Mass.) and Abner J. Mikva (D-Ill.). The NRA also made $98,257 in positive independent expenditures on behalf of senatorial candidates. Two other gun groups, the Gun Owners of America Campaign Committee and the Minnesota Gun Owners' Political Victory Fund, spent slightly more than $5,000 combined. One antigun group, Handgun Control, Inc., spent $43,055 in independent expenditures, all of it against House candidates.

Finally, three health-related groups spent $194,953 independently, all of it in favor of House candidates. Most of the expenditures, $172,397, were made by AMPAC, the largest independent spender supporting House candidates. Two state committees, the Texas Medical Association PAC and the Louisiana Medical Association PAC, together made more than $22,000 in independent expenditures.

The health groups appear to fall into a category different from the other groups discussed to this point. Whereas the New Right, abortion, and gun groups all focus on ideological issues, the health groups represent the sort of special interest that is commonly a direct contributor to congressional campaigns. According to one account, AMPAC first turned to independent expenditures in 1978 because it collected more than it could legally contribute to favored candidates.[217] With its even larger 1980 budget, AMPAC undertook a parallel television campaign in favor of preferred candidates.

Corporate Speech

The constitutional rights of corporations have been debated in the courts for nearly as long as the nation has been in existence. Recent breakthroughs in what is called corporate speech mark a move by the Supreme Court to affirm greater First Amendment freedoms for corporations by invoking rights secured under the Fourteenth Amendment.

The Court's opinion in *Buckley* v. *Valeo* (1976) made a new opening toward greater corporate speech when it ruled that the First Amendment could not permit the restriction of one group's right of expression in order to increase the opportunity for expression by another group.[218] The implication was that entities and groups such as corporations and trade associations that possess the financial resources to engage in substantial political speech could not be barred from spreading its message simply because opposition groups lacked the resources to be heard. In fact, during oral arguments Justice Potter Stewart blurred the demarcation between money and speech, asking whether an expenditure for speech is substantially the same as speech itself in an age when money is necessary to reach large audiences by the purchase of air time or space in the print media. The Court did, however, uphold the FECA's individual and group contribution limits, pronouncing them justifiably marginal restrictions of political speech. The Court's reasoning in *Buckley* was promulgated in the 1976 amendments.

First National Bank of Boston v. Bellotti

In 1978, the Court further defined its position on corporate speech in *First National Bank of Boston* v. *Bellotti*. In striking down a Massachusetts state law prohibiting corporations from making political expenditures on ballot questions that did not directly pertain to the corporation's business, Justice Lewis F. Powell, writing for the majority, said that political speech should not be judged from the point of view of the speaker but rather from the point of view of the audience since "the inherent worth of speech in terms of its capacity for informing the public does not depend upon the identity of its source, whether corporation, association, union or individual."[219]

This framing of the First Amendment—contending that the true value of freedom of speech is the freedom to hear such speech, no matter what its source—was never fully enunciated by the Court prior to *Bellotti*. The significance of the decision was recognized almost immediately by academicians and the corporate sector alike. In a special report it published regarding the *Bellotti* decision, the National Chamber Litigation Center of the Chamber of Commerce of the U.S.A. outlined five areas in which the decision was bound to make an impact.

First, the decision had the immediate effect of invalidating laws in eighteen states proscribing corporate expenditures on ballot and referendum issues. Second, it raised questions over the constitutionality of special treatment of corporate lobbyists. Third, it opened to challenge several IRS revenue rulings that took a narrow view of deductible corporate communications. Among others, communications to shareholders on legislative matters and communications going beyond the membership of a trade association were held nondeductible. Fourth, the decisions in *Buckley* and *Bellotti* appeared to favor an interpretation of section 441b of the FECA that would permit corporations to make independent expenditures. Last, some observers believed that the *Bellotti* decision marked a turn toward permitting corporations to participate directly in federal elections.[220]

Within several months of the decision, suit was brought against the FEC by Martin Tractor Co., two other midwestern corporations, and the National Chamber Alliance for Politics. The plaintiffs challenged section 201(a) of the 1976 amendments, which placed limitations on a corporation's right to solicit contributions to its PAC from its employees by dividing them into two classes: executive and administrative personnel (paid on a salaried basis) and other employees (paid on an hourly basis). Corporations could solicit executive and administrative personnel as often as they wished; hourly personnel, however, could be solicited only twice yearly. The latter provision prompted the suit. The FEC's motion to dismiss was granted by the U.S. District Court for the District of Columbia on October 18, 1978, with the court saying that the corporations lacked standing under a provision of the FECA.[221] The Chamber Litigation Center and the corporations pressed the matter, however, and took the case to the U.S. District Court of Appeals for the District of Columbia, which ruled that the complaints lacked ripeness for adjudication.[222] The court said the complaints failed to show that they had been or would be caused specific injury by the FECA amendment; however, the decision did note that the act's definition of solicitation was ambiguous enough to have a possible "chilling" effect on First Amendment rights. It suggested that the litigants use the FEC's advisory opinion process. Instead, the chamber took its case to the Supreme Court; Martin Tractor and the other corporations did not. On November 3, 1980, the Supreme Court declined to review the case, thereby upholding the appeals court decision.[223]

In December 1981, the Court continued to support broader First Amendment rights for corporations, voting eight to one to invalidate a Berkeley, California, city ordinance that placed a $250 limit on contributions to ballot-issue committees. In *Citizens Against Rent Control* v. *City of Berkeley*, Chief Justice Warren E. Burger said a key issue in overturning the statute was that it posed no limitations on individual expenditures and said it was "clearly a restraint on the right of association."[224] His opinion affirmed that there can be no limits on contributions to committees that are created to support or defeat a ballot measure. One political trade magazine called it a decision "which removes the last obstacle to potential corporate domination of state and local ballot issues."[225]

In a related 1981 decision, the Supreme Court ruled in *CBS* v. *Federal Communications Commission* that section 312(a)(7) of the 1934 Communications Act created an enforceable right of access to broadcasting facilities for individual candidates seeking elective office; however, the Court decided that the First Amendment never mandated a general right of media access. The 1934 act empowered the FCC with the authority to revoke any broadcaster's license for willful or repeated failure to allow reasonable access, paid or otherwise, to candidates for federal office. The Court linked the *Bellotti*-given rights of the audience to hear the message with the candidates' right of speech in order to grant First Amendment priority over the broadcasters.[226] The case stemmed from a complaint by the Carter Committee to the FCC after the three major television networks refused then-President Carter half-hour segments of prime time to announce his candidacy for reelection. The commission sided with Carter, prompting the suit.

Federal Election Commission

The FEC inevitably has become a center of controversy in the trend toward greater corporate First Amendment rights. It has been both a leader and a follower in this area. The most-notable intraagency movement has been in nonpartisan communications. The impetus came indirectly from *Bellotti* and directly from the agency's first advisory-opinion reversal in the case of Rexnord, Inc., and, according to some observers, the U.S. Circuit Court of Appeals' 1979 decision in *FEC* v. *CLITRIM* in which the Court criticized the FEC for insensitivity toward First Amendment rights.[227]

Whatever the causes, the vehicle for the commission's change of position on nonpartisan communications was the advisory opinion request in 1979 by Rexnord, Inc., which asked whether it could legally pay for an advertisement in a general-circulation newspaper carrying the message "Please Register to Vote" and including the identification of "Rexnord, Inc." in a lower corner of the advertisement. In advisory opinion 1979-48, the commission replied that although Rexnord's PAC could legally pay for the advertisement, the corporation could not.[228] In its interpretation of the FECA, the commission stated that a corporation may undertake voter-registration activity only if it is restricted to the corporation's shareholders and executive or administrative personnel (and their families), or if the activity is jointly sponsored by a civic or nonprofit organization that does not support or endorse candidates or political parties.

The commission reversed itself May 1, 1980, on a four-to-two vote, with chairman Robert O. Tiernan and commissioner Thomas E. Harris dissenting. Both maintained that the 1979 opinion, in which they both took part, was correct. According to the majority, however, Rexnord could be permitted to pay for the advertisement with corporate funds because:

1. Rexnord's activity involved a communication urging only nonpartisan participation, not personal services such as driving people to the polls, which would require joint sponsorship with a nonpartisan organization.
2. The Rexnord advertisement lacked any suggestion that the reader designate a political-party preference when registering to vote.
3. The advertisement did not appeal for political participation on the part of any identifiable group to ensure the well-being of a particular political party.

4. By placing the advertisement in a general-circulation newspaper, Rexnord did not try to determine the political preference of the audience
reading the advertisement.[229]

The majority concluded that the activities in question could be legally
undertaken because the FECA, among its exceptions in 11 CFR 114.4, permits activities that are "materially indistinguishable" from those otherwise
allowed. Another section of the code permits "simple communication
which urges individuals to vote."[230]

One month later, on June 2, 1980, the commission affirmed broader
Rexnord nonpartisan rights for trade associations in an advisory opinion requested by the National Association of Realtors. In advisory opinion
1980-33, the commission stated that the nonprofit, incorporated trade
association could legally finance voter-registration and get-out-the-vote
programs directed to both association members and the general public.[231]
On June 25, the commission reaffirmed the newly won nonpartisan speech
rights of corporations in advisory opinion 1980-55, ruling that Connecticut's Office of Secretary of State, which administers the state's elections,
could accept corporate assistance in undertaking nonpartisan voter-registration activities, including the reprint and distribution of voter-registration
information and the organization of voter-registration drives. Materials
reprinted by the corporations could include a company logo or other identification noting the company's participation.[232]

The commission also had an opportunity to issue an advisory opinion
covering an issue almost exactly the same as that in *Bellotti*. On September
19, 1980, the commission ruled unanimously that the First National Bank of
Florida could legally make a contribution to "5 for Florida's Future," a
fund whose express purpose was to promote adoption of five amendments
to the state constitution. Because the spending was restricted to the proposed amendments, the commission considered it immaterial that the questions appeared on the same ballot as a primary runoff election.[233]

But the commission was not completely permissive in the area of corporate speech during the election year of 1980. In an unissued opinion requested by the Sun Oil Co. on June 11, the FEC planned to uphold the
FECA regulations governing corporate contributions to federal campaigns.
Sun Oil had asked the commission if it would be possible to invite the three
major candidates for president—Jimmy Carter, Ronald Reagan, and John
Anderson—to "Super Senior Sunday," a company-sponsored event, but
withdrew its request before a negative opinion could be issued. In the
absence of a contrary opinion, the company proceeded with its plans and
held the event September 7, with Republican candidate Reagan in atten-
dance. President Carter was represented by his son, Chip, and independent
candidate Anderson was represented by his wife, Keke.[234]

A second oil company request—made by the Atlantic Richfield Co.—was denied by the FEC when it issued advisory opinion 1980-90 stating that presidential candidates could not be invited to appear on the company's "Energy Update" television show. The Atlantic Richfield matter differed from that of Sun Oil in that the former company argued that the television appearances would be exempt from corporate-contribution restrictions because of the FECA's exemption for media corporations presenting news stories. However, the commission rejected this argument, saying, "This is an inaccurate interpretation of the news story exemption . . . [it] was intended to apply to election-related communications by a broadcaster, newspaper or other form of recognized public media."[235] The "Energy Update" broadcast was produced by the company's public relations department and distributed to 145 television stations throughout the country.

Nonpartisan Speech Rules

By mid-1980, the FEC decided that the Supreme Court's *Bellotti* decision, plus the commission's own advisory opinions broadening the corporate role of nonpartisan speech, called for an examination of 11 CFR 114.3 and 114.4 of the FECA, which governed corporate and union nonpartisan political communications. In particular, the commission sought advice on the following matters: contributions or expenditures by corporations or unions to their respective "restricted classes" (executive and administrative employees and shareholders and their families for corporations and members and their families for unions); candidate and party appearances on corporate and union premises; and nonpartisan voter-information, -registration, and -turnout, drives. The commission's call for comments appeared in the *Federal Register* on August 25, 1980.[236] By December the commission had received, and subsequently released, comments pertaining to changing the status quo in the area of nonpartisan activities, which allowed corporations and unions to undertake such activities only in conjunction with a nonpartisan, nonprofit organization. Of course, corporate and labor PACs were free to engage in such activities.

In its comments to the FEC, for example, Common Cause expressed concern that voter-registration and -turnout activities could be used in a way subtle enough to stay within the letter of the law, claiming that such activities can be "targeted or steered towards or away from particular identifiable voting blocs." Business-oriented groups, such as the National Association of Manufacturers (NAM), generally favored all efforts to reach the electorate, in targeted groups or at large, with nonpartisan information, registration, and turnout drives.[237]

During the first half of 1981, the commission weighed the comments received and drew up new rules for proposal. On August 27, 1981 the FEC approved a notice of proposed rulemaking for publication in the *Federal Register*. The proposed rules would continue to allow corporations and unions to make partisan communications to persons within their restricted classes. Also, corporations and unions would still not be allowed to make partisan communications to the general public. However, corporate and union treasuries could fund nonpartisan communications and activities if the following qualifications were met:

1.   Registration and get-out-the-vote drives: Such communications may not assume or depict any candidate unless all candidates for a particular office are mentioned. No single candidate may be favored. Parties can be mentioned only as candidate identification. The message is restricted only to voting and registering. The wording cannot be directed at any particular group, and issues cannot be linked to any candidate.
2.   Voting records: All members of Congress from a particular state must be included. Such materials must cover a variety of issues, express no editorial opinion, cannot include which candidates are running for reelection, and should be timed to the adjournment of legislative sessions, not elections.
3.   Voter guides: All candidates for office must be included on a variety of issues. Answers must be verbatim. Biographical information may be included.

The proposed rules also would be extended to trade associations.[238]

Business did not act as a monolith in its comments on the proposed rules. For instance, while most business groups, such as the NAM, applauded the greater leeway proposed in nonpartisan matters, others in the business sector were wary. In all, the FEC received thirty-three written comments in advance of the public hearing held October 26, 1981. In addition, six persons gave live testimony. None of the witnesses appearing in person opposed permitting corporations and labor unions from participating in nonpartisan voter-registration and get-out-the-vote drives.

On December 2, 1981, the commission held a special all-day meeting at the request of general counsel Charles N. Steele and assistant general counsel Susan E. Propper to discuss possible revisions of the FEC's rulemaking proposal. Steele and Propper sought guidance and a consensus on changes to be made in the staff's upcoming agenda document. These changes were initiated to reflect both the feelings of the commission and the comments it received from the public. Among the points the commission told the general counsel to revise were the following:

1. Labor organizations' restricted class could be broadened to include union administrative and executive personnel; corporate restricted class could include the incidental solicitation of necessary nonmanagerial employees and news-media personnel present at company functions.
2. Nonpartisan communications could be limited to any portion of a restricted class.
3. Provisions relating to registration and turnout drives could be narrowed by deleting the allowance that issues of public concern could be mentioned in connection with such drives.[239]

The commission also discussed several other matters without bringing any motions or taking any votes, including the possibility of scrapping the requirement in section 114.3(c)(2) that federal candidates could be invited only to a "regularly scheduled meeting" of a corporation or union. Also in this regard, the commission suggested that a time limitation, perhaps thirty days, could be set in connection with a candidate requesting to appear at a corporate or union function or meeting. A mechanism for ensuring the invitation of the other candidates once one is set to appear at a function also was discussed.

Discussion on voting records under sections 114.4(b)(4)(ii) and 114.4(b)(4)(v) suggested that such communications could be permitted without provisions requiring that they include all members of Congress from a particular state and that a variety of issues be presented. In particular, the commission showed sentiment for giving corporations and unions the option of including only representatives from the corporation or union's geographic area, as opposed to entire states.[240]

These points produced differing opinions among the commission members. At the close of the meeting, the commission directed the general counsel to draft alternative proposals along the lines of the suggested changes. These proposed changes were incorporated into agenda document 81-197, presented to the commission on December 9.

The commission held another special meeting on January 26, 1982. Assistant counsel Propper outlined the changes made in AD 81-197 and sought further guidance from the commission. The matter was discussed further at the FEC's regular meeting on January 28. No motions were made or votes taken at the earlier meeting. At the conclusion of the January 28 meeting, it was agreed that the staff would continue working on the proposed revisions and that a new document would be submitted to the commission in March.[241]

The staff's next draft, AD 82-26, reached the FEC on February 17. Propper appeared at the regular commission meeting on March 11 to outline the latest revisions. According to vice-chairman Frank P. Reiche, some of the commissioners were reluctant to submit such legislation to Congress in an election year. At his suggestion, the proposals were set aside until after the 1982 congressional elections.

Concurrently the solicitation rights of trade associations were receiving attention from both Congress and the Supreme Court. BreadPAC, the separate segregated fund of the American Bakers Association, and two other PACs, the Restauranteurs PAC and the Lumber Dealers PAC, brought suit in the U.S. District Court for the Northern District of Illinois on April 5, 1977, against a provision of the 1976 amendments to the FECA that imposed restrictions on the manner in which trade associations could solicit money. Under the FECA, trade associations must gain annual permission to solicit corporate members; corporations, which may belong to several trade associations, may give permission to only one such association each year. The plaintiffs argued that the provisions violated their First Amendment rights of speech and association and their Fifth Amendment right to equal protection. In September 1977 the district court ruled that the plaintiffs lacked standing to bring suit under the FECA provision allowing the court to certify all questions of constitutionality of the FECA to the U.S. court of appeals sitting en banc.[242]

The court of appeals, however, granted the associations and PACs standing on January 12, 1979, but rejected their argumentation.[243] This decision was overruled by the U.S. Supreme Court on March 8, 1982, with the Court unanimously holding that the plaintiffs lacked standing under an FECA provision that limits those authorized to bring suit "for declaratory judgment as may be appropriate to construe the constitutionality of any provision" of the act to "the commission, the national committee of any paticular party, or any individual eligible to vote in any election for the office of President of the United States."[244] This obstacle was circumvented in October 1982 by the Athens Lumber Co., which was granted certification after its president was included as a plaintiff. The suit, which seeks to have all restrictions on contributions and expenditures by corporations and national banks in connection with federal elections struck down on First and Fifth Amendment grounds, was referred to a twelve-judge en banc appeals court panel. The case was scheduled to be heard early in 1983.[245] This, in turn, has brought new life to BreadPAC and its collaborators. According to a BreadPAC spokesman, individuals will be included as plaintiffs when the case is again heard by the U.S. District Court for the Northern District of Illinois in 1983.[246]

Trade associations have seen the momentum move their way in both the FEC and the Ninety-seventh Congress. The commission issued legislative recommendations in 1980 and 1982 calling for a relaxation of the solicitation rule. In particular, the FEC has recommended that the annual permission provision be amended to allow associations to obtain permission to solicit until further notice.[247] This point has been included in two FECA amendment bills introduced into the Ninety-seventh Congress: SB 1851, authored by Sen. Charles Mathias (R-Md.), and HR 6479, authored by Rep. Bill Frenzel (R-Minn.). The Frenzel bill would help association PACs additionally by freezing funds given to defray establishment, solicitation, and administration from the act's definition of a contribution. As of late 1982, hearings had not been held on either proposal.

Conclusion

The trend toward greater corporate speech appears to be embedded in both the recent decisions of the FEC and the courts. New FEC regulations, advisory opinions that allow greater corporate speech,[248] and court decisions sensitive to First Amendment arguments will likely continue to be the main vehicles for this trend. Heavy activity was expected in this area in 1983. Athens Lumber and BreadPAC were expected to revive their cases in the courts. The FEC was expected to continue review of its nonpartisan speech regulations following the 1982 congressional elections. It will meet with pressure to change its rules, not only by business-oriented groups but by such right-leaning groups as the Heritage Foundation, which has published an agenda proposing that any group be allowed to publish candidate voting records without FEC interference.[249] Only in Congress, where the Democratic House majority was increased in 1982 by twenty-six seats, is widespread resistance to the general trend toward increased corporate First Amendment rights expected to occur.

Corporate Disclosure

On April 26, 1978, in the case of *First National Bank of Boston* v. *Bellotti*, the Supreme Court declared unconstitutional a Massachusetts law that had limited a corporation's First Amendment rights to those issues "that materially affect its business, property or assets."[250] By a five-to-four vote the Court greatly strengthened the right of banks and corporations to speak out on political issues by holding that they have the right to spend treasury funds to publicize their views in opposition to ballot questions. Writing for the majority, Associate Justice Lewis F. Powell indicated how corporations might determine whether to speak out on issues: "Ultimately, shareholders may decide, through the procedures of corporate democracy, whether the corporations should engage in debate on public issues."[251] The Court appears to imply that although corporations may well enjoy greater First

Amendment guarantees in the future, they will gain them at the price of increased corporate democracy. Since the exercise of democracy depends on
an informed electorate, corporations may be required to expand their
disclosure policies to include information about the operation of corporate
PACs and the conduct of advocacy advertising.

Currently a corporation need not disclose any information to shareholders about the corporation's PAC or PACs. Although PACs must make
substantial disclosures to the FEC, their corporate or union sponsors are
not required to report the amount of treasury funds flowing to the sponsored PACs for establishment, administration, and fund-raising costs.
These costs are significant. The associate executive director of AMPAC has
estimated that operating a successful PAC can cost between $200,000 and
$1 million.[252] The Institute for Public Representation (IPR), a group con-
nected with the Georgetown Law Center, estimates the amount of corporate
treasury funds spent annually on PAC establishment, administration, and
fund raising at approximately $20 million.[253]

Corporate Accountability Project

On behalf of the Corporate Accountability Project, a public-interest group,
the IPR has sought greater disclosure of corporate PAC activity to
shareholders. First, it has submitted shareholder proxy proposals to four
major American corporations: General Motors, AT&T, Coca-Cola, and
Union Carbide. Second, it has proposed an amendment to the Securities
and Exchange Commission's (SEC) rule 14a-3(b) that would require reporting corporations to state whether they or any of their subsidiaries have
established or are establishing a PAC. Under this amendment, corporations
with PACs would have to furnish the following information: the PAC's
name; the names of the PAC's principal officers and a description of their
positions, the process for selecting them, and their duties; the names and
positions within the corporation of the persons to whom the principal officers of the PAC report; the involvement of the corporation's board of
directors with the PAC; the names and positions within the corporation of
persons whose duty it is to select the recipients of the PAC contributions;
exactly who is solicited by the PAC; whatever action may be taken by the
corporation to ensure that contributions to the PAC are truly voluntary; the
total amount received by the PAC, on an annual basis, from the persons
solicited; the total costs attributable to soliciting contributions and to the
administration and operation of the PAC; the total amount contributed by
the PAC to candidates and committees involved in election campaigns; and

a description of any cooperative activities or agreements with other PACs.[254]

In arguing for its proposal, the IPR echoed the Supreme Court's finding in *Bellotti*, saying "Investors need more detailed information to evaluate the soundness of their investment as well as to make use of their corporate democracy rights."[255] Furthermore, the IPR charged that some corporate PACs do not solicit shareholders, a potentially lucrative source of income, in order to avoid any accountability to or input from the owners of the corporation.[256] It also asserted that the absence of shareholder control enables management to make contributions "to further management's own view of how the nation's political order should be structured."[257]

The IPR's proposal was favorably reported in the SEC's *Staff Report on Corporate Accountability* made to the Senate Banking, Housing and Urban Affairs Committee in September 1980. The staff report recommended that the SEC issue a "concept release" to solicit public comment on several issues, including whether the commission should adopt requirements concerning disclosure of information on corporate political activities and expenditures consistent with the assumptions of corporate democracy made in *Bellotti*.[258] As of late 1982, however, the SEC had not made such a release although the IPR's appeal was still before the commission.

Shareholder Proposals

The IPR also has sought its objective of corporate disclosure by approaching individual corporations through the proxy proposal process. Attention has focused on four large firms with PACs: General Motors, AT&T, Coca-Cola, and Union Carbide. The IPR's first attempt was a shareholder proposal made to General Motors on behalf of the Project on Corporate Accountability (which owned twelve shares of GM stock) in January 1980. The proposal asked the company to include in its annual report the names of persons administering the company PAC (Civic Involvement Plan), the criteria for deciding which candidates to support, the total amount of PAC funds contributed to candidates and political committees in the preceding year, and the total amount of corporate treasury funds spent to defray PAC administration and fund raising.[259] A formal agreement was reached on March 12, 1980, making GM the first major American corporation to disclose PAC information to shareholders. The settlement, according to the IPR's report, marked one of the few times increased corporate disclosure had been achieved through "negotiations with a public interest group, rather than through a court fight or administrative battle."[260]

In exchange for withdrawal of the IPR's shareholder proposal, GM agreed to:

1. Include a discussion in its 1980 Public Interest Report on the background, objectives, and candidate-selection process used by the Civic Involvement Plan.
2. Disclose in the Public Interest Report how the PAC is funded, candidate-selection criteria, method of choosing PAC officers, who is solicited for funds and the total amounts disbursed in 1978 and 1979 by the PAC; and outline the procedures used to ensure confidentiality of all persons solicited.
3. Include the same disclosures in the PAC's annual report, which is distributed to all participants in the program.
4. Make the 1979 GM PAC annual report available to any shareholder upon written request; the report would contain exact amounts given by the PAC to each candidate.
5. Include a reference in the proxy report noting the availability of the Public Interest Report and note that the PAC is established and administered by company funds.
6. Announce the availability of the report at annual stockholder meetings.
7. Respond to any reasonable shareholder inquiry regarding the overall operating policies of the PAC and the general criteria and guidelines under which the PAC makes contributions in the best interests of the employer and the corporation.[261]

PAC information was first disclosed in the company's 1980 Public Interest Report, sent to approximately 60,000 shareholders. By the end of 1980, PAC information had reached all 1.2 million shareholders by the company's quarterly and proxy reports.[262] The Public Interest Report disclosed that the Civic Involvement Plan disbursed $193,500 in 1978 and $95,000 in 1979, that contributors could earmark contributions to a specific candidate or party, and that nonearmarked contributions were disbursed by seven executives on the candidate-selection committee. According to the report, the committee used as criteria for determining which candidates were to receive contributions "the party's or candidate's record on business and on automotive industry issues" and whether and how well a candidate represents a GM plant city.[263]

On November 5, 1980, a political trade publication reported that the IPR, still acting on behalf of the Project on Corporate Accountability, had submitted identical shareholder proxy proposals to AT&T, Coca-Cola, and Union Carbide. Through 1981 and the first half of 1982, the IPR made no major breakthroughs in regard to the last three proxy proposals. The proposals were submitted to stockholder votes at the annual meetings of all three corporations in 1981. Although they received only a small percentage of the vote on all three occasions, the proposals did poll more than 3 percent in each case, meaning it could be reintroduced in 1982. In March 1982 the IPR's disclosure proposal was reintroduced at the AT&T shareholders' meeting, where it received a 7.27 percent affirmative vote, qualifying it for yet another resubmission in 1983.[264]

In all four instances, the corporations gave no sign of invoking SEC rule 14a-8(c)(5), which states that corporations may omit from their proxy materials proposals dealing with matters that are "not significantly related to the issuer's business." If a corporation wishes to exclude a proposal on the grounds of the "not significantly related" rule, the onus is on the corporation to show the cause.

Legislative Proposals

On April 1, 1980, Rep. Benjamin S. Rosenthal (D-N.Y.) and others introduced the Corporate Democracy Act of 1980. The bill, HR 7010, would require disclosure of information concerning corporate social performance, regardless of the materiality of such information to investors. PAC information would be disclosed in corporate annual reports under this proposal. The reports, in turn, would be available to the public on request. Under the disclosure section of the act, each corporation would publish in its annual report the amounts spent on political activities (as defined by the Internal Revenue Service Code), including a description of each activity; contributions to federal candidates, including the exact amount of each contribution; and paid political or advocacy advertising, including payments made to media consulting firms for this purpose.[265] The bill was submitted to several committees in the Ninety-sixth Congress but did not reach the public hearing stage in any of them. As of mid-1982, it had not been reintroduced in the Ninety-seventh Congress.

The FECA, however, has come under legislative scrutiny in the Ninety-seventh Congress. On November 2, 1981, Sen. Charles M. Mathias (R-Md.) submitted a bill, S 1851, that would amend section 304(c) of the FECA to require corporations, national banks, and labor organizations with PACs to disclose the following in reports to the FEC: costs incurred for the establishment, administration, and solicitation of contributions to the company or union PAC; costs incurred for nonpartisan registration and get-out-the-vote campaigns by corporations or unions; and costs attributable to partisan communications (thereby eliminating the current $2,000 reporting threshhold).[266]

Communication Costs

On October 5, 1981, the FEC released its *Index of Communication Costs* covering the 1979-1980 election cycle.[267] The compilation is based on information made available under the 1976 FECA amendments, which require corporations, labor and membership organizations, and trade associations to report costs of partisan communications made to their respective stockholders, executive and administrative personnel, or members, and their families, when the costs exceed $2,000 per election. Partisan communications relating to federal candidates may include such activities as distributing literature promoting a certain candidate or advocating his or her defeat (this material cannot be a reproduction of any candidate's own literature); inviting a candidate to appear at a regularly scheduled meeting or event attended by select personnel or members; paying for phone banks to contact select personnel or members to urge them to vote for a particular candidate; and conducting get-out-the-vote drives aimed at select personnel or members urging them to vote for a particular candidate. Expenditures for such activities, known as communications costs, are made directly from corporate or union treasuries and are made in addition to and separate from the contributions and independent expenditures made by the PACs of corporations, unions, membership groups, and trade associations.

Of the sixty-two organizations that filed such reports with the commission during the 1979-1980 cycle, fifty-seven were labor organizations, four were membership groups, and only one was a corporation.[268] For the 1975-1976 cycle, the corresponding totals were sixty-six labor organizations, one membership group, and four corporations.[269] The sixty-two filers spent $3,971,559 in 1980, $3,193,479 supporting the election of candidates and $778,080 advocating their defeat. Labor organizations spent about three-fourths of the total, or about $3 million. Membership groups spent approximately $1 million. The sole corporation, Mesa Petroleum of Amarillo, Texas, spent less than $4,000. By comparison, some $2.1 million was spent for communication costs during the 1975-1976 cycle. Labor accounted for 93.9 percent of the total.

Some $480,343 in communication costs were reported to the FEC for the 1977-1978 congressional-election cycle. Of this total, 96 percent was spent in connection with primary races. Labor accounted for slightly more than half of the total reported spending.

The most-notable difference over the four-year period is the increase in communication costs by membership groups. This growth is due largely to the increased spending of one group: the Institute for Legislative Action, an arm of the NRA. The NRA group had spent $120,423 in 1975-1976 and was the only membership organization in the 1976 FEC Index. In 1977-1978 the group supplanted the AFL-CIO as the largest communications spender, paying out $213,837. In 1979-1980 it reported spending $803,839, against the largest total. The U.S. Chamber of Commerce is the only other nonlabor group among the top ten spenders, as measured by communications costs, in the 1979-1980 election cycle:

1. National Rifle Association (Institute for Legislative Action), $803,839.
2. American Federation of State, County and Municipal Employees, $532,538.
3. AFL-CIO, $441,064.
4. United Auto Workers, $402,280.
5. United Steelworkers of America, $209,512.
6. National Education Association, $183,636.
7. Chamber of Commerce of the U.S., $158,650.
8. Ohio AFL-CIO, $149,439.
9. Communications Workers of America, $91,475.
10. International Union of Bricklayers and Allied Craftsmen, $85,555.

Democrats were the beneficiaries of most of the internal communications spending. President Carter was the focus of more than $1.6 million in partisan communications; all but $125,469 of it advocated his candidacy. Sen. Edward Kennedy was the object of slightly less than $600,000 in communications costs; all but $155,500 (spent by the NRA) advocated his nomination. Ronald Reagan drew mostly opposition spending: $254,130 was spent opposing his candidacy and $64,784 was spent in his favor.

Carter-Kennedy

Kennedy was the clear favorite of labor organizations to win the Democratic nomination for president, based upon communication costs by those organizations. The Massachusetts senator benefited from $442,242 in communication costs advocating his nomination. In comparison, $163,476 was spent during the primary season on internal communications supporting President Carter. Funds also were spent in opposition to the two candidates: the NRA's Institute for Legislative Action spent $155,500 in communications to its members opposing the Kennedy candidacy,[270] and the American Federation of State, County and Municipal Employees—a pro-Kennedy organization during the primaries—spent $79,860 in communications opposing President Carter's renomination.[271]

In all, eleven labor organizations supported President Carter with partisan internal communications during the primary season. Five of the eleven were education related, accounting for 35.7 percent of the pro-Carter prenomination communication costs. Six spent more than $5,000:

1. Communications Workers of America, $50,646.
2. National Education Association, $45,454.
3. UA Plumbing and Pipe Fitting Industry, $25,067.
4. United Mine Workers PAC, $11,762.
5. International Union of Operating Engineers, $8,235.
6. International Association of Bridge, Structural and Ornamental Iron Workers, $7,769.

Six labor organizations supported the Kennedy candidacy. Three of the six—including the sole teachers' group, the American Federation of Teachers—were connected with the AFL-CIO; they accounted for $289,887, or 65.5 percent, of the money spent on pro-Kennedy internal communications:

1. American Federation of State, County and Municipal Employees (AFL-CIO), $228,132.
2. International Union of Bricklayers and Allied Craftsmen, $83,654.
3. Pennsylvania UAW CAP Council, $44,782.
4. American Federation of Teachers (AFL-CIO), $40,072.
5. Brotherhood of Railway and Airline Clerks, $23,919.
6. Service Employees International Union COPE, $21,683.

Some labor organizations, the United Auto Workers in particular, supported President Carter only half-heartedly during the prenomination period.[272] Furthermore, labor organizations that supported Kennedy for the Democratic nomination provided comparatively weak support for President Carter during the general-election campaign; combined, they spent $94,761 in communications supporting Carter.[273] They also reported an additional $71,980 in communication costs dated after the election as part of their postelection and year-end reports.

Carter-Reagan

After the Democratic convention, labor organizations stepped up their internal communications advocating President Carter's reelection and opposing the Reagan candidacy. Forty organizations reported pro-Carter internal communications costing $1,345,249 in the postconvention period, including five groups that spent more than $50,000 each:

1. AFL-CIO COPE, $382,120.
2. United Steelworkers of America, $195,739.
3. National Education Association, $133,034.

4. United Auto Workers, $119,278.
5. Ohio AFL-CIO, $57, 983.

Only the NRA reported costs for internal communications opposing the Democratic candidate, spending $45,609.

In comparison, nine organizations spent $253,809 opposing Ronald Reagan in their internal communications during this period, including five that spent more than $5,000 each:

1. United Auto Workers, $198,424.
2. AFL-CIO COPE, $19,574.
3. United Mine Workers PAC, $11,497.
4. Ohio AFL-CIO, $9,748.
5. New Jersey State AFL-CIO, $8,790.

Only Mesa Petroleum and the NRA reported pro-Reagan communication costs, spending $260 and $64,524, respectively.

No communication costs supporting the independent candidacy of John Anderson were reported to the FEC, but $60,003 was spent on communications opposing him. The UAW was the largest anti-Anderson spender, accounting for $22,229. The UAW Coal Miners' PAC was the second-largest spender, paying out $9,076. Both unions supported President Carter.

Spending on Congressional Races

In the senatorial contests, Birch Bayh (D-Ind.), John Glenn (D-Ohio), Donald Stewart (D-Ala.), Gaylord Nelson (D-Wis.), and Charles Mathias (R-Md.), in that order, drew the most attention from organizations spending for internal communications. Nelson was the only senatorial candidate to have more than $1,000 spent on such communications opposing his candidacy. He was the target of $12,895 in negative communication costs. In the House, Les Aspin (D-Wis.), Edward Beard (D-R.I.), Frank Thompson (D-N.J.), and Royden Dyson (D-Md.) drew the most in communication costs. Dyson was the object of $8,169 in negative communications, the highest total.[274]

Altogether 397 congressional and 42 senatorial candidates were favored by such spending, and 146 congressional and 20 senatorial candidates were opposed. Roughly two-thirds of the monies—about $2.6 million—were spent on the presidential candidates. Some $940,000 was spent on House candidates, slightly less than one-quarter of the total. Just under 10 percent, about $392,000, was spent on senatorial candidates.[275]

Modes of Communication

The 1976 FEC report stated that direct mailings comprised some 87.1 percent of these communications. Other modes of communication were brochures, leaflets, and flyers, 6.2 percent; phone banks, 2.7 percent; posters and banners, 2 percent; and miscellaneous, 1.9 percent.[276] The 1980 report does not contain a similar breakdown, but given the decrease in reported internal communications costs by corporations and the increase in such costs by membership organizations (notably the NRA), in 1980 the percentage of communications by direct mail probably was even higher than in 1976.

The FEC code concerning partisan communications has drawn criticism. Joseph J. Fanelli, president of BIPAC, testifying on November 24, 1981, before the Senate Committee on Rules and Administration, objected to the sections of the code that divide employees into two classes, managerial and nonmanagerial, saying it creates "an artificial and unnatural caste system."[277] Fanelli suggested that corporations be allowed to make partisan communications to all of their employees.

Following the 1980 election, the FEC pressed forward with its proposed revisions in the area of communications costs. On August 27, 1981, the FEC approved a notice of proposed rulemaking for publication in the *Federal Register*. Although the issues raised in this proposal had not been resolved as of late 1982, steps taken by the commission have indicated that the new rules will offer a greater latitude to labor, corporate, membership, and trade-association groups making communications to their respective restricted classes.

Patterns in Political Giving

Despite the widely reported post-Watergate disillusionment with elective politics among large segments of the electorate, in 1980 the proportion of the population contributing money to political candidates and causes increased significantly. Although a provision of the FECA that prohibits private contributions to publicly funded presidential general-election candidates may have served to decrease the number of political contributors, another provision of the law may have served, at least indirectly, to increase that number. By limiting contributors to a maximum donation of $1,000 per candidate per election, the law prompted candidates and committees to develop alternative fund-raising techniques, such as television appeals and sophisticated direct-mail solicitations, which seek relatively small contributions from large numbers of people. These techniques and the groups that have employed them the most successfully, notably the national Republican party committees and the New Right PACs, probably are responsible in great part for the increase in political giving in the most recent presidential-election year.

Furthermore, survey findings spanning more than four decades indicate that despite the inroads made by the New Right and other PACs, a reservoir of untapped potential for campaign funds continues to exist. From time to time, the Gallup Poll has asked people whether they would contribute $5 to a party campaign if they were asked. Throughout the 1940s and 1950s, approximately one-third of those surveyed said they would be willing to contribute; in the 1960s, this segment increased to more than 40 percent. A June 1981 Gallup Poll indicated that 39 percent of those surveyed expressed a desire to join one or more special-interest groups.[278] Even with the enormous costs of presidential elections, only a small portion of such potential would have to be tapped to eliminate many of the financial problems of candidates and parties.

Surveys taken between 1952 and 1976 indicated that from 8 to 12 percent of the total adult population contributed to politics at some level in presidential-election years, with the figure standing at 9 percent in 1976. A survey by the Center for Political Studies at the University of Michigan indicates that 13.4 percent of the adult population gave to candidates and causes during the 1980 presidential election year.[279] Survey data suggest that the increase registered in 1980 is due to the increased number of persons giving to interest groups. Of those surveyed, 6.8 percent gave to candidates, 3.8 percent gave to parties, and 6.8 percent gave to interest groups. Since those three figures add up to well over 13.4 percent, it is obvious that a significant number of persons contributed in two or all three categories.

Although only 3.8 percent gave to parties, nearly half of those contributors did so at the federal level, with 29.8 percent giving to local parties, 22.1 percent giving to state parties, and 48.1 percent giving to national parties. In addition to those contributing directly to candidates and committees, some 25 to 30 percent of federal income taxpayers show a willingness to earmark $1 of their tax liability for the presidential campaign fund through the checkoff procedure.

Survey results compiled by the Gallup Poll and the Survey Research Center over the last quarter-century also show a surge in the number of political contributors during the 1950s (see table 8-3). The number remained relatively steady in 1960 and 1964, fell off in 1968, and in 1972 climbed back to about the level of eight years earlier. This number increased slightly in 1976 before rising by nearly 5 million in 1980. Applying survey percentages to the adult, noninstitutionalized civilian population suggests the following numbers of contributors in each presidential-election year listed: 3 million in 1952, 8 million in 1956, 10 million in 1960, 12 million in 1964, 8.7 million in 1968, 11.7 million in 1972, 12.2 million in 1976, and 17.1 million in 1980.

Table 8-3

Percentage of National Adult Population Solicited and Making Political Contributions, 1952-1980

Year	Polling Organization	Solicited by			Contributed to		
		Republican	Democrat	Total[a]	Republican	Democrat	Total[a]
1952	SRC				3	1	4
1956	Gallup	8	11	19	3	6	9
1956	SRC				5	5	10
1960	Gallup	9	8	15	4	4	9
1960	Gallup						12
1960	SRC				7	4	11
1964	Gallup				6	4	12
1964	SRC	8	4	15	6	4	11
1968	SRC	9	7	23[a]	4	4	9[c]
1972	SRC				4	5	10[d]
1974	SRC				3	3	8[e]
1976	Gallup				3	3	8[f]
1976	SRC				4	4	9[g]
1980	CPS[h]				7	3	13.4[i]

Source: Survey Research Center, University of Michigan; data direct from center or from Angus Campbell, Philip E. Converse, Warren E. Miller, and Donald E. Stokes, *The American Voter* (New York: John Wiley and Sons, 1960), p. 91; 1980 data from Ruth S. Jones, Center for Political Studies, University of Michigan; Gallup data direct or from Roper Opinion Research Center, Williams College, and from American Institute of Public Opinion (Gallup Poll).

[a]The total percentage may add to a total different from the total of Democrats and Republicans because of individuals solicited by or contributing to both major parties, nonparty groups, or combinations of these.

[b]Includes 4 percent who were solicited by both major parties and 1.4 percent who were solicited by Wallace's American Independent Party (AIP).

[c]Includes 0.7 percent who contributed to Wallace's AIP.

[d]Includes contributors to American Independent Party.

[e]Includes 0.7 percent who contributed to both parties and 0.8 percent who contributed to minor parties.

[f]Includes 1 percent to another party and 1 percent Do Not Know or No Answer.

[g]Republican and Democratic figures are rounded. The total includes 0.6 percent who gave to both parties, 0.4 percent to other, and 0.3 percent Do Not Know.

[h]The Center for Political Studies (CPS), located at the University of Michigan, is the successor to the Survey Research Center (SRC).

[i]Includes persons giving to special-interest groups. As some 6.8 percent of those surveyed fell into this category, it appears that many persons contributed in two or all three categories.

Presidential Election Campaign Fund

The success of public financing in the 1976 and 1980 presidential campaigns depended on taxpayers' willingness to earmark a small portion of their tax liabilities—$1 for individuals, $2 for married persons filing jointly—for the Presidential Election Campaign Fund by using the federal income-tax checkoff. This procedure provided more than enough funds to

Table 8-4
Federal Income Tax Checkoff

Tax Year	Approximate Percentages of Taxpayers Using Checkoff[a]	Approximate Amount[b]
1972[c]	7.0	$ 12,900,000
1973	13.6	17,300,000
1974	24.2	31,900,000
1975	25.8	33,700,000
Total available for 1976 presidential election (approx.)		95,900,000
Total payout to candidates and conventions		70,800,000
Total remaining after 1976 election		$ 25,100,000
1976	27.5	36,600,000
1977	28.6	39,200,000
1978	25.4	35,900,000
1979	27.4	38,800,000
Total available for 1980 presidential election (approx.)		$175,600,000
Total payout to candidates and conventions		100,600,000
Total remaining after 1980 election		$ 75,000,000
1980	28.7	41,000,000
Balance		$116,000,000

Source: Testimony of Thomas E. Harris before the Committee on Rules and Administration, U.S. Senate, *Federal Election Reform Proposals of 1977,* appendix B, p. 430. Figures for 1976-1981 are from the FEC.

[a]Percentage figures are compiled by the IRS on the basis of fiscal years. Therefore they are not directly comparable to the tax-year dollar figures.

[b]Subject to minor discrepancies due to the unresolved status of some repayments and miscellaneous disbursements, as well as to rounding.

[c]In its first year, the tax checkoff form was separate from the 1040 form and was not readily available. In 1974 the tax checkoff form was included on the front page of the 1040 form. It also allowed taxpayers who had not checked off for 1972 to do so retroactively, for a total of $12.9 million.

cover the more than $100 million certified to 1980 presidential prenomination- and general-election candidates and to the major parties for their national nominating conventions. By the end of 1981, taxpayers had shown sufficient support for the tax checkoff to ensure adequate funds for the 1984 payouts to eligible candidates and parties.

The extent of support for the program is indicated in table 8-4, which shows both the approximate percentages of taxpayers using the checkoff and the amount checked off for each year since the program began in 1972. The number of persons using the checkoff increased greatly starting in 1974 when the checkoff began to be included on the front page of the 1040 form.

About $176 million was available for the 1980 payout of nearly $101 million. Including a carryover of more than $75 million following the 1980 payout, the presidential campaign fund may be expected to have approximately $225 million on hand to finance the 1984 presidential elections.[280]

Notes

1. Democratic Study Group, *Special Report: Special Interest Money in the 1980 Congressional Election* (September 30, 1980) p. 1.

2. FEC, "FEC Releases Final PAC Report for 1979-80 Election Cycle," press release, February 21, 1982, p. 3.

3. Joseph E. Cantor, *Political Action Committees: Their Evolution and Growth and Their Implications for the Political System* (Washington, D.C.: Congressional Research Service, May 7, 1982), p. 56.

4. Ibid.

5. "Total PAC Collection Reached $140 Million, FEC Data Shows," *Political Finance/Lobby Reporter*, March 4, 1981, p. 49.

6. FEC, "FEC Releases Final Statistics on 1979-80 Congressional Races," press release, March 7, 1982, p. 3.

7. Edward Roeder, *PACs Americana* (Washington, D.C.: Sunshine Services Corp., 1982), p. D-1.

8. FEC press release, March 7, 1982, p. 3.

9. Cantor, *Political Action Committees*, p. 116.

10. Ibid. Since the New Right PACs relied largely on independent expenditures to unseat the targeted senators, this anti-incumbent spending would not show up in an analysis of PAC giving.

11. FEC, press release, October 5, 1981, p. 1.

12. Larry Light, "The Game of PAC Targeting: Friends, Foes and Guesswork," *Congressional Quarterly Weekly Report*, November 21, 1981, p. 2268. A corresponding figure for 1976 is difficult to determine due to differences in categorization in the compiling of 1976 and 1980 figures. Total corporate PAC expenditures are listed at $5.8 million in 1976. The figure

for PAC giving, then, would be somewhat lower. See Cantor, *Political Action Committees*, p. 83.

13. Cantor, *Political Action Committees*, p. 86.

14. Democratic Study Group, *Special Report*, p. 5.

15. Cantor, *Political Action Committees*, p. 85.

16. Ibid., p. 82.

17. Cantor, *Political Action Committees*, p. 83. Here, too, because of the differences in the categorizations between 1976 and 1980, direct comparisons between the two years are difficult. According to one source, however, contributions by ideological groups to congressional elections in 1976 reached $1.5 million. See Common Cause, "Campaign Reports for 1976 Show Near Doubling of Interest Group Contributions to Candidates for Congress," press release, February 15, 1977.

18. "Total PAC Collection," p. 49.

19. During the 1979-1980 election cycle, Helms's Congressional Club, for example, contributed just $157,879 to federal candidates; NCPAC did only slightly better, contributing $235,515. Between them, the two PACs directed less than 3 percent of their expenditures into contributions to federal candidates. Ed Zuckerman, "PACs: Where Did $76 Million Go?" *Political Finance/Lobby Reporter*, October 28, 1981, p. 277.

20. "PACs Contributed 22% of Total Raised by 1980's Candidates," *Political Finance/Lobby Reporter*, August 19, 1981, p. 212.

21. Cantor, *Political Action Committees*, p. 182.

22. See "Campaign Costs Boom at State Level, Too," *Memo from COPE*, September 21, 1981, p. 2.

23. Edwin M. Epstein, "Business and Labor Under the Federal Election Campaign Act of 1971," in Michael J. Malbin, ed., *Parties, Interest Groups, and Campaign Finance Laws* (Washington, D.C.: American Enterprise Institute for Public Policy Research, 1979), p. 143.

24. Cantor, *Political Action Committees*, p. 212. For more information on the growth of Corporte PACs, see Don R. Kendall, "Corporate PACs: Step-by-Step Formation and Troublefree Operation," *Campaigns and Elections* (Spring 1980): 14; Andrew Mollison, "Business Groups Outspend Labor in the Political Field," *Atlanta Journal-Constitution*, July 3, 1978; and "Corporations Increase Their Role in Politics through Contributions and Grass-Roots Lobbying," *News for Investors* (October 1979):185.

25. Cantor, *Political Action Committees*, p. 136.

26. Ibid., pp. 173-174.

27. For example, Cantor uses the term *business oriented* and defines it as all corporate PACs plus one-half of all trade, membership, and health, nonconnected, cooperative, and corporation-without-stock PACs. Ibid., p. 61.

28. Ibid., pp. 121-122. In 1980, corporate PACs gave 65 percent of their contributions to Republican candidates, with the remaining 35 percent going

to Democrats. Trade, membership, and health PACs gave 57 percent to Republicans and 43 percent to Democrats. Nonconnected groups gave 71 percent of their contributions to Republicans, with the remaining 29 percent going to Democrats. Labor is far more partisan in its giving, allocating 93 percent of its 1979-80 contributions to Democrats and 7 percent to Republicans. See Charles W. Hucker, "Corporate Political Action Committees Are Less Oriented to Republicans Than Expected," *Congressional Quarterly Weekly Report*, April 8, 1978, p. 849; and Larry Light, "Democrats May Lose Edge in Contributions from PACs," *Congressional Quarterly*, November 22, 1980, p. 3405. See also, "Corporate PACs: Some Improvement, But Still Disgraceful," *New Right Report*, July 31, 1979, p. 1.

29. These three groups were the AMPAC, the National Association of Realtor's Political Action Committee, and the Automobile and Truck Dealers' Association Political Action Committee. See "An Embarrassment of Riches," *Memo from COPE*, April 28, 1980, p. 2.

30. Total labor contributions to congressional candidates in 1980 were about $13.2 million; trade, membership, and health PAC contributions were approximately $15.9 million. See Cantor, *Political Action Committees*, p. 87.

31. Ibid. Contributions by nonconnected PACs to congressional candidates in 1980 amounted to about $4.9 million.

32. Ibid., p. 106.

33. The four targeted senators who were defeated were George McGovern (D-S.D.), Birch Bayh (D-Ind.), Frank Church (D-Idaho), and John Culver (D-Iowa). Also originally targeted were Thomas Eagleton (D-Mo.) and Alan Cranston (D-Calif.).

34. FEC press release, February 21, 1982, p. 3.

35. The total number of PACs increased by some 14 percent between December 31, 1980, and December 31, 1981, whereas corporate PACs increased 10.2 percent during that period. "At Year's End, 2,901 PACs," *Political Finance/Lobby Reporter*, January 20, 1982, p. 11. By July 1, 1982, there were 3,149 PACs, up 8.5 percent over December 31, 1981. Over the six-month period, labor PACs registered a higher percentage increase, 10.1 percent, than corporate PACs, 6.6 percent. "3,149 PACs," *Political Finance/Lobby Reporter*, July 28, 1982, p. 192. These figures are still below the six-month growth rates of 11 to 14 percent registered between 1978 and 1980. See "PACs Hit 2,678 as Growth Rate Slows," *Political Finance/Lobby Reporter*, July 29, 1981, p. 192.

36. Edwin M. Epstein, "The Irony of Electoral Reform: The Business PAC Phenomenon," *Regulation* (May-June 1979):39.

37. "Business PAC Activity in the 1980 Election: A Study of PACs Sponsored by Fortune 500 Companies," *BIPAC Politikit* (November 1981):35. The PAC growth reflected in this study parallels a study by the

Conference Board showing that corporate executives have become increasingly active in political affairs. See "40% of Leading Executives Called Political Activists," *Los Angeles Times*, March 27, 1980.

38. Marvin I. Weinberger and David U. Greevy, *The PAC Directory* (Cambridge, Mass.: Ballinger, 1982), p. III-113.

39. Quoted in Alan Berlow and Laura Weiss, "Oil, Gas Political Groups Mushroom," *Los Angeles Times*, November 15, 1979. The auto and truck dealers raised $1,274,000 in 1979-1980 and $916,000 during the first eighteen months of the 1981-1982 election cycle.

40. The average corporate PAC contributed $8,730 during the 1979-1980 election cycle, and labor PACs contributed an average of $23,600. Fraser Associates, *The PAC Handbook* (Washington, D.C.: Fraser Associates, 1981), p. 26. A Survey by Civic Service Inc. of 275 PACs formed by Fortune 500 companies revealed those PACs averaged $31,818 in contributions during the 1979-1980 election cycle. "Summary of Corporate PAC Survey," *BIPAC Politikit* (December 1981):33.

41. "Small Business PACs Have Muscle Too!" *Political Action Report*, October 30, 1980, p. 8. The *Wall Street Journal* has gone so far as to suggest that small business, organized through various organizations, wields far more political power than large corporations. See "Big Is Powerless," *Wall Street Journal*, September 8, 1981.

42. Survey by Civic Service Inc. for BIPAC, November 1981. Of the 275 PACs that participated in the survey, some listed as few as three to five donors and others numbered donors in the thousands. See also "Survey Shows 1/3 Respond to Corporate PAC Solicitations," *Political Finance/Lobby Reporter*, November 18, 1981, p. 296.

43. This survey found that PACs soliciting fewer than 200 persons had an average contribution of $141.77, while PACs soliciting more than 1,400 persons received average contributions of $83.97. Public Affairs Council, *PAC News*, July 27, 1979. By comparison, union members contribute very nominal amounts. For example, a successful payroll checkoff plan instituted by the Communications Workers of America netted an average contribution of $1 per month. Only 10 percent of the union's members used the checkoff at all. See "AT&T Checkoff Could Net Millions for Union Political Funds," *Political Finance/Lobby Reporter*, April 15, 1981, p. 89. The United Steelworkers PAC contribution program asks for only 2 cents per workday or $5 per year. See "Union PAC Activity High: Spending More, Earlier," *Campaign Practices Reports*, September 28, 1981, p. 2. AFL-CIO members in 1982 began to pay a mandatory 2 cents per month levy for COPE activities. See John Herling, "Kirkland's Debut," *New Republic*, December 16, 1981, p. 17.

44. Public Affairs Council, *PAC News*. This seems to explain the apparent discrepancies in various reports of the participation level of cor-

porate PACs. While some sources peg participation at the 20 to 30 percent level, the *New York Times* stated that "statistics gathered at some large companies show that 70 or 80 percent of high-level executives contribute . . . an extraordinarily high rate of return for any solicitation." "Politics: Business Antes Up," *New York Times*, January 13, 1980. The BIPAC survey of Fortune 500 companies shows a 32.9 percent response rate among solicited employees of those companies. "Summary of Corporate PAC Survey," *BIPAC Politikit* (December 1981):32.

45. Civic Service Inc. survey for BIPAC, p. 32.

46. Ibid., p. 10.

47. Ibid., p. 12.

48. Ibid.

49. 11 CFR 114.1 (b). Although this appears to be a large loophole for corporations in particular, the opportunity may be minimized by the IRS, which in a technical advisory opinion disallowed a federal income-tax deduction by a corporation for PAC sponsorship costs. Although the advisory affects only the unnamed corporation receiving it, some PAC authorities believe a general revenue ruling may be in the offing. See "Ruling Could Affect PACs' Tax Status," *U.S. Chamber News* (March 1982); Ed Zuckerman, "IRS Tells Auditors to Disallow Deductions for PAC Support," *Political Finance/Lobby Reporter*, January 27, 1982, p. 15; and "IRS Questions Corporate Deductions of PAC Costs," *Campaign Practices Reports*, February 1, 1982, p. 3.

50. FEC, advisory opinion 1980-59.

51. Cantor, *Political Action Committees*, p. 69.

52. Zuckerman, "PACs: Where Did $76 Million Go?" p. 276.

53. Reported in ibid. The article noted that during the 1979-1980 cycle, PACs spent $133.2 million, of which $57.2 million was given to federal candidates. Said the article, "From that, it would seem, PACs spent the remaining $76 million on various other purposes, presumably including a significant amount for expenses which otherwise could have been paid for by their sponsors."

54. Civic Service Inc. survey for BIPAC, p. 15.

55. Ibid., p. 16.

56. Ibid., p. 27.

57. Quoted in Douglas N. Dickson, "Corpacs: The Business of Political Action Committees," *Across the Board* (November 1981):22.

58. Quoted in "Political Action Roundup," *Political Action Report* (June 1979):11. See also "Does the Public Really Mistrust Business?" *Public Affairs Report* (May 1979):4, and "Ethics: Some Practical Considerations for Business PACs," *Political Action Report*, January 15, 1980, p. 10.

59. Cantor, *Political Action Committees*, p. 109. For example in 1980 AT&T sponsored twenty-three separate PACs whose gross expenditures totaled $895,437 and whose contributions to federal candidates were $652,679. Had the PACs been under one banner, AT&T would have been the tenth-largest contributor to federal candidates.

60. *Political Action Report* (January 1979):3. The Civic Involvement Program at General Motors is a PAC that follows this practice.

61. "Ethics and Business Public Affairs," *Impact* (March 1979). See also Fraser Associates, *The PAC Handbook*, p. 24.

62. Quoted in Dickson, "Corpacs," p. 13. For other examples of pro-business PAC views, see Terry Atlas and James O'Shea, "Business Promotes Views by 'Investing' in Politics," *Chicago Tribune*, October 26, 1980; "Corporate Political Action Committees Said Not to Be the Threat Many Claim," *Campaigning Reports*, October 3, 1979, p. 8; Joseph J. Fanelli, "Political Action Committees," *Corporate Director* (January-February 1980):14; and John Mercer, "Political Action Committees: A Good Cause," *Los Angeles Times*, October 5, 1979.

63. BIPAC, in particular, has spent substantial sums for research, survey, and polling information. For more information about BIPAC, see "Pro-Industry PAC Has Difficult Act to Follow," *Campaign Practices Reports*, December 21, 1981, p. 5. For further information on the U.S. Chamber Alliance for Politics, see "PAC Looks to Future with Satellite Network," *Campaign Practices Reports*, March 29, 1982, p. 5.

64. FEC, advisory opinion 1975-23.

65. Stephen J. Sansweet, "Political Action Units at Firms Are Assailed by Some over Tactics," *Wall Street Journal*, July 24, 1980. Epstein's full quote was: "Most companies are quite concerned that their PACs survive the fishbowl test. They know they're being closely watched."

66. See Nathan J. Muller, "Interview of John A. Kochevar," *Public Affairs Report* (January 1980):4.

67. Quoted in Sansweet, "Political Action Units."

68. Quoted in "Corporation Executive Urges Greater Business Participation in Politics," *Campaign Insight*, October 1, 1978, p. 8. As evidence that his company does not use coercion in soliciting for its PAC, Dart notes that only about 20 percent of those persons contacted actually contribute. He adds, "We could get that up to 50 percent if we wanted to push." Quoted in Sansweet, "Political Action Units."

69. Cantor, *Political Action Committees*, p. 44.

70. FEC, advisory opinion 1979-21.

71. William T., Mayton, "Nixon's PAC America: What CREEP Proposed, Congress Has Perfected," *Washington Monthly* (January 1980):56.

72. Civic Service Inc. survey for BIPAC, p. 11.

73. 2 U.S.C. 441b(b)(4)(D); 11 C.F.R. 114.8.

74. Civic Service Inc. survey for BIPAC, p. 15.

75. "Percentage of Corporate PACs Soliciting Shareholders May Increase," *Campaigning Reports*, July 11, 1979, p. 9.

76. Fraser Associates, *PAC Handbook*, p. 42.

77. Richard E. Cohen, "Congressional Democrats Beware—Here Come the Corporate PACs," *National Journal*, August 9, 1980, p. 1306.

78. Civic Service Inc. survey for BIPAC, p. 14.

79. Cantor, *Political Action Committees*, p. 15.

80. Civic Service Inc. survey for BIPAC, p. 15.

81. Cited by "Employee Attitudes and PACs," *Impact* (February 1980):2.

82. Civic Service Inc. survey for BIPAC, p. 26.

83. This concern was fueled in September 1981 when the Senate scrapped its $25,000 annual limit on honorariums, although it retained its $2,000 limit on the amount a candidate may receive per honorarium. "Senate Lifts Honoraria Limit; Panel OKs 1982 FEC Funding," *Campaign Practices Reports*, September 28, 1981, p. 3. For a broader overview of a variety of payments to key members of Congress, see Common Cause, *Money, Power & Politics in the 97th Congress* (Washington D.C.: Common Cause, 1981). For an academic viewpoint, see Edward Handler and John R. Mulkern, *Business in Politics* (Lexington, Mass.: Lexington Books, D.C. Heath and Company, 1982).

84. See Democratic Study Group, "Special Report: Special Interest Money in the 1980 Congressional Election," September 30, 1980; James Barron, "How Grumman Spends Its Campaign Fund," *New York Times*, October 26, 1980; Barbara R. Bergmann, "Lobbying: Shakedown on Capitol Hill," *New York Times*, April 4, 1981; John S. Lang, "When Special Interests Put Heat on Candidates," *U.S. News & World Report*, September 29, 1980, p. 25; Ward Sinclair, "Congress Gets the Message on Billboards," *Los Angeles Times*, November 14, 1979; Patricia Theiler, "Can the Used Car Lobby Sell Congress?" *Washington Post*, November 22, 1981; Warren Weaver, "Special-Interest Units Contributed $927,000 to 8 Leaders in Congress," *New York Times*, January 4, 1979; "PACs Vobiscum," *Nation*, July 7, 1979, p. 4; "Top Leaders on Hill Got $6.5 Million from PACs in Last Campaigns," *Washington Post*, April 8, 1981; Elizabeth Drew, A Reporter at Large, "Politics and Money—I," *New Yorker*, December 6, 1982, p. 54. Another view is that corporate PACs do not attempt to buy access so much as they give to counteract labor's influence. See Dickinson McGaw and Richard McCleary, "The Corporate-Labor PAC Struggle: A Vector ARIMA Time Series Analysis" (paper presented to the American Political Science Association, annual meeting, Denver, September 2-5, 1982).

85. Edward Roeder, "18 Finance Panel Members Got $300,000 from Chemical Industry," *Washington Post*, November 17, 1980. The two panel members who did not receive such contributions were Abraham Ribicoff (D-Conn.), who was retiring, and David Boren (D-Okla.), who accepted no PAC contributions.

86. Ibid.

87. Edward Cowan, "Taxes, Debt and Mr. Jones," *New York Times*, February 3, 1980. Rep. Jones became chairman of the House Budget Committee in 1981.

88. Mark Green and Jack Newfield, "Who Owns Congress: A Guide to Indentured Politicians," *Village Voice,* April 21, 1980.

89. Common Cause, "Members of House Committee Received $101,000 from Leading Interest Group Opponent to Carter Health Legislation [,] Common Cause Study Shows," August 3, 1978, p. 1.

90. Ibid., p. 2. The average amount received by representatives who supported the AMA position was $4,482, compared with an average of $1,007 received by members who opposed the AMA position.

91. Common Cause, "Tower and Krueger Receive Campaign Contributions from Same Special Interest Groups in Texas Senate Race, Common Cause Analysis Reveals," October 20, 1978, p. 1.

92. "Common Cause Hoodwinked the Public," *Political Action Report* (January 1979):1.

93. Quoted in ibid., p. 2.

94. "Business Gives $280,000 to Tax Panel, Gets $1/2 Trillion, Nader Group Says," *Public Citizen*, October 14, 1981, p. 1. See also Morton Mintz, "House Tax-Cutters Got Large Donations from Business Pals," *Washington Post*, July 2, 1981.

95. "Nonsense," *BIPAC Politikit* (November 1981):31.

96. Ibid., pp. 31-32. BIPAC concluded, "The result of the study, even if it were construed as accurate, is unimpressive."

97. Robert Shogan, "Democrats Seek More Business Political Funds," *Los Angeles Times*, April 9, 1981.

98. Quoted in "Democrat Heads PAC Which Might Help GOP," *Political Finance/Lobby Reporter*, May 19, 1982, p. 131.

99. Quoted in Dickson, "Corpacs," p. 13.

100. Jack Bass, "For Regulating Corporate Political Action Committees," *New York Times*, May 30, 1979.

101. FEC press release, February 21, 1982, p. 3.

102. Cantor, *Political Action Committees*, p. 26.

103. Epstein, "Business and Labor," p. 125.

104. Cantor, *Political Action Committees*, pp. 83, 87. For other perspectives on labor's declining role between 1976 and 1980, see Michael J. Malbin, "Labor, Business and Money—A Post-Election Analysis," *National Journal*, March 19, 1977, p. 412; "Special Report: Organized

Labor's 303 PACs Spend $20 Million in 1976," *Campaign Practices Reports*, February 6, 1978, p. 8; and "Special Report: Organized Labor in the New Political Environment," *Baron Report*, December 22, 1980, pp. 2-4.

105. As a rough measure of business-related PACs, Epstein includes all corporate PACs plus one-half of all trade, membership, and health, non-connected, cooperative, and corporation-without-stock PACs. Epstein, "Business and Labor," p. 116.

106. FEC, "Election Unit Announces Drop in PAC Growth," press release, July 17, 1981.

107. *Memo from COPE*, December 9, 1980.

108. Quoted in Philip Shabecoff, "Labor Political Action Groups Mobilize in Bid to Defeat Reagan in Pennsylvania," *New York Times*, October 8, 1980.

109. Cantor, *Political Action Committees*, p. 58.

110. Laura B. Weiss, "Labor Unions, Split by Battle for Democratic Nomination, Worry about Reagan Inroads," *Congressional Quarterly Weekly Report*, June 21, 1980, p. 1733.

111. Harry Bernstein, "Labor's Fear of Reagan Bars Support of Kennedy," *Los Angeles Times*, May 2, 1980.

112. Ibid.

113. Quoted in ibid.

114. Quoted in Harry Bernstein, "Labor Leaders Reluctantly Back Carter," *Los Angeles Times*, June 6, 1980.

115. Cited by "Longshoremen for Carter, But with Reservations," *New York Times*, October 15, 1980.

116. Quoted in James W. Singer, "Closing Ranks behind Carter," *National Journal*, July 5, 1980, p. 1108.

117. Quoted in Bernstein, "Labor Leaders Reluctantly."

118. Quoted in ibid.

119. Quoted in Jerry Flint, "Labor Outlook on Presidency," *New York Times*, February 22, 1979.

120. Quoted in Weiss, "Labor Unions Split," p. 1733.

121. Quoted in Bernstein, "Labor's Fear of Reagan." For other accounts of labor's split in 1980 between Carter and Kennedy, see Harry Bernstein, "Unionists' View of 1980: No One They Can Back," *Los Angeles Times*, May 28, 1979; Jack W. Germond and Jules Witcover, "Winpisinger Pressing Move to Dump Carter," *Washington Star*, February 22, 1979; Jack W. Germond and Jules Witcover, "Carter and Labor," *Washington Star*, September 3, 1979; Philip Shabecoff, "Carter Seen Gaining Some Labor Support," *New York Times*, September 30, 1979; Philip Shabecoff, "Labor Uneasy Over Carter," *New York Times*, April 30, 1980; Ed Townsend, "AFL-CIO Faces a Split If Kennedy Opposes Carter," *Christian*

Science Monitor, October 23, 1979; and "Labor's Plans for Presidential Politics," *Baron Report*, March 30, 1979, p. 2.

122. "Council Panel to Study Action in Primaries," *Memo from COPE*, March 9, 1981, p. 4.

123. Philip Shabecoff, "Race for President Stirring AFL-CIO," *New York Times*, November 18, 1980.

124. Philip Shabecoff, "Officers of Six Large Unions Set Up a Carter-for-President Committee," *New York Times*, July 31, 1979.

125. Quoted in Richard Bergholz, "Reagan Wins Teamsters' Endorsement," *Los Angeles Times*, October 9, 1980.

126. Quoted in Weiss, "Labor Unions Split," p. 1733. See also William Clairborne, "New Right Leaders Reach Out to Unions," *Washington Post*, February 6, 1978; and "AFL-CIO Trying to Stem Worker Drift to Reagan," *Washington Post*, July 3, 1980.

127. Ed Townsend, "Liberal Losses at Polls 'Disappoint' AFL-CIO," *Christian Science Monitor*, November 20, 1980.

128. Quoted in Philip Shabecoff, "Labor Vote: Democratic Ties Weaker," *New York Times*, November 11, 1980, p. 11.

129. Ibid.

130. Townsend, "Liberal Losses at Polls."

131. "Labor and Democrats: Finances and Politics," *New York Times*, November 20, 1981.

132. Quoted in Shabecoff, "Labor Vote."

133. "Poll Shows Union Members Don't Fear GOP Victories," *New York Times*, October 16, 1980.

134. Rhodes Cook, "Reagan and Realignment," in Alan Ehrenhalt, ed., *Politics in America* (Washington, D.C.: Congressional Quarterly Press, 1981), pp. 9-10.

135. Townsend, "Liberal Losses at Polls." COPE also reported below-average results in 1978. See Ed Townsend, "U.S. Labor Less Than Happy with Look of New Congress," *Christian Science Monitor*, November 17, 1978; and "How COPE Fared," *Memo from COPE*, November 27, 1978.

136. Damon Stetson, "Unions Viewing Payroll Checkoff as Funds Source," *New York Times*, October 26, 1980. For views critical of union political payroll checkoffs, see Glenn Fowler, "Koch Opposes Payroll Checkoffs by City for Union Political Funds," *New York Times*, September 11, 1980; and "Can Political Influence be Democratized?" *Political Action Report* (September 1979):8.

137. Ibid.

138. See Herbert E. Alexander, *Financing the 1976 Election* (Washington, D.C.: Congressional Quarterly Press, 1979), p. 109.

139. "Unions Can't Have Dues Checkoff Plan," *Political Finance/Lobby Reporter*, December 24, 1980, p. 2.

140. FEC, advisory opinion 1980-133. See *FEC Record*, February 1981, p. 4.

141. "FEC Action May Help Unions Increase Use of PAC Checkoffs," *Campaign Practices Reports*, April 13, 1981, p. 4.

142. The FEC rules that only one of a company's subsidiaries need have a company PAC withholding option to enable the company's labor PACs to ask for a similar plan in all of the company's subsidiaries.

143. "AT&T Checkoff Could Net Millions for Union Political Funds," *Political Finance/Lobby Reporter*, April 15, 1981, p. 89.

144. "FEC OK's Union, Corporation Payroll Deduction Proposal," *Campaign Practices Reports*, October 12, 1981, p. 9.

145. "PAC of Union Local May Solicit Members of an Affiliated Local," *Campaign Practices Reports*, July 7, 1980, pp. 6-7.

146. "Union PAC Activity High: Spending More, Earlier," *Campaign Practices Reports*, September 28, 1981, p. 2.

147. "Council Urges Political Checkoff," *Memo from COPE*, March 5, 1979, p. 1.

148. FEC, "FEC Study Shows Independent Expenditures to Top $16 Million," press release, November 29, 1981, p. 4.

149. "Independent Spending Soars for 1980 Presidential Race," *National Journal*, December 5, 1981, p. 2171.

150. Jane Stone, "Have Calumny, Will Travel," *Nation*, October 10, 1981, p. 345.

151. Robert Shaw, "New Right Gave Candidates Little," *Miami Herald*, March 29, 1981.

152. "Political Action Roundup," *Political Action Report*, May 15, 1981, p. 5.

153. Ibid.

154. Edward Walsh, "GOP-NCPAC Marriage of Convenience Fails," *Washington Post*, June 27, 1981.

155. See, for example, Stone, "Have Calumny," p. 345.

156. Ibid.

157. Larry Light, "Surge in Independent Campaign Spending," *Congressional Quarterly Weekly Report*, June 14, 1980, pp. 1638-1639.

158. 2 USC 431(17)

159. *American Civil Liberties Union* v. *Jennings*, 424 U.S. 1030 (1976).

160. Joseph E. Cantor, "The Evolution and Issues Surrounding Independent Expenditures in Election Campaigns," Congressional Research Service, May 5, 1982, p. 7.

161. Quoted in ibid., pp. 10-11.

162. Quoted in Michael J. Malbin, "What Should Be Done about Independent Campaign Expenditures?" *Regulation* (January-February 1982):42.

163. *Buckley* v. *Valeo*, 424 U.S. 1 (1976), at 261-262.

164. Cantor, "Evolution and Issues," p. 15.

165. Ibid., p. 17.

166. Ibid., p. 24.

167. Ibid., p. 26.

168. Ibid., p. 19.

169. Quoted in ibid., p. 52.

170. Quoted in Malbin, "What Should Be Done," p. 43.

171. See, for example, Richard A. Viguerie, *The New Right: We're Ready to Lead* (Falls Church, Va.: Viguerie Co., 1981): see also Kevin Philips, *The Emerging Republican Majority* (New York: Arlington House, 1969).

172. See, for example, Alan Crawford, *Thunder on the Right* (New York: Pantheon Books, 1980); also Peter Ross Range, "Thunder from the Right," *New York Times Magazine*, February 8, 1981, pp. 23-25.

173. Crawford, *Thunder on the Right*, p. 4.

174. Quoted in Viguerie, *New Right*, p. 56.

175. Quoted in Richard J. Cattani, "Democratic Left Doesn't Open Wallets for Kennedy," *Christian Science Monitor*, December 17, 1979.

176. Cited by Herbert E. Alexander, *Financing the 1964 Election* (Princeton, N.J.: Citizens' Research Foundation, 1966), p. 71.

177. Ibid.

178. Ibid.

179. Robert D. Shaw, Jr., "Direct-Mail Pleas Raise Thousands for Fundraisers, Little for Causes," *Miami Herald*, March 30, 1981.

180. Ibid.

181. "Hatfield Puts Direct Mail Firms under Scrutiny for Campaign 'Loans,' " *Campaigning Reports*, July 26, 1979, p. 3.

182. E.J. Dionne, Jr., "The Mail Order Campaigners," *New York Times*, September 7, 1980.

183. L.J. Davis, "Conservatism in America," *Harper's* (October 1980):24.

184. See Shaw, "New Right Gave."

185. Ibid.

186. Ibid.

187. Viguerie, *New Right*, p. 92.

188. Quoted in Shaw, "New Right Gave."

189. Quoted in "Hatfield Puts Direct Mail."

190. Warren Weaver, Jr., "Reagan Aided by 'Independent' Donors," *New York Times*, November 30, 1980.

191. The four other such groups—the National Congressional Club, the Fund for a Conservative Majority, Americans for an Effective Presidency, and Americans for Change—spent independently only on the presidential race.

192. Adam Clymer, "Conservative Political Action Committee Evokes Both Fear and Adoration," *New York Times*, May 31, 1981.

193. Malbin, "What Should Be Done," p. 41.

194. "Conservative NCPAC Has Its Own Man at White House," *White House Weekly*, July 20, 1981, p. 3.

195. Cantor, "Evolution and Issues," p. 23.

196. Jack Anderson, "McGovern Target of Election Smears," *Washington Post*, August 14, 1980.

197. Clymer, "Conservative Political Committee."

198. Light, "Surge in Independent," p. 1639.

199. "PACs Are Independent Expenditure Leaders," *Congressional Quarterly Weekly Report*, June 14, 1980, p. 1637.

200. "NCPAC's Negative Campaign," *Political Action Report* (November 1979):5.

201. Stone, "Have Calumny," p. 345.

202. Anderson, "McGovern Target."

203. "Conservatives on the Attack with Ad Campaigns," *Broadcasting*, March 10, 1980, p. 89.

204. NCPAC originally budgeted $500,000 for its anti-Kennedy effort but actually spent less than $250,000.

205. Weaver, "Reagan Aided."

206. Maxwell Glen, "How to Get Around Campaign Spending Limits," *National Journal*, June 23, 1979, p. 1046.

207. "Campaign Accountability," *Washington Post*, December 10, 1980.

208. "Loopholes: The Campaign Finance Act Has Some Million-Dollar Deficiencies," *Detroit Free Press*, December 5, 1981.

209. James M. Perry, "Liberal Incumbents Are Main Targets of TV Ads as Political-Action Groups Exploit Court Ruling," *Wall Street Journal*, January 25, 1980.

210. "Conservatives on the Attack," p. 89.

211. Perry, "Liberal Incumbents."

212. Ibid.

213. Shaw, "New Right Gave"; see also Zuckerman, "Where Did $76 Million," p. 275.

214. FEC, *FEC Index of Independent Expenditures, 1979-80* (Washington, D.C.: November 1981).

215. "Cheap Shots or Fair Play?" (advertisement), *Los Angeles Times*, November 2, 1980. This advertisement attacked the negative campaigns waged against Cranston and added an endorsement of him at the bottom of the page.

216. The Life Amendment PAC distributed what were described as "lurid" photos of dead fetuses displayed next to a photo of McGovern.

These photos were mailed to voters and placed on the windshields of cars parked outside Sunday church services. See Anderson, "McGovern Target."

217. Perry, "Liberal Incumbents."

218. *Buckley* v. *Valeo*, 424 U.S. 1 (1976).

219. *First National Bank of Boston* v. *Bellotti* 435 U.S. 765, at 777 (1978).

220. National Chamber Litigation Center, "Special Litigation Report: *The First National Bank of Boston et. al.* v. *Bellotti*" (Supreme Court No. 76-1172), 1978, p. 5.

221. Under 2 USC 437h of the FECA, only the FEC, the national committee of a political party, or any individual eligible to vote for president may bring action to interpret the constitutionality of the FECA. See *Martin Tractor* v. *Federal Election Commission*, 460 F. Supp. 1017 (D.D.C. 1978).

222. *Martin Tractor* v. *Federal Election Commission*, 627 F.2d 375 (D.C. Cir.).

223. *National Chamber Alliance for Politics* v. *Federal Election Commission*, 449 U.S. 954 (1980).

224. *Citizens against Rent Control* v. *City of Berkeley*, 102 S.Ct. 434, quoted at 437 (1981).

225. "Berkeley Ruling Gives Corporations Unlimited Spending in Ballot Issues," *Political Finance/Lobby Reporter*, September 23, 1981, p. 331.

226. *CBS, ABC and NBC* v. *Federal Communications Commission* 347 U.S. 284 (1981). See also David M. Ifshin and Roger E. Warin, "Litigating the 1980 Election," *American University Law Review* 31 (Spring 1982):545.

227. *Federal Election Commission* v. *CLITRIM*, CA-2, 79-3014. See also "FEC Proposals to Let Firms Spend More on Nonpartisan Activities Prove Controversial," *Campaign Practices Reports*, December 8, 1980, p. 5.

228. The specific rule cited by the commission was 11 CFR 114.4(d)(1). See "AO 1979-48: Voter Registration Advertisement," *FEC Annual Report 1979*, p. 80.

229. "AO 1980-20: Nonpartisan Voter Registration Communication," *FEC Annual Report 1980*, p. 83.

230. For a discussion of this point as it relates to the events following the opinion, see "FEC to Propose New Corporation, Union Rules for Nonpartisan Ads," *Campaign Practices Reports*, September 14, 1981, p. 6.

231. "AO 1980-33 and Supplement: Trade Association's Nonpartisan Voter Drive," *FEC Annual Report 1980*, p. 86.

232. "AO 1980-55: Corporate Assistance for Secretary of State's Voter Registration Drive," *FEC Annual Report 1980*, p. 94.

233. "AO 1980-95: National Bank's Contribution to State Political Fund," *FEC Annual Report 1980*, pp. 103-104.

234. See "Sun Oil Invites Candidates Despite Unissued Opinion,"

Political Finance/Lobby Reporter, September 20, 1980, p. 6.

235. FEC, advisory opinion 1980-90 (full text), p. 3. See also "Presidential Candidates Can't Appear on Oil Company's Television Show," *Political Finance/Lobby Reporter*, September 10, 1980, p. 7.

236. "11 CFR Part 114 Nonpartisan Communications by Corporations or Labor Organizations," *Federal Register*, August 25, 1980, p. 56349. See also "FEC to Review Rules on Nonpartisan Communications by Corporations, Unions," *Campaign Practices Reports*, September 15, 1980, p. 7.

237. "FEC Proposals to Let Firms and Unions Spend More on Nonpartisan Activities Prove Controversial," *Campaign Practices Reports*, December 8, 1980, p. 3.

238. Under section 437(f) of the FECA, the FEC is empowered to propose rules. Under section 438(d), the commission must submit such proposed rules to both houses of Congress, along with a detailed explanation and justification of each rule. Either house may disapprove by resolution any proposed rule within thirty legislative days of receipt. The FEC's notice of proposed rulemaking first appeared on September 8, 1981. See "11 CFR Part 114 Communications by Corporations and Labor Organizations," *Federal Register*, September 8, 1981, p. 44964.

239. FEC, "Minutes of a Special Meeting of the Federal Election Commission," agenda document 82-6, December 2, 1981, pp. 3-4.

240. Ibid., p. 7.

241. FEC, "Minutes of a Regular Meeting of the Federal Election Commission," agenda document 82-24, January 28, 1982, p. 7.

242. *BreadPAC* v. *Federal Election Commission*, United States District Court, Northern District of Illinois, Civil Action No. 77-C-947, October 6, 1977.

243. *BreadPAC* v. *Federal Election Commission*, 7 U.S. District Court of Appeals, No. 80-1146, December 5, 1980.

244. Sec. 437h(a); see *BreadPAC* v. *Federal Election Commission*, 50 U.S.L.W. 4291 (1982).

245. *Athens Lumber Co.* v. *FEC*, U.S. Court of Appeals, 11th Circuit, No. 82-8102. See also, "Corporate Contribution Case on the Move Again in Georgia," *Campaign Practices Reports*, November 8, 1982, p. 4; and "Athens Lumber Headed for En Banc Court," *PACs & Lobbies*, November 3, 1982, p. 1.

246. Telephone interview, November 16, 1982.

247. FEC, press release, June 8, 1982.

248. In this regard, see especially FEC, advisory opinion 1982-44. In this decision, the FEC allowed the Turner Broadcasting System to give free air time on cable television to the Republican and Democratic National Committees. See Ed Zuckerman, "FEC Approves Corporate Gift of Free TV Time for Parties," *Political Finance/Lobby Reporter*, September 1,

1982, p. 230; "Party Committees May Accept Free Broadcast Time," *Campaign Practices Reports*, August 30, 1982, p. 9; and "Campaigning on Cable: A Question of Potential," *Campaign Practices Reports*, September 13, 1982, p. 1.

249. James Shoener, "Federal Election Commission," in Charles L. Heatherly, ed., *Mandate for Leadership* (Washington, D.C.: Heritage Foundation, 1981), pp. 745-750.

250. *First National Bank of Boston* v. *Bellotti*, 435 U.S. 765 (1978).

251. Ibid., at p. 794.

252. "SEC Asked to Write Corporate Disclosure Rule to Help Keep Shareholders Informed," *Political Finance/Lobby Reporter*, August 6, 1980, p. 3.

253. Ibid.

254. "Georgetown Group Asks Commission to Propose Rule Requiring Corporations to Provide PAC Disclosure," *Securities Regulation & Law Report* 563, July 23, 1980, pp. 8-9.

255. Ibid.

256. "SEC Asked to Write," p. 3.

257. Ibid.

258. Staff Report on Corporate Accountability (Washington, D.C. Securities and Exchange Commission, September 4, 1980), p. 201.

259. "Corporations: GM Agrees to Shareholder Proposal to Disclose More about Its Political Action Committee," regulatory and legal analysis, DNA's Daily Reporter System, March 28, 1980.

260. Ibid.

261. Ibid.

262. "Georgetown Group Asks Commission," p. A-9.

263. Morton Mintz, "GM Offers Stockholders Key Data on Workings of Political Action Panel," *Washington Post*, April 8, 1980. See also 1980 General Motors Public Interest Report, pp. 116-117.

264. A shareholder proxy proposal must receive at least 6 percent on its second and subsequent attempts to qualify for further submissions.

265. HR 7010, 96th Cong., 2d sess.

266. S 1851, 97th Cong., 1st sess., sec. 8(4)(A)(B)(C).

267. FEC, *Index of Communication Costs, 1979-80* (Washington, D.C., 1981).

268. FEC, press release, October 5, 1981, p. 1.

269. See Alexander, *Financing the 1976 Election*, p. 566.

270. The NRA spent no funds during the primary season opposing President Carter, however, the group did begin to spend for communications opposing President Carter once he had won the Democratic nomination.

271. This labor organization was the only one listed by the FEC in

1979-1980 to have spent in opposition to President Carter in the primaries and then to have switched to advocacy of Carter once he captured the nomination.

272. The UAW International Union made a $1,638 communications expenditure supporting President Carter on July 11, 1980, more than one month after the conclusion of the primary season, a time by which President Carter had virtually secured his renomination.

273. An example of the weak support for President Carter from the former Kennedy camp is provided by the American Federation of State, County and Municipal Employees, which spent only $33,597 during the general-election campaign after spending more than $300,000 during the preconvention period on communications supporting Kennedy or opposing President Carter.

274. FEC press release, October 5, 1981, p. 3. The figures in this section represent a combined figure for both primary and general elections.

275. Ibid.

276. *FEC Disclosure Series No. 5: Index of Communication Costs* (Washington, D.C., 1977), p. 7.

277. 11 CFR 114.3 (a) states, "A corporation may make partisan communications in connection with a Federal election to its stockholders and executive administrative personnel and their families, or by a labor organization to its members and their families." 11 CFR 114.4 (a) places similar restrictions on corporations and labor unions undertaking nonpartisan communications. Text of statement by Joseph J. Fanelli, president, BIPAC, before the Committee on Rules and Administration of the U.S. Senate, November 24, 1981, p. 6.

278. Gallup Poll, "Participation in Interest Groups High," *Gallup Report* (August 1981):45.

279. This figure was obtained directly from Ruth S. Jones, Center for Political Studies, University of Michigan.

280. For more information about state experiences with political tax checkoff funds, see Jack L. Noragon, "Political Finance and Political Reform: The Experience with State Income Tax Checkoffs," *American Political Science Review*, (September 1981):667; reprinted in Herbert E. Alexander and Jennifer W. Frutig, *Public Financing of State Elections: A Data Book and Election Guide to Public Funding of Political Parties and Candidates in Seventeen States* (Los Angeles: Citizens' Research Foundation, 1982), p. 295.

9 Aftermath

Reagan Transition

Prior to 1964, the transition from one presidential administration to another was largely dependent on funds from the president-elect's party and on the work of unpaid volunteer staff. For most of the nation's history, new presidents took office with relatively little specific preparation or substantive communication with the outgoing administration. As the nation grew in size and presidential responsibilities grew more complex, however, the need to maintain effective continuity in the executive branch of government increased accordingly. In 1962 the bipartisan Commission on Campaign Costs, which had been appointed by President John F. Kennedy, recommended that federal funds be made available to pay costs incurred in promoting an orderly change of presidential administrations. Congress responded by enacting the Presidential Transition Act of 1963, which directed government officials to promote orderly transitions in administrations and authorized Congress to appropriate funds to cover some of the costs involved in doing so.

In 1976 Congress, at the repeated urging of the General Services Administration (GSA), raised the appropriation for transition funds for the incoming administration from $450,000 to $2 million.[1] In 1980 $2 million once again was authorized for the administrator of the GSA to provide facilities and services needed by the incoming Reagan administration from the day following the general election until inauguration day. These funds were to be used to pay for office space and equipment for the president-elect and the vice-president-elect, for transition-team salaries and consultant fees, for travel expenses and subsistence allowances, and for communication services, printing and binding, and postage.

GAO Report

According to a report prepared by the GAO at the request of Rep. John D. Dingell (D-Mich.), chairman of the House Committee on Energy and Commerce, transition-related expenses incurred by the Reagan-Bush transition team actually were paid for both from funds appropriated under the Presidential Transition Act and from funds furnished by two private foundations

441

established on behalf of the Reagan team.[2] In addition, the GSA spent more than $100,000 in Public Building Fund monies to provide office space to the transition team, and government agencies from which the transition team sought information spent other funds on transition-related work.

According to the GAO report, as of December 31, 1981, the Reagan transition team had spent $1,746,544 of the $2 million appropriated under the Transition Act.[3] Of this amount, about $1.3 million was used to pay staff salaries and benefits. The transition team included 1,559 members who were located both at transition-team headquarters and at some one hundred different federal agencies. Of those staff members, 311 received salaries from appropriated funds, 331 received token payments of $1 each, and 917 received no payment from those funds. The remaining $400,000 of Transition Act funds spent by the Reagan transition team was used to pay for rent, communications, and utilities; travel for the president-elect, the vice-president-elect, and transition-team members; printing and photocopying costs; office supplies; transportation; and other services.

In addition to the $1.75 million in appropriated funds spent by the Reagan transition team, about $117,000 was spent by the GSA to provide office space for the president-elect in a building already leased by the GSA.[4] The figure represents the agency's cost for the portion of the building used by the office of the president-elect from November 5, 1980, to January 20, 1981. Additional space was provided at no cost to the vice-president-elect in federally owned buildings. Only the costs of space acquired specifically for transition purposes were charged to the Transition Act funds. Since the office space provided to both Reagan and Bush already was in the GSA's inventory, the agency determined, under the authority of the Federal Property and Administrative Services Act of 1949, that it would be infeasible or impractical to charge rent for the space.

The federal agencies from which Reagan transition-team members sought information also absorbed costs in the process of complying with transition team requests. According to the GAO report, six agencies that fall within the jurisdiction of the House Committee on Energy and Commerce—the Department of the Interior, the Department of Transportation, the Environmental Protection Agency, the Nuclear Regulatory Commission, the SEC, and the Federal Trade Commission—reported having incurred about $235,000 in such transition-related expenses as salaries of professional and clerical staff, office supplies, and photocopying.[5] Since the agencies were not required to maintain records of such expenses, the expense figures were based largely on recollections by agency personnel of the time that agency staff members spent working on transition-related matters. Of the six agencies listed, the Department of the Interior reported the highest amount for transition-related expenses—almost $183,000—and the SEC the lowest—approximately $5,000.

Private Funding

The GAO report to the Committee on Energy and Commerce notes that private funds were used in addition to appropriated funds to pay transition-related costs. Although the GAO was denied access to records and accounts of the private funds, the agency's report indicates that two private foundations were established to fund some transition activities. According to the report, the Presidential Transition Trust was established to undertake some transition-related activities prior to the November 4 general election. The report cited a Trust document that listed among the foundation's purposes: to receive contributions from individuals not to exceed $5,000 per person; to pay for costs of gathering information about particularly important administration jobs and of identifying personnel to fill those jobs; to pay costs involved in liaison with the GSA in preparation for possible postelection transition activities; and to provide reports to the general public regarding monies raised and spent. By November 30, 1981, however, no such reports had been forthcoming. The GAO examined files maintained by the GSA and discovered that Reagan-Bush representatives had been in communication with the GSA on numerous occasions prior to the general election; the GAO suggested such Reagan-Bush activities may have been funded by the Presidential Transition Trust. At least one news report, however, indicated that some Reagan-Bush preelection transition activities were financed out of general-election campaign funds and thus counted toward the Republican campaign's overall spending limit. According to the early October 1980 report, the campaign established a planning task force, staffed by three full-time workers and by volunteers, to prepare lists of potential appointees, to consider legislative and policy initiatives to be taken by Reagan in his first ninety days in office, to lay groundwork for organization of the White House staff and its relationship with the cabinet and the Congress, and to examine the mechanics of the budget-making process.[6] The article also noted that Reagan aides, including Edwin Meese, Reagan-Bush campaign chief of staff who later headed the Reagan transition team, were keeping in touch with a number of organizations involved in privately funded transition studies, including the Heritage Foundation, a conservative, public-policy think tank; the Institute of Politics at Harvard University's John F. Kennedy School of Government; and the National Academy of Public Administration.

According to the GAO report, on November 5, 1980, a second private fund, the Presidential Transition Foundation, Inc., was established "to facilitate an orderly transfer of the power of the executive branch" and "to receive funds from any lawful source" for that purpose.[7] The government agency report cited a June 1981 newspaper report that $500,000 had been contributed to the foundation and that the funds were spent on the same kinds of items and services as the appropriated funds: salaries, travel, and so forth. The newspaper report did not indicate the sources of funds donated to the Transition Foundation, but according to the FEC's audit of the Reagan for President Committee, the candidate's prenomination-campaign committee, $250,000 in leftover contributions, some of which the committee received after Reagan had been formally nominated, was transferred by the committee to the Presidential Transition Fund.[8] The committee informed the FEC of its action on December 22, 1980.

Inaugural Activities

Ronald Reagan's inauguration was an elaborate affair stretching out over four days and costing about $16.3 million, reportedly the most expensive inauguration celebration in U.S. history.[9] President Carter's inaugural celebration four years earlier had cost a reported $3.5 million.[10] The entire cost of the Reagan inaugural celebration was covered by private funds raised from contributions and from the sale of souvenirs and tickets to inaugural events. In fact the inaugural committee, headed by Robert K. Gray, a public-relations specialist, and Charles Z. Wick, a prominent Reagan campaign fund raiser, took in $1 million more than needed to cover its costs. Most of the excess was slated to found an Inaugural Scholars Program to help disadvantaged youths.

The 1981 Presidential Inaugural Committee raised more than $1 million in tax-deductible contributions to a separate Inaugural Trust Fund established by the committee to construct a parade viewing stand for the president and the press and to stage a fireworks show. The committee spent nearly $900,000 for those purposes. It raised $12.3 million from sales of tickets to various inaugural events, with some tickets priced as high as $500, but refunded $1.4 million because tickets had been oversold. It also raised $2.3 million from the sale of such memorabilia as inaugural license plates and cuff links.

Appointments

As with previous incoming administrations, the new Reagan administration was roundly criticized by the American Foreign Service Association (AFSA) for making too many political appointments to foreign-service posts. According to the AFSA, whose membership includes some 5,000 active-duty foreign-service officers and about 2,000 retired officers, Reagan named a larger proportion of noncareer officers to ambassadorial posts than any other president since World War II. And, claimed the association, the vast majority of such appointees were "relatively undistinguished as public figures."[11] Career foreign-service officer Malcolm Toon, who left his post as U.S. ambassador to the Soviet Union and retired from the foreign service in 1979, was particularly critical of the incoming administration's political appointments. The outspoken Toon disapproved not only of the number of political appointees but also of their quality, and he maintained that the trend under President Reagan would have a damaging effect on the service as a whole.[12] Toon criticized four of Reagan's appointments in particular: Hollywood actor John Gavin as ambassador to Mexico; Johnson's Wax heir and Republican contributor John Lovis as ambassador to Great Britain; financier Evan Griffin Galbraith as ambassador to France; and banker-lawyer Maxwell Rabb as ambassador to Italy. The Reagan administration, claimed Toon, was using U.S. diplomatic posts as "a dumping ground for defeated politicians and Republican financial backers."[13]

The administration's appointments were defended by E. Pendleton James, who became White House personnel director after Reagan's inauguration. James argued that political appointees generally were better ambassadors because they have greater access to the president and high-level administration officials.[14] According to James, by early April 1982, forty of the ninety-six ambassadors appointed by Reagan—42 percent of the total— were political appointees. About 27 percent of the Carter administration's choices for ambassadorial posts were political appointments.

Other Reagan-administration appointees drew fire for alleged financial indiscretions. In two cases the criticisms that resulted led the appointees to resign their positions. On January 4, 1982, national security adviser Richard Allen resigned from the White House staff while he was under investigation for having accepted $1,000 from a Japanese magazine in conjunction with the magazine's postelection interview of Nancy Reagan, for having accepted expensive watches from Japanese friends, and for having made errors in his financial-disclosure form required by the 1978 Ethics in Government Act. On February 10, 1982, Joseph W. Canzeri, a deputy assistant to President Reagan, resigned in the wake of publicity surrounding his receipt of a $400,000 loan on favorable terms from Laurence S. Rockefeller and from California real-estate developer Donald M. Koll. Additional negative publicity regarding Canzeri's submission of expense claims to the government and to the RNC for the same trips also contributed to Canzeri's resignation. He claimed the double billing was a mistake and noted he had reimbursed the RNC for $800 since the trips were for official business.

Reagan's choice for secretary of labor, Raymond J. Donovan, was the subject of investigations regarding alleged organized-crime connections, but twice federal prosecutors concluded there was no prosecutable evidence of such connections. One of the allegations against Donovan was that he had taken part in distributing $20 million from the Teamsters union to Reagan's presidential campaign in exchange for a promise to pardon two imprisoned organized-crime figures who had served in high union positions.[15] Since that figure represented more than two-thirds of the Reagan prenomination campaign's gross receipts, the federal prosecutor dismissed the allegation. Donovan himself maintained he had raised no more than $600,000 for the Reagan campaign, and White House officials said his fund-raising activities had not influenced Donovan's appointment.[16]

A GAO review of the effects of the Reagan transition on the Senior Executive Service was conducted at the request of Rep. Patricia Shroeder (D-Colo.), chairwoman of the House Subcommittee on Civil Service. In a report released on March 23, 1982, the GAO noted that a survey and other oversight activities conducted by the Office of Personnel Management indicated there had been "no problems with the reassignment or detail of career SES members"[17] and that a survey conducted by the Merit System Protection Board found "no instances of forced resignations, retirements, reassignments, or details."[18]

Republican Party Aftermath

After their candidates' stunning victories in the 1980 general elections—a net gain of twelve Senate seats and thirty-three House seats in addition to Ronald Reagan's presidential victory—the Republican party's national committees continued to assert their organizational and fund-raising superiority over their Democratic counterparts. In 1979-1980, the three principal Republican national-party groups—the RNC, the National Republican Congressional Committee ((NRCC), and the National Republican Senatorial Committee (NRSC)—raised a combined total of $112.3 million, compared with the corresponding Democratic national committees' total of only $18.9 million. During the final five weeks of the general-election year, customarily an extremely slow period for political fund raising, the three Republican national committees raised $5.2 million of their total.[19] Their success, no doubt, was due in some measure to the desire of contributors to prepare the way for access to new and returning Republican officeholders. During the same five-week period, the Democratic national committees received only $174,777 in contributions.[20]

Direct mail accounted for a substantial percentage of the RNC's receipts during the 1979-1980 election cycle. Direct-mail appeals also were prominent in the fund-raising strategies of the other two Republican committees. In fact the three committees coordinated their mailings according to an annual master schedule and were careful not to solicit the same contributors too frequently. Wyatt Stewart, NRCC finance director, estimated that the committees netted $3 to $4 for every dollar they spent. "There's not a business in the world that does that well," he said.[21]

1981-1982 Fund Raising

For the 1981-1982 election cycle, the three Republican committees established a combined fund-raising goal of more than $95 million: $30 million for the RNC in 1981 alone, $40 million for the NRCC for the complete election cycle, and $25 million for the NRSC for the election cycle.[22]

According to reports filed with the FEC, the three committees met or surpassed their 1981-1982 fund-raising goals during the first fifteen months of the election cycle. As of March 31, 1982, the RNC had raised $54 million and spent $45.3 million; the NRCC had raised $39.6 million and spent $24.7 million; and the NRSC had raised $26.4 million and spent $21.3 million.[23] The three committees collectively had more than $33 million cash in hand. As indicated in table 9-1, direct mail accounted for the lion's share of the RNC's 1981 total cash receipts of $33.5 million. Major contributors accounted for only about $5.7 million of that total, in keeping with the party's concerted effort to build a broad financial base. Nevertheless the national committee did not neglect its large contributors, especially contributors of at least $10,000 a year, known as Eagles. For example, RNC national finance chairman Richard DeVos arranged White House receptions hosted by

Table 9-1
Republican National Committee Receipts and Expenditures, 1981

Receipts		
Direct response	$26,710,400	
Major contributors	5,651,800	
Miscellaneous	1,149,000	
Total		$33,511,200
Expenditures		
Chairman's office	$ 347,100	
Co-chairman's office	218,200	
Deputy chairman-liaison	331,600	
Deputy chairman-political	271,000	
Fund raising	8,845,000	
Political	5,979,700	
Administration	1,959,000	
Communications	2,488,900	
Redistricting	1,318,700	
Media	1,401,000	
White House support	1,898,700	
RNC meetings	160,500	
Polling	880,300	
1980 obligations	1,492,800	
Total		$27,592,500

Source: Information provided by the RNC.

President Reagan for large contributors. That the large donors appreciated the extra attention is apparent from a $10,000-a-table formal dinner party the Republican Eagles threw to celebrate the one-year anniversary of the Reagan administration. The event drew 2,000 persons who sat at tables that had been purchased by Standard Oil Co. of California, the Atlantic Richfield Corp., the American Gas Association, the American Bankers Association, and other business and banking interests, as well as individuals.[24]

Included in the Republican House and Senate campaign committees' receipts were receipts from an April 7, 1981, fund-raising dinner that took in $3 million and netted about $2.6 million.[25] President Reagan had been scheduled to address the $1,000-a-plate dinner audience, but with Reagan hospitalized after the March 30 attempt on his life, Vice-President George Bush stepped in and used the occasion to plead for support for the administration's economic-recovery program. In May the following year, President Reagan did address a $1,000-a-plate unity dinner cosponsored by the two committees. The event raised $3 million,[26] but those receipts are not included in the fifteen-month totals.

For the remainder of its funds, the NRCC depended primarily on receipts from direct-mail appeals. The committee also organized a Leadership Council, whose 400 members were to pay $2,500 annually and to receive four day-long briefings.[27] As in the past, funds raised by the committee were used in part to pay for the costs of recruiting and training candidates and to make direct financial contributions to the candidates' campaign committees. The NRSC was less dependent on direct-mail solicitations, although it did plan to raise $10 million of its 1981-1982 goal of $25 million by that means.[28] The remainder of its funds were to come from large contributors who could participate in a number of programs: the Senate Republican Trust, made up of donors of $10,000 annually; the Inner Circle, whose members were asked to contribute $1,000 annually; and the Business Advisory Board, whose 4,000 small-business owners were asked to donate $250 to $750 a year.[29] Members of each group were to receive briefings and other communications about Senate legislative and political activities. NRSC funds, like those of its House counterpart, were to be used in part to provide candidate services and direct financial aid.

Some Republican state-party committees echoed the fund-raising success of the national-level committees. For example, the California Republican party netted more than $1 million from an April 23, 1981, fund-raising dinner at which Vice-President Bush substituted for President Reagan, wounded in an assassination attempt.[30] State Republican committees later benefited from a series of three appearances by the president at fund-raising events expected to raise an additional $400,000 for state legislative candidates.[31]

White House Intervention

Despite notable fund-raising successes, the Republican national committees were guilty of some embarrassing tactics that elicited White House intervention to stop their use. Shortly after Reagan's inauguration on January 20, 1981, the NRCC mailed a fund-raising letter that said, "Winning Republican control of the House in the next election [is] our party's No. 1 priority." The letter, dated January 21 and sent out over a facsimile of Reagan's signature, reportedly angered the House Democratic leadership, then being wooed to support Reagan's first legislative initiative, a request to increase the national debt ceiling.[32] According to White House spokesmen Larry Speakes, Reagan had understood the letter would be sent out prior to his taking office. "We regret it was sent out in this manner," said Speakes, who noted an apology had been conveyed to majority leader Jim Wright (D-Tex.).[33]

Late in the year the NRSC sent out a fund-raising letter that Lyn Nofziger, Reagan's political director, reportedly described as "about the limit of fund-raising letter hyperbole."[34] The letter, signed by NRSC chairman Sen. Robert Packwood of Oregon, appeared to scold reluctant Republican contributors. President Reagan, wrote Packwood, "personally asked me to find out why you're holding back."[35] The appeal repeated an earlier offer of a variety of incentives to contributors of $120 a year, including "President Reagan's personally commissioned Medal of Merit," a full-sized American flag, and an embossed membership card with a toll-free hot-line number for members only. Soon after Nofziger was shown a copy of the letter, he said he asked the committee to stop sending it and was told the appeal would cease.

Senator Packwood

NRSC chairman Packwood later was the focal point of some in-party controversy that almost surely had a negative effect on party fund raising. In the fall of 1981, Packwood had incurred the administration's displeasure by opposing its ultimately successful effort to win approval for sale of sophisticated surveillance planes to Saudi Arabia. Early in March 1982, it was widely reported that the outspoken Packwood had become dismayed over what he called President Reagan's "idealized concept of America," as white, Anglo-Saxon Protestant.[36] He worried that if that view prevailed, the Republican party would lose its appeal among women, blacks, Hispanics, and Jews. Packwood also expressed concern that the president tended to respond to problems raised by Republican congressional leaders in GOP leadership meetings with anecdotes "on a totally different track" from the problems raised.[37]

Packwood's candid remarks were quickly followed by a storm of protest, some from fellow Republicans calling upon him to resign his NRSC
chairmanship. Senate majority leader Howard Baker met with Packwood
and urged him to apologize to the president, which Packwood did, to both
the president and the Republican Policy Committee. Nevertheless, Packwood did not deny that he had made the remarks he apologized for.

Despite the apology, the furor continued. RNC chairman Richards told
reporters that Packwood's presence as chairman of the NRSC "is going to
cost us, and cost us money."[38] Richards maintained that he had received
complaints from campaign contributors who said they would no longer contribute to the Senate committee. As the controversy continued, Republican
contributors received a fund-raising letter over Reagan's signature appealing for donations to the Republican Presidential Task Force chaired by Sen.
Packwood and mentioning Packwood's name several times. At the beginning of April, the letter was abruptly withdrawn by the White House, whose
spokespersons objected that the letter and the use of the president's
signature had not been authorized and that the letter and accompanying
literature were not presidential enough.[39] Packwood insisted the letter had
been approved by Lyn Nofziger, when Nofziger was White House political
director, but Nofziger's successor, Ed Rollins, in a tense meeting with
Packwood, maintained that only a small test mailing had been approved.
The NRSC was forced to destroy eight million copies of the letter, reportedly
produced at a cost of $2 million.[40] As a result, the committee announced it
would be forced temporarily to cut in half a number of support services it
had been providing to individual senators, to put a moratorium on hiring
political consultants, and to cut back on travel expenditures.

The setback to the NRSC's fund-raising drive did not deter Packwood
from criticizing the president on additional matters. By abandoning his
campaign goal of balancing the federal budget, said the Oregon senator in
a mid-April speech in his home state, the president "removed the glue that
held everyone together in the Republican Party."[41] At about the same
time, Joseph Coors, head of a Colorado brewery and often described as
an archconservative, mailed a letter to about 2,500 fellow Republican contributors urging them to join him in withholding support from the Senate
campaign committee until Packwood was removed from his chairmanship.[42] Majority leader Baker, who had failed in an attempt to persuade
Coors not to send his letter, reportedly intervened with President Reagan,
who subsequently made a statement assuring Republicans he wanted contributions made to the Senate committee.[43] Late in May it was reported
that the brochure that had accompanied the original task force letter was
reprinted to include a picture of Sen. Baker in place of Sen. Packwood
and that the letter itself, whose basic wording remained the same, though
Packwood's name was removed, was sent out over Baker's signature
rather than the president's.

Media Advertising

In addition to providing candidate services and direct financial aid, the money raised by the Republican national committees was used in a number of other ways to support Republican candidates and the Republican program. In July 1981 party officials announced the RNC and the NRCC would sponsor a half-million dollar media advertising program to promote President Reagan's tax-cut plan.[44] Although the RNC had sponsored a television advertising campaign in support of the party's candidates in 1980, the 1981 program marked the first time a major political party had bought advertisements to lobby for pending legislation. The budget announced for the program included $250,000 to buy advertising time on nationwide radio networks, about $220,000 for additional radio time in targeted congressional districts, and about $30,000 on television and radio commercials in the Washington area.[45] In mid-October it was reported that the Republicans were spending approximately $2.3 million on a television advertising campaign that would run through early November and would give Republican officeholders credit for having passed the tax cut.[46] The advertisements were scheduled to run on network television and in all congressional districts.

In May 1982 the RNC and the NRCC contracted with Korey, Kay and Partners, a New York advertising agency, to produce advertisements for a proposed $1.7 million advertising campaign, the first phase of a $10 million campaign planned by the Republicans. The firm borrowed from what appeared to be an effective campaign run by the GOP in 1980 that had used a look-alike actor to portray House Speaker Thomas O'Neill running out of gas on a highway. One of the 1982 advertisements used look-alike actors to portray both O'Neill and President Carter sitting by as a third actor portraying a lawyer read a "last will and testament" bequeathing Ronald Reagan "a recession." The advertisement, which did run on at least one network, drew fire from the Democratic leadership and from editorialists around the country. Democrats called the message "a lie" and encouraged stations and networks to refuse to broadcast it. In mid-June it was announced that the advertisement, and another produced by the agency, were being withdrawn and that the two Republican committees were severing their relationship with Korey, Kay.[47] Rep. Guy Vander Jagt, chairman of the NRCC, insisted that the advertisements had not been prematurely withdrawn but that they had "run their course."[48]

One of the replacement advertisements also was criticized by the Democrats as deceptive. It suggested that Reagan had promised that Social Security recipients would continue to receive their automatic annual cost-of-living increases and delivered on his promise despite the opposition of unnamed "sticks-in-the-mud." In fact Reagan had attempted on at least three occasions to have the increase delayed for three months in order to trim federal spending.[49]

Other Programs

In 1981 the RNC spent some $1.3 million in party funds to fight battles over the redistricting of congressional and state legislative seats (see table 9-1). The California state GOP received $100,000 of those funds from the national-party committee to help support the state-party's drive to collect signatures needed to qualify a referendum proposed for the June 1982 ballot that would overturn the Democratic remapping of congressional and legislative districts.[50] In addition the RNC spent about $880,000 for polling in 1981. About $820,000 of that amount was slated to go to Decision Making Information, whose president, Richard Wirthlin, had served as deputy campaign manager in the Reagan-Bush Committee and had conducted polling operations and devised strategy for the campaign.[51] Wirthlin conducted both national and state polls for the party's national committee.

The national committee spent about $1 million in cash and in-kind contributions to help Republican Thomas Kean win a November 1981 gubernatorial race in New Jersey.[52] It purchased a video satellite teleconference system that would allow party leaders to confer on television with Republican gatherings and conducted seminars around the country for party political operatives and candidates. The biggest category of expenditure for the RNC in 1981 was fund raising, on which the committee spent $8.8 million. The committee also purchased new hardware to increase the effectiveness of its fund-raising operation, including high-speed printing presses and a computerized phone bank system.

Chairman Richards

During his term as GOP chairman, Richard Richards was the subject of considerable criticism. More than once in 1981 Richards clashed with White House political director Lyn Nofziger and later with his successor, Edward Rollins, over the role of independent expenditures in election campaigns. Nofziger and Rollins were favorable to such expenditures, which in 1980 appeared to benefit Republicans far more than Democrats, but Richards found them "obnoxious."[53]

Late in 1981 Richards commented in an off-the-record question-and-answer session overheard by reporters at a GOP fund raiser that Reagan aides Richard Allen and David Stockman would soon be forced to resign their positions. Allen's credibility had been called into question because of alleged improprieties surrounding, among other things, his acceptance of money from a Japanese magazine. OMB director Stockman's influence appeared to be on the wane in the wake of disparaging remarks he had made about Reagan's economic program, which were published in the *Atlantic*

Monthly. Richards, who also speculated that President Reagan would not seek a second term, subsequently was rebuked by White House chief of staff James Baker, and, shortly afterward, Richard Bond, a top aide to Vice-President Bush, was named chief political operative at the RNC. Although it was reported that Richards was assured his job was not in jeopardy,[54] the appointment of Bond was widely interpreted as an effort by the White House to rein in the party's candid chairman and to exert greater control over the activities of the national committee.

Early in 1982 Richards's woes were compounded by the revelation that he and a business partner were delinquent on about $300,000 in loans guaranteed by the federal government. Although White House spokespersons shrugged off the matter as a private affair, the disclosure did nothing to help Richards's standing with administration officials. Finally, on October 4, 1982, Richards announced he would resign his post when his term was completed in January 1983. Richards said that criticism of his performance by White House aides had been "disruptive to the Republican Party and to the Republican National Committee."[55]

Democratic Party Aftermath

"We have been out-conceptualized, out-organized and out-financed," said new DNC chairman Charles T. Manatt of the 1980 general-election campaign.[56] In a single sentence, he summarized the agenda for the Democratic party in the wake of its overwhelming defeat at the hands of the Republicans: to develop more-compelling ideas, more-effective structures, and more-productive approaches to fund raising. Manatt's summary, however, did not determine the order in which those tasks were to be accomplished, and debate over priorities may have slowed the Democrats from accomplishing the renewal they obviously needed.

During the first few months after the election, the Democrats appeared unable to develop a central theme or to agree upon a central spokesman in their attempts to counter initiatives taken by a highly popular president and in their efforts to begin rebuilding the party. Some Democratic leaders were convinced it was time to redefine the party's goals and ideology. Said Massachusetts Sen. Paul E. Tsongas, "The old liberal dogma doesn't work any more."[57] And Harold Ickes, a campaign organizer for Sen. Edward Kennedy in the 1980 prenomination contest, said that the Democratic party had "to develop a new core of ideas."[58] Others were reluctant to abandon the party's long-time goals. In a resolution adopted immediately after the 1980 general elections, the national board of Americans for Democratic Action declared it would continue to support liberal values and fight to preserve liberal programs, which, it maintained, represented significant advancements over previous periods.[59] Still others proposed avoiding debate over party ideology and concentrating on organization and fund raising. Said long-time party activist Robert Strauss, who served as President Carter's 1980 campaign chairman, "First thing, the party has to elect itself a chairman. Then he has to find a good, professional staff and raise money."[60]

In fact debate over the direction in which the party should move and efforts to rebuild party structures and the party's fund-raising apparatus proceeded simultaneously, although not as quickly as some observers thought necessary. Throughout the year following the 1980 general election, Democratic leaders met in a variety of forums to consider the future of the party. In July 1981, members of the DNC elected in February of that year met in Denver to consider how the party could respond with better results to President Reagan's initiatives. Discussion ranged from how to achieve more effective coordination of state- and national-party fund raising to whether the party has any relevance in major elections. In October more than one hundred Democratic leaders met in Oregon to consider whether the traditional Democratic ideology was still valid. Claimed party veteran Ted Van Dyke, "We've been running on the intellectual capital left us 50 years ago by Franklin Roosevelt."[61] Forty-one Democratic senators chose West Virginia's mountains as the site of their party strategy session, which also took place in October. Democratic leaders, including senators, representatives, governors, and mayors, met in Baltimore in a National Strategy Council.[62]

New groups were formed to deal with issues, including the Center for National Policy, a Democratic think tank, formed by attorneys David M. Ifshin, William Oldaker, and others, to advise Democrats on a whole range of policy issues.[63] It is difficult to measure the results of this Democratic party self-scrutiny. The meetings were part of an extended process of introspection forced on the party by its poor performance in the 1980 elections.

Party Structures

In the meantime, the party had to turn its attention to more practical matters. Clearly party structures had to be reexamined and party leadership roles redefined. The first step in that process was the selection of a new DNC chairman to replace the outgoing John C. White, who decided not to seek another term. White had been criticized by some party members as too openly favorable to President Carter during the primary season, and the national committee itself had been blamed for contributing to the downfall of a number of Democratic candidates by paying too much attention to the presidential race.

Several groups, including the nation's Democratic governors and a number of politically active labor unions, made it clear soon after the elections that they intended to play a much stronger role in party affairs, including the selection of a party chairman.[64] A number of candidates emerged as possible contenders, particularly Charles T. Manatt, a Los Angeles attorney and banker who was serving as chairman of the party's National Finance Council; Arkansas Gov. Bill Clinton, who had been defeated in his reelection bid in November 1980; New York attorney Pat Cunningham, a former state-party chairman; and Kansas City investment banker Charles E. Curry. Manatt waged a vigorous campaign, reportedly spending $75,000 in the effort.[65] Much of the money, said to have been raised in part through contributions from personal friends, was used to fund travel costs and other expenses involved in regional meetings with DNC members.[66] Manatt promised to remain scrupulously neutral in the 1984 Democratic presidential primary contests and to expand the party's fund-raising base. He received the support of AFL-CIO president Lane Kirkland and a number of other union leaders and of Democrats of differing philosophies, such as California Gov. Jerry Brown and Texas Sen. Lloyd Bentsen. By the time the election took place in late February 1981, Manatt's opponents had withdrawn, and the California lawyer was elected by acclamation. Charles Curry was elected party treasurer, and Peter Kelly, who had served as party treasurer, was selected as national finance chairman.

Once elected, Manatt turned his attention to both the organizational and the fund-raising problems that had plagued the party. Although the new chairman played an active role in a number of the party's self-examination sessions, he moved quickly to prevent the party's midterm conference from becoming "a debating society after the general election."[67] Despite opposition from some party liberals, Manatt succeeded in scaling down the size of the conference, which was held in Philadelphia, and in moving it from December 1982 to late June 1982. He argued successfully that a larger conference, such as the one held in Memphis in 1978, would divert energy and money from the 1982 congressional elections. The Memphis conference, attended by about 1,600 delegates, reportedly cost the party about $800,000.[68] Several prominent Democrats then attracting media attention as possible presidential contenders addressed the Philadelphia conference, including Sen. Kennedy and Vice-President Mondale, as well as Sens. Alan Cranston of California, John Glenn of Ohio, Ernest Hollings of South Carolina, and Gary Hart of Colorado. Although their speeches were greeted with varying degrees of enthusiasm, none of the potential candidates emerged as the clear favorite of conference participants.

Hunt Commission

Following a mandate of the party's 1980 convention, Manatt appointed a commission to examine the presidential-selection process. The Commission on Presidential Nominations, chaired by North Carolina Gov. James B. Hunt, conducted hearings in locations throughout the nation and early in 1982 submitted to the DNC a draft of its recommendations. Late in March the DNC accepted a number of wide-ranging proposals designed to strengthen the role of the party establishment in the presidential-selection process, making it more difficult for an outsider like Jimmy Carter to capture the nomination. The new nominating rules create a special group of 550 delegates—about 15 percent of the projected total for the 1984 Democratic convention—who will be free to back the candidate of their choice regardless of the preference of voters in their states. These uncommitted delegates will include party leaders and elected officials, including up to three-fifths of the Democratic members of Congress. The new rules also permit the return of loophole primaries, which will allow states to award all of the delegates in a congressional district to the presidential candidate winning a plurality of the vote in the district. This rule undercuts the proportional-representation rule in effect in 1980, which awarded delegates on the basis of the percentage of the vote a candidate received.

The national committee accepted a Hunt Commission recommendation that the campaign calendar be shortened by requiring that all primaries and caucuses, with the exception of those in Iowa and New Hampshire, take place during a thirteen-week period between the second Tuesday in March and the second Tuesday in June. The Iowa caucuses are to start no earlier than fifteen days before the beginning of the period, and the New Hampshire primary must take place no earlier than seven days before the period begins.

Although the effort to change the party's nominating rules was intended by party officials who supported it to make the nominating process more responsive to the needs of party regulars, it also became a vehicle for the 1984 presidential contest. Backers of Walter Mondale, for example, advocated the creation of an uncommitted bloc of delegates made up of party and elected officials because they thought Mondale would have support among those officials. Backers of Sen. Edward Kennedy were less responsive to the proposal but acquiesced after the size of the uncommitted bloc was reduced from 30 percent to 15 percent. Supporters of both candidates advocated shortening the primary calendar and allowing what had been called loophole primaries because they thought both proposals would make it more difficult for lesser-known candidates to mount successful campaigns.

Party Fund Raising

Manatt and the new DNC also turned their attention to building a more effective fund-raising apparatus, particularly to broadening the party's financial base. During the 1979-1980 election cycle, the three Republican national committees enjoyed a nearly six-to-one fund-raising advantage over their Democratic counterparts. In order to begin making up the difference, DNC officials turned, as the Republicans had some years earlier, to direct mail. Early in February, before the new party chairman was chosen, Craver, Mathews, Smith & Co., a direct-mail firm that had conducted direct-mail fund drives for a number of prominent liberal groups, as well as for John Anderson's independent presidential campaign, turned down a bid from Capitol Hill Democrats to launch a fund drive on their behalf.[69] Firm president Roger Craver said he preferred to wait and see how the new party leadership evolved. Early in May, however, the firm agreed to a DNC request that it prepare the committee's direct-mail plea and materials and coordinate its drive with those of the Democratic Senate and House committees. It was agreed that the three committees initially would reinvest all of the money they received in response to direct-mail appeals in further efforts to build up their contributor files rather than use the money to pay other bills.[70] Craver hoped to expand the national committee's list from 60,000 to 250,000 by 1982 and to 500,000 by 1984[71] with the help of a list of more than 200,000 moderate-to-liberal political contributors his firm had developed during the Anderson independent campaign.

The first mailing by Craver's firm on behalf of the DNC went to 60,000 past contributors to the party's national committee. The letter, cosigned by New York's Sen. Patrick Moynihan and Arizona's Rep. Morris Udall, appealed for funds to help defeat the forces of the New Right, who, it claimed, "now control the Republican Party."[72] A later mailgram sent out over Manatt's name to 2 million persons warned of dire consequences for the Social Security system unless Democrats took action.[73] Other letters targeted to specific interest groups, such as environmentalists and feminists, contained similar messages.

Large Contributors: In order to fund party operations while they sought to broaden the party's financial base, party officials tried to increase income from larger contributors. Chairman Manatt was instrumental in establishing the Lexington Group, a new fund-raising project to be composed of 1,000 emerging young professionals and executives who would be expected to contribute $1,000 annually and raise an additional $4,000 per year for the national party.[74] In return the members of the new group, named after the Kentucky home town of its first chairman, Larry Townsend, were to par-

ticipate in meetings and seminars with party and elected officials. Manatt
hoped a new generation of party leaders and professionals would develop
from the group's membership. On behalf of the Democrats' Senate campaign committee, California's Sen. Alan Cranston organized the Leadership Circle with the goal of enlisting 200 members who would contribute

Table 9-2
Democratic National Committee Receipts and Expenditures, 1981

Receipts		
Direct mail	$1,722,423	
Prospect mail	1,001,349	
Major contributor and fund-raising events	1,919,724	
Joint fund-raising contributions	32,275	
Contributions for payment of pre-1975		
indebtedness	220,000	
Nonfederal contributions	1,093,389	
Other	118,930[a]	
Total		$6,108,090
Expenditures		
Fund-raising expenses		
Direct mail	820,812	
Prospect mail	1,277,811	
Major contributor and fund-raising events	1,080,486	
Total fund-raising expenses	3,179,109	
General and administrative expenses		
Payroll and related expenses	1,407,776	
Office and equipment rental	312,300	
Telephone and telegraph	168,565	
Professional services	407,901	
Travel	299,887	
Printing and office supplies	124,878	
Postage	72,158	
Depreciation, repairs, and maintenance	20,846	
Interest, insurance, and other taxes	38,135	
Other	82,034	
Total general and administrative expenses	2,934,480	
Political projects and constituency building		
Transfers for voter registration	15,000	
Contributions and campaign support	273,214	
Other	8,433	
Total political projects and		
constituency building	296,647	
Total expenditures		$6,410,236

Source: Information provided by the DNC.
[a]DNC officials determined that a reserve for possible vendor claims arising out of previous national conventions was excessive and recorded the balance of $68,000 as other income.

and solicit $15,000 a year and would be invited to frequent Washington meetings for in-depth briefings.[75] By the end of May 1981, Cranston, with the help of some colleagues, reportedly had reached about half his goal.[76] House Democrats created a Speaker's Club, coordinated by Rep. Frederick W. Richmond of New York, which had a goal of 600 members contributing $5,000 each. House Democrats also established a task force with the ultimate goal of gaining a bigger share of business PAC contributions for Democratic lawmakers.[77]

National Committee Receipts: The DNC's overall fund-raising goal for the 1981-1982 election cycle was $18 million, and the goals of the Democratic House and Senate campaigns for the same period were $6 million each.[78] According to reports filed with the FEC covering the first fifteen months of the cycle, however, all three committees were falling considerably short of their goals. During the period from January 1, 1981, through March 31, 1982, the DNC raised $8.9 million and spent $8.8 million; the Democratic Senatorial Campaign Committee raised $1.3 million and spent the same amount; and the Democratic Congressional Campaign Committee raised $2.8 million and spent $2.7 million.[79] The three committees combined reported a cash balance of $1 million.[80]

As indicated in table 9-2, $2.7 million of the DNC's 1981 total revenues of $6.1 million came from direct and prospect mail and $1.9 million from major contributors and fund-raising events. Nonfederal contributions accounted for an additional $1.19 million. The national committee, however, incurred significant expenses of $3.2 million in raising the money. The committee spent an additional $2.9 million on general and administrative expenses and only about $297,000 on political projects and constituency building.

The Democrats did manage to pay off at last campaign debts that the party's national committee had assumed from the 1968 prenomination campaign of Sen. Robert F. Kennedy and the general-election campaign of Vice-President Hubert H. Humphrey. According to former DNC chairman Robert Strauss, the existence of the debts, which at one time amounted to $9.3 million, had made it "harder to raise money for other things."[81] The final portion of the debt was paid off with the purchase of annuities for four remaining creditors: the American Telephone and Telegraph Company, Eastern Airlines, Trans World Airlines, and Emery Air Freight. The annuities cost the DNC $420,000; upon maturity they would pay the corporations more than $600,000 due them.[82] Federal regulations prohibited airlines and telephone companies from settling for anything less than full payment of outstanding political debts. At the time repayment of the 1968 debts was announced in June 1982, however, the DNC had an operating debt of $500,000 and was in the process of assuming responsibility for up to

$640,000 of debts left over from President Carter's 1980 general-election campaign.[83]

Because it did not enjoy the financial strength of the Republican party, the Democratic party was unable to fund activities such as the media advertising campaigns conducted by the Republicans. The Democrats, however, did accept an offer from the Turner Broadcasting System of two hours of free air time on WTBS, which was carried on 4,100 cable television systems nationwide. The June 10, 1982, program produced by the Democrats was the first political program aired on national cable television.[84] It combined discussion of issues by party leaders with party fund raising. The RNC planned to use the time offered by the cable network later.

Other Democratic Groups

In addition to the fund raising conducted by Democratic party organizations, a number of prominent Democrats organized their own fund-raising committees not formally connected with the party.

The 13.5 million member AFL-CIO, traditionally a strong source of support for Democratic candidates, also took steps after the 1980 elections to bolster its political influence. At the labor federation's convention in February 1982, organization spokesmen announced creation of the Institute of Public Affairs to assist unions in improving their communications with their own members and with the public at large through such means as public-opinion polling, direct-mail campaigns, and television programs. The new organization was to be funded from an increase in dues money from nineteen cents per member per month to twenty-seven cents by 1983.[85] The dues increase, which was expected to add about $14 million a year to the federation's treasury, also was to cover an increase in the amount allocated to the federation's COPE from $1.7 million to $3.5 million a year.[86] Finally, AFL-CIO president Lane Kirkland appointed fourteen members to a new committee created by the union organization's executive council to work out the details of involving the union directly in presidential primary campaigns and in party politics. Kirkland insisted the organization would try to work with both major political parties, but retiring political director Alexander Barkan said that although the AFL-CIO worked closely with some individual Republican candidates, "the Republicans don't want us in their operations as a national party."[87] According to a late November 1981 news report, labor unions belonging to the AFL-CIO had made direct contributions of $616,555 to the DNC and had pledged enough in addition to bring total 1981 contributions to $1 million.[88]

The 1.7 million member NEA sought to continue its program of political action, which in 1980 had put it squarely in the camp of President

Carter. The theme of its July 1982 convention was "Political Power for Educational Excellence." Said NEA political director Ken Melley, "The whole theme of [the convention] and our whole thrust this year is political activity."[89] Melley said the union was undertaking a major political training program to teach teachers how to raise funds, recruit, and get out the vote. At the time of the education group's convention, he estimated the NEA would spend between $1.5 million and $2 million on the fall 1982 campaigns.[90]

Anderson Campaign Aftermath

After sixteen months in pursuit of the presidency, the last six as an independent candidate, John Anderson understandably was reluctant to leave presidential politics behind. Although he was disappointed he had polled less than 7 percent of the nation's vote, the former Illinois congressman was aware that his election results made him eligible to receive more than $4 million in federal funds at the outset of a 1984 campaign, if he chose to run again. Shortly after the November 4 general election, it was reported that Anderson backers already were talking about possible formation of a "coalition for new ideas for responsive, far-sighted government," to keep Anderson supporters together and provide a springboard for a 1984 presidential bid.[91]

Early in the following year, Anderson let it be known he might consider a second presidential try.[92] Unlike in 1980, however, he seriously considered a possibility he had rejected outright: formation of a third party. In addition to federal subsidy money, Anderson made it clear that he would count on financial support of his 1980 contributors and avowed he was guarding his contributor list carefully.[93]

By mid-1982 Anderson still had made no firm decision about whether to form a third party and run again for the presidency. But, he claimed, the possibility never was far from his mind. In November 1982, after the midterm elections, it was reported that Anderson had sent a fund-raising letter to 50,000 persons proposing the organization of a third party in 1984.[94]

Independent Committees

Next to ceilings placed upon individual contributions to federal candidates by the FECA, the primary catalyst in the growth of independent expenditures, according to Joseph E. Cantor of the Congressional Research Service, has been the publicity generated by large independent spenders.[95] If

Cantor is right, NCPAC's Terry Dolan has made shrewd use of the media in the afterglow of his group's well-publicized efforts in the 1980 election.

One week after the defeat of NCPAC-targeted Senators McGovern, Bayh, Church, and Culver, Dolan held a well-attended news conference in Washington to announce the names of twenty senators—three of them Republicans—who were potential targets for 1982. In addition, he said some House members could be targeted. Said Dolan, "If these individuals would move noticeably to the right, they would improve their chances substantially" of avoiding a target campaign.[96]

NCPAC's actions throughout 1981-1982 seemed bent on creating enthusiasm within right-wing circles, concern among more-orthodox Republicans, and a high profile in the media. Its 1981 fund-raising letter described the senators named as targets "dangerous" because of "their liberal records" and asked contributors to help pick the 1982 targets.[97] Atop the list was Sen. Edward M. Kennedy, whom Dolan insisted could be defeated. But media reports speculated that Kennedy's name appeared mainly as a fund-raising device. Furthermore, the Massachusetts Republican party asked NCPAC to stay out of the race, fearing that a target campaign would only make a martyr of Kennedy and attract sympathy votes.[98] By August 1982, NCPAC's list was not yet complete, although most of the senators mentioned as possible targets had been dropped from consideration. Seven remained, however: Kennedy, Robert C. Byrd (D-W.Va.), Paul S. Sarbanes (D-Md.), John Melcher (D-Mont.), Lloyd Bentsen (D-Tex.), Lowell P. Weicker (R-Conn.), and Howard W. Cannon (D-Nev.). NCPAC also expanded its activities into House races. At what one commentator described as a "brassy" Washington press conference on July 22, 1981, Dolan announced that NCPAC planned to spend $500,000 to target thirteen representatives, with the goal of coercing them into voting for the Reagan tax-cut bill.

In addition to these highly publicized activities, according to the AFL-CIO newsletter *A Memo from COPE*, NCPAC had a secret "invasion" plan for Texas in 1982.[99] The newsletter said that NCPAC had budgeted $800,000 for a "destabilization" of "liberal incumbents." The program would offer friendly candidates financial support, a campaign school, instruction in the use of direct mail, and support from incumbent members of Congress. *Washington Post* columnist Jack Anderson corroborated the story in October 1981.[100]

Meantime, NCPAC was increasing its visibility by producing "American Forum," a televised interview show with Terry Dolan as its host and Rep. Robert K. Dornan (R-Calif.) as cohost. Produced as a thirteen-week series, the program aired in forty-one media markets during the 1981-1982 television season, including six of the top ten markets. For 1982-1983 the show's producers attempted to place the program in media markets representing more than 50 percent of the national viewing public.[101]

The Sarbanes Campaign

By mid-1981 NCPAC's negative advertising campaign was focused mainly
on Senators Kennedy and Sarbanes. Some $550,000 was budgeted for the
anti-Sarbanes effort; no corresponding number was set for the anti-
Kennedy campaign.[102] For NCPAC, the Sarbanes campaign represented a
chance to flex its muscles in a state within commuting distance of
Washington, D.C. For NCPAC critics, the negative campaign, which began
in March 1981, offered an opportunity to discredit the organization long
before the general-election campaigns were in full swing.

By the end of 1981 it appeared that Democrats were rallying to Sarbanes's defense and that NCPAC's campaign was making little, if any,
headway. Maryland Republicans said NCPAC failed to bring down Sarbanes because Marylanders do not like outsiders or negativism. Republican
Rep. Marjorie Holt, identified in NCPAC polls as the person most able to
defeat Sarbanes, briefly showed interest in mounting a challenge during the
summer of 1981 but then backed off. According to a Holt aide, NCPAC
advertising created a backlash that "did Sarbanes more good than it did
us."[103] In addition, Democrats for the '80s, an independent-expenditure
group created at least partly in response to NCPAC, made Sarbanes its first
cause, spending $20,000 on a radio campaign on his behalf during spring
1981 and making a direct-mail solicitation for his campaign. The Progressive Political Action Committee (ProPAC) also produced pro-Sarbanes
advertisements. Meantime NCPAC's Dolan claimed that the target campaign produced results. NCPAC polls in late 1981 showed Sarbanes's
favorable rating down 4.4 percent and his unfavorable rating up 3.6 percent.[104] NCPAC budgeted an additional $150,000 for the anti-Sarbanes
campaign in May 1982.[105]

NCPAC also found rougher going in its other 1981-1982 target campaigns. NCPAC dropped its campaign against Sen. Daniel P. Moynihan
(D-N.Y.) in August 1982 after making $77,338 in independent expenditures
for advertisements accusing Moynihan of being "a big spender." According to NCPAC spokesman Joseph Steffen, Moynihan was "stronger than
we'd thought."[106] Just one week earlier, NCPAC was effectively shut out of
the Senate race in Connecticut where liberal Sen. Lowell P. Weicker was the
focus of more than $100,000 in negative independent spending. Although
his Republican challenger, Prescott Bush, Jr., brother of the vice-president,
drew enough support at the state convention to prompt a runoff, Bush
abruptly withdrew his candidacy, leaving Weicker to run against liberal
Democratic Rep. Toby Moffett. NCPAC refused to terminate its Connecticut campaign, headed by Margaret K. "Peg" Dolan, Terry Dolan's
mother, and backed Conservative party candidate Lucien DiFazio. NCPAC
also found itself backing a long shot in Ohio after the sudden death of Rep.

John M. Ashbrook, a candidate for the Republican U.S. Senate nomination. Ashbrook, a New Right favorite, would have challenged targeted Sen. Howard M. Metzenbaum (D-Ohio) had he won the nomination. NCPAC responded by running a $60,000 advertising campaign to aid the primary write-in effort of former state Rep. Bill Ress. Ress was unsuccessful, and NCPAC pulled out of Ohio.

Nor was NCPAC having an easy time with its House target campaigns. In Oklahoma, NCPAC got off to a disastrous start in its campaign against Rep. James R. Jones (D-Okla.), chairman of the House Budget Committee, when all three of Tulsa's major television stations rejected its advertising. Although NCPAC had been turned down by stations before, Tulsa was the first market it was shut out of completely. NCPAC was forced to run its advertising on Tulsa Cable Television.[107] Furthermore, NCPAC's vaunted public-opinion polls appeared to backfire when one showed that Rep. Jones would breeze to a 59 to 20 percent victory if matched against Tulsa's conservative mayor, Jim Inhofe. Far from being encouraged to run, Inhofe complained about the poll to Dolan. In addition, the local media chided NCPAC about its issue polls, charging that they misstated Jones's positions on military and social spending. Despite these gaffes, the Jones campaign was still wary enough to form a group, Oklahomans for Truth, to respond to NCPAC's charges whenever necessary.[108]

Legal Challenges

Understandably NCPAC has been at the center of considerable legal controversy. One objection continually raised against it is that it engages the services of persons who also have worked for opponents of targeted candidates. In advisory opinion 1979-80, the FEC ruled that NCPAC was permitted to have a relationship with a vendor who also was an agent for a Republican candidate for office while the organization ran an independent campaign against a Democrat running for the same office during the primary season. The FEC reasoned that primary winners are not elected to legal office but, rather, are awarded the nomination of their parties. Therefore Democrats and Republicans do not run against each other until they receive their respective parties' nominations. In addition, the opinion noted that to prove coordination between an independent group and a campaign, the common vendor must be an agent of a federal candidate. An agent is defined as a person who has authorization to make expenditures for the federal candidate.[109] A similar complaint was filed against NCPAC in 1981.[110]

NCPAC has had to defend itself against other charges that it is not truly independent of federal political campaigns. In May 1980, the South Dakota

Democratic party filed a formal complaint with the FEC asking it to strip NCPAC of its independent expenditure rights on the grounds that it was connected with the campaign of McGovern's opponent and eventual successor, James Abdnor. People for an Alternative to McGovern, a group funded by NCPAC, began its anti-McGovern advertising campaign just two days before Abdnor announced his candidacy. The Democrats felt the timing between the two events was too close to be coincidental.[111] The complaint was dismissed by the FEC on a four-to-two vote, despite the recommendation of the FEC's legal counsel that there was reason to believe that the law was violated and that the case warranted further examination.[112]

NCPAC's target campaign of House opponents of the Reagan tax-cut bill also produced a legal backlash. Rep. Stephen L. Neal (D-N.C.) accused NCPAC of blackmail and bribery after the independent group contacted him in July 1981 and said it would spend $40,000 in positive advertising if he were to vote for the tax cut; the advertising would be used against him if he did not vote in that way. Neal charged that NCPAC violated the federal statute regarding bribery of public officials, which makes it illegal to give anything of value to a public official "for or because of any official act performed or to be performed."[113] Noting that Neal voted against the tax-cut bill anyway, the Justice Department said the offer would have constituted a bribe if it had caused him to change his mind and vote for the tax cut.[114]

Advisory Opinion Requests

Instead of complaining to the Justice Department, Rep. Les Aspin (D-Wis.), another tax-cut target, requested an advisory opinion from the FEC. According to Robert Henzl, Aspin's campaign committee chairman, the Congressman received a letter from NCPAC chairman Dolan shortly before the group planned to run advertisements criticizing Aspin for what they presumed would be his vote against the tax cut. According to Henzl, Dolan offered to withdraw the advertisements if Aspin voted in favor of the tax cut and to run newspaper and radio advertisements applauding him for his vote.[115] Aspin contended that Dolan's offer constituted a contribution because it promised to run a given amount of advertising, positive or negative, depending on the course of action Aspin took. Henzl noted that federal campaign law does not specify that a campaign contribution be positive; it merely defines it as "something of value" given to influence election to any federal office. The FEC, however, sided with NCPAC in advisory opinion 1981-44, saying there was no contribution made by NCPAC because Aspin did not accept "anything of value."[116]

NCPAC also survived a request to the FEC by the Democratic Senatorial Campaign Committee asking that groups making negative independent expenditures be required to inform their contributors that tax credits might not be available if the group makes substantial negative independent expenditures. This request followed a 1980 IRS letter ruling that made the tax status of groups making substantial negative expenditures questionable.[117] Also, critics have claimed that NCPAC should be deprived of its favorable tax status because it has engaged in lobbying activities. According to one political trade publication, a NCPAC staff member "exposed his organization's tax status to challenge" when he registered as a lobbyist.[118]

NCPAC has been charged with compromising its independent status by collaborating with the White House and by its practice of first recruiting candidates to run against Democrats and then, after breaking ties with the recruited candidates, conducting polls, mailings, and advertisements on their behalf as an independent committee. The first action was touched off by a comment made by Edward J. Rollins in November 1981, shortly after he replaced Lyn Nofziger as deputy assistant to the president for political affairs. Said Rollins of NCPAC and similar New Right groups, "We will be meeting with them regularly, to tell them where we're heading" and to find out what they are doing.[119]

NCPAC has responded to its critics with charges of its own. On December 15, 1981, it filed a $5 million lawsuit in federal court charging thirteen television stations with conspiring with various political figures to keep NCPAC commercials off the air. Named as defendants were Senators Thomas F. Eagleton (D-Mo.), Wendell Ford (D-Ky.), Edward M. Kennedy, Daniel P. Moynihan, and John Melcher; Representatives Tony Coelho (D-Calif.) and James Wright (D-Tex.); and Eagleton aide Ed Quick.[12] NCPAC also filed separate $5 million suits against each legislator. Two complaints were filed with the FCC pertaining to the broadcasters asking the regulatory body to guarantee NCPAC access to the airwaves. The FCC refused.[121]

New Right Fund Raising

Despite these problems, NCPAC, and the New Right in general, continued to generate large sums of money in the 1981-1982 election cycle. NCPAC raised $4,143,000 during 1981 and $4,781,000 during the first ten months of 1982. This figure was exceeded only by the National Congressional Club, which raised $9,054,000 during 1981 and the first ten months of 1982. This robust financial picture held true for the five largest New Right PACs—the National Congressional Club, NCPAC, Fund for a Conservative Majority, Citizens for the Republic, and the Committee for the Survival of a Free Congress—which raised a combined total of $12,576,000 in 1981 and added

$12,319,000 during the first ten months of 1982.[122] Also, nonconnected PACs continued to make heavy use of the independent expenditure tool in 1981 and the first half of 1982. Such groups spent $228,000 independently in favor of federal candidates and $2,473,000 against such candidates.[123]

Although corporate PACs may make independent expenditures, few chose to do so in 1980, spending only $18,190 overall, and just $14,161 on congressional races. Figures for the first eighteen months of the 1981-1982 cycle show little change in this pattern. A somewhat greater amount likely will come from business-related trade associations, which spent $292,000 on independent expenditures in 1980; some $271,000 of that total went toward congressional races. The leader among nonideological committees making independent expenditures probably will be AMPAC, which spent $172,000 on independent expenditures for fourteen congressional candidates in 1980. Corporations and trade, membership, and health groups made independent expenditures totaling $5,035 and $59,632, respectively, through mid-1982.[124]

Independent expenditures favoring Democratic candidates in 1980 lagged far behind such expenditures on behalf of Republicans. Labor unions were not large independent spenders in 1980; union PACs spent $54,000 independently in 1980, most of it on the presidential race. Only $16,087 in independent expenditures were made on congressional races.[125] Through the first eighteen months of the 1981-1982 election cycle, independent expenditures by labor totaled only $10,971.[126] The task of offsetting the independent power of the New Right, and specifically NCPAC, in congressional campaigns appears to have fallen to a handful of pro-Democrat independent committees.

Democratic Response

The loss of the presidency, thirty-three House seats, and twelve Senate seats in 1980 sent Democrats of the center and left searching for both the causes and the cure. Some media reports credited the staggering Democratic losses to the activity of New Right independent-expenditure groups, which skillfully collected hundreds of thousands of mostly small donations nationwide using a combination of computerized direct mailings and impassioned political rhetoric. With its sometimes-outrageous fund-raising letters and hard-hitting independent target campaigns, the New Right found it could defy the normal laws of American political gravity: the more extreme NCPAC and the others became, the more wealthy and powerful they became.

More thoughtful members of the media and most of the Democratic establishment largely disputed the influence of the New Right in all but a handful of races. Instead they point to the lack of a coherent party ideology and a shortage of new ideas. Furthermore, while the Republicans were rebuilding their party apparatus in the wake of Watergate, the Democrats were allowing theirs to atrophy.

These two strains represent the Democratic response to the Republican gains of 1980. On the one hand, independent groups have sprung up specifically to counteract the New Right. This reaction, too, has two variants. First, there is the approach of the Progressive PAC, or ProPAC, which targeted a handful of conservative Republicans for negative independent expenditure campaigns. Second, groups such as Democrats for the '80s take a defensive approach. Instead of mimicking New Right tactics, these groups aim to defend targeted Democrats through a combination of positive independent expenditures, direct contributions, and counterattacks against the New Right groups themselves.

The large 1980 losses have given rise to a number of PACs, think tanks, and quasi-party committees designed to revitalize the ideological and intellectual underpinnings of the party. These groups have two purposes, one internal and the other external. Externally, several of these groups are attempting to construct a coherent alternative program to that of the Reagan administration; internally, they seek to concentrate intraparty dialogue on particular ideological positions or, in the case of PACs founded by Sen. Edward M. Kennedy and former Vice-President Walter Mondale, around particular party leaders.

The new groups join the well-established National Committee for an Effective Congress, the sole liberal independent PAC showing substantial financial activity during the 1979-1980 election cycle. Founded in 1948 by New York reform forces, the NCEC raised $1,571,000 and spent $1,420,000 during the 1979-1980 election cycle. Traditionally the organization has aided candidates with direct contributions and services that include polling data and precinct voter-targeting studies. The NCEC also has recruited candidates and provided campaign workers,[127] activities that would make any independent expenditures undertaken by the group open to legal challenge. The NCEC continued to be the leading independent liberal fundraiser in the 1981-1982 cycle, collecting $2,132,000 through October 1982.[128]

For 1981-1982 the NCEC hoped to contribute $1.2 million in cash and campaign services. Such in-kind services are subject to the contribution limits imposed by the FECA: $5,000 for the primary and $5,000 for the general election. In addition to supporting seventy House and twelve Senate candidates up for reelection in 1982, all Democrats, the group's Target 1982 campaign selected for defeat five Republican senators and sixty-three congressmen, twenty-one Democrats, most from the South, and forty-two Republicans. Because the NCEC does not make independent expenditures, the organization's target effort amounts to a virtual declaration of support for candidates opposing the targeted Democrats in the primary or opposing the targeted Republicans in the general election, providing they share the NCEC's liberal philosophy.[129]

New Democratic Groups

Several new groups joined the NCEC in support of moderate and liberal Democratic candidates in 1982. The Progressive Political Action Committee was established in January 1981 by labor-oriented political consultant Victor Kamber as a direct opponent to NCPAC. ProPAC formed its own list of targeted Senate and House candidates in 1982, including Senators Orrin G. Hatch (R-Utah) and Harrison "Jack" Schmitt (R-N.M.), and Representatives Phil Gramm (D-Tex.) and John LeBoutillier.[130] In addition, ProPAC launched a target campaign against New Right Sen. Jesse Helms (R-N.C.), although he is not up for reelection until 1984. The group also ran advertisements critical of its arch-rival, NCPAC.

But ProPAC's plan for adopting the negative independent campaign tactics of the New Right appears not to have captured the enthusiasm of liberal political figures or contributors weary of such practices. For example, in response to ProPAC's target campaign against Sen. Hatch, Utah Democratic chairman Michael T. Miller has demanded that the independent group stay out of the state, charging that ProPAC's negative campaigning could likely backfire and reduce the chances of defeating Hatch.[131] And although it had hoped to raise $1.5 million by early 1982, ProPAC could manage only to take in $312,000 through October 1982. The group's plans began to go awry early in 1981 when ProPAC asked thirty liberal political figures and celebrities to sign its hard-hitting fund-raising letter. All of them declined, and the letter was eventually signed by Mathews.[132]

Democrats for the '80s, founded by Pamela Harriman and her husband, Democratic elder statesman W. Averell Harriman, has sought to defend Democrats targeted by the New Right in two ways: by running advertising campaigns defending the candidates' records and by publishing materials that call attention to alleged inaccuracies, half-truths, and overheated rhetoric from the New Right. Democrats for the '80s responded to NCPAC's negative campaign against Sen. Paul Sarbanes with a $20,000 radio campaign defending the senator. In addition, the group published a brochure, "The New Right: A Threat to America's Future," which outlines from a Democratic perspective the activities of various New Right groups.[133]

Democrats for the '80s relies on two methods of fund raising: $1,000-a-plate dinner parties and direct mailings undertaken by Roger Craver. Each of the group's dinner parties focuses on one issue—taxes, energy, the federal budget, defense—and includes well-known experts and Democratic political figures. A March 31, 1981 panel on the economy featured economist Walter Heller, Sen. Lloyd Bentsen (D-Tex.), and former Vice-President Mondale.[134] The group's most successful fund raiser to date was a $500-a-plate ninetieth birthday celebration for Averell Harriman, held November 11, 1981, a well-publicized event that grossed more than $750,000. The DNC received a little more than half that gross after expenses.[135] Democrats for the '80s raised $963,000 through October 1982; its share of the birthday celebration, itemized as a separate fund, was $365,000.[136] The group expected to have about $500,000 to give to fifty to sixty House candidates and ten to fifteen Senate candidates.[137]

Capitalizing on its position deep within the Democratic establishment, Democrats for the '80s published at a cost of $70,000 a 400-page "Democratic Fact Book." It represents an attempt to lay out a party-line criticism of the Reagan administration and the Republican Senate while offering an alternative Democratic agenda. Written as an issue manual for Democratic candidates, copies of the book were handed out to delegates to the party's June 1982 midterm convention in Philadelphia.[138]

The Fund for a Democratic Majority (FDM) was founded by Sen. Edward M. Kennedy in 1981 and was considered by many to be a stalking horse for a 1984 Kennedy presidential campaign. Building upon a mailing list of 50,000 contributors to Kennedy's 1980 presidential campaign, the San Francisco firm of Parker-Dodd sent out FDM's first mailing in May 1981. According to Jack Leslie, the group's director, some 30,000 new contributors had been located by early 1982.[139] FDM seeks to aid progressive candidates through direct contributions and endorsements by Kennedy. Through mid-1982, the group had contributed $49,812 to federal candidates.

The benefits of FDM to Kennedy, had he made another presidential bid, would have been fourfold. First, he could help elect liberal Democrats to office who not only share his basic political philosophy but who, once elected, would be in his debt. Second, FDM could legally pay travel costs for Kennedy if he chose to fly around the country endorsing various candidates, thereby keeping his name before the public. Third, the group could find new potential Kennedy contributors. And last, FDM serves as a magnet for experienced campaign workers who worked for Kennedy in his 1980 presidential bid.[140] FDM surpassed its 1981 fund-raising goal of $500,000, collecting $861,000. It raised $1,265,000 during the first ten months of 1982.[141]

Similarly the Committee for the Future of America is considered a launching pad for former Vice-President Walter Mondale's presidential aspirations. In addition to making direct contributions to candidates, the commitee plans to assist its friends with campaign strategy, research, and fund raising.[142] Although the committee raised most of its early money at two receptions—once in Minneapolis, the other in Chicago—featuring Mondale as the speaker, it also mailed 250,000 fund-raising letters in 1981. The committee raised $678,000 in 1981 and $1,293,000 during the first ten months of 1982.[143] But more than anything, the Committee for the Future of America serves to keep Mondale on the road campaigning for his political allies and himself. The former vice-president was scheduled to begin full-time campaigning on July 1, 1982.

Independent Action was founded in 1981 by direct-mail specialist Roger Craver; Rep. Morris K. Udall signed the group's early fund-raising letters and is considered to be instrumental in its establishment. Although the group netted $10,000 at a 1981 fund-raising event in Washington, it has since relied exclusively upon direct mailings. Independent Action sent out forty to fifty mailings in 1981 totaling about 1.5 million letters. These mailings, plus the lone fund raiser, brought in $684,000 in 1981 and an additional $415,000 through October 1982.[144] Coyle said the group hoped to aid fifty to sixty candidates. Contributions totaled $55,479 through mid-1982.[145] In addition, Independent Action planned to make some minor independent expenditures for favored candidates plus one long-range negative campaign against Sen. Jesse Helms, who is not up for reelection until 1984. The anti-Helms mailings in December 1981 and January 1982, totaling 30,000 letters each, were at least partly motivated by a desire to stimulate fund raising.[146]

The Parker-Coltrane PAC was founded by Rep. John Conyers (D-Mich.), to further the political careers of southern Blacks, who Conyers feels receive disproportionately few PAC dollars. Although the need seemed to exist for such a PAC, Conyers realized the group could not survive through direct-mail solicitation: blacks have never been big political givers, mainly for economic reasons. Conyers devised an alternative method of fund raising: he asked a number of prominent black entertainers to donate their time and talents. The response was positive, and the Parker-Coltrane PAC (named after jazz saxophonists Charlie Parker and John Coltrane) was registered with the FEC in May 1981.[147] The PAC's first fund raiser was held January 18, 1982, with singer Nancy Wilson at the Blues Alley jazz club in Georgetown. At $100 per ticket, the event raised more than $10,000. Additional events were scheduled in Chicago, New York, Los Angeles, and Atlanta. Parker-Coltrane also planned a modest direct-mail campaign, hoping to raise $100,000 through the mail in 1982.[148]

The Senate Democratic Leadership Circle, founded by Sen. Alan Cranston, was qualified as a party committee with the FEC and is an adjunct to the Democratic Senatorial Campaign Committee. Cranston, who has made known his presidential aspirations, is seeking a membership of 200 persons who will donate $15,000 annually. According to Theodore Waller, executive director of the DSCC, members are invited to frequent

Washington meetings where they receive "unique, in-depth exposure in the political process."[149] By the end of 1981, the group was more than halfway to reaching its goal of $3 million, having raised $1,526,000.[149]

Americans for Common Sense (ASC), a group founded by former Sen. George McGovern, is attempting to build grass-roots support for its liberal agenda through more than 400 state and local chapters, most of them located in the West and Midwest. According to executive director George Cunningham, a former McGovern administrative assistant, ACS is intended "to act as a counterforce against the conservatives, raising a dialogue on the issues."[150]

In 1981 McGovern, Cunningham, and other ACS members pursued this goal by giving hundreds of speeches and interviews and by participating in radio call-in shows rebutting the New Right's politics and tactics. In addition, McGovern visited thirty states in 1981 for fund-raising purposes. So far, the group has claimed 427 active chapters with more than 100,000 members paying an average of $18 to join.[151] In 1982 the group planned to distribute a greater number of policy papers to its membership and the media on major political issues.

People for the American Way, a group founded by television producer Norman Lear, seeks to build grass-roots support to counteract the right-wing religious movement spawned by the Moral Majority and similar groups. People for the American Way has attempted to build a sort of moral popular front, uniting secular and religious leaders who oppose efforts by the religious Right to impose their moral codes upon the public at large. In addition, the group has formed a separate agency, the Project for Electoral Accountability, to monitor independent expenditure campaigns.[152]

Growing Pains

The largest problem the new liberal PACs faced in 1981-1982 was that of simultaneously attempting to build a large contributor list and committing large sums to candidates in order to offset the immediate threat posed by the New Right. In particular, the new liberal PACs, relying on fund raising by direct mail, are finding that process so expensive that it drastically cuts the amount available to aid candidates. In this respect, the liberal PACs are at a severe disadvantage compared with the New Right PACs, which have had several years to build and refine their mailing lists. For example, Sen. Kennedy's FDM spent some $636,000 in 1981, but about 55 percent of that figure went toward direct-mail costs. A similar story is reported by Roger Craver, the direct-mail specialist who helped found Independent Action. In 1981 the group was able to raise $684,000 against expenditures of $673,000; of the amount spent, only $16,150 was contributed to candidates. Even the well-established NCEC spent more than it took in during 1981, largely because of the expensive list-building process. This spending allowed the NCEC to identify approximately 17,000 new contributors in 1981; the group had about 80,000 contributors during the 1979-1980 election cycle. In an attempt to cut costs and pool influence, account executives at the direct-mail firm of Craver, Mathews and Smith, which directs the mailings for both the NCEC and Independent Action, have suggested that the two PACs undertake joint mailings and other efforts.[153]

Reform

Nearly all sides in the independent-expenditure controversy agree on one point: there is room for substantial reform. The main concern of many reform advocates is that the FECA, in reducing the influence of large contributors to candidates, has instead created a new type of "fat cat." William C. Oldaker, a former general counsel to the FEC, maintains that the large sums of money accumulated by independent committees amplifies the clout of the committees' leaders rather than the voices of individual contributors. "The leaders of these so-called 'independent committees' are the new 'fat cats.' "[154]

NCPAC's Dolan believes independent expenditures are the unfortunate consequence of an overregulated political system and sees the rise of liberal PACs as a logical outcome of the system. He suggests that severe restriction, or abolition, of the FEC should be considered before independent groups become an institutionalized part of campaign financing. According to Dolan, if individuals and committees were permitted to make larger contributions directly to candidates, there would be no need for independent expenditure programs.[155] Other conservatives maintain that only the disclosure provisions of the FECA should be allowed to stand.[156]

RNC chairman Richard Richards claimed that New Right target campaigns "hurt us more than [they] help us."[157] Richards's continued criticism prompted DNC chairman Charles T. Manatt to write to Richards in early 1981 suggesting that the two committees undertake a bipartisan study on ways to curb independent expenditure campaigns. Richards replied that he would not join a study that singled out independent groups but would agree to "a joint effort to study election reform across the board."[158] Some campaign experts feel Richards's interest in curbing independent expenditure groups is linked to a desire to divert New Right money to the party. Plans for the joint study fell apart, however, in May 1981, and the committees decided to undertake separate investigations. Manatt chose Theodore Sorenson, former counsel to President Kennedy, to head the DNC probe. Richards tapped Ernest Angelo, the GOP's Texas national committeeman, to lead its Election Reform Committee.[159]Sorenson reported his group's findings to the House Administration Committee task force on elections on July 28, 1982, telling the committee that independent expenditure groups "are accountable to no one" and use "big money for their extreme ideological ends."[160]

Joseph E. Cantor of the Congressional Research Service says that although most observers agree that FEC regulations are part of the problem, the majority propose a more moderate solution than Dolan's. Raising the individual and committee contribution limits has been widely suggested, as has a lifting of restrictions for candidates against whom independent expenditures are used.[161] Another suggestion has been to limit the use of broadcast time to candidate-authorized announcements, but this would certainly encounter objections on First Amendment grounds. A more constitutionally acceptable method of reducing the effects of negative independent spending has been suggested by Sen. Eagleton, who asked the FCC to provide equal time to any candidate attacked in a paid advertisement by an independent group, even if the advertisement does not directly support the candidate's opponent.[162]

The liberal Committee for American Principles submitted a rulemaking petition to the FEC in November 1981, asking for a more narrowly constructed interpretation of activities a group may engage in and remain independent. It asked the IRS to work with the FEC in promulgating such a rule. The FEC, in turn, asked for comments.[163] In arguing for a broader rule addressing what constitutes a link between PACs and independent expenditure committees, former Senator McGovern commented, "A federal election campaign is not a closely held enterprise," and noted that almost any campaign staff person could reveal to "independent parties" how so-called independent expenditures might be helpful.[164]

Two other former NCPAC targets, Birch Bayh and Frank Church, criticized the FEC's definition of an agent as a person who has expenditure responsibilities on a political campaign committee. Under the current rules, an independent expenditure committee must be linked with such an agent to forfeit its independent status. According to the two former senators, the regulations make it possible for independent committees to coordinate their expenditures with a campaign with the help of information from campaign staff persons or volunteers not authorized to spend campaign funds.[165]

Another proposal for reform has been made by Sen. Daniel K. Inouye. In November 1981 Inouye, a member of the Joint Leadership Task Force, asked the Senate Rules Committee to draw tighter limits on independent expenditures. In a letter to Rules Committee chairman Charles McC. Mathias (R-Md.), Inouye said that the current independent-expenditure regulations are "threadbare, offering little guidance to candidates, political committees or the general public."[166]

Inouye suggested legislation that would deny independence to a group making any contact with a candidate or his agents at any time, including the period prior to the candidate's decision to seek federal office. (In 1980, NCPAC was able to encourage several Republicans to run after showing them polling data and promising financial support; once these candidates announced, NCPAC switched over to making independent expenditures.) Inouye also proposed an FEC mechanism for resolving charges of unfair campaign tactics. The FEC would make public any complaints upon their receipt and appoint a fact finder from the American Arbitration Association. The fact finder would have the same investigatory power as the FEC and would make a report within sixty days, or fifteen days if within two months of the election. The FEC would then make the report public within three days. Those persons making the complaints would be liable for the fact-finding costs, but candidates could raise funds separately to cover these costs. Any interested party would be able to present evidence to the fact finders.[167]

Media Coverage of the Election

Throughout this book, the use of media advertising by candidates, particularly broadcast media advertising, has been amply noted. According to the Television Bureau of Advertising, about $90.6 million was spent in 1980 to buy advertising time on television alone for candidates, political parties, and ballot issues, $20.7 million of it on the networks.[168] The bureau estimated that close to $100 million would be spent for that purpose in 1982 in conjunction with the midterm elections.[169] But the media spent far greater amounts covering the 1980 elections. According to one television commentator, the three commercial television networks alone spent some $150 million to cover the 1980 campaigns, and other news organizations spent "countless tens of millions of dollars" more.[170] There is no doubt that media advertising is a pivotal component in most federal-election campaigns, particularly presidential campaigns, and a significant factor in increasing campaign costs. Nor is there any doubt that the media remain fascinated with election contests and are willing to spend prodigious amounts to cover them.

As in other election years, in 1980 the media were criticized for their campaign coverage, often by the candidates themselves,[171] but also by others.[172] One element of media coverage that was the subject of widespread criticism was the commercial networks' practice of projecting a winner in the presidential contest before all the polls were closed.

As early as four o'clock on the afternoon of November 4, the three commercial televison networks knew, as a result of their exit pollings

throughout the day, that Ronald Reagan would decisively win the presidential contest.[173] The decision, then, was when to announce the results.
Custom and good sense required that the announcement be delayed until
projections based on polls and computer analyses could be certified as fact.
At 8:15 P.M. Eastern Standard Time, NBC, unable to hold back any
longer, announced that Reagan was indeed the projected winner. The other
two networks followed suit in relatively short order. At 9:52 EST, despite
objections from House Speaker Thomas O'Neill that polls in California
were still open, President Carter officially conceded victory to his
Republican opponent.

Early in the following year, senators and congressmen concerned about
the possible effect the network's early projections and Carter's early concession may have had on the election results, particularly in senatorial and congressional races, held a number of hearings on the influence of media
coverage on the national electoral process.[174] A flurry of legislation was introduced to eliminate the problems perceived to be caused by media projections of election results before polls close. Some of the proposed legislation
would have required that polls open and close at the same time across the
country. Other legislation would restrict the release of election results until
all the polls close.

A study conducted by the University of Michigan, commissioned in part
by ABC News, seemed to legitimate the concern that motivated the congressional hearings and the proposed legislation. According to the study, about
one-fourth of those who planned to vote in the 1980 presidential election
later in the day decided not to after they had heard the network projections
or Carter's subsequent concession.[175] It was not clear at the time the study
was released whether the networks would voluntarily change their coverage
techniques or be hindered from continuing them by force of legislation.

The Financial Future

The 1980 election results brought a decade of election reform to an
undeniable close. In the early 1970s, election reform had occupied center
stage. Reformers succeeded in having enacted into law several far-reaching
measures designed to open federal campaign financing to public scrutiny, to
encourage political giving from a broader constituency, and to reduce the
influence of large contributors and special interests on electoral outcomes.
Their successes, however, created a backlash that led to efforts to enact
amendments designed to lighten the burden the laws imposed on candidates

and political committees and to litigation designed to temper the new laws by testing their constitutionality. By the end of the 1970s, the initiative clearly had passed from the reformers to those most directly affected by the reform laws: officeholders, political parties, and major interest groups.

The 1980 elections, which brought to office a national administration pledged to alleviate the burdens imposed by government regulations, further eclipsed the cause of election reform. There is a widespread perception among reform advocates that energies once devoted to supporting passage of reform policies must now be concentrated on activities to forestall countermeasures that threaten to reverse those policies.

Paradoxically, the 1980 elections, which caused a good measure of dismay among the ranks of political campaign reformers, may hold the key to the most likely reform in the near future: political-party renewal. The renewal of partisan Republicanism is best exemplified in the painstaking development of a potent and well-financed RNC, which probably proved more important in determining many races in 1980 than other, more highly publicized factors, such as increased PAC giving and the activities of the New Right and its evangelical allies. This renewal recalls the useful role parties once played in election campaigns and suggest they might be able to do so once again, given the opportunity. The response of the Democratic party in the wake of the 1980 elections to strengthen its fund-raising and party-building programs indicates the party has taken that lesson of the elections to heart.

The Decline of the Parties

Several factors that have contributed to the decline of the political parties —replacement of party-controlled patronage by civil service, the ascendancy of television as a means of reaching voters, a more highly educated electorate, the democratization of the presidential nominating process— have received ample description and analysis.[176] The decline of the parties also is a story of missed opportunities. In the many years that the Democratic party controlled Congress and occasionally the White House, the party never built stable financial constituencies but continued to depend on labor support, large contributors, and the power of incumbency to see it through in election after election. The Republican party, particularly in the years of the Nixon presidency, existed largely to serve the needs of the party's presidential wing, while problems faced by the party at other levels suffered from inattention.

Political-party decline also is, in part, a consequence of election reform gone awry. Reform laws intended to increase citizen participation in election campaigns and decrease so-called special-interest influence have served to reinforce candidate-centered politics to the detriment of the parties and the purposes they serve. The Revenue Act of 1971 allowed tax credits or deductions for contributions to candidates and parties. (The Revenue Act of 1978 eliminated the tax deduction while increasing the tax credit.) Since the act made no distinction between the two types of contributions, parties have been forced to compete with their own candidates for available campaign money. In addition the FECA of 1971 made federal candidates self-contained units for purposes of disclosure of monies received and spent. The 1971 Revenue Act and the FECA amendments of 1974 had the same effect on presidential candidates for purposes of public financing, thus isolating them from their parties. The 1974 amendments also imposed limits on the amount of money national- and state-party organizations may contribute to federal-election campaigns. (Some limits on state and local party groups subsequently were lifted by the 1979 FECA amendments.) The 1976 FECA amendments imposed an annual limit on the amount an individual may contribute to the national committee of a political party.

Curbing the PACs?

There is little doubt that candidate-centered politics and growing interest-group pressure on members of Congress have made it increasingly difficult to mobilize effective congressional majorities. Some critics have proposed solving the problem by extending public funding to congressional campaigns, thus reducing the possibility that interest groups could curry favor through political contributions. Efforts to enact such legislation, however, have reached an impasse, and it is clear that in this era of fiscal conservatism, a new spending program to help fund political campaigns will not be enacted.

Other critics propose to diminish the perceived influence of PACs by lowering the amount the committees may contribute to federal candidates, now $5,000 per candidate per election, and placing an aggregate limit on the amount candidates may receive from all PACs. The fate of legislation introduced in both the ninety-sixth and the ninety-seventh congresses to accomplish those purposes was described in chapter 2. There is little chance such bills regarding PACs will be enacted in the near future, given the permissive atmosphere, the nonregulatory mode, that currently prevails at the federal level. Further, such legislation would be counterproductive in the face of rising campaign costs and the unlikely prospect that a budget-conscious Congress would enact legislation providing for alternative sources of funds. Finally, the impact of contribution limitations on certain groups would be greater than on others, causing more disparity and imbalance than now exists between business and labor PACs and between conservative and liberal PACs.

A better means of offsetting the development of PACs without unduly restricting their growth or limiting their contributions would be to increase the $1,000 individual contribution limit to $5,000 and to repeal the annual $25,000 overall contribution limit for individuals. This approach not only would compensate for the damaging effect of inflation on the ability of individuals to participate financially in political campaigns; it also would begin to counterbalance PAC contributions and reduce financial pressures on candidates by providing them with alternatives to PAC donations. At the same time, it would respect the right of interest groups to organize and to seek to influence the political process and the values of diversity and increased participation that PACs bring to our political system. Further, raising the contribution limits for individuals would make independent expenditure committees less attractive to contributors because it would open up to them a direct channel of support for the candidates of their choice.

Strengthening the Parties

Reducing special-interest influence in election campaigns by increasing the amount individuals may contribute to candidates still leaves unaddressed the matter of achieving effective congressional majorities, of establishing coherent public policies. Clearly parties can become more effective, broadly based groups to which candidates can turn for the support they currently receive from narrowly focused PACs. Parties can be conceptualized as intermediate structures between policymakers and the individuals and organized groups who help them achieve office by supporting them financially and who then seek to make their voices heard.

Political parties once served such a mediating purpose, and the revival of the Republican party in the 1980 elections suggests they can do so once again. This is not to suggest a return to the days of Tammany Hall and smoke-filled rooms but rather the development of modern parties based on democratic principles, open and welcoming, interested in issues, but seeking to accommodate conflicting interests.

Several proposals already have been offered to help accomplish this goal. The recommendations of the Democratic party's Hunt Commission are clearly intended to give the party establishment greater control over the selection of its presidential nominee. In addition, although the campaign finance reforms of the early 1970s are by no means the sole, or even the major, cause of the decline of the parties, some proposals include suggestions to amend the FECA in ways that would strengthen the parties. For example, former RNC chairman Richard Richards suggested the following changes:

> Eliminate limits on party committee spending on behalf of candidates or substantially increase those expenditure limits.

> Allow all party committees to spend unlimited amounts on such items as buttons and bumper stickers for voluntary activity on behalf of candidates and on such activities as get-out-the-vote drives. (Currently only state- and local-party groups are allowed to do so.)

> Increase party committee contribution limits to House and Senate candidates.

> Exempt party committee legal, accounting, and administration expenses from the law's definition of contribution or expenditure.[177]

Other advocates of political-party renewal go even further. For example, participants in discussions held in April 1982 on the future of political parties sponsored by the American Assembly agreed that all limits on contributions to parties ought to be eliminated, as well as limitations on how much parties can contribute to candidate committees.[178] A recent study of presidential campaign financing conducted by the Campaign Finance Study Group of Harvard's Institute of Politics recommends that qualified national-party committees be given a modest level of public funding at the start of the election year, which might be used to underwrite party-building activities.[179] The study group earlier recommended that a separate tax credit be established for contributions to political parties and that taxpayers be allowed to deduct 100 percent of such contributions from their total tax liability up to a maximum of $50.00.[180]

In mid-1982, Rep. Bill Frenzel (R-Minn.) introduced legislation that would revise a number of FECA provisions. Among the changes he sought were several he intended to strengthen the role of the political parties.[181] Under Frenzel's bill, a new PAC category would be created for political parties, and the parties would be permitted to raise money from any source without limit for the purpose of establishing and administering their PACs and raising funds for them. Parties would be required to make semiannual disclosures of their party PAC fund raising, and the PACs themselves would be allowed to contribute up to $15,000 per election to federal candidates. In keeping with Richards's recommendations, Frenzel's bill also would extend to national-party committees the permission state- and local-party committees already have to spend unlimited amounts on campaign materials used in conjunction with volunteer activities. It would extend to political parties at all levels permission to spend unlimited amounts on voter-registration and get-out-the-vote drives. The bill also would raise the amount national political-party committees could spend on behalf of presidential candidates from two cents to three cents per voting-age population.

Advocates of such measures maintain they would help the parties assist candidates not only through direct contributions but also through provision of services and the latest in campaign technology. Parties are ongoing organizations that, in an era of high campaign costs, can provide economies of size by pooling computer, polling, and other campaign services for use by presidential and other candidates on the ticket, thus saving candidates significant funds. Such party assistance would diminish some of the dependence candidates now have on interest-group contributions, as well as the appearance of undue interest-group influence. Currently PACs often have direct access to successful candidates they support, once those candidates are elected, without the mediation of the party acting as honest broker to reconcile the conflicting claims of all the individuals and groups seeking to influence public policy.

Parties with more funds to help candidates might earn the respect, and eventually the loyalty, of party candidates. Stronger parties would strengthen the political system by encouraging elected representatives not only to serve their constituencies but also to serve the public interest as formulated by their parties in terms of reasonably coherent programs.

Political scientist Michael J. Malbin proposes an alternative approach to building up the parties.[182] Malbin would build up the parties by first strengthening the parties' grass roots. To do so he advocates extending the provisions contained in the 1979 FECA amendments that allow state- and local-party committees to spend unlimited amounts on volunteer activities on behalf of presidential candidates to include such activities on behalf of congressional candidates as well. This change in the law would encourge parties to establish ongoing, grass-roots volunteer networks for use every two years instead of every four. Starting the task of party rebuilding at the grass-roots level by encouraging volunteer activity, suggests Malbin, is preferable to strengthening the parties first at the national level. He fears that unlimited spending by national committees would give them enormous power over congressional candidates and would unduly emphasize the influence of the campaign technologies—mass-media advertising, professionally run voter-registration and turnout drives—which the Republican party, at least, has mastered, to the detriment of personalized campaigning and grass-roots activity.

Participants in the Sixty-second Annual Assembly on the future of political parties suggested another avenue for strengthening the parties at the state level: the use of the tax checkoff at the state level to provide for public funding of the party machinery and of candidates through party auspices. Eight states already do so. The participants also recommended that taxpayers in such states have the opportunity to direct their support to the political party of their choice.

Whatever approach is chosen, efforts to strengthen the parties may encounter opposition from PAC managers, not only because stronger parties would decrease candidate need for direct PAC contributions but also because they would take the edge off PAC activities on behalf of candidates. Many PACs have expanded their activities into voter education and mobilization. Some, mainly issue-oriented or ideological PACs, have been active in candidate recruitment, in providing field assistance, and, particularly in the 1980 elections, in direct parallel campaigning through independent expenditures. PACs will not readily surrender the traditional functions of parties a number of them have now assumed.

There is danger, clearly, in our pluralistic society if groups are overly restricted in their political activity. Efforts to strengthen the political parties should not include restrictive legislation regarding interest groups that currently compete with the parties. It is useful to recall that five of the most significant movements of the last two decades—the civil-rights movement, the Vietnam peace movement, the political-reform movement, the women's-rights movement, and the movement toward fiscal restraint—originated in the private sector, where the need for action was perceived and where needed interest organizations were established to carry it out. Hence, there is a strong case for the continued existence of interest groups, which are simply aggregations of like-minded persons whose political power is strengthened when they combine forces. An equally strong case may be made for vigorous and competitive political parties that can build coalitions among various interest groups and effectively adjudicate their competing claims.

Notes

1. For information about amounts authorized and spent on presidential transitions between 1964 and 1965 and 1980 and 1981, see Herbert E. Alexander, *Financing the 1976 Election* (Washington, D.C.: Congressional Quarterly Press, 1976), pp. 675-679.

2. U.S. GAO, *The Reagan-Bush Transition Team's Activities at Six Selected Agencies* (Washington, D.C., January 28, 1982).

3. Ibid., p. 28.

4. Ibid., p. 30.

5. Ibid., p. 33.

6. William Endicott, "'Think Tank' Drawing Up Plans to Achieve Conservative Goals in Reagan Presidency," *Los Angeles Times*, October 4, 1980.

7. GAO, *Reagan-Bush Transition*, p. 32.

8. FEC, *Report of the Audit Division on Reagan for President* (Washington, D.C., February 3, 1981), p. 20.

9. Pete Earley, "Reagan Inaugural the Most Costly at $16.3 Million," *Washington Post*, April 22, 1982.

10. Ibid.

11. Quoted in Jack Nelson, "Reagan to Name More Political Ambassadors," *Los Angeles Times*, April 8, 1982.

12. See "Diplomat Wants Diplomats Abroad," *New York Times*, May 8, 1982.

13. Quoted in Nelson, "Reagan to Name."

14. Ibid.

15. Ralph Blumenthal, "Inquiry on Donovan Again Yields 'Insufficient Evidence' to Prosecute," *New York Times*, September 14, 1982.

16. Ibid.

17. Memorandum to the Honorable Patricia Schroeder from Clifford I. Gould, director, Federal Personnel and Compensation Division, United States General Accounting Office, regarding the Effects of the Presidential Transition on the Senior Executive Service, March 23, 1982, p. 2.

18. Ibid.

19. Morton Mintz, "Republicans Far Ahead in Harvesting Cash," *Washington Post*, February 22, 1981.

20. Ibid.

21. Quoted in ibid.

22. Richard E. Cohen, "Democrats Take a Leaf from GOP Book with Early Campaign Finance Start," *National Journal*, May 23, 1981, p. 923.

23. "Big Gap in Party Fund Raising," *Political Finance/Lobby Reporter*, July 14, 1982, p. 182.

24. Betty Cuniberti, "Dinner-Dance Celebrates Reagan's First Year," *Los Angeles Times*, January 22, 1982.

25. George Skelton and Don Irwin, "Bush Subs for Reagan, Speaks at Shooting Site," *Lost Angeles Times*, April 8, 1981.

26. Lou Cannon, "President Lends a Hand Raising Campaign Funds for Congressional Races," *Washington Post*, May 5, 1982.

27. Cohen, "Democrats Take a Leaf," p. 923-924.

28. Ibid.

29. Ibid.

30. Richard Bergholz, "State GOP's Fund Event to Set Mark," *Los Angeles Times*, April 23, 1981.

31. George Skelton, "Reagan to Make 3 Fund-raising Stops in Southland," *Los Angeles Times*, August 9, 1981.

32. See Mintz, "Republicans Far Ahead."

33. Quoted in "White House Apologizes for Priority Letter," *San Diego Union*, February 6, 1981.

34. "Honor Roll Letter Gets Presidential F," *Los Angeles Times*, October 7, 1981.

35. Ibid.

36. See, for example, Donald M. Rothberg, "Reagan Is Alienating Minorities: Packwood," *Baltimore Evening Sun*, March 2, 1982.

37. "Reagan's Views Damage GOP, Packwood Says," *Los Angeles Times*, March 2, 1982.

38. Quoted in Adam Clymer, "Leader of G.O.P. Bids Party Oust Packwood from Post," *New York Times*, March 5, 1982.

39. "GOP Withdraws Fund-Raising Letter after Reagan Objects," *Los Angeles Times*, April 1, 1982.

40. Bill Peterson, "Rift over Fund Letter Costs GOP $2 Million," *Washington Post*, April 16, 1982.

41. Quoted in ibid.

42. Rowland Evans and Robert Novak, "Shoving Packwood from the Pack," *Washington Post*, April 19, 1982.

43. Adam Clymer, "Fracas: White House and Packwood," *New York Times*, April 23, 1982.

44. George Skelton, "GOP Plans Media Blitz to Promote Reagan's Tax Plan," *Los Angeles Times*, July 24, 1981.

45. Ibid.

46. "Republicans Kick Off 1982 Advertising Blitz," *Campaign Practices Reports*, October 12, 1981, p. 2.

47. Bill Peterson, "In a New Beginning, GOP Ads Will Retire Democratic Look-Alikes," *Washington Post*, June 20, 1982.

48. "G.O.P. Campaign Official Says a TV Ad Had Run Its Course," *New York Times*, June 17, 1982.

49. See "White House Answers Criticism of TV Ad," *Los Angeles Times*, July 9, 1982.

50. George Skelton, "GOP Opens Drive for Remapping Measure," *Los Angeles Times*, September 23, 1981.

51. Dom Bonafede, "As Pollster to the President, Wirthlin Is Where the Action Is," *National Journal*, December 12, 1981, p. 2186.

52. Paul Taylor, "RNC Can't Spend Money As Fast As It's Pouring In," *Washington Post*," November 13, 1981.

53. "GOP Chief Wants Contribution Law Eased for Parties," *Washington Post*, November 21, 1981.

54. Bill Peterson, "White House Tightens Its Control over GOP," *Washington Post*, December 11, 1981.

55. Quoted in Robert Shogan, "GOP Chief Richards Quits, Cites Criticism," *Los Angeles Times*, October 5, 1982.

56. Quoted in Robert Shogan, "Manatt Vows to Lead Democrat 'Comeback,'" *Los Angeles Times*, February 28, 1981.

57. Quoted in Robert Shogan, "Democrats Seek Formula for Regrouping in the 1980s," *Los Angeles Times*, December 12, 1980.

58. Quoted in ibid.

59. Quoted in ibid.

60. Quoted in Dom Bonafede, "For the Democratic Party, It's a Time for Rebuilding and Seeking New Ideas," *National Journal*, February 21, 1981, p. 319.

61. Quoted in Robert Shogan, "Democrats Take a Meeting near a Mountaintop Looking for a Way out of Their Valley," *Los Angeles Times*, October 12, 1981.

62. See ibid.

63. See "Think Tank to Review Campaign Law, Aid Democratic Party," *Campaign Practices Reports*, February 16, 1981, pp. 4-5.

64. See, for example, Bill Stall, "Democratic Governors Plan Stronger Role in Party Operation," *Los Angeles Times*, December 9, 1980, and Robert Shogan, "Unions Seek Bigger Democratic Role," *Los Angeles Times*, February 3, 1981.

65. Shogan, "Manatt Vows."

66. Kenneth Reich, "Manatt Working to Win Party Post," *Washington Post*, January 24, 1981.

67. Quoted in Robert Shogan, "Smaller Democratic Conference Proposed," *Los Angeles Times*, April 8, 1981.

68. Ibid.

69. See Richard J. Cattani, "Democratic Leaders Quietly Draft Blueprint for Party Resurgence," *Christian Science Monitor*, February 5, 1981.

70. See Cohen, "Democrats Take a Leaf," p. 922.

71. Ibid.

72. Cited by David S. Broder, "Democrats' Fund Letter Assails GOP Right Wing," *Washington Post*, July 22, 1981.

73. Cited by Adam Clymer, "Mailings by Democrats Assail White House," *New York Times*, September 3, 1981.

74. "Money Politic/Kentucky Fried Style," *The Political Animal*, May 15, 1981.

75. Cohen, "Democrats Take a Leaf," p. 923.

76. Ibid.

77. See Shogan, "Democrats Seek More Business."

78. Cohen, "Democrats Take a Leaf," p. 923.

79. "Big Gap in Party Fundraising," p. 182.

80. Ibid.

81. Quoted in Adam Clymer, "Democrats Repay '68 Contest Debts," *New York Times*, June 4, 1982.

82. Ibid.

83. Ibid.

84. "DNC's Cablecast," *Campaign People*, June 2, 1982, p. 8.

85. Harry Bernstein, "Kirkland Leading Major Shifts by Labor," *Los Angeles Times*, November 18, 1981.

86. Ibid.

87. Quoted in Harry Bernstein, "AFL-CIO to Seek Stronger Political Role," *Los Angeles Times*, February 19, 1981.

88. Adam Clymer, "Labor and the Democrats: Finances and Politics," *New York Times*, November 20, 1981.

89. Quoted in David C. Savage, "Teachers Union Learning Political Muscle," *Los Angeles Times*, July 4, 1982.

90. Ibid.

91. George B. Merry, "Next for Anderson: A Coalition for New Ideas Aimed at 1984?" *Christian Science Monitor*, November 11, 1980.

92. See Richard E. Meyer, "Anderson Ponders a Third Party," *Los Angeles Times*, February 4, 1981.

93. Quoted in ibid.

94. The Nation, *Los Angeles Times*, November 21, 1982.

95. Joseph E. Cantor, "The Evolution and Issues Surrounding Independent Expenditures in Election Campaigns" (Congressional Research Service, May 5, 1982), p. 24.

96. "Conservative Group Names 20 Senators, May Add Congressmen for Defeat in 1982," *Los Angeles Times*, November 12, 1980.

97. David S. Broder, "Sen. Melcher Gets Apology from NCPAC over Record," *Washington Post*, May 30, 1981.

98. Peter Goldman and Howard Fineman, "The War of the Wolf PACs," *Newsweek*, June 1, 1981, p. 38.

99. "NCPAC's Texas Takeover," *Memo from COPE*, June 1, 1981, p. 1.

100. Jack Anderson, "Here's NCPAC: Slick, Cynical Manipulators," *Washington Post*, October 6, 1981.

101. See Jack W. Germond and Jules Witcover, "Conservatives Super-Skilled Media Users," *Washington Star*, July 9, 1981.

102. "Political Action Roundup," *Political Action Report*, May 15, 1981, p. 5. See also "Washington Focus," *Campaign Practices Reports*, May 24, 1982, p. 1.

103. Quoted in Dale Russakoff, "NCPAC Bid to Beat Him Proves Boon to Sarbanes," *Washington Post*, November 16, 1981.

104. Ibid.

105. "Washington Focus," May 24, 1982, p. 1.

106. Quoted in Jane Perlez, "Moynihan Fight by Action Panel Is Put in 'Limbo,'" *New York Times*, August 6, 1982.

107. Paul J. Cleary, "NCPAC Lays an Egg," *New Republic*, May 23, 1981, p. 10.

108. Ibid.

109. "Conservative PAC Gets Instructions from FEC on Independent Expenditures," *Campaign Practices Reports*, March 17, 1980, p. 3.

110. See Alan Emory, "Democrats Doubt Independence of Conservative Money Baggers," *Washington Post*, January 31, 1981.

111. "McGovern Challenges NCPAC Activities," *Political Finance/Lobby Reporter*, May 14, 1980, pp. 1, 3.

112. "Complaint Dismissed: FEC, by 4-2 Vote, Saw No Collusion in S.D. Senate Race," *Political Finance/Lobby Reporter*, August 27, 1980, p. 5.

113. Robert G. Kaiser, "2 on Hill Call for Probe of NCPAC," *Washington Post*, July 30, 1981.

114. "NCPAC Offer to Rep. Neal Found Not a Bribe," *Washington Post*, September 26, 1981.

115. "Did Dolan's Offer Destroy NCPAC's Independent Status?" *Political Finance/Lobby Reporter*, September 23, 1981, p. 246.

116. "AO 1981-44: Multicandidate Committee's Expenditures Advocating Candidate's Defeat," *FEC Record* (December 1981):4.

117. "FEC Will Not Publicize IRS Letter Ruling Denying Tax Credits to Negative Campaigns," *Campaign Practices Reports*, September 29, 1980, pp. 2-3.

118. "NCPAC Lobby Registration May Jeopardize Tax Status," *Political Finance/Lobby Reporter*, December 9, 1981, p. 318.

119. Quoted in David S. Broder and Bill Peterson, "Democrats to Demand Investigation of NCPAC," *Washington Post*, November 21, 1981.

120. Quick allegedly held seminars for Democratic candidates in which he outlined tactics for getting rid of negative independent expenditures. See "Democrats, TV Stations Conspired, NCPAC Claims," *Campaign Practices Reports*, December 21, 1981, p. 4.

121. "FCC Rejects NCPAC's Air Waves Access Claim," *Campaign Practices Reports*, April 12, 1982, p. 7.

122. See FEC, "PAC Contributions Exceed $22 Million," press release, June 30, 1982, p. 6; "By Election Eve, Nation's PAC Spending Hit $164.2 Million," *PACs & Lobbies*, November 17, 1982, p. 1; and FEC, *FEC Reports on Financial Activity, 1981-1982*, vol. 4: *Non-Party Detailed Tables* (Washington, D.C.: FEC, October 1982).

123. FEC, *FEC Reports*, vol. 1: *Summary Tables* (Washington, D.C.: FEC, October 1982).

124. Ibid., pp. 118-127.

125. FEC, "FEC Releases Final PAC Report for 1979-80 Election Cycle," press release, February 21, 1982, p. 3. See also FEC, *FEC Index of Independent Expenditures, 1979-80* (Washington, D.C.: FEC, November 1981), p. 3.

126. FEC, *FEC Reports*, vol. 4, pp. 118, 127.

127. Maxwell Glen and James K. Popkin, "Liberal PACs Learning It Won't Be Easy to Stem the Conservative Tide," *National Journal*, March 20, 1982, p. 500.

128. "By Election Eve," p. 5.

129. See "NCEC Targets 68 for Defeat," *Political Finance/Lobby Reporter*, May 6, 1981, p. 113; and Warren Weaver, Jr., "Group for Effective Congress to Stress Aid to Democrats," *New York Times*, April 26, 1981.

130. "PACs & Lobbies: Dispatches from the Front," *Political Finance/Lobby Reporter*, March 31, 1982, p. 89.

131. Phil Gailey, "A Political Action Unit of the Left," *New York Times*, February 10, 1982.

132. Glen and Popkin, "Liberal PACs Learning," p. 501.

133. "The New Right: A Threat to America's Future," brochure, Democrats for the '80s.

134. Larry Light, "New Liberal Money Groups Compete for Campaign Funds," *Congressional Quarterly Weekly Report*, October 3, 1981, p. 1905.

135. Jack Erickson, "The Democrats: Rebuilding with Support Groups," *Campaigns & Elections* (Spring 1982):5.

136. "Nation's PACs Raise $81.9 Million in 1981," *Political Finance/Lobby Reporter*, March 3, 1982, p. 52.

137. Erickson, "The Democrats," p. 6.

138. *Washington Post*, June 20, 1982.

139. Erickson, "The Democrats," p. 10.

140. Adam Clymer, "Democrats Forming Fund-Raising Units," *New York Times*, February 13, 1981.

141. "By Election Eve," p. 5.

142. Steven Dornfeld, "Mondale Forms Political Committee to Pursue 1984 Presidential Aims," *Philadelphia Inquirer*, February 14, 1981.

143. "By Election Eve," p. 5.

144. Ibid.

145. FEC, *FEC Reports*, vol. 4, pp. 113-114.

146. Erickson, "The Democrats," p. 7.

147. Ibid., p. 11.

148. Ibid.

149. FEC, Committee Index of Disclosure Documents, p. 210.

150. Quoted in "These Liberal Groups Are Keeping the Voters on Their Toes," *National Journal*, July 4, 1981, p. 1200.

151. Erickson, "The Democrats," p. 8.

152. "These Liberal Groups," p. 1200.

153. Glen and Popkin, "Liberal PACs Learning," p. 501.

154. William C. Oldaker, "The Rise of Political Fat Cats," *Los Angeles Times*, February 17, 1982.

155. "Hit List: NCPAC Has a 'Score' to Settle in 1982," *Political Finance/Lobby Reporter*, November 19, 1980, p. 5.

156. See Michael J. Malbin, "What Should Be Done About Independent Expenditures?" *Regulation* (January-February 1982):44.

157. Quoted in Robert Shogan, "GOP Chairman Condemns Negative Ad Campaigns," *Los Angeles Times*, April 28, 1981.

158. Quoted in David S. Broder, "Parties Won't Conduct Joint Campaign Study," *Washington Post*, May 19, 1981.

159. See "Campaign Expenditure Reform," *The Political Animal*, May 8, 1981, p. 1; Lou Cannon, "GOP Chief Decries Independent Efforts to Target Democrats on 'Single Issues,'" *Washington Post*, April 28, 1981; and "Richards Sees Danger in Independent Expenditures," *Political Finance/Lobby Reporter*, May 6, 1981, p. 112.

160. Quoted in David Hoffman, "Growth of Independent PACs Worries Both Parties," *Washington Post*, July 29, 1982.

161. Cantor, "Evolution and Issues," pp. 40-42.

162. This solution also has the backing of Fred Wertheimer, president of Common Cause. See David S. Broder, "Equal Time for Targets," *Washington Post*, August 26, 1981.

163. "FEC Invites Comment on Independent Expenditure Petition," *Political Finance/Lobby Reporter*, December 9, 1981, p. 318.

164. Quoted in "Former Senators Ask FEC to Revise 'Independent' Rules," *Political Finance/Lobby Reporter*, February 17, 1982, p. 36.

165. Ibid.

166. "Inouye Offers Legislative Proposals to Assure Greater Campaign Fairness," *Political Finance/Lobby Reporter*, December 9, 1981, p. 319.

167. Ibid.

168. "Parties Spend Sums," *Los Angeles Times*, September 2, 1982.

169. Ibid.

170. Jeff Greenfield, *The Real Campaign* (New York: Summit Books, 1982), p. 268.

171. See Dom Bonafede, "The Press Makes News in Covering the 1980 Primary Election Campaign," *National Journal*, July 12, 1980, pp. 1132-1135; Jonathan Friendly, "Aides to Candidates Criticize the Media," *New York Times*, November 20, 1980.

172. See Greenfield, *Real Campaign*.

173. See Theodore H. White, *America in Search of Itself: The Making of the President, 1956-1980* (New York: Harper & Row, 1982), p. 411ff.

174. U.S. Congress, House, House Administration Committee and the Energy and Commerce Committee, *Early Election Returns and Projections Affecting the Electoral Process* (Washington, D.C.: Government Printing Office, 1981).

175. Brad Knickerbocker, "Did TV Change Election '80?" *Christian Science Monitor*, October 21, 1981.

176. See, for example, Robert A. Goldwin, ed., *Political Parties in the Eighties* (Washington, D.C.: American Enterprise Institute for Public Policy Research and Kenyon College, 1980); David Broder, *The Party's Over* (New York: Harper & Row, 1972); and Sidney Blumenthal, *The Permanent Campaign* (Boston: Beacon Press, 1980).

177. "GOP Chief Wants Contribution Law Eased for Parties," *Washington Post*, November 21, 1981.

178. See Joel Fleishman, ed., *The Future of American Political Parties* (Englewood Cliffs, N.J.: Prentice-Hall, 1982).

179. *Financing Presidential Campaigns, A Research Report by the Campaign Finance Study Group to the Committee on Rules and Administration of the United States Senate* (Cambridge, Mass.: Institute of Politics, John F. Kennedy School of Government, Harvard University, January 1982).

180. U.S. Congress, House, Committee on House Administration, *An Analysis of the Impact of the Federal Election Campaign Act, 1972-78*, Institute of Politics, John F. Kennedy School of Government, Harvard University (Washington, D.C.: Government Printing Office, 1979).

181. See "Frenzel Introduces GOP Bill to Overhaul Election Law," *Political Finance/Lobby Reporter*, June 2, 1982, pp. 145-147.

182. Michael J. Malbin, "What Should Be Done about Independent Expenditures," *Regulation* (January-February 1982):41-46.

Appendix

Federal Election Campaign Act of 1971

The Federal Election Campaign Act of 1971 (FECA) was the first comprehensive revision of federal campaign legislation since the Corrupt Practices Act of 1925. The act established detailed spending limits and disclosure procedures. P.L. 92-225 contained the following major provisions:

General

Repealed the Federal Corrupt Practices Act of 1925.

Defined "election" to mean any general, special, primary or runoff election, nominating convention or caucus, delegate-selection primary, presidential preference primary or constitutional convention.

Broadened the definitions of "contribution" and "expenditure" as they pertain to political campaigns, but exempted a loan of money by a national or state bank made in accordance with applicable banking laws.

Prohibited promises of employment or other political rewards or benefits by any candidate in exchange for political support, and prohibited contracts between candidates and any federal department or agency.

Provided that the terms "contribution" and "expenditure" did not include communications, nonpartisan registration and get-out-the-vote campaigns by a corporation aimed at its stockholders or by a labor organization aimed at its members.

Provided that the terms "contribution" and "expenditure" did not include the establishment, administration and solicitation of voluntary contributions to a separate segregated fund to be utilized for political purposes by a corporation or labor organization.

Contribution Limits

Placed a ceiling on contributions by any candidate or his immediate family to his own campaign of $50,000 for president or vice president, $35,000 for senator and $25,000 for representative.

Herbert E. Alexander, *Financing Politics: Money, Elections and Political Reform,* 2d ed. (Washington, D.C.: Congressional Quarterly, Inc., 1980), pp. 163-176. Reprinted with permission.
    Some provisions have been declared unconstitutional and some have been superseded by later amendments or repealed.

491

Spending Limits

Limited the total amount that could be spent by federal candidates for advertising time in communications media to 10 cents per eligible voter or $50,000, whichever was greater. The limitation would apply to all candidates for president and vice president, senator and representative, and would be determined annually for the geographical area of each election by the Bureau of the Census.

Included in the term "communications media" radio and television broadcasting stations, newspapers, magazines, billboards and automatic telephone equipment. Of the total spending limit, up to 60 percent could be used for broadcast advertising time.

Specified that candidates for presidential nomination, during the period prior to the nominating convention, could spend no more in primary or nonprimary states than the amount allowed under the 10-cent-per-voter communications spending limitation.

Provided that broadcast and nonbroadcast spending limitations be increased in proportion to annual increases in the Consumer Price Index over the base year 1970.

Disclosure and Enforcement

Required all political committees that anticipated receipts in excess of $1,000 during the calendar year to file a statement of organization with the appropriate federal supervisory officer, and to include such information as the names of all principal officers, the scope of the committee, the names of all candidates the committee supported and other information as required by law.

Stipulated that the appropriate federal supervisory officer to oversee election campaign practices, reporting and disclosure was the Clerk of the House for House candidates, the Secretary of the Senate for Senate candidates and the Comptroller General for presidential candidates.

Required each political committee to report any individual expenditure of more than $100 and any expenditures of more than $100 in the aggregate during the calendar year.

Required disclosure of all contributions to any committee or candidate in excess of $100, including a detailed report with the name and address of the contributor and the date the contribution was made.

Required the supervisory officers to prepare an annual report for each committee registered with the commission and make such reports available for sale to the public.

Required candidates and committees to file reports of contributions and expenditures on the 10th day of March, June and September every year, on the 15th and fifth days preceding the date on which an election was held and on the 31st day of January. Any contribution of $5,000 or more was to be reported within 48 hours after its receipt.

Required reporting of the names, addresses and occupations of any lender and endorser of any loan in excess of $100 as well as the date and amount of such loans.

Required any person who made any contribution in excess of $100, other than through a political committee or candidate, to report such contribution to the commission.

Prohibited any contribution to a candidate or committee by one person in the name of another person.

Authorized the office of the Comptroller General to serve as a national clearinghouse for information on the administration of election practices.

Required that copies of reports filed by a candidate with the appropriate supervisory officer also be filed with the secretary of state for the state in which the election was held.

Miscellaneous

Prohibited radio and television stations from charging political candidates more than the lowest unit cost for the same advertising time available to commercial advertisers. Lowest unit rate charges would apply only during the 45 days preceding a primary election and the 60 days preceding a general election.

Required nonbroadcast media to charge candidates no more than the comparable amounts charged to commercial advertisers for the same class and amount of advertising space. The requirement would apply only during the 45 days preceding the date of a primary election and 60 days before the date of a general election.

Provided that amounts spent by an agent of a candidate on behalf of his candidacy would be charged against the overall expenditure allocation. Fees paid to the agent for services performed also would be charged against the overall limitation.

Stipulated that no broadcast station could make any charge for political advertising time on a station unless written consent to contract for such time had been given by the candidate, and unless the candidate certified that such charge would not exceed the spending limit.

Revenue Act of 1971

The Revenue Act of 1971, through tax incentives and a tax checkoff plan, provided the basis for public funding of presidential election campaigns. P.L. 92-178 contained the following major provisions:

Tax Incentives and Checkoff

> Allowed a tax credit of $12.50 ($25 for a married couple) or a deduction against income of $50 ($100 for a married couple) for political contributions to candidates for local, state or federal office. [NOTE: The Revenue Act of 1978, P.L. 96-600, raised the tax credit to $50 on a single tax return, $100 on a joint return. As in the 1971 Act, the credit equaled 50 percent of the contribution, up to those limits. The 1978 law eliminated the tax deduction for political contributions while increasing the tax credit.]

> Allowed taxpayers to contribute to a general fund for all eligible presidential and vice presidential candidates by authorizing $1 of their annual income tax payment to be placed in such a fund.

Presidential Election Campaign Fund

> Authorized to be distributed to the candidates of each major party (one which obtained 25 percent of votes cast in the previous presidential election) an amount equal to 15 cents multiplied by the number of U.S. residents age 18 or over.

> Established a formula for allocating public campaign funds to candidates of minor parties whose candidates received 5 percent or more but less than 25 percent of the previous presidential election vote.

> Authorized payments after the election to reimburse the campaign expenses of a new party whose candidate received enough votes to be eligible or to a minor party whose candidate increased its vote to the qualifying level.

> Prohibited major-party candidates who chose public financing of their campaign from accepting private campaign contributions unless their share of funds contributed through the income tax checkoff procedure fell short of the amounts to which they were entitled.

Prohibited a major-party candidate who chose public financing and all campaign committees authorized by the candidate from spending more than the amount to which the candidate was entitled under the contributions formula.

Provided that if the amounts in the fund were insufficient to make the payments to which each party was entitled, payments would be allocated according to the ratio of contributions in their accounts. No party would receive from the general fund more than the smallest amount needed by a major party to reach the maximum amount of contributions to which it was entitled.

Provided that surpluses remaining in the fund after a campaign be returned to the Treasury after all parties had been paid the amounts to which they were entitled.

Enforcement

Provided penalties of $5,000 or one year in prison, or both, for candidates or campaign committees that spent more on a campaign than the amounts they received from the campaign fund or who accepted private contributions when sufficient public funds were available.

Provided penalties of $10,000 or five years in prison, or both, for candidates or campaign committees who used public campaign funds for unauthorized expenses, gave or accepted kickbacks or illegal payments involving public campaign funds, or who knowingly furnished false information to the Comptroller General.

Federal Election Campaign Act Amendments of 1974

The 1974 Amendments set new contribution and spending limits, made provision for government funding of presidential prenomination campaigns and national nominating conventions, and created the bipartisan Federal Election Commission to administer election laws. P.L. 93-443 contained the following major provisions:

Federal Election Commission

> Created a six-member, full-time bipartisan Federal Election Commission to be responsible for administering election laws and the public financing program.

> Provided that the president, Speaker of the House and president pro tem of the Senate would appoint to the commission two members, each of different parties, all subject to confirmation by Congress. Commission members could not be officials or employees of any branch of government.

> Made the Secretary of the Senate and Clerk of the House ex officio, nonvoting members of the FEC; provided that their offices would serve as custodian of reports for House and Senate candidates.

> Provided that commissioners would serve six-year, staggered terms and established a rotating one-year chairmanship.

Contribution Limits

> $1,000 per individual for each primary, runoff or general election, and an aggregate contribution of $25,000 to all federal candidates annually.

> $5,000 per organization, political committee and national and state party organization for each election, but no aggregate limit on the amount organizations could contribute in a campaign nor on the amount organizations could contribute to party organizations suporting federal candidates.

> $50,000 for president or vice president, $35,000 for Senate and $25,000 for House races for candidates and their families to their own campaign.

> $1,000 for independent expenditures on behalf of a candidate.

> Barred cash contributions of over $100 and foreign contributions.

Spending Limits

Presidential primaries—$10 million total per candidate for all primaries. In a state presidential primary, limited a candidate to spending no more than twice what a Senate candidate in that state would be allowed to spend.

Presidential general election—$20 million per candidate.

Presidential nominating conventions—$2 million each major political party, lesser amounts for minor parties.

Senate primaries—$100,000 or eight cents per eligible voter, whichever was greater.

Senate general elections—$150,000 or 12 cents per eligible voter, whichever was greater.

House primaries—$70,000.

House general elections—$70,000.

National party spending—$10,000 per candidate in House general elections; $20,000 or two cents per eligible voter, whichever was greater, for each candidate in Senate general elections; and two cents per voter (approximately $2.9 million) in presidential general elections. The expenditure would be above the candidate's individual spending limit.

Applied Senate spending limits to House candidates who represented a whole state.

Repealed the media spending limitations in the Federal Election Campaign Act of 1971 (P.L. 92-225).

Exempted expenditures of up to $500 for food and beverages, invitations, unreimbursed travel expenses by volunteers and spending on "slate cards" and sample ballots.

Exempted fund-raising costs of up to 20 percent of the candidate spending limit. Thus the spending limit for House candidates would be effectively raised from $70,000 to $84,000 and for candidates in presidential primaries from $10 million to $12 million.

Provided that spending limits be increased in proportion to annual increases in the Consumer Price Index.

Public Financing

Presidential general elections—voluntary public financing. Major-party candidates automatically would qualify for full funding before the campaign. Minor-party and independent candidates would be eligible to receive a proportion of full funding based on past or current votes received. If a candidate opted for full public funding, no private contributions would be permitted.

Presidential nominating conventions—optional public funding. Major parties automatically would qualify. Minor parties would be eligible for lesser amounts based on their proportion of votes received in a past election.

Presidential primaries—matching public funds of up to $5 million per candidate after meeting fund-raising requirement of $100,000 raised in amounts of at least $5,000 in each of 20 states or more. Only the first $250 of individual private contributions would be matched. The matching funds were to be divided among the candidates as quickly as possible. In allocating the money, the order in which the candidates qualified would be taken into account. Only private gifts, raised after January 1, 1975, would qualify for matching for the 1976 election. No federal payments would be made before January 1976.

Provided that all federal money for public funding of campaigns would come from the Presidential Election Campaign Fund. Money received from the federal income tax dollar checkoff automatically would be appropriated to the fund.

Disclosure and Enforcement

Required each candidate to establish one central campaign committee through which all contributions and expenditures on behalf of a candidate must be reported. Required designation of specific bank depositories of campaign funds.

Required full reports of contributions and expenditures to be filed with the Federal Election Commission 10 days before and 30 days after every election, and within 10 days of the close of each quarter unless the committee received or expended less than $1,000 in that quarter. A year-end report was due in nonelection years.

Required that contributions of $1,000 or more received within the last 15 days before election be reported to the commission within 48 hours.

Prohibited contributions in the name of another.

Treated loans as contributions. Required a cosigner or guarantor for each $1,000 of outstanding obligation.

Required any organization that spent any money or committed any act for the purpose of influencing any election (such as the publication of voting records) to file reports as a political committee.

Required every person who spent or contributed more than $100, other than to or through a candidate or political committee, to report.

Permitted government contractors, unions and corporations to maintain separate, segregated political funds.

Provided that the commission would receive campaign reports, make rules and regulations (subject to review by Congress within 30 days), maintain a cumulative index of reports filed and not filed, make special and regular reports to Congress and the president, and serve as an election information clearinghouse.

Gave the commission power to render advisory opinions, conduct audits and investigations, subpoena witnesses and information and go to court to seek civil injunctions.

Provided that criminal cases would be referred by the commission to the Justice Department for prosecution.

Increased existing fines to a maximum of $50,000.

Provided that a candidate for federal office who failed to file reports could be prohibited from running again for the term of that office plus one year.

Miscellaneous

Set January 1, 1975, as the effective date of the act (except for immediate preemption of state laws).

Removed Hatch Act restrictions on voluntary activities by state and local employees in federal campaigns, if not otherwise prohibited by state law.

Prohibited solicitation of funds by franked mail.

Preempted state election laws for federal candidates.

Permitted use of excess campaign funds to defray expenses of holding federal office or for other lawful purposes.

**Federal Election Campaign Act
Amendments of 1976**

The 1976 Amendments revised election laws following the Supreme Court
decision in *Buckley* v. *Valeo*. The Amendments reopened the door to large
contributions through "independent expenditures" and through corporate
and union political action committees. P.L. 94-283 contained the following
major provisions:

Federal Election Commission

Reconstituted the Federal Election Commission as a six-member panel
appointed by the president and confirmed by the Senate.

Prohibited commission members from engaging in outside business activities; gave commissioners one year after joining the body to terminate outside business interests.

Gave Congress the power to disapprove individual sections of any
regulation proposed by the commission.

Contribution Limits

Limited an individual to giving no more than $5,000 a year to a political
action committee and $20,000 to the national committee of a political
party (the 1974 law set a $1,000-per-election limit on individual con-
tributions to a candidate and an aggregate contribution limit for individuals of $25,000 a year, both provisions remaining in effect).

Limited a multicandidate committee to giving no more than $15,000 a
year to the national committee of a political party (the 1974 law set only
a limit of $5,000 per election per candidate, a provision remaining in ef-
fect).

Limited the Democratic and Republican senatorial campaign committees to giving no more than $17,500 a year to a candidate (the 1974 law
set a $5,000-per-election limit, a provision remaining in effect).

Allowed campaign committees organized to back a single candidate to
provide "occasional, isolated, and incidental support" to another candidate. (The 1974 law had limited such a committee to spending money
only on behalf of the single candidate for which it was formed.)

Restricted the proliferation of membership organization, corporate and union political action committees. All political action committees established by a company or an international union would be treated as a single committee for contribution purposes. The contributions of political action committees of a company or union would be limited to no more than $5,000 overall to the same candidate in any election.

Spending Limits

Limited spending by presidential and vice presidential candidates to no more than $50,000 of their own, or their families', money on their campaigns, if they accepted public financing.

Exempted from the law's spending limits payments by candidates or the national committees of political parties for legal and accounting services required to comply with the campaign law, but required that such payments be reported.

Public Financing

Required presidential candidates who received federal matching subsidies and who withdrew from the prenomination election campaign to give back leftover federal matching funds.

Cut off federal campaign subsidies to a presidential candidate who won less than 10 percent of the vote in two consecutive presidential primaries in which he ran.

Established a procedure under which an individual who became ineligible for matching payments could have eligibility restored by a finding of the commission.

Disclosure and Enforcement

Gave the commission exclusive authority to prosecute civil violations of the campaign finance law and shifted to the commission jurisdiction over violations formerly covered only in the criminal code, thus strengthening its power to enforce the law.

Required an affirmative vote of four members for the commission to issue regulations and advisory opinions and initiate civil actions and investigations.

Required labor unions, corporations and membership organizations to report expenditures of over $2,000 per election for communications to their stockholders or members advocating the election or defeat of a clearly identified candidate. The costs of communications to members or stockholders on issues would not have to be reported.

Required that candidates and political committees keep records of contributions of $50 or more. (The 1974 law had required records of contributions of $10 or more.)

Permitted candidates and political committees to waive the requirement for filing quarterly campaign finance reports in a nonelection year if less than a total of $5,000 was raised or spent in that quarter. Annual reports would still have to be filed. (The exemption limit was $1,000 under the 1974 law.)

Required political committees and individuals making an independent political expenditure of more than $100 that advocated the defeat or election of a candidate to file a report with the election commission. Required the committee and individual to state, under penalty of perjury, that the expenditure was not made in collusion with a candidate.

Required that independent expenditures of $1,000 or more made within 15 days of an election be reported within 24 hours.

Limited the commission to issuing advisory opinions only for specific fact situations. Advisory opinions could not be used to spell out commission policy. Advisory opinions were not to be considered as precedents unless an activity was "indistinguishable in all its material aspects" from an activity already covered by an advisory opinion.

Permitted the commission to initiate investigations only after it received a properly verified complaint or had reason to believe, based on information it obtained in the normal course of its duties, that a violation had occurred or was about to occur. The commission was barred from relying on anonymous complaints to institute investigations.

Required the commission to rely initially on conciliation to deal with alleged campaign law violations before going to court. The commission was allowed to refer alleged criminal violations to the Department of Justice for action. The attorney general was required to report back to the commission within 60 days an action taken on the apparent violation and subsequently every 30 days until the matter was disposed of.

Provided for a one-year jail sentence and a fine of up to $25,000 or three times the amount of the contribution or expenditure involved in the violation, whichever was greater, if an individual was convicted of knowingly commiting a campaign law violation that involved more than $1,000.

Provided for civil penalties of fines of $5,000 or an amount equal to the contribution or expenditure involved in the violation, whichever was greater. For violations knowingly committed, the fine would be $10,000 or an amount equal to twice the amount involved in the violation, whichever was greater. The fines could be imposed by the courts or by the commission in conciliation agreements. (The 1974 law included penalties for civil violations of a $1,000 fine and/or a one-year prison sentence.)

Miscellaneous

Restricted the fund-raising ability of corporate political action committees. Company committees could seek contributions only from stockholders and executive and administrative personnel and their families. Restricted union political action committees to soliticing contributions only from union members and their families. However, twice a year the law permitted union and corporate political action committees to seek campaign contributions only by mail from all employees not initially included in the restriction. Contributions would have to remain anonymous and would be received by an independent third party that would keep records but pass the money to the committees.

Permitted trade association political action committees to solicit contributions from member companies' stockholders, executive and administrative personnel and their families.

Permitted union political action committees to use the same method to solicit campaign contributions that the political action committee of the company uses. The union committee would have to reimburse the company at cost for the expenses the company incurred for the political fund raising.

Federal Election Campaign Act Amendments of 1979

The 1979 Amendments were enacted to lighten the burden the law imposed
on candidates and political committees by reducing paperwork, among
other changes. P.L. 96-187 contained the following major provisions:

Disclosure

Required a federal candidate to file campaign finance reports if he or
she received or expended more than $5,000. Previously any candidate,
regardless of the amount raised or spent, had to file.

Allowed local political party organizations to avoid filing reports with
the FEC if expenditures for certain voluntary activities (get-out-the-
vote and voter registration drives for presidential tickets and purchase
of buttons, bumper stickers and other materials) were less than $5,000 a
year. If other types of expenditures were more than $1,000 a year, then
such a group would be required to file. Previously local political party
organizations were required to file when any class of expenditure exceeded $1,000 a year.

Permitted an individual to spend up to $1,000 in behalf of a candidate
or $2,000 in behalf of a political party in voluntary expenses for pro-
viding his home, food or personal travel without it being counted as a
reportable contribution.

Eliminated the requirement that a political committee have a chairman,
but continued the requirement that each have a treasurer.

Allowed 10 days, instead of the previous five, for a person who received
a contribution of more than $50 on behalf of a candidate's campaign
committee to forward it to the committee's treasurer.

Required a committee's treasurer to preserve records for three years.
Previously, the FEC established the period of time that committee
treasurers were required to keep records.

Required a candidate's campaign committee to have the candidate's
name in the title of the committee. Also, the title of a political action
committee was required to include the name of the organization with
which it was affiliated.

Reduced to six from 11 the categories of information required on
registration statements of political committees. One of the categories
eliminated was one requiring political action committees to name the
candidates supported. That requirement meant that PACs were forced

frequently to file lists of candidates to whom they contributed when that information already was given in their contribution reports.

Reduced to nine from 24 the maximum number of reports that a candidate would be required to file during a two-year election cycle. Those nine reports would be a preprimary, a pregeneral, a postgeneral, four quarterly reports during an election year and two semiannual reports during the nonelection year. The preelection reports would be due 12 days before the election; the postgeneral report would be due 30 days after the election; the quarterly reports would be due 15 days after the end of each quarter and the semiannual reports would be due July 31 and January 31.

Required presidental campaign committees to file monthly reports, as well as pre- and postgeneral reports, during an election year if they had contributions or expenditures in excess of $100,000. All other presidential campaign committees would be required to file quarterly reports, as well as pre-and postgeneral reports, during an election year. During a nonelection year presidential campaign committees could choose whether to file monthly or quarterly reports.

Required political committees other than those affiliated with a candidate to file either monthly reports in all years or nine reports during a two-year election cycle.

Provided that the FEC be notified within 48 hours of contributions of $1,000 or more that were made between 20 days and 48 hours before an election. Previously the period had been between 15 days and 48 hours before an election.

Required the names of contributors to be reported if they gave $200 or more instead of $100 or more.

Required expenses to be itemized if they were $200 or more instead of $100 or more.

Increased the threshold for reporting independent expenditures to $250 from $100.

Federal Election Commission

Established a "best effort" standard for the FEC to determine compliance by candidates' committees with the law. This was intended to ease the burden on committees, particularly in the area of meeting the requirement of filing the occupations of contributors.

Allowed any person who had an inquiry about a specific campaign transaction—not just federal officeholders, candidates, political committees and the national party committees—to request advisory opinions from the FEC.

Required the FEC to respond to advisory opinion requests within 60 days instead of within a "reasonable time." If such a request were made within the 60-day period before an election, the FEC would be required to issue an opinion within 20 days.

Provided that within five days of receiving a complaint that the election campaign law had been violated the FEC must notify any person alleged to have committed a violation. The accused has 15 days in which to respond to the complaint.

Required a vote of four of the six members of the FEC to make the determination it had "reason to believe" a violation of the law had occurred. An investigation then would be required, and the accused had to be notified.

Provided that four votes of the FEC were necessary to determine "probable cause" that a violation had occurred. The commission then would be required to attempt to correct the violation by informal methods and to enter into a conciliation agreement within 90 days. Commission action required the vote of four FEC members.

Narrowed the scope of the FEC's national clearinghouse function from all elections to federal elections.

Eliminated random audits of committees by the FEC and required a vote of four FEC members to conduct an audit after it had determined that a committee had not substantially complied with the election campaign law.

Required secretaries of state in each state to keep copies of FEC reports on file for only two years compared with the previous requirement that all House candidate reports be retained for five years and all other reports for 10 years.

Provided an expedited procedure for the Senate, as well as for the House, to disapprove a regulation proposed by the FEC.

Enforcement

Retained the substance of the existing law providing for civil and criminal relief of election campaign law violations.

Continued the prohibition on the use of the contents of reports filed with the FEC for the purpose of soliciting contributions or for commercial purposes, but added the exception that the names of PACs registered with the FEC may be used for solicitation of contributions.

Permitted political committees to include 10 pseudonyms on each report to protect against illegal use of the names of contributors. A list of those names would be provided to the FEC and would not be made public.

Political Parties

Allowed state and local party groups to buy, without limit, buttons, bumper stickers, handbills, brochures, posters and yard signs for voluntary activities.

Authorized state and local party groups to conduct voter registration and get-out-the-vote drives on behalf of presidential tickets without financial limit.

Public Financing

Increased the allotment of federal funds for the Democrats and Republicans to finance their nominating conventions to $3 million from $2 million.

Miscellaneous

Permitted buttons and similar materials, but not commercial advertisements, that promoted one candidate to make a passing reference to another federal candidate without its being treated as a contribution to the second candidate.

Permitted leftover campaign funds to be given to other political committees, as well as charities.

Prohibited anyone, with the exception of members of Congress at the time of P.L. 96-187's enactment, to convert leftover campaign funds to personal use.

Continued the ban on solicitation by candidates for Congress or members of Congress and by federal employees of other federal workers for campaign contributions, but dropped the prohibition on the receipt of such contributions by federal employees. An inadvertent solicitation of a federal employee would not be a violation.

Permitted congressional employees to make voluntary contributions to members of Congress other than their immediate employers.

Continued the ban on solicitation and receipt of contributions in a federal building. But it would not be a violation if contributions received at a federal building were forwarded within seven days to the appropriate political committee and if the contribution had not been directed initially to the federal building.

Index

About the Author

Herbert E. Alexander is professor of political science at the University of Southern California and since 1958 has been director of the Citizens' Research Foundation. He received the B.S. from the University of North Carolina, the M.A. from the University of Connecticut, and the Ph.D. in political science from Yale University. Dr. Alexander has taught at Princeton University, the University of Pennsylvania, and Yale University. He also has held a number of government posts, including executive director of the president's Commission on Campaign Costs and consultant to the Office of Federal Elections at the General Accounting Office. In 1973-1974, Dr. Alexander undertook a consultancy with the U.S. Senate Select Committee on Presidential Campaign Activities.

Dr. Alexander has written extensively on matters relating to money in politics. In addition to his five books on the financing of the presidential-election campaigns since 1960, he has authored *Financing Politics: Money, Elections, and Political Reform* and *Money in Politics.* He is the editor of *Campaign Money: Reform and Reality in the States* and coauthor of *The Federal Election Campaign Act: After a Decade of Political Reform.*